THE DICTIONARY OF JEWISH BIOGRAPHY

For my students

THE DICTIONARY OF JEWISH BIOGRAPHY

DAN COHN-SHERBOK

OXFORD
UNIVERSITY PRESS
2005

OXFORD
UNIVERSITY PRESS

Oxford University Press, Inc., publishes works that further
Oxford University's objective of excellence
in research, scholarship, and education.

Oxford New York
Auckland Cape Town Dar es Salaam Hong Kong Karachi
Kuala Lumpur Madrid Melbourne Mexico City Nairobi
New Delhi Shanghai Taipei Toronto

With offices in
Argentina Austria Brazil Chile Czech Republic France Greece
Guatemala Hungary Italy Japan Poland Portugal Singapore
South Korea Switzerland Thailand Turkey Ukraine Vietnam

Published by Oxford University Press, Inc.
198 Madison Avenue, New York, New York 10016
www.oup.com

First published by Continuum in the United Kingdom

Library of Congress cataloging-in-publication data is available.

0-19-522391-8

1 3 5 7 9 8 6 4 2

Printed in the U.K
on acid-free paper

CONTENTS

MAPS

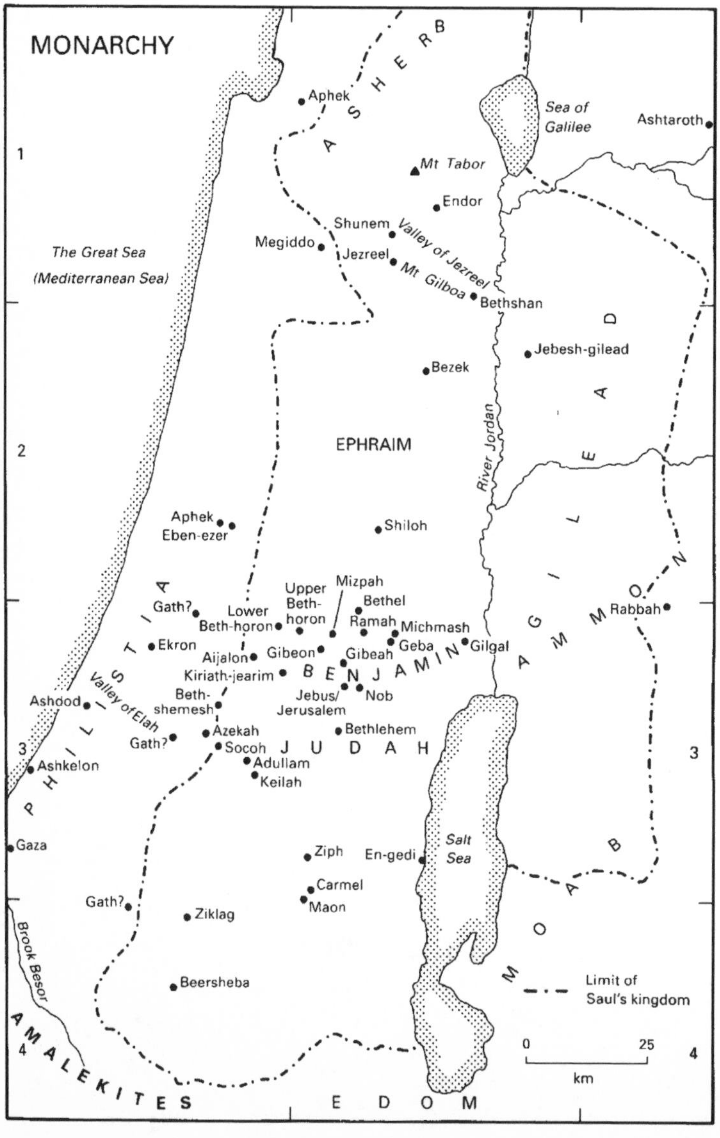
MONARCHY
The Great Sea
(Mediterranean Sea)
ASHER
Aphek
Sea of
Galilee
Ashtaroth
Mt Tabor
Endor
Shunem
Valley of Jezreel
Megiddo
Jezreel
Mt Gilboa
Bethshan
Jebesh-gilead
Bezek
EPHRAIM
River Jordan
GILEAD
Aphek
Eben-ezer
Shiloh
Mizpah
Upper
Beth-
horon
Bethel
Gath?
Lower
Beth-horon
Ramah
Michmash
Rabbah
Ekron
Geba
Gilgal
Aijalon
Gibeon
Gibeah
AMMON
Kiriath-jearim
BENJAMIN
Ashdod
Valley of Elah
Beth-
shemesh
Jebus/
Jerusalem
Nob
Gath?
Azekah
Bethlehem
Socoh
JUDAH
Ashkelon
PHILISTIA
Adullam
Keilah
Gaza
Ziph
En-gedi
Salt
Sea
Carmel
Maon
Gath?
Ziklag
MOAB
Brook Besor
Beersheba
Limit of
Saul's kingdom
0
25
km
AMALEKITES
EDOM
1
2
3
4
3
4

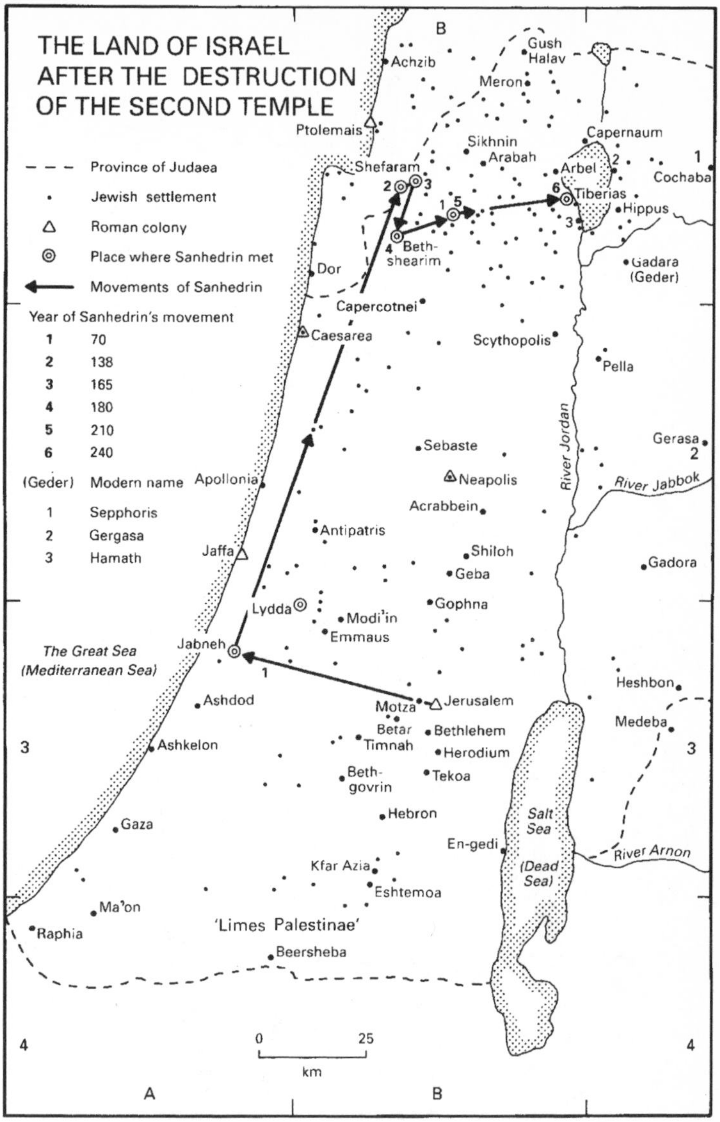
THE LAND OF ISRAEL
AFTER THE DESTRUCTION
OF THE SECOND TEMPLE
Province of Judaea
Jewish settlement
Roman colony
Place where Sanhedrin met
Movements of Sanhedrin
Year of Sanhedrin's movement
1 70
2 138
3 165
4 180
5 210
6 240
(Geder) Modern name
1 Sepphoris
2 Gergasa
3 Hamath
The Great Sea
(Mediterranean Sea)
Achzib
Gush Halav
Meron
Ptolemais
Sikhnin
Arabah
Capernaum
Shefaram
Arbel
Cochaba
Tiberias
Hippus
Beth-shearim
Gadara
(Geder)
Dor
Capercotnei
Caesarea
Scythopolis
Pella
River Jordan
Sebaste
Gerasa
Neapolis
River Jabbok
Apollonia
Acrabbein
Antipatris
Shiloh
Jaffa
Geba
Gadora
Gophna
Lydda
Modi'in
Emmaus
Jabneh
Heshbon
Ashdod
Motza
Jerusalem
Medeba
Betar
Bethlehem
Ashkelon
Timnah
Herodium
Beth-govrin
Tekoa
Hebron
Salt Sea
Gaza
En-gedi
River Arnon
Kfar Azia
(Dead Sea)
Eshtemoa
Ma'on
Raphia
'Limes Palestinae'
Beersheba
0 25
km
A
B
1
2
3
4

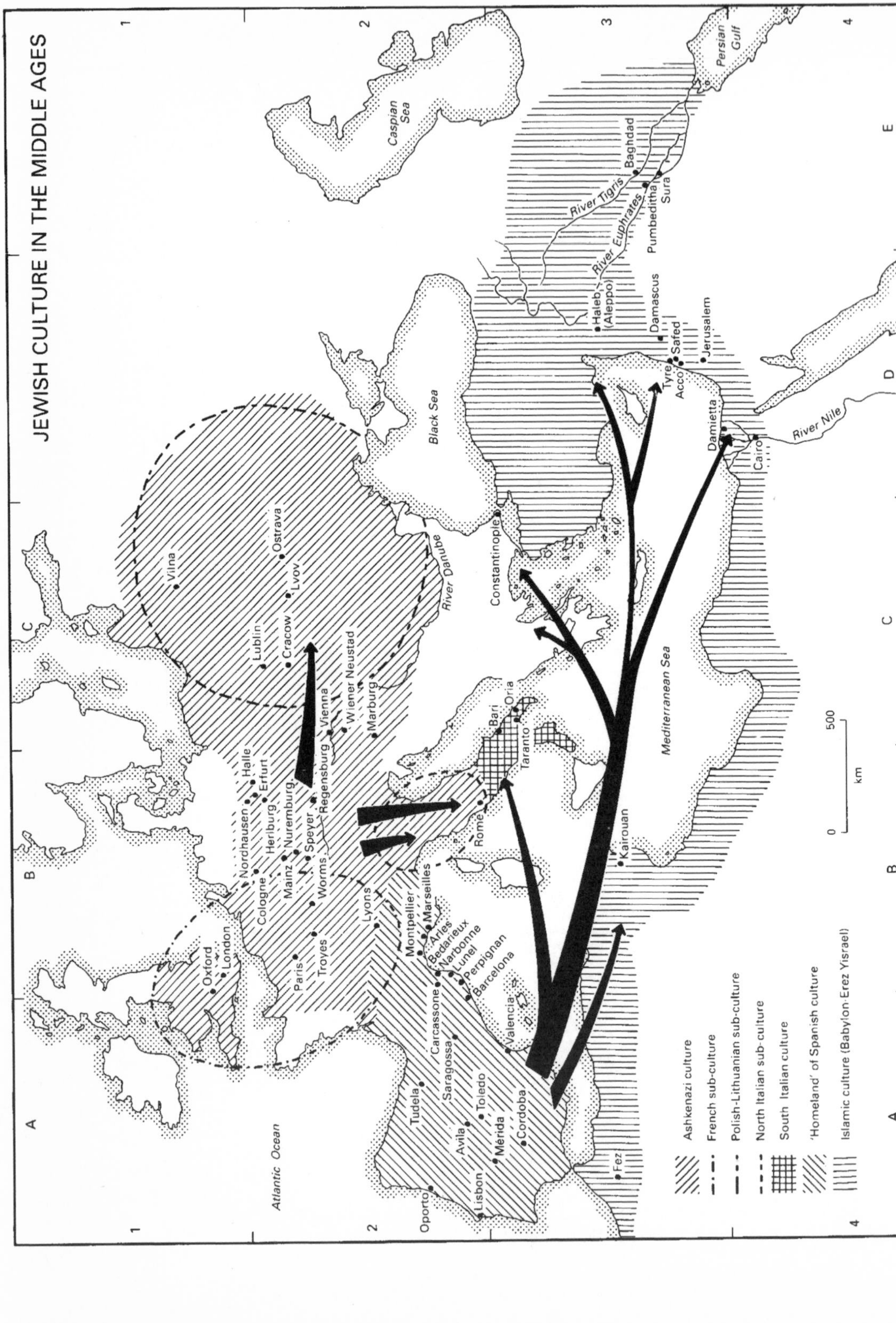
JEWISH CULTURE IN THE MIDDLE AGES
Ashkenazi culture
French sub-culture
Polish-Lithuanian sub-culture
North Italian sub-culture
South Italian culture
'Homeland' of Spanish culture
Islamic culture (Babylon-Erez Yisrael)
Atlantic Ocean
Mediterranean Sea
Black Sea
Caspian Sea
Persian Gulf
River Danube
River Nile
River Tigris
River Euphrates
0
500
km
Oxford
London
Paris
Troyes
Cologne
Mainz
Worms
Speyer
Nordhausen
Heriburg
Nuremburg
Regensburg
Halle
Erfurt
Vienna
Wiener Neustad
Marburg
Lublin
Cracow
Lvov
Ostrava
Vilna
Lyons
Montpellier
Marseilles
Arles
Bedarieux
Narbonne
Lunel
Perpignan
Barcelona
Carcassone
Saragossa
Tudela
Toledo
Avila
Merida
Cordoba
Valencia
Lisbon
Oporto
Fez
Kairouan
Rome
Bari
Oria
Taranto
Constantinople
Haleb (Aleppo)
Damascus
Tyre
Acco
Safed
Jerusalem
Damietta
Cairo
Baghdad
Pumbeditha
Sura
A
B
C
D
E
1
2
3
4

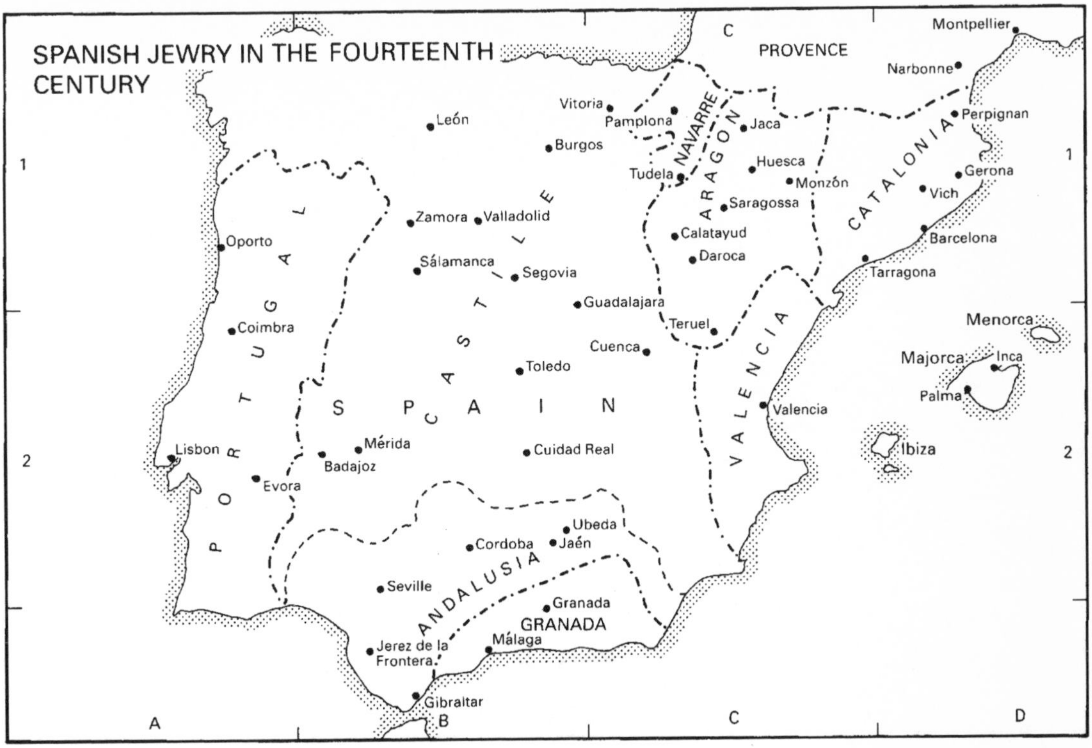
SPANISH JEWRY IN THE FOURTEENTH CENTURY
PROVENCE
Montpellier
Narbonne
Perpignan
Vitoria
Pamplona
NAVARRE
Jaca
León
Burgos
ARAGON
Huesca
Monzón
Tudela
CATALONIA
Gerona
Vich
Saragossa
Zamora
Valladolid
CASTILE
Oporto
Calatayud
Daroca
Barcelona
Tarragona
Sálamanca
Segovia
Guadalajara
PORTUGAL
Coimbra
Teruel
Menorca
Cuenca
Majorca
Inca
Toledo
Palma
SPAIN
Valencia
VALENCIA
Lisbon
Mérida
Badajoz
Cuidad Real
Ibiza
Evora
Ubeda
Cordoba
Jaén
ANDALUSIA
Seville
Granada
GRANADA
Jerez de la Frontera
Málaga
Gibraltar
A
B
C
D
1
2

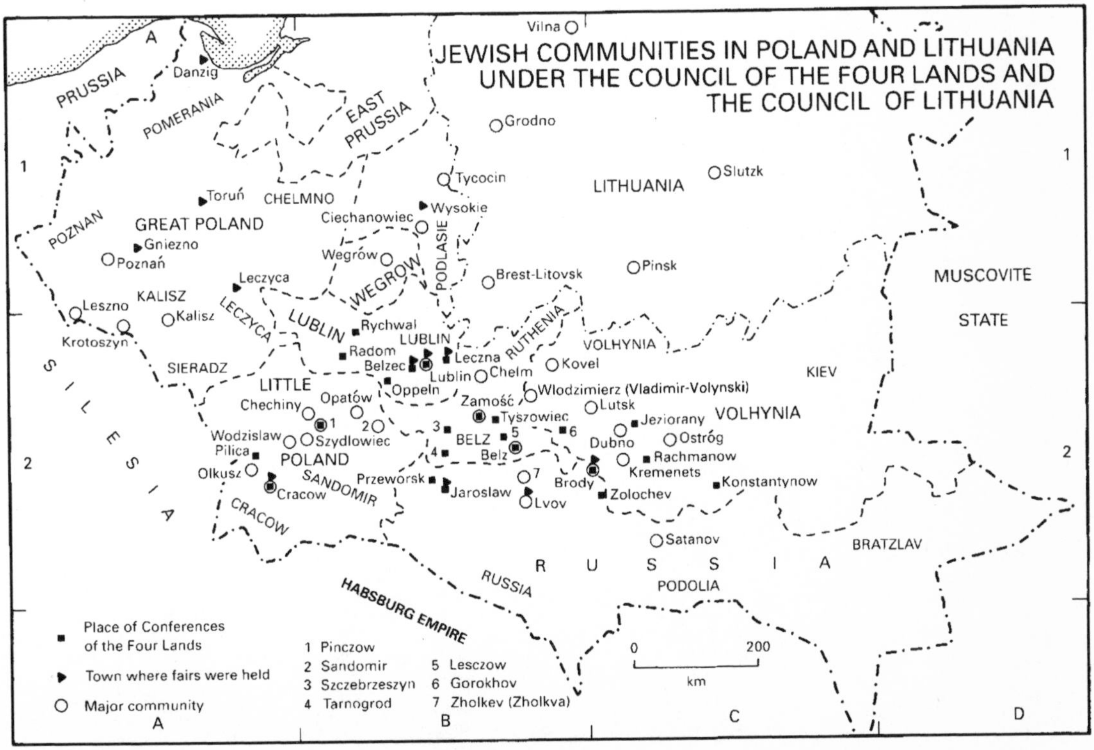
JEWISH COMMUNITIES IN POLAND AND LITHUANIA UNDER THE COUNCIL OF THE FOUR LANDS AND THE COUNCIL OF LITHUANIA
Vilna
Danzig
PRUSSIA
POMERANIA
EAST PRUSSIA
Grodno
Tycocin
LITHUANIA
Slutzk
Toruń
CHELMNO
Wysokie
GREAT POLAND
Ciechanowiec
POZNAN
PODLASIE
Gniezno
Poznań
Wegrów
WEGROW
Brest-Litovsk
Pinsk
MUSCOVITE STATE
Leczyca
KALISZ
Leszno
Kalisz
LECZYCA
LUBLIN
Rychwal
RUTHENIA
Krotoszyn
Radom
LUBLIN
VOLHYNIA
Leczna
Belzec
Kovel
SIERADZ
Lublin
Chelm
KIEV
SILESIA
LITTLE
Oppeln
Opatów
Zamość
Wlodzimierz (Vladimir-Volynski)
Chechiny
Lutsk
Tyszowiec
Jeziorany
VOLHYNIA
BELZ
Wodzislaw
Szydlowiec
Dubno
Ostróg
Pilica
Belz
POLAND
Rachmanow
Kremenets
Olkusz
SANDOMIR
Przeworsk
Brody
Konstantynow
Cracow
Jaroslaw
Lvov
Zolochev
CRACOW
Satanov
BRATZLAV
RUSSIA
RUSSIA
PODOLIA
HABSBURG EMPIRE
Place of Conferences of the Four Lands
Town where fairs were held
Major community
1 Pinczow
2 Sandomir
3 Szczebrzeszyn
4 Tarnogrod
5 Lesczow
6 Gorokhov
7 Zholkev (Zholkva)
0 200 km
A
B
C
D
1
2

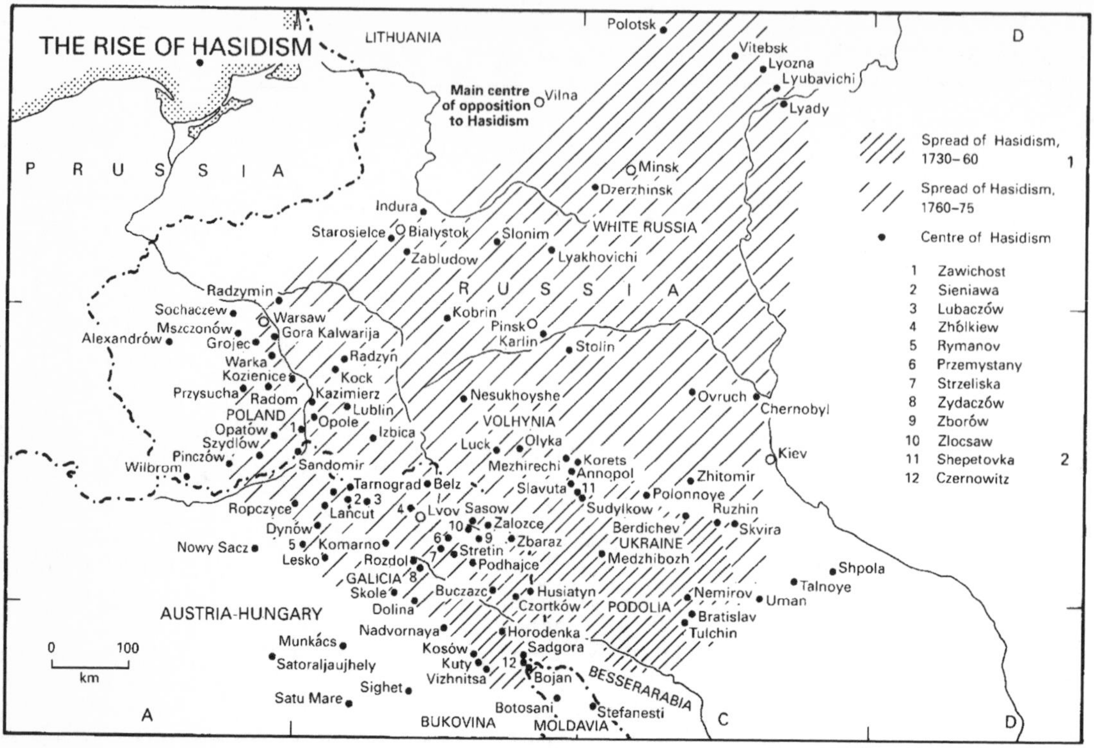
THE RISE OF HASIDISM
LITHUANIA
PRUSSIA
Main centre of opposition to Hasidism
Vilna
Polotsk
Vitebsk
Lyozna
Lyubavichi
Lyady
Minsk
Dzerzhinsk
WHITE RUSSIA
Indura
Starosielce
Bialystok
Zabludow
Slonim
Lyakhovichi
RUSSIA
Radzymin
Sochaczew
Warsaw
Mszczonów
Alexandrów
Grojec
Gora Kalwarija
Warka
Radzyn
Kozienice
Kock
Przysucha
Radom
Kazimierz
POLAND
Lublin
Opatów
Opole
Szydlów
Izbica
Pinczów
Wilbrom
Sandomir
Kobrin
Pinsk
Karlin
Stolin
Nesukhoyshe
VOLHYNIA
Luck
Olyka
Mezhirechi
Korets
Annopol
Slavuta
Ovruch
Chernobyl
Kiev
Zhitomir
Polonnoye
Sudylkow
Ruzhin
Skvira
Berdichev
UKRAINE
Medzhibozh
Tarnograd
Belz
Ropczyce
Lancut
Lvov
Sasow
Zalozce
Dynów
Zbaraz
Nowy Sacz
Komarno
Stretin
Lesko
Rozdol
Podhajce
GALICIA
Skole
Buczazc
Husiatyn
Czortków
Dolina
PODOLIA
Nemirov
Uman
Bratislav
Tulchin
Shpola
Talnoye
AUSTRIA-HUNGARY
Nadvornaya
Horodenka
Munkács
Kosów
Sadgora
Satoraljaujhely
Kuty
Vizhnitsa
Bojan
BESSERABIA
Sighet
Satu Mare
Botosani
Stefanesti
BUKOVINA
MOLDAVIA
0 100 km
Spread of Hasidism, 1730–60
Spread of Hasidism, 1760–75
Centre of Hasidism
1 Zawichost
2 Sieniawa
3 Lubaczów
4 Zhólkiew
5 Rymanov
6 Przemystany
7 Strzeliska
8 Zydaczów
9 Zborów
10 Zlocsaw
11 Shepetovka
12 Czernowitz

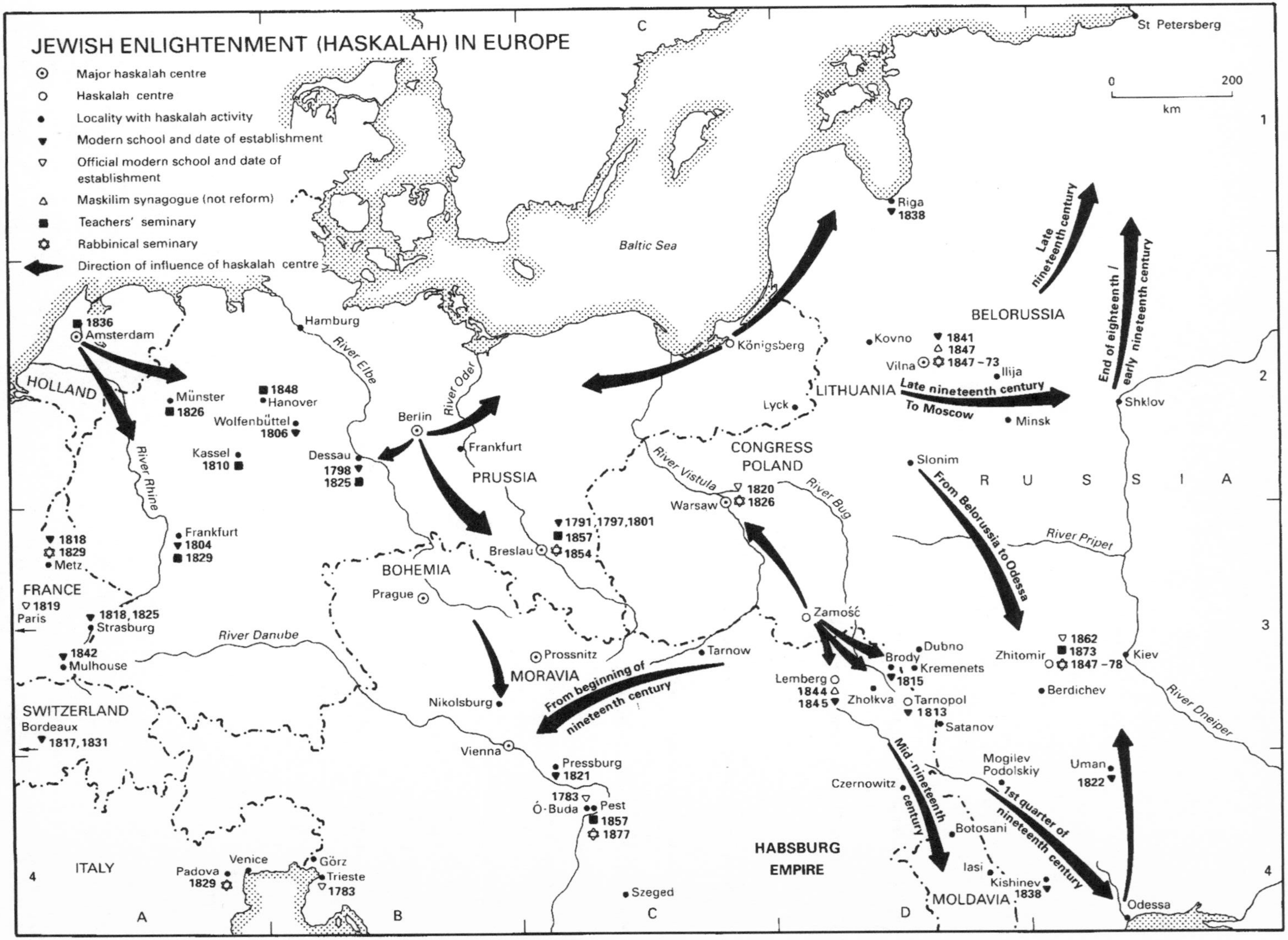
JEWISH ENLIGHTENMENT (HASKALAH) IN EUROPE
Major haskalah centre
Haskalah centre
Locality with haskalah activity
Modern school and date of establishment
Official modern school and date of establishment
Maskilim synagogue (not reform)
Teachers' seminary
Rabbinical seminary
Direction of influence of haskalah centre
0
200
km
Baltic Sea
St Petersberg
Riga 1838
Amsterdam 1836
HOLLAND
Hamburg
River Elbe
River Oder
Berlin
Frankfurt
Münster 1826
Hanover 1848
Wolfenbüttel 1806
Kassel 1810
Dessau 1798 1825
PRUSSIA
River Rhine
Frankfurt 1804 1829
Metz 1818 1829
FRANCE
Paris 1819
Strasburg 1818, 1825
Mulhouse 1842
SWITZERLAND
Bordeaux 1817, 1831
River Danube
BOHEMIA
Prague
Breslau 1791, 1797, 1801 1857 1854
Prossnitz
MORAVIA
Nikolsburg
Vienna
Pressburg 1821
Ó-Buda 1783
Pest 1857 1877
Szeged
ITALY
Padova 1829
Venice
Görz
Trieste 1783
Königsberg
Lyck
CONGRESS POLAND
River Vistula
Warsaw 1820 1826
River Bug
Tarnow
From beginning of nineteenth century
Zamość
Lemberg 1844 1845
Zholkva
Brody 1815
Dubno
Kremenets
Tarnopol 1813
Satanov
Czernowitz
Mid-nineteenth century
HABSBURG EMPIRE
Botosani
Iasi
Kishinev 1838
MOLDAVIA
Mogilev Podolskiy
1st quarter of nineteenth century
Odessa
Uman 1822
LITHUANIA
Kovno
Vilna 1841 1847 1847–73
Ilija
Late nineteenth century To Moscow
Minsk
BELORUSSIA
Late nineteenth century
End of eighteenth / early nineteenth century
Shklov
Slonim
From Belorussia to Odessa
RUSSIA
River Pripet
Zhitomir 1862 1873 1847–78
Berdichev
Kiev
River Dneiper
A
B
C
D
1
2
3
4

ADVISORS

Dr Glenda Abramson, University of Oxford

Professor Marc Ellis, Baylor University

Professor Menahem Kellner, University of Haifa

Professor Dovid Katz, University of Vilnius

Professor Oliver Leaman, University of Kentucky

Professor Norbert Samuelson, Arizona State University

PREFACE

Who are the Jews? This *Dictionary of Jewish Biography*, which contains brief accounts of nearly 4000 individuals, presents a wide range of Jewish figures – from talmudists to film stars, from poets to theologians, from novelists to kabbalists, from scientists to rabbinic sages – who have made a major contribution to the life and thought of the Jewish people, or who have played an important role in modern history. Until the period of the Enlightenment Jewish existence centred around the religious tradition: for this reason the majority of those included in this volume contributed to the religious life of the nation. However, with the destruction of ghetto existence in the 18th and 19th centuries, Jews were free to enter the mainstream of society. As a result, a significant number of Jews engaged in scientific activities, industry, art, sports, literature, business activities and politics – because of their importance, these persons are included as well. Throughout my intention is that this volume should provide the type of information most commonly sought by students and teachers as well as the general reader.

Any scholar working in Jewish studies owes an enormous debt to those lexicographers who have already published Jewish reference works. All of the following have been consulted in checking and cross-checking the information contained in this Dictionary: Geoffrey Wigoder, *The New Standard Jewish Encyclopedia* (London: W. H. Allen, 1977), *Jewish Encyclopedia* (New York: Funk and Wagnalls, 1901–5); *Encyclopedia Judaica* (Jerusalem: Keter, 1972–), Yacov Newman and Gavriel Sivan, *Judaism A–Z: Lexicon of Terms and Concepts* (Jerusalem: Department for Torah Education and Culture in the Diaspora of the World Zionist Organization, 1980); Raphael Jehudah Zwi Werblowsky and Geoffrey Wigoder, eds, *The Encyclopedia of Jewish Religion* (London: Phoenix House, 1967), Glenda Abrahamson, ed., *The Blackwell Companion to Jewish Culture* (Oxford: Blackwell, 1989), Geoffrey Wigoder, ed., *The Encyclopedia of Judaism* (New York: Macmillan, 1989); David Bridger and Samuel Wolk, eds, *The New Jewish Encyclopedia* (New York: Behrman House, 1976), Dan Cohn-Sherbok, *The Blackwell Dictionary of Judaica*, (Oxford: Blackwell, 1992), Joan Comay, *Who's Who in Jewish History* (London: Routledge, 2002). Geoffrey Wigoder, *Dictionary of Jewish Biography* (New York: Simon and Schuster, 1991).

The entries in this work are ordered alphabetically and in matters of orthography, terminology and punctuation the Dictionary generally follows British practice. An effort has been made to identify small places by naming a larger place nearby, or by locating it within a state or area. Where a place name has changed in the course of history, the name current at the time under discussion has been used. In article headings, the following abbreviations are used: b. = born; d. = died; fl. = flourished; c. = circa; cent. = century. The use of a question mark indicates uncertainty about the date or dates to which it is attached. Throughout the Dictionary BCE is used for dates before the year l, and CE for dates from the year 1 onward. Hebrew words have been transliterated generally according to the Sephardi pronunciation. For purposes of tracing entries in the Dictionary, readers should note that 'ḥ' (not 'ch') and 'ph' (not 'f') are used. Titles of works generally appear in italic type. All articles begin with a name, in inverted form; brackets are used for alternative names; bold for cross-references. Those included in this volume are either Jewish by birth or conversion, as well as those Jews who converted to another faith.

CHRONOLOGY

BCE

c. 1900–1600 Age of the Patriarchs
c. 1250–1230 Exodus from Egypt
c. 1200–1000 Period of the Judges
c. 1030–930 United Monarchy
1110–970 David
c. 930 Division of the Kingdom
c. 8th century **Amos, Hosea**
722 Destruction of the Northern Kingdom by the Assyrians
c. 7th century **Zephaniah, Jeremiah**
c. 6th century **Ezekiel, Second Isaiah, Haggai, Zerubbabel, Zechariah**
586 Destruction of the Southern Kingdom by the Babylonians
c. 586 Babylonian Exile begins
538 Return of the Exiles
c. 520–515 Rebuilding of the Temple in Jerusalem
c. 5th century **Malachi**
c. 450–400 **Ezra** and **Nehemiah**'s reforms
c. 450 End of prophecy
400–300 Greek domination
333–63 Hellenistic period
c. 200 Prophets given scriptural status
c. 2nd century **Daniel**
167–164 Hasmonean revolt
c. 146–400 CE Roman period
c. 100–200 CE Mishnaic period
20–50 CE **Philo**

CE

c. 50–90 New Testament
66–70 Jewish rebellion against Rome
70 Siege and destruction of Jerusalem and the Second Temple
132–5 **Bar Kokhba** revolt
c. 150 Hagiographa given scriptural status
c. 200 *Mishnah* compiled
c. 200–600 Talmudic period
c. 5th century Jerusalem *Talmud*
c. 6th century Babylonian *Talmud*
600–700 End of the Academies
700–800 Rise of Karaism
800–900 Conversion of Khazars to Judaism, Era of Karaite biblical scholars
c. 8th century Messianic Jewish movements
882–942 **Saadyah Gaon**
900–1000 Golden age of Spain
1021–56 **Solomon ibn Gabirol**
1040–1105 Rashi
1078–1141 **Judah ha-Levi**
1096 First Crusade
1100–1200 First example of blood libel, Era of the Ḥasidei Ashkenaz, Kabbalistic study in Provence
1135–1204 **Moses Maimondes**
1145–47 Second Crusade
1182–98 Expulsion of French Jews
1189–90 Third Crusade
1194–1270 **Naḥmanides**
c. 1230 Establishment of the Inquisition
1240 Disputation of Paris
1263 Disputation of Barcelona
c. 1286 Zohar
1288–1344 **Levi ben Gershon**
1290 Expulsion of Jews from England
1340–1412 **Ḥasdai Crescas**
1380–1445 **Joseph Albo**
1413–15 Disputation of Tortosa
1437–1508 **Isaac Abravanel**
1492 Expulsion of the Jews from Spain

1500–1600 Era of Safed mystics, Council of the Four Lands
1534–72 **Isaac Luria**
1542–1620 **Ḥayyim Vital**
1555 Ghetto in Italy
1600–1700 Chmielnicki massacres
1626–76 **Shabbetai Tzevi**
1650–1700 Golden age of Dutch Jewry
1700–1800 Rise of Ḥasidism, opposition of mitnaggedim
1700–60 Baal Shem Tov
1707–47 **Moses Ḥayyim Luzzatto**
1710–72 **Dov Baer of Mezhirech**
1726–86 **Jacob Frank**
1729–86 **Moses Mendelssohn**
1750–1800 Beginning of the Haskalah
1768–1828 **Israel Jacobson**
1772–1811 **Naḥman of Bratzlav**
1795–1874 **Tzevi Hirsch Kalischer**
1808–1874 **Samson Raphael Hirsch**
1810–1875 **Abraham Geiger**
1812–1875 **Moses Hess**
1821–1891 **Judah Loeb Pinsker**
1842–1918 **Hermann Cohen**
c. 1850 Reform Judaism founded
1856–1922 **Aaron David Gordon**
1860–1904 **Theodor Herzl**
1865–1935 **Avraham Yitzḥak Kook**
1873–1956 **Martin Buber**
1880–1940 **Vladimir Jabotinsky**
1880–1900 Pogroms in Russia, Dreyfus case, mass emigration to the USA
1881–1983 **Mordecai Kaplan**
c. 1895 Conservative Judaism founded
1897 First Zionist Congress
1900–20 Pogroms in Russia, mass emigration from Eastern Europe, Jewish settlement in Palestine
1902–44 **Menaḥem Mendel Schneersohn**
c. 1905 Modern Orthodoxy founded
1907–72 **Abraham Joshua Heschel**
1920–40 Emigration restrictions to Palestine, Western Europe and the USA, Rise of Nazism
c. 1935 Reconstructionist Judaism founded
1942–5 Holocaust
1948 Founding of the State of Israel
1965 Humanistic Judaism founded
1967 Six Day War
1973 Yom Kippur War
1982 Israeli advance into Southern Lebanon
1992 Labour Party under **Yitzḥak Rabin** wins election in Israel and engages in dialogue with the PLO
1996 **Benjamin Netanyahu** becomes Prime Minister of Israel
2001 **Ariel Sharon** elected Prime Minister of Israel

HISTORICAL BACKGROUND

Jews in the Ancient World

The history of the Jewish people began in Mesopotamia where successive empires of the ancient world flourished and decayed before the Jews emerged as a separate people. The culture of these civilizations had a profound impact on the Jewish religion – ancient Near Eastern myths were refashioned to serve the needs of the Hebrew people. It appears that the Jews emerged in this milieu as a nation between the 19th and 16th centuries BCE. According to the Bible, **Abraham** was the father of the Jewish people. Initially known as Abram, he came from Ur of the Chaldees. Together with his family he went to Haran and subsequently to Canaan, later settling in the plain near Hebron. Abraham was followed by **Isaac** and **Jacob**, whose son **Joseph** was sold into slavery in Egypt. There he prospered, becoming a vizier in the house of Pharaoh. Eventually the entire Hebrew clan moved to Egypt, where they remained and flourished for centuries until a new Pharaoh decreed that all male Hebrew babies should be put to death.

To persuade Pharaoh to let the Jewish people go, God sent a series of plagues upon the Egyptians. After this devastation **Moses**, the leader of the people, led his kinsfolk out of Egypt; after wandering in the desert for 40 years, the Hebrews finally entered into the land God had promised them. Under **Joshua**'s leadership, the Hebrews conquered the existing inhabitants. After Joshua's death the people began to form two separate groups. At first there were 12 tribes named after the sons of **Jacob**: **Joseph**, **Benjamin**, **Levi**, **Simeon**, **Reuben**, **Judah**, **Issachar**, **Zebulun**, **Dan**, **Naphtali**, **Gad** and **Asher**. When **Levi** became a special priestly group excluded from this territorial division, the tribe of **Joseph** was divided into two and named after this sons, **Ephraim** and **Manasseh**. During this period the Hebrews were ruled over by 12 national heroes who served successively as judges. In Scripture the sagas of the major judges (**Othniel**, **Ehud**, **Deborah**, **Gideon**, **Jephthah** and **Samson**) are recounted at length.

Frequently the Covenant between God and his chosen people – first formulated by **Moses** – was proclaimed at gatherings in such national shrines as Shechem. Such an emphasis on covenantal obligation reinforced the belief that the Jews were the recipients of God's loving kindness. Now in a more settled existence, the Covenant expanded to include additional legislation, including the provisions needed for an agricultural community. During this period it became increasingly clear to the Jewish nation that the God of the Covenant directed human history: the Exodus and the entry into the Promised Land were viewed as the unfolding of a divine plan.

Under the judges, God was conceived as the supreme monarch. When some tribes suggested to **Gideon** that he deserved a formal position of power, he declared that it was impossible for the nation to be ruled by both God and a human king. Nonetheless, **Saul** was subsequently elected as king despite the prophet **Samuel**'s warnings against the dangers of usurping God's rule. In later years the Israelite nation divided into two kingdoms. The northern tribes, led by Ephraim, and the southern tribes, led by Judah, had been united only by their allegiance to King **David**. But when his successor King **Solomon**, and his son **Rehoboam**, violated many of the ancient traditions, the northern tribes revolted. The reason they gave for this rebellion was the injustice of the monarchy, but in fact they sought to recapture the simple ways of the generation that had escaped from Egypt. Then there had been no monarch, and leadership was exercised on the basis of charisma. What the north looked for was allegiance and loyalty to the King of Kings, who had brought them from Egyptian bondage into the Promised Land. It is against this background that the pre-exilic prophets (**Elijah**, **Elisha**, **Amos**, **Hosea**, **Micah** and **Isaiah**) endeavoured to bring the nation back to the true worship of God. Righteousness, they declared, is the standard by which all people are to be judged, especially kings and rulers.

During the first millennium BCE the Jews watched their country emerge as a powerful state only to see it sink into spiritual and moral decay. Following the Babylonian conquest in 586 BCE the Temple lay in ruins, Jerusalem was demolished, and they despaired of their fate. This was God's punishment for their iniquity, which the prophets had predicted. Yet despite defeat and exile, the nation rose phoenix-like from the ashes of the old kingdoms. In the centuries which followed, the Jewish people continued their religious traditions and communal life. Though they had lost their independence, their devotion to God and his law sustained them through suffering and hardship and inspired them to new heights of creativity. In Babylonia the exiles flourished, keeping their religion alive in the synagogues. These institutions were founded so that Jews could meet together for worship and study; no sacrifices were offered since that was the prerogative of the Jerusalem Temple. When in 538 BCE King Cyrus of Persia permitted the Jews to return to their former home, the nation underwent a transformation. The Temple was rebuilt and religious reforms were enacted. This return to the land of their fathers led to national restoration and a renaissance of Jewish life which was to last until the first century CE.

The period following the death of King **Herod** in 4 BCE was a time of intense anti-Roman feeling among the Jewish population in Judea as well as in the diaspora. Eventually such hostility led to war, only to be followed by defeat and destruction, once again, of the Jerusalem Temple. In 70 CE, thousands of Jews were deported. Such devastation, however, did not quell the Jewish hope of ridding the Holy Land of its Roman oppressors. In the second century a messianic rebellion led by **Simeon Bar Kokhba** was crushed by Roman forces, who killed multitudes of Jews and decimated Judea. Yet despite this defeat, the Pharisees carried on the Jewish tradition through teaching and study at Javneh, near Jerusalem.

Rabbinic Judaism

From the first century BCE Palestinian rabbinic scholars engaged in the interpretation of Scripture. The most important scholar of the early rabbinic period was **Judah ha-Nasi**, the head of the Sanhedrin, whose main achievement was the redaction of the *Mishnah* (a compendium of the oral Torah) in the second century CE. This volume consisted of the discussions and rulings of sages whose teachings had been transmitted orally. According to the rabbis, the law recorded in the *Mishnah* was given orally to **Moses** along with the written law: 'Moses received the Torah from Sinai, and handed it down to Joshua, and Joshua to the elders, and elders to the prophets, and the prophets to the men of the Great Assembly.' This view recorded in the *Mishnah* implies that there was an infallible chain of transmission from **Moses** to the leaders of the nation and eventually to the Pharisees.

The *Mishnah* is an almost entirely legal document, consisting of six sections. The first section ('Seeds') begins with a discussion of benedictions and required prayers and continues with the other tractates dealing with various matters such as the tithes of the harvest to be given to the priests, Levites and the poor. The second section ('Set Feasts') contains 12 tractates dealing with the Sabbath, Passover, the Day of Atonement and other festivals as well as shekel dues and the proclamation of the New Year. In the third section ('Women') seven tractates consider matters affecting women, such as betrothal, marriage contracts and divorce. The fourth section ('Damages') contains ten tractates concerning civil law: property rights, legal procedures, compensation for damage, ownership of lost objects, treatment of employees, sale and purchase of land, Jewish courts, punishments and criminal proceedings. In addition a tractate of rabbinic moral maxims ('Sayings of the Fathers') is included in this section. In the fifth section ('Holy Things') there are 11 tractates on sacrificial offerings and other Temple matters. The final section ('Purifications') treats the various types of ritual uncleanliness and methods of legal purification. In addition to the

Mishnah, the rabbis engaged in the composition of scriptural commentaries. This literature (known as midrash) was written over centuries and is divided into works connected directly with the books of the Bible and those dealing with readings for special festivals as well as other topics.

The Sanhedrin, which had been so fundamental in the compilation of the *Mishnah*, met in several cities in Galilee, but later settled in the Roman district of Tiberius. Simultaneously other scholars established their own schools in other parts of the country where they applied the *Mishnah* to everyday life, together with old rabbinic teachings which had not been incorporated in the *Mishnah*. During the third century the Roman empire encountered numerous difficulties, including inflation, population decline and a lack of technological development to support the army. In addition, rival generals struggled against one another for power, and the government became increasingly inefficient. Throughout this time of upheaval, the Jewish community underwent a similar decline as a result of famine, epidemics and plunder.

At the end of the third century the emperor Diocletian inaugurated reforms that strengthened the empire. In addition, Diocletian introduced measures to repress the spread of Christianity which had become a serious challenge to the official religion of the empire. But Diocletian's successor, Constantine the Great, reversed his predecessor's hostile stance and extended official toleration to Christians. By this stage Christianity had succeeded in gaining a substantial number of adherents among the urban population; eventually Constantine became more involved in church affairs and just before his death he himself was baptized. The Christianization of the empire continued throughout the century and by the early 400s, Christianity was fully established as the state religion.

By the first half of the fourth century Jewish scholars in Israel had collected together the teachings of generations of rabbis in the academies of Tiberius, Caesarea and Sepphoris. These extended discussions of the *Mishnah* became the Palestinian *Talmud*. The text of this multi-volume work covered four sections of the *Mishnah* ('Seeds', 'Set Feasts', 'Women' and 'Damages'), but here and there various tractates were omitted. The views of these Palestinian teachers had an important influence on scholars in Babylonia, though this work never attained the same prominence as that of the Babylonian *Talmud*.

Paralleling the development of rabbinic Judaism in Palestine, Babylonian scholars founded centres of learning. The great third-century teacher **Rav** established an academy at Sura in central Mesopotamia; his contemporary **Samuel** was head of another Babylonian academy at Nehardea. After Nehardea was destroyed in an invasion in 259 CE, the school at Pumbedita also became a dominant Babylonian academy of Jewish learning. The Babylonian sages carried on and developed the Galilean tradition of disputation, and the fourth century produced two of the most distinguished scholars of the talmudic period, **Abbaye** and **Rava**, who both taught at Pumbedita. With the decline of Jewish institutions in Israel, Babylonia became the most important centre of Jewish scholarship.

By the sixth century Babylonian scholars completed the redaction of the Babylonian *Talmud* – an editorial task begun by Rav **Ashi** in the fourth to fifth century at Sura. This massive work parallels the Palestinian *Talmud* and is largely a summary of the rabbinic discussions that took place in the Babylonian academies. Both *Talmuds* are essentially elaborations of the *Mishnah*, though neither commentary contains material on every *Mishnah* passage. The text itself consists largely of summaries of rabbinic discussions: a phrase of the *Mishnah* is interpreted, discrepancies are resolved and redundancies are explained. In this compilation, conflicting opinions of the earlier scholars are contrasted, unusual words are explained and anonymous opinions are identified. Frequently individual teachers cite specific cases to support their views and hypothetical eventualities are examined to reach a solution on the discussion. Debates between outstanding scholars in one generation are often cited, as are differences of opinion between contemporary members of an academy or a teacher and his students. The range of talmudic exploration is much broader than that of the *Mishnah* itself and includes a wide range of rabbinic teachings about such subjects as theology, philosophy and ethics.

Judaism in the Middle Ages

By the sixth century the Jews had become largely a diaspora people. Despite the loss of a homeland, they were unified by a common heritage: law, liturgy and shared traditions bound together the scattered communities stretching from Spain to Persia and Poland to Africa. Though sub-cultures did form during the Middle Ages which could have divided the Jewish world, Jews remained united in their hope for messianic redemption, the restoration of the Holy Land, and the ingathering of the exiles. Living among Christians and Muslims, the Jewish community was reduced to a minority group and their marginal status resulted in repeated persecution. Though there were times of tolerance and creative activity, the threats of exile and death were always present in Jewish consciousness during this period.

Within the Islamic world, Jews along with Christians were recognized as 'Peoples of the Book' and were guaranteed religious toleration, judicial autonomy and exemption from the military. In turn they were required to accept the supremacy of the Islamic state. Such an arrangement was formally codified by the Pact of Omar dating from about 800. According to this treaty, Jews were restricted in a number of spheres: they were not allowed to build new houses of worship, make converts, carry weapons or ride horses. In addition, they were required to wear distinctive clothing and pay a yearly poll tax. Jewish farmers were also obliged to pay a land tax consisting of a portion of their produce. Despite these conditions, Jewish life prospered. In various urban centres many Jews were employed in crafts such as tanning, dyeing, weaving, silk manufacture and metal work; other Jews participated in interregional trade and established networks of agents and representatives.

During the first two centuries of Islamic rule under the Ummayad and Abbasid caliphates, Muslim leaders confirmed the authority of traditional Babylonian institutions. When the Arabs conquered Babylonia, they officially recognized the position of the exilarch who for centuries had been the ruler of Babylonian Jewry. By the Abbasid period, the exilarch shared his power with the heads of the rabbinical academies which had for centuries been the major centres of rabbinic learning. The head of each academy was known as the gaon, who delivered lectures as well as learned opinions on legal matters.

During the eighth century messianic movements appeared in the Persian Jewish community which led to armed uprisings against Muslim authorities. Such revolts were quickly crushed, but an even more serious threat to traditional Jewish life was posed later in the century by the emergence of an anti-rabbinic sect, the Karaites. This group was founded in Babylonia in the 760s by **Anan ben David**. The guiding interpretative principle formulated by Anan, 'Search thoroughly in Scripture and do not rely on my opinion', was intended to point to Scripture itself as the source of law. After the death of the founder, new parties within the Karaite movement soon emerged, and by the tenth century Karaite communities were established in Israel, Iraq and Persia. The growth of Karaism provoked the rabbis to attack it as a heretical movement since these various groups rejected rabbinic law and formulated their own legislation.

By the eighth century the Muslim empire began to undergo a process of disintegration; this process was accompanied by a decentralization of rabbinic Judaism. The academies of Babylonia began to lose their hold on the Jewish scholarly world, and in many places rabbinic schools were established in which rabbinic sources were studied. The growth of these local centres of scholarship enabled individual teachers to exert their influence on Jewish learning independent of the academies of Sura and Pumbedita. In the Holy Land, Tiberias was the location of an important rabbinical academy as well as the centre of the masoretic scholars who produced the standard text of the Bible. In Egypt Kairouan and Fez became centres of scholarship. But it was in Spain that the Jewish community attained the greatest level of achievement in literature, philosophy, theology and mysticism.

In their campaigns the Muslims did not manage to conquer all of Europe – many countries remained under Christian rule, as did much of the Byzantine empire. In Christian Europe Jewish study took place in a number of important towns such as Mainz and Worms in the Rhineland and Troyes and Sens in northern France. In such an environment the study of the *Talmud* reached great heights: in Germany and northern France scholars known as 'the tosafists' utilized new methods of talmudic interpretation. In addition, Ashkenazic Jews of this period composed religious poetry modelled on the liturgical compositions of fifth and sixth-century Israel.

Despite such an efflorescence of Jewish life, the expulsion of the Jews from countries in which they lived became a dominant policy of Christian

Europe. In 1182 the king of France expelled all Jews from the royal domains near Paris, cancelled nearly all Christian debts to Jewish moneylenders, and confiscated Jewish property. Though the Jews were recalled in 1198, they were burdened with an additional royal tax and in the next century they increasingly became the property of the king. In 13th-century England the Jews were continuously taxed and the entire Jewish population was expelled in 1290, as was that in France some years later. At the end of the 13th century the German Jewish community suffered violent attack. In the next century Jews were blamed for bringing about the Black Death by poisoning the wells of Europe, and from 1348–9 Jews in France, Switzerland, Germany and Belgium suffered at the hands of their Christian neighbours. In the following two centuries Jewish massacre and expulsion became a frequent occurrence. Prominent Spanish Jewish thinkers of this period were **Solomon ibn Gabirol**, **Baḥya ibn Pakuda**, **Judah ha-Levi**, **Moses Maimonides**, **Ḥasdai Crescas**, and **Joseph Albo**. During this period the major mystical work of Spanish Jewry, the Zohar, was composed by Moses ben Shem Tov de León.

Jewry in the Early Modern Period

By the end of the fourteenth century political instability in Christian Europe led to the massacre of many Jewish communities in Castile and Aragon. Fearing for their lives, thousands of Jews converted to Christianity in 1391. Two decades later Spanish rulers introduced the Castilian laws which segregated Jews from their Christian neighbours. In the following year a public disputation was held in Tortosa about the doctrine of the Messiah; as a result increased pressure was applied to the Jewish population to convert. Those who became apostates (marranos) found life much easier, but by the 15th century, anti-Jewish sentiment again became a serious problem. In 1480 King Ferdinand and Queen Isabella established the Inquisition to determine whether former Jews practised Judaism in secret. In the late 1480s inquisitors used torture to extract confessions, and in 1492 the entire Jewish community was expelled from Spain. In the next century the Inquisition was established in Portugal.

To escape such persecution many Spanish and Portuguese marranos sought refuge in various parts of the Ottoman empire. Some of these Sephardic immigrants prospered and became part of the Ottoman court, such as **Gracia Nasi** and her nephew **Joseph Nasi**. Prominent among the rabbinic scholars of this period was **Joseph Caro** who emigrated from Spain to the Balkans. In the 1520s he commenced a study of Jewish law, *The House of Joseph*, based on previous codes of Jewish law. In addition he composed a shorter work, the Shulḥan Arukh, which became the authoritative code of law in the Jewish world.

While working on the *Shulḥan Arukh*, Caro emigrated to Safed in Israel which had become a major centre of Jewish religious life. In the 16th century this small community had grown to a population of over 10,000 Jews. Here talmudic academies were established and small groups engaged in the study of kabbalistic literature as they piously awaited the coming of the Messiah. In this centre of kabbalistic activity one of the greatest mystics of Safed, **Moses Cordovero**, collected, organized and interpreted the teachings of earlier mystical authors. Later in the 16th century kabbalistic speculation was transformed by the greatest mystic of Safed, **Isaac Luria**.

By the beginning of the 17th century Lurianic mysticism had made an important impact on Sephardic Jewry, and messianic expectations had also become a central feature of Jewish life. In this milieu the arrival of self-proclaimed messianic-king, **Shabbetai Tzevi**, brought about a transformation of Jewish life and thought. After living in various cities, he travelled to Gaza where he encountered **Nathan of Gaza** who believed he was the Messiah. In 1665 his messiahship was proclaimed and Nathan sent letters to Jews in the diaspora asking them to recognize **Shabbetai Tzevi** as their redeemer. In the following year **Shabbetai** journeyed to Constantinople, but on the order of the grand vizier he was arrested and put into prison. Eventually he was brought to court and given the choice between conversion and death. In the face of this alternative he converted to Islam. Such an act of apostasy scandalized most of his followers, but others continued to revere him as the Messiah. In the following century the most important Shabbetaian sect was led by **Jacob Frank** who believed himself to be the incarnation of **Shabbetai**.

During this period Poland had become a great centre of scholarship. In Polish academies scholars collected together the legal interpretation of previous authorities and composed commentaries on the *Shulḥan Arukh.* To regulate Jewish life in the country at large Polish Jews established regional federations that administered Jewish affairs. In the midst of this general prosperity, the Polish Jewish community was subject to a series of massacres carried out by the Cossacks of the Ukraine, Crimean Tartars and Ukrainian peasants. In 1648 Bogdan Chmielnicki was elected hetman of the Cossacks and instigated an insurrection against the Polish gentry. As administrators of noblemen's estates, Jews were slaughtered in these revolts.

As the century progressed, Jewish life in Poland became increasingly more insecure due to political instability; nonetheless the Jewish community increased in size considerably during the 18th century. In the 1730s and 1740s Cossacks known as Haidemaks invaded the Ukraine, robbing and murdering Jewish inhabitants, and finally butchering the Jewish community of Uman in 1768. In Lithuania on the other hand, Jewish life flourished and Vilna became an important centre of Jewish learning. Here **Elijah ben Solomon Zalman**, referred to as the Vilna Gaon, lectured to disciples on a wide range of subjects and composed commentaries on rabbinic sources.

Elsewhere in Europe this period witnessed Jewish persecution and oppression. Despite the positive contact between Italian humanists and Jews, Christian anti-Semitism frequently led to persecution and suffering. In the 16th century the Counter-Reformation Church attempted to isolate the Jewish community. The *Talmud* was burned in 1553, and two years later Pope Paul IV reinstated the segregationist edict of the Fourth Lateran Council, forcing Jews to live in ghettos and barring them from most areas of economic life. In addition, marranos who took up the Jewish tradition were burned at the stake, and Jews were expelled from most church domains.

In Germany the growth of Protestantism frequently led to adverse conditions for the Jewish population. Though Martin Luther was initially well-disposed to the Jews, he soon came to realize that the Jewish community was intent on remaining true to its faith. As a consequence he composed a virulent attack on the Jews. Nonetheless some Jews, known as Court Jews, attained positions of great importance among the German nobility. A number of these favoured individuals were appointed by the rulers as chief elders of the Jewish community and acted as spokesmen and defenders of German Jewry.

In Holland some Jews had also attained an important influence on trade and finance. By the mid-17th century both marranos and Ashkenazi Jews came to Amsterdam and established themselves in various areas of economic activity. By the end of the century there were nearly 10,000 Jews in Amsterdam; there the Jewish community was employed on the stock exchange, in the sugar, tobacco and diamond trades, and in insurance, manufacturing, printing and banking. In this milieu Jewish cultural activity flourished: Jewish writers published works of drama, theology and mystical lore. Though Jews in Holland were not granted full rights as citizens, they nevertheless enjoyed religious freedom, personal protection and the liberty of participating in a wide range of economic affairs.

Jews in the Modern World

By the middle of the 18th century the Jewish community had suffered numerous waves of persecution and was deeply dispirited by the conversion of the 17th-century false messiah **Shabbetai Tzevi.** In this environment the Ḥasidic movement – grounded in kabbalah – sought to revitalize Jewish life. The founder of this new sect was Israel ben Eleazer, known as the **Baal Shem Tov** (Besht). Born in southern Poland, he travelled to Medzibozh in Polodia, Russia in the 1730s, where he performed various miracles and instructed his disciples in kabbalistic lore. By the 1740s he attracted a considerable number of disciples who passed on his teaching. After his death, **Dov Baer of Mezhirich** became the leader of his sect and Ḥasidism spread to southern Poland, the Ukraine and Lithuania. The growth of this movement engendered considerable hostility on the part of rabbinic authorities, and by the end of the century the Jewish religious establishment of Vilna denounced Ḥasidism to the Russian government.

During the latter part of the century the treatment of Jews in central Europe greatly improved due to the influence of Christian polemicists who argued that Jewish life should be improved. The Holy Roman Emperor Joseph II embraced such views; he abolished the Jewish badge as well as taxes imposed on Jewish travellers and proclaimed an edict of toleration which granted the Jews numerous rights. As in Germany, reformers in France during the 1770s and 1780s ameliorated the situation of the Jewish population. In 1789 the National Assembly issued a declaration stating that all human beings are born and remain free and equal and that no person should be persecuted for his opinions as long as they do not subvert civil law. In 1791 a resolution was passed which bestowed citizenship rights on all Jews. This change in Jewish status occurred elsewhere in Europe as well – in 1796 the Dutch Jews of the Batvian republic were granted full citizenship rights, and in 1797 the ghettos of Padua and Rome were abolished.

In 1799 Napoleon became the First Consul of France and five years later he was proclaimed Emperor. Napoleon's Code of Civil Law propounded in 1804 established the right of all individuals to follow any trade and declared equality for all. After 1806 a number of German principalities were united in the French kingdom of Westphalia, where Jews were granted equal rights. In the same year Napoleon convened an Assembly of Jewish notables to consider a series of religious issues.

In the following year he summoned a Grand Sanhedrin consisting of rabbis and laymen to confirm the views of the Assembly. This body pledged its allegiance to the emperor and nullified any features of the Jewish tradition that conflicted with the particular requirements of citizenship.

After Napoleon's defeat and abdication, the map of Europe was redrawn by the Congress of Vienna between 1814–15, and in addition the diplomats at the Congress issued a resolution that instructed the German confederation to improve the status of the Jews. Yet despite this decree the German governments disowned the rights of equality that had previously been granted to Jews by the French. In 1830, however, a more liberal attitude prevailed, and various nations advocated a more tolerant approach. The French Revolution in 1848 which led to outbreaks in Prussia, Austria, Hungary, Italy and Bohemia forced rulers to grant constitutions which guaranteed freedom of speech, assembly and religion.

Within this environment Jewish emancipation gathered force. At the end of the 18th century the Jewish philosopher **Moses Mendelssohn** advocated the modernization of Jewish life, and to further this advance he translated the Torah into German so that Jews would be able to speak the language of the country in which they lived. Following **Mendelssohn**'s example a number of Prussian followers, known as maskilim, fostered a Jewish Enlightenment – the Haskalah – which encouraged Jews to abandon medieval forms of life and thought. By the 1820s the centre of this movement shifted to the Austrian empire, where journals propounding the ideas of the Enlightenment were published. In the 1840s the Haskalah spread to Russia where writers made important contributions to Hebrew literature and translated textbooks and European fiction into Hebrew.

Paralleling this development, reformers encouraged the modernization of the Jewish liturgy and the reform of Jewish education. At the beginning of the 19th century the Jewish financier and communal leader **Israel Jacobson** initiated a programme of reform. In 1801 he founded a boarding school for boys in Seesen, Westphalia, and later created other schools throughout the kingdom. In these new foundations general subjects were taught by Christian teachers while a Jewish instructor gave lessons about Judaism. Subsequently, **Jacobson** built a Reform Temple next to the school and another in Hamburg. Although such changes were denounced by the Orthodox establishment, Reform Judaism spread throughout Europe. In 1844 the first Reform Synod took place in Brunswick; this consultation was followed by another conference in 1845 in Frankfurt. At this gathering one of the more conservative rabbis, **Zacharias Frankel**, expressed dissatisfaction with progressive reforms to Jewish worship, and resigned from the Assembly, establishing a Jewish theological seminary in Breslau. In 1846 a third Synod took place in Breslau, but the Revolution and its aftermath brought about the cessation of these activities until 1868 when another Synod took pace at Cassel.

In the United States, Reform Judaism had also become an important feature of Jewish life. The most prominent of the early reformers was **Isaac Mayer Wise** who came from Bavaria to Albany, New York, in 1846. Later he went to Cincinnati, Ohio, where he published a new Reform prayerbook as well as several Jewish newspapers. In addition he attempted to convene a Reform Synod. In 1869 the first conference of the Central Conference of American Rabbis was held in Philadelphia; this was followed in 1873 by the founding of the Union of American Hebrew Congregations. Two years later the Hebrew Union College was established to train rabbinical students for Reform congregations. In 1885 a conference of Reform rabbis met in Pittsburgh, which produced a formal list of principles, the Pittsburgh Platform.

In Eastern Europe conditions were less conducive to emancipation. In 1804 Alexander I specified territory in western Poland as an area in which Jews would be allowed to reside (the Pale of Settlement). After several attempts to expel Jews from the countryside, the tsar in 1817 initiated a new policy of integrating the Jewish community into the population by founding a society of Israelite Christians which extended legal and financial concessions to baptized Jews. In 1824 the deportation of Jews from villages began. In the same year Alexander I died and was succeeded by Nicholas I who adopted a severe attitude to the Jewish commmunity. In 1827 he initiated a policy of inducting Jewish boys into the Russian army for a 25-year period to increase the number of converts to Christianity. Nicholas I also deported Jews from villages in certain areas. In 1844 the tsar abolished the kehillot (Jewish commual bodies) and put Jewry under the authority of the police as well as municipal government. Between 1850 and 1851 the government attempted to forbid Jewish dress, men's sidecurls, and the ritual shaving of women's hair. After the Crimean War of 1853–6 Alexander II emancipated the serfs, modernized the judiciary and established a system of local self-government. In addition he allowed certain groups to reside outside the Pale of Settlement. As a result Jewish communities appeared in St Petersburg and Moscow. Furthermore a limited numbers of Jews were allowed to enter the legal profession and participate in local government.

Jews in the 20th and 21st Centuries

After the pogroms of 1881–2 many Jews emigrated to the United States, but a significant number were drawn to Palestine. By the late 1880s the idea of a Jewish homeland had spread throughout Europe. At the first Zionist Congress at Basle in 1887 **Theodor Herzl** called for a national home based on international law. After establishing the basic institutions of the Zionist movement, **Herzl** embarked on a range of diplomatic negotiations. At the beginning of the 20th century a sizeable number of Jews had emigrated to Palestine. After World War I Jews in Palestine organized a National Assembly and Executive Council. By 1929 the Jewish community numbered 160,000 with 110 agricultural settlements. In the next ten years the population increased to 500,000 with 223 agricultural communities. About a quarter of this population lived in co-operatives. Tel Aviv had 150,000 settlers, Jerusalem 90,000 and Haifa 60,000. Industrialization was initiated by the Palestinian Electric Corporation and developed by the Histadrut. In 1925 the Hebrew University was opened. During this period Palestine was 160 miles long and 70 miles wide; its population was composed of about one million Arabs consisting of peasants and a number of landowners, in addition to the Jewish population. In 1929 the Arab community rioted following a dispute concerning Jewish access to the Western Wall of the ancient Temple. This conflict caused the British to curtail Jewish immigration as well as the purchase of Arab land.

By the 1920s Labour Zionism had become the dominant force in Palestinian Jewish life; in 1930 various socialist and Labour groups joined together in the Israel Labour Party. Within the Zionist movement a right-wing segment criticized the President of the World Zionist Organization, **Chaim Weizmann**, who was committed to co-operation with the British. **Vladimir Jabotinsky**, leader of the Union of Zionist Revisionists, stressed that the central aim of the Zionist movement was the establishment of an independent state in the whole of Palestine. At several Zionist Congresses, the Revisionists founded their own organization and withdrew from the militia of the Haganah to form their own military force. In 1936 the Arabs, supported by Syria, Iraq and Egypt, launched an offensive against Jews, the British, and moderate Arabs. In 1937 a British royal commission proposed that Palestine be partitioned into a Jewish and Arab state with a British zone; this recommendation was accepted by Zionists but rejected by the Arabs. Eventually the British government published a White Paper in 1939 which rejected the concept of partition, limited Jewish immigration to 75,000 and decreed that Palestine would become independent in ten years.

As these events unfolded in the Middle East, Jews in Germany were confronted by increasing hostility, amounting to antipathy. Once the Nazis gained control of the government, they curtailed civil liberties. In 1935 the Nuremburg Laws made Jews into second-class citizens, and all intermarriage and sexual liaisons between Jews and non-Jews were described as crimes against the state. In 1938 Jewish community leaders were put under the control of the Gestapo, and Jews were forced to register their property. From 9 to 10 November of that year, the Nazi party organized an onslaught against the Jewish population in which Jews were killed and Jewish property destroyed. This event, known as Kristallnacht, was a prelude to the Holocaust and precipitated the next stage of hostility.

The first stage of Hitler's plan for European Jewry had already begun with the invasion of Poland. In September 1939 Hitler decided to incorporate much of Poland into Germany, and more than 600,000 Jews were gathered into a large area in Poland. When the Jewish population was ghettoized into what Hitler referred to as a huge Polish labour camp, a massive work programme was initiated. Jews worked all day, seven days a week, dressed in rags and fed on bread, soup and potatoes. Officially, these workers had no names, only numbers tattooed on their bodies; if one died, a replacement was sought without any inquest into the cause of death.

With the invasion of Russia in 1941 the Nazis used mobile killing battalions of 500–900 men (Einsatzgruppen) to destroy Russian Jewry. Throughout the country these units moved into Russian towns, sought out the rabbi or Jewish court and obtained a list of all Jewish inhabitants. The Jews were then rounded up in market places, crowded into trains, buses and trucks and taken to woods where graves had been dug. They were then machine-gunned to death. Other methods were also employed by the Nazis. Mobile gas units were supplied to the Einsatzgruppen. Meanwhile these mobile killing operations were being supplanted by the development of fixed centres – the death camps. The six major death camps constituted the major areas of killing. Over 2,000,000 died at Auschwitz; 1,380,000 at Majdanek; 800,000 at Treblinka; 600,000 at Belzec; 340,000 at Chelmno and 250,000 at Sobibor.

Despite acts of resistance against the Nazis such as occurred in 1942 in Warsaw, 6,000,000 Jews died in this onslaught. In Poland more than 90 per cent of Jews were killed. The same percentage of the Jewish population died in the Baltic states, Germany and Austria. More than 70 per cent were murdered in the Bohemian protectorate, Slovakia, Greece and the Netherlands. More than 50 per cent were killed in White Russia, the Ukraine, Belgium, Yugoslavia and Norway.

During the war and afterwards, the British prevented illegal immigrants from entering the Holy Land. Campaigning against the policy, in 1946 the Haganah blew up the King David Hotel in Jerusalem, where part of the British administration was housed. Later in the same year the British Foreign Secretary, Ernest Bevin, handed over the Palestinian problem to the United Nations.

On 29 November 1947 the General Assembly of the United Naitons endorsed a plan of partition. Once this proposal was endorsed, the Arabs attacked Jewish settlements. In March 1948 David Ben-Gurion read out the Scroll of Independence of the Jewish state. Immediately a government was formed, the Arabs stepped up their assault. Following the War of Independence, armistice talks were held and later signed with Egypt, the Lebanon, Transjordan and Syria. Later President Gamal Abdel Nasser refused to allow Israeli ships to cross to the Gulf of Aqaba in 1956, and siezed the Suez Canal, and formed a pact with Saudi Arabia and various Arab states. In response Israel launched a strike conquering Sinai and opening the sea route to Aqaba. In 1967 Nasser began another offensive against Israel which resulted in the Six Day War in which Israel emerged victorious. This was followed by another, the Yom Kippur War in 1973, and in the 1980s by an Israeli offensive against the Palestinian Liberation Organization in Southern Lebanon in 1982.

In 1985 the Palestinian Intifada began in Israeli-occupied Gaza and the West Bank. Several years later Israel engaged with the PLO in dialogue, however, Prime Minister **Yitzḥak Rabin** was assassinated in 1995. In the ensuing years **Benjamin Netanyahu** was elected Prime Minister, followed by **Ariel Sharon**, and Palestinians engaged in suicide bombings of Israel despite Israel's determination to construct a wall to protect the country from attack.

GLOSSARY

Aggadah: Rabbinic teaching which amplifies the biblical narrative
Agudah: International organization of Orthodox Jews
Aḥdut ha-Avodah: Israeli Socialist Party
Amora: Palestinian sage (200–500 CE)
Apocrypha: Non-canonical writings from the Second Temple period
Ashkenazim: Eastern European Jews
Av bet din: Head of a rabbinic court
Avot: Sayings of the Fathers
Baraitot: Tannaitic sayings not contained in the *Mishnah*
Bet Din: Rabbinic court
Bet Midrash: House of study
B'nai B'rith: International Jewish service organization
Bund: Jewish socialist party
Cantor: Official in charge of music in the synagogue
Dayyan: Rabbinic judge
Derash: Rabbinic commentary on Scripture
Dybbuk: Evil spirit
Essenes: Jewish ascetic sect living by the Dead Sea during the Hellenistic period
Ethnarch: Ruler of a people
Exilarch: Head of the Jewish community in Babylonia
Gaon: Head of a Babylonian academy
Gemara: *Talmud*
Genizah: Place for storing old sacred books
Ghetto: Residential area where Jews were confined
Ḥabad: Hasidic movement
Hadassah: Women's Zionist Organization
Haganah: Israeli defence force
Haggadah: Passover prayerbook
Hakham: Wise person
Halakhah: Jewish law
Hannukah: Festival of Lights
Ha-Poel ha-Tzair: Religious Zionist labour movement
Ḥasidism: Mystical Jewish movement founded in the 18th century
Haskalah: Jewish Enlightenment
Hasmoneans: Priestly dynasty founded in the 2nd century BCE
Ḥeder: Jewish primary school
Herem: Excommunication
Herut: Israeli political party founded by the Irgun Tzevai Leumi
Hevra Kaddisha: Burial society
Ḥibbat Zion: International Zionist movement
Histadrut: Israeli federation of trade unions
Hovevei Zion: Early Zionist organization
ICA: Jewish Colonization Association
Irgun Tzevai Leumi: Revisionist party
Jewish Agency: Executive body of the World Zionist Organization
Kabbalah: Jewish mysticism
Karaism: Anti-rabbinic movement
Kashrut: Laws concerning ritually fit food
Kehillah: Jewish communal body
Knesset: Israeli parliament
Kollel: Advanced rabbinical academy
Likud: Israeli right-wing party
Maggid: Popular preacher
Mahzor: Festival prayerbook
Mapai: Israeli labour party
Marrano: Jews who converted to Christianity (Spain and Portugal)
Maskil: Follower of the Jewish Enlightenment
Masorah: Rules developed by 6th–9th century scholars (Masoretes) to preserve the biblical text

Merkavah: Divine chariot
Midrash: Rabbinic commentary on Scripture
Mishnah: Compendium of oral law compiled by Judah ha-Nasi at the end of the second century
Mitnaggedim: Rabbinic opponents of Ḥasidism
Mizraḥi: Religious Zionist organization
More Judaico: Jewish oath
Moshavim: Agricultural villages
Musar: Movement of return to traditional ethics
Nagid: Head of Jewish community in Islamic lands
Nasi: President of the Sanhedrin
Neoplatonism: Hellenistic philosophical system
Novellae: Commentaries on the *Talmud* and later rabbinic literature
Oral law: Interpretation of the written Torah
ORT: Society for the Encouragement of Handicraft
Palmaḥ: Mobilized striking force of the Haganah
Pardes: Paradise
Paytan: Liturgical Hebrew poet
Peshat: Basic type of scriptural interpretation
Pseudepigrapha: Jewish religious literature written between the 2nd century BCE and the 2nd century CE
Pharisees: Sect of the Hellenistic period
Pilpul: Interpretation of the oral law based on dialectical reasoning
Piyyutim: Hymns
Poale Zion: Socialist Zionist movement
Purim: Festival commemorating the rescue of Jewry through the mediation of Esther
Rabbanites: Name given by the Karaites to their political opponents
Responsa: Answers to specific legal questions
Revisionists: Zionist political movement founded by Vladimir Jabotinsky
Rosh Ha-Shanah: New Year
Rosh Yeshivah: Head of a Yeshviah
Sabbateans: Followers of Shabbetai Tzevi
Sadducees: Hellenistic sect
Sanhedrin: Assembly of 71 rabbinic scholars which acted as supreme court and legislature
Semikah: Rabbinic ordination
Sephardim: Jews originating in Spain or North Africa
Sepher Torah: Torah scroll
Sepher Yetzirah: Mystical tract
Sephirot: Divine emanations
Sevoraim: Babylonian scholars
Shulḥan Arukh: Code of Jewish law
Shtetl: Jewish village in Eastern Europe
Siddur: Jewish prayerbook
Takkanot: Regulations which supplement the laws in the Torah
Talmud: Compilation of the legal discussions based on the *Mishnah*
Tanna: Jewish sage (70–200 CE)
Targum: Aramaic translation of the Bible
Tetrarch: Subordinate ruler
Torah: Five books of Moses
Tzaddik: Spiritual leader
WIZO: Women's Internationalist Zionist Organization
Written law: Law contained in the Torah
Yeshivah: Rabbinical academy
Yiddish: Language spoken by Ashkenazi Jews from the Middle Ages
Yishuv: Jewish community in Israel
YIVO: Yiddish Scientific Institute
Yom Kippur: Day of Atonement
Zealots: Jewish political party active during the Second Temple period
Zionism: Movement for a Jewish homeland in Israel
Zohar: Medieval mystical text
Zugot: Pairs of Palestinian sages

LIST OF ENTRIES

Baruch of Tulchin **see** Baruch of Medzibozh
Bar-Yehudah, Eliezer (1858–1922)
Barzillai (fl. 11th–10th BCE)
Basch, Victor (1863–1944)
Bashyazi, Elijah (1420–90)
Basir ha-Roeh **see** Basir, Yosef ben Avraham
Basir, Yosef ben Avraham (c. 980–c. 1040)
Baskin, Leonard (b. 1922)
Bass, Shabbetai ben Joseph (1641–1718)
Bassani, Giorgio (1916–2000)
Bassevi, Jacob (1570–1634)
Bathsheba (fl. 11th–10th BCE)
Bauer, Herbert **see** Balazs, Bela
Bauer, Otto (1881–1938)
Baum, Oscar (1883–1941)
Baum, Vicki (1888–1960)
Bavli, Hillel (1863–1961)
Baylis, Lillian Mary (1874–1937)
Bearsted, Marcus Samuel **see** Bearsted, Samuel Marcus
Bearsted, Samuel Marcus (1853–1927)
Beck, Karl Isidor (1817–79)
Bedersi, Abraham ben Isaac (c. 1230–c. 1300)
Bedersi, Jedaiah (c. 1270–c. 1340)
Be'er, Haim (b. 1945)
Beer, Jakob Liebmann **see** Meyerbeer, Giacomo
Beer, Rachel (1858–1927)
Beer, Richa **see** Beer, Rachel
Beer, Wilhelm (1797–1850)
Beer-Hofmann, Richard (1866–1945)
Begin, Menaḥem (1913–92)
Behar, Nissim (1848–1931)
Behrman, Samuel Nathan (1893–1973)
Beilis, Menahem Mendel (1874–1934)
Bein, Alex (b. 1903)
Beit, Alfred (1853–1906)
Bekhor Shor, Joseph **see** Bekhor Shor, Joseph ben Isaac
Bekhor Shor, Joseph ben Isaac (fl. 12th cent.)
Belkin, Samuel (1911–76)
Belkind, Israel (1861–1929)
Bellow, Saul (b. 1915)
Belzer, Nissan (1824–1906)
Benaiah ben Jehoiada (fl. 11th–10th cent. BCE)
Ben-Ammi (1854–1932)
Benamozegh, Elijah (1822–1900)
Ben Asher, Aaron ben Moses (fl. first half of the 10th cent.)
Ben-Avi, Ittamar (1882–1943)
Ben Avigdor (1867–1921)
Ben Azzai, Simeon (fl. early 2nd cent.)
Benda, Julien (1867–1956)
Bendemann, Eduard (1811–99)
Benedictus, David (b. 1938)
Benedikt, Moritz (1849–1920)
Benet, Mordecai (1753–1829)
Ben-Gorion, Micah Joseph **see** Berdichevsky, Micah Joseph
Ben-Gurion, David (1886–1973)
Ben-Haim, Paul (1897–1984)
Benjacob, Isaac Eisik (1801–1863)
Benjamin (i) (fl. ?19th–16th cent. BCE)
Benjamin (ii) (1818–64)
Benjamin, Israel ben Joseph **see** Benjamin (ii)
Benjamin, Judah Philip (1881–84)
Benjamin, Walter (1892–1940)
Benjamin ben Moses Nahavendi (fl. 9th cent.)
Benjamin of Tudela (fl. second half of 12th cent.)
Ben Kalab Shabbua (fl. 1st cent.)
Ben Naphtali, Moses ben David (fl. 10th cent.)
Ben-Ner, Yitzḥak (b. 1937)
Benny, Jack (1894–1974)
Bensew, Judah Lob **see** Ben-Zeev
Ben Sira (fl. 2nd cent. BCE)
Ben Solomon, Menahem **see** Alroy, David
Bentov, Mordekhai (b. 1900)
Bentwich, Norman (1883–1971)
Ben-Tzevi, Yitzhak **see** Ben-Zvi, Yitzḥak
Benveniste, Abraham (1406–54)
Benveniste, Ḥayyim ben Israel (1604–73)
Benveniste, Immanuel (fl. 7th cent.)
Ben-Zeev, Judah Löb (1764–1811)
Ben-Zion, Simḥah (1870–1932)
Ben Zoma, Simeon (fl. 2nd cent.)
Ben-Zvi, Yitzḥak (1884–1963)
Berab, Jacob (1474–1546)
Berdichevsky, Micah Joseph (1865–1921)
Berechiah (fl. 4th cent.)
Berechiah ben Natronai ha-Nakdan (fl. 12th–13th century)
Berechiah of Nicole (d. 1278)
Berenice I (fl. late 1st cent. BCE)
Berenice II (b. 28)
Berenson, Bernard (1865–1959)
Bergelson, David (1884–1952)
Bergman, George (1900–79)
Bergmann, Samuel Hugo (1883–1975)
Bergner, Elisabeth (1897–1986)
Bergner, Herz (1907–70)
Bergner, Yosl (b. 1920)

Brahinski, Mani Leib **see** Mani Leib
Brainin, Reuben (1862–1939)
Bramson, Leon (1869–1941)
Brand, Joel (1906–64)
Brandeis, Louis Dembitz (1856–1941)
Brandes, Carl (1847–1931)
Brandes, Georg (1842–1927)
Brandstätter, Mordecai David (1844–1928)
Brann, Marcus (1849–1920)
Braudes, Reuben Asher (1851–1902)
Brauer, Erich (b. 1929)
Braunstein, Menaḥem Mendel (1858–1944)
Braunstein, Mibashan **see** Braunstein, Menahem Mendel
Brenner, Yoseph Ḥayyim (1881–1921)
Breslau, Lina Bauerlin **see** Morgenstern, Lina
Breuer, Isaac (1883–1946)
Breuer, Joseph (1842–1925)
Breuer, Solomon (1850–1926)
Brice, Fanny (1891–1951)
Brill, Jehiel (1836–86)
Brill, Joel ben Judah Loeb **see** Loewe, Joel ben Judah Loeb
Brill, Joseph (1839–1914)
Briscoe, Robert (1894–1969)
Brittan, Leon (b. 1939)
Broch, Hermann (1886–1951)
Brod, Max (1884–1968)
Broder, Berl (1815–68)
Broderson, Moses (1860–1956)
Brodetsky, Selig (1888–1954)
Brodie, Israel (1895–1979)
Brodski, Iosif Aleksandrovich (b. 1940)
Brodski, Joseph **see** Brodski, Iosif Aleksandrovich
Brody, Heinrich (1868–1942)
Bródy, Sándor (1863–1924)
Broner, Esther (b. 1930)
Bronfman, Samuel (1891–1971)
Bronstein, Lev Davidovich **see** Trotsky, Leon
Brooks, Mel (b. 1926)
Brown, Saul **see** Pardo, Saul
Bruce, Lenny (1925–66)
Bruckner, Ferdinand (1891–1958)
Bruggen, Carry van (1881–1932)
Brüll, Nehemiah (1843–91)
Brunner, Constantin (1862–1937)
Bruno, Leonhard **see** Rathaus, Karol
Brunschvicg, Leon (1869–1944)
Buber, Martin (1878–1965)
Buber, Solomon (1827–1906)
Bublick, Gedaliah (1875–1948)
Buchalter, Lepke **see** Buchalter, Louis
Buchalter, Louis (1897–1944)
Büchler, Adolf (1867–1939)
Budko, Yoseph (1888–1940)
Bunin, Ḥayyim Isaac (1875–1943)
Burla, Yehudah (1886–1969)
Burns, Arthur (1904–87)
Burnshaw, Stanley (b. 1906)
Burton, Montague (1885–1952)
Bustanai, Ben-Chaninai (c. 618–70)
Buttenwieser, Moses (1862–1939)
Buxtorf, Johannes (i) (1564–1629)
Buxtorf, Johannes (ii) (1599–1664)

Caballeria, Bonafos **see** Caballeria, Pedro de la
Caballeria, Pedro de la (c. 1450)
Caceres, Abraham (fl. 18th cent.)
Caceres, Francisco de (b. c. 1580)
Caceres, Jacob **see** Caceres, Simon de
Caceres, Joseph **see** Caceres, Francisco de
Caceres, Samuel de (1628–60)
Caceres, Simon de (d. 1704)
Cahan, Abraham (1860–1951)
Cahan, Israel Meir **see** Ḥaphetz Ḥayyim
Cahan, Yaahov (1881–1961)
Caiaphas, Joseph (fl. 1st cent.)
Caleb (fl. ?19th–16th cent. BCE)
Calisher, Hortense (b. 1911)
Calvin, Melvin (b. 1922)
Canetti, Elias (1905–94)
Cantarini, Isaac Cohen (1644–1723)
Cantor, Eddie (1892–1964)
Capa, Robert (1913–54)
Capsali, Elijah (1483–1555)
Capsali, Moses (1420–96/97)
Cardozo, Abraham (1626–1706)
Cardozo, Benjamin (1870–1918)
Cardozo, Issac (1604–81)
Carigal, Raphael Ḥayyim Isaac (1733–77)
Carlebach, Azriel (1908–56)
Carlebach, Joseph (1882–1942)
Carmi, Tcharney (1925–94)
Carmoly, Eliakim (1802–75)
Caro, Anthony (b. 1924)
Caro, Heinrich (1834–1910)
Caro, Joseph (1488–1575)
Caro, Nikodem (1871–1935)
Carrion, Santob de (fl. 14th cent.)
Carvajal, Antonio Fernandez (c. 1590–1659)

Elijah Be'er ben Shabbetai (fl. 14th–15th cent.)
Elijah ben Judah of Chelm (1514–83)
Elijah ben Solomon Zalman (1720–97)
Elijah of Chelm **see** Elijah ben Judah of Chelm
Elijah Sabot **see** Elijah Be'er ben Shabbetai
Elijah the Tishbite **see** Elijah
Elimelech (fl. 12th–11th cent. BCE)
Elimelech of Lizensk (1717–87)
Eliphaz (fl. 19th–16th cent. BCE)
Eliphaz the Temanite (fl. 19th–16th cent. BCE)
Elisha (fl. 9th cent. BCE)
Elisha ben Avuyah (fl. 2nd cent.)
Eliya, Joseph (1901–31)
Elkan, Benno (1877–1960)
Elkanah (fl. 11th cent. BCE)
Elkin, Stanley (1930–95)
Elkus, Abram Isaac (1867–1947)
Elman, Mischa (1891–1967)
Elon, Amos (b. 1926)
Elyashar, Jacob Saul ben Eliezer Jeroham (1817–1906)
Elyashev, Isidor **see** Baal Makhshoves
Emden, Jacob Israel (1697–1776)
Emin Pasha (1840–92)
Enelow, Hyman Gershon (1877–1934)
Engel, Yoel (1868–1927)
Ephraim (fl. 19th–16th cent. BCE)
Ephraim ben Jacob of Regensburg (1110–75)
Ephraim ben Jacob of Bonn (1132–c. 1175)
Ephraim ben Shemariah (c. 980–1060)
Ephraim Moses Ḥayyim of Sodilkov **see** Moses of Sodilkov
Ephraim Veitel Heine (1703–75)
Ephron, Elia (1847–1915)
Epstein, Abraham (1841–1918)
Epstein, Eliahu **see** Elath, Eliahu
Epstein, Isidore (1894–1962)
Epstein, Jacob (1880–1959)
Epstein, Jacob Nahum (1878–1952)
Epstein, Louis M. (1887–1949)
Epstein, Yitzḥak (1862–1943)
Epstein, Zalman (1860–1936)
Erikson, Erik (1902–2004)
Erlanger, Camille (1863–1919)
Erhlanger, Joseph (1874–1965)
Erter, Isaac (1791–1851)
Esau (fl. 19th–16th cent. BCE)
Eshbaal **see** Ish-bosheth
Eshkol, Levi (1895–1969)
Espinoza, Benedict **see** Spinoza, Benedict
Espinoza, Enrique (1898–1987)
Esther (i) (fl. 4th cent. BCE)
Esther (ii) (1880–1943)
Ethan the Ezrahite (fl. 10th cent. BCE)
Ettinger, Akiva Yaakov (1872–1945)
Ettinger, Solomon (1803–56)
Ettlinger, Jacob (1798–1871)
Euchel, Isaac (1756–1804)
Even-Shoshan, Avraham (b. 1906)
Eydoux, Emmanuel (b. 1913)
Ezekiel (fl. 6th cent. BCE)
Ezekiel, Jacob (1812–99)
Ezekiel, Moses Jacob (1844–1917)
Ezra (fl. 5th cent. BCE)

Fackenheim, Emil (1916–2003)
Factor, Max (1877–1938)
Faitlovitch, Jacques (1881–1955)
Fajans, Kasimir (1887–1975)
Falaquera, Shemtov ben Joseph (c. 1225–95)
Falk, Ḥayyim Samuel Jacob (c. 1708–82)
Falk, Jacob Joshua ben Tzevi Hirsch (1680–1756)
Falk, Joshua ben Alexander ha-Cohen (1555–1614)
Faludy, György (b. 1910)
Fano, Jacob (fl. 16th cent.)
Fano, Joseph (c. 1550–1630)
Fano, Menaḥem Azariah (1548–1620)
Farbstein, David Tzevi (1868–1953)
Farbstein, Joshua Heschel (1870–1948)
Farḥi, Estori (1280–?1355)
Farḥi, Ḥayyim Mu'Allim (c. 1760–1820)
Farrisol, Abraham (c. 1451–c. 1525)
Fast, Howard (1914–2003)
Feder, Tobias Guttman (1760–1817)
Fefer, Itzik (1900–52)
Feierberg, Mordecai Ze'ev (1874–99)
Feiffer, Jules (b. 1929)
Feigenbaum, Benjamin (1860–1932)
Feinberg, Abraham L. (1899–1986)
Feinberg, Avshalom (1889–1917)
Feinstein, Elaine (b. 1930)
Feinstein, Moses (1895–1986)
Feiwel, Berthold (1875–1937)
Feldman, Louis (1896–1975)
Felix, Eliza Rachel **see** Rachel (iii)
Fels, Mary (1863–1953)
Felsenthal, Bernard (1822–1908)
Ferber, Edna (1887–1968)
Ferenczi, Sandor (1873–1933)
Feuchtwanger, Lion (1884–1958)

Frigeis, Lazaro de (fl. 16th century)
Frischmann, David (1859–1922)
Fromm, Erich (1900–80)
Frug, Simon Samuel (1860–1916)
Frumkin, Aryeh Leib (1845–1916)
Frumkin, Israel Dov (1850–1914)
Frumkin, Michael **see** Rodkinson, Michael
Frumkin, Sidney **see** Franklin, Sidney
Fuchs, Daniel (1909–93)
Fuchs, Ernst (b. 1930)
Fuchs, Eugen (1856–1923)
Funk, Casimir (1884–1967)
Fünn, Samuel Joseph (1818–90)
Fürst, Julius (1805–73)
Furstenthal, Raphael Jacob (1781–1855)
Furtado, Abraham (1756–1817)
Füst, Milán (1888–1967)

Gabor, Dennis (1900–79)
Gabirol, Solomon **see** Ibn Gabirol, Solomon
Gad (i) (fl. 19th–16th cent. BCE)
Gad (ii) (fl. 11th–10th cent. BCE)
Gadi **see** Johanan
Galante, Abraham (1873–1961)
Galante, Abraham ben Mordecai (fl. 16th cent.)
Galante, Moses ben Jonathan (1620–89)
Galante, Moses ben Mordecai (fl. 16th cent.)
Galich, Alexander (1919–77)
Galili, Israel (1910–86)
Gallico, Abraham Jagel ben Hananiah (fl. 16th cent.)
Gama, Gaspar da (c. 1440–1510)
Gamaliel the Elder (fl. 1st cent.)
Gamaliel II (fl. 1st–2nd cent.)
Gamaliel III (fl. 3rd cent.)
Gamoran, Emanuel (1895–1962)
Gance, Abel (1889–1981)
Gans, David ben Solomon (1541–1613)
Gans, Eduard (1798–1839)
Ganzfried, Solomon (1804–86)
Gardner, Herb (b. 1934)
Gardosh, Kariel (1921–2000)
Gary, Romain (1914–80)
Gasser, Herbert (1888–1963)
Gaster, Moses (1856–1939)
Gaster, Theodor Herzl (1906–92)
Gavsie, Charles (1906–67)
Geber, Hana (1910–90)
Gebirtig, Mordecai (1877–1942)
Gedaliah (fl. 6th cent BCE)
Gehazi (fl. 9th cent. BCE)
Geiger, Abraham (1810–74)
Geiger, Lazarus (1829–70)
Geiger, Ludwig (1848–1919)
Gelber, Nathan Mikhael (1891–1966)
Gell-Mann, Murray (b. 1929)
Gélleri, Andor Endre (1907–45)
Gelman, Aryeh Leon (b. 1887)
Gentili, Gershom ben Moses (1683–1700)
Gentili, Moses ben Gershom (1663–1711)
George, Manfred (1893–1965)
Gerchunoff, Alberto (1884–1950)
Gerondi, Isaac ben Zerachiah (fl. 13th cent.)
Gerondi, Jacob ben Sheshet (fl. 13th cent.)
Gerondi, Jonah ben Abraham (fl. 13th cent.)
Gerondi, Nissim ben Reuben (fl. 14th cent.)
Gerondi, Samuel ben Meshullam (fl. ?12th–13th cent.)
Gerondi, Zerachiah ben Isaac (fl. 12th cent.)
Geronimo de Santa Fé **see** Lorki, Joshua
Gershom ben Judah (c. 960–1028)
Gershom ben Solomon (fl. 13th cent.)
Gershuni, Grigori (1870–1908)
Gershwin, George (1898–1937)
Gersonides **see** Levi ben Gershon
Gertler, Mark (1891–1939)
Gestetner, Sigmund (1897–1956)
Ghazzati, Nathan Benjamin **see** Nathan of Gaza
Ghirondi, Mordecai Samuel (1799–1852)
Gideon (fl. 12th cent. BCE)
Gideon, Miriam (1906–96)
Gikatilla, Isaac (fl. 10th cent.)
Gikatilla, Moses ben Samuel (fl. 11th cent.)
Gilbert, Martin (b. 1936)
Gilboa, Amir (1917–84)
Gimbel, Adam (1817–96)
Ginsberg, Allen (1926–97)
Ginsberg, Asher **see** Ahad ha-Am
Ginsberg, Harold Louis (1903–1990)
Ginsburg, Christian David (1831–1914)
Ginsburg, Jekuthiel (1889–1957)
Ginsburg, Ruth (b. 1933)
Ginsburg, Saul (1866–1940)
Ginzburg, Louis (1873–1953)
Ginzburg, Natalia (1916–91)
Gittelsohn, Roland (1910–95)
Glanz, Leib (1898–1964)
Glaser, Donald (b. 1926)
Glaser, Eduard (1855–1908)
Glatstein, Jacob (1896–1971)

Gronemann, Sammy (1875–1952)
Gropper, William (1897–1979)
Gross, Charles (1857–1909)
Gross, Haim (1904–91)
Gross, Heinrich (1835–1910)
Grossbard, Batia (b. 1910)
Grossberg, Yitzroch Loiza **see** Rivers, Larry
Grossman, David (b. 1954)
Grossman, Elias Mandel (1898–1947)
Grossman, Meir (1888–1964)
Grossman, Vasily Semyonovich (1905–64)
Gruening, Ernst (1887–1974)
Grumberg, Jean-Claude (b. 1939)
Grünbaum, Max (1817–98)
Grünbaum, Yitzḥak (1879–1970)
Grünberg, Carlos (1903–68)
Grünthal, Yoseph **see** Tal, Yoseph
Grunwald, Max (1871–1953)
Grusenberg, Oscar (1866–1940)
Grynszpan, Herschel (b. 1921)
Güdemann, Moritz (1835–1918)
Guedalla, Philip (1899–1944)
Guggenheim, Meyer (1828–1905)
Guggenheim, Peggy (1898–1979)
Guglielmo da Pesaro **see** Guglielmo, Ebreo
Guglielmo, Ebreo (fl. 15th cent.)
Gumplowicz, Ludwig (1838–1909)
Günzburg, David (1857–1910)
Günzburg, Horace (1833–1909)
Günzburg, Jekuthiel **see** Ginsburg, Jekuthiel
Günzburg, Joseph Yozel (1812–78)
Günzburg, Mordecai Aaron (1795–1846)
Günzburg, Pesaḥ (1894–1947)
Günzburg, Shimon (1890–1944)
Günzburg, Yevsel (1812–78)
Günzig, Azriel (1868–1931)
Guri, Ḥayyim (b. 1922)
Guston, Philip (1913–80)
Gutmacher, Elijah (1796–1874)
Gutman, Naḥum (1898–1980)
Guttmann, Jacob (1845–1919)
Guttmann, Julius (1880–1950)
Guttmann, Michael (1872–1942)
Gutmann, Simhah Alter **see** Ben-Zion, Simhah

Haan, Jacob Israel de (1881–1924)
Haas, Jacob de (1872–1937)
Haber, Fritz (1868–1934)
Habermann, Avraham Meir (1901–80)
Ḥabib **see** Ibn Ḥabib, Jacob
Habshush, Chaim (d. 1899)
Ha-Cohen, Mordecai ben Hillel (1856–1936)
Ha-Cohen, Shalom **see** Cohen, Shalom ben Jacob
Hadamard, Jacques (1865–1963)
Hadassi, Judah ben Elijah (fl. 12th cent.)
Haffkine, Waldemar (1860–1930)
Haggai (fl. 6th cent. BCE)
Ḥagiz, Jacob (1620–74)
Ḥagiz, Moses (1672–?1751)
Hai Gaon (939–1038)
Haim, Victor (b. 1935)
Ḥakham Tzevi **see** Ashkenazi, Tzevi
Halberstamm, Hayyim (1793–1876)
Halberstamm, Solomon Zalman Hayyim (1832–1900)
Halévy, Élie (1760–1826)
Halévy, Isaac (1847–1914)
Halévy, Jacques François Fromental (1799–1862)
Halévy, Joseph (1827–1917)
Halévy, Léon (1802–83)
Halévy, Ludovic (1834–1908)
Halkin, Abraham (b. 1903)
Halkin, Shemuel (1897–1960)
Halkin, Simon (1898–1987)
Halper, Ben Zion (1884–1924)
Halprin, Rose Luria (1896–1978)
Halter, Marek (b. 1932)
Ḥama bar Ḥanina (fl. 3rd cent.)
Hambro, Joseph (1780–1848)
Hamburger, Jacob (1826–1911)
Hamburger, Michael (b. 1924)
Ha-Meiri, Avigdor (1890–1970)
Hammerstein, Oscar II (1895–1960)
Hamnuna (fl. 4th cent.)
Hamnuna Saba (fl. 3rd cent.)
Hamnuna Zuta (fl. 4th cent.)
Ha-Nagid **see** Samuel ibn Nagrela
Hanamel (fl. 1st cent. BCE)
Hananel ben Ḥushiel (d. 1055)
Hananiah (fl. 2nd cent.)
Hananiah ben Ḥakhinai (fl. 2nd cent.)
Hananiah ben Teradyon (fl. 2nd cent.)
Ha-Natziv **see** Berlin, Naphtali Tzevi Judah
Handler, Simon **see** Hevesi, Simon
Ḥanina bar Ḥama (fl. 3rd cent.)
Ḥanina ben Dosa (fl. 1st cent.)
Ḥankin, Yehoshua (1864–1945)
Hannah (fl. 11th cent. BCE)
Hannover, Nathan Nata (fl. 17th cent.)
ha-Parhi, Estori **see** Farhi, Estori

Jonah (ii) (fl. 4th cent.)
Jonathan (i) (fl. 11th cent. BCE)
Jonathan (ii) (fl. 2nd cent. BCE)
Jonathan ben Amram (fl. 2nd–3rd cent.)
Jonathan ben David ha-Cohen of Lunel (c. 1135–after 1210)
Jonathan ben Eleazar (fl. 3rd cent.)
Jonathan ben Uzziel (fl. 1st cent. BCE–1st cent. CE)
Jong, Erica (b. 1942)
Joram (i) **see** Jehoram (i)
Joram (ii) **see** Jehoram (ii)
Josel of Rosheim **see** Joselman of Rosheim
Joselewicz, Berek (c. 1768–1809)
Joselman of Rosheim (1480–1544)
Joseph (fl. ? 19th–16th cent. BCE)
Joseph abu Jacob **see** Joseph ben Abraham ha-Cohen
Joseph, Keith (1918–94)
Joseph, Morris (1848–1930)
Joseph bar Ḥiyya (fl. 9th cent.)
Joseph ben Abraham ha-Cohen (fl. 11th cent.)
Joseph ben Gorion (fl. 1st cent.)
Joseph ben Isaac ha-Levi (fl. 17th cent.)
Joseph ben Isaac Kimḥi **see** Kimḥi, Joseph
Joseph ben Jacob bar Staya (fl. 10th cent.)
Joseph ben Joshua ha-Cohen (1496–c. 1575)
Joseph ben Mattathias **see** Josephus, Flavius
Joseph ben Nathan (fl. 13th cent.)
Joseph ben Tanḥum Yerushalmi (b. 1262)
Josephs, Wilfred (b. 1927)
Josephus, Flavius (c. 38–after 100)
Joshua (fl. ?13th cent. BCE)
Joshua ben Gamla (d. 69/70)
Joshua ben Hananiah (fl. 1st–2nd cent.)
Joshua ben Jehozadak (fl. 6th cent. BCE)
Joshua ben Korḥa (fl. 2nd cent.)
Joshua ben Levi (fl. 3rd cent.)
Joshua ben Peraḥyah (fl. 2nd cent. BCE)
Joshua Heshel ben Jacob of Lublin (1595–1663)
Josiah (fl. 7th cent. BCE)
Josiah ben Zakkai (fl. 10th cent.)
Jost, Isaac Marcus (1793–1860)
Jotham (i) (fl. c. 12th cent. BCE)
Jotham (ii) (fl. 8th cent. BCE)
Judah (fl. ?19th–16th cent. BCE)
Judah bar Ezekiel (d. 299)
Judah ben Asher (1270–1349)
Judah ben Barzillai al-Bargeloni (fl. 11th–12th)
Judah ben Bathyra I (fl. 1st cent.)
Judah ben Bathyra II (fl. 2nd cent.)
Judah ben Bava (fl. 1st–2nd cent.)
Judah ben Ilai (fl. 2nd cent.)
Judah ben Isaac (1166–1224)
Judah ben Jehiel **see** Leon, Judah Messer
Judah ben Kalonymos (d. 1196/1199)
Judah ben Samuel he-Ḥasid of Regensburg (c. 1150–1217)
Judah ben Simon (fl. 4th cent.)
Judah ben Tabbai (fl. 1st cent. BCE)
Judah ha-Levi (before 1075–1141)
Judah ha-Nasi (fl. c. 2nd–3rd cent.)
Judah Ḥasid ha-Levi (?1660–1700)
Judah ibn Balam **see** Ibn Balam, Judah ben Samuel
Judah Löw ben Bezalel (c. 1525–1609)
Judas Maccabee (fl. 2nd cent. BCE)
Judah Nesiah (fl. 3rd cent.)
Judah the Galilean (d. c. 6)
Judith (fl. 7th–6th cent. BCE)
Jung, Leo (1892–1987)
Juster, Jean (c. 1886–1916)
Justus of Tiberias (fl. 1st cent.)

Kabak, Ahron Avraham (1880–1944)
Ka'b Al-Aḥbár (fl. 7th cent.)
Kadoorie, Ellis (1865–1922)
Kadoorie, Elly Silas (1867–1944)
Kafka, Franz (1883–1924)
Kaganovich, Lazar Moiseyevich (1893–91)
Kahan, Israel Meir **see** Ḥaphetz Ḥayyim
Kahan, Ya'akov (1881–1960)
Kahana (i) (fl. 2nd–3rd cent.)
Kahana (ii) (fl. 3rd cent.)
Kahana (iii) (fl. 4th cent.)
Kahana (iv) (d. 414)
Kahana, Aharon (1905–67)
Kahana, Avraham (1874–1946)
Kahana, David **see** Kogan, David
Kahana, pupil of Rav **see** Kahana (ii)
Kahana, pupil of Rava **see** Kahana (iii)
Kahanovitz, Phinehas (1884–1952)
Kahane, Meir (d. 1990)
Kahn, Bernhard (1876–1955)
Kahn, Gustave (1859–1936)
Kahn, Louis (1901–74)
Kahn, Zadok (1839–1905)
Kaidanover, Aaron Samuel (1614–76)
Kaidanover, Tzevi Hirsch (d. 1712)
Kalich, Bertha Rachel (1875–1939)
Kalinsky, René (1936–81)
Kalischer, Tzevi Hirsch (1795–1874)

Kalisher, Abraham **see** Abraham ben Alexander Katz of Kallisk
Kallen, Horace Meyer (1882–1974)
Kallir, Eleazar (fl.? 7th cent.)
Kalmanovitch, Zelig (1881–1944)
Kalonymous ben Kalonymous (1286–after 1328)
Kaminer, Isaac (1834–1910)
Kaminka, Armand Aharon (1866–1950)
Kaminka, Esther Rachel (1870–1925)
Kaminski, Ida Kaminska (1899–1980)
Kaminsky, David Daniel **see** Kaye, Danny
Kaminsky, Melvin **see** Brooks, Mel
Kaniuk, Yoram (b. 1930)
Kann, Jacobus Henricus (1872–1945)
Kaplan, Eliezer (1891–1952)
Kaplan, Jacob (b. 1895)
Kaplan, Mordecai Menaḥem (1881–1983)
Kaplansky, Shelomoh (1884–1950)
Kappel, Alexander **see** Mukdoni, Alexander
Kara, Abigdor ben Issac (d. 1439)
Kara, Joseph ben Simeon (c.1060–c.1130)
Karavan, Dani (b. 1930)
Kardos, Gyorgy (b. 1925)
Karkasani, Abu Yusuf Yakub (fl. 10th cent.)
Karkasani, Jacob **see** Karkasani, Abu Yusuf Yakub
Karlitz, Avraham Yeshayahu (1878–1953)
Karman, Theodore Von (1881–1963)
Karni, Yehuda (1884–1949)
Karo, Joseph **see** Caro, Joseph
Karpleles, Gustav (1848–1909)
Kasher, Menaḥem (1895–1983)
Kassovsky, Hayyim Yehoshua (1873–1960)
Kastein, Joseph (1890–1946)
Kasztner, Rezso (1906–57)
Katsch, Abraham (b. 1908)
Katz, Ben-Tziyyon (1875–1958)
Katz, Bernard (1911–2003)
Katz, Jacob (b. 1904)
Katz, Menke (1906–91)
Katzenelson, Isaac (1886–1944)
Katzenelson, Judah Löb Benjamin (1864–1917)
Katzenstein, Julius **see** Kastein, Joseph
Katzir, Aharon (1914–72)
Katzir, Ephraim (b. 1916)
Katznelson, Berl (1887–1944)
Kaufman, Bel (b. 1911)
Kaufman, George S. (1889–1961)
Kaufman, Shirley (b. 1923)
Kaufmann, David (1852–99)
Kaufmann, Isidor (1854–1921)
Kaufmann, Yeḥezkel (1889–1963)
Kaye, Danny (1913–87)
Kayserling, Meyer (1829–1905)
Kayyara, Simeon (fl. 9th cent.)
Kazin, Alfred (1915–98)
Keesing, Nancy (b. 1923)
Kellner, Leon (1859–1928)
Kemelman, Harry (1908–96)
Kemph, Franz (b. 1926)
Kern, Jerome (1885–1945)
Kessel, Joseph (b. 1898–1979)
Kesten, Hermann (1900–96)
Kestenberg, Leo (1882–1962)
Ketav Sopher **see** Schreiber, Abraham Samuel Benjamin
Kimḥi, David (?1160–?1235)
Kimḥi, Dov (1889–1961)
Kimḥi, Joseph (c.1105–c.1170)
Kimḥi, Moses (d. c.1190)
Kingsly, Sidney (1906–95)
Kipnis, Menachem (1878–1942)
Kirchheim, Raphael (1804–89)
Kirkisani, Jacob **see** Karkasani, Abu Yusuf Yakub
Kirsch, Olga (b. 1924)
Kirschen, Ya'akov (b. 1938)
Kisch, Alexander (1848–1917)
Kisch, Egon (1885–1948)
Kisch, Frederick Hermann (1888–1943)
Kisch, Guido (1889–1986)
Kishon, Ephraim (b. 1924)
Kisling, Moïse (1891–1953)
Kiss, Joseph (1843–1921)
Kissinger, Henry (b. 1923)
Kitaj, R. B. (b. 1932)
Klaczko, Julian (1825–1906)
Klatzkin, Jacob (1882–1948)
Klausner, Yoseph Gedaliah (1874–1958)
Klein, Abraham M. (1909–72)
Klein, Melanie (1882–1960)
Klein, Shemuel (1886–1940)
Kleinbaum, Mosheh **see** Sneh, Mosheh
Klemperer, Otto (1885–1973)
Kluger, Solomon ben Judah Aaron (1785–1869)
Klutznick, Philip Morris (1907–99)
Kobrin, Leon (1873–1946)
Koenig, Leo (1889–1970)
Koestler, Arthur (1905–83)
Kogan, David (1838–1915)
Kohen, Gershom ben-Solomon (d. 1544)
Kohen, Tzedek ben Joseph (fl. 10th cent.)

A

Aaron (fl. ?13th cent. BCE) Israelite leader, elder brother of **Moses**. He and Moses freed the Jews from Egyptian bondage. He made the Golden Calf to placate the people when **Moses** did not come down from Mount Sinai (Exodus 32). When the Tabernacle was established, he and his sons became priests.

Aaron ben Elijah (?1328–69) Karaite philosopher and exegete. Born in Nicomedia in Asia Minor, he lived in Constantinople. He used **Maimonides**' *Guide for the Perplexed* as a basis for his defence of Karaism in *The Tree of Life* (1346). He believed that the Mosaic law is immutable and should not be supplemented by rabbinic ordinances.

Aaron ben Jacob ha-Cohen of Lunel (fl. late 13th–early 14th cent) French talmudist. When the Jews were expelled from France in 1306 he emigrated to Majorca. He wrote a compilation of Jewish law based on earlier legal works. This was abbreviated by an anonymous editor known as Kol Bo (1490).

Aaron ben Joseph ha-Cohen Sargado (fl. 9th cent.) Babylonian gaon and head of the academy at Pumbedita from 942 to 960. He joined the campaign against **Saadyah Gaon** led by the exilarch **David ben Zakkai**. He wrote an Arabic commentary on the Torah.

Aaron ben Joseph ha-Levi [R'ah] (1235–1300) Spanish talmudist. He was a student of **Naḥmanides** in Barcelona. He wrote *Repair of the House* consisting of critical comments on *Law of the House* by **Solomon ben Adret**. In reply **Adret** wrote *Guard of the House.*

Aaron ben Joseph ha Rofe (1250–1320) Crimean Karaite scholar and liturgical poet. His commentary on the Pentateuch, *Sepher ha-Mivḥar* (1293), was used by Karaites in the 14th and 15th centuries. Aaron's redaction of the Karaite liturgy was adopted by most Karaite congregations.

Aaron [Abu Ahron] ben Samuel (fl. 9th cent.) Italian mystic He left Baghdad and taught kabbalah in Italy. His pupil Moses ben Kalonymos of Lucca carried on his teaching in Germany. He is regarded as the father of kabbalistic study in Europe.

Aaron ha-Levi of Barcelona (fl. 14th cent.) Spanish talmudist. His *Book of Education* analyses the 613 commandments.

Aaronson, Aaron (1849–1939) Palestinian leader. He studied agronomy in France and from 1895 worked as an expert for **Edmond de Rothschild**. During World War I he organized an underground intelligence service (Nili) in Palestine. He promoted Zionist concerns at the Paris Peace Conference in 1919.

Abba [Ba] (fl. late 3rd–early 4th cent.) Babylonian amora. He was the disciple of **Huna** and **Judah**. In Tiberius he studied with **Eleazar** and **Simeon ben Lakish**. He frequently visited Babylonia and passed on Babylonian teachings in Israel.

Abbahu (c. 300) Palestinian amora. He was the disciple of **Johanan**, and also studied with **Simeon ben Lakish** and **Eleazar ben Pedat**. He lived in Caesarea when it was the Roman administrative centre. He was an important halakhic figure, and his aggadic sayings deal with theology, philosophy and ethics.

Abba Mari ben Moses ha-Yarḥi [Don Astruc of Lunel] (fl. 13th–14th cent.) French scholar. He and **Asher ben Jehiel** persuaded **Solomon ben Adret** to issue a ban in 1305 prohibiting students under 30 from studying philosophy. **Jacob ibn Tibbon** issued a counter-ban. This controversy is discussed in Abba Mari's *The Offering of Zeal.*

Abba Shaul (fl. 2nd cent.) Palestinian scholar. He was the colleague of **Judah ben Illai** and **Meir**. He described himself as a gravedigger and explained various burial customs. He also transmitted traditions concerning pathology and growth of the human embryo. He often used his own terminology and different versions of tannaitic texts from those of his contemporaries.

Abba Sikra (fl. 1st cent.) Israelite Zealot leader. He helped **Johanan ben Zakkai** escape from Jerusalem when it was besieged by the Romans.

Abbaye [Naḥmani bar Kaylil] (278–338) Babylonian amora. He developed talmudic dialectic as head of the academy at Pumbedita. His arguments with **Rava** are recorded in the Babylonian Talmud. In his teaching Abbaye distinguished between the literal meaning of the biblical text ('peshat') and the figurative interpretation ('derash').

Abendana, Isaac (1640–1710) English Hebrew scholar. He taught Hebrew at the universities of Cambridge and Oxford, and translated the Mishnah into Latin.

Abiathar (fl. 11th–10th cent. BCE) Israelite, chief priest at Nob. He was loyal to **David** during **Absalom's** unsuccessful rebellion. At the end of **David**'s reign he supported **Adonijah's** claim to become king in opposition to **Solomon. Solomon** later banished him from Jerusalem and transferred his priestly rights to **Zadok** (I Kings 1:2; I Chronicles 15).

Abiathar ben Elijah ha-Cohen (1040–1109) Last Palestinian gaon. He left Palestine after quarreling with the Egyptian exilarch David ben Daniel. His travail is depicted in the *Scroll of Abiathar.*

Abigail (fl. 11th–10th cent. BCE) Israelite woman, wife of **David**. After the death of her husband, **Nabal**, she became **David**'s wife. (I Samuel 25).

Abihu (fl. ?13th cent. BCE) Israelite priest, second son of **Aaron**. With his brother, Nadab, he ascended Mount Sinai to behold God's revelation (Exodus 24:1–11). Later they made a fire sacrifice on the altar against God's command and were struck dead by fire as punishment (Leviticus 10:1–3).

Abijah (fl. 10th cent. BCE) King of Judah (914–912 BCE). He engaged in continuous battle with **Jeroboam**, King of Israel (I Kings 15; II Chronicles 13).

Abimelech (fl. 12th cent. BCE) Israelite king. Supported by the chiefs of Shechem, he ruled for three years before he was killed in a revolt (Judges 9).

Abiram (fl. ?13th cent. BCE) Israelite rebel leader. With **Dathan** and **Koraḥ**, he led an unsuccessful revolt against **Moses** in the wilderness (Numbers 16).

Abishag (fl. 11th–10th cent. BCE) Shunamite woman who ministered to **David** (I Kings 1:1–4).

Abishai (fl. 11th–10th cent. BCE) Israelite general. He was commander of **David**'s army. He fought heroically and once saved **David**'s life in battle (II Samuel 21:16–17).

Abner ben Ner (fl. 11th cent. BCE) Israelite general. He was commander of **Saul**'s army. He supported **Ish-bosheth**'s claim to the throne when Saul died. Subsequently he became a member of **David**'s court. He was killed by Joab (I Samuel 3).

Abner of Burgos [Alfonso of Valladolid] (1270–1340) Spanish scholar. A convert to Christianity, he wrote anti-Jewish polemical tracts and engaged in disputes with Jewish scholars. He formulated an ideological justification for his conversion in *Epistle on Fate.*

Aboab, Immanuel (1555–1628) Spanish scholar. He wrote *Nomologia, o discursos legales*, a defence of the divine origin of the oral law and the Jewish tradition.

Aboab, Isaac (i) (fl. 14th cent.) Spanish writer on ethics. He collected aggadic teaching and homiletical literature concerned with Jewish ethics in the *Candlestick of Light.*

Aboab, Isaac (ii) (1433–93) Spanish rabbinic scholar. He is known as the last gaon of Castile. He was the head of the Toledo yeshivah.

Aboab, Isaac de Fonseca (1605–93) Portuguese rabbi. He was the first rabbi in the western hemisphere. Born a marrano in Portugal, he emigrated to Holland. In 1641 he travelled to Recife, Brazil. He later went to Amsterdam where he was appointed ḥakham. He was a follower of **Shabbetai Tzevi**, and a member of the tribunal which excommunicated **Benedict Spinoza**.

Aboab, Samuel (1610–94) Italian rabbi. He was an opponent of the Sabbetaians. He was among the rabbis who interrogated **Nathan of Gaza** in Venice in 1668. He wrote *Devar Shemuel.*

Abraham [Abram] (fl. ?19th–16th cent. BCE) Israelite patriarch. He left Ur and travelled to Canaan. God appeared to him and promised that his offspring would inherit the earth. The Lord made a covenant with Abraham and tested his faith by asking him to sacrifice his son **Isaac** (Genesis 11:26—25:10).

Abraham Abele of Gombin [Gombiner, Abraham Abele] (c. 1635–83) Polish talmudist. His commentary on the Code of Jewish Law, *Magen Avraham*, influenced religious practice among the Ashkenazim.

Abraham bar Ḥiyya [Judaeus, Abraham; Savasdora, Abraham Kalisk] (fl. 12th cent.) Spanish scholar. He established the foundations of Hebrew scientific terminology and transmitted Greco-Arabic science to the Christian world. His *Meditation of the Sad Soul* is an ethical treatise influenced by Neoplatonism.

Abraham ben Alexander Katz of Kallisk [Kalisher, Abraham] (1741–1810) Polish Ḥasidic rabbi. He represented popular elements of the Ḥasidic movement, but the odd customs of his followers evoked opposition. With **Menaḥem Mendel of Vitebsk**, he led a group of Ḥasidim from Russia to Palestine in 1777.

Abraham ben David of Posquières [Ravad] (1125–98) French talmudist. His strictures on the writings of **Maimonides**, **Isaac Alfasi** and **Zerahiah ben Issac ha-Levi** were widely read. He objected to **Maimonides**' *Mishneh Torah* because he believed such codes might take the place of talmudic study.

Abraham ben Elijah of Vilna (1750–1808) Polish scholar. His edition of *Aggadat Bereshit* was the first complete history of midrashic literature. He wrote a critical index to 130 midrashim, *Rav Pealim.*

Abraham ben Isaac ben Garton (fl. 15th cent.) Spanish printer. He produced the first dated Hebrew book (**Rashi**'s commentary on the Pentateuch) at Reggio di Calabria in 1475.

Abraham ben Isaac of Narbonne [Ravad II] (1110–79) French talmudist. He was the spiritual leader of the Jews in Provence. He produced the first code of Jewish law in southern France, *Ha-Eshkol.*

Abraham ben Moses ben Maimon [Maimon, Abraham ben Moses] (1186–1237) Egyptian rabbinic scholar. He succeeded his father as head of the Egyptian Jewish community. His *Comprehensive Guide for the Servants of God*, is an encyclopaedic work on the Jewish faith.

Abraham ben Nathan ha-Yarḥi (1155–1215) French talmudist. In his *Sepher ha-Manhig*, he describes synagogue practices in France, Germany, England and Spain.

Abraham Joshua Heshel of Apta [Apt (Opatav), Rabbi of] (1745–1825) Polish Ḥasidic leader. He opposed the maskilim for spreading heretical ideas among Russian Jewry. He recounted fantastic reminiscences about what he had witnessed in former incarnations as high priest, king of Israel, nasi and exilarch.

Abraham, Karl (1877–1925) German psychoanalyst. Born in Germany, he completed his medical studies in 1901. In 1905 he began to work as a psychiatrist at the Burgholzi clinic in Zurich where he came into contact with C. G. Jung and Eugen Bleuler. In 1907 he met **Sigmund Freud** and became a member of his inner circle. He was the founder of the German Psychoanalytic School and Institute. He analysed many of the early analysts including **Melanie Klein**, Sandor Rado and Helene Deutsch.

Abrahams, Harold Maurice (1899–1978) British athlete. He studied law and became a senior civil servant. A brilliant athlete, he set a British long-jump record in 1924. At the Olympic Games in the same year he won the gold medal in the 100-yard sprint.

Abrahams, Israel (1858–1924) English scholar. He was reader in rabbinics at Cambridge University. With **Claude Montefiore** he founded (1888) and edited the *Jewish Quarterly Review*. His most important works were *Jewish Life in the Middle Ages*, *Studies in Pharisaism and the Gospels*, and *Hebrew Ethical Wills*.

Abramowitsch, Shalom Jacob [Sephorim, Mendel Mocher] (1836–1917) Russian Hebrew and Yiddish author. He was born in Belorussia. With **Ḥayyim Naḥman Bialik** and **Yehoshua Ḥana Ravnitzky**, he translated the Pentateuch into Yiddish; he also wrote short stories. He is the father of prose literature in Hebrew and Yiddish.

Abrams, Lionel (b. 1931) South African artist. Born in Johannesburg, he held his first exhibition in 1957. His interest in the Lubavitch movement in the early 1970s led to a four-year period of work on Jewish themes: he produced a series of pastel portraits of five generations of Lubavitcher rebbes, and painted a number of traditional Jewish themes.

Abramsky, Chimen (b. 1917) British scholar of Russian origin. Born in Minsk, he emigrated to the UK, where he became professor of Hebrew and Jewish studies at University College, London. His publications include *Karl Marx and the English Labour Movement*, *First Illustrated Grace after Meals*, and *The Jews in Poland*.

Abravanel [Abrabanel], Isaac ben Judah (1437–1508) Portuguese biblical exegete and statesman. He was treasurer to Alfonso V of Portugal and served King Ferdinand and Queen Isabella of Castile. His writings include a commentary on the Bible, philosophical studies of an anti-rationalist nature, and theological treatises stressing the primacy of Judaism.

Abravanel [Abrabanel], Judah [Leone Ebero] (1460–after 1523) Portuguese philosopher. His *Dialoghi di amore* combines Judaism and Neoplatonism and stresses love as the foundation of the world.

Absalom (i) (fl. 10th cent. BCE) Israelite, son of **David**. He killed his brother **Amnon** who had raped his sister **Tamar**. He led an unsuccessful rebellion against **David**, in which his army was defeated and he was killed by **Joab** (II Samuel 13–19).

Absalom (ii) (fl. 1st cent.) Israelite, Jewish patriot. He joined **Menaḥem ben Judah** in the revolt against Rome.

Abse, Dannie (b. 1923) Welsh poet and playwright. He was born in Cardiff. He published his first volume of poetry while still a medical student. His *Collected Poems, 1948–76* draw together his roles as Jew, Welshman, British poet, doctor, bourgeois family man, bohemian observer, pragmatist and mystic. In the collections *Way Out in the Centre* and *Ask the Bloody Horse*, he displays an affinity with midrashic, Ḥasidic, and kabbalistic legends.

Abse, Leo (b. 1917) British politician. Born in Cardiff, he is the brother of **Dannie Abse**. He served as a member of parliament for Pontypool (1958–83), and Torfaen (1983–7).

Abudarham, David ben Joseph (fl. 14th cent.) Spanish talmudist. His commentary on synagogue liturgy, *The Book of Abudarham* is based on numerous rabbinic sources.

Abu Issa al-Isfahani [Isfahani] (fl. 8th cent.) Persian, self-proclaimed Messiah. He claimed to be the Messiah ben Joseph, the last of the five forerunners of the Messiah ben David. He prohibited divorce, eating meat, and drinking wine. He recognized the prophecies of **Jesus** and Mohammed and decreed seven daily prayers. In a rebellion against the Abbasid rulers, he was killed in battle.

Abulafia, Abraham ben Samuel (1240–after 1291) Spanish kabbalist and pseudo-messiah. In 1280 he went to Rome to persuade Pope Nicholas III to help the Jews. He evoked hostility from **Solomon ben Adret** by prophesying his own messiahship and redemptive powers. He believed his kabbalistic practices, based on letter manipulation, enabled one to receive prophetic gifts and commune with God.

Abulafia, Ḥayyim ben Jacob (1580–1668) Palestinian talmudist. In 1666 he was one of the delegation who went to Gaza to investigate the authenticity of **Nathan of Gaza**'s prophecies about **Shabbetai Tzevi**.

Abulafia, Meir ben Todros Ha-Levi (?1170–1244) Spanish talmudist and poet. He wrote about halakhah, masorah and the controversy over **Maimonides**' opinion on the subject of resurrection. He also composed Hebrew poetry.

Abulafia, Todros ben Joseph (1220–98) Spanish kabbalist. He was the spiritual leader of the Jewish community in Castile. His *Oẓar ha-Kavod* combines kabbalistic doctrines of gnostic circles in Castile with those of the Gerona school.

Abulafia, Todros ben Judah (1247–after 1298) Spanish Hebrew poet. His poems throw light on contemporary conditions in Castile. His *Garden of Apologues and Saws* contains more than 1000 poems.

Achan (fl. 13th cent. BCE) Israelite. He took some of the consecrated spoil when Jericho was captured. Because of this sacrilege the Israelites were unable to capture Ai. Achan and his family were put to death as a punishment for his sin (Joshua 7).

Achron, Joseph (1886–1943) American composer of Lithuanian origin. He was a founder of the Society for Hebrew Folk Music in St Petersburg. He composed *Hebrew Melody* (1911), as well as violin concertos and string quartets inspired by Jewish motifs.

Acosta, Uriel (1585–1640) Spanish heretic. He lived first in Spain and later in Amsterdam and Hamburg. He wrote against the Jewish faith and was excommunicated. Before his death he published a brief autobiography, *Exemplar humanae vitae.*

Acsady, Ignac (1845–1906) Hungarian historian and writer. He fought for equal rights for Hungarian Jews. In 1883 he published *Jewish and Non-Jewish Hungarians after the Emancipation.*

Adler, Alfred (1870–1937) Austrian psychiatrist. Born in Vienna, he studied medicine and opened a practice there. After meeting **Sigmund Freud**, he became a member of his inner circle. Later he disagreed with **Freud** about the role of sexual factors in neurosis and developed a psychology based on the role of environment and society.

Adler, Cyrus (1863–1940) American scholar. He was president of the Jewish Theological Seminary and Dropsie College, and served as editor of the *Jewish Quarterly Review.* His publications include *Lectures, Selected Papers, Addresses* and *I Have Considered the Days.*

Adler, Dankmar (1844–1900) US architect and engineer. Born in Stadtlengsfeld, Germany, he went with his family to the US at the age of 10. He lived in Detroit, and later in Chicago. Initially he worked as a draftsman; after the war he became an architect. He is best known for collaborative work with Louis Sullivan.

Adler, Elkan Nathan (1861–1946) English bibliophile. His library contained some 4500 Hebrew manuscripts. They are summarized in the *Catalogue of Hebrew Manuscripts in the Collection of E. N. Adler.*

Adler, Felix (1851–1933) American philosopher and educator. He founded the Society for Ethical Culture in 1876, and in 1902 was appointed professor of social ethics at Columbia University. He viewed ethical culture as a way of applying morality to modern life. An elaboration of his philosophy is contained in *An Ethical Philosophy of Life.*

Adler, Hermann (1839–1911) English rabbi. He was principal of Jews College. In 1891 he was elected chief rabbi. A selection of his sermons were published in *Anglo-Jewish Memories.*

Adler, Jacob (1855–1926) American actor of Russian origin. He began his acting career in Russia. In 1888 he went to the US where he became the most important actor on the Yiddish stage.

Adler, Nathan ben Simeon (1741–1800) German pietist. He founded a yeshivah in Frankfurt am Main. He conducted services in his home using

Isaac Luria's prayerbook. A ban was imposed on these prayer meetings under threat of excommunication.

Adler, Nathan Marcus (1803–90) English rabbi. Appointed chief rabbi in 1844, he modernized the British rabbinate and paved the way for the establishment of Jews College in 1855 and the United Synagogue in 1870. He wrote a commentary on *Targum Onkelos*.

Adler, Samuel (1809–91) American Reform rabbi of German origin. He was born in Worms and settled in the US in 1857. An early European reformer, he became rabbi of Temple Emanuel in New York in 1857.

Adler, Samuel H. (b. 1928) American composer, conductor and educator of German origin. Born in Mannheim, he moved to the US in 1939. He was music director at Temple Immanuel in Dallas (1953–66), then became professor of composition at the Eastman School of Music in Rochester, New York. He has composed cantatas dealing with Jewish themes as well as synagogue services.

Adler, Saul Aaron (1895–1966) Israeli parasitologist. Born in Russia, he moved to Britain and qualified as a specialist in tropical medicine. He emigrated to Palestine and in 1927 was appointed professor and director of the Institute of Parasitology at the Hebrew University.

Adler, Victor (1852–1918) Austrian politican. He was born in Prague. Even though he qualified as a physician, he devoted his life to the cause of the working class. He was a member of the Austrian parliament from 1905 to 1918. He converted to Christianity and opposed the idea of Jewish nationhood.

Adler, Yankel (1895–1949) Polish painter. Born in Lódź, he taught in Düsseldorf and later lived in France and England. His style was based on Jewish folk traditions.

Adonijah (fl. 10th cent.) Son of **David**. When **David** was dying, Adonijah attempted to prevent **Solomon** from becoming king. But under the influence of **Nathan** the prophet, **David** decreed that **Solomon** should reign after him. When Adonijah desired to marry **David**'s concubine **Abishag**, **Solomon** regarded this as an act of rebellion and had him executed (I Kings 1–2).

Adorno, Theodor Wiesengrund (1903–69) German philosopher and sociologist. He taught at the University of Frankfurt in 1931 and later lived in the US. In 1949 he returned to Germany, where he served as director of the Institute for Social Research in Frankfurt and professor of sociology and philosophy at the university. In his later works he discussed the nature of modern anti-Semitism.

Adret [Abraham], Solomon ben [Adret, Solomon Ibn; Rashba] (1235–1310) Spanish scholar. He studied under **Naḥmanides** and was later the leader of Spanish Jewry. His legal decisions were viewed as authoritative because of his stature as a scholar; they constitute a primary source of information about the history of the Jews from the period. He defended Judaism from Christian and Muslim detractors and disputed the messianic claims of **Abraham ben Samuel Abulafia**.

Afendopolo, Caleb ben Elijah (?1464–1525) Karaite scholar and poet. He lived most of his life in Kramariya near Constantinople. He wrote on biblical, theological, ethical and scientific subjects, and composed liturgical poetry.

Agam, Yakov (b. 1928) Israeli painter and sculptor. He was born in Rishon le Zion. He was the first to introduce geometrical abstraction into Israeli art. From the early 1950s he produced experimental works involving techniques and concepts of his own invention, such as 'simultaneous writing' in which superimposed words suggested multiple ideas to the viewer. In later works he used electrical motors to produce movement and change of composition, as well as light and sound effects. Some of his work contains traditional Jewish symbols.

Agnon, Shemuel Yosef (1888–1970) Galician Hebrew writer. He settled in Palestine and published novels and short stories dealing with life in Galicia and Palestine. Regarded as the greatest epic writer of modern Hebrew literature, he was awarded the Nobel Prize. His writings include *The Bridal Canopy* and *A Guest for the Night*.

Agron [Agronsky], Gershon (1894–1959) Jerusalem editor and mayor, of Ukrainian orign. His family went to the US when he was 13. He settled in Palestine during World War I. In 1932 he became the founder and editor of the *Palestine Post.* In 1949 he organized and directed the Israel Government Information Services, and later became mayor of Jerusalem.

Aguilar, Diego d' [Pereira, Moses Lopez (1699–1759) Marrano financier. Born in Portugal, he settled in Vienna. He used his influence at court to assist Jews, preventing their expulsion from Moravia in 1742 and from Prague in 1744. When the Spanish Inquisition asked for his extradition, he went to London where he was active in the Jewish community.

Aguilar, Grace (1816–47) English writer. She was born in London. In 1842 she published *The Spirit of Judaism: In Defence of her Faith and its Professors.* Her *Records of Israe1: Two Tales and Women of Israel* presented idealized pictures of Jewish life in Spain and women in the Bible. Her own beliefs are contained in *The Jewish Faith, its Spiritual Consolation, Moral Guidance and Immortal Hope.* She also published popular novels dealing with Jewish life.

Agus, Jacob (1911–86) American rabbi and philosopher of Polish origin. He was a rabbi in Cambridge (Massachusetts), Chicago, and Dayton (Ohio). Later he was appointed professor of religion at Temple University and was a member of the faculty of the Reconstructionist Rabbinical College. He also served as rabbi of Beth El Synagogue in Baltimore. His writings include *Modern Philosophies of Judaism, Guideposts in Modern Judaism, The Meaning of Jewish History* and *Dialogue and Tradition.*

Ahab (fl. 9th cent. BCE) King of Israel (874–852 BCE). He was reproved by **Elijah** for seizing **Naboth**'s vineyard. When his wife, **Jezebel**, introduced the worship of Baal into Israel, a struggle took place between **Elijah** and the prophets of Baal. Ahab was victorious over Ben-Hadad of Damascus and later formed an alliance with him against the Assyrians (I Kings 16:29—22:40).

Aḥad ha-Am [Ginsberg, Asher] (1856–1927) Ukrainian Hebrew essayist. Born in the Ukraine, he lived in Odessa and Tel Aviv. He advocated spiritual Zionism, which he believed would lead to the founding of a national spiritual centre. His writings include six volumes of collected essays.

Aḥa of Shabḥa (680–752) Babylonian scholar. When he failed to be appointed gaon of the academy at Pumbedita, he moved to Palestine. His *Book of Questions* contains lectures in Aramaic on weekly portions of the Torah.

Ahaz (fl. 8th cent. BCE) King of Judah (743–727 BCE). When he introduced Assyrian cults into the Temple worship, he was criticized for doing evil in the eyes of the Lord (II Kings 16:3–4).

Ahaziah (i) (fl. 9th cent. BCE) King of Israel (853–852 BCE). He was influenced by his mother, **Jezebel**, who introduced the cult of Baal into Israel. He was injured in a fall from an upper chamber in his palace and asked for an oracle from Baal-Zebub; **Elijah** reproved him and prophesied his death (II Kings 1:2–17).

Ahaziah (ii) (fl. 9th cent. BCE) King of Judah (842–841 BCE). He and **Jehoram**, King of Israel, went to war against Hazael, King of Aram (II Kings 8:28–29; II Chronicles 22:5–6). When **Jehoram** was injured in battle, Ahaziah visited him in Jezreel. Both kings were assassinated by **Jehu** (II Kings 9:27–28; II Chronicles 22:9).

Ahijah (fl. 11th cent. BCE) Chief priest at Shiloh during **Saul**'s reign. He wore an ephod when **Saul** fought against the Philistines (I Samuel 14:3).

Ahijah the Shilonite (fl. 10th cent. BCE) Israelite prophet. He prophesied during **Solomon**'s reign and the concurrent reigns of **Rehoboam** and **Jeroboam** (I Kings 11–14).

Ahimaaz ben Paltiel (1017–60) Italian chronicler and poet. In 1054 he compiled a genealogy of his family in rhymed prose, preserved in *The Ahimaaz Scroll.*

Ahithophel (fl. 11th–10th cent. BCE) Adviser to **David**, he joined **Absalom** in his unsuccessful revolt against **David** (II Samuel 15–17).

Aizman, David (1869–1922) Russian writer. He wrote about the Jewish poor and about revolutionary-minded Jewish intellectuals. An eight-volume edition of his work appeared in Russian between 1911 and 1919.

Akavia ben Mahalalel (fl. 1st cent.) Palestinian scholar. He disagreed with other sages about legal issues. He was offered the position of president of the court on condition that he change his views; when he refused he was excommunicated.

Akiva (50–135) Palestinian scholar, patriot and martyr. He developed a method of biblical exegesis, systematized the oral law, and established an academy at Bene Berak. He believed that **Simeon bar Kokhba** was the Messiah. He was imprisoned by the Romans for teaching Torah and was tortured to death.

Albalag, Isaac (fl. 13th cent.) Spanish translator and philosopher. He translated into Hebrew Al-Ghazzali's *Tendencies of the Philosophers*. He believed that there are two sources of knowledge: philosophical thought and prophetic intuition.

Albeck, Ḥanokh (1890–1972) German talmudist. He lectured on Talmud in Germany and later became professor of Talmud at the Hebrew University. His work covers almost all areas of talmudic research.

Albo, Joseph (fl. 15th cent.) Spanish philosopher. He was a pupil of **Ḥasdai Crescas** and participated in the Disputation of Tortosa (1413–14). His *Book of Dogmas* reduces the Jewish faith to three central principles: God's existence, divine revelation, and reward and punishment.

Alcimus (fl. 2nd cent. BCE) Judean high priest. He served as high priest during the Maccabean revolt (162–159 BCE). Appointed by the Syrian king Demetrius I to succeed **Menelaus** after the victories of **Judah Maccabee**, he favoured Hellenism.

Alexander (i) (80–49 BCE) Son of **Aristobulus II**, King of Judea. He was taken captive with his father by the Romans in 63 BCE. He later organized unsuccessful resistance in Judea.

Alexander (ii) (35–7 BCE) Son of **Herod the Great**. He and his brother **Aristobulus** were accused of plotting to kill their father. They were killed by strangulation.

Alexander, Abraham (1743–1816) British settler in the American colonies. He emigrated to Charleston, South Carolina from London where he was a lay minister for the small Jewish congregation. After the American revolution, he served as a customs clerk and auditor.

Alexander, Haim (b. 1915) Israeli composer and pianist. He was born in Berlin but emigrated to Palestine in 1936. He taught at the Academy of Music in Jerusalem. In addition to composing choral, chamber and orchestral works, he made a series of arrangements of traditional Jewish melodies.

Alexander, Samuel (1859–1938) British philosopher. Born in Sydney, Australia, he taught at Oxford and later served as professor of philosophy at the University of Manchester. In 1920 he published *Space and Deity*. After his retirement, he published *Beauty and Other Forms of Value*. His *Philosophical and Literary Pieces* was published posthumously.

Alexander Yannai (fl. 2nd–1st cent. BCE) King of Judea and high priest (103–76 BCE). He added the coastal region to his kingdom. During his reign the Pharisees rebelled against him for violating Pharisaic law concerning Temple practice. A massacre took place and many leading Pharisees went into exile.

Alexandra (i) (fl. 1st cent. BCE) Daughter of Aristobulus II, King of Judea. She married Philippion, son of Ptolemy of Chalcis. Ptolemy had his son killed and married her.

Alexandra (ii) (d. 28 BCE) Daughter of **Hyrcanus II**. When her son **Aristobulus III** was drowned, she accused **Herod** of murder. **Herod** had her executed after she attempted to seize power.

Alfasi, David [David ben Abraham Alfasi] (fl. 10th cent.) Karaite grammarian and commentator. Originally from Fez, he settled in Palestine. He composed a Hebrew–Arabic lexicon of the Bible.

Alfasi, Isaac ben Jacob [Rif] (1013–1103) North African talmudist. He lived in Fez. He was the author of a code of Jewish law, *Sepher ha-Halakhot*, the most important code before the *Mishneh Torah* of **Maimonides**.

Alfayyumi, Jacob (fl. 12th cent.) Leader of the Yemenite Jewish community to whom **Maimonides** addressed his *Letter to the Yemen* in 1172.

Alfonsi, Petrus [Sephardi, Moses] (1062–1110) Spanish writer and translator. He converted to Christianity and wrote a polemic against Judaism in the form of a dialogue. His collection of pious anecdotes for preachers, *Training for the Clergy*, introduced oriental tales to European readers.

Al-Ḥarizi, Judah [Taḥkemoni] (1170–1235) Spanish Hebrew poet and translator. He travelled widely through Mediterranean countries. His *Taḥkemoni* consists of 50 narratives in rhymed prose – it throws light on the culture of the period and describes the scholars and leaders he met on his travels. He translated **Maimonides**' *Guide for the Perplexed* from Arabic into Hebrew.

Alkabetz, Solomon ben Moses (1505–84) Palestinian kabbalist and poet. Born in Salonica, he lived in Adrianople and Safed. He wrote on biblical and kabbalistic subjects. His Sabbath hymn, 'Lekhah dodi' ('Come, my beloved') is recited on Friday evenings.

Alkalai, Abraham ben Samuel (?1750–1811) Bulgarian codifier. He was the head of a yeshivah in Dupnitsa and later settled in Safed. His *Zekhor le-Avraham* contains the laws of the Shulḥ-an Arukh arranged alphabetically. He also wrote a collection of responsa, *Ḥesed le-Avraham*.

Alkalai, Isaac ben Abraham Alcalay (1881–1978) Yugoslav rabbi. He was chief rabbi of Yugoslavia, and the country's first Jewish senator. When the Germans invaded, he escaped to the US where he became chief rabbi of the Sephardi congregations.

Alkalai, Judah Solomon Ḥai (1798–1878) Bosnian Zionist. He was born in Sarajevo. As rabbi to the Sephardi congregation in Semlin, near Belgrade, he encouraged Jewish settlement in Palestine. In 1874 he settled in Jerusalem. His writings supported a return to Israel on religious grounds.

Alkan, Charles Henri-Valentin (1813–88) French pianist and composer. Born in Paris, he studied at the Paris Conservatoire. A friend of Chopin, George Sand and Liszt, he became a recluse, devoting himself to religious studies and compositions. His works include: *Storm at Sea*, *The Dying Man* and *Grande Sonate*.

Allen, Woody (b. 1935) American film director and actor. He was born in Brooklyn. From the first his films used Jewish humour. Later he explored a range of American Jewish issues, including the role of the Jew in American life and Jewish paranoia and self-hatred.

Allon, Gedaliah (1902–50) Russian historian. Born in Kobin, he emigrated to Palestine in 1924. He taught Talmud and Jewish history at the Hebrew University. His writings include *History of the Jews in Palestine in the Period of the Mishnah and the Talmud*.

Allon, Yigal (1918–80) Israeli statesman and soldier. Born at Kefar Tavor in Lower Galilee, he served in the Haganah and was a founder and commander of the Palmaḥ In 1954 he was elected to the Knesset and served as minister of labour, 1961–8. After 1969 he was appointed deputy prime minister. His writings include *Curtain of Sand* and *Palmaḥ Campaigns*.

Alman, Samuel (1877–1947) Russian liturgical composer. Born in Sobolevka, Podolia, he studied in Odessa and Kishinev, and later settled in London and served as choirmaster of London synagogues and Jewish choral groups. He wrote musical works for cantor, choir, chorus and organ.

Almanazi, Joseph (1801–60) Italian Hebrew poet and bibliophile. He was born in Padua. He wrote poems of a moralistic character, and collected thousands of Hebrew manuscripts.

Almosnimo, Moses (1515–80) Greek scholar. He was born in Salonica. He was part of a delegation sent to Sultan Selim II to obtain the privileges and exemptions gained by Suleiman the Magnificent to the Salonican Jewish community. His writings include a description of Constantinople, *Extremos y grandezas de Constantinopla*.

Al-Mukammas, David ben Merwan [David ibn Merwan al-Mukammas] (fl. c. 900) Iraqi philosopher. He translated Christian commentaries on Genesis and Ecclesiastes and wrote on different religions and sects. His *Twenty Treatises* contains most of his theological and philosophical work. He was the first to introduce the methods of Arabic philosophy into the Jewish world.

Alnakawa, Ephraim (d. 1442) Spanish spiritual leader. He was born in Spain, and emigrated to North Africa in 1391, where he became spiritual leader of the Tlemcen Jewish community.

Alnakawa, Israel ben Joseph (d. 1391) Spanish writer. He composed an ethical treatise, *Candlestick of Light*. When the Toledans attacked the Jewish community of the city in 1391, he was dragged through the streets. He subsequently killed himself.

Aloni, Nissim (1926–98) Israeli playwright and short-story writer. He was born in Tel Aviv. He was the first playwright to eschew the social realism characteristic of Israeli drama in the early 1950s. In 1963 he established his own theatre in Tel Aviv. His plays synthesize Israeli consciousness and European cultural sources. The Sephardi working-class quarter in Tel Aviv is the setting for his short stories.

Alotin, Yardena. Israeli composer. Born in Tel Aviv, she was composer-in-residence at Bar-Ilan University in 1976. Much of her work has a Hebraic flavour.

Alroy, David [Ben Solomon, Menaḥem] (fl. 12th cent.) Leader of a messianic movement in Kurdistan. He was proclaimed Messiah among the Jews living in the mountains of the north-east Caucasus. He was subsequently murdered. He is the subject of *The Wondrous Tale of David Alroy* by **Benjamin Disraeli**.

Alshekh, Moses ben Ḥayyim (fl. 16th cent.) Palestinian biblical commentator and talmudist. Born in Adrianople, he settled in Safed. He was a halakhic authority, a teacher in talmudic academies, a preacher, and a member of the rabbinical court of **Joseph Caro**. He reworked his sermons into commentaries on most of the books of the Bible.

Alter, Abraham Mordecai, of Gur (1864–1948) Polish leader of Agudat Israel. He urged his followers to participate in building Palestine, where he settled after World War II.

Alter, Isaac Meir, of Gur (1799–1866) Founder of a dynasty of Ḥasidic rabbis in Gur near Warsaw. He published numerous halakhic works.

Alter, Judah Aryeh Loeb, of Gur (1847–1905) Polish anti-Zionist. He persuaded Polish Ḥasidim not to join the Zionist movement.

Alter, Robert (b. 1935) American scholar. Born in New York, he became professor of Hebrew and comparative literature at the University of California, Berkeley. He has written on Hebrew and Jewish literature and the literary form and content of the Bible. His works include *The Art of Biblical Narrative*, *The Art of Biblical Poetry*, and *The Literary Guide to the Bible*.

Alterman, Nathan (1910–70) Israeli Hebrew poet. Born in Warsaw, he settled in Tel Aviv in 1925. Influenced by French and Russian symbolists, he became the leading imagist poet of his generation. He also wrote satirical poetry related to political events. His collected works are contained in four volumes, *Kol Shirei Alterman*.

Altman, Nathan (1889–1970) Ukrainian painter, sculptor and stage designer. He settled in St Petersburg and became head of the city's section of the Department of Fine Arts. From 1918–22 he developed a constructivist style. After 1929 he lived in France, but later returned to the USSR. His work was influenced by Jewish themes and includes paintings, sculptures, graphic art and stage-designs.

Altmann, Alexander (1906–88) Rabbi and scholar of Hungarian origin. He served as rabbi in Berlin and taught philosophy at the Rabbinical Seminary there. In 1938 he settled in Manchester, England, where he founded the Institute of Jewish Studies. In 1959 he became professor of Jewish philosophy at Brandeis University. He wrote studies on Jewish philosophy and mysticism, including *Saadya Gaon: The Book of Doctrines and Beliefs*, *Isaac Israeli* and *Studies in Religious Philosophy and Mysticism*.

Altschuler, David (fl. 18th cent.) Galician biblical exegete. He planned a commentary on the Prophets and Hagiographa based on the work of earlier commentators; his son, **Jahiel Hillel Altschuler**, continued the work. His commentary on Psalms, Proverbs and Job was published in 1753–4.

Altschuler, Jahiel Hillel (fl. 18th cent.) Galician scholar. He completed the biblical commentary on the Prophets and Hagiographa (1780–2) begun by his father, **David Altschuler**.

Alvarez, Alfred (b. 1929) British author. Born in London, his writings include: *The Shaping Spirit, The School of Donne, Under Pressure, Beyond All This Fiddle, Beckett, The Savage God, Life after Marriage, The Biggest Game in Town, Offshore, Feeding the Rat, Rain Forest, Night, Lost, Apparition, Day of Atonement* and *The New Poetry*.

Amasa (fl. 11th–10th cent. BCE) Israelite commander. He led **Absalom**'s army in the unsuccessful rebellion against **David**. After the suppression of this uprising, **David** appointed Amasa his general. He was later killed by **Joab** (II Samuel 17–20).

Amatus Lusitanus (1511–68) Portuguese physician. Born in Portugal of marrano parents, he went to Antwerp, where he published a book on medicinal botany, *Index dioscorides*. He later taught medicine at the University of Ferrara and treated Pope Julius III. His major work was *Centuriae curationum* in seven volumes.

Amaziah (fl. 8th cent. BCE) King of Judah (796–780 BCE). He put to death the assassins who murdered his father **Joash**. He waged war against Edom and the kingdom of Israel (II Kings 14; II Chronicles 25).

Amichai, Yehuda (1924–2000) Israeli poet and novelist. Born in Germany, he settled in Palestine in 1936. His poetry reflects the changes in the Hebrew language during World War II and the Israeli War of Independence: he introduced airplanes, tanks, fuel trucks and administrative contracts into Hebrew poetry. His writings include *Shirim: 1948–1962* and *Not of this Time, Not of this Place*.

Amiel, Moses Avigdor (1893–1946) Israeli rabbi and writer. After serving as a rabbi in Poland and Antwerp, he became chief rabbi of Tel Aviv in 1936. He established the first modern high school yeshivah in Tel Aviv. His writings include *Ha-Middot le-Ḥeker ha-Halakhah, Derashot el Ammi* and *Hegyonot el Ammi*.

Amittai (fl. c. 800) Italian Hebrew liturgical poet. Several piyyutim, signed Amittai, are credited to him including the hymn 'Lord I remember thee and am sore amazed'. This is included in the concluding service for the Day of Atonement according to the Ashkenazi rite.

Amittai ben Shephatiah (fl. 9th cent.) Italian Hebrew liturgical poet. Several of his poems were incorporated into the Italian and Ashkenazi liturgies. His poems contain references to contemporary Jewish persecutions and Jewish–Christian disputations.

Ammi bar Nathan (fl. late 3rd cent.) Palestinian amora. He and **Assi** headed the yeshivah at Tiberias. Together with **Ḥiyya bar Abba**, they acted as education inspectors in Palestine with authority to introduce reforms.

Amnon (fl. 11th–10th cent. BCE) Israelite, eldest son of David. He raped his half-sister **Tamar**. Her brother **Absalom** had him killed for this offence (II Samuel 13).

Amnon of Mainz (fl. 10th cent.) German martyr. After attempts by the Bishop of Mainz to convert him, he asked for three days to consider the matter. When he failed to appear he was brought by force; his arms and legs were amputated and salt was poured on his wounds. On Rosh ha-Shanah he was carried to the synagogue where he recited the hymn 'U-Netannah Tokeph' ('Let us declare the mighty importance') and died. He later appeared to Kalonymus ben Meshullam in a dream and taught him the entire prayer. It is recited in synagogues on Rosh ha-Shanah.

Amos (fl. 8th cent. BCE) Israelite prophet. He prophesied during the reign of Jeroboam II. He was disturbed by the corruption in the country resulting from the exploitation of the poor. At Bethel he foretold the destruction of Israel; **Amaziah**, the priest of Bethel, told him to return to Judah, but he insisted on fulfilling his mission.

Amram (fl. 13th cent. BCE) Israelite, the father of **Moses**, **Aaron** and **Miriam** (Exodus 6:18, 20; Numbers 26:58–59).

Amram bar Sheshna (d. c. 875) Babylonian gaon. He was gaon of Sura. He wrote numerous responsa and the oldest suriving order of prayer: his *Seder Rav Amram* contains the text of the prayers for the entire year, as well as laws and customs pertaining to the different prayers.

Anan ben David (fl. 8th cent.) Babylonian biblical scholar, founder of the Karaites. When his younger brother was appointed exilarch, he founded his own sect which opposed the talmudic tradition. In his *Sepher ha-Mitzvot* he argues that the Bible was the sole basis of Judaism. He was strict in his application of biblical law.

Ananias (fl. 1st cent.) Israelite, high priest. Appointed by **Herod of Chalcis**, he was involved in the prosecution of **Paul** (Acts 24). He was killed by Jewish extremists at the outset of the rebellion against Rome in the late 60s.

Ananu, Phinehas Ḥai (1693–1768) Italian rabbi. He was rabbi in Ferrara. He became involved in a controversy about the correct pronunciation of the Priestly Blessing. His *Givat Pinḥas* is a collection of responsa.

Anatoli, Jacob ben Abba Mari (fl. 13th cent.) French translator and philosopher. Originally from Provence, he settled in Naples, where he was physician to Emperor Frederick II. He translated Arabic philosophical and astronomical works into Hebrew. His *Malmad ha-Talmidim* consists of popular sermons.

Anav, Benjamin ben Abraham (c. 1215–c. 95) Italian scholar and poet. His poetry is concerned with historical events. He also wrote treatises on Jewish law, notes on **Rashi**'s biblical commentary, and a satire on rich Jewish families in Rome.

Anav, Jehiel ben Jekuthiel (fl. c. 1250–1300) Roman copyist and author. His *Maalot ha-Middot* deals with ethical conduct and is based on midrashic and talmudic sources. The only complete, extant manuscript of the Jerusalem Talmud was copied by him in 1289. He also wrote a liturgical poem about the burning of a Rome synagogue in 1268.

Anav, Judah ben Benjamin (fl. 13th cent.) Roman author. In 1280 he completed a treatise on the laws of ritual slaughter with special reference to Roman customs.

Anav, Zedekiah (fl. 13th cent.) Italian talmudist. His *Shibbolei ha-Leket* contains ritual law and regulations.

Angoff, Charles (1902–79) American novelist of Russian origin. He was editor of the *American Mercury* and the *Literary Review*. He wrote a series of autobiographical novels: *Journey to the Dawn*, *In the Morning Light*, *The Sun at Noon*, *Between Day and Dark*, *The Bitter Spring*, *Summer Storm*, *In Memory of Autumn* and *Winter Twilight*.

Anilewicz, Mordecai (1919–43) Polish Zionist. He was born in Wyszków. He became an active Zionist and, as a member of Ha-Shomer ha-Tzair, was arrested by the Soviet authorities in 1939 for organizing the emigration of Jews to Palestine. As commander of the Jewish Fighting Organization, he led the uprising in the Warsaw Ghetto in April 1943.

An-Ski, S. [Rapoport, Solomon Seinwil] (1863–1920) Russian author. He was born in Belorussia and settled in Paris in 1894. In 1905 he returned to Russia and joined the Social Revolutionary Party. He composed the party's hymn (*Di Shvue*) and wrote folk legends, Ḥasidic tales, and stories about Jewish poverty. His play *The Dybbuk* was translated into Hebrew by **Ḥayyim Naḥman Bilalik**. His Yiddish works were published in five volumes.

Antigonus II (fl. 1st cent. BCE) Israelite, last king of the Hasmoneans (40–37 BCE). When Pompey captured Jerusalem in 63 BCE, Antigonus was taken to Rome. In 40 BCE he captured Jerusalem, put to death Herod the Great's brother **Phasael**, and cut off **Hyrcanus II**'s ears so he would be disqualified from the high priesthood. He then ruled as king and high priest. From 39 to 37 BCE Herod besieged his army in Judea and was eventually victorious. Antigonus was executed by the Romans.

Antigonus of Sokho (fl. early 2nd cent. BCE) Palestinian sage. Only one of his statements has been preserved: 'Be not like servants who minister to their master in order to receive a reward, but be like servants who minister to their master not in order to receive a reward: and let the fear of Heaven be upon you.' His pupils Zadok and Boethus interpreted it as a denial of the after-life and founded the Sadducees and Boethusians.

Antin, Mary (1881–1949) American author of Belorussian origin. Her autobiographical work *The Promised Land* contrasts her early life with her experiences in the US.

Antipater I (fl. 1st cent. BCE) Edomite administrator, governor of Idumea. He was a convert to Judaism. He served under **Alexander Yannai** and **Salome Alexandra**.

Antipater II (fl. 1st cent. BCE) Edomite administrator, ruler of Judea (63–43 BCE). He supported **Hyrcanus II** in his war against **Aristobulus II**. Julius Caesar made him financial administrator of Judea in 44 BCE. He appointed his sons **Phasael** and **Herod** to administrative positions.

Antipater III (fl. 1st cent.) Son of **Herod** the Great. When Herod executed his other sons, **Alexander** and **Aristobulus**, Antipater was made **Herod**'s heir. He was executed when his plan to murder **Herod** was revealed.

Antokolski, Mark (1843–1902) Russian sculptor. Born in Vilna he created bas-reliefs dealing with Jewish subjects. Later he chose themes from Russian history. During waves of anti-Semitism prior to the pogroms of the 1880s, he was criticized by the Russian national press.

Appelfeld, Aharon (b. 1932) Israeli writer. Born in Czernowitz, Bukovina, he settled in Palestine in 1947. His stories concern the Holocaust, which he often saw allegorically. They are collected in *Smoke*, *In the Fertile Valley*, *Frost upon the Land*, and *In the Wilderness*.

Aptowitzer, Avigdor (1871–1942) Galician rabbinical scholar. He taught Talmud at the Hebrew Teachers College in Vienna from 1919 until 1938, when he settled in Jerusalem. He published studies on various aspects of rabbinic literature and Jewish history.

Arama, Isaac ben Moses [Isaac Arama] (1420–94) Spanish rabbi, philosopher and preacher. As rabbi of various Spanish communities, he delivered sermons on the principles of Judaism. He also engaged in public disputations with Christian scholars. After the Jews were expelled from Spain 1492, he settled in Naples. His *Akedat Yitzḥak* is a philosophical commentary on the Pentateuch.

Arazi, Yehuda (1907–54) Israeli Haganah leader. Born in Lódź, Poland he emigrated to Palestine. In 1936 he was sent by the Haganah to Poland and organized the purchase of arms. After returning to Palestine, he worked with the Haganah. In 1947 he was sent to the United States to obtain arms for the yishuv.

Archivolti, Samuel (1515–1611) Italian Hebrew grammarian and poet. From 1568 he lived in Padua, where he was secretary of the community, principal of a yeshivah, and av bet din. His writings include a Hebrew grammar, *Arugat ha-Bosem*, and numerous poems and piyyutim. His poetry reflects the attitudes of Jews to their Christian neighbours.

Ardon, Mordecai (1896–1992) Israeli painter. Born in Poland, he settled in Palestine in 1933 and became director of the Bezalel School of Arts and Crafts in 1940. From 1952 to 1962 he was artistic adviser to the ministry of education.

Arendt, Hannah (1906–75) Amerian political and social philosopher of German origin. Born in Hanover, she lived in Paris after Adolf Hitler came to power. In 1941 she escaped to the US. From 1963 to 1967 she taught at the University of Chicago, and then at the New School for Social Research. Her writings include *The Origins of Totalitarianism*, *Rachel Varnhagen: The Life of a Jewess*, *Between Past and Future*, *On Revolution*, *Eichmann in Jerusalem* and *Men in Dark Times*.

Aristobulus (c. 35–7 BCE) Son of **Herod** the Great. He and his brother **Alexander** were accused of plotting to kill their father. They were killed by strangulation.

Aristobulus I (fl. 2nd cent. BCE) King of Judah (104–103 BCE). Under the will of his father, **John Hyrcanus I**, he was to become high priest while his mother was to receive the throne. He put her in prison where she died, and also imprisoned all his brothers except **Antigonus**; he later put him to death for treachery.

Aristobulus II (d. 49 BCE) King of Judea (67–63 BCE). He usurped the throne of his brother **Hyrcanus II** in 67 BCE and civil war broke out. In 63 both brothers urged their claims to the throne before Pompey. He ordered Aristobulus to surrender Jerusalem, but his supporters refused. Pompey besieged the city, captured the Temple, and took him prisoner. When Julius Caesar came to power, Aristobulus was released and given troops to attack Pompey's men, but he was poisoned before he could embark on this campaign.

Aristobulus III (d. 35 BCE) Hasmonean high priest. At the time he was due to become high priest, **Herod** the Great appointed **Hananel** in his place. Aristobulus' mother, **Alexandra** (daughter of **Hyrcanus II**) asked Cleopatra to intercede for him with **Herod. Hananel** was subsequently dismissed and Aristobulus appointed in his place. He was later drowned in the baths at Jericho by **Herod**'s soldiers.

Arlosoroff, Ḥaim (1899–1933) Ukrainian Zionist leader. He lived in Germany where he was active in the Ha-Poel ha-Tzair party. He emigrated to Palestine in 1924 and became editor of the monthly journal *Mapai*. In 1931 he was elected to the executive of the Jewish Agency for Israel and headed its political department in Jerusalem. In 1933 he aided the emigration of German Jews to Palestine. His writings, *Kitvei Ḥaim Arlosoroff*, were published in seven volumes.

Arnshteyn Mark (1879–1943) Polish Yiddish playwright. He initially wrote Polish plays on Jewish themes for the Warsaw stage. From 1912 to 1924 he directed and wrote for the Yiddish theatre in Russia, Britain, and North and South America. After returning to Poland, he translated and directed popular Yiddish plays. He founded and directed the New Chamber Theatre in the Warsaw Ghetto.

Arnstein, Fanny von (1757–1818) Viennese hostess. She was the daughter of the Berlin banker **Daniel Itzig**; she married Nathan Adam von Arnstein, court purveyor to Joseph II. During the Congress of Vienna, her balls and receptions attracted leading political figures.

Aron, Raymond (1905–83) French philosopher. Born into a Parisian family, he taught at various institutions before World War II. He wrote works on international relations, industrial society, Algerian independence, and historical knowledge. His writings include *Peace and War*, *The Great Debate: Theories of Nuclear Strategy* and *Main Currents in Sociological Thought*.

Aronsohn, Zalman Yitzḥak [Anokhi, Z. I.; Onochi, Z. I] (1878–1947) Hebrew and Yiddish author of Russian origin. Born in Belorussia, he lived in Argentina and later settled in Palestine. His stories describe Jewish life in eastern Europe. His collected works, *Between Heaven and Earth*, appeared in 1945.

Aronson, Solomon (1862–1935) Zionist leader and rabbi, of Ukrainian origin. He was chief rabbi of Kiev from 1906 to 1921. After the Russian Revolution, he sponsored the nationalist-religious Aḥdut Israeli movement. In 1921 he escaped to Berlin and later emigrated to Palestine, where he served as chief rabbi to the community of Tel Aviv and Jaffa.

Arragel, Moses (fl. 15th cent.) Spanish scholar. Together with Arias de Enciena (of the Franciscan order in Toledo), he translated the Bible into Spanish with a commentary in 1433.

Arrow, Kenneth (b. 1921) US economist. Born in New York, he served as professor of economics at Stanford University (1949–68), and at Harvard. He was awarded the Nobel Prize in 1972.

Artapanus (fl. 2nd cent. BCE) Hellenistic Jewish writer. He wrote *On the Jews*, the purpose of which was to demonstrate that the foundations of Egyptian culture were laid by **Abraham**, **Jacob**, **Joseph** and **Moses**. Fragments of it are preserved n the writings of the Church Fathers.

Artom, Isaac (1829–1900) Italian diplomat. Born into a distinguished Piedmontese family, he played an active role in the Risorgimento, the Italian struggle for independence from Austria. He was the first Jew to be elected to the Senate of the Italian kingdom.

Aryeh Leib ben Samuel (1640–1718) Polish rabbi. He served as rabbi in various Polish communities. In 1666 he met **Shabbetai Tzevi** in Constantinople. His *Shaagat Aryeh* is a collection of responsa.

Aryeh Leib of Shpola (1725–1812) Ukrainian Ḥasid. He was known as a miracle worker, and was called 'Sabba' ('grandfather') by his followers. He and **Naḥman of Bratzlav** engaged in a dispute over Shabbataism, which was continued by their disciples.

Arey Leib Sarahs (c. 1730–91) Russian Ḥasidic tzaddik. He was the subject of various legends.

Asa (fl. 10th–9th cent. BCE) King of Judah (908–867 BCE). He restored the worship of the Lord in Jerusalem and built fortified cities in Judah (II Chronicles 14:5–6). There was warfare between the kingdoms of Israel and Judah during his reign.

Asaph ben Berechiah (fl. 11–10th cent. BCE) Israelite musician. He was one of the Levites appointed by **David** to supervise music in the Sanctuary. Psalms 50 and 73–83 are attributed to him. The sons of Asaph were singers in the Temple during the reign of the kings of Judah (10th–6th cent. BCE) and at the time of **Ezra** and **Nehemiah**.

Asaph the Physician (fl. 6th cent.) Syrian physician. He is allegedly the author of a Hebrew book on medicine, *Sepher Asaph ha-Rophe*. This work is a source of information about Jewish medical ethics, ancient Jewish remedies and medical terminology.

Asch, Sholem (1880–1957) Polish Yiddish author. He lived in the US, France and Israel. In short stories, novels and plays he depicted shtetl life in eastern Europe, as well as the American Jewish experience. His later novels deal with the Jewish–Christian idea of messianic redemption. His writings include *Motke the Thief, Kiddush ha-Shem, Three Cities, Salvation, East River, Moses, The Prophet, Mary, The Nazarene* and *The Apostle*.

Ascher, Saul (1767–1822) German philosopher. In his early writings he encouraged Jews to abandon their traditional lifestyle in order to obtain civic emancipation. In *Leviathan, oder Ueber Religion in Ruecksicht des Judentums* he argues that the uniqueness of Judaism arises from its philosophical worldview rather than the revelation of divine law.

Ascoli, David (fl. 16th cent.) Italian writer. In *Apologia Hebraeorum* he protested against the anti-Jewish legislation of Pope Paul IV. He was imprisoned as a result.

Ascoli, Graziadio (1829–1907) Italian philologist. He was professor of linguistics at the University of Milan. He published studies of Hebrew, Latin and Greek inscriptions on early medieval Jewish tombstones in southern Italy.

Asenath (fl. ?19th–16th cent. BCE) Israelite woman, wife of **Joseph**. She was the mother of **Manasseh** and **Ephraim**. (Gen. 41. 50; 46. 20.)

Asher (fl. 19th–16th cent. BCE) Israelite, son of **Jacob**. His mother was **Zilpah**, **Leah**'s handmaid (Genesis 30:12). One of the tribes of Israel was named after him.

Asher ben Jehiel [Rosh] (1250–1327) German talmudist. He was a pupil of **Meir of Rothenberg** and became the spiritual leader of German Jewry. In 1303 he settled in Toledo. His responsa reflect the cultural life of Spanish and German Jews. In *Piske ha-Rosh* he recorded the decisions of earlier codifiers and commentators.

Ashi (335–427) Babylonian amora. He was head of the academy at Sura. With the help of other sages, he assembled and arranged in appropriate tractates the sayings of earlier amoraim.

Ashkenazi, Berman (fl. 16th cent.) Polish rabbi. He was the author of *Matenot Kehunnah*, a commentary on Midrash Rabbah. His *Mareh Cohen* is a key to scriptural references to the Zohar.

Ashkenazi, Bezalel (c. 1520–91) Palestinian talmudist. Born in Israel, he settled in Egypt, where he became chief of the Egyptian rabbis. After he excommunicated the nagid of Egyptian Jewry, this office was abolished. He later lived in Jerusalem, where again he was chief rabbi. He travelled extensively to collect money for the community and encourage immigration. His *Shittah Mekubbetzet* is a collection of medieval talmudic commentaries.

Ashkenazi, Jacob (1550–1626) Polish rabbinic scholar. He wrote (in Yiddish) the *Tz'enah u-Re'enah*, a compendium of rabbinic commentaries on the Pentateuch. His *Sepher ha-Maggid* is based on the Prophets and Hagiographa.

Ashkenazi, Tzevi [Ḥakham Tzevi] (1660–1718) Moravian talmudist. He travelled widely and became head of the rabbinic academy in Altona, then in 1710 he settled in Amsterdam, where he was head of the Ashkenazim. After a controversy concerning **Nehemiah Ḥayyon**, a follower of **Shabbetai Tzevi**, he resigned his position in 1714. He subsequently settled in Lvóv. His *Ḥakham Tzevi*, after which he was known, is a collection of responsa.

Assaf Simḥah (1889–1953) Israeli historian and rabbinic scholar. From 1915 to 1919 he taught Talmud and was director of a yeshivah in Odessa. In 1921 he settled in Jerusalem. He later became a professor and rector at the Hebrew University and a member of the Israeli Supreme Court. He wrote many studies of the gaonic period, the history of Jewish law, medieval Jewish culture, and the history of the Jewish community in Palestine.

Asscher-Pinkhof, Clara (1896–1984) Dutch author. Born in Amsterdam, she lived there and in Groningen. She emigrated to Palestine in 1944. Her novels depict pre-war Holland, the experience of European Jewish children during the German occupation, and Israeli life.

Asser, Tobias Michael Carel (1838–1911) Dutch statesman. He came from a distinguished family of Dutch jurists, and served as professor of international law at the University of Amsterdam (1862–93). He was a member of the Council of State in the Netherlands from 1893, and chairman of the Royal Commission on Private International Law in 1898. He was awarded the Nobel Peace Prize in 1911.

Assi (fl. late 3rd–early 4th cent.) Palestinian amora. Born in Babylonia, he settled in Tiberius. He and **Ammi bar Nathan** were the most distinguished sages of their generation.

Assi, Rav (fl. early 3rd cent.) Babylonian amora. He was a contemporary of **Rav** and **Samuel**.

Astruc, Levi (fl. late 14th–early 15th cent.) Spanish rabbi. He participated in the Disputation of Tortosa in 1413–14.

Athaliah (fl. 9th cent. BCE) Queen of Judah (842–836 BCE). When her son **Ahaziah** was murdered by **Jehu** she seized power and murdered all her rivals except **Joash**. Six years later she was killed when **Joash** was crowned king in the Temple (II Kings 11:4–16; II Chronicles 23:1–5).

Athias, Isaac (fl. 16th–17th cent.) German rabbi. He was Ḥakham of the Sephardic community in Hamburg. His *Tesoro de preceptos* is a study of Jewish religious practices.

Athias, Joseph (fl. 17th cent.) Dutch publisher and printer. He founded a publishing house in Amsterdam. His first publication was a Sephardic prayerbook (1658). In 1659 he produced a commentary on the Pentateuch and in 1661 a Bible. In 1689 he announced that he had reprinted more than a million Bibles for England and Scotland.

A-Tiflisi, Abu Imran [Abu Imran of Tiflis] (fl. 9th cent.) Russian religious leader, founder of a dissident Karaite sect. He was born near Baghdad, and was taught by **Ishmael of Akbara**, who greatly influenced him. His followers were known as 'Abu-Imranists' or 'Tiflisists'; the sect persisted until the 12th century.

Atlan, Jean-Michel (1913–60) French-Algerian painter and poet. Born in Constantine, Algeria, he went to Paris and studied at the Sorbonne. He published collections of poems, but from 1946 worked as a painter. His works include *The Magic Mirrors of King Solomon* and *The Lion of Judah.*

Atlan, Liliane (b. 1932) French dramatist and poet. She was born in Montpellier. She went into hiding during World War II. After the war, she became interested in metaphysical issues. One of her plays, *Mister Fugue*, or *Earth Sick*, depicts the fantasies of children sent to the crematorium in the concentration camps.

Atlas, Samuel (b. 1889) US philosopher of Lithuanian origin. Born in Kamai, Lithuania, he went to the US in 1942. He taught at the Hebrew Union College in Cincinnati, and later in New York. His writings include *From Critical to Speculative Idealism: The Philosophy of Solomon Maimon.*

Attar, Ḥayyim ben Moses ben (1696–1743) North African kabbalist. Born in Morocco, he lived in Livorno and later settled in Jerusalem, where he founded the Midrash Keneset Israel Yeshivah. His *Or ha-Ḥayyim* is a commentary on the Pentateuch.

Auer, Leopold (1845–1930) Russian violinist and teacher, of Hungarian origin. Born in Veszprem, Hungary, he studied at the Vienna Conservatory. He served as concertmaster at Düsseldorf from 1863–5, and then at Hamburg. In 1868 he became professor of violin at the Imperial Conservatory, St Petersburg. In 1894 he was knighted by Nicholas II. After the Revolution, he went to New York where he taught violin.

Auerbach, Berthold (1812–82) German author. Born at Nordstetein in Würtemberg, he was an active supporter of Jewish Emancipation. He wrote short stories and novels, and translated **Benedict Spinoza**'s works.

Avidan, David (1934–95) Israeli poet. He was born in Tel Aviv. From the start his work was highly experimental, using composite words, loan words, and neologisms in Hebrew. He played an important role in the development of a modern style in Hebrew poetry.

Avidom, Menaḥem (1908–95) Israeli composer. Born in Poland, he settled in Palestine in 1925, where he taught music. From 1945 to 1952 he was general secretary of the Israel Philharmonic Orchestra, and then became adviser on the arts to the Ministry of Tourism. He was appointed director-general of the Israeli Performing Rights Society in 1955, and was also chairman of the Israel Composers' League. His works include *Alexandra the Hasmonean* and the symphony *David.*

Avigur, Shaul (b. 1899) Israeli political figure. Born in Dvinsk, Russia, he went to Palestine in 1912 and joined the Haganah. He spearheaded the Haganah initiative to bring illegal immigrants into the country. During World War II he helped organize illegal immigration from Middle Eastern countries. When the war ended, he headed the underground operation for the transportation of the survivors of European Jewry.

Avinoam, Reuben (1905–74) Israeli poet and translator. Born in Chicago, he settled in Palestine in 1929, where he taught English. In 1950 he became supervisor of English studies at the Israeli ministry of education and culture. He published poetry, translations and a collection of literary writings of those who died in the Israeli War of Independence.

Avi-Yonah, Michael (1904–74) Israeli archaeologist and art historian. Born in Galicia, he emigrated to Palestine in 1919. He was professor of classical and Byzantine architecture at the Hebrew University. His writings concern the late-Hellenistic, Roman and Byzantine periods, and the topography of Palestine.

Avni, Ahron (1906–51) Israeli painter. Born in the Ukraine, he emigrated to Palestine in 1925. In 1936 he founded the Histadrut Seminary for Painting and Sculpture in Tel Aviv, of which he was director until his death. He painted members of the Haganah and later soldiers on the battlefield during the Israeli War of Independence.

Avtalyon (fl. 1st cent. BCE) Palestinian scholar. He and **Shemaiah** constituted the fourth of the zugot in Palestine. He served as av bet din of the Sanhedrin.

Axelrod, Julius (1912–83) US biochemist. Born in New York City, he was awarded the Nobel Prize in Medicine in 1970 for research on nerve impulses and the treatment of nervous disorders.

Axenfeld, Israel (1787–1866) Russian Yiddish writer. He was born in Nemirov. He originally was a follower of **Naḥman of Bratzlav**, but after contact with the maskilim, he became anti-Ḥasidic. He wrote 30 novels and plays which satirize Ḥasidic life.

Ayllon, Solomon ben Jacob (1655–1728) Greek rabbi and kabbalist. He was born in Salonica. He became a follower of **Shabbetai Tzevi**. In 1689 he was appointed Ḥakham in London. He later served as rabbi to the Portuguese Jews in Amsterdam, where he came into conflict with Tzevi Ashkenazi.

Azleff, Yevno (1869–1918) Russian revolutionary. He was born in Lyskovo, and moved to Rostov with his family. He worked as a reporter for a local newspaper, and later as a clerk. His activities in the revolutionary movement were observed by the authorities, and he fled to Germany where he settled at Karlsruhe. Later he returned to Russia where he worked in a general-supply company, and was a member of the Union of Social Revolutionaries underground. Appointed to the party's first triumvirate, he became leader of the Battle Organization. He was instrumental in the assassination of Grand Duke Sergei. Later he planned to blow up the Ochrana (Russian secret police) headquarters in St Petersburg. Under suspicion as an informer, he fled to Paris, and later to Germany. He was imprisoned because of his revolutionary leanings during World War I, but subsequently released.

Azriel of Gerona (fl. early 13th cent.) Spanish kabbalist. His work reflects the process whereby Neoplatonism permeated the kabbalistic tradition. He wrote a commentary on the ten sephirot, the Sepher Yetzirah, talmudic aggadot, and the liturgy, as well as several treatises on mysticism.

Azulai, Abraham (1570–1643) North African kabbalist. Born in Fez, he emigrated to Hebron. He wrote three treatises on the Zohar and a kabbalistic work, *Ḥessed le-Avraham.*

Azulai, Ḥayyim Joseph David (1724–1806) Palestinian emissary and writer. He was born in Jerusalem. He came to be regarded as the leading scholar of his generation, and also travelled abroad as an emissary of the Jewish community in Israel. His *Maagal Tov* is a literary diary covering the years 1753–78. His *Shem ha-Gedolim* contains 1300 brief biographies.

B

Baal Shem Tov, Israel ben Eliezer [Besht; Israel ben Eliezer] (1700–60) Polish spiritual leader, founder of Ḥasidism. He was born in Podolia and lived in the Carpathian mountains. He emerged as a healer and spiritual leader and travelled about curing the sick and expelling demons and evil spirits. In the course of these journeys his influence grew. Prayer rather than study was his major approach to God. He attracted many followers and has remained the inspiration for Ḥasidim to the present day.

Baasha (fl. 10th–9th cent. BCE) King of Israel (906–883 BCE). He assassinated **Nadab** (son of **Jeroboam I**), proclaimed himself king, and killed all the members of the royal family. He lived at Tirzah. Throughout his reign he was at war with King **Asa** of Judah (I Kings 15:16, 32).

Babel, Isaac (1894–?1939) Ukrainian writer. He was born in Odessa. He served on the Romanian front after the Russian Revolution. From 1923 he devoted himself to literature and many of his stories contain Jewish themes. He was arrested and disappeared in 1939. His writings include *Red Cavalry*, *Collected Stories* and *The Lonely Years, 1925–1939.*

Bacharach, Jair Ḥayyim (1638–1702) German talmudist. He served as rabbi in Koblenz and Worms. Thirteen scholars met under his leadership to study and prepare themselves for redemption. He collected writings connected with **Shabbetai Tzevi**. His *Ḥavvot Yair* consists of responsa demonstrating an extensive knowledge of secular subjects.

Bacher, Simon (1823–91) Hungarian poet and translator. He lived in Budapest, where he was the treasurer of the Jewish community. He wrote poems in the florid style of the Haskalah and translated German and Hungarian poetry into Hebrew; his *Zemirot ha-Aretz* (Songs of the Land) is an anthology of translations from Hungarian poetry. His translation of Gotthold Ephraim Lessing's *Nathan the Wise* appeared in Vienna in 1865.

Bacher, Wilhelm (1850–1913) Hungarian Semitic scholar. He was professor and head of the rabbinic seminary in Budapest, where he taught biblical exegesis, midrash, homiletics and Hebrew poetry and grammar. He published on various aspects of Judaism; his works include studies of talmudic aggadah, Hebrew grammarians, medieval biblical exegesis, and Judeo-Persian literature.

Bader, Gershom (1868–1953) Polish Hebrew and Yiddish author. Born in Kraków, he lived in Lemberg from 1893 until 1912. He founded the first Yiddish daily in Galicia, the *Togblat* in 1904. In 1896 he established the *Yidisher folks-kalender*, which he edited until 1912; in that year he settled in New York. His writings include a life of Jesus, a lexicon of Galician Jewish cultural figures, and a dictionary of talmudic abbreviations.

Baeck, Leo (1873–1956) German rabbi and religious leader. He served as rabbi in Berlin, where he lectured on midrashic literature and homiletics at the Hochschule für Wissenschaft des Judentums. From 1933 he was president of the Reichsvertretung or representative body of German Jews. He was deported to Theresienstadt in 1943. After the war, he settled in London where he served as chairman of the World Union for Progressive Judaism. He was visiting professor at the Hebrew Union College. His writings include *The Essence of Judaism.*

Baer, Max (1909–59) American world heavyweight champion. Born in Omaha, Nebraska, he appeared with a Star of David on his shorts.

Baer, Seligmann (1825–1897) German masorah scholar and linguist. He taught in the Jewish community school in Biebrich. Together with Franz Delitzsch he published the Psalms and other books of the Bible with masorah texts. His *Avodat Yisrael* (Service of Israel) became the standard prayerbook text for most subsequent editions of the siddur.

Baer, Werner (1914–92) German composer. He studied piano composition and conducting at the Hochschule für Musik Berlin. Before the First World War, he was the organist at the Church of St Thomas, Leipzig and served as choirmaster and organist for the Liberal synagogue group in Berlin. In 1938 he left Germany and settled in Singapore. He subsequently emigrated to Australia. His compositions include: *Test of Strength, Life of the Insects, Harvester's Song* and *Psalm 8.*

Baer, Yitzḥak (1888–1980) German historian. He was born in Halberstadt. He became professor of medieval history and head of the history department at the Hebrew University. His writings include studies of the Jews in Christian Spain and the period of the second Temple. He was one of the founders and editors of the Jewish historical review *Zion.*

Baerwald, Paul (1871–1961) American banker and communal leader. Born in Frankfurt, he went to the United States in 1896. In 1908 he became a partner in Lazard Frères. After he retired, he served as treasurer of the American Joint Distribution Committee. In 1938 he joined President Roosevelt's Advisory Committee on Political Refugees, was active in the JDC rescue work during World War II, and arranged for funds for the War Refugee Board. After the war, the JDC helped more than half a million refugees to reach Israel. In 1957 the Paul Baerwald School of Social Work was established at the Hebrew University.

Baeyer, Adolf von (1835–1917) German chemist. He was a professor of organic chemistry in Berlin. He won the Nobel Prize for chemistry in 1905.

Baginsky, Adolf Aron (1843–1918) German founder of modern paediatrics. Born in Ratibor, Silesia, he studied medicine at the University of Berlin. In 1881 he joined the faculty of paediatrics and later became professor. Together with Rudolf Virchow, he founded the chidren's hospital, Kaiser und Kaiserin Friedrich Krankenhaus. In 1879 he founded and served as editor of the journal *Archiv für Kinderheilkunde.* His writings include *Lehrbuch der Kinderheilkunde.*

Baḥya ben Asher ibn Halawa (fl. 13th cent.) Spanish exegete and kabbalist. He lived in Zaragoza where he was dayyan and preacher. In his commentary on the Torah he used literal, philosophical, homiletical and mystical interpretations.

Bahya ben Joseph ibn Pakuda [Ibn Bakuda, Ibn Pakuda, Baḥya] (fl. 11th cent.) Spanish moral philosopher. He lived in Zaragoza. In *Duties of the Heart* he examined the obligations of the inner life which he regarded as having equal importance with ritual and ethical observances; this work draws on Islamic mysticism and Neoplatonism.

Bakst, Leon [Rosenberg Lev Samuilovich] (1867–1924) Russian artist. Born in St Petersburg, he was baptized and later returned to Judaism. He was employed by Sergey Diaghilev as chief designer of costumes for his ballets. He had an deep influence on **Marc Chagall.**

Balaban, Barney (1887–1983) American motion picture executive. Born in Chicago, he founded the Balaban and Katz company in 1908. In 1926 the company was bought by Paramount Pictures, and he and his brother remained as managers. In 1936 he was elected president of the company.

Balaban, Meir (1877–1942) Polish historian. He was born in Lemberg. He became director of the Taḥkemoni rabbinical seminary in Warsaw and lectured in Jewish history at the University of Warsaw. He was the founder of the historiography of Polish Jewry. His writings deal with the history of the Jews in Poland and Russia.

Balázs, Béla [Bauer Herbert] (1884–1949) Hungarian writer. His first collection of poetry appeared in 1910. Later he emigrated to Vienna where he continued to write poetry and became interested in film. Subsequently he moved to Berlin and directed films and wrote film scenarios. In 1931 he moved to Moscow where he taught at the Academy of Cinematography. He returned to Hungary in 1945 and was Professor at the Budapest Academy of Theatrical and Cinematographic Arts.

Balcon, Michael (1896–1977) British film producer. He helped establish Gainsborough Pictures, and was regarded as elder statesman of the British film industry. His daughter was the actress Jill Balcon, and his grandson Daniel Day-Lewis.

Ballin, Albert (1857–1918) Hamburg shipping magnate. After building up the steamship company that his father established, he took advantage of the opportunities afforded by the transatlantic passenger trade. From 1886 he transformed the Hamburg-Amerika Line into Germany's foremost shipping concern with a fleet of 400 vessels. During World War I he organized the shipping of foodstuffs to Germany, circumventing the Allied blockade.

Bal-Makhshoves [Isidor Elyashev] (1873–1924) Lithuanian Yiddish author. Born in Lithuania, he studied medicine in Heidelberg and Berlin, and practised medicine in Russia. He edited a daily Yiddish newspaper in Riga and eventually settled in Berlin. His five-volume collected writings appeared in Berlin from 1910–15.

Balmes, Abraham ben Meir de (1440–1523) Italian physician and grammarian. He was born in Lecce. He became court physician to King Ferdinand I of Naples. He translated a number of medieval Arabic works from the Hebrew versions into Latin. His *Mikneh Avraham* is a standard work on Hebrew grammar.

Balogh, Thomas (1905–85) English economist of Hungarian origin. He studied economics and law at the universities of Budapest and Berlin and was later invited to the United States as a Rockefeller Fellow at Harvard University. During the 1930s he worked in France and Germany. In 1934 he was appointed a lecturer at University College, London and later at Balliol College, Oxford. During World War II he was chairman of the Mineral Development Committee. After the war he became deputy chief of a United Nations mission to Hungary. In the 1950s he served as advisor to the UN's Food and Agriculture Organization. Subsequently he became an advisor on economic affairs for the Labour government. In 1968 he received a peerage.

Bamberger, Fritz (1902–84) German philosopher. He was born in Frankfurt am Main. He was professor of philosophy at the College of Jewish Studies in Chicago from 1937 to 1942, then until 1961 was professor of intellectual history at the Hebrew Union College-Jewish Institute of Religion in New York. His writings include studies of **Moses Mendelssohn** and **Benedict Spinoza**.

Bamberger, Ludwig (1823–99) German economist and politician. He was a Mainz lawyer with liberal views. He was condemned to death for his part in the 1848–9 uprisings and fled to Switzerland. The amnesty of 1866 allowed him to return to Germany where he was elected to the Riechstag. He became an expert on financial issues. His articles and essays were published in five volumes.

Bamberger, Seligmann Bär (1807–78) Leader of German Orthodoxy. He was born in Wiesenbronn. He served as rabbi in Würzburg, where he founded a teachers' training college. His writings were devoted to subjects of practical halakhah.

Bamberger, Simon (1846–1926) American industrialist and politician. Born in Germany, he emigrated to the US at the age of 14. He eventually moved to Salt Lake City, Utah. He served in the State Senate (1903–7), and was governor of Utah.

Bambus, Willi (1863–1904) German Zionist. He was a leading member of the Ezra Society in Berlin, which supported agricultural settlements in Palestine. He was opposed to political Zionism. In 1901 he was a co-founder of the Hilfsverein der deutschen Juden. His writings include *Palaestina, Land und Leute*, *Die Kriminalität der Juden* and *Die Juden als Soldaten*.

Banco, Anselmo del (d. c. 1532) Italian banker. He was the founder of the Jewish community in Venice. His financial assistance to the government and skill at negotiation led to the community's formal recognition.

Band, Arnold (b. 1929) American literary scholar. He was born in Boston, Massachusetts. He served on the faculty of the University of California at Los Angeles from 1959, becoming professor of Hebrew literature and chairman of the Department of Comparative Literature. His publications include a study of **Shemuel Yosef Agnon**.

Bandes [Miller], Louis E. (1866–1927) American Yiddish journalist. Born in Russia, he settled in the US, where he became a leader of the socialist movement. In 1890 he founded the Yiddish Marxist weekly *Die arbeiter zeitung*, and in 1897 helped to establish the labour daily newspaper *Forverts*. In 1905 he founded *Die varheit*, which later altered its ideology from socialism to Zionism.

Baneth, David Tzevi Hartwig (1893–1973) Israeli Arabist, son of **Eduard Baneth**. He was born in Krotoszyn, Poland. He settled in Palestine, where he became professor of Arabic language and literature at the Hebrew University. His writings concern the influence of Arabic thought on medieval Jewish philosophy.

Baneth, Eduard (1855–1930) Prussian talmudist. He was born in Liptó-Szent-Miklós, Hungary. He served as rabbi in Krotoszyn and lectured on Talmud at the Lehranstalt für die Wissenschaft des Judentums in Berlin. His work was concerned primarily with talmudic and rabbinic literature, the development of halakhah, and the Jewish calander.

Baneth, Ezekiel (1773–1854) Hungarian rabbi. He was born in Alt-Ofen. He served as rabbi of Paks, Belassagyarmat and Nyitra, and his yeshivah was attended by students from all over the country. He was a halakhic authority and an eloquent preacher.

Barak ben Abinoam (fl. 12th cent. BCE) Israelite commander. He served **Deborah** in the war against the Canaanites, doing battle at her instigation with King Jabin of Hazor (Judges 4–5).

Barany, Robert (1876–1936) Austrian otologist. Born in Vienna, he became lecturer in the Otological Clinic in Vienna. He won the Nobel Prize in 1914. During World War I he served in the Austro-Hungarian army. In 1917 he became professor of otology at the University of Uppsala.

Barash, Asher (1889–1952) Hebrew author of Galician origin. Born in Eastern Galicia, he emigrated in 1914 to Palestine, where he taught high school in Tel Aviv and Haifa. He wrote novels, short stories, poems, essays and translations. His fictional works depict life among Galician Jewry and the pioneering efforts in Palestine.

Bar Giora, Simon [Simeon] (fl. 1st cent.) Palestinian military leader in the war against Rome in 66–70. He fought in the battle at Beth-Horon in 66, in which the Jews defeated the Romans. He gathered together a band of patriots who attacked opponents of the revolt and Roman sympathizers. He opposed the moderate Jewish government in Jerusalem, which wished to come to terms with Rome. When Titus' forces reached Jerusalem in 70 he fought with the rebels against him. He eventually surrendered, was taken prisoner to Rome, and executed.

Bar-Hanina (fl. 4th cent.) Palestinian scholar. He lived in Bethlehem and was a teacher of Jerome. He introduced the Church Fathers to rabbinic exegesis and influenced the translation of the Hebrew Scriptures into Latin.

Bar-Hebraeus, Gregorius (1226–86) Syrian scholar of Jewish origin. He was appointed Archbishop of Mesopotamia and Persia in 1252. He wrote a Syriac grammar, commentaries on the Bible and Aristotle, and a history of the world.

Bar-Ilan [Berlin], Meir (1880–1949) Zionist leader of Russian origin. He was born in Volozhin. He represented the Mizraḥi movement at the seventh Zionist Congress in 1905. In 1926 he settled in Jerusalem, where he became President of the World Mizraḥi Centre. Opposed to the Palestinian partition plan and the British White Paper of 1939, he advocated civil disobedience. After the establishment of the State of Israel, he organized a group of scholars to examine the legal probelms of the state in the light of Jewish law. He was editor of the Mizraḥi daily newspaper and organized the publication of the *Talmudic Encyclopaedia*.

Bar Kappara (fl. 3rd cent.) Palestinian scholar. A disciple of **Judah ha-Nasi**, he was the author of a compilation of Jewish law. This collection explains obscure passages in the Mishnah and transmits traditions that differ from it. He valued natural science and encouraged the use of Greek, but was opposed to metaphysical speculation. He founded an academy in the south of Israel.

Bar Kokhba, Simeon [Bar Kosiba, Simeon] (d. 135) Palestinian military leader in the war against Rome in 132–5. At the outbreak of the war, **Akiva** proclaimed him Messiah; the appelation Bar Kokhba (Son of the Star) was given to him because of his messianic role. His forces captured Jerusalem, but in 133 the Romans counterattacked with an army of 35,000 under Hadrian and the commander Julius Severus. In 134–5 they besieged Bar Kokhba's stronghold Betar, and he was killed.

Bar-Lev, Ḥayyim (b. 1924) Israeli military commander. Born in Vienna, he settled in Palestine in 1939. In 1946 he was in charge of blowing up the Allenby Bridge during the struggle with the British. In the War of Independence and the Sinai Campaign of 1956 he served as military commander of various units. In 1964 he was appointed head of the General Staff Branch at GHQ. From 1968 to 1971 he was chief of staff of the Israeli Defence Forces. In 1972 he became minister of commerce and industry.

Barna, Victor (1911–72) Hungarian table tennis champion. He dominated the sport in the 1920s and 1930s. Between 1929 and 1939 he won five singles, eight doubles, and two mixed doubles world titles.

Barnato, Barney (1852–97) South African mining magnate. Born in London, he went to the Jews' Free School. In 1873 he went to South Africa during the diamond rush. He initially ran a theatrical company, and later worked in the diamond industry. Together with his brother, he bought diamond claims, and they founded the Barnato Mining Company. In 1888 Barnato amalgamated with De Beers. He then turned to finance and became a member of the Johannesburg Stock Exchange.

Barnett, Lionel David (1871–1960) English orientalist. Born in Liverpool, he was Keeper of the Department of Oriental Printed Books and Manuscripts at the British Museum from 1908 to 1936. His writings include *Antiquities of India*, *Hindu Gods and Heroes*, and the English translation of *A History of Greek Drama and Brahma-Knowledge*. He edited Bevis Marks Synagogue records of the contributions made to history by members of the congregation.

Barnett, Richard David (1909–86) English orientalist, son of **Lionel David Barnett**. He was born in London and became head of the Department of Western Asiatic Antiquities at the British Museum. From 1959 to 1961 he was president of the Jewish Historical Society of England. His publications include *Assyrian Palace Reliefs and their Influence on the Sculptures of Babylonia and Persia* and *Illustrations of Old Testament History*.

Baron, Salo Wittmayer (1896–1989) Galician Jewish historian. He taught history at the Jewish Teachers College in Vienna (1919–26), at the Jewish Institute of Religion in New York (1927–30), and at Columbia University (1930–62). He served as president of the American Academy for Jewish Research and as a member of other academic bodies. His writings include the multi-volume *Social and Religious History of the Jews*.

Barondess, Joseph (1867–1928) American labour and communal leader. Born in the Ukraine, he emigrated to New York in 1888. He helped lead the cloakmakers' strike in 1890 and was sentenced to imprisonment as a result. He was active in the Socialist Labour Party and later in the Zionist movement. He was a founder of the American Jewish Congress and a member of the American Jewish delegation to the Versailles peace talks in 1919.

Barrios, Daniel Levi [Miguel] de (1635–1701) Spanish poet and playwright. He was born in Montilla of a Portuguese marrano family. He served as captain in the Spanish Netherlands, living in Brussels and Amsterdam. He was a follower of **Shabbetai Tzevi**. In his writing he initially emphasized classical and pagan allusions, but later stressed his Jewishness. His poems contain extensive information about contemporary Jewish life.

Barros Basto, Arturo Carlos de (1887–1961) Portuguese leader of the marrano revival. He was born in Amarante near Oporto. He entered the military, and in the revolution of 1910 it was he who hoisted the Republican flag on the town hall of Oporto. After World War I he embraced Judaism and was active in the regeneration of the marrano community. His periodical *Ha-Lappid* spread Jewish ideas among the marranos. He also edited handbooks of religious guidance and wrote a history of Jewry in Oporto.

Barsimon, Jacob (fl. 17th cent.) Dutch emigrant, the first Jewish resident of New Amsterdam (New York). He arrived in the New World in July 1654 aboard the Dutch ship 'Peartree'. In 1655 he joined **Asser Levy** in petitioning for the right to stand guard instead of paying a special tax. The Dutch West India Company overruled Governor Peter Stuyvesant, who had rejected the petition.

Barth, Aaron (1890–1957) Israeli banker and Zionist leader. He was born in Berlin. He became active in the Mizraḥi movement in Germany; from 1921 to 1938 he was attorney for the Zionist Congress court and from 1946 its chairman. He settled in Palestine in 1933 and became director-general of the Anglo-Palestine Bank in 1947. His writings include *The Modern Jew Faces Eternal Problems*, in which he advocated a modern interpretation of Orthodoxy.

Barth, Jacob (1831–1941) German Semitic linguist. He was born in Flehingen, Baden. He taught Hebrew, biblical exegesis, and Jewish philosophy at the Orthodox Rabbinic Seminary in Berlin. From 1847 he also lectured on Semitic philology at the University of Berlin. He published studies on Semitic linguistics and edited grammatical, poetic and historical texts.

Bartov, Hanokh (b. 1926) Israeli novelist. Born in Petaḥ Tikvah, he served in the Jewish Brigade during World War II and in the Israeli army during the War of Independence. He was cultural attaché at the Israeli embassy in London from 1966 to 1968. His writings include stories, novels, plays and journalism.

Baruch (fl. 7th cent. BCE) Israelite scribe of the book of **Jeremiah**. He set down in writing Jeremiah's prophecies and may have composed the biographical narrative about him (Jeremiah 36:4).

Baruch, Bernard (1870–1965) American statesman. He served as chairman of the War Industries Board and as an adviser to President Wilson and later to President Roosevelt. In 1944 he was a member of a committee that studied postwar adjustment issues. His writings include *American Industry in the War*, *My Own Story* and *Public Years*.

Baruch ben David Yavan (d. 1780) Polish financier. He exercised influence at the Polish court, by means of which he protected the Jewish community and discredited the Sabbetaians and the Frankist movement.

Baruch ben Samuel of Mainz (c. 1150–1221) German talmudist and liturgical poet. He was dayyan of Mainz. His responsa were incorporated in his *Sepher ha-Ḥokhmah* (The Book of Wisdom). He wrote commentaries on several talmudic tractates, and piyyutim on persecutions of the Jews.

Baruch ben Samuel of Safed (d. 1834) Russian physician and rabbinic emissary. He settled in Palestine in 1819. In 1830 he went to Yemen to find the Ten Lost Tribes of Israel.

Baruch of Medzibozh [Baruch of Tulchin] (1757–1810) Ukrainian Ḥasidic tzaddik. He was the grandson of the **Baal Shem Tov**, and regarded himself as the heir to his leadership. He held court in Medzibozh in a luxurious fashion and aroused the opposition of other Ḥasidic leaders. He believed the tzaddik could save the whole world. He was the first to institute payments to the tzaddik from the Ḥasidim.

Baruch of Shklov [Schick, Baruch] (1752–1810) Polish talmudist and scientist. He studied medicine in England and later lived in Berlin, where he wrote on astronomy, mathematics and medicine. He was dayyan at Slutsk and physician to Prince Radziwill.

Bar-Yehuda, Yisrael [Idelson, Yisrael] (1895–1965) Israeli political leader. Born in Russia, he settled in Palestine in 1926. From 1949 he was a member of the Knesset. After the split in Mapam in 1954, he became a member of the Aḥdut ha-Avodah-Poale Zion party. From 1955 to 1959 he was minister of the interior, and from 1962 to 1965 minister of communications.

Barzillai (fl. 11th–10th BCE) Gileadite who ministered to **David**. When **David** fled to Gilead because of **Absalom**'s rebellion, Barzillai welcomed him with food and sustained him throughout his stay. He later sent his son to live in **David**'s court in Jerusalem (I Kings 2:7).

Basch, Victor (1863–1944) French philosopher. Born in Budapest, he was professor at the universities of Nancy, Rennes and Paris. He championed **Alfred Dreyfus**. In 1926 he served as president of the League for the Rights of Man. During World War II he was a member of the central committee of the French Resistance. His writings concern literature, philosophy and political issues.

Bashyazi, Elijah (1420–90) Turkish Karaite scholar. He was the ideologist of the Karaite rapproachement with the rabbis, and a codifier of Karaite law. His *Adderet Eliyahu* is a code of Karaite law.

Basir, Yosef be Avraham [Basir ha-Roeh] (c. 980–c. 1040) Iraqui Karaite author. He travelled to Jerusalem to join the Karaite community. He was one of the few Karaites who wrote responsa on theological and legal subjects. His major theological work is *Kitab al-Muhtawi*. His most important legal work is *Kitab al-Istibsar*. He also wrote polemical works against Islam, the Samaritans and the Rabbanites.

Baskin, Leonard (b. 1922) American artist. He was born in New Jersey. He taught printmaking and sculpture at Smith College from 1953. He was influenced in his early years by **Ben Shahn** and many of his drawings and prints concern Jewish subjects.

Bass, Shabbetai ben Joseph (1641–1718) Polish cantor and publisher. He became the first Jewish bibliographer. When his parents were killed in a pogrom, he fled to Prague, where he served as an assistant cantor. From 1674 to 1679 he visited libraries in Poland, Germany and Holland. His *Siftei Yeshenim* is a list of Hebrew of some 2200 items of Hebraica and Judaica.

Bassani, Giorgio (1916–2000) Italian writer. Born in Bologna, he lived in Ferrara until 1943, when he moved to Rome. He edited *Bolteghe oscure*, an international literary review, from 1948 to 1960. His *Garden of the Finzi-Continis* depicts an aristocratic Italian Jew unable to come to terms with Fascism.

Bassevi [von Treuenberg], Jacob (1570–1634) Court Jew. He engaged in large scale trading and business transactions. In 1622 Friedrich II granted him a coat-of-arms. As head of the Jewish community in Prague he took an active role in Jewish communal life and defended the Jews from persecution.

Bathsheba (fl. 11th–10th cent. BCE) Israelite woman, wife first of **Uriah**, then of **David**. When **David**, from his rooftop, saw her bathing, he had **Uriah** her husband killed in battle by placing him in the front lines. Bathsheba was the mother of **Solomon** (II Samuel 11–12; I Kings 1–2).

Bauer, Otto (1881–1938) Austrian socialist leader. Born in Vienna, he studied at the University of Vienna and co-founded the monthly *Der Kampf*. As a leader of the neo-Marxian school in Vienna, he was secretary to the socialist faction in the Austrian Parliament. During World War I he fought in the Austrian army and was a prisoner-of-war in Russia. In 1918 he became the first foreign minister of the Austrian Republic. In 1934 he took a leading part in the uprising of the workers in Vienna. He was forced to find refuge in Czechoslovakia and Paris.

Baum, Oscar (1883–1941) Czech author. He was a member of the Prague circle of **Max Brod** and **Franz Kafka**. He lost his sight as a boy and therefore dictated his short stories. His *Die böse Unschuld* (1913) documents Jewish life in Bohemia against the background of the Czech nationalist struggle. His last novel, *Das Volk des harten Schlafes* (1937), portrays Jewish life in the early years of Nazi rule.

Baum, Vicki (1888–1960) American author. Born in Vienna, she attended a music school and appeared as a harpist at the age of 11. She played in various orchestras in Vienna. In 1916 she married the conductor Richard Lert and gave up her musical career. Her first book, *Falling Star,* was published only after a friend discovered her mansucripts in 1920. In 1921 she worked as an editor for the Ullstein publishing house. Some of her novels were serialized in illustrated weeklies. In 1928 she published *Helen Willfür*; this was followed by *Menschen in Hotel* which was made into a film starring Gerta Garbo. In 1938 she became an American citizen.

Bavli, Hillel (1863–1961) American Hebrew poet and educator of Lithuanian origin. He settled in the US in 1912 and taught modern Hebrew literature at the Jewish Theological Seminary. He was one of the first Hebrew poets to deal with the American milieu. His poems have been collected in several volumes. He translated Dicken's *Oliver Twist* and Shakespeare's *Antony and Cleopatra* into Hebrew.

Baylis, Lillian Mary (1874–1937) Founder of the Old Vic theatre company in London. Born in London, she spent many years in South Africa teaching dancing, violin and banjo. In 1898 she returned to London and joined her aunt who ran the Coffee Music Hall in the Victoria Theatre. In 1912 she became the manager of the theatre. From 1931 she also managed the Sadler's Wells opera and ballet companies.

Bearsted, Marcus Samuel [Samuel, Marcus] (1853–1927) English industrialist. In 1878 he founded companies in London and Japan. He began transporting oil to the Far East from Russia. In 1897 he founded the Shell Transport and Trading Company which amalgamated with the Royal Dutch Petroleum Company in 1901 to form the British-Dutch Oil Company. In 1921 he was granted a peerage.

Beck, Karl Isidor (1817–79) Hungarian-born poet. His writing gave voice to the Hungarian people's struggle against the Austrian empire, and is filled with despair over the state of Jewry and the world. Although he was baptized in 1843 he continued to be haunted by the fate of the Jewish people. After the failure of the Hungarian uprising in 1848, he renounced his radical activities and made peace with the Austrian government.

Bedersi, Abraham ben Isaac (c.1230–c. 1300) French Hebrew poet. He lived most of his life in Perpignan. His poems and satires contain numerous historical details and provide an insight into the contemporary cultural scene. His *Ḥotam Tokhnit* was the first dictionary of Hebrew synonyms in the Bible.

Bedersi, Jedaiah [Jedaiah ha-Penini] (c.1270–c.1340) French philosopher and poet. He lived in Perpignan and Barcelona. His *Examination of the World* is an ethical work stressing the worthlessness of the world and indicating the way to attain eternal happiness. Among his poems is the prayer *Eleph Alaphim,* each word of which begins with the letter aleph. His *Apologetic Letter* addressed to **Solomon ben Adret** vindicates philosophical studies.

Be'er, Haim (b. 1945) Israeli poet and novelist. He served in the chaplaincy corps of the Israeli army. He published poems and short stories from an early age. His collection of poems *Shashuim Yom-Yom* (Day to Day Delights) portrays a religious upbringing in Jerusalem in the early years of the State of Israel. His novel *Notzot* (Feathers) depicts the memories of an Orthodox boy from Jerusalem who, as a soldier, served in a burial unit at the Suez Canal. *Et Hazamir* (The Time of Trimming) is a political satire about the religious nationalist movement.

Beer, Rachel [Richa] (1858–1927) British newspaper publisher and editor. Born in Bombay, she was brought to England at an early age. After serving as a voluntary hospital nurse, she married F. A. Beer. In 1893 she bought the *Sunday Times* and became its editor. She was also a gifted musician.

Beer, Wilhelm (1797–1850) German astronomer. Born in Berlin, his brother, **Giacomo Meyerbeer**, became a composer. At the age of 16 he volunteered for the military and served in the campaigns of

1813 and 1815 against Napoleon. Later he joined his father's banking house, succeeding him in 1826. Beer pursued astronomy as a hobby and built a private observatory in the garden of his villa. Together with Johann Heinrich von Müdler, he observed Mars and they published their results. From 1834 to 1836 they compiled a map of the moon.

Beer-Hofmann, Richard (1866–1945) Austrian poet and playwright. Born in Vienna, he emigrated to New York in 1939 after the Nazi occupation of Austria. Much of his work deals with Jewish themes. In a trilogy of biblical plays he sought to restate in modern terms the Hebraic position on fundamental questions of human existence.

Begin, Menaḥem (1913–92) Israeli statesman. He was the leader of Betar in Poland. In 1942 he emigrated to Palestine and became commander of the Irgun Tzevai Leumi. From 1944 to 1948 he led the Irgun's underground war against the British. In 1948 he founded the Ḥerut party. He led the Likud party to victory in the general elections of 1977 and became prime minister. His writings include *The Revolt* and *White Night.*

Behar, Nissim (1848–1931) Palestinian educator, the founder of modern Hebrew education in Palestine. He was born in Jerusalem. He organized schools in the Near East on behalf of the Alliance Israélite Universelle, and from 1882 to 1887 he directed their school in Jerusalem, where he introduced Hebrew as a spoken language. He later settled in the US and directed the National Liberal Immigration League from 1906 to 1924.

Behrman, Samuel Nathan (1893–1973) American playwright. Initially he wrote book reviews, short stories and articles. Later he produced a series of plays, and in the 1950s wrote essays for the *New Yorker*, as well as a novel *The Burning Glass.* He also collaborated on film scripts.

Beilis, Menaḥem Mendel (1874–1934) He was the victim of a blood libel charge in Russia in 1911, having been accused of the ritual murder of a 12-year-old boy. In 1913 a trial was held and he was acquitted. This event was the subject of the novel *The Fixer* by **Bernard Malamud**.

Bein, Alex (b. 1903) German historian of Zionism. Born in Steinach, he served on the staff of the German State Archives from 1927 to 1933. In 1933 he settled in Palestine, where he became director of the General Zionist Archives. In 1956 he became state archivist of Israel. He published works on Zionism and anti-Semitism.

Beit, Alfred (1853–1906) German-British financier. Born to a Portuguese family in Hamburg, his parents were baptized after their marriage. Educated in Hamburg, he went to work with a firm importing wool and diamonds; in 1871 he went to Holland, and in 1875 joined a relative's firm in South Africa as a diamond buyer. In 1890 he established the firm of Wernher, Beit and Company. He also set up and controlled the Pretoria Waterworks, the Pretoria Electric Lighting Company, and the National Bank of South Africa. In 1888 Beit and Cecil Rhodes formed De Beers Consolidated Mines Limited.

Bekhor Shor, Joseph ben Isaac [Joseph Bekhor Shor] (fl. 12th cent.) French scholar. He lived in Orléans. His commentary on the Torah was based on a literal and rationalistic understanding of the text. He opposed the allegorization of the commandments, and the christological interpretation of Scripture.

Belkin, Samuel (1911–76) American rabbi and educator of Polish origin. He settled in the US in 1929. In 1943 he became president of the Rabbi Isaac Elchanan Theological Seminary and Yeshiva College. At Yeshiva he launched an extensive programme of academic and physical expansion. In 1945 the college became Yeshiva University. He published studies on **Philo**, rabbinic literature, and traditional Jewish thought.

Belkind, Israel (1861–1929) Zionist leader of Belorussian origin. He was a leader of the first Bilu group to go to Palestine in 1882. He founded the first Hebrew school in Jaffa in 1889 and an agricultural school for orphans of the first Kishinev pogroms. After World War I he established another agricultural school for orphans of the Ukrainian pogroms. He was the author of Hebrew, Yiddish and Russian textbooks on Jewish subjects.

Bellow, Saul (b. 1915) American novelist. Born in Quebec, he lived in Montreal and Chicago. Many of his novels deal with Jewish life. *The Victim* (1947) is a treatment of anti-Semitism. *The Adventures of Augie March* (1953) deals with the experience of a Jewish boy from Chicago during the Depression of the 1930s. *Herzog* (1964) portrays a Jewish professor who attempts to relate humanistic values to the modern world.

Belzer [Spivak], Nissan (1824–1906) Ukrainian cantor. He was active in Belz, Kishinev and Berdichev. He was a leading ḥazzan and also wrote liturgical compositions.

Benaiah ben Jehoiada (fl. 11th–10th cent. BCE) Israelite commander. He was one of **David**'s warriors; after **David**'s death he supported **Solomon** and became commander of his army (I Kings 2).

Ben-Ammi [Rabinowicz, Mordecai] (1854–1932) Russian author. He became a maskil and organized Jewish defence in Odessa. He emigrated to Geneva and later settled in Palestine. His stories portray traditional Jewish life.

Benamozegh, Elijah (1822–1900) Italian rabbi and theologian. He was born in Livorno and served there as rabbi and professor of theology at the rabbinical school. In his writings he presented a systematic exposition of the doctrines of Judaism and defended the kabbalah.

Ben Asher, Aaron ben Moses (fl. first half of the 10th cent.) Palestinian masoretic scholar. He lived in Tiberias. He produced a biblical manuscript incorporating vocalization and accentuation, which formed the basis for the accepted Hebrew text of the Bible. He also wrote grammatical works in the tradition of the scholars of Tiberias.

Ben-Avi, Ittamar (1882–1943) Palestinian Hebrew journalist. He initially wrote for Hebrew periodicals edited by his father, **Eliezer Ben-Yehuda**. During World War I he lived in the US, but later returned to Palestine, where he founded the daily newspaper *Doar ha-Yom*. From 1924 he was editor of *The Palestine Weekly*.

Ben Avigdor [Shalkovitz, Leib; Shelkowitz, Abraham Leib] (1867–1921) Polish Hebrew writer and publisher. He lived in Warsaw, where he founded the series of small booklets called 'Penny Books', which contained Hebrew belles-lettres. These introduced European literary trends into Hebrew literature. In 1893 he established the Aḥiasaph publishing company and later the Tushiyyah company, which published hundreds of Hebrew books. He founded the children's weekly *Olam Katan* in 1901, and the Aḥisepher publications in 1913.

Ben Azzai, Simeon (fl. early 2nd cent.) Palestinian rabbinic scholar. He lived in Tiberias. He was one of the four sages who engaged in esoteric speculation (thereby entering Pardes); according to tradition he was one of the ten martyrs who died during the Hadrianic persecutions.

Benda, Julien (1867–1956) French writer. Born into an assimilated Parisian family, he studied at the Sorbonne. He believed poets and philosophers had betrayed their mission of upholding rational and human values: this was a theme of his writings: literary, historical, journalistic and philosophical.

Bendemann, Eduard (1811–99) German painter. He was born in Berlin. He converted to Christianity in 1835 and later was appointed professor at the Academy of Fine Arts in Dresden. In 1856 he became director of the Academy in Düsseldorf. Some of his paintings depict biblical scenes.

Benedictus, David (b. 1938) English writer. Born in London, he was commissioning editor of Channel 4 (1984–6) and produced plays and various works. His writings include: *The Fourth of June*, *You're a Big Boy Now*, *The Guru and the Golf Club*, *The Rabbi's Wife*, *The Antique Collector's Guide*, *Lloyd George*, *Local Hero*, *The Streets of London* and *The Stamp Collector*.

Benedikt, Moritz (1849–1920) Austrian journalist. From 1881 he was editor of the *Neue Freie Presse* in Vienna. He was an anti-Zionist and would not allow **Theodor Herzl** to publish anything in support of Zionism in his newspaper.

Benet, Mordecai (1753–1829) Bohemian rabbi and talmudist. In 1789 he was appointed chief rabbi of Moravia. He had a broad secular knowledge and was temperate in his attitude towards Reform

Judaism and the Haskalah. He wrote several works of responsa.

Ben-Gurion, David (1886–1973) Israeli statesman. Born in Poland, he joined the Zionist movement and settled in Palestine in 1906. He was among the labour leaders who founded the Aḥdut ha-Avodah party in 1919 and Mapai in 1930. From 1921 to 1935 he was general secretary of the Histadrut. He was chairman of the Zionist executive and the Jewish Agency executive from 1935 to 1948. In April 1948 he became head of the provisional government in which he served as prime minister and minister of defence. In 1956 he was responsible for the Sinai Operation. His writings include speeches, articles and memoirs.

Ben-Haim, Paul (1897–1984) Israeli composer. Born in Munich, he settled in Tel Aviv in 1933. He helped create the eastern Mediterranean school of composition. His compositions evoke the pastoral atmosphere of the Israeli countryside and the youthful spirit of the people. They include *Hymn from the Desert*, *Sweet Psalmist of Israel*, *Liturgical Cantata*, *Vision of the Prophet*, *Three Psalms* and *Kabbalat Shabbat*.

Benjacob, Isaac Eisik (1801–63) Lithuanian Hebrew author and bibliographer. He lived in Vilna. He published an edition of the Bible incorporating **Moses Mendelssohn**'s German translation. His *Otzar ha-Sepharim* lists and describes about 8500 Hebrew manuscripts and 6500 Hebrew books.

Benjamin (i) (fl. ?19th–16th cent. BCE) Israelite, youngest son of **Jacob**. The tribe of Benjamin occupied territory between Ephraim and Judah, which included Jerusalem.

Benjamin (ii) [Benjamin, Israel ben Joseph] (1818–64) Romanian explorer and writer. He journeyed in the Near East, Asia, North Africa and North America. He attempted to discover the Ten Lost Tribes of Israel and published an account of his travels. His *Drei Jahre in Amerika* is the first comprehensive account of Jewish communities in the US.

Benjamin, Judah Philip (1818–84) American lawyer and statesman. He was born in the Virgin Islands. He was elected to the US Senate in 1852. In 1861 he became attorney-general of the Confederate government and later served as secretary of state until the collapse of the Confederacy. After the Civil War he settled in England, where he had a distinguished career as a barrister.

Benjamin, Walter (1892–1940) German philosopher. Born in Berlin, he worked as a critic, translator and reviewer. In 1924 he was involved with a Latvian actress whose radical communism inspired him. When Hitler came to power, he went to the Baleric Isles and then to Paris. At the outbreak of World War II he was interned as a German citizen, but released in November 1939. He fled to the south of France, and then crossed the Spanish border. When threatened with deportation, he committed suicide. His writings include a study of the origin of German drama.

Benjamin ben Moses Nahavendi [Nahavendi, Benjamin] (fl. 9th cent.) Persian Karaite scholar. He lived in Nahavend in Persia, where he established a community that observed Karaite principles and methods of biblical study. He was the first Karaite author to write in Hebrew, and was responsible for the use of the name 'Karaites' to designate the members of the sect (in place of the former 'Ananites').

Benjamin of Tudela (fl. second half of 12th cent.) Spanish traveller. A resident of Tudela, he set out on his travels in about 1167 and returned in 1172 or 1173. He visited France, Italy, Greece, Syria, Palestine, Iraq, the Persian Gulf, Egypt and Sicily. His *Book of Travels* is an important source for Jewish history of the period.

Ben Kalab Shabbua (fl. 1st cent.) Israelite, citizen of Jerusalem. He was active during the Roman conquest in 70. According to the Talmud, he possessed sufficient grain to feed Jerusalem for several years, but this was destroyed by the Zealots.

Ben Naphtali, Moses ben David (fl. 10th cent.) Palestinian masoretic scholar. He lived in Tiberias. Like his contemporary **Aaron ben Moses Ben Asher**, he edited the punctuation and accentuation of the Hebrew Bible. His version differs only in small details in about 850 instances from **Ben Asher**'s text.

Ben-Ner, Yitzḥak (b. 1937) Israeli writer. He was born in Kfar Yehoshua. His novel *Eretz Rehokah* (A

Distant Land) contrasts an idyllic portrayal of New Zealand with contemporary Israeli life. His other writings include *Shekiah Kafrit* (Rustic Sunset) and *Protokol.*

Benny, Jack [Kublesky, Benjamin] (1894–1974) American comedian. Born in Waukegan, Illinois, he studied violin and entered vaudeville. His first film appearance took place in 1929, but he gained success on radio and later on television.

Ben Sira [Jesus ben Sira] (fl. 2nd cent. BCE) Palestinian sage. He lived in Jerusalem. He was the author of the apocryphal book known as Ecclesiasticus or The Wisdom of Ben Sira.

Bentov, Mordekhai (b. 1900) Israeli politician. Born in Poland, he settled in Palestine in 1920. He was editor of the Mapam daily from 1943 to 1948. In the 1948 provisional government he served as minister of labour and reconstruction. He sat in the Knesset as a member for Mapam from 1949 to 1965, then from 1966 to 1969 he was minister of housing. He published books and articles on politics and economics.

Bentwich, Norman (1883–1971) English Zionist. Born in London, he practised law from 1908–12. In 1913 he became commissioner of courts in Egypt and taught at the Cairo Law School. During World War I he served in the British Army on the Palestine front. From 1920–31 he was attorney general of the Mandate government in Palestine. Later he became professor of international relations at the Hebrew University. In 1951 he retired and returned to England. He wrote studies of Zionism as well as works dealing with international relations. He was also the author of a number of biographies as well as an autobiography.

Benveniste, Abraham (1406–54) Spanish rabbi. He was rabbi to the court in Castile and financial agent to John II of Aragon. In 1432 he was appointed chief justice and tax superintendent of Castilian Jewry. In the same year he convened a synod at Valladolid which encouraged Jewish education, the correct administration of Jewish courts, and equitable tax apportionment.

Benveniste, Ḥayyim ben Israel (1604–73) Turkish rabbinic codifier. He was born in Constantinople and served as a rabbi in Smyrna. He was opposed to the Shabbetaian movement. His *Keneset ha-Gedolah* is a guide to the halakhah embodying decisions made after the completion of the Shulḥan Arukh.

Benveniste, Immanuel (fl. 7th cent.) Netherlands printer of Hebrew texts. Active in Amsterdam, he printed the Midrash Rabbah, Mishnah, **Alfasi**'s *Halakhot*, and the Talmud.

Ben-Yehudah [Perelmann], Eliezer (1858–1922) Hebrew writer and lexicographer of Lithuanian origin. He went to Paris in 1878 to study medicine and in 1879 he published articles encouraging Jewish settlement in Palestine. In 1881 he emigrated to Jerusalem, where he edited Hebrew journals. He advocated the acceptance of Hebrew as a spoken language and in 1890 founded the Hebrew Language Council of which he was chairman. He wrote a comprehensive dictionary of ancient and modern Hebrew.

Ben-Zeev [Bensew], Judah Löb (1764–1811) Polish Hebrew grammarian. Born in Poland, he lived in Berlin, Breslau, Kraków and Vienna. His writings included a Hebrew grammar, a biblical lexicon, and an introduction to the Bible, as well as Hebrew poetry.

Ben-Zion, Simḥah [Gutmann, Simḥah Alter] (1870–1932) Hebrew author. He was born in Bessarabia and settled in Palestine in 1905. He wrote short stories as well as novels, and translated German classics into Hebrew.

Ben Zoma, Simeon (fl. 2nd cent.) Palestinian sage. He was a contemporary of **Akiva**. It appears that he studied under **Joshua ben Hananiah**. The Mishnah declares that he was the last of the authoritative biblical expositors. Many of his sayings became proverbs. He was one of the sages who was concerned with mystical speculation concerning creation and the divine chariot.

Ben-Zvi [Ben-Tzevi], Yitzḥak [Shimshelevitz, Yitzḥak] (1884–1963) Israeli statesman. Born in the

Ukraine, he was one of the pioneers of the Poale Zion movement in Russia. In 1907 he settled in Palestine, where he was active in the Jewish defence movement. He was a founder of the Aḥdut ha-Avodah party in 1919, of Histradrut in 1921, and of Mapai in 1930. He succeeded **Chaim Weizmann** as president of the state in 1952. His wife, Rachel Yanait (1886–1979), was involved with the Palestinian labour movement, Jewish self-defence, and agricultural training for women.

Berab, Jacob (1474–1546) Talmudist of Spanish origin. He lived in North Africa before settling in Safed. He initiated a plan to reintroduce ordination (semikhah) in order to establish an authoritative Jewish leadership and reconstitute the Sanhedrin. This project was opposed by **Levi ibn Ḥaviv**. A controversy ensued and the plan failed.

Berdichevsky [Ben-Gorion], Micah Joseph (1865–1921) Ukranian Hebrew writer. He lived in Breslau and Berlin. In his writings he attacked the limited scope of Hebrew literature, the inadequacy of Haskalah, the ideology of **Aḥad ha-Am**, and **Ḥibbat Zion**. Influenced by Nietzsche, he called for a re-evaluation of Judaism and Jewish history and the expansion of the canons of Hebrew literary taste. His fiction depicts Jewish towns of eastern Europe at the end of the 19th century and the life of eastern European Jewish students in the cities of central and western Europe.

Berechiah (fl. 4th cent.) Palestinian amora. His aggadic sayings are found mostly in the midrashim and the Jerusalem Talmud. In his homilies he stressed the virtues of charity and the uniqueness of the Jewish people.

Berechiah ben Natronai ha-Nakdan (fl. 12th–13th century) French translator and writer. He lived in Normandy and England. His *Fox Fables* were collected largely from non-Jewish sources. He translated into Hebrew the *Quaestiones naturales* of Abelard of Bath and wrote ethical treatises. He has been identified with Benedictus le Puncteur, who lived in Oxford at the end of the 12th century.

Berechiah of Nicole (d. 1278) English financier and scholar. In 1255 he was arrested in connection with the murder of Hugh of Lincoln, but was later released.

Berenice I (fl. late 1st cent. BCE) Judean woman, daughter of **Salome**. She married her cousin **Aristobulus**. After his death she married Theudion, brother-in-law of **Herod** the Great. She was the mother of **Herod Agrippa I**.

Berenice II (b. 28) Judean woman, eldest daughter of **Herod Agrippa I**. She married her uncle Herod of Chalcis. After his death in 48 she was suspected of incest with her brother **Herod Agrippa II** and was induced to marry Polemon II of Cilicia. In 60 she rejoined **Herod Agrippa II** and supported his efforts to suppress the revolt against Rome. She fled with him to the protection of the Romans and became the mistress of Titus. Because of the adverse reaction of the Roman populace, she was forced to part from Titus.

Berenson, Bernard [Bernhard Valvrojenski] (1865–1959) American art historian. Born in Vilna in Lithuania, his family moved to the US. After graduating from Harvard University, he went to London, Oxford, Berlin and finally settled in Italy. In 1907 he began a long relationship with the art dealer, Joseph Duveen. He published a number of works dealing with art history.

Bergelson, David (1884–1952) Ukrainian writer. He initially wrote in Russian and Hebrew but later published Yiddish novels, plays and stories. His works depict Russian Jewish urban life in the early 20th century. After living in Berlin for 11 years, he returned to the USSR, where he published realistic novels with a pro-communist emphasis.

Bergman, George (1900–79) Australian historian and biographer. He was born in Germany, where he worked as a lawyer. In 1933 he went to France and served in the Foreign Legion in World War II. After moving to Australia he entered public service and wrote about Australian Jewish history. He was co-author of *Australian Genesis: Jewish Convicts and Settlers*.

Bergmann, Samuel Hugo (1883–1975) Czech philosopher. He was born in Prague. He was active in the Czech Zionist movement and in 1920 he settled in Palestine. He directed the National and University

Library in Jerusalem and from 1928 he taught philosophy at the Hebrew University, where he was rector from 1936 to 1938. His writings include *Faith and Reason: An Introduction to Modern Jewish Thought* and *Philosophy of Solomon Maimon.*

Bergner, Elisabeth (1897–1986) Austrian actress of Galician origin. Born in Drohobycz, Galicia, she studied at the Vienna Conservatory. She made her debut in 1919 in Zurich. In 1928 she went on a tour of Holland, Denmark, Sweden, Germany and Austria playing in works by Shakespeare, Ibsen and others. From 1923 she appeared in films. In 1933 she emigrated with her husband to Britain where she appeared in plays and films.

Bergner, Herz (1907–70) Australian Yiddish novelist. He emigrated from Galicia to Australia in 1938 and settled in Melbourne. From 1928 he published Yiddish short stories in Europe, Israel, Australia and the US. His later novels and short stories deal with Jewish immigrants in Australia.

Bergner, Yosl (b. 1920) Israeli painter of Austrian origin. Born in Vienna, he studied at the Melbourne Academy of Art and travelled extensively. In 1950 he settled in Israel and lived in Safed. His earlier works depict the life of early Israeli pioneers. After 1957 his paintings were concerned with the Holocaust.

Bergson, Henri (1859–1941) French philosopher. Born in Paris, he taught philosophy at the Angers Lycée and later at Clermont-Ferrard. In 1889 he returned to Paris and in 1900 became professor at the Collège de France. In 1928 he received the Nobel Prize for Literature. His works include *Time and Free Will, Creative Evolution* and *Two Sources of Morality and Religion.*

Berkman, Alexander (1870–1936) US anarchist. Born in Vilna, he emigrated to the US in 1888. He was a member of the Pioneers of Freedom, a Jewish anarchist group. Together with **Emma Goldman**, he led the anarchist movement in the US. In 1892, he shot the director of the steelworks as a protest against the treatment of workers. He was imprisoned, but later released. During World War I he was convicted of engaging in propaganda against conscription, and later deported to the USSR. He later left for Germany, and in 1925 settled in France.

Berkovits, Eliezer (1900–92) American theologian. Born in Oradea, Transylvania, he served as a rabbi in Berlin and later went to England where he was a rabbi in Leeds. He eventually moved to the US and served as a rabbi in Boston. Later he became chairman of the department of Jewish philosophy at the Hebrew Theological College in Chicago. His writings include *Faith after the Holocaust* and *With God in Hell.*

Berkowitz, Yitzḥak Dov (1885–1967) Israeli author. Born in Slutsk, Belorussia, he served as a literary editor of *Ha-Zeman.* In 1906 he married **Sholem Aleichem**'s daughter. Later he went to Warsaw where he edited the literary page of a Yiddish journal. He eventually settled in the USA where he edited *Ha-Toren* and *Miklat.* In 1928 he settled in Palestine and became an editor of *Moznayim.* He published a translation of the works of **Sholom Aleichem**.

Berl, Emmanuel (1892–1976) French journalist. Born in Paris, he published novels, essays and pamphlets, and after World War II he wrote essays about Israel.

Berlin, Irving [Balin, Israel] (1888–1989) American songwriter. Born in Tumen, Siberia, he was the son of a cantor. His family went to the US, and he founded his own music publishing company. He composed more than 1000 songs and wrote songs for numerous films as well as Broadway shows.

Berlin, Isaiah (1909–97) British philosopher. Born in Latvia, he was the first Jewish fellow of All Souls at Oxford, and later became professor of social and political theory and president of Wolfson College, Oxford. He published a range of works concerning philosophy and Marxism. He was knighted in 1957 and received the Order of Merit in 1971. His works include *Karl Marx: His Life and Environment, Four Essays on Liberty, Against the Current* and *The Crooked Timber of Humanity.*

Berlin, Isaiah ben Judah Loeb [Pick, Isaiah] (1725–99) German talmudist. He was born in Hungary and lived in Berlin and Breslau. He wrote on a wide range of rabbinic literature. His emendations have been added to editions of the Talmud since 1800.

Berlin, Naphtali Tzevi Judah [Ha-Natziv] (1817–93) Lithuanian talmudist. He was born in Mir and was head of the yeshivah at Volozhin for 40 years. He was one of the first rabbis to support Zionism. His *Haamek Sheelah* concerns the *Sheiltot of Aḥa of Shabha.*

Berlin, Saul (1740–94) German rabbi. He served as rabbi of Frankfurt an der Oder but later retired from the rabbinate and settled in Berlin. He wrote a volume of responsa containing radical views which he attributed to **Asher ben Jehiel** and his contemporaries.

Berliner, Abraham (1833–1915) German literary historian. Born in Posen he taught Jewish history and literature at the Berlin Rabbinical Seminary. His publications include an edition of **Rashi**'s commentary on the Pentateuch, studies of medieval Bible commentators, an edition of *Targum Onkelos*, studies of Jewish life in the Middle Ages, and a history of the Jewish community of Rome.

Berliner, Emile (1851–1929) American inventor. He emigrated to the US at the age of 19, and showed aptitude in scientific subjects and technological fields. His inventions made possible the long-distance use of the telephone and the practical use of the phonograph. Later he designed helicopters.

Berlinski, Herman (1910–2001) American composer, conductor and organist. Born in Leipzig, he emigrated to the US in 1946. He held positions at Temple Emanuel in New York and the Washington Hebrew Congregation. He was also professor of comparative history of sacred music at the Catholic University of America. His compositions include *The Burning Bush* (1957), *Avodat Shabbat* (1958) and *Job* (1971).

Berman, Hannah (1883–1955) English novelist and translator of Lithuanian origin. She translated novels by **Sholem Aleichem** and I. A. Lisky as well as Yiddish short stories. She also wrote two novels in English, which describe Jewish life in Lithuania under the rule of Nicholas I.

Bermann, Issachar (fl. 17th–18th cent.) German actor. He was a pioneer of the Yiddish folk theatre, founding a Yiddish drama group in Frankfurt am Main in 1708.

Bermant, Chaim (1929–98) British writer of Polish origin. After settling in the UK, he worked as a schoolteacher, economist, television writer and journalist. His writings include *Jericho Sleep Alone, Diary of an Old Man, Israel, Troubled Eden: An Anatomy of British Jewry, The Cousinhood: The Anglo-Jewish Gentry, Point of Arrival: A Study of London's East End, Coming Home* and *The Jews.*

Bernard-Lazare [Lazare, Bernard] (1865–1903) French writer. Born in Nîmes into a prosperous family of traders, he rebelled against the education he received and settled in Paris in 1886. He soon gained notoriety as a critic of the establishment. His Jewish journey is found in his epic: *Le Fumier de Job.* He also wrote a history of anti-Semitism. He sought to demonstrate that Dreyfus was innocent of the charges brought against him.

Bernays, Isaac (1792–1849) German rabbi. He was born in Mainz and served as rabbi in Hamburg from 1821. In his struggle against Reform Judaism, he denounced the Reform prayerbook. His modern approach to Orthodoxy influenced his disciple **Samson Raphael Hirsch**.

Bernfeld, Simon (1860–1940) Galician scholar. He was appointed chief rabbi of Belgrade in 1886. In 1894 he settled in Berlin, where he wrote on Jewish history and philosophy.

Bernhardt, Sarah (1844–1923) French actress. She was baptized at an early age. She began her career at the Comédie-Française in 1862; in 1866 she joined the Odéon theatre. In 1872 she returned to the Comédie-Française and later toured Europe, the United States, South America and Australia. Her writings include *Petite idol* and *Ma double vie.*

Bernstein, Eduard (1850–1932) German propagandist. Born in Berlin, he joined the Marxist wing of the labour movement in 1872. He later left Germany for Switzerland and became editor of *Der Sozialdemokrat* in 1881. In 1888 he was expelled from the country, and emigrated to London where he published *Evolutionary Socialism*. He subsequently settled in Germany and became the theoretician of the revisionist school of the reformist labour movement. In 1902 he became a member of the Reichstag, sitting until 1906 and again from 1912–18. During World War I he sided with the Independent Socialists, and from 1920–8 he served as a Social Democrat in Parliament.

Bernstein, Ignaz (1836–1909) Polish Yiddish folklorist. As a rich merchant of Warsaw, he travelled for 35 years through Europe, North Africa and Palestine, collecting Yiddish proverbs, which he published in several volumes.

Bernstein, Julius (1839–1917) German scientist. Born in Berlin, he studied medicine in Breslau and Berlin. From 1864 he served as an assistant in Heidelberg, later becoming associate professor in physiology at the University of Halle, and eventually professor.

Bernstein, Leonard (1918–90) American composer and conductor. He was born in Lawrence, Massachusetts. He became director and conductor of the New York Philharmonic. His many works on Jewish subjects include the symphonies *Jeremiah* and *Kaddish*.

Ber of Bolechov [Birkenthav, Ber] (1723–1805) Galician writer. As one of the first maskilim, he took part in a debate with the Frankists at Lvov in 1759. He wrote a polemic against the Shabbetaians and the Frankists. His memoirs are a major source for the study of the economic and cultural conditions of Galician Jews in this period.

Bershadski, Isaiah (1817–1908) Russian Hebrew novelist. He was born in Belorussia and lived in Russia. His novel *To No Purpose* depicts Jewish life in the Pale of Settlement, and *Against the Stream* describes the collapse of traditional Russian Jewish life.

Bertinoro, Obadiah of (c. 1450–1510) Italian scholar. In 1485 he went to Palestine and settled in Jerusalem, where he founded a yeshivah. He was recognized as the chief halakhic authority in Palestine and Egypt. His writings include a commentary on the Mishnah, in which he incorporated the explanations of the Talmud as well as medieval commentators.

Beruryah (fl. 2nd cent.) Palestinian scholar. She was the wife of **Meir**. She is the only woman in talmudic literature whose views on legal matters were recognized by contemporary scholars.

Bettelheim, Bruno (1903–90) American psychologist and educator. He was born in Vienna. In 1938 he was transported to the Dachau concentration camp and then to Buchenwald. In 1939 he was released and settled in the US. He was principal of the University of Chicago's Orthogenic School for children with severe psychological problems and professor of educational psychology at the university. His psychological theories were based on his experiences in the concentration camps. His *The Children of the Dream* is an analysis of the rearing of kibbutz children.

Bezalel (fl. ?13th cent. BCE) Israelite craftsman who constructed and decorated the Ark of the Covenant (Exodus 36:2).

Bezem, Naftali (b. 1924) Israeli artist. He was born in Essen, Germany, and went to Palestine in 1939. In 1947 he was a teacher of painting in the detention camps in Cyprus. A number of his works deal with biblical and Jewish themes. After the death of his son (caused by a booby trap) in Jerusalem, he worked in Paris, where he painted a series of pessimistic paintings.

Bialik, Ḥayyim Naḥman (1873–1934) Russian Hebew poet, essayist, storywriter and translator. He was born in Zhitomir and lived in Volozhin, Odessa, Korostyshev, Sosnowiec and Warsaw. In 1924 he settled in Palestine. His poetry is infused with Jewish hopes, memories and national aspirations; written in a simple lyric style, it uses Hebrew metrics and biblical parallelism. His essays trace the course of Jewish culture, the state of Hebrew literature, and the development of language and style. Together with **Yehoshua Ḥana Ravnitzky** he published *Sepher ha-Aggadah*, which classified midrashic material according to subject matter.

Bibago, Abraham ben Shemtov (fl. 15th cent.) Spanish philosopher and writer. He was born in Aragon and became head of the yeshivah in Zaragoza. He engaged in disputations with Christian scholars at the court of Juan II, King of Aragon. His *The Path of Faith* examines the principal tenets of Judaism. He also wrote commentaries on Aristotle's works.

Bickerman, Elias J. (1897–1981) American historian. He was born in Kishinev in the Ukraine. He taught at the University of Berlin from 1929 to 1932, when he emigrated to France. He later settled in the US, where he taught at the New School for Social Research, the Jewish Theological Seminary, the University of Judaism in Los Angeles, and Columbia University. His published writings cover ancient history, law, religion, epigraphy, chronology, and the political history of the Hellenistic world.

Bilhah (fl. ?19th–16th cent. BCE) Israelite woman, concubine of **Jacob**. She was the mother of **Dan** and **Naphtali. Rachel**, whose servant she was, gave Bilhah to **Jacob** when she herself proved to be barren (Genesis 30:18; 32:25–26).

Binder, A. W. (1865–1966) American composer. He was born in New York. He became instructor in Jewish music at the Jewish Institute of Religion in 1921 and music director at the Stephen Wise Free Synagogue the following year. In 1948 he was appointed professor of Jewish liturgical music at the Hebrew Union College-Jewish Institute of Religion. He wrote synagogue services and songs, Hebrew and Yiddish songs, cantatas and oratorios, as well as chamber and orchestral music.

Birnbaum, Eduard (1855–1920) Polish liturgical composer and cantor. He was born in Kraków and served as cantor in Beuthen and Königsberg. He composed liturgical works, catalogued synagogue melodies thematically and collected references to music in rabbinic texts.

Birnbaum, Nathan [Acher, Mattathias] (1864–1937) Austrian political philosopher. He was born in Vienna. An advocate of Jewish nationalism, he co-operated with **Theodor Herzl** and served as general secretary of the World Zionist Organization. However after the Third Zionist Congress in 1899, he became an opponent of the Zionist movement. He regarded cultural and political autonomy in the diaspora as the means of attaining Jewish national existence. He was a convenor of the conference at Czernowitz in 1908 which proclaimed Yiddish as a national language. Later he embraced Orthodoxy.

Birnbaum, Solomon (1891–1990) British palaeographer and Yiddish philologist of Austrian origin. He was born in Vienna. He lectured in Yiddish at Hamburg University from 1922 to 1933, when he emigrated to England. He taught Yiddish and Hebrew palaeography at the London School of Oriental Studies and the School of Slavonic and East European Studies. He wrote for Yiddish newspapers and journals and published works on Yiddish grammar. His major work is in the field of palaeography.

Blank, Samuel Leib (1893–1962) American Hebrew novelist and author of short stories, of Ukrainian origin. He lived in Bessarabia and settled in the US in 1922. His writings depict Jewish farmers in Bessarabia, the pogroms in the Ukraine, and immigrant life in the US.

Blankfort, Michael (1907–82) American novelist, playwright and screenwriter. He was born in New York. He taught psychology at Bowdoin College and Princeton, and worked as a clinical psychologist. He subsequently was a freelance novelist, dramatist and screenwriter. His novel *The Juggler* portrays the disturbance and eventual recovery of a Holocaust survivor in Israel. *Behold the Fire* deals with the Nili, a secret group of Palestinian Jews who served as spies for the British.

Blaser, Isaac ben Moses Solomon (1837–1907) Lithuanian rabbi and educator. He was born in Vilna. A disciple of Israel Salanter, he served as rabbi in St Petersburg and later settled in Kovno, Lithuania, where he headed the advanced talmudic academy. He helped to found the yeshivah of Slobodka. In 1904 he emigrated to Palestine and settled in Jerusalem. He made an important contribution to the Musar movement in his emphasis on acquiring piety by emotional meditation on works of musar.

Blau, Amram (1894–1974) Palestinian religious leader. He was born in Jerusalem. He was a founder of the anti-Zionist Ḥevrat Ḥayyim and refused to recognize the State of Israel when it was established in 1948. When Ḥevrat Ḥayyim was reconstituted as the ultra-Orthodox sect Neturei Karta he became its leader. After his first wife's death, he married a proselyte, Ruth Ben-David.

Blau, Lajos (1861–1936) Hungarian talmudist. He was a professor and director of the Jewish Theological Seminary of Budapest. He served as editor of the *Hungarian Jewish Review* and was a founder of the Hebrew review *Ha-Tzopheh.* He wrote on Jewish history and literature.

Blaustein, Jacob (1892–1970) American industrialist. He was the son of Louis Blaustein, the founder of American Oil Company, and worked with his father. He served as president of the American Jewish Committee and was a leading member of the Conference on Jewish Claims Against Germany. In 1956 he was a member of the US delegation to the United Nations General Assembly, dealing with social and economic affairs.

Bleichröder, Gerson von (1822–93) German banker. Born in Berlin, he entered his father's banking business and eventually became head of the firm. He became involved in the metallurgical industry and in railroads. In 1859 he was co-founder of a syndicate to finance Prussian mobilization during the Franco-Austrian war. When Bismark became premier in 1862, he became his financial adviser. In 1872 he was raised to the hereditary noblility and was appointed British consul general in Berlin.

Blitzstein, Marc (1905–64) American composer. Born in Philadelphia, he studied with Nadia Boulanger in Paris and **Arnold Schoenberg** in Berlin. He composed works of social conciousness and also wrote film music and music for Shakespearean plays.

Bloch, Edward (1816–81) American publisher. An immigrant from Bohemia, he learned the printing trade in Albany and founded the Bloch Publishing Company in Cincinnati. Eventually the press was transferred to New York City by his son Charles.

Bloch, Ernest (1830–1959) American composer of Swiss origin. He was professor of composition at the Geneva Conservatory. In 1917 he settled in the US, where he served as director of the San Francisco Conservatory of Music. His works include *Trois poèmes juifs* (1913), *Israel Symphony* (1912–16), the rhapsody *Shelomoh* (1915–16), and *Avodat ha-kodesh* (1930–3).

Bloch, Ernst (1885–1977) German Marxist-humanist philosopher. Born in the Rhineland city of Ludwigshafen, he began a teaching career at the University of Leipzig in 1918. In 1933 he fled to Switzerland and later emigrated to the US where he completed *Das Prinzip Hoffnung.* After World War II he returned to the University of Leipzig to teach philosophy. In 1960 he defected to West Germany and became a visiting professor at the University of Tübingen.

Bloch, Felix (1905–83) Swiss-American physicist. Born in Zurich, he studied engineering at the Swiss Federal Institute of Technology. With the rise of Hitler, he settled in the US and took up a position at Stanford University. During World War II he was involved with the Manhattan Project. In 1952 he received the Nobel Prize for his work on nuclear induction.

Bloch, Ivan (1836–1901) Russian pacifist, financier and writer. Born in Radom, Poland, he became a banker and was involved in the construction and operation of the Russian railway system. As a pacifist, he published a study of war; this multi-volume work helped convince Tsar Nicholas II to convene the 1899 Hague Peace Conference. Although he converted to Calvinism, he was concerned with Russian Jewry and campaigned on their behalf. A friend of **Theodor Herzl**, he introduced him to important Russian authorities.

Bloch, Jean-Richard (1884–1947) French author. He was born in Paris. When the Germans occupied France, Bloch escaped to Moscow, but later returned. His writings deal with the place of Jewry in contemporary society. His novel *Lévy* (1911) concerns the effects of the **Dreyfus** case on a Jewish family in a provincial French town. In *& Co.* (1918) he describes a Jewish cloth merchant from Alsace, who moves to a small town in western France.

Bloch, Joseph Samuel (1850–1923) Austrian rabbi. He was born in Galicia. He served as a lecturer in the Vienna bet midrash. In 1882 he accused August Rohling of perjury for his allegation that Jews practised ritual murder. Rohling sued Bloch, but later withdrew his suit. Bloch was a member of the Austrian parliament. In 1885 he established the Union of Austrian Jews to Combat Anti-Semitism. His *Israel and the Nations* (1922) is a defence of Judaism.

Bloch, Konrad (1912–2000) American biochemist, of German origin. He emigrated to the US in 1936 and taught at Columbia and Harvard universities. In 1964 he was awarded the Nobel Prize in Physiology and Medicine for the discovery of the mechanism of cholesterol and fatty acid metabolism.

Bloch, Marc (1886–1944) French historian. Born in Lyons, he studied at the École Normale Supérieure in Paris. He then studied in Germany and returned to France to work in Paris. He influenced a generation of French historical scholarship through his teaching and the journal *Annales d'Historie Economique et Sociale.* He was a professor at Strasbourg University and at the Sorbonne. After the defeat of France, he taught in Vichy France for three years and then joined the French resistance. In 1944 he was arrested by the Nazis and executed.

Blondes, David (fl. late 19th–early 20th cent.) Lithuanian barber. He was accused of wounding a girl in order to use her blood for ritual purposes. He was convicted of injurious intent and sentenced to prison. On appeal in 1902 he was acquitted of all charges.

Bloom, Harold (b. 1930) American literary critic and editor. He was born in New York and taught at Yale. In his literary work he has been influenced by the kabbalah and by **Martin Buber**. His publications include *Kabbalah and Criticism*, *Poetry and Repression* and *Agnon: Towards a Theory of Revisionism.*

Bloom, Hyman (b. 1913) American painter. He was born in Bounoviski, Lithuania, and emigrated to the US in 1920. Following the Depression he was employed by the Federal Arts Project in Boston. Early in his career he painted works dealing with European Jewry and he later returned to themes of the synagogue and Jewish observance.

Bloom, Sol (1870–1949) American politician and businessman. He was born in Pekin, Illinois, but in 1875 moved to San Francisco with his family. At the age of 13 he became a bookkeeper. Later he worked in San Francisco theatres, performing various jobs. With his brother he began a retail business. In 1903 he moved to New York City where he entered the real estate and construction business. In 1923 he was elected to the House of Representatives. A supporter of the United Nations, he was appointed by Franklin D. Roosevelt to serve as a delegate to the San Francisco Conference in 1945. Later he served on the delegation committee to the Rio de Janeiro Conference.

Bloomgarden, Solomon [Jehoash; Yehoash] (1870–1927) American Yiddish poet and author of Lithuanian origin. He emigrated to the US in 1890. He wrote dramas, poems, fables, folktales and stories, and translated the Bible into Yiddish. With C. D. Spivak he compiled a dictionary of Hebrew and Aramaic elements in the Yiddish language.

Blue, Lionel (b. 1930) English rabbi and writer. He was born in London. He served as convenor of the Reform bet din in London, and taught at Leo Baeck College. His publications include *To Heaven with Scribes and Pharisees*, *A Taste of Heaven*, *A Backdoor to Heaven*, *Simply Divine*, *Bolts from the Blue* and *Blue Heaven.*

Blum, Julius (1843–1919) Austrian financier. In 1869 he was sent to Egypt to take charge of the Alexandria branch of an Austrian bank. In 1877 he became under-secretary of finance. In 1890 he resigned, returned to the bank in Vienna and became its president.

Blum, Léon (1872–1950) French statesman. He first worked as a literary critic and author. He was premier in the Popular Front government of 1936–7, vice-premier from 1937–8, and premier in 1938. In 1943 he was handed over to the Germans, who deported him to Buchenwald, but he survived the war and was liberated in 1945. In 1946–7 he was head of an interim government and he became vice-premier in 1948. He was active in Jewish affairs and served on the council of the Jewish agency.

Blumenfeld, Kurt Yehudah (1884–1963) German Zionist leader. He was born in Trüburg. He was one of the founders of Keren ha-Yesod and was president of the German Zionist Federation from 1923 to 1933. In that year he settled in Palestine and became a member of the Keren ha-Yesod directorate.

Blumenfeld, Simon (1907–89) English novelist, journalist and playwright. His novels include *Jew Boy*, *Phineas Kahn* and *They Won't Let You Live*. Later he turned to journalism and drama. After the war he held various editorial jobs before working for the theatrical magazine *Stage*.

Blumenkranz, Bernhard (b. 1913) French historian. He lectured on the social history of the Jews at the École Pratique des Hautes Études in Paris and was president of the French Commission on Jewish Archives. His writings deal with Jewish Christian relations in the Middle Ages and the history of the Jews in medieval France.

Blumenthal, Nissan (1805–1903) Ukrainian cantor. He was chief cantor at the Brody Synagogue in Odessa, where he founded a choir school to develop choral singing in four voices. He introduced melodies from German classical music into the liturgy.

Boas, Franz (1858–1942) American anthropologist. Born in Minden, Westphalia, he studied the Eskimos in Baffin Island. After teaching at Berlin University, he went to the US where he taught at Clark University, later becoming professor of anthropology at Columbia and in 1901 curator of the American Museum of Natural History. From 1908–25 he edited the *Journal of American Folklore*. Later he led a campaign against Nazi racism.

Boaz (fl. 12th cent. BCE) Israelite landowner, husband of **Ruth**. When **Ruth** came to glean in his fields, Boaz saw and admired her devotion to her widowed mother-in-law **Naomi**. As a kinsman of **Elimelech** (Ruth's father-in-law), Boaz undertook to marry her (Ruth 2–4).

Bodenheimer, Max Isador (1865–1940) German Zionist leader. A Cologne lawyer, he was an associate of **Theodor Herzl**, and became one of the delegation that accompanied him in 1898 to Constantinople and Palestine to meet the kaiser. At the first Zionist Congress, he helped draft the Basle Programme and the statutes of the World Zionist Organization. He later was president of the German Zionist Federation (1897–1910), and chairman of the Jewish National Fund (1907–14). He eventually joined the Revisionist movement, but resigned when it succeeded from the World Zionist Organization. In 1935 he settled in Jerusalem. His memoirs *Prelude to Israel* were published posthumously.

Bodo-Eleazer (fl. 1st cent.) Spanish apostate. He served as a deacon at the court of Louis the Pious and the emperor's confessor. When he converted to Judaism, he took the name Eleazar. Much of what is known of him is based on his exchange of correspondence with Paolo Alvaro, a Christian layman from Cordova. Using his knowledge of anti-Jewish polemics, he attacked his former faith.

Bograshov, Chaim (1876–1963) Israeli educator. He grew up in the Ukraine, where he taught in Jewish schools. He served as a delegate to the Sixth Zionist Congress, and in 1904 was asked to go to Palestine and survey the possiblity of a high school with Hebrew as its means of instruction. Two years later he helped found the Herzliah Gymnazia where he became a teacher. He was a founder of Tel Aviv. After the Arab riots of 1921, he estabished its Nordia quarter to house Jews who had fled from Arab Jaffa. He served in the Knesset from 1951 to 1955.

Bogrov, Grigori (1825–85) Russian author. He wrote historical novels which were critical of Jewish leadership, and advocated reform. He was baptized before his death.

Böhm, Adolf (1873–1941) Bohemian Zionist historian and leader. He lived in Vienna, where he advocated practical work in Palestine. He wrote about Palestinian financial and agrarian problems, edited *Palästina*, the German monthly for Palestinography, and wrote a history of Zionism.

Bohr, Niels (1885–1962) Danish physicist. Born in Copenhagen, he was the son of a non-Jewish father. He became professor of chemical physics at the University of Copenhagen, and in 1920 head of the Institute of Theoretical Physics. In 1922 he was awarded the Nobel Prize.

Bomberg, Daniel (d. between 1533 and 1549) Hebrew printer. Born in Antwerp, he founded a Hebrew publishing firm in Venice in 1516 which published about 200 books, including the first complete editions of the Palestinian and Babylonian Talmuds, the Tosephta, and the Rabbinic Bible. His pagination of the Talmud has become standard.

Bomberg, David (1890–1957) English painter. He was born in Birmingham and lived in the East End of London. A number of his paintings were influenced by scenes in the Whitechapel area. From 1923 to 1927 he lived in Palestine and later travelled widely. He returned to England and taught at the Borough Polytechnic in London from 1945 to 1953. His paintings include 'Ghetto Theatre', 'The Talmudist' and 'Hear, O Israel'.

Bonfils, Joseph ben Samuel [Tov Elem; Tuv Elem] (fl. 11th cent.) French talmudist. He was born in Narbonne and lived at Limoges and Anjou. He wrote religious poems, biblical and talmudic commentaries, and codifications of Jewish law.

Boraisha, Menaḥem (1888–1949) American Yiddish poet of Polish origin. He emigrated to the US in 1914. His poem *Polyn* expresses the tense relationship between Jews and Poles. He published a number of collections, including a *A ring in der keyt*, *Zamd*, a book of lyrics, one of which is on **Theodor Herzl**, and *Zavl rimer*, a rhymed chronicle exposing the horror of post-war Russian pogroms. His *The Wayfarer* is a spiritual autobiography.

Borchardt [Hermann], Georg (1871–1943) German author and art historican. He was born in Berlin and lived there until 1933, when he emigrated to Holland. After the Nazi invasion he was deported to Auschwitz, where he died. He published essays on fine art, sketches, novels and short stories. His fictional works portray cultivated Berlin Jews in the 19th century and modern Jewish intellectual life.

Born, Max (1882–1970) German physicist. He was born in Breslau, and lectured on physics in Berlin, Frankfurt and Göttingen. He later moved to Britain and taught at Edinburgh University. On his retirement, he returned to Germany. He played a major role in the development of modern theoretical physics.

Börne, Ludwig (1786–1837) German writer. Born in Frankfurt am Main, he studied medicine in Giessen and Berlin. Later he studied law, political science, and administration in Heidelberg. He became a police actuary in Frankfurt, but lost his position with the defeat of Napoleon. He converted to Protestantism. With **Heinrich Heine**, he was the initiator of the German feuilleton. His volumes of *Briefe aus Paris* first appeared in 1832. His writings in favour of Jewish emancipation include *Für die Juden* and *Der ewige Jude*.

Borochov, Dov Ber (1881–1917) Ukrainian Socialist Zionist leader and writer. He was a founder of Poale Zion in 1906 and served as secretary of the World Confederation of Poale Zion. Having left Russia, he was from 1914 a spokesman for the American Poale Zion and for the World and American Jewish Congress movements. He later returned to the USSR. He analysed the economic and social situation of the Jewish people along Marxist lines, and argued for their settlement in Palestine.

Borowitz, Eugene (b. 1924) American theologian. He was born in New York. He became professor of education and Jewish religious thought at the Hebrew Union College-Jewish Institute of Religion in New York in 1962. He is the author of numerous books about contemporary Jewish thought and has served as visiting professor at various universities including Princeton, Columbia and Harvard.

Boscovitch, Alexander Uriah (1907–64) Israeli composer. He was born in Cluj, Transylvania, and conducted the Jewish Goldmark Orchestra there. In 1938 he settled in Palestine, and later became a music critic for the daily paper *Ha-Aretz*. He advocated the development of a nationalist school of composition in which the composer would represent the new reality of life in Palestine.

Bostanai ben Ḥanina (fl. 7th cent.) Babylonian exilarch. He was the first exilarch after the Arab conquest and his office was confirmed by the caliph Omar. He was appointed a member of the Council of State, and married a daughter of Chosroes, the former Persian king.

Boteach, Shmuel (b. 1966) American writer and broadcaster. Born in Los Angeles, he studied at

Yeshiva Toras Emes in Jerusalem and at the Central Lubavitch Yeshiva. He is the author of books dealing with Judaism and modernity, and a radio host.

Brafman, Jacob (c. 1825–79) Russian scholar. He was born in Kletsk. He converted to Christianity, joining the Greek Orthodox Church, and served as a teacher of Hebrew at the government theological seminary in Minsk. Later he was censor of Hebrew and Yiddish books in Vilna and St Petersburg. His *The Book of the Kahal* is a translation into Russian of the minutes of the kehillah of Minsk; it describes how Jews acquire power over gentiles and it was used to justify anti-Jewish acts.

Brainin, Reuben (1862–1939) American Hebrew and Yiddish author of Russian origin. He was born in Belorussia and lived for a time in Vienna and Berlin. At the beginning of the 20th century he encouraged the infusion of humanistic themes and new literary forms into Hebrew literature. From 1909 he lived in the US and Canada. During his later years he devoted himself to journalism, through which means he supported Jewish settlement in the Russian province of Birobidjan. He edited a number of Hebrew and Yiddish periodicals.

Bramson, Leon (1869–1941) Russian communal worker and writer. He was born in Kovno. He was active in the Society for the Dissemination of Enlightenment Among the Jews, and served as director of the Jewish Colonization Association from 1899 to 1906. During World War I, the Russian Revolution and the Civil War, he was an organizer of the Central Committee for the Relief of Jewish War Sufferers. When he left Russia in 1920 he worked in western Europe on behalf of ORT.

Brand, Joel (1906–64) Hungarian Zionist. Born in Hungary, he grew up in Germany but settled in Budapest in the 1930s. He was active in Jewish rescue efforts. In 1944 he was associated with Rudolf Kasztner in negotiations with Adolf Eichmann for the release of Hungarian Jews in exchange for military trucks and other material. He went to Constantinople to discuss the matter with Jewish Agency leaders, but was arrested in Syria by the British authorities on the allegation he was a German spy and was interned in Egypt. In 1944 he was released when the Hungarian Jews were rounded up and transported to concentration camps. He settled in Palestine and sought to track down Nazi criminals.

Brandeis, Louis Dembitz (1856–1941) American lawyer and Zionist leader. He was born in Louisville, Kentucky. He served as justice to the Supreme Court from 1916 to 1939, its first Jewish member. He was active in American Zionsm and the World Zionist Organization. Brandeis University was named after him.

Brandes, Carl (1847–1931) Danish writer. The brother of **Georg Brandes**, he studied at the University of Copenhagen. He specialized in Persian and Sanskrit, but later turned to literature and politics. With his brother, he produced the periodical *Det 19. Aahundrede.* He also was a journalist for the Radical party. Later he founded and edited *Politiken.* He subsequently served as minister of finance.

Brandes, Georg (1842–1927) Danish literary critic and writer. He was born in Copenhagen. He advocated the acceptance by Jews of the work of Ibsen, Björnsen, Strindberg and Nietzsche. His writings include *Main Currents of Nineteenth-Century Literature* and studies of Lassalle, Disraeli, Shakespeare, Goethe, Voltaire, Michelangelo and Julius Caesar. Although he defended **Dreyfus**, he did not embrace Zionism until after World War I.

Brandstätter, Mordecai David (1844–1928) Galician Hebrew novelist. He was a successful manufacturer and owing to the circles in which he moved, became interested in Haskalah. He contributed stories about Ḥasidic life in Galicia to the Hebrew journal *Ha-Shaḥar.* In his writing he ridiculed the Ḥasidim and the materialism of Galician Jewry. He later joined the Ḥibbat Zion movement and extolled Zionism in his stories.

Brann, Marcus (1849–1920) Polish historian. He was appointed successor to **Heinrich Graetz** at the Breslau Rabbinical Seminary. He wrote studies of Jewish history, literature and bibliography, and served as co-editor of *Germania Judaica*, a topographical encyclopaedia of German Jewish history.

Braudes, Reuben Asher (1851–1902) Lithuanian Hebrew novelist and reformer. He was born in Vilna and lived in Odessa, Warsaw and Lemberg where he edited the monthly journal *Ha-Boker Or*. He later lived in Romania and Vienna. His novel *Two Extremes* depicts the limitations of Haskalah and Orthodoxy, and endorses Jewish nationalism. His writings, which advocate social and religious reform, reflect the intellectual changes taking place in eastern European Jewish society at the end of the 19th century.

Brauer, Erich (b. 1929) Austrian painter. He was born in Vienna. From 1938 to 1945 he was interned in a concentration camp. After the liberation he travelled extensively, and lived in Austria and Israel. His paintings depict crimes against the Jews, such as pogroms and the Holocaust.

Braunstein, Menaḥem Mendel [Mibashan] (1858–1944) Romanian Hebrew writer. He was one of the founders in Jassy of Doresh le-Zion, an organization which sought to revive the movement of Romanian Jews to Palestine. He edited the newspaper *Jüdischer Volksfreund* and taught Hebrew subjects in Jewish schools throughout Romania. He published a history of the Jewish people, as well as poems and stories for young people. He settled in Palestine in 1914.

Brenner, Yoseph Ḥayyim (1881–1921) Hebrew author and editor of Ukrainian origin. He edited the Bund newspaper in Homel in 1898. His sketches of Jewish poverty in Russia appeared in 1900 and were followed by his novels *In Winter* and *Around the Point*. From 1904 to 1907 he lived in London, where he published the journal *Ha-Meorer*, which criticized Jewish political life. Later he lived in Lemberg, where he edited *Revivim*. In 1909 he settled in Palestine and became a leader of the workers' movement; his stories of this period describe contemporary Palestinian life. In 1919 he became the editor of the journal *Ha-Adamah*. He was murdered by the Arabs.

Breuer, Isaac (1883–1946) He was the leader of Orthodox Jewry of Hungarian origin, the son of **Solomon Breuer**. He lived in Frankfurt am Main where he was active in Jewish organizations. When Agudat Israel was founded in 1912 he became one of its ideologists. He settled in Jerusalem in 1936 and he served as president of Poale Agudat Israel. He published works on Judaism and Jewish problems.

Breuer, Joseph (1842–1925) Austrian physician. Born in Vienna, he studied medicine in Vienna and later taught at the University of Vienna. In addition to his clinical work, he was involved in neurological, respiratory and otic research. His most important case was that of Anno O. Under his influence, **Sigmund Freud** developed his theory of psychoanalysis.

Breuer, Solomon (1850–1926) German rabbi. He served as rabbi in Frankfurt am Main and founded the Association of Orthodox Rabbis in Germany. He was president of the Free Union for the Advancement of Orthodoxy and co-founder of the Agudat Israel movement. In 1890 he founded and directed a yeshivah. With Phinehas Kohn he published the periodical *Jüdische Monatshefte* from 1913 to 1920.

Brice, Fanny (1891–1951) American entertainer. Born in New York City, she was heard by Florenz Ziegfeld in a burlesque show and became a regular performer in the Ziegfeld Follies. She appeared in musical shows in the 1920s and 1930s. Her career was the basis of the film *Funny Girl*.

Brill, Jehiel (1836–86) Hebrew journalist of Russian origin. He settled in Palestine, where he edited the journal *Ha-Levanon* in 1863–4. The periodical reappeared under his editorship in Paris in 1865, and later in Mainz from 1872 to 1882. It supported Jewish law and the Jerusalem rabbis, and attacked the Haskalah and religious reform. After the Russian pogroms of 1881, Brill returned to Palestine and helped to found the colony of Ekron. As a result of a dispute he left the country and settled in London, where he founded the Yiddish newspaper *Ha-Shulamit*. He also published editions of several medieval texts.

Brill, Joseph [Iyyov of Minsk] (1839–1914) Russian Hebrew author. He was born in Gorki. He published critical essays as well as satirical feuilletons and parodies modelled on midrashic and talmudic texts.

Briscoe, Robert (1894–1969) Irish politician. He was an IRA member, and later became a member of the Dail in De Valera's Finna Fail Party. He held his seat until he retired in 1965. He twice served as Lord Mayor of Dublin.

Brittan, Leon (b. 1939) British politician. Born in London, he served as minister of state, home office, secretary of state for trade and industry, and vice-president commissioner of the European Communities.

Broch, Hermann (1886–1951) Austrian writer. Born in Vienna, he went to Realschule and was later given a vocational training. In 1909 he married and converted to Catholicism. He studied at the University of Vienna, while director of the family factory. He commenced his trilogy, *Die Schlafwandler*, in 1927. He then worked on a religious novel. His most important work is *Der Tod des Vergil* which was written in American exile.

Brod, Max (1884–1968) Austrian author and composer. He was born in Prague. He was a founder of the National Council of Jews of Czechoslovakia and became active in the Zionist movement. In 1939 he settled in Palestine, where he worked as a music critic and drama adviser to the Ha-Bimah theatre. His writings include a trilogy of historical novels, a story of the Israeli War of Independence, and studies of Judaism. He was the discoverer and biographer of **Franz Kafka**, whose works he edited. His musical compositions include *Requiem Hebraïcum* and Israeli dances.

Broder [Margulies], Berl (1815–68) Galician composer. He organized the first troupe of professional Yiddish folk singers. They toured Galicia, Hungary and Romania in the 1860s and sang many of his songs.

Broderson, Moses (1860–1956) Russian Yiddish poet and theatre director. He was born in Moscow and lived in Lódź from 1918 to 1938. He was a journalist, poet and writer of songs for children. He founded a number of small theatres and wrote modest plays and librettos for operas. He was confined to a Siberian labour camp from 1948 to 1955. His wife, Sheyne, Miriam Broderson, described their years of misery in *My Tragic Road with Moshe Broderson.*

Brodetsky, Selig (1888–1954) British mathematician and Zionist leader, of Ukrainian origin. He was professor of mathematics at the University of Leeds from 1920 to 1949 and served as president of the Board of Deputies of British Jews from 1939 to 1949. In that year he became president of the Hebrew University, but returned to England in 1952.

Brodie, Israel (1895–1979) British rabbi. He was born in Newcastle upon Tyne. He served as senior minister in Melbourne, Australia, from 1923 to 1937. After several years as senior chaplain in the British Army, he was appointed chief rabbi of the British Commonwealth and continued in that office until 1965.

Brodski, Iosif [Joseph] Aleksandrovich (b. 1940) Russian poet. After having been arrested several times, he left the USSR in 1972, and settled in the US. His publications include the poem *Isaak i Avraam*, which deals with the sacrifice of **Isaac**. He also wrote a poem about the Jewish cemetery near Leningrad.

Brody, Heinrich (1868–1942) Hebrew scholar of Hungarian origin. He was appointed chief rabbi of Prague in 1912. He settled in Palestine in 1933 and was appointed head of the Schocken Institute for Hebrew Poetry. He was co-founder and editor of the *Zeitschrift für hebraïsche Bibliographie* and edited the poems of **Judah Ha-Levi**, **Moses ibn Ezra** and **Immanuel of Rome**.

Bródy, Sándor (1863–1924) Hungarian novelist and playwright. He prepared the ground for the development of Hungarian prose in the 20th century. A number of his stories and plays introduce Jewish characters. His collection of short stories *Misery* was the first work of Hungarian literature to describe the Jewish worker, and his play *Timár Liza* depicts the decadence of assimilated Jews in Hungary.

Broner, Esther (b. 1930) American novelist, playwright and essayist. She was born in Detroit, and taught at Wayne State University and Sarah Lawrence College.

Her novels include *Her Mothers*, *Unafraid Women* and *A Weave of Women*. She was also the co-author with Naomi Nimrod of *A Woman's Passover Haggadah*.

Bronfman, Samuel (1891–1971) Canadian liquor and oil magnate. Born in Brandon, Manitoba, he left school at the age of 15. He later joined his brothers in the hotel business, and in his early 20s took charge of a hotel in Winnipeg. The Bronfman family subsequently entered the liquor trade. By 1929 the Bronfmans had joined the Distillers Corporation-Segram Ltd and became one of the largest distillers. With the end of prohibition, Bronfman expanded his business; later he took the firm into the petroleum business. During World War II he set up the Canadian Jewish Congress Refuge Committee.

Brooks, Mel [Kaminsky, Melvin] (b. 1926) American film director, writer and actor. He was born in New York, and first worked as a comedian in the Borscht Belt of New York's Catskill Mountain resorts. Later he was one of a team of comedy writers for *The Sid Caesar Show* and *Your Show of Shows*. He also wrote, directed and produced, and acted in a number of films. He is one of those comic writers and performers who see humour as a traditional Jewish response to adversity and a way of effacing anger.

Bruce, Lenny [Schneider, Leonard Alfred] (1925–66) American entertainer. Born in Long Island, New York, he studied drama in Los Angeles. At the height of his career, he performed throughout the US. In 1962 he faced narcotics and obscenity charges, and attempted to defend himself in court. From 1964 he was banned from stages in New York. He later committed suicide.

Bruckner, Ferdinand [Tagger, Theodor] (1891–1958) Austrian playwright. Born in Vienna, he studied in Vienna, Paris and Berlin. He founded the Berlin Renaissance Theater which he directed. He wrote a number of successful plays, and adapted and modernized various plays. With the rise of Hitler, he went into exile and spent 17 years in America writing scripts for Hollywood as well as historical and poetic drama. In 1951 he returned to Germany and settled in Berlin.

Bruggen, Carry van (1881–1932) Dutch novelist and philosopher. She was born in Smilde near Amsterdam. She expressed an ambivalent and occasionally antagonistic attitude to Jewish tradition and nationalism. Her novels include *The Little Jew*.

Brüll, Nehemiah (1843-91) German scholar. He was rabbi of the Reform synagogue in Frankfurt am Main from 1870. He founded and edited the journal *Jahrbücher für jüdische Geschichte und Literatur*, in which he published Jewish studies.

Brunner, Constantin [Wertheimer, Leopold] (1862–1937) German philosopher. He lived in Potsdam until 1933, and then emigrated to the Netherlands. His philosophy was influenced by Plato and **Spinoza**. As part of his theory of society he opposed Zionism and argued for the assimilation of the Jews.

Brunschvicg, Leon (1869–1944) French philosopher. He was a professor at the Sorbonne. He wrote a critical edition of Blaise Pascal's *Pensées*.

Buber, Martin (1878–1965) Austrian theologian, grandson of **Solomon Buber**. He was born in Vienna. He joined the Zionist movement and became editor of *Die Welt* in 1901. He founded the Jewish National Council in Berlin during World War I and in 1916 established the monthly journal *Der Jude*. With **Franz Rosenzweig** he translated the Bible into German. From 1924 to 1933 he taught at the University of Frankfurt am Main and then became head of the Jüdisches Lehrhaus in Frankfurt. He settled in Palestine in 1938 and became professor of social philosophy at the Hebrew University. His writings include *I and Thou*, *For the Sake of Heaven*, *Between Man and Man*, *Tales of the Ḥasidim*, *The Prophetic Faith* and *Two Types of Faith*.

Buber, Solomon (1827–1906) Galician rabbinic scholar. He was born in Lemberg and was a governor of the Austro-Hungarian Bank and the Galician Savings Bank. He published scholarly editions of midrashim, edited works by medieval scholars, and wrote on the history of the Jewish of Poland.

Bublick, Gedaliah (1875–1948) American Yiddish journalist and Zionist leader. He was born in Russia. In 1900 he helped to lead a group of 50 Jewish families to Argentina. He settled in New York in 1904, where he became editor of the Yiddish *Jewish Daily News*. He was a founder of the American Jewish Congress and served as president of the Mizraḥi Organization of America from 1928 to 1932.

Buchalter, Louis [Lepke] (1897–1944) American labour racketeer. Born in New York City, he embarked on a life of crime. He was first part of a juvenile gang that rolled drunks, picked pockets, and robbed pushcarts. In the 1920s he went into labour racketeering. His gangs' weapons included acid, bludgeons, blackjacks, knives, fire, ice picks and pistols. Adopting the lifestyle of a multi-millionaire, he lived in mid-Manhatten and maintained chauffeur-driven cars for trips to race tracks and night clubs. In 1941, he was indicted and convicted for the killing of a garment worker and executed.

Büchler, Adolf (1867–1939) Historian and theologian of Hungarian origin. He became principal of Jews College in London in 1907. His writings include studies of the Second Temple period, rabbinic literature of the 1st century, and the history of the synagogue.

Budko, Yoseph (1888–1940) Polish painter and graphic artist. He was born in Płońsk then lived in Berlin from 1910 to 1933, when he settled in Jerusalem. He served as director of the Bezalel School of Arts from 1935. His work was influenced by eastern European Jewish life and scenes in Jerusalem.

Bunin, Ḥayyim Isaac (1875–1943) Belorussian author and teacher. He settled in Warsaw in 1929. A follower of the Ḥabad movement, he published studies of Ḥabad Ḥasidism. His *Mishneh Ḥabad* describes Ḥabad doctrines and applies them to modern life.

Burla, Yehudah (1886–1969) Israeli novelist. He was born in Jerusalem. He became head of the Arab Department of the Histadrut, an envoy of Karen Hayesod to Latin American countries, and director of Arab affairs in the Israeli Ministry of Minorities. He wrote stories and novels depicting the life of the Middle Eastern Sephardim.

Burns, Arthur (1904–87) American economist, of Austrian origin. Born in Stanislau, Austria, he studied at Columbia University. He served as economic adviser to presidents Eisenhower, Nixon, Carter and Ford. His publications include *Economic Research and the Keynesian Thinking of Our Times*, *Measuring Business Cycles*, *Frontiers of Economic Knowledge* and *Prosperity Without Inflation*.

Burnshaw, Stanley (b. 1906) American poet and publisher. His father, Ludwig Burnshaw was a teacher of Greek and Latin who become director of an orphanage, and later of a boarding school. After studying at Columbia University, he went to the University of Pittsburgh. When working as an advertising apprentice for a still mill, he founded Poetry Folio. He later studied in France. His writings include *André Spire and His Poetry: Two Essays and Forty Translations*, *The Iron Land*, *Early and Late Testament*, *Caged in an Animal's Mind*, *In the Terrified Radiance* and *Mirages: Travel Notes in the Promised Land: A Public Poem*.

Burton, Montague (1885–1952) British industrialist. Born in Russia, he settled in Leeds. He was the founder of a large chain of clothing shops, and a pioneer of improved labour conditions in England. He was knighted in 1931.

Bustanai, Ben-Chaninai (c. 618–70) Babylonian exilarch. His marriage to a captive Persian princess had halakhic implications in later gaonic literature, where the descendants of his Jewish wives wished to assert their precedence over those of a Persian wife. It was later acknowledged that Bustanai had first freed her and converted her to Judaism.

Buttenwieser, Moses (1862–1939) American biblical scholar of German origin. He became professor of biblical exegesis at the Hebrew Union College in 1897. He wrote studies of the prophets, Psalms and Job.

Buxtorf, Johannes (i) (1564–1629) Swiss Hebraist. He was professor of Hebrew at the University of Basle. He edited *Biblia Hebraica Rabbinica* (the Hebrew Bible with rabbinic commentaries) and compiled the *Bibliotheca Rabbinica* (a rabbinic bibliography). He also wrote a Hebrew grammar and a Hebrew and Aramaic lexicon.

Buxtorf, Johannes (ii) (1599–1664) Swiss Hebraist, son of **Johannes Buxtorf (i)**. He was professor of Hebrew and biblical exegesis at the University of Basle. He wrote studies of the Hebrew alphabet and Hebrew pronunciation, and translated **Maimonides**' *Guide for the Perplexed* and **Judah ha-Levi**'s *Kuzari* into Latin.

C

Caballeria, Pedro [Bonafos] de la (c.1450) Spanish financial official. He lived and worked in Aragon. He converted to Christianity and wrote the anti-Jewish work *Zelus Christi adversus Judaeos.*

Caceres, Abraham (fl. 18th cent.) Dutch composer of Portuguese origin. He was the leading musician of the Portuguese community of Amsterdam. In 1726 he provided music for the consecration of the Ḥonen Dal synagogue in The Hague.

Caceres, Francisco [Joseph] de (b. c.1580) Spanish marrano writer. After leaving Spain, he lived in France and Amsterdam. His writings include *Nuevos fieros espãnoles, Dialogos satýricos* and *Visión deleytable y sumario de todas las sciencias.*

Caceres, Samuel de (1628–60) Dutch scholar. He was the spiritual leader of the Jewish community of Amsterdam. He edited and revised a Spanish translation of the Bible.

Caceres, Simon [Jacob] de (d. 1704) English merchant. He was born in Amsterdam and settled in London before 1656. He lived openly as a Jew and urged marranos in London to practise Judaism. He advised Oliver Cromwell during the conquest of Jamaica. He was one of the signatories of a petition organized by the Jews of London requesting freedom of worship, and he helped with the acquisition of the first congregational cemetery in 1657.

Cahan, Abraham (1860–1951) American Yiddish journalist and author. He was born in Lithuania and settled in the US in 1882. He organized the first Jewish tailors' union and founded Yiddish periodicals to propagate his theories of socialism and Americanization. From 1897 he was editor-in-chief of the Yiddish newspaper the *Forverts.* His novel *The Rise of David Levinsky* portrays the urban immigrant experience in America.

Cahan [Cohen], Yaakov (1881–1961) Hebrew author of Russian origin. He taught at the Institute for Jewish Studies in Warsaw from 1927 to 1933. The following year he settled in Palestine. He wrote lyrics, ballads, epic poems, folk stories and novels. Many of his poems and ballads were influenced by Jewish folklore.

Caiaphas, Joseph (fl. 1st cent.) High priest. Appointed by the procurator Valerius Gratus, he also served under Pontius Pilate. The New Testament portrays him as largely responsible for the prosecution of **Jesus** (Matthew 26).

Caleb (fl. ?19th–16th cent. BCE) Israelite, one of the 12 spies sent to explore Canaan. He and **Joshua** were the only two spies to bring back a favourable report. As a result Caleb was allowed to enter the Promised Land. He captured Hebron and expelled its inhabitants, the Anakim (Numbers 13–14; Joshua 14–15).

Calisher, Hortense (b. 1911) American writer of short stories and novels. She was born in New York. Her numerous publications include *The Rabbi's Daughter.*

Calvin, Melvin (b. 1912) American biochemist. He worked at the University of California on the chemical details of photosynthesis. He used the Carbon 14 isotope as a research tool. He was awarded the Nobel Prize for Chemistry in 1961.

Canetti, Elias (1905–94) Austrian novelist, essayist and dramatist. He was born in Ruse in Bulgaria. He was a freelance writer and translator and in 1938 he went to London, where he settled. His works include *Auto da Fé*, *Crowds and Power*, *The Tongue Set Free*, *The Torch in My Ear* and *The Play of the Eyes*. In 1981 he received the Nobel Prize for Literature.

Cantarini, Isaac Cohen (1644–1723) Italian rabbi and physician. He lived in Padua and his *Pahad Yitzḥak* describes the anti-Jewish outbreaks in the city in 1684. His *Vindex Sanguinis* is a refutation of the blood libel charge.

Cantor, Eddie [Iskowitz, Edward Israel] (1892–1964) American entertainer. Born in New York, he began to tour with a comedy blackface act; eventually he went on the vaudeville circuits. He starred in various musicals and films. During the early years of television, he became a frequent performer.

Capa, Robert [Friedmann, Andrei] (1913–54) American photographer, of Hungarian origin. Born in Hungary, he settled in the US in the 1930s and became famous for his photographs of the Spanish Civil War, China, North Africa, and Normandy landings in World War II as well as the Israeli War of Independence. He was one of the founders of the international photographic agency, Magnum Photos.

Capsali, Elijah (1483–1555) Cretan rabbi and historian. He was head of the Jewish community in Crete. His *Seder Eliyahu Zuta* contains a survey of the history of the Jewry in the Ottoman empire down to his day, as well as an account of Spanish Jewish history. His *Divrei ha-Yamim le-Malkhut Venezia* depicts the conditions of the Jews in Venice and the Venetian dominions. It is a central source for the social, cultural and political history of north Italian Jewry in the early 16th century.

Capsali, Moses (1420–96/97) Turkish rabbi. He was born in Crete. He served as a rabbi in Constantinople under Byzantine rule. After the conquest of the city by the Turks in 1453, he was the most important rabbi in the Ottoman empire and became the spiritual and communal leader in the city.

Cardozo, Abraham (1626–1706) Spanish marrano physician and mystic. He was born in Rio Seco. He became an adherent of **Shabbetai Tzevi**, supporting him even after his apostasy; he expounded Shabbetaian doctrines in a number of published works. His theology was based on gnostic dualism. He disparaged the value of the hidden First Cause and placed supreme importance on the God of Israel.

Cardozo, Benjamin (1870–1918) American Supreme Court Justice. Born in New York, he practised law until he was elected to the Supreme Court of New York. Eventually he became chief judge of the Court of Appeals, and in 1932 was appointed to the United States Supreme Court. A defender of the New Deal social legislation, he wrote a range of legal studies including *The Nature of the Judicial Process*, *The Growth of Law*, *Paradoxes of Legal Science* and *Law and Literature*.

Cardozo, Issac (1604–81) Portuguese marrano physician and philosopher. He was physician at the Royal Court of Madrid. Persecuted by the Inquisition, he fled to Venice where he embraced Judaism. He later settled in Verona. In his *Philosophia Libera* he opposed the teachings of the kabbalah and **Shabbetai Tzevi**. His *Las excelencias y calumnias de los Hebreos* describes ten virtues of the Jewish people and refutes ten calumnies.

Carigal, Raphael Ḥayyim Isaac (1733–77) Palestinian rabbi and emissary. He was born in Hebron. He served as an emissary to Jewish communities in the Near East, Europe and the US; there he became a friend of Ezra Stiles (later president of Yale University), with whom he maintained an extensive correspondence.

Carlebach, Azriel (1908–56) Israeli journalist. He was born in Leipzig. He was secretary of the International Sabbath League. After serving as a foreign correspondent for several newspapers, he founded and edited *Maariv*, the most important Hebrew newspaper in Israel.

Carlebach, Joseph (1882–1942) German rabbi and educator. After teaching in Jerusalem, he founded a Hebrew high school in Kovno, Lithuania. He then succeeded his father, Solomon Carlebach, as rabbi of Lübeck. He became chief rabbi of Altona and later of Hamburg. He published commentaries on the Song of Songs, the Prophets and Ecclesiastes, as well as a study of **Levi ben Gershon**.

Carmi, Tcharney (1925–94) Israeli poet and literary historian. He was born in New York, but in 1946 he left the US for France, where he worked with Jewish war orphans. In 1947 he emigrated to Palestine. His publications include *There Are No Black Flowers*, *Snow in Jerusalem* and *At the Stone of Losses*. He edited the *Penguin Book of Hebrew Verse*, and was one of the editors of *The Modern Hebrew Poem Itself*. In addition he has translated numerous classic works into Hebrew.

Carmoly, Eliakim (1802–75) German rabbi, writer and editor. He was born in Alsace. He served as a rabbi in Brussels in 1832 and later settled in Frankfurt am Main, where he published articles about ancient manuscripts and books. His other publications include a work on the Ten Lost Tribes, descriptions of his travels in Palestine, a genealogy of the Rapoport family, and a coronation poem in praise of Louis Philippe of France. He was a pioneer in the study of Jewish medicine and Jewish physicians.

Caro, Anthony (b. 1924) English sculptor. Born in London, he studied at Cambridge University, and the Royal Academy Schools in London. From 1951–3 he worked as an assistant to Henry Moore. He later taught at Bennington College in Vermont. He has exhibited widely in Europe and the US.

Caro, Heinrich (1834–1910) German chemist. Born in Posen, Prussia, he moved to Berlin and trained as a dyer in Gewerbeinstitut. From 1852–5 he was a lecturer at the University of Berlin. In 1859 he went to England to work as an analytical chemist for Roberts, Dale and Co. in Manchester, where he became a partner. He subsequently returned to Germany and served as a director of Badische Analin und Soda-Fabrik from 1869–89, and became a leading spokesman for the chemical industry.

Caro [Karo], Joseph (1488–1575) Spanish talmudic codifier. He was born in Toledo, then settled in Turkey after the expulsion of the Jews from Spain in 1492. In 1536 he left Turkey for Safed where he was the head of a large yeshivah. His *Bet Yoseph* (House of Joseph) is a commentary on **Jacob ben Asher**'s *Arbaah Turim*. He also compiled its classical abbreviation, *Ṣhulhan Arukh* (The Prepared Table). His codes were criticized by Ashkenazi scholars, who claimed that they ignored French and German traditions. Nevertheless, the *Ṣhulhan Arukh* (printed with **Moses Isserles**' strictures) became the authoritative code for Orthodox Jewry.

Caro, Nikodem (1871–1935) German chemist, of Polish origin. Born in Lódź, Poland, he studied at Berlin University. He set up his own laboratory, and later became a consultant to the chemical industry and director of Stickstoffwereke A. G. He took out numerous patents, and published *Handbuch für Acetylen*.

Carrion, Santob de (fl. 14th cent.) Spanish poet. His *Proverbios morales* is a collection of aphorisms dedicated to King Pedro of Castile. It is the principal work by a medieval Jew to enter Spanish literature. Santob de Carrion has been identified with the Hebrew poet Shem Tov ibn Ardutial.

Carvajal, Antonio Fernandez (c. 1590–1659) Portuguese merchant. He settled first in the Canary Islands and later in Rouen. He eventually lived in London, where he engaged in trade with the East and West Indies. He organized a foreign information service for Oliver Cromwell. He was head of the crypto-Jewish community at the time that **Manasseh ben Israel** requested the readmission of the Jews to England (1655–6).

Caspi, Joseph ben Abba Mari (1280–c. 1340) French commentator, philosopher and grammarian. He was born in L'Argentière and lived at Tarascon in southern France. He wrote commentaries on **Maimonides**' *Guide for the Perplexed*. As a follower of Aristotle and Averroes, he equated their teaching with Judaism. He evoked the opposition of many rabbis who regarded his views as heretical.

Cassel, David (1818–93) German scholar. He was born in Silesia. He lectured at the Hochschule für die Wissenschaft des Judentums in Berlin. His publications include a history of Jewish literature,

German translations of the Apocrypha and **Judah ha-Levi**'s *Kuzari*, and critical editions of classical texts.

Cassel, Ernst (1852–1921) British financier. In 1869 he went to Liverpool where he worked as a clerk; later he was employed by the Anglo-Egyptian Bank in Paris. Returning to England, he joined the London financial house of Bischoffheim and Goldschmidt. In 1884 he founded his own banking business. Later he became a Catholic. By 1896 he was one of the wealthiest and most important financiers in Britain.

Cassel, Paulus Stephanus (1821–92) German theologian and historian. After he converted to Christianity in 1855, he was librarian at the Royal Erfurt Library, and was elected as a conservative member to the Prussian Landtag. From 1868 to 1891 he served as a researcher at the Christuskirche in Berlin and as a missionary for the London Society for Promoting Christianity Among the Jews. His publications include an account of Jewish history based on non-Jewish sources, and studies of the books of Judges, Ruth and Esther, as well as the *Targum Sheni* to Esther.

Cassin, René (1887–1976) French statesman. He was born in Bayonne. He was professor of law at the universities of Lille and Paris, and French delegate to the League of Nations from 1924 to 1938. He served as National Commissioner for Justice and Education under De Gaulle (1941–3) and head of the French delegate to the UN General Assembly (1946–51). He was awarded the Nobel Peace Prize in 1968. He also served as president of the Alliance Israélite Universelle.

Cassirer, Ernst (1874–1945) Philosoher of Polish origin. Born in Breslau, he studied under **Hermann Cohen** at the University of Marburg. In 1903 he began teaching at the University of Berlin. He published studies of Leibniz, as well as a four-volume treatment of the problem of knowledge. Later he was offered chairs at the universities of Frankfurt and Hamburg where he developed theories of symbolic form and myth. In 1929 he was elected rector of the University of Hamburg. With Hitler's rise to power, he left Germany and subsequently settled in the US.

Cassuto, Moses David [Umberto] (1883–1951) Italian biblical scholar. He was born in Florence and became chief rabbi there and director of the Collegio Rabbinico Italiano. He was professor of Hebrew at the University of Rome, and from 1939 professor of Bible at the Hebrew University. He was editor-in-chief of the *Biblical Encyclopaedia* and prepared the *Jerusalem Bible* for publication. His other publications include studies of Italian history and **Immanuel of Rome**, and catalogues of the Hebrew manuscripts in Florentine libraries.

Castel, Moshe (b. 1909) Israeli painter. He was born in Jerusalem. He was a member of the New Horizons group of Israeli painters. Judaism and Israel were dominant themes in his art. He produced a stained-glass window for the synagogue of the SS Shalom in 1956. His later paintings are reminiscent of ancient steles, in which writing is incorporated into the subject-matter.

Castelnuovo-Tedesco, Mario (1895–1965) American composer of Italian origin. He was a member of an old Florentine family. He settled in Hollywood, where he wrote film music. In 1925 he found a notebook of Jewish melodies in his grandfather's house, which encouraged him to write Jewish compositions; his works on Jewish subjects include *La danza del Rè David*, *Tre corali su melodie ebraiche*, *The Prophets*, *Sacred Service*, *Ruth*, *Jonah*, *Naomi and Ruth* and *Saul*.

Castro, Abraham de (fl. 16th cent.) Egyptian financial administrator. He was director of the mint in Cairo and supervisor of economic affairs in Egypt. When the Egyptian pasha (in revolt against Sultan Suleiman I) ordered Castro to issue a new coinage bearing his name, Castro refused. He escaped to Constantinople and informed the sultan of the pasha's rebellion; as a result the pasha was put to death. Egyptian Jews commemorate the date of the pasha's execution (28 Adar) as a feast day (Purim of Egypt).

Castro, Balthasar Orobio de (1620–87) Spanish philosopher and physician. He was imprisoned and tortured by the Spanish Inquisition. He later went to Toulouse where he practised Judaism. He wrote polemical works in Latin and Spanish, including a critique of **Spinoza**'s writings.

Castro, Benedict Nehemias de (1597–1684) German physician of Portuguese origin. He practised medicine in Hamburg from 1625, and in 1645 became physician to the Queen of Sweden. He served as president of the Portuguese congregation in Hamburg and was a follower of **Shabbetai Tzevi**.

Castro, David Henriques de (1832–98) Dutch historian. He published a study of the Sephardi cemetery in Ouderkerk and a bicentennial history of the Amsterdam synagogue.

Castro, Jacob de (1758–1824) English comedian. He was born in London. He acted in traditional Purim plays and in 1786 joined Philip Astley's troupe known as 'Astley's Jews'. In 1803 he was appointed manager of the Royal Theatre, London. His *Memoirs* casts light on English Jewish life.

Castro, Moses de (fl. 16th cent.) Egyptian rabbi. He settled in Jerusalem in 1530. He opposed **Jacob Berab**'s initiative to reintroduce Jewish ordination into Palestine.

Castro Tartas, Isaac (c. 1625–47) Portuguese marrano martyr. He was the son of Portuguese New Christians (i.e. Jews converted to Christianity), who settled in Tartas in southern France. He lived in Amsterdam and Brazil before moving to Bahia. There he lived outwardly as a Catholic, but his pretence was detected and he was arrested. He was condemned and burned alive in Lisbon in 1647. He recited the Shema before he died, and his memory inspired many marranos in the diaspora.

Cattaui, Joseph Aslan (1861–1942) Egyptian politican, nephew of **Moses Cattaui**. He was an official in the ministry of public works, directed a sugar factory, and set up other industrial plants. In 1915 he became a member of the Egyptian delegation to London to negotiate the independence of Egypt. In 1924 he was appointed minister of finance, and in the following year minister of communications. He served as a senator (1927–36), and as president of the Jewish community of Cairo.

Cattaui, Moses (1850–1924) Egyptian communal leader. He was president of the Jewish community of Cairo, and during the last year of his life was elected to the Egyptian parliament. He was decorated by the Egyptian and Austrian governments.

Celan, Paul (1920–70) German poet. He was born in Czernowitz and after the war lived in Bucharest, where he worked as a translator. In 1947 he escaped and went to Vienna and Paris, continuing to translate and also teaching languages. Several of his poems commemorate the victims of the Holocaust.

Celler, Emanuel (1888–1981) American politician. Born in Brooklyn, he studied at Columbia Law School. He began his political career in 1922 when he was asked to run as the Democratic candidate for the tenth congressional district. He supported Franklin D. Rossevelt's New Deal, and Harry S. Truman's Fair Deal. After World War II, he was a supporter of political Zionism. In 1948 he became head of the House Judiciary Committee.

Cerf, Bennet (1898–1971) American publisher. He began his career as a writer for the *New York Tribune*. Several years later he helped found Random House. He edited a number of anthologies including *Great German Short Novels and Stories*, *Bedside Book of Famous British Stories* and *Encyclopedia of Modern American Humour*.

Cerfberr, Herz (1726–94) Alsatian Jewish leader. He worked as an army contractor and employed many Jews in his factories. In 1780 he asked **Moses Mendelssohn** to help him in his efforts to improve the position of the Jews in Alsace. He commissioned a translation into French of Christian Wilhelm von Dohm's book encouraging Jewish emancipation. This resulted in the appointment of a commission to report to the king concerning the legal position of the Jews. As a consequence the poll tax for Jewry was abolished.

Chagall, Marc (1887–1985) French artist of Russian origin. He was born in Vitebsk and studied in St Petersburg and Paris. In May 1914 he had a one-man show in Berlin. In 1917 he was appointed commissar for fine arts in Vitebsk and director of the Free Academy of Art. Later he became designer for the Chamber State Jewish Theatre. He settled in France in 1923, and emigrated to New York in 1941, but later returned to France. Eastern European Jewish life is a dominant theme of his work.

Chain, Ernst Boris (1906–79) Biochemist of German origin. Born in Berlin, he studied at the Pathological Institute of Berlin. Following the rise of the Nazis, he settled in England. In 1945 he received the Nobel Prize for his work on penicillin.

Chajes, Tzevi Hirsch (1805–55) Galician rabbi and scholar. He was rabbi at Zolkiev (1829–52) and Kalisz (1852–5). He was influenced by **Naḥman Krochmal** and corresponded with leading maskilim of Galicia and Italy (such as **Solomon Judah Rapoport**, **Samuel David Luzzatto** and **Isaac Samuel Reggio**). Although he introduced modern critical methods into talmudic and cognate studies, he was a defender of Orthodoxy. He wrote on the principles of the written and oral law, the Targums and midrash, and the Talmud.

Chajes, Tzevi Peretz (1876–1927) Galician rabbi and scholar, grandson of **Tzevi Hirsch Chajes**. He taught at the Collegio Rabbinico Italiano in Florence. In 1912 he was appointed chief rabbi at Trieste. From 1918 until his death he was chief rabbi in Vienna. He served as chairman of the Zionist Actions Committee from 1921 to 1925. He published studies of biblical exegesis, archaeology, the Talmud, and Hebrew poetry.

Chao Yng Che'eng (d. 1657) Chinese civil servant. He was born in Kaifeng. He entered public service as a mandarin and served at Fukien (1650–3), and in Hukwang (1656–7). He was largely responsible for rebuilding the Kaifeng synagogue in 1653. Although he was regarded as a Confucian mandarin when in Fukien, he lived as a religious Jew when in Honan, his home province.

Charles, Gerda (1915–96) English novelist. She was born in Liverpool. Her novels deal with various Jewish themes and include *The True Voice*, *The Slanting Light*, *A Logical Girl*, *The Crossing Point* and *The Destiny Waltz*.

Charney, Daniel (1888–1956) Belorussian Yiddish poet and journalist. He was born in Minsk. He suffered from illness from early childhood and when he attempted to emigrate to the US in 1925 he was refused entry because of ill-health, and was forced to return to Europe. He finally settled in New York after the rise of Nazism. His stories, fables and articles (including a series on the conditions of Jews in Lithuania, Latvia and Poland) were printed in newspapers in Russia, Poland and the US.

Chasanowitsch, Leon [Schub, Kasriel] (1882–1925) Labour Zionist leader, of Lithuanian origin. He was born near Vilna. He became active in Labour Zionism in 1905, and in 1908 was forced to flee from the Russian police to Galicia. He served as secretary of the world Poale Zion movement from 1913 to 1919. He published studies on the Polish and Ukrainian pogroms and represented Labour Zionism at international socialist congresses.

Chayefsky, Paddy (1923–81) American playwright. He was born in New York. His work draws on Jewish life and tradition. His *The Tenth Man* is based on the legend of the dybbuk, and *Gideon* was inspired by the biblical account of the Hebrew judge's victory over the Midianites.

Chazanovitz, Joseph (1844–1919) Lithuanian Zionist. He practised medicine in Grodno, Bialystock and Yekaterinoslav. He was one of the first members of Ḥovevei Zion. He helped to establish a central Jewish library in Jerusalem, which became the basis of the Jewish National Library.

Cherniakov [Tcherniakov; Tchernikhovski], Adam (1881–1942) Polish labour leader. He was head of the organization of Jewish craftsmen in Poland after World War I. Under Nazi occupation, he was chairman of the council of the Warsaw Ghetto. In 1942, when confronted by the demand to supply the names of Jews for deportation, he committed suicide. His diary is an important historical source about the Warsaw Ghetto.

Chocrón, Isaac (b. 1930) Venezuelan novelist and dramatist. His publications include *Break in Case of Fire*, *The Fifth Circle of Hell* and *Wild Animals*.

Chomsky, Noam (b. 1928) American linguist. He studied at the University of Pennsylvania and was professor of linguistics at Massachusetts Institute of Technology. In addition to Studies of Linguistics, he wrote works critical of American foreign policy.

Chomsky, William (1896–1977) American educator of Russian origin. He settled in the US in 1913.

From 1922 he was on the faculty of Gratz College and from 1954 he lectured at Dropsie College. He wrote about Jewish education, stressing the importance of classical Hebrew language and literature.

Chouraqui, Nathan André (b. 1917) Israeli author and politician. He was born in Algeria. From 1959 to 1963 he was an adviser to **David Ben-Gurion** on the immigration to Israel of ethnic minorities. He was later deputy mayor of Jerusalem (1965–9). His publications include *Between East and West: A Hisory of the Jews of North Africa.*

Christiani, Pablo (fl. 13th cent.) French Dominican monk. He was born in Montpellier. He converted to Christianity and joined the Dominican order. In 1263 a public disputation took place in Barcelona between him and **Naḥmanides** in the presence of King James I of Aragon. In 1269 he persuaded Louis IX of France to compel Jews to listen to his sermons and to wear the Jewish badge.

Churgin, Pinkhos M. (1894–1957) Scholar of Belorussian origin. He emigrated to Palestine in 1907 and later settled in the US. He was professor of Jewish history and literature at Yeshiva University and dean of its teachers' institute. In 1955 he emigrated to Israel and published studies of the Targumim and the history of the Second Temple period.

Chwolson, Daniel (1819–1911) Russian orientalist of Lithuanian origin. He converted to Christianity in 1855. He was professor of Hebrew, Syriac and Chaldaic philology at the University of St Petersburg and at the Russian Orthodox and Roman Catholic theological academies in the same city. He defended the Jewish community against anti-Semitic allegations and intervened with Russian authorities on their behalf. He published studies of the Sabians, Syriac inscriptions, **Jesus**' trial, and the Semitic peoples.

Citroen, André Gustave (1878–1935) French engineer. Born in Paris, he became responsible for the Mors automobile company. After the war, he converted his munitions plant into an automobile manufacturing company.

Cohen, Abraham (1887–1957) English scholar. He was born in Reading. He served as minister to the Birmingham Hebrew Congregation and was the first minister to preside over the Board of Deputies of British Jews. He edited the Soncino Books of the Bible.

Cohen, Albert (1895–1981) French novelist. He was born in Corfu. He wrote poems and novels about modern Jewry, including *Solal of the Solals*, *Mangeclous* and *Belle du Seigneur*; he also edited the journal *Revue juive*. He served as an official in international organizations in Geneva.

Cohen, Alfred Morton (1859–1949) American lawyer. He was born in Cincinnati. He was president of B'nai B'rith from 1925 to 1938 and chairman of the Board of Governors of the Hebrew Union College from 1918 to 1937.

Cohen, Benjamin Victor (1894–1983) American lawyer. Born in Muncie, Indiana, he studied at Harvard University. During World War I he worked as an attorney for the US Shipping Board. Later he opened a law practice in New York. Subsequently he joined President Roosevelt's group of advisers, and was a member of the US delegation to the United Nations General Assembly.

Cohen, Boaz (1899–1968) American rabbinic scholar. He was born in Bridgeport, Connecticut. He served as chairman of the Rabbinical Assembly of America from 1945 to 1948. His *Kunteres ha-Teshuvot* is an annotated bibliography of rabbinic responsa of the Middle Ages. He published biographies of **Israel Friedlaender**, **Louis Ginzberg** and **Alexander Marx**, as well as studies of comparative law.

Cohen, Eli (1924–65) Israeli spy. Born in Alexandria, he settled in Israel. Serving with the Israel intelligence service, he was arrested in Damascus as an Israeli secret agent. Convicted on a charge of espionage, he was sentenced to death. Despite efforts to commute his sentence, he was hanged.

Cohen, Francis Lyon (1862–1934) English rabbi and scholar. He was born in Aldershot. He served as senior Jewish chaplain to the Australian army from 1914 to 1934. He edited collections of Jewish music including *A Handbook of Synagogue Music for Congregational Singing* and *The Voice of Prayer and Praise.*

Cohen, Harriet (1901–67) British pianist. She was active in Jewish and Zionist affairs. In 1934 she performed at a concert in aid of German Jewish refugee scientists together with **Albert Einstein**. She also appeared with the Palestine Symphony Orchestra before World War II. Her memoirs *A Bundle of Time* was published posthumously.

Cohen, Henry (1863–1952) American rabbi. He was born in London. He became rabbi of Temple Beth Bnai Israel in Galveston, Texas. He was involved in numerous humanitarian activities.

Cohen, Hermann (1842–1918) German philosopher. He was born in Coswig. He was professor of philosophy at the University of Marburg until 1912 and later taught at the Hochschule für Wissenschaft des Judentums. In 1880 he began to resume his hitherto lapsed links with Judaism and to defend the Jewish people and tradition. His writings include *Religion der Vernunft aus den Quellen des Judentums.*

Cohen, Israel (1879–1961) English writer. He was born in Manchester. From 1922 he was secretary of the Zionist Organization in London, on whose behalf he visited Jewish communities in Egypt, Australia, China, Manchuria, Japan, Java and India. His writings include *Jewish Life in Modern Times, The Zionist Movement, A Short History of Zionism* and *Theodor Herzl: Founder of Political Zionism.*

Cohen, Jeffrey (b. 1940) English rabbi and writer. He was born in Manchester. He served various congregations and lectured at Jews College and Glasgow University. His publications include *Understanding the Synagogue Service, A Samaritan Chronicle, Festival Adventure, Understanding the High Holyday Services, Yizkor, Horizons of Jewish Prayer* and *Moments of Insight.*

Cohen, Leonard (b. 1934) Canadian poet. Born in Montreal, he graduated from McGill University. He lived in Greece, England and the US. In the late 1980s he returned to Montreal. His works include *Beautiful Losers, Let Us Compare Mythologies, The Spice-Box of Earth, Flowers for Hitler, Parasites of Heaven, Selected Poems* and *Book of Mercy.*

Cohen, Lionel (1888–1973) British jurist. Born in London, he studied at Oxford and became a successful barrister. He was a draftsman of the amended Companies Act of 1948. In 1943 he became a judge, and later Lord Justice of Appeal. From 1946–56 he was head of the Royal Commission.

Cohen, Morris [Moishe] Abraham [Two Gun Cohen] (1887–1970) Military adviser to Chiang Kai-shek. A Londoner, he worked in the Chinese quarter of Edmonton, Alberta, and became a friend of the Chinese communist leader, Sun Yat-sen in exile. He joined him in China in 1922, and helped reorganize the army. He fought against Japanese invaders and communist rebels. Later he settled in Manchester.

Cohen, Morris Raphael (1880–1947) American philosopher, of Russian origin. Born in Minsk in Belorussia, he moved to the US in 1892 and studied at the City College of New York, and then at Columbia and Harvard. After teaching in the New York public school system, he taught mathematics and philosophy at City College of New York. Later he taught at the University of Chicago. His writings include: *Reflections of a Wandering Jew* and *A Dreamer's Journey* as well as *Reason and Nature, Law and the Social Order, Introduction to Logic and Scientific Method, Faith of a Liberal* and *The Meaning of Human History.*

Cohen, Naphtali ben Isaac (1649–1719) German rabbi and kabbalist. He served as rabbi at Ostrog, Posen and Frankfurt am Main, where he was known as a practical kabbalist. He resigned his post when it was alleged that his kabbalistic experiments were responsible for the destruction of the Frankfurt Ghetto by fire. He died at Constantinople on his way to Palestine. He was an opponent of the Shabbetaians.

Cohen, Robert Waley [Cohen, Waley] (1877–1952) English Jewish communal leader. He was managing director of the Shell Transport and Trading Company and chairman of the Palestine Corporation. He served as president of the United Synagogue and vice-president of the Board of Deputies of British Jews.

Cohen, Shalom ben Jacob [Ha-Cohen, Shalom] (1772–1845) German Hebrew poet of Polish origin. He joined the circle of maskilim in Berlin. In 1809 he revived the journal *Ha-measseph*, then in 1821, after settling in Vienna, he founded the annual *Bikkure ha-Ittim*. He later lived in Hamburg. He wrote poems on biblical themes and Jewish textbooks.

Cohen, Tobias [Tobias the Doctor] (1652–1729) Turkish physician and author, of German origin. He was born in Metz. He served as court physician in Turkey until he was 62. He then went to Jerusalem to concentrate on the study of Torah. His *Maaseh Tovyah* is an encyclopaedia dealing with theology, astronomy, cosmography, geography, botany and medicine; it also contains references to **Shabbetai Tzevi**.

Cohn, Ferdinand Julius (1828–93) German botanist and bacteriologist. Born in Breslau, he studied at the universities of Breslau and Berlin. In 1850 he became a lecturer at Breslau University, and later professor. In 1854 he published the first monograph on bacteriology, and in 1874 the first major classification of bacteria. In 1888 he founded the Institute of Plant Physiology and the Botanical Museum at Breslau University.

Cohn, Haim (b. 1911) Israeli lawyer. He was born in Lübeck and settled in Palestine in 1930. From 1953 to 1960 he was attorney general and contributed to the founding of the Israeli legal and judicial system. He was minister of justice in 1952–3, and in 1960 was appointed a justice of the Israeli Supreme Court. His publications include *Foreign Laws of Marriage and Divorce* and *The Trial and Death of Jesus*.

Cohn, Harry (1891–1958) American film executive. Born in New York, he formed a vaudeville partnership with Harry Rubinstein. Later he joined his brother at Universal Studios. In 1920 the brothers along with Joe Brandt formed their own company which later became Columbia Pictures.

Cohon, Samuel Solomon (1888–1959) American theologian. He was born in Minsk. He became professor of theology at the Hebrew Union College in 1923. He was active in the Central Conference of American Rabbis and served as the principal draftsman of the Columbus Platform, the statement of principles of Reform Judaism. He was an editor of the *Union Haggadah* and the *Rabbis' Manual*, and his writings include *What We Jews Believe*.

Colon, Joseph (c. 1420–80) Italian rabbinic scholar. He was born in France. He served as rabbi in various Italian communities, including Pavia, which he made the centre of Italian talmudic learning. After his death his responsa were collected and published. His decisions had considerable influence on later Italian halakhah.

Columbus, Christopher (1451–1500) Explorer of Italian origin, discoverer of America. He was possibly of marrano extraction. He boasted about his connection with King David and was interested in Jewish and marrano society. His name was not unknown among Italian Jews of the late medieval period. On his journeys he used nautical instruments perfected by Jews such as **Joseph Vecinho** and nautical tables drawn up by **Abraham Zucato**.

Comtino, Mordecai ben Eliezer (1420–before 1487) Turkish rabbinic scholar and scientist. He was born in Constantinople and became one of the leaders of the Hebrew cultural movement there. Two of his hymns were incorporated into the Karaite liturgy.

Conforte, David (1618–c. 90) Greek rabbi and literary historian. He was born in Salonica. He founded a bet midrash in Jerusalem, and served as rabbi in Cairo. His *Kore ha-Dorot* is a chronicle of authors and works from post-talmudic times until the 17th century.

Copland, Aaron (1900–91) American composer. He was born in Brooklyn. He served as head of the composition department of the Berkshire Music Centre in Tanglewood from 1940 to 1965. His compositions include symphonies, ballets, film scores, orchestral works and operas. His chamber work *Vitebsk* is based on a Jewish melody.

Cordovero, Moses ben Jacob [Ramak; Remak] (1522–70) Palestinian kabbalist, of Spanish origin. He was the most important kabbalist in Safed before **Isaac Luria**. His first systematic work, *Pardes Rimmonim*, covers a wide range of kabbalistic problems. He also wrote a second systematic work, *Elimah Rabbati*, and a commentary on the Zohar.

Costa, Isaac de (1798–1860) Dutch writer and poet. The son of a distinguished Sephardi family in Amsterdam, he converted to Christianity in 1822. He published studies of Jews in Spain, Portugal and the Netherlands. His *Israel and the Gentiles* is a history of the Jewish people written from a Christian point of view. Many of his poems have biblical themes.

Costa, Uriel da (1585–1640) Portuguese rationalist. He was born in Oporto into a marrano family. After moving to Amsterdam in c.1615 he returned to Judaism, but he was later excommunicated because of his heretical views about rabbinic doctrine and practice. His subsequent attack on the Bible led to a second ban.

Cowen, Philip (1853–1943) American journalist and author. He was born in New York. In 1879 he founded the weekly *American Hebrew*, which he edited and published for 27 years. From 1905 he served as an official of the US Immigration Service at Ellis Island, and in 1906 he went to Russia on a special mission to report on the causes of immigration from eastern Europe.

Cowen, Zelman (b. 1919) Australian jurist and legal scholar. Born in Melbourne, he served as vice-chancellor of the University of Queensland, and later as vice-chancellor of the New England University in New South Wales. In 1977 he became governor-general of Australia. He was appointed provost of Oriel College, Oxford in 1982. He published various studies of legal topics.

Creizenach, Michael (1789–1842) German educator and proponent of Reform. He was born in Mainz and founded a Jewish boys' school there based on the principles of Reform Judaism. In 1825 he was appointed teacher and preacher at the Philanthropin high school in Frankfurt am Main. With **Isaac Marcus Jost** he edited the Hebrew periodical *Zion*. In his writings he attempted to show that since talmudic Judaism represented a reform of biblical Judaism, Reform Judaism is a legitimate approach to the Jewish tradition.

Crémieux, Isaac-Adolphe (1796–1880) French lawyer and statesman. He fought for the abolition of the oath *more judaico*. In 1843 he was elected president of the Central Consistory of French Jews. On several occasions he intervened with the government in an attempt to gain protection of Jewish rights in other countries. From 1864 to 1880 he served as president of the Alliance Israélite Universelle.

Crescas, Ḥasdai ben Abraham (c.1340–c.1412) Spanish rabbi and theologian. He was born in Barcelona and was active as a merchant and communal leader there. In 1367 he was imprisoned on a charge of desecrating the Host, but was later released. With the accession of John I in 1387 he became associated with the royal household of the Court of Aragon. He later settled in Zaragoza where he served as rabbi. In 1391 his son was killed in anti-Jewish riots in Barcelona, which he described in a Hebrew account. His *Light of the Lord* is a refutation of **Maimonides**.

Cresques, Abraham (fl. 14th cent.) Majorcan cartographer. He was Master of Maps and Compasses to the King of Aragon. In 1375–7 he and his son **Judah Cresques** made the *Catalan Atlas*, which was sent as a gift to the king of France. In 1381 they were granted royal protection and exemption from wearing the Jewish badge.

Cresques, Judah [Ribes, Jaime] (fl. 14th–15th cent.) Majorcan cartographer, son of **Abraham Cresques**. He made maps for John I and Martin of Aragon. During the anti-Jewish outbreaks in Spain in 1391, he converted to Christianity and changed his name to Jaime Ribes. He settled in Barcelona in 1394. From 1399 he is referred to in documents as 'magister cartarum navegandi'.

Cresson, Warder [Israel, Michael Boaz] (1798–1860) American religious zealot and Zionist. He was born in Philadelphia and emigrated to Palestine, where he converted to Judaism. On his return to the US he was declared insane by a court, but successfully appealed against the decision. He returned to Jerusalem as Michael Boaz Israel and undertook propaganda campaigns against Christian missionary groups and on behalf of the agricultural colonization by Jews of Palestine. Many of his writings were published in the journal *The Occident.*

Cukerman, Yitzḥak [Antek] (1915–81) Polish communal leader in the Warsaw Ghetto. He was one of the four commanders of the Jewish Fighting Organization set up in Warsaw on 22 July 1942. During the ghetto uprising in April 1943 he took part in the battle against the Germans. He helped to organize the Jewish National Council, a Jewish underground resistance movement among Jews hiding on the Aryan side of the ghetto boundary. He emigrated to Israel in 1946 and served as a prosecution witness at the Eichmann trial in 1961.

D

Da Costa, Isaac (1721–83) American merchant and shipping agent. He was born in London and emigrated to Charleston, South Carolina in the late 1740s. He was a founder in 1749 of Congregation Beth Elohim, where he served as cantor. Later he settled in Philadelphia, where he helped establish Congregation Mikveh Israel.

Dahlberg, Edward (1900–77) American novelist. Born in Boston, he lived a vagabond existence and eventually settled in Europe. His novels *Bottom Dogs* and *From Flushing to Calvary* reflect his early childhood experiences. His *Those who Perish* deals with the impact of Nazism on a small American Jewish community. His later works include *Can these Bones Live*, *Flea of Sodom*, *The Sorrows of Priapus* and *Truth Is More Sacred*.

Daiches, David (b. 1912) British literary critic, nephew of **Samuel Daiches**. He was born in Sunderland. He taught at the universities of Chicago, Cornell, Cambridge and Sussex. His *Two Worlds: An Edinburgh Jewish Childhood* depicts his rebellion against Orthodox Judaism personified by his father. His interest in Hebrew matters is reflected in *The King James Version of the English Bible*.

Daiches, Israel Ḥayyim (1850–1937) British Orthodox rabbi and scholar. He was born in Darshunishek, Lithuania, and eventually settled in England, where he served as a rabbi in Leeds. He founded the Union of Orthodox Rabbis of England. His writing includes annotations on the Jerusalem Talmud, responsa and sermons.

Daiches, Samuel (1878–1949) British rabbi and scholar, son of **Israel Ḥayyim Daiches**. He was born in Vilna. He served as rabbi in Sunderland, England, and later became a lecturer in the Bible, Talmud and midrash at Jews College. He took an active part in the work of B'nai B'rith, the Anglo-Jewish Association, the Board of Deputies of British Jews, the Jewish Agency, and Jewish relief organizations. His published works include studies of Babylonian antiquity and its influence on Judaism, the Psalms, the Talmud in Spain, and Jewish divorce law.

Dainow, Tzevi Hirsch [Maggid of Slutsk] (1832–77) Russian preacher. He was born in Slutsk. He advocated combining Torah with the haskalah, and upheld the efficacy of manual labour and the need for educational reform. He was active on behalf of the Society for the Promotion of Culture Among the Jews of Russia. Due to opposition to his views, he emigrated to England and settled in London, where he preached to Russian and Polish immigrants.

Damrosch, Leopold (1832–85) American musician, of Polish origin. Born in Posen, Prussia, he studied medicine but devoted himself to music. He initially was a violinist in small towns and spas. Later he began to conduct at small theatres; subsequently he became a violinist to the court orchestra at Weimar under Franz Liszt. In 1858 he became conductor of the Breslau Philharmonic Concerts and founded the Orchestral Society and Choral Union in Breslau. In 1871 he became a conductor of the Arion Male Choral Union in New York, and founded the Oratorio Society and the New York Symphony Society.

Damrosch, Walter Johannes (1862–1950) American conductor of Polish origin. Born in Breslau, he studied harmony, piano and conducting with his father **Leopold Damrosch**. In 1871 he moved to New York with his family, and in 1881 became conductor of the Newark, New Jersey Harmonic Society. In 1885 he succeeded his father at the New York Oratorio Society and the New York Symphony Society. In 1894 he organized the Damorsch Opera company. Subsequently he conducted the New York Symphony Society in the first network broadcast over NBC, and was appointed musical adviser for the network.

Dan (fl. ?19th–16th cent BCE) Israelite, fifth son of **Jacob** and the firstborn of **Bilhah**, **Rachel**'s maid (Genesis 30:1–6). One of the 12 tribes of Israel took this name.

Dan, Joseph (b. 1935) Israeli scholar. He was born in Bratislava, Czechoslovakia, and went to Palestine in 1938. He taught at the Hebrew University, where in 1983 he was appointed the Gershom Scholem Professor of Kabbalah. His publications include *Ideological Movements and Conflicts in Jewish History.*

Daniel (fl. 7th–6th century BCE) He was a Judean exile in Babylon. Several miraculous experiences occurred to him and his friends at the courts of Nebuchadnezzar, Darius the Mede and Belshazzar. The second half of the book of Daniel contains visions of the rise and fall of empires from Babylon to Macedon and beyond. Daniel is also the hero of the story of Susanna and the Elders and two other tales in the book of Bel and the Dragon.

Daniel, Brother [Rufeisin, Oswald] (b. 1922) Carmelite monk in Israel. A Polish Jew who, during the Nazi occupation, was hidden in a Catholic convent. He was baptized, became a Carmelite monk, yet viewed himself as a Jew. He applied for citizenship under the Law of Return, but his application was rejected, and he brought the case before the Supreme Court but the ruling was upheld.

Daniel ben Moses al-Kumisi [Al-Damagani] (fl. 9th–10th cent.) Karaite scholar and leader of the Avele Zion (Mourners of Zion). He was born in Damghan in northern Persia, and was the first eminent Karaite scholar to settle in Jerusalem. His *Pitron Sheneim-Asar* is a commentary on the Minor Prophets, which contains criticism of the rabbinate.

Daniel, Menachem Salih (1846–1940) Baghdad leader. He was elected to the Ottoman parliament in 1876, and from 1925 represented Iraqi Jewry in the senate.

Daniel, Yuli Markovich [Arzhak, Nikolai] (1925–88) Russian poet and writer. He grew up in an environment of revolutionary ideas. In the 1950s he began to develop as a poet and also translated poetry from Ukrainian, Armenian, the Balkan languages and Yiddish. In 1965 he was arrested for publishing seditious works and sentenced to five years in prison.

Danziger, Itzchak (1916–78) Israeli sculptor. He was born in Berlin and settled in Palestine in 1923. He later taught at the Haifa Technicon. His early sculptures achieved a balance between Near Eastern sculpture and a modern concept of human form. He was awarded the Israeli Prize for Sculpture in 1968.

Danzig, Abraham ben Jehiel Michael (1748–1820) Polish rabbinic scholar. He was born in Danzig and served as dayyan in Vilna from 1794 to 1812. His *Ḥayye Adam* (Human Life) and *Ḥokhmat Adam* (Human Wisdom) contain succinct presentations of parts of the *Shulḥan Arukh.*

Da Ponte, Lorenzo [Conegliano, Emanuelle] (1749–1838) Italian poet and adventurer. His parents abandoned Judaism in 1763 and changed their names. He was trained for the Roman Catholic priesthood, but at the age of 21 he sought a more adventurous life in Venice. He turned to writing, was a friend of Casanova, and became involved in various love affairs. In 1779 he was expelled from Venice; later he settled in Vienna and became the imperial opera's Italian librettist. His librettos were used by Mozart. He later lived in London and the US.

Dari, Moses (12th–13th cent.) Egyptian Karaite scholar. Born in Alexandria, he lived in Damascus and Jerusalem. He worked as a physician and composed more than 500 poems. His work was influenced by the Spanish school of Hebrew poetry.

Darmesteter, Arsène (1846–88) French philologist, brother of **James Darmesteter**. He was born at Château-Salins. He was appointed lecturer in French language and literature at the Sorbonne in 1877 and also taught at the École Rabbinique. He was a founder of the Société de Études Juives and the *Revue des Études Juives.* His writings include a dictionary of 11th-century French, based on medieval Jewish commentators, and a dictionary of **Rashi**'s French glosses in his commentaries on the Bible and the Talmud.

Darmesteter, James (1849–94) French orientalist, brother of **Arsène Darmesteter**. He was born at Château-Salins. He became professor at the Collège de France. He translated the sacred books of the Zoroastrian religion into French and English and published material concerning the relationship between Zoroastrianism and Judaism.

Dassault, Marcel [Bloch, Marcel] (1892–1986) French aircraft designer. Born in Paris, he studied electricity and worked in a car factory. He later studied in an aeronautical school. During World War I he designed propellers. In the 1930s he continued to design planes. During the war he was arrested as a Jew and deported to Buchenwald. Later he was the head of an aircraft factory. In 1951 he entered politics.

Dathan (fl. ?13th cent. BCE) Israelite rebel leader, head of a family of the tribe of **Reuben**. He and **Abiram**, also of the tribe of **Reuben**, joined **Koraḥ** in his rebellion against **Moses**, whom they attacked for assuming the leadership; as descendants of **Jacob**'s eldest son, they claimed the leadership for themselves. Later they were swallowed up by the earth (Numbers 16).

Daube, David (1909–89) British jurist and biblical scholar. He was born in Freiburg, Germany. He taught at the universities of Cambridge, Aberdeen and Oxford, and at the University of California. He wrote studies of biblical and rabbinic law, the New Testament and rabbinic Judaism, and various themes in Scripture.

David (fl. 11th–10th BCE) King of Israel (c. 1001–986 BCE). David's life is divided into three main phases: the first when Saul was alive; the second when he was king in Judah (c. 1008–1001 BCE); the third when he was king over all Israel. A warrior king, he succeeded in uniting the tribes of Israel and created a kingdom that dominated surrounding peoples and attained power and riches. The Psalms were supposed to have been written by him. The account of his life appears in I Samuel 16ff., II Samuel, I Kings 1–2, and I Chronicles 10ff.

David ben Judah he-Ḥasid (fl. 14th cent.) Spanish kabbalist, grandson of **Naḥmanides**. He wrote commentaries on the Zohar and the order of the prayers, and a treatise on the mysteries of the alphabet.

David ben Samuel ha-Levi (1586–1667) Polish rabbi and halakhic authority. He was born in the Ukraine. He established his own bet midrash in Kraków, and later served as a rabbi in Posen and Ostrog, where he maintained a yeshivah. During the Chmielnicki pogroms (1648–9), he escaped to a fortress in Ulick. In 1654 he was appointed rabbi of Lwów. His *Ture Zahav* (*Taz*) is a commentary on the *Shulḥan Arukh.*

David ben Zakkai I (fl. 10th cent.) Babylonian exilarch (917–40). He appointed **Saadyah ben Joseph** gaon of Sura, but later quarrelled with him and had him deposed. The supporters of **Saadyah** attempted to appoint a new exilarch, Josiah-Ḥasan. After a bitter dispute the two parties reached a compromise.

Davidson, Israel (1870–1939) American Hebrew scholar. He was born in Lithuania and emigrated to the US in 1888. He became professor of medieval Hebrew literature at the Jewish Theological Seminary. His *Thesaurus of Medieval Hebrew Poetry* lists in alphabetical order the initial words of more than 35,000 poems and prayers from post-biblical times to the present.

Davidson, Jo (1883–1952) American sculptor. Born in New York, he studied art at Yale and at the Art Students League. Later he enrolled in the École des Beaux-Arts in Paris. During World War I he served as an artist-correspondent. He sculpted presidents of the United States as well as made busts of leading statesmen and generals.

Davin [David] de Caderousse (fl. 15th cent) French dyer. He was the first Jew to attempt the printing of Hebrew. He lived in Avignon, where he met a Christian goldsmith (Pocop Waldvogel) from Prague. He promised to teach Waldvogel the art of dyeing, in return for which Waldvogel was to give him 27 iron letters of the Hebrew alphabet as well as instruments for printing. This arrangement broke down, and no specimen of the earliest Hebrew printing press has survived.

Davis, Edward (1816–41) Australian bushranger. Born in London, in 1832 he was sentenced to deportation for theft. In Australia he was confined, but escaped; later he was recaptured. After his fourth escape he took refuge in the bush and became a leader of bushrangers. Known as Teddy the Jewboy, he ranged over northern New South Wales. He was captured and hung.

Dayan, Moshe (1915–81) Israeli military commander and politician, son of **Shemuel Dayan**. He was born in Deganyah Alef. During the War of Independence in 1948 he commanded the defence of Jewish settlements in the Jordan Valley. In 1952 he was appointed chief of operations at GHQ and later became commander-in-chief. In 1959 he was elected to the Knesset as a member of the Mapai party. Later he was elected to the Sixth Knesset representing Rafi. He conducted the Six Day War in 1967 and the Yom Kippur War in 1973 as minister of defence.

Dayan, Shemuel (1891–1968) Israeli pioneer and politician. He was born in the Ukraine and settled in Palestine in 1908. He was a founder of Deganyah and Nahalal and a leader of the moshavim co-operative settlement organization. He represented Mapai in the Knesset from 1949 to 1959. His writings include *Nahalal, Moshav Ovedim, Pioneers in Israel* and *Man and the Soil.*

Deborah (fl. 12th cent. BCE) Israelite woman, judge and prophetess. She promoted the war of liberation from the oppression of Jabin, King of Canaan (Judges 4). She was the author of the Song of Deborah (Judges 5), which describes the battle and victory of the Israelites over the Canaanites.

De Haan, Jacob Israel (1881–1924) Dutch author. Despite having married a non-Jewish woman, he returned to Orthodox Judaism. In 1912 he joined Mizraḥi, the Orthodox party of the Zionist Organization and emigrated to Palestine in 1919. He later became a lecturer in commercial and criminal law at the Law School in Jerusalem. Subsequently he became affiliated with the Agudah, the Orthodox party critical of Zionism and served as the spokesman of the movement to the British authorities. In 1924 he was murdered by a Zionist terror group.

De Haan, Jacob Meijer (1852–95) Dutch painter. He was born in Amsterdam, where he ran a biscuit factory with his brothers. They also formed a string quartet which gained a reputation throughout the Netherlands. A disciple of Gauguin, he was a popular painter of Jewish subjects.

Deinard, Ephraim (1846–1930) Bibliographer and Hebrew author of Latvian origin. He worked for much of his life as a bookseller in Odessa. In 1897 he tried unsuccessfully to found an agricultural settlement in Nevada. In 1913 he settled in Palestine, but was expelled three years later by the Turks. He then returned to the US and continued his bibliographic work. His writings include: *Or Mayer: Catalogue of Old Hebrew Manuscripts and Printed Books of the Library of the Hon. Mayer Sulzberger of Philadelphia* and *Koheleth America,* and a list of Hebrew books published in America between 1735 and 1926. He also wrote polemical books and pamplets on a variety of Jewish topics.

De Leon, Daniel (1852–1914) American socialist. Born in Curaçao, he studied in Europe. In 1872 he went to the US and taught at the Columbia Law School. He was drawn into the labour movement, left Columbia, and devoted himself to labour. He became editor of *The Weekly People,* and founded the Socialist Trade and Labour Alliance. Later he organized the Workers' International Industrial Union.

Della Torre, Lelio (1805–71) Italian rabbi and scholar. He was born in Cuneo in Piedmont. He became professor of Talmud at the Padua Rabbinical College. He published volumes of Hebrew poetry, sermons and a commentary on the Pentateuch;

he also translated and annotated the Psalms, and rendered the prayers according to Ashkenazi custom into Italian.

Delmedigo, Elijah ben Moses Abba (c.1460–97) Greco-Italian philosopher and talmudist. He was born in Crete and emigrated to Italy, where he served as head of the yeshivah in Padua. He engaged in a bitter controversy on a halakhic question with Judah Mintz, the rabbi of Padua. Subsequently he left Italy and returned to Crete, where he completed his major work, *The Examination of Religion.*

Delmedigo, Joseph Solomon ben Elijah [Medigo, Joseph Solomon ben Elijah del] (1591–1655) Cretan rabbi, philosopher, mathematician and astronomer. He studied astronomy and mathematics under Galileo at the University of Padua, then travelled widely, visiting Egypt, Turkey, Poland, Germany, Holland and Bohemia. He wrote studies of religious, metaphysical and scientific topics.

Dembitz, Lewis Naphtali (1833–1907) American lawyer. He was born in Prussia and emigrated to the US in 1849. Initially he was involved with Reform Judaism, but later joined the Conservative movement and helped to establish the Jewish Theological Seminary. He contributed articles on Talmudic jurisprudence and liturgy to the *Jewish Encyclopedia*, and prepared the translations of Exodus and Leviticus for the revised English Bible. He also wrote *Jewish Services in Synagogue and Home.*

Dembitzer, Ḥayyim Nathan (1820–92) Polish talmudist and historian. He was born in Kraków and became dayyan there. He was active in financial support of the old yishuv in Palestine. He published works on responsa literature, the tosaphists, and talmudic and rabbinic literature; he also wrote biographies of the rabbis of Lwów/Lemberg and neighbouring communities.

De Pass, Aaron (1815–77) South African industrialist. He arrived in South Africa in 1846 and played an important role in the development of coastal shipping. He founded the sealing, whaling and island gauano industries off the Cape Province. He brought the first Sepher Torah to Cape Town and helped build the synagogue there.

Derenbourg, Hartwig (1844–1908) French orientalist, son of **Joseph Derenbourg**. He lectured in Arabic at the École des Langues Orientales Vivants in Paris, and on oriental languages at the École Rabbinique. In 1885 he became professor of Arabic at the École des Hautes Études. He wrote studies of Arabic grammar, literature and religion, and of Semitic manuscripts and inscriptions.

Derenbourg, Joseph (1811–95) French orientalist. He worked as a domestic tutor in Amsterdam in 1835–8, and then settled in Paris. In 1852 he became corrector of the Imprimerie Nationale, and also catalogued the Hebrew manuscripts at the Bibliothèque Nationale. In 1877 he was appointed to a chair for rabbinic Hebrew language and literature at the École Pratique des Hautes Études. He published studies of oriental languages and inscriptions as well as works on various Jewish subjects.

Derenbourg, Tzevi Hirsch (fl.18th cent.) German Hebrew writer. He was born in Offenbach and went to Mainz in 1789, where he kept a restaurant and was a private tutor of Hebrew. His *Yoshevei Tevel* is a didactic moral drama.

Derrida, Jacques (1930–2004) French philosopher. Born in Algiers, he taught at the École Normale Superieure and later at the École des Hautes Études en Sciences Sociales. His works include *Speech and Phenomena, Writing and Difference, Margins of Philosophy, Dissemination, Glas, Truth in a Painting, The Post Card, Shibboleth, Feu la Cendre* and *Ulysse Gramophone.*

Déry, Tibor (1894–1977) Hungarian writer. Born into a wealthy family of assimilated Hungarian Jews, he joined the communist party. After leaving Hungary, he lived in Czechoslovakia, Vienna, Paris and Italy. In 1926 he returned to Hungary where he was a co-editor of an activist review. When the Germans occupied Hungary in 1944, he went into hiding. After the war he rejoined the Hungarian communist party and published a cycle of stories. Later he published a two-volume novel, *Felelet* which was attacked by the communist authorities.

De-Shalit, Amos (1926–69) Israeli nuclear physicist. He studied in Switzerland and later at Princeton.

He returned to Israel in 1953 and became head of the nuclear physics department of the Weizmann Institute. In 1965 he recived the Israel Prize for Natural Sciences.

Desnos, Robert (1900–54) French poet. Born into a Parisian-Jewish bourgeois family, he caused a scandal with two works: *De L'Erotisme Considéré dan ses Manifestations Écrites* and *La Liberté ou l'Amour*. Later he pursued a career in journalism and radio broadcasting. He was eventually deported to Terezín where he died.

Dessau, Paul (1894–1979) German composer. Born in Hamburg, he began as a violinist, but eventually turned to conducting and composing. He was appointed to a number of posts in German opera houses. During the 1920s he wrote for the cinema. Eventually he emigrated to New York, but in 1948 settled in Berlin and served as professor of the German Academy of Arts.

Deutsch, Babette (1895–1982) American writer. Born in New York of German-Jewish parents, she studied at Barnard College. She collaborated with her husband Avraham Yarmolinsky on the translation of Blok's *The Twelve* and *Modern Russian Poetry*. Her works include a philosophical poem, *Epistle to Prometheus*, and a novel about Socrates, *Mask of Silenus*. From 1933–5 she taught at the New School for Social Research, then at Queens College, and later at Columbia. From 1960–6 she was Honorary Consultant to the Library of Congress.

Deutsch, Bernard Seymour (1884–1935) American lawyer and communal leader. He was born in Baltimore. In 1933 he was elected president of the Board of Aldermen of New York. He was president of the American Jewish Congress and led campaigns with **Stephen Samuel Wise** to arouse public opinion on behalf of the rights of German Jews.

Deutsch, Emanuel Oscar Menaḥem (1829–73) British orientalist. He was born in Upper Saxony. He became assistant in the oriental department of the British Museum in 1855. He wrote studies of Phoenician inscriptions, the Targumim, the Samaritan Pentateuch, and the Jewish background of Jesus.

Deutsch, Gotthard (1859–1921) American historian and theologian of Moravian origin. He became professor of Jewish history and philosophy at the Hebrew Union College, Cincinnati, in 1891. In 1901 he succeeded **Isaac Mayer Wise** as editor of *Deborah*. He published studies of Jewish history and served as editor of the modern Jewish history division of the *Jewish Encyclopedia*.

Deutsch, Leo (1855–1941) Russian revolutionary. He was born in Tylchin. In 1877 he led a revolt of Ukrainian peasants. He was exiled to Siberia in 1884, but escaped in 1901. Later he moved to the US, where he edited a workers' journal, but he returned to Russia in 1917. In 1923 he published in Berlin a study of Jews in the Russian revolutionary movement.

Deutsch, Moritz (1818–92) German cantor and teacher of Moravian origin. He became second cantor of the Liberal Temple in Vienna. He later served as chief cantor in the Reform synagogue in Breslau. He taught cantorial music at the Breslau Theological Seminary for 30 years and composed original arrangements of liturgical music.

Deutscher, Isaac (1907–67) British historian and political scientist. He was born in Kraków. He was a member of the communist party in Poland, but was expelled, and in 1939 went to London, where he was on the editorial staff of the *Economist* and the *Observer*. Later he devoted himself to historical research. He wrote political bibliographies of Stalin and **Trotsky** and published works on Stalin, Soviet Russia and communism. His *The Non-Jewish Jew and Other Essays* describes the contributions of such Jews as **Spinoza**, **Freud**, **Marx** and **Trotsky**.

Dhu Nuwas, Yusuf (c. 490–525) South Arabian king and convert. Before ascending to the throne, he was converted to Judaism by rabbinic emissaries from Tiberias.

Diamond, David (b. 1915) American composer. His compositions include violin concertos, symphonies, chamber music, ballets, film scores and choral music. His *Ahavah* for narrator and orchestra is based on Jewish themes.

Dick, Isaac Meir (1814–93) Polish Yiddish author. He was born in Vilna. As an exponent of the Haskalah, he advocated reforms in Jewish life. He was the first popular writer of Yiddish fiction, producing more than 300 stories and short novels, which introduced sentimental and realistic storytelling into Yiddish literature. He also popularized knowledge of the Bible, wrote on the Passover Haggadah, and composed a popular version of the Shulḥan Arukh.

Diesendruck, Tzevi Hirsch Wolf (1890–1940) American philosopher and scholar of Galician origin. He taught at the Jewish Pedagogium in Vienna (1918–27), the Jewish Institute of Religion in New York (1927), the Hebrew University (1928–30), and the Hebrew Union College, Cincinnati (1930–40). He published Hebrew translations of Plato's writings and worte studies of **Maimonides**' philosophy.

Dilon [Zhuravitski], Avrom-Moyshe (1883–1934) Yiddish poet. Born in Zhetl, near Grodna, he emigrated to New York in 1904. He joined the group of poets, *Yunge*. His works include *Gele bleter* and *Di lider*.

Dimanstein, Simon (1886–1937) Russian communist. Born in Vitebsk, he studied in a Ḥasidic yeshivah. At the same time he studied Russian and joined the revolutionary movement. Later he was arrested, but managed to escape to Minsk and then to Riga but was arrested again in 1908 and sentenced to hard labour in Sibera. In 1913 he escaped and went to France. Later he returned to Russia where he became minister of labour in Lithuania. In 1918 he helped create the Yevsektsiya, the Jewish wing of the communist party, and became commissar of Jewish affairs. He also edited the Yiddish journal *Der Emes*, and served as director of the Institute for National Minorities.

Dinah (fl. ?19th–16th cent. BCE) Israelite woman, daughter of **Jacob** and **Leah**. She was raped by Shechem. Jacob's sons **Simeon** and **Levi** avenged their sister by slaughtering the male poplulaton of the town of Shechem, carrying off their women and children, and taking their goods and livestock as spoil (Genesis 34).

Dinesohn, Jacob (1856–1919) Russian Yiddish novelist. He was born in the district of Kovno. His first Yiddish novel, *For the Parents' Sins*, was banned by the Russian censor. His second, *The Beloved and the Pleasant*, or *The Black Youth* sold more than 200,000 copies. In 1885 he settled in Warsaw. He was the pioneer of the Yiddish sentimental novel and also helped to modernize elementary Jewish education by founding secular schools.

Dinur, Benzion [Dinaburg, Ben Zion] (1884–1973) Israeli historian and educator of Ukrainian origin. He emigrated to Palestine in 1921. From 1923 to 1948 he taught at the Jewish Teachers' Training College in Jerusalem, of which he later became head. In 1948 he was appointed professor of modern Jewish history at the Hebrew University. He was elected to the first Knesset (1949–51) as a Mapai delegate and from 1951 to 1955 was minister of education and culture. He edited the Jewish historical quarterly *Zion* and wrote on Jewish and Zionist history.

Diskin, Yehoshua Leib (1817–98) Russian rabbi and halakhist. He was born in Grodno and served as a rabbi in various Russian cities. He opposed the religious authorities, was imprisoned, and in 1887 emigrated to Palestine. He settled in Jerusalem, where he served as a rabbi and was in the vanguard of Orthodox activism. He founded an orphanage and directed the Ohel Moshe yeshivah.

Disraeli, Benjamin (1804–81) English statesman and novelist. His father, Isaac d'Israeli, quarrelled with the London Sephardi community and had his children baptized. Disraeli was already an established novelist when he was elected to parliament in 1837 as a Tory. In 1868 he became prime minister. Although he was defeated in the next general election, he became prime minister again in 1874. In 1876 he was created Earl of Beaconsfield. Jewish figures and themes appear in several of his novels.

Dizengoff, Meir (1861–1937) Politician of Russian origin. He was born in Bessarabia. He became active in Russian revolutionary circles and later in the Ḥovevei Zion movement. In 1892 he was sent by Baron Edmond de Rothschild to establish a bottle factory in Palestine. He returned to Russia, but in 1905 went back to Palestine and settled in Jaffa. He was a founder of Tel Aviv and became its first mayor in 1921. He published his memoirs, *With Tel Aviv in Exile*, in 1931.

Döblin, Alfred (1878–1957) German poet and novelist. He was born in Stettin and became a psychiatrist. His first novels were expressionist in nature. In 1933 he fled from Germany to France and then to the US. In his novels of this period he criticized Jewish assimilationists and Zionists. In 1940 he converted to Catholicism. After World War II he returned to Germany, where he continued his literary activity.

Doctorow, Edgar Lawrence (b. 1931) American writer. Born in New York, he began his career as an editor, but later taught at the University of California, Sarah Lawrence College, Yale and New York University. His works include *Welcome to Hard Times*, *Big as Life*, *The Book of Daniel*, *Loon Lake*, *World's Fair* and *Billy Bathgate*.

Dolitzki, Menaḥem Mendel (1856–1931) American Hebrew and Yiddish writer of Russian origin. He was born in Bialystok. He was Hebrew secretary to **Kalonymos Ze'ev Wissotzky** in Berlin from 1882 to 1892, when he emigrated to the US and settled in New York. In his early works he described the sufferings of Jewish people in Russia; later he wrote poems of yearning for Zion. He also published a biography of **Wissotsky**. In the US his descriptions of Jewish persecution in Russia appeared in the journal *Ha-Ivri*.

Doniach, Nakdimon (b. 1907) British lexicographer. Born in London, he studied at London University and Jews College. Later he studied Arabic at the School of Oriental Studies. After travelling to Palestine, he returned to London where he became a freelance scholar. His works include a dictionary of English and Arabic.

Donin, Nicholas (fl. 13th cent.) French Franciscan monk. He was a pupil of **Jehiel ben Joseph of Paris**, who excommunicated him for his heretical ideas. He joined the Franciscan order and compiled a list of 35 accusations against the Talmud. He was the main instigator of the Disputation of Paris in 1240, as a consequence of which 24 cartloads of copies of the Talmud were burned in 1242.

Donnolo, Shabbetai (913–c. 982) Italian physician. He was born in Oria. He travelled widely and served as physician to the Byzantine governor in Calabria and to church officials. He wrote a commentary on the Sepher Yetzirah. His *Book of Remedies* was the first Hebrew treatise on medicine written in Christian Europe.

Dori, Ya'akov (1899–1973) Israeli military leader. He was born in Odessa and was taken to Palestine in 1906. From 1931 to 1939 he was commander of the Haganah in the Haifa district. In September 1939 he became the first chief of staff of the Haganah. With the establishment of the State of Israel, he became chief of staff of the Israeli Defence Forces. He was president of the Haifa Technion from 1951 to 1965.

Dormido, David Abravanel (fl. 17th cent.) One of the founders of the modern English Jewish community. Born in Spain, he was arrested by the Inquisition in 1627 and eventually escaped to Bordeaux. In 1640 he reached Amsterdam. He accompanied Samuel Soeiro, the son of **Manasseh ben Israel**, to London in 1654, where he petitioned Oliver Cromwell to readmit the Jews to England. When the Jewish community was organized in 1663, he served as its presiding warden.

D'Orta, Gracia (c. 1500–68) Portuguese marrano scientist and physician. He was born in Castelo de Vide, and taught at Lisbon University. In 1534 he left Portugal for India, where he served in Goa as a physician to Portuguese viceroys, Christian dignitaries, and the Muslim ruler. His *Coloquios dos simples e drogas he cousas medicinais da India* laid the foundation for the study of tropical diseases. He was posthumously condemned by the Inquisition.

Dosa ben Saadyah (930–1017) Babylonian communal leader and head of the academy of Sura. He wrote a biography of his father, responsa, commentaries on the Talmud, and philosophical works.

Dositheus (fl. 1st cent.) Samaritan pseudo-messiah. He was the founder of a sect that resembled Judaism.

Doubrovsky, Serge (b. 1928) French critic and novelist. In a number of works of fiction (*Fils*, *Un amour de soi*, *La vie l'instant*), he discussed his Jewish past and origins, World War II, and the treatment of Jews in France during the Nazi period.

Dov Ber of Mezhirich [Ber [Maggid] of Mezhirich]. (c. 1710–72) Russian Ḥasidic teacher. Originally a folk preacher (maggid), he became a disciple of the **Baal Shem Tov**, after whose death he became leader of the Ḥasidim. He transferred the movement from Medzhibozh to Mezhirich and under his leadership it spread into the Ukraine, Lithuania and central Poland. Many of his homilies are included in works written by his disciples. He provided Ḥasidism with a speculative-mystical system based on the kabbalah.

Drach, David Paul (1791–1865) French scholar. He was born in Strasbourg. In 1819 he was appointed head of the Paris Jewish School, but in 1823 he was baptized into the Catholic Church. He worked in Paris as an expert in Hebrew and took part in the publication of the Venice Bible. From 1832 to 1842 he served as librarian of the Congregation for the Propagation of the Faith in Rome and published poems in honour of the pope and the cardinals. Returning to Paris, he collaborated with the Abbé J. P. Migne in the publication of his *Patrologia* and edited Origen's *Hexapla*. He also published books and pamphlets justifying his conversion.

Drachman, Bernard (1861–1945) American Orthodox rabbi. He was born in New York and served as an Orthodox rabbi there and in Newark, New Jersey. He was the first Orthodox rabbi to preach in the vernacular in the US and was one of the founders of the Jewish Theological Seminary, where he taught from 1887 to 1902. He later taught at Yeshiva College and from 1908 to 1920 served as president of the Union of Orthodox Jewish Congregations. He translated **Samson Raphael Hirsch**'s *Nineteen Letters of Ben Uziel* into English.

Dreyfus, Alfred (1859–1935) French soldier. He was born in Alsace. He became a captain on the general staff of the French army in 1892. In 1894 he was accused of treason, found guilty, and sentenced to life imprisonment. He protested his innocence and was eventually exonerated, but the case plunged France into a state of virulent anti-Semitism for a decade. The so-called Dreyfus Affair deeply influenced **Theodor Herzl** and contributed to the development of Zionism. Dreyfus' *The Letters of Captain Dreyfus to His Wife* and *Five Years of My Life* depict his ordeal.

Dreyfus, Ferdinand-Camille (1851–1905) French journalist. He was a founder of the liberal newspaper *La nation* and general secretary of *La grande encyclopédie*. He was twice elected to the chamber of Deputies. He fought several duels with anti-Semites.

Dreyfus, George (b. 1928) Australian composer and arranger. He was born in Wuppertal, Germany, and went to Australia in 1939. A number of his works reflect his Jewish background.

Dreyfuss, Barney (1865–1932) American baseball executive, and creator of the modern World Series. Born in Freiburg, he emigrated to the US in 1881 and settled in Paducah, Kentucky. He worked in a distillery. Later he acquired an interest in the Pittsburgh Pirates. In 1903 he proposed that the American League's leading Boston team should meet the Pirates in the best of nine series. This led to the creation of the World Series.

Druyanow, Alter (1870–1938) Polish Hebrew writer and Zionist leader. He was born in Druya in the district of Vilna. He was a member of the Ḥibbat Zion movement and secretary of its Odessa committee from 1890–1905. He lived in Palestine in 1906–9 and from 1923. He edited the Zionist organ *Ha-Olam* and wrote a history of Ḥibbat Zion. He also published a collection of Jewish folk humour, *The Book of Jokes and Witticisms*.

Dubinsky, David (1862–1982) American labour leader. He was born in Belorussia, and emigrated to the US in 1910. He became president of the International Ladies Garment Workers' Union in 1932, and vice-president of the American Federation of Labour in 1934. After World War II he was a founder of the International Confederation of Free Trade Unions. He was a supporter of Israel, and in particular the Histadrut.

Dubno, Solomon (1738–1813) Dutch Bible scholar and Hebrew poet of Ukrainian origin. He lived in Amsterdam and Berlin, where he served as a tutor for **Moses Mendelssohn**'s son. He helped with **Mendelssohn**'s German translation of the Bible and commentary. He eventually returned to Amsterdam, where he published a commentary on the Torah as well as Hebrew poetry.

Dubnow, Simon (1860–1941) Russian historian. Born in Belorussia, he lived in St Petersburg, Odessa, Vilna, Berlin and Riga. He wrote a ten-volume history of the Jewish people, a history of the Jews in Russia and Poland, and a history of Ḥasidism. In his writings he propounded the doctrine of national autonomy. He believed that the Jews are a nation spiritually and should aspire to social and cultural, rather than political, independence.

Dujovne, Leon (1899–1984) Argentine philosopher and communal leader. He was born in Russia and went to Argentina as a child. He taught at the University of Buenos Aires and published studies of **Benedict Spinoza** and **Martin Buber**. He also translated the writings of a number of medieval Jewish philosophers into Spanish. He served as president of the Sociedad Hebraica Argentina and the Instituto de Intercambio Cultural Argentina-Israel.

Dukas, Paul (1865–1935) French composer. Born in Paris, he studied at the Paris Conservatoire. After serving in the military, he returned to composing. His works include *Polyeucte*, *Symphony in C Major*, *L'Apprenti Sorcier*. He taught orchestration at the Paris Conservatoire and later composition.

Duker, Abraham Gordon (1907–87) American educator and historian. He was born in Poland and went to the US in 1923. From 1956 to 1962 he was president of the Chicago Spertus College of Judaica. In 1963 he became director of the libraries and professor of history and social institutions at Yeshiva University. He wrote studies of Polish–Jewish relations and American Jewish sociology.

Dukes, Leopold (1810–91) Hungarian historian. He was born in Pressburg. He visited libraries in Europe and uncovered many unknown medieval works. His research covered aggadic literature, Bible exegesis, medieval Jewish literature, Hebrew grammar and masoretic texts, and talmudic maxims and truisms. He translated **Rashi**'s Torah commentary into German and published studies of the poetry of **Solomon ibn Gabirol** and **Moses ibn Ezra**.

Dunash ben Labrat [Ibn Labrat, Dunash] (c.920–990 BCE) Iraqi Hebrew poet and grammarian. He was born in Baghdad, studied at Fez, and later settled in Córdoba. He applied Arabic forms of Hebrew to poetry and laid the foundation for medieval Hebrew poetry. He wrote 200 criticisms of **Menaḥem ben Saruk**'s dictionary, the *Maḥberet*. This led to a controversy which influenced the development of Hebrew philology and grammar.

Dunash ben Tamim (c.860–after 955/6) North African scholar. He wrote studies of philology, mathematics, astronomy and medicine, as well as a commentary on the Sepher Yetzirah.

Dünner, Joseph Hirsch (1833–1911) Dutch rabbi and talmudist. He was born in Kraków. He was appointed director of the rabbinical seminary in Amsterdam in 1862. In 1874 he became chief rabbi of the Ashkenazi community in the city, and later a leader of the Mizraḥi party. He published glosses to 19 tractates of the Talmud as well as an enquiry into the origin of the Tosephta.

Duran, Profiat [Ephodi] (fl. 13th–14th cent.) Spanish scholar and polemicist. He was born in Perpignan. He was forcibly converted to Christianity in 1391 but later reverted to Judaism. He wrote two polemical tracts against Christianity, a Hebrew grammar, a commentary on **Maimonides**' *Guide for the Perplexed*, and a history of the persecutions and expulsions of the Jews from the destruction of the Second Temple until his own time.

Duran, Simeon ben Tzemaḥ [Rashbatz] (1361–1444) North African rabbinic scholar, philosopher and scientist. He was born in Majorca and worked as a physician and surgeon in Palma. After the massacre there in 1391 he settled in Algiers, where he served as chief rabbi. His writings include an encyclopaedic philosophical work, *Magen Avot*. His responsa deal with religious and legal problems as well as grammar, philology, exegesis, literary history, philosophy, kabbalah, mathematics and astronomy.

Duran, Solomon ben Simeon [Rashbash] (c.1400–47) North African scholar, son of **Simeon ben Tzemah Duran**. He was born in Algiers. He joined his father's bet din at an early age and became the head of the yeshivah. His *Milhemet Mitzvah* is a defence of the Talmud against the accusations made by the apostate **Joshua Lorki** (Geronimo de Santa Fé).

Durkheim, Émile (1858–1917) French sociologist. He was born in Épinal. He became professor of sociology at the University of Bordeaux in 1887, and in 1902 he was appointed professor of sociology and education at the Sorbonne. He founded and edited *L'année sociologique* and wrote numerous sociological works including *The Elementary Forms of the Religious Life*. Although he did not write directly on Jewish topics, his work reflects his Jewish background.

Duschak, Moritz (1815–90) Moravian rabbi, teacher and writer. He served as a rabbi in Aussee and Gaya. From 1877 he occupied the post of preacher and teacher in Kraków. He published studies on talmudic topics and Jewish scholarship.

Dushkin, Alexander (1890–1976) American educator. He was born in Poland and was taken to the US in 1901. He was director of Chicago's Board of Jewish Education (1923–34) and executive director of the Jewish Education Committee in New York (1939–49). From 1962 he headed the Department of Jewish Education in the Diaspora at the Hebrew University Institute of Contemporary Jewry. He published numerous studies of Jewish education.

Duveen, Joseph (1869–1939) Art dealer. Born in Hull, he began investing in art. Later he settled in the US where he educated a small group of collectors and encouraged the public to visit museums. He established galleries in New York, Paris and London. He was knighted and later made a peer.

Dymov, Ossip [Perelmann, Joseph] (1878–1959) Russian Yiddish author and playwright. He was born in Bialystok. He first wrote fiction in Russian, blending symbolism, irony and wit. His plays deal with Jewish suffering and experience. After he emigrated to the US he wrote for the Yiddish theatre.

E

Eban, Abba (1915–2002) Israeli statesman and diplomat. He was born in Cape Town. He lectured in Arabic at Cambridge University from 1938 to 1940. After World War II he settled in Israel. He was a member of the Jewish Agency delegation to the UN (1947–8) and then represented Israel at the UN (1948–9) before serving as Israeli ambassador to the US. He was president of the Weizmann Institute from 1948 to 1966. Elected to the Knesset as a Mapai delegate, he was successively minister of education and culture (1960–3), deputy prime minister (1963–6), and foreign minister (1966–74).

Edelman, Gerald Maurice (b. 1929) American scientist. Born in New York, he taught at Rockefeller University. He shared the Nobel Prize for Medicine and Physiology for research on the nature of antibodies.

Edels, Samuel Eliezer [Maharsha] (1555–1631) Polish talmudist. He was born in Kraków and settled in Posen, where he married the daughter of Moses Ashkenazi Heilpern. His mother-in-law Edel (by whose name he became known) supported him and his disciples for years. He was later a rabbi in Chelm, Lublin and Ostrog, where he founded a yeshivah. His *Ḥiddushe Halakhot* is a talmudic commentary which is included in most editions of the Talmud.

Edelstein, Jacob (d. 1944) Czech Zionist. Born in Galicia, he became a Zionist socialist leader in Czechoslovakia and director of the Palestine office of the Jewish Agency in Prague. During the German occupation, he encouraged the idea of a Jewish labour camp at Theresienstadt. In 1941 he became Jewish elder of the Theresienstadt ghetto. In 1943 he was arrested for falsifying the lists in order to help some Jews to escape and was shot in Auschwitz.

Eder, Montagu David (1865–1936) English psychoanalyst and physician. He was born in London. He was a founder of the Psychoanalytical Association in England; he also established a children's clinic and edited the journal *School Hygiene*. He was active in Zionist affairs and served on the Zionist Commission in Palestine from 1918 to 1921. He later served on the World Executive Committee of the Zionist Organization in Jerusalem and London.

Edidin, Ben M. (1899–1948) American educator. He was prominent in Jewish educational activities in New York. He wrote several textbooks on Jewish and Zionist education.

Efros, Israel (1891–1981) American Hebrew scholar. He was born in the Ukraine and emigrated to the US in 1905. He was professor at Johns Hopkins University, Buffalo University, Hunter College and Dropsie College. In 1955 he settled in Israel and served as rector and later honorary president of Tel Aviv University. He published studies of medieval Jewish philosophy, translated Hamlet into Hebrew and **Ḥayyim Naḥman Bialik**'s poetry into English, co-authored an English–Hebrew dictionary, and wrote volumes of poetry.

Eger, Akiva ben Moses (1761–1837) German rabbi. He was born in Eisenstadt and served as a rabbi at Märkisch-Friedland in 1791, and from 1814 at Posen, where he established a yeshivah. As one of the foremost rabbinic authorities in Europe, he opposed the Reform movement. He published glosses on the Mishnah and the Talmud, as well as numerous responsa.

Eger, Akiva ben Simḥa Bunem (c. 1720–58) German rabbi and author. He was born in Halberstadt and served as rabbi of Zuelz in Upper Silesia. In 1756 he became head of the yeshivah of Pressburg. He was one of the foremost talmudic scholars of his generation. He published novellae on the Talmud and responsa.

Eger, Judah Leib (1816–88) Polish Ḥasidic leader. He was born in Warsaw and led a Ḥasidic congregation in Lublin. After the death of Menaḥem Mendel of Kotsk in 1859, he assumed the role of tzaddik and propounded his own teaching. He spent much time in prayer, devoting himself to it with fervour accompanied by weeping and loud cries. His teachings on the law and festivals were arranged by his son Abraham in *Torat Emet* and *Imrei Emet.*

Eger, Samuel Levin ben Judah Leib (1769–1842) German talmudist. He was born in Halberstadt and served as rabbi of Braunschweig. An opponent of the Reform movement, he insisted on the retention of Hebrew in prayer. He wrote talmudic novellae, homiletic discourses and responsa.

Eger, Solomon ben Akiva (1786–1852) Polish rabbi and communal leader. He was born in Lissa and served as rabbi of Kalisz and Posen. He encouraged Jews to move away from commerce into farming, solicited contributions for Palestine, and campaigned for the emancipation of the Jews in his own country. He was an opponent of the Reform movement. He published notes on the Talmud and **Isaac ben Jacob Alfasi**'s code.

Ehrenburg, Ilya Grigoryevich (1891–1967) Russian author and journalist. He was born in Kiev. He was exiled from 1908 to 1917 for revolutionary activities. On his return to Russia in 1917 he opposed the Bolsheviks and again left the country in 1921. He returned once more in 1941 and became a spokesman for Stalin. He wrote against Nazi anti-Semitism and Zionism. He was awarded the Stalin Prize in 1942 for his novel *The Fall of Paris* and in 1948 for *The Storm*. His autobiography appeared in six volumes.

Ehrenkranz, Benjamin Wolf [Velvel of Zbahrz] (1819–83) Galician Yiddish and Hebrew poet. He travelled to various European cities as a singing bard. His poems were concerned with nature and man, poverty and wealth, and the struggle of light and darkness (symbolizing the opposition of the maskilim and the Ḥasidim). Much of his poetry employs parody and satire. His collected poems appeared between 1865 and 1878.

Ehrenpreis, Marcus (1869–1951) Swedish rabbi and author. He was born in Lemberg, and served as rabbi in Djakovo, Croatia from 1869 to 1900. He later became chief rabbi of Sofia, and from 1914 of Stockholm. At the request of **Theodor Herzl** he translated the invitation to the First Zionist Congress into Hebrew; he acted as consultant on cultural matters at Zionist congresses. He translated modern Hebrew literature into Swedish, founded a Jewish Swedish journal, and edited a Jewish encyclopaedia in Swedish.

Ehrenstein, Albert (1886–1950) Austrian poet and author. He was born in Vienna. He lived in Berlin, travelled widely in Europe, and eventually settled in New York in 1941. His poetry was pessimistic in character and occasionally bears witness to a yearning for the oriental world; he published several volumes of Chinese poetry in his own free adaptations, as well as narrative works and essays.

Ehrlich, Arnold Bogumil (1848–1919) American biblical exegete of Polish origin. He was born in Wlodawa near Lublin. He worked as a librarian in the Semitics department of the Berlin Royal Library. At the age of 30 he settled in the US. He helped Franz Delitzsch to translate the New Testament into Hebrew and later published Hebrew and German commentaries on the Bible.

Ehrlich, Joseph (1842–99) Austrian writer. He was born in Brody, Galicia. He worked as a poet and journalist in Vienna. His autobiography, *My Life's Way*, describes the life of the Jewish community of Brody in the 1840s and 1850s.

Ehrlich, Paul (1854–1915) German scientist. Born in Silesia, he discovered bacterial strains and also a new variety of white blood corpuscles as a research student. Later he became a professor at the University of Berlin. In 1908 he shared the Nobel Prize in Medicine and Physiology.

Ehud (fl. 12th cent. BCE) Judge of the tribe of **Benjamin**. He delivered Israel from Eglon, King of Moab. Under the pretext of having a secret message for the king, he drew a dagger and killed him. This ended Moabite rule over Israel for several generations (Judges 3).

Eibeschütz, Jonathan (c.1690–1764) Bohemian talmudist and kabbalist. He was head of a yeshivah in Prague and became the rabbi in Metz in 1741. From 1750 he officiated in turn at Altona, Hamburg and Wandsbeck. He was accused of being a follower of **Shabbetai Tzevi** but denied the charge. He was one of the greatest talmudic scholars of his time.

Eichelbaum, Samuel (1894–1967) Argentine playwright and short-story writer. He was born in Dominguez, Entre Riós. His play *El Judio Aarón* is based on a Jewish theme, and his short story *Una buena cosecha* is set in Rosh Pinnah, Israel.

Eichenbaum, Jacob (1796–1861) Polish Haskalah poet, educator and mathematician. He was born in Krystianopol, Galicia. He was married at 11, but divorced when his father-in-law suspected him of secular leanings. He married again in 1815, lived in Zamość, and later settled in Odessa, where he established a Jewish school. In 1844 he was appointed director of the Kishinev Jewish school, and in 1850 inspector of the Zhitomir Rabbinical Seminary. A collection of poems by him was one of the first books of poetry published in the Haskalah period.

Einhorn, David (1809–70) American Reform rabbi of German origin. He was born in Bavaria and succeeded **Samuel Holdheim** as chief rabbi of Mecklenburg-Schwerin. In 1855 he became rabbi of the Har Sinai Congregation of Baltimore, and later served as rabbi of Kenesseth Israel in Philadelphia and Congregation Adath Israel in New York. He was the leader of the extreme Reform wing of American Jewry. His *Olat Tamid* served as the model of the *Union Prayer Book* of the Reform movement.

Einhorn, Ignaz [Horn, Éduard] (1825–75) Hungarian Reform rabbi and economist. He was born in Nove Mesto. He organized the society for the Reform of Judaism in Pest in 1847; later he served as rabbi of the society's first Reform Temple. He also helped to found the Society for the Propagation of Hungarian Language and Culture, and edited the first Jewish-Hungarian yearbook. After the suppression of the Hungarian uprising in 1849 he settled in Paris, where he published works on economic problems. In 1867 he returned to Budapest and was elected to the Hungarian parliament.

Einhorn, Moses (1896–1966) American physician and editor. He was born in Russia, and was taken to Palestine in 1908. He was forced to emigrate by the Turkish authorities in 1916 and later settled in the US. He was head of the gastroenterological department of the Bronx Hospital in New York. In 1926 he founded (with Asher Goldstein) the Hebrew medical journal *Ha-Rophe ha-Ivri.*

Einstein, Albert (1879–1955) German physicist. He was born in Ulm. He worked in the patent office at Berne, and later was professor at the University of Prague and at the Prussian Academy of Science in Berlin. In 1921 he received the Nobel Prize for Physics in recognition of his work on relativity, quantum physics and Brownian motion. In 1933 he settled in the US and became professor of theoretical physics at the Princeton Institute for Advanced Studies. He was an active supporter of Zionism.

Eisendrath, Maurice Nathan (1902–73) American Reform rabbi. He was born in Chicago, and served as rabbi in Charleston, South Carolina and Toronto. In 1943 he became president of the Union of American Hebrew Congregations. He was active in interfaith activities and social action. His publications include *Spinoza*, *Never Failing Stream* and *Can Faith Survive?*

Eisenstadt, Benzion (1873–1951) American rabbi and Hebrew writer of Belorussian origin. He settled in the US in 1903. He published lexicographic and biographical works on contemporary rabbis and writers.

Eisenstadt, Meir ben Issac [Maḥaram Ash] (c.1670–1744) Polish rabbinic authority. He served as rabbi in Szydlowiec, Poland and later settled in Worms, where he became head of yeshivah. When the French occupied Worms in 1701 he went to Prossnitz, Moravia, where he served as rabbi. In 1714 he was appointed rabbi of Eisenstadt and its seven communities, where he established a yeshivah. His *Panim Meirot* contains responsa and novellae on the Talmud.

Eisenstein, Ira (1906–2001) American rabbi. He was born in New York. He led the Society for the Advancement of Judaism and subsequently served as rabbi to Anshe Emet synagogue in Chicago. Later he became president of the Reconstructionist Foundation and editor of the *Reconstructionist*. In 1968 he was appointed president of the Reconstructionist Rabbinical College. His writings include *Creative Judaism*, *What We Mean by Religion* and *Judaism Under Freedom*.

Eisenstein, Judah David (1854–1956) American Hebrew writer and editor of Polish origin. He emigrated to the US in 1872, where he became a coal manufacturer. He was a founder in 1880 of Shoḥarei Sefat Ever, the first Hebrew society in the US. He published in Hebrew a Jewish encyclopaedia in ten volumes (*Otzar Yisrael*) as well as several anthologies of Jewish literature.

Eisenstein, Sergei Mikhailovich (1898–1948) Russian film director. Born in Riga, Latvia, he studied architecture at the Petrograd Institute of Civil Engineering. Later he joined the Red Army. In 1920 he became a set director of the Moscow Proletkult Theatre. His films include *Strike*, *Battleship Potemkin*, *October*, *The General Line*, *Alexander Nevsky* and *Ivan the Terrible*.

Eisler, Moritz (1823–1902) Moravian educator and historian of Jewish philosophy. He founded and served as president of an organization for the support of disabled Jewish teachers and their widows and children. His *Lectures on Jewish Philosophy in the Middle Ages* was one of the first attempts to summarize and present the main systems of medieval Jewish philosophy.

Eisner, Kurt (1867–1919) German journalist and statesman. His father was a merchant in Berlin. He became a journalist and published a book about Nietzsche. In 1892 he went to Marburg where he studied with **Hermann Cohen**, and later became the editor of the Social Democrats' newspaper. In 1916 he founded a weekly discussion group with an anti-war slant. Two years later he was arrested and imprisoned. Upon his release, he became involved in the revolution which overthrew the Bavarian monarchy, becoming prime minister of the Bavarian Republic.

Elah (fl. 9th cent.) King of Israel (883–882 BCE), son of **Baasha**. He was murdered while in a state of intoxication, by **Zimri**, the captain of his chariots. His murder arose from the army's dissatisfaction with his indifference to the campaign against the Philistines near Gibbethon.

Elath [Epstein], Eliahu (b. 1903) Israeli diplomat. He was born in Russia and settled in Palestine in 1924. From 1934 to 1945 he was director of the Middle East section in the Jewish Agency's Political Department, and from 1945 to 1948 head of its Political Office in Washington. In 1949 he served as ambassador in Washington, and was then ambassador in London (1950–9). He was president of the Hebrew University from 1962 to 1968. His writings include *Israel and Its Neighbours*.

Elazari-Volcani [Volkani; Wilkanski; Wilkansky], Yitzḥak Avigdor (1880–1955) Israeli agronomist. He was born in Lithuania and settled in Palestine in 1908, where he became one of the leaders of the Ha-Poel ha-Tzair party. He founded and directed workers' farms at Ben Shemen and Ḥulda from 1909 to 1918, and in 1921 he established the Agricultural Experiment Station at Ben Shemen. He was appointed professor of agricultural economics at the Hebrew University in 1938.

Elbogen, Ismar (1874–1943) American scholar. He was born in Schildberg, in the Posen district. He began teaching Jewish history and biblical exegesis at the Collegio Rabbinico Italiano in Florence in 1899. In 1903 he joined the faculty of the Hochschule für die Wissenschaft des Judentums in Berlin. In 1938 he emigrated to New York, where he was appointed research professor at the Jewish Theological Seminary, Hebrew Union College, Jewish Institute of Religion, and Dropsie College.

He published studies in Jewish history and the history of the Jewish liturgy.

Eldad (fl. 13th cent. BCE) Elder of Israel. He was one of the 70 Israelite elders appointed by **Moses** to aid him in governing the people (Numbers 11:16ff). He and Medad aroused the suspicion of **Joshua** by prophesying within the camp, but their conduct was approved by **Moses** (Numbers 11:26–29).

Eldad ha-Dani (fl. 9th cent.) Traveller. His origins are obscure. He claimed to belong to the tribe of Dan, and asserted that the tribes of Dan, Naphtali, Gad and Asher formed an independent kingdom in Africa. He visited Jewish communities in North Africa and Spain. The Kairouan community sought the opinion of the gaon Tzemaḥ about the halakhic practices described by him.

Eleazar (i) (fl. 13th cent. BCE) Israelite, third son of **Aaron** (Exodus 6:23). After his father's death, he was appointed high priest (Exodus 20:28; Deuteronomy 10:6). The priestly family of Zadok traces its descent from him.

Eleazar (ii) [Auran] (fl. 2nd cent. BCE) Hasmonean warrior and brother of **Judah Maccabee**. At the battle of Bet Zechariah, he stabbed an elephant of the enemy's army, believing that its rider was Antiochus Eupator, the Syrian ruler. He was killed when the animal fell on him.

Eleazar (iii) (fl. 2nd cent. BCE) Judean martyr. During the religious persecution instigated by Antiochus Epiphanes in 167 BCE, he chose death rather than submit to eating pork (II Maccabees 16:18–31; IV Maccabees 5–6).

Eleazar ben Arakh (fl. 1st cent.) Palestinian tanna. He was the most outstanding of the inner circle of the five disciples of **Johanan ben Zakkai**. He engaged in mystical speculation concerning the divine chariot ('merkavah'). He later settled in Emmaus.

Eleazar ben Azariah (fl. 1st–2nd cent.) Palestinian tanna. He traced his ancestry back ten generations to **Ezra**. When **Rabban Gamaliel II** was temporarily deposed as nasi, Eleazar ben Azariah was chosen to succeed him; the school of Jabneh, the centre of rabbinic learning, was opened to all who wished to study, and no longer restricted to those considered worthy. According to tradition, Eleazar ben Azariah went on a mission to Rome with **Rabban Gamaliel II**. He was a halakhist and an aggadist.

Eleazar ben Dinai (f. 1st cent.) Palestinian Zealot leader. He ravaged Judea for 20 years until he was captured by the procurator Felix and sent to Rome.

Eleazar ben Hananiah (fl. 1st cent.) Palestinian scholar. He was a leader of the school of **Shammai**.

Eleazar ben Jair (fl. 1st cent.) Palestinian Zealot leader. After the assassination of **Menaḥem ben Judah** in 66, he led Jewish forces to the fortress of Masada and held it for seven years. When it was surrounded by the Romans, he persuaded the Jews to kill one another rather than be captured.

Eleazar ben Judah of Worms [Rokeaḥ, Eleazar] (c. 1165–c. 1230) German talmudist, kabbalist and liturgical poet. Born in Mainz, he spent most of his life in Worms. He witnessed the murder by crusaders of his wife and children. He published works on halakhah, liturgical poetry, theology, ethics and exegesis. His *Sepher ha-Rokeaḥ* was intended to educate the common reader in the details of halakhic law. He was the last major scholar of the Ḥaside Ashkenaz movement.

Eleazar ben Parta (fl. 2nd cent.) Palestinian tanna. He was one of the sages arrested by the Romans for contravening Hadrian's decree forbidding the public teaching of Torah and observance of the commandments. Although the offence carried the death penalty, he was miraculously delivered from execution.

Eleazar ben Pedat (fl. 3rd cent.) Palestinian amora. He was born in Babylonia and settled in Palestine. After the death of **Johanan** in 279, he was appointed head of the council in Tiberias. He was a major exponent of the oral law and a prolific aggadist.

Eleazar ben Shammua (fl. 2nd cent.) Palestinian tanna. He was one of the last pupils of **Akiva**. After **Simeon Bar Kokhba**'s revolt (132–5), he was ordained by **Judah ben Bava**. Several of his teachings were incorporated into the Mishnah by his pupil **Judah ha-Nasi**. He is included among the Ten Martyrs of the Hadrianic persecutions.

Eleazar ben Simeon (i) (fl. 1st cent.) Palestinian Zealot leader. He played an important role in the war against Cestius Gallus. He was responsible for the entry of the Idumeans to Jerusalem and the subsequent massacre of the opponents of the Zealots. He fought against John of Giscala until the beginning of the siege of the city by Titus.

Eleazar ben Simeon (ii) (fl. 2nd cent.) Palestinian tanna. He was the son of **Simeon ben Yoḥai**, with whom he escaped from the Romans by hiding in a cave for 13 years. He engaged in halakhic controversy with **Judah ha-Nasi** as well as in halakhic and aggadic discussions with other scholars. He eventually accepted a position in the Roman administration as an official responsible for the apprehension of thieves and robbers.

Elhanan (i) (fl. 10th cent. BCE) Israelite warrior. According to II Samuel 21:19 he killed Goliath; in I Chronicles 20:5 it is stated that he killed Lahmi, the brother of Goliath.

Elhanan (ii) Legendary Jewish pope. According to tradition, he was the son of Simeon the Great of Mainz.

Eli (fl. 11th cent. BCE) Israelite, head priest in the Sanctuary at Shiloh during the period of the Judges. When Elkanah made an annual pilgrimage to Shiloh, his wife, **Hannah**, made a vow in the presence of Eli and received the assurance that her prayer for a son would be answered (I Samuel 1:11ff). After her son, **Samuel**, was weaned **Hannah** brought him to Eli to serve in the Sanctuary. Eli's family was subsequently deprived of the priesthood (I Kings 2:26–27) because of the immoral conduct of Eli's sons, **Hophni** and **Phinehas** (I Samuel 2:11–36; 3:11–14).

Elias, Brian (b. 1948) English composer. Born in Bombay, he went to school in England. He entered the Royal College of Music, travelled to the US and studied at the Juilliard School of Music, and eventually returned to England. His works include *Proverbs of Hell*, *At the Edge of Time* and *L'Eylah*.

Elias, Samuel [Dutch Sam] (1775–1816) Boxing champion. Beginning in 1801, he had many victories, but died in poverty.

Eliashib (fl. 5th cent. BCE) Israelite, high priest in the time of **Ezra** and **Nehemiah**. He and his priestly colleagues were responsible for rebuilding the wall guarding the north-western approach to the Temple Mount: their portion was the Tower of Hananel, the Tower of the Hundred, and the Sheep Gate (Nehemiah 3:1).

Eliezer (i) (fl. ?19th–16th cent. BCE) Israelite, steward of **Abraham**'s household (Genesis 15:2). He was to have been **Abraham**'s heir in the absence of any offspring. But when **Abraham** complained to God that material goods were of little use to him since he had no chidren to whom to bequeath them, God responded with the promise of a son (Genesis 15:4ff). Eliezer was identified by the rabbis with the servant sent by **Abraham** to find a wife for **Isaac**.

Eliezer (ii) (fl. 13th cent. BCE) Israelite, second son of Moses (Exodus 18:4).

Eliezer (iii) (fl. 9th cent. BCE) Israelite, prophet of Mareshah. He denounced **Jehoshaphat**'s alliance with **Ahaziah** (II Chronicles 20:37).

Eliezer ben Hyrcanus (fl. 1st–2nd cent.) Palestinian tanna. He was a pupil of **Johanan ben Zakkai** and teacher of **Akiva**. After the destruction of the Temple in 70, he was among the important scholars of the great bet din of Jabneh. Later he established an academy at Lydda. He was a member of a delegation to Rome led by the nasi to obtain concessions for the Jews. He also travelled to Antioch on behalf of the scholars.

Eliezer ben Joel ha-Levi [Rabiyah] (1140–1225) German scholar. He wandered from place to place, visiting Bonn, Worms, Würzburg, Mainz, Metz, Cologne and Regensburg. He refused to accept rabbinic office in order not to derive material benefit from his learning. Eventually he accepted the rabbinate of Cologne in 1200. His *Sepher ha-Rabiyah* contains halakhot and legal decisions according to the order of the tractates in the Talmud, and also responsa.

Eliezer ben Nathan of Mainz [Raben] (c. 1090–c.1170) German scholar. He lived in Slavic countries, then settled in Mainz. His *Sepher ha-Raban* (also called *Even ha-Ezer*) is the first complete book emanating from the German Jewish community to have survived. It contains responsa, and various extracts and halakhic rulings following the order of talmudic tractates. He was also the first commentator on liturgical poetry in Germany. Some of his own piyyutim were influenced by the terrors of the First Crusade.

Eliezer ben Yose ha-Galili (fl. 2nd cent.) Palestinian tanna. He was one of the last pupils of **Akiva** and was among those who re-established the academy in Jabneh, and then in Usha after the Hadrianic persecutions. He wrote the *Baraita of Thirty-Two Rules*, which enables the aggadah to be expounded like the halakhah by fixed hermeneutical rules. He was one of the greatest aggadists of his time.

Eliezer of Touques (fl. 13th cent.) French tosaphist. He edited most of the tosaphot incorporated in standard editions of the Babylonian Talmud. The disciples of **Meir of Rothenburg** used his tosaphot extensively, and it was through them that his versions became accepted in France and Germany.

Elijah [Elijah the Tishbite] (fl. 9th cent. BCE) Israelite prophet. He prophesied during the reigns of **Ahab** and **Ahaziah**. He attempted to restore the purity of the worship of the God of Israel when **Ahab**'s wife, **Jezebel**, introduced the cult of Baal into the country. In a contest with the prophets of Baal, he emerged victorious (I Kings 18). According to II Kings 2:1–11, Elijah did not die but was carried to heaven in a chariot of horses and fire. In the rabbinic tradition he is viewed as the harbinger of the Messiah. At the Passover seder a glass of wine is traditionally poured for him.

Elijah Be'er ben Shabbetai [Elijah Sabot] (fl. 14th–15th cent.) Italian physician. He taught at the University of Padua, and was in the service of several popes (Innocent VII, Martin V and Eugene IV) as well as Italian rulers. He was summoned to England in 1410 to attend on Henry IV.

Elijah ben Judah of Chelm [Baal Shem, Elijah of Chelm] (1514–83) Polish rabbi and kabbalist. He was known for his miracle cures by means of charms and amulets. According to legend, he created a golem.

Elijah ben Solomon Zalman [Vilna Gaon] (1720–97) Lithuanian talmudist. After travelling throughout Poland and Germany he eventually settled in Vilna. He encouraged the translation of works on natural science, but was opposed to philosophy and the Haskalah. He also led the oppositon to the Ḥasidic movement and was regarded as the spiritual leader of the Mitnaggedim. He wrote commentaries on the Bible; annotations on the Talmud, midrash and Zohar; and works on mathematics, the geography of Palestine, and Hebrew grammar. In his studies of halakhah he sought to establish critical texts of rabbinic sources; he avoided pilpul and based his rulings on the plain meaning of the text.

Elimelech (fl. 12th–11th cent. BCE) Israelite, husband of **Naomi** and father of Mahlon and Chilion. Owing to the famine during the time of the Judges, he crossed over from Judah to Moab, where he and his sons died. Following their deaths, his wife **Naomi** returned to Judah with her daughter-in-law **Ruth**. (Ruth 1:1–3; 2:1, 3; 4:3, 9)

Elimelech of Lizensk (1717–87) Galician rabbi. He was one of the founders of Ḥasidism in Galicia. A disciple of **Dov Ber of Mezhirich**, he is regarded as the theoretician and creator of practical tzaddikism. His *Noam Elimelekh* describes the role of the tzaddik in the Ḥasidic movement; it stresses the holiness and perfection of the tzaddik and his influence in the earthly and spiritual realms.

Eliphaz (fl. 19th–16th cent. BCE) Israelite, the eldest son of **Esau** and his wife Adah (Genesis 36:2–4).

Eliphaz the Temanite (fl. 19th–16th cent. BCE) One of the three friends of **Job**.

Elisha (fl. 9th cent. BCE) Israelite prophet. He prophesied during and after the reign of **Jehoram**. He was the disciple and successor of **Elijah**. He foretold Hazael's accession to the Syrian throne, and anointed **Jehu** king over Israel.

Elisha ben Avuyah [Aḥer] (fl. 2nd cent.) Palestinian tanna. He was born in Jerusalem. He came to doubt the unity of God, divine punishment, and ultimately renounced Judaism. Although befriended by **Meir**, the rabbis dissociated themselves from him and referred to him as Aḥer (the other). He was the subject of several historical novels including *As a Driven Leaf* by **Milton Steinberg**.

Eliya, Joseph (1901–31) Greek poet and scholar. He was born in Janina and taught French at the Alliance Israélite Universelle school there. He wrote poetic love songs dedicated to **Rebekah** and also produced Greek translations of Isaiah, Job, the Song of Songs, Ruth and Jonah, as well as the works of medieval and modern Jewish writers.

Elkan, Benno (1877–1960) German sculptor. He was born in Dortmund, went to Paris in 1905, and returned to Germany in 1911. In 1933 he settled in England. His seven-branched candelabrum embellished with biblical scenes was presented by members of the British Parliament to the Israeli Knesset.

Elkanah (fl. 11th cent. BCE) Israelite, father of **Samuel** (I Samuel 1:1ff).

Elkin, Stanley (1930–95) American short-story writer and novelist. A number of protagonists in his writings are Jews.

Elkus, Abram Isaac (1867–1947) American lawyer. He was born in New York. He served as special US attorney to prosecute bankruptcy in 1908. In 1911 he was counsel for the New York State Factory Investigating Commission. He was ambassador in Turkey from 1916 to 1919, and then president of the New York Free Synagogue until 1927.

Elman, Mischa (1891–1967) American violinist. He was accepted at the Odessa music academy at the age of six, and made his debut in St Petersburg. In 1908 he went to the US where he was known for his purity of tone and technique. He also composed light opera.

Elon, Amos (b. 1926) Israeli journalist and writer. He was born in Vienna and emigrated to Palestine as a child. He was a journalist, editorial writer, and columnist for *Ha-Aretz*. His books include *Journey through a Haunted Land, The Israelis: Founders and Sons* and *A Certain Panic*. He also wrote a biography of **Theodor Herzl** and a play entitled *Herzl*.

Elyashar, Jacob Saul ben Eliezer Jeroham (1817–1906) Palestinian Sephardi rabbi. He was born in Safed. He was appointed dayyan in Jerusalem in 1853 and became head of the bet din in 1869. In 1893 he became Sephardi chief rabbi of Palestine. He wrote thousands of responsa to questions from Ashkenazim and Sephardim throughout the world.

Emden, Jacob Israel [Yavetz] (1697–1776) Danish halakhic authority. He was born in Altona. He served as rabbi at Emden from 1728 to 1733, when he returned to Altona and set up a printing press. He regarded Shabbetaianism as a danger to Judaism and engaged in a prolonged dispute about this movement with **Jonathan Eibeschütz**. He wrote studies on halakhic subjects as well as polemical pamphlets.

Emin Pasha [Schnitzer, Eduard] (1840–92) African explorer. Born in Silesia, he was baptized when young. He worked in the Sudan as a doctor, and became governor of the Equatorial Province in 1878. He was cut off by the Mahdi rebellion of 1881 until an expedition reached him. He subsequently served in the German colonial service in Africa, but was murdered in 1892 by slave traders.

Enelow, Hyman Gershon (1877–1934) American Reform rabbi and scholar. He was born in Lithuania and went to the US as a youth. He served as a rabbi in Kentucky and at Temple Emanuel in New York from 1912 to 1934. He was president of the Central Conference of American Rabbis from 1927 to 1929. His writings include *The Synagogue in Modern Life, The Faith of Israel* and *A Jewish View of Jesus*. He also edited **Israel Alnakawa**'s *Menorat ha-Maor* as well as the *Midrash of 32 Hermeneutical Rules* ascribed to **Eliezer ben Hyrcanus**.

Engel, Yoel (1868–1927) Russian composer. He was music critic of the journal *Russkiye Vedomosti* for 20 years. In 1900 he began to adapt Jewish folk songs. In 1912 he took part with **S. An-Ski** in an expedition to southern Russia to collect folk songs among the Jewish population. He later contributed the music to **An-Ski**'s play *The Dybbuk*. He settled in Tel Aviv in 1924, where he composed Hebrew songs.

Ephraim (fl. 19th–16th cent. BCE) Israelite, younger son of **Joseph**. His name became that of one of the tribes of Israel and of the more northern of the two Israelite kingdoms. During the period of the Judges, the tribe of Ephraim claimed priority. When the northern tribes seceded after **Solomon**'s death, the first king of the northern kingdom of Israel (**Jeroboam I**) belonged to this tribe. The prophets later referred to the House of Judah and the House of Ephraim.

Ephraim ben Isaac of Regensburg (1110–75) German tosaphist and liturgical poet. As a youth he lived in France, where he was among the first pupils of **Jacob ben Meir Tam**. He wrote piyyutim which reflect the hardships suffered by the Jews of Germany in the Regensburg massacre of 1137 and during the Second Crusade (1146–7).

Ephraim ben Jacob of Bonn (1132–c. 1175) German liturgical poet and commentator. When Joel ben Isaac ha-Levi left Bonn, Ephraim ben Jacob succeeded him as av bet din. He also taught in Mainz and Speyer. He wrote the *Book of Remembrance* and dirges on the sufferings of Jews during the Second Crusade. He also composed liturgical poems for the festivals, responsa, tosaphot and commentaries on benedictions and various customs.

Ephraim ben Shemariah (c. 980–1060) Egyptian rabbi. He was leader of the Palestinian community in Fostat (Old Cairo). Although he was engaged in commerce, he became the community's rabbi in about 1020. He corresponded with the gaon Solomon ben Judah for many years.

Ephraim Veitel Heine (1703–75) German court jeweller and community leader. In 1745 he was appointed court jeweller to the King of Prussia. Three years later he was elected head of the Berlin Jewish community. He built a school for the children employed in his factories and set up an educational foundation.

Ephron, Elia (1847–1915) Russian publisher. With P. Brockhaus he founded the Brockhaus-Ephron publishing house, which published a general Russian encyclopaedia in 86 volumes. It also participated in the publication of the 16-volume Russian Jewish encyclopaedia, *Yevreyskaya Entziklopedia*.

Epstein, Abraham (1841–1918) Austrian rabbinic scholar of Russian origin. He travelled to western Europe in 1861, where he met some of the leading figures in Jewish scholarship. Eventually he sold his shares in the family business and devoted himself to research. In 1876 he settled in Vienna, where he wrote studies on a wide range of Jewish topics.

Epstein, Isidore (1894–1962) English rabbi and scholar. He was born in Lithuania and emigrated first to France and then (in 1911) to England. He served as rabbi in Middlesbrough from 1921 to 1928. In 1928 he began teaching Semitics at Jews College, and became principal there in 1948. His publications include *Studies in the Communal Life of the Jews of Spain, as Reflected in the Responsa of Rabbi Solomon ben Adreth and Rabbi Simeon ben Zemach Duran*, *Faith of Judaism* and *Judaism*. He also supervised the English translation of the Babylonian Talmud.

Epstein, Jacob (1880–1959) British sculptor. He was born in New York and settled in England in 1905. His works include a number of sculptures on Jewish themes.

Epstein, Jacob Nahum (1878–1952) Israeli talmudist. He was born in Brest-Litovsk. He became a lecturer at the Hochschule für die Wissenschaft des Judentums in Berlin in 1923, and in 1925 he was appointed professor of talmudic philology at the Hebrew University. He published studies on the Mishnah and Talmud and edited the journal *Tarbitz* from 1930 to 1952.

Epstein, Louis M. (1887–1949) American Conservative rabbi. He was born in Lithuania and emigrated to the US in 1904. He was appointed rabbi of Kehilath Israel in Brookline, Massachusetts, in 1925. He served as president of the Rabbinical Assembly and chairman of its committee on Jewish law. His writings include *The Jewish Marriage Contract*, *Marriage Laws in the Bible and Talmud* and *Sex Laws and Customs in Judaism*.

Epstein, Yitzḥak (1862–1943) Writer and teacher of Belorussian origin. He settled in Palestine in 1886. From 1908 to 1915 he directed the Alliance Israélite Universelle school in Salonica. After World War I, he returned to Palestine and engaged in educational activities. He was a pioneer in teaching Hebrew by the direct method. He wrote studies on Hebrew language problems and Arab-Jewish relations, and a Hebrew textbook, *Ivrit be-Ivrit.*

Epstein, Zalman (1860–1936) Russian Hebrew essayist and critic. He was born in Belorussia and moved to Odessa in 1876, where he lived for 30 years. Later he lived in St Petersburg, Warsaw and Moscow; he eventually settled in Palestine in 1925. He published studies on Zionism and the settlement of Palestine as well as Hebrew and general literature. He also wrote a number of poetic sketches.

Erikson, Erick (1902–2004) American psychoanalyst. He was born in Frankfurt am Main and emigrated to the US in 1933. He taught at Harvard, Yale and the University of California. In 1960 he was appointed professor of human development and psychiatry at Harvard. His publications include *Childhood and Society*, in which he discusses anti-Semitism and the role of Jews in society.

Erlanger, Camille (1863–1919) French composer. In addition to operas, orchestral music and songs, he composed *Le juif polonais.*

Erhlanger, Joseph (1874–1965) American physiologist. He was a professor of physiology at Washington University in St Louis. He received the 1944 Nobel Prize for Medicine and Physiology.

Erter, Isaac (1791–1851) Galician Hebrew satirist. He was born in Koniuszek and lived in various cities before settling in Brody in 1831. In addition to his literary work, he was active in Haskalah circles. *The Watchman of the House of Israel* consists of five satires on Jewish society in Galicia and Poland in the first half of the 19th century.

Esau (fl. 19th–16th cent. BCE) Israelite, firstborn son of **Isaac** and **Rebekah** and twin brother of **Jacob**. After **Jacob** obtained Esau's birthright and the firstborn's blessing, Esau became **Jacob**'s enemy and **Jacob** fled to Haran. When he returned 20 years later, his brother greeted him affectionately (Genesis 35ff). The Bible identifies him with Edom (Genesis 36:1). In the Talmud, he was associated with wickedness and violence.

Eshkol, Levi (1895–1969) Israeli politician. He was born in Oratov, in the Ukraine, and settled in Palestine in 1914. After World War I he became director-general of the ministry of defence. He represented Mapai in the Knesset from 1949. In 1951 he joined **David Ben-Gurion**'s government as a minister of agriculture and development and the following year he became minister of finance. In 1963 he succeeded **Ben-Gurion** as prime minister, remaining in office until his death.

Espinoza, Enrique (1898–1987) Argentine writer, editor and journalist. He was born in Kishinev and was taken to Argentina as a child. He edited monthly literary reviews in the 1920s. In 1928 he helped to found the Argentine Writers' Association. From 1935 he lived in Chile. His writings include *Ruth y Noemi, El angel y el leon, El Castellano y Babel* and *Cuadernos de oriente y occidente.*

Esther (i) (fl. 4th cent. BCE) Israelite woman, wife of Ahasuerus, King of Persia, and niece of **Mordecai**. Through her intervention, the plan of Haman (the prime minister) to annihilate the Jewish community was thwarted.

Esther (ii) [Lifschitz, Malkah] (1880–1943) Russian writer and communist leader. She was born in Minsk. She edited Bundist periodicals after the revolution of 1905. She was one of the main promoters in the Bund of Jewish education in Yiddish. After the Russian Revolution in February 1917 she became a member of the central committee of the Bund. From 1921 to 1930 she was a leader of the Yevsektzia. She published a Yiddish edition of Lenin's writings, and edited the Moscow Yiddish daily *Emes.*

Ethan the Ezrahite (fl. 10th cent. BCE) Israelite sage, spoken of as one whom **Solomon** surpassed in wisdom (I Kings 5:11). Psalm 89 is attributed to him.

Ettinger, Akiva Yaakov (1872–1945) Zionist leader of Belorussian origin. He went to London as an adviser on settlement matters during the negotiations over the Balfour Declaration. He settled in Palestine in 1918 and served as director of the agricultural settlement department of the Jewish National Fund until 1924. From 1924 to 1932 he played a prominent role in the purchase of land

and the drafting and implementation of Jewish settlement plans. He wrote many articles on agriculture and settlement in Palestine.

Ettinger, Solomon (1803–56) Polish Yiddish poet and dramatist. He was born in Warsaw and settled in Zhdanov near Zamość. He wrote parables, satirical ballads, epigrams, poems and dramas. His *Serkele* portrays an amibitious woman who pursues power and wealth.

Ettlinger, Jacob (1798–1871) German rabbi and champion of neo-Orthodoxy. In 1826 he was appointed district rabbi for the districts of Ladenburg and Ingolstadt and settled in Mannheim, where he founded a yeshivah. He was appointed chief rabbi of Altona in 1836. He wrote numerous studies of Jewish law.

Euchel, Isaac (1756–1804) German Hebrew author and Bible commentator of Danish origin. He became a leader of the Haskalah in Germany. He was born in Copenhagen and in 1787 settled in Berlin, where he managed the printing press of the Jüdische Freischule. His writings include a comedy, satirizing Orthodoxy, a study of **Moses Mendelssohn**, a translation of and commentary on the book of Proverbs, and a German translation of the prayerbook.

Even-Shoshan, Avraham (b. 1906) Hebrew educator of Russian origin. He was born in Minsk and emigrated to Palestine in 1925. From 1954 to 1968 he was director of the Bet ha-Kerem Teachers' Institute in Jerusalem. He published stories, poems and plays for children, translated children's books into Hebrew, and compiled a Hebrew dictionary.

Eydoux, Emmanuel [Eisinger, Roger] (b. 1913 French author. He was born in Marseilles. He taught Jewish history and thought in an ORT school and was active in the Marseilles Jewish community. He wrote poems, as well as plays, and books on the history of Judaism.

Ezekiel (fl. 6th cent. BCE) Israelite prophet. He prophesied among the Babylonian exiles from 592 to 570 BCE. After the destruction of Jerusalem, he consoled and encouraged those in captivity.

Ezekiel, Jacob (1812–99) American communal leader. He was born in Philadelphia, and moved to Baltimore and then to Richmond, Virginia, where he was active in Jewish affairs. He fought against legislation which discriminated against Jews. Later he moved to Cincinnati, where he served as secretary to the board of governors of the Hebrew Union College.

Ezekiel, Moses Jacob (1844–1917) American sculptor. He served in the Civil War, only later becoming a sculptor. His *Religous Liberty* is a large marble group commissioned by the B'nai B'rith for the Centennial Exposition of 1876.

Ezra (fl. 5th cent. BCE) Israelite prophet. He served as a scribe in the Persian government. Later he received permission from Artaxerxes I to lead the Jewish exiles back to Jerusalem. Together with **Nehemiah**, he persuaded the people to return to the Torah, observe the Sabbath and sabbatical year, pay Temple dues, and refrain from intermarriage. The story of Ezra is contained in the books of Ezra and Nehemiah.

F

Fackenheim, Emil (1916–2003) Canadian theologian. He was born in Halle, Germany. He emigrated to Canada in 1940, where he became professor of philosophy at the University of Toronto. His major work concerns the religious response to the Holocaust. His writings include: *God's Presence in History*, *The Jewish Return Into History* and *To Mend the World*.

Factor, Max (1877–1938) American manufacturer of cosmetics, of Polish origin. He emigrated from Poland to the US at the age of 27. He began a cosmetics firm which became one of the largest in the US.

Faitlovitch, Jacques (1881–1955) Polish researcher and activist on behalf of the Falashas. He went to Ethiopia in 1904 and spent 18 months among the Falashas. He published *Notes of a Voyage Among the Falashas* and organized committees in Italy and Germany to raise money for their education. Later he continued with his activities on the Falashas' behalf in the US and Israel, and published books on their literature.

Fajans, Kasimir (1887–1975) American chemist of Polish origin. Born in Warsaw, he studied at the University of Leipzig. From 1911–17 he was at the Technische Hochschule in Karlsruhe, Germany, and later at the University of Munich. Subsequently he became director of the Institute for Physical Chemistry in Munich. After the victory of the Nazis, he emigrated to the US and in 1936 became professor of chemistry at the University of Michigan.

Falaquera, Shemtov ben Joseph [Ibn Falaquera] (c.1225–95) Philosophical author. Born in Spain, he lived there and in the border provinces of Spain and France. His writings include a defence of **Maimonides**' *Guide for the Preplexed*, a compilation of ethical aphorisms, an introduction to the study of the sciences, an encyclopaedia of the sciences, and translations of sections of **Solomon ibn Gabirol**'s *Fountain of Life*.

Falk, Ḥayyim Samuel Jacob (c.1708–82) English mystic. He was born in Podolia and settled in England in about 1742. He was reputed to be a miracle-worker and became known as the Baal Shem of London.

Falk, Jacob Joshua ben Tzevi Hirsch (1680–1756) Polish rabbi and halakhic authority. He was born in Kraków and lived and worked in Lwów before serving as rabbi in the communities of Tarnów, Kurów and Lesko. In 1717 he became rabbi of Lwów; from 1730 to 1734 he was rabbi of Berlin, and he later became rabbi of Metz and Frankfurt am Main. His *Penei Yehoshua* is an outstanding work of novellae on the Talmud.

Falk, Joshua ben Alexander ha-Cohen [Walk, Joshua] (1555–1614) Polish educationalist and communal leader. He was born in Lublin. He devoted his life to teaching and took an active part in the Council of the Four Lands. His *Bet Yisrael* is a commentary on **Jacob ben Asher**'s Turim. In *Sepher Meirat Enayim*, he amended and interpreted part of the text of the Shulḥan Arukh. He also wrote responsa as well as commentaries on the Pentateuch and Talmud.

Faludy, György (b. 1910) Hungarian poet. Born in Hungary, he studied in Vienna. In 1938 he left

Hungary for France; later he went to Casablanca, and eventually to the US. In 1945 he returned to Hungary and became the literary editor of the Social Democratic daily *Népszava*. After the failure of the 1956 uprising, he settled in London where he was editor of *Irodalmi Ujság*. He then lived in Florence, Malta and Toronto. He subsequently taught Hungarian literature at Columbia University.

Fano, Jacob (fl. 16th cent.) Italian scholar and poet. He lived in Cento, Ferrara and Bologna. His elegy on the marrano martyrs of Ancona of 1555 provoked church authorities. He was punished and his book was burned.

Fano, Joseph (c. 1550–1630) Italian communal leader. He was on familiar terms with dukes of Mantua and Ferrara and occasionally acted as their intermediary. Some time before 1628 he was raised to the rank of Marquis of Villimpenta. He was the first Jew to be ennobled in Europe.

Fano, Menaḥem Azariah (1548–1620) Italian rabbi and kabbalist. He was active in Ferrara, Venice, Reggio nell'Emilia and Mantua. He published a collection of 130 responsa and also wrote works on the kabbalah, prayer and the transmigration of the soul.

Farbstein, David Tzevi (1868–1953) Swiss lawyer and Zionist. He was born in Warsaw and settled in Zurich in 1894. He served as a member of the Swiss parliament after World War I until 1939. He was the first president (from 1920) of the Keren ha-Yesod in Switzerland. When the State of Israel was founded, he suggested that its legislation be based on the model of the Swiss republic.He wrote studies of Judaism, Zionism and law.

Farbstein, Joshua Heschel (1870–1948) Polish communal leader. He was born in Warsaw. He was president of the Zionist Organization in Poland from 1915 to 1918. A founder of Mizraḥi in Poland, he was its president from 1918 to 1931; he was also president of the Keren ha-Yesod in Poland and of the Warsaw Jewish community from 1926 to 1931. He moved to Jerusalem, where he led the Community Council from 1938 to 1945.

Farḥi [Parḥi], Estori [Estori ha-Parḥi] (1280–?1355) Palestinian topographer. Born in Provence, he lived in various cities in Spain, and later settled in Palestine. His *Kaphtor va-Pheraḥ* presents the results of his travels throughout Palestine: it establishes the names of Palestinian towns and villages, describes the geography and natural history of the country, and identifies ancient sites.

Farḥi, Ḥayyim Mu'Allim (c. 1760–1820) Palestinian statesman. He entered the service of Aḥmad al-Jazzar Pasha in Damascus and was responsible for Palestine's treasury affairs. He participated in the city of Acre's stand against Napoleon in 1799. Later he was imprisoned, but was restored under Al-Jazzar's successor, Suleiman Pasha (ruled 1805–18). He acted as the protector of the Jews of Palestine.

Farrisol, Abraham (c. 1451–c. 1525) Italian biblical scholar, geographer and polemicist. He was born in Avignon and lived in Ferrara and Mantua, working as a cantor and copyist. He represented Judaism before the Duke of Ferrara in a religious dispute with two Dominican monks. He wrote a commentary on the Torah, Ecclesiastes and Job, a defence of Judaism, and the first modern Hebrew work on geography.

Fast, Howard (1914–2003) American author. He was born in New York. He wrote novels about American history, injustice and oppression. He also published books on Jewish themes, including *Haym Solomon: Son of Liberty*, *Picture Book of History of the Jews*, *My Glorious Brothers* and *Moses, Prince of Egypt*.

Feder, Tobias Guttman (1760–1817) Galician Haskalah scholar. He was born in Przedbórz and later wandered through Galicia, Poland and Russia. He wrote plays and satires, as well as studies in linguistics and grammar, and was one of the pioneers of Hebrew literary criticism.

Fefer, Itzik (1900–52) Ukrainian Yiddish poet. He was born in Shpola. He made his debut as a Yiddish poet in 1920 and became prominent in Soviet Yiddish literature. The majority of his poems are propaganda for the communist party. He also wrote poetry about Birobidjan, the Jewish autonomous region in eastern Siberia. He was arrested in 1948 in the Stalinist anti-Jewish purges.

Feierberg, Mordecai Ze'ev (1874–99) Russian Hebrew author. He wrote essays and lyrical novels. In his novels he expressed the plight of eastern European youth at the end of the 19th century, who were disillusioned with the Haskalah movement but were unable to accept traditional Judaism.

Feiffer, Jules (b. 1929) American playwright and cartoonist. He grew up in New York and contributed cartoons to the *Village Voice* in the 1950s. Much of his satire is based on Jewish sensibility; his characters are often victims at the mercy of a hostile world. He also wrote a number of plays dealing with Jewish themes.

Feigenbaum, Benjamin (1860–1932) American Yiddish writer and activist. He was born in Warsaw. He became a militant atheist and agitator for socialism. He settled in London in 1887, where he published pamphlets on socialism, then in 1891 he emigrated to the US. He attempted to win support for socialism and atheism among Jewish workers and in 1900 became general secretary of the Workmen's Circle.

Feinberg, Abraham L. (1899–1986) American Reform rabbi. He was born in Bellaire, Ohio. He served congregations in Niagra Falls, New York, Denver and Toronto. He was an advocate of liberal social causes, a supporter of nuclear disarmament, and an opponent of the Vietnam War. His works include *Storm the Gates of Jericho* and *Hanoi Days*.

Feinberg, Avshalom (1889–1917) Palestinian writer and leader of the Nili. He was born in Gedera. He founded the Nili movement with **Aaron Aaronsohn**. He was shot and killed by a Bedouin on a journey to Egypt. His writings depict the world of the first generation born in Jewish settlements in Palestine.

Feinstein, Elaine (b. 1930) British poet and novelist. Born in Merseyside, she began composing poetry in the early 1960s. Her works include *The Circle, The Magic Apple Tree, At the Edge, The Celebrants and Other Poems, The Amberstone Exit, The Glass Alembic, Children of the Rose, The Ecstasy of Dr Miriam Garner, The Shadow Master, The Survivors, The Border, Badlands* and *Mother's Girl.*

Feinstein, Moses (1895–1986) Orthodox scholar of Belorussian origin. Born in Uzda, Belorussia, he became rabbi of Luban, Belorussia. Later he emigrated to the US and became the rosh yeshivah of the Metivta Tifereth Yerushalayim. He served as president of the Union of Orthodox Rabbis of the United States and Canada. He wrote numerous responsa dealing with a wide range of problems.

Feiwel, Berthold (1875–1937) German Zionist leader. He was born in Moravia. He was a close associate of **Theodor Herzl** and helped to organize the first Zionist Congress in 1897. In 1901 he became editor-in-chief of the central organ of the Zionist Organization, *Die Welt*. He translated Hebrew and Yiddish works into German and was a founder of the Judischer Verlag in Berlin. In 1933 he settled in Palestine.

Feldman, Louis (1896–1975) South African Yiddish writer. He was born in Lithuania and went to South Africa in 1910, where he worked as a businessman. His publications include *Jews in South Africa, Oudtshoorn: the Jerusalem of Africa, Jews in Johannesburg* and *Israel as I See it.*

Fels, Mary (1863–1953) American Zionist. She was born in Bavaria and was taken to the US in 1869. She organized the Joseph Fels Foundation in 1925 to promote human welfare through education and cultural exchange, particularly between the US and Palestine.

Felsenthal, Bernard (1822–1908) American rabbi. He was born in Germany and settled in the US in 1854. He served as rabbi in Chicago from 1861 to 1887. He was a founder of the Jewish Publication Society of America and the American Jewish Historical Society.

Ferber, Edna (1887–1968) American novelist. Born in Kalamazoo, Michigan, she worked first as a journalist. Her works include *Show Boat, Giant, So Big, Dawn O'Hara, The Girls, Cimarron, Come and Get It* and *Saratoga Trunk.* Together with **George S. Kaufmann**, she wrote a number of plays.

Ferenczi, Sandor (Fraenkel, Sandor] (1873–1933) Hungarian psychiatrist. He met Sigmund Freud in 1908 and went with him to the US the next year. In 1913 he founded the Hungarian Psychoanalytic Society. He was the first to stress the importance of loving, physical contact with the mother.

Feuchtwanger, Lion (1884–1958) German historical novelist. He was born in Munich. He wrote plays as a young man and in 1926 his novel *Jud Süss* was published. Eventually he settled in the US. His novel *The Oppermanns* deals with a German Jewish family during the rise of Nazism. He also wrote a historical trilogy on the life of **Josephus**.

Feuerberg, Mordecai Ze'ev (1874–99) Ukrainian Hebrew writer. He was born in Novograd Volynskiy. His literary career began in 1896, when he went to Warsaw. He broke with his Ḥasidic background and wrote short stories about the conflict between traditional Judaism and modern secular culture.

Feuermann, Emanuel (1902–42) Cellist of Galician origin. Born in Kolomea, Galicia, he made his debut at the age of ten. His official debut with the Vienna Philharmonic took place in 1914. He made regular appearances with numerous orchestras, and in 1929 he became professor at the Hochschule für Musik in Berlin. With the rise of Hitler, he left Germany and went on a world tour appearing with leading orchestras.

Feuerring, Maximillan (1896–1985) Polish-Australian painter. Born in Lvov, Poland, he studied at the art school in Berlin, Florence, the Royal Academy of Fine Arts in Rome, and Paris and Warsaw. He taught at the Academy of Fine Arts, Warsaw from 1934–9. From 1947 to 1950 he taught at the Universität International, Munich. He later settled in Australia.

Feynman, Richard (1918–88) American physicist. Born in New York City, he worked on the atom bomb project. In 1965 he shared the Nobel Prize for Physics. From 1950 he was professor at the California Institute of Technology.

Fichman, Yaakov (1881–1958) Palestinian Hebrew poet, critic and literary editor. He was born in Bessarabia and lived in various cities in Russia and western Europe before settling in Palestine in 1912. He edited literary periodicals, anthologies and textbooks, and wrote poetry.

Fiedler, Leslie A. (1917–2003) American writer and critic. He was born in Newark, New Jersey. He taught at the University of Montana and the State University of New York at Buffalo. Jewish themes have played an increasing role in his later work. His writings include *Image of the Jew in American Fiction* and *The Jew in the American Novel.*

Filipowksi, Herschell Phillips (1816–72) British Hebraist, editor and actuary. He was born in Lithuania and emigrated to London in 1839, where he taught at a Jewish school. He was the editor of the Hebrew annual *Ha-Asif* from 1847 to 1849. In 1851 he founded a Jewish antiquarian society for the purpose of publishing medieval Hebrew texts on which he wrote various studies. In 1862 he printed a pocket edition of the prayerbook. His *Biblical Prophecies* discusses the Jewish view of prophecy and messianism.

Fineman, Irving (b. 1893) American novelist. He was born in New York and worked as an engineer until 1929, when he turned to writing. Of his later novels *Jacob* and *Ruth* deal with biblical themes. He also wrote a biography of **Henrietta Szold**, *Woman of Valor.*

Finkelkraut, Alain (b. 1949) French philosopher. His parents survived the Holocaust, and he studied in Paris. In *Le Juif imaginaire* he deals with the question how the Holocaust deformed his Jewish identity. His other works include *Réflexions sur la question juive, Anti-Semite and Jew, L'Avenir d'une négation* and *La Défaite de la pensée.*

Finkelstein, Louis (1895–1991) American Conservative rabbi, scholar and educator. He was born in Cincinnati. He began teaching at the Jewish Theological Seminary in 1920 and later became president and chancellor there. He served as president of the Rabbinical Assembly from 1928 to 1930. He wrote and edited books and articles on general problems in religion, sociology, culture, and ethics. His publications include *Pharisees, Jews:*

Their History, Culture and Religion and *Jewish Self-Government in the Middle Ages.*

Finzi, Angelo Mordecai (d. 1476) Italian banker and scientist. He lived in Bologna and Mantua. He wrote studies on mathematics and astronomy, translated various works on mathematics, geometry and astronomy into Hebrew, explained recently invented astronomical instruments, and published treatises on grammar and mnemonics.

Finzi, Isaac Raphael (1728–1812) Italian preacher. He served as a rabbi in Padua and was widely acclaimed as a preacher. He was a member of the French Sanhedrin in 1806 and served as its vice-president.

Finzi, Solomon (fl. 16th cent.) Italian rabbinical scholar. He served as a rabbi in Forli and Bologna. His methodological work *Mafteaḥ ha-Gemara* was reprinted in 1697 in Helmstedt with a Latin translation and notes, and again reprinted in the 18th century in *Clavis Talmudica maxima.*

Firkovich, Abraham (1786–1874) Palestinian Karaite leader of Polish birth. He engaged in bitter disputes with rabbinic authorities. In 1830 he accompanied Simḥah Bobowich to Palestine, where he collected numerous manuscripts. When in 1839, the governor general of the Crimea addressed a series of questions dealing with Karaite origins to Bobowich, he recommended Firkovich, who initiated archaeological expeditions to the Crimea and the Caucasus to uncover ancient tombstones and manuscripts. Firkovich's travels and discoveries are described in his *Avnei Zikkaron.*

Fischel, Harry (1865–1948) American philanthropist. He was born in Russia and emigrated to the US in 1885. He settled in New York, where he was active as a businessman in the construction and real estate industry. He was associated with a number of Jewish institutions, and endowed the Harry Fischel Foundation for Research in Talmud in Palestine.

Fischer, Bobby (b. 1943) American chess master. He won the US chess championship seven times, and in 1972 defeated the Russian Boris Spassky, becoming the world chess champion.

Fishberg, Maurice (1872–1934) American physician and anthropologist. He was born in Russia and emigrated to the US in 1889. He was professor of clinical medicine at New York University and Bellevue Hospital Medical College. His publications include *The Jews: A Study of Race and Environment.*

Fishman, Jacob (1878–1946) American Yiddish editor and Zionist leader of Polish origin. After he emigrated to the US he was active in Zionist societies that pre-dated those founded under the influence of **Theodor Herzl**. He was a founder of the Zionist Organization of America. He co-edited the New York Yiddish dailies *Tageblat* (1893–1914) and *Varhayt* (1914–16). Later he served as managing editor of the *Jewish Morning Journal.*

Fleckeles, Eleazar ben David (1754–1826) Bohemian rabbi and author. He was born in Prague and served as a rabbi there; he was also head of a large yeshivah and president of a three-man rabbinate council. When the Frankists made their appearance in the city in 1800, he led the opposition to them. He published a collection of sermons on halakhic and aggadic themes, as well as a volume of responsa.

Fleg, Edmond (1874–1963) French poet, playwright and essayist. He lived in Paris, where he worked as a theatre critic and playwright. Jewish themes are found throughout his work. his writings include *Écoute Israel, Pourquoi je suis Juif, Ma Palestine, L'anthologie juive,* and *Jésus, raconté par le Juif Errant.*

Fleischer, Max (1885–1972) American producer of animated cartoons. Born in Australia, he went to the US at the age of five and studied at various schools in New York. He initially worked as a cartoonist for the Brooklyn *Daily Eagle* and as art editor of *Popular Science Monthly.* In 1919 he founded the Fleischer Studios. Later the studio became a major enterprise.

Fleischmann, Gisi (1897–1944) Slovak underground leader during the Holocaust. She served as the head of WIZO in Slovakia before the war. She was deported from Slovakia in March 1942, and became one of the founders of the Committee of Six which was a precursor to the Working Group. During the period of the deportations, the Working

Group sought to end the flow of transports to the East.

Fleisher, Ezra (b. 1928) Israeli poet and scholar. He was born in Transylvania and emigrated to Israel in 1960. He became a lecturer on medieval Hebrew literature at Bar Ilan University, and then at the Hebrew University. His writings include *Mershalim* and *Be-Heḥalek Laylah.*

Flexner, Abraham (1866–1959) American educationalist. Born in Louisville, Kentucky, he published a review of higher education: *The American College: A Criticism.* In 1910 he published *Medical Education in the United States and Canada.* His other works include: *Medical Education in Europe* and *Prostitution in Europe.* He founded and organized the Institute for Advanced Study at Princeton University and served as its director.

Flexner, Bernard (1865–1945) American lawyer and Zionist leader. He was born in Louisville, Kentucky, and practised law in Kentucky, Chicago and New York. He was concerned with social welfare and labour problems as well as the Zionist movement. In 1919 he was counsel to the Zionist delegation at the Paris Peace Conference. He later served as president and chairman of the board of the Palestine Economic Corporation.

Flusser, David (1917–2000) Israeli New Testament scholar. In 1962 he became professor of comparative religions at the Hebrew University. His research was in the origins of Christianity. He was also known for his work on the Dead Sea Scrolls.

Foa, Eleazar Naḥman (d. after 1641) Italian rabbi and kabbalist. He lived at Reggio nell'Emilia and became chief rabbi of the duchy of Modena. He was head of Ḥevrat ha-Aluvim, which sponsored the printing of a commentary on the Haggadah. He also wrote a philosophical and kabbalistic commentary on the Torah.

Foa, Moses Benjamin (1729–1822) Italian bibliophile and bookseller. Living in Reggio nell'Emilia, he supplied books to the ducal library at Modena and became one of the most important booksellers of his day. He wrote a Hebrew grammar and copied several Hebrew manuscripts.

Fonseca, Daniel de (1672–c. 1740) Turkish physician and diplomat. He was born in Portugal and was brought up as a Christian. Although he became a priest, he adhered to Judaism in secret. He was pursued by the Inquisition and fled to France. In 1702 he arrived in Constantinople, where he embraced Judaism. He later became medical attendant to Prince Mavrocordato at Bucharest. After returning to Constantinople, he became physician to the sultan and eventually settled in Paris.

Ford, Aleksander (1908–80) Polish film director. Born in Lodz, he studied at Warsaw Univeristy. His first feature film, *Mascot,* was made in 1930. At this time he became a co-founder of the Society of the Devotees of the Artistic film. His 1932 film *The Street Legion* was set in Warsaw. The next year he made *Sabra in Palestine.* In 1937 he founded the Co-operative of Film Authors in Poland. From 1939 he was in the Soviet Union where he produced films for the Red Army. Later he became head of Film Polski, and eventually head of the Lodz film school. In 1970 he emigrated to Israel.

Formstecher, Solomon (1808–89) German philosopher and rabbi. He was born in Offenbach and served as rabbi there from 1842. He was active in the Reform movement and edited *Der Freitagabend* and *Die Israelitische Wochenschrift.* His *Die Religion des Geistes* presents a basis for the aims of the Emancipation and Reform movements in Judaism.

Fortas, Abe (1910–82) American lawyer. Born in Memphis, Tennessee, he taught at Yale University. Later he entered the Department of the Interior becoming its undersecretary. In 1965 he became a member of the US Supreme Court. In 1968 he was nominated to succeed retiring Chief Justice Earl Warren, but this was opposed by a coalition of Republican and Southern Democrats.

Foss, Lucas (b. 1922) American musician of German origin. Born in Berlin, he moved to Paris with his family at the onset of Nazism. In 1937 he went to the US. He studied at the Curtis Institute of Music and at Yale. After 1950 he studied in Rome, returning two years later. He taught composition at the University of California at Los Angeles. He was the conductor of the Buffalo Philharmonic

Orchestra (1963–70), and later music director of the Milwaukee Symphony Orchestra.

Fould, Achille (1800–67) French financier. He served as a minister of finance under Louis Napoleon. He introduced a number of reforms and reorganized the postal service. In 1852 he was appointed to the French Senate.

Fox, William (1879–1952) American film executive. He was brought to the US from Hungary. He established the Box Office Attractions Film Rental Company and opened a studio in Hollywood. He was eventually ousted from his own company. He was convicted of attempting to bribe a judge at his bankruptcy hearing and spent several months in jail.

Fram, David (1903–88) South African Yiddish poet. He was born in Lithuania and became a member of the Yung Vilne school of poets. In 1927 he settled in South Africa, where he published poems about Jewish life in Lithuania. His later poetry deals with South Africa, but is rooted in the tradition of Lithuanian Jewry. He served as editor of the Johannesburg Yiddish periodical *Der yidisher ekspres.*

Frances, Immanuel ben David (1618–c. 1710) Italian Hebrew poet. He was born in Livorno. He led an unsettled life, wandering from town to town and suffering many misfortunes, including the death of his family. He later served as a rabbi in Florence. He wrote love poems, satirical epigrams, polemics against the Shabbetaians, and religious poetry.

Frances, Jacob ben David (1615–67) Italian poet. He was born in Mantua. Some of the poetry attributed to him has also been ascribed to his brother, **Immanuel ben David.** Both men opposed the Shabbetaians.

Franck, Adolphe (1809–93) French philosopher and writer. He was born at Liocourt. He taught philosophy at several lycées and lectured at the Sorbonne. He was later appointed to the Collège de France as professor of ancient philosophy and then professor of law. He served as president of the Alliance Israélite Universelle. His writings include *The Kabbalah, or The Religious Philosophy of the Hebrews.*

Franck, Henri (1888–1912) French poet. He was born in Paris. He wrote philosophical essays, literary criticism and poetry. His poem *La danse devant l'Arche* seeks to harmonize biblical inspiration with the French Cartesian traditions; in this work he saw himself as the new **David** dancing before the Ark of the Covenant.

Franck, James (1882–1964) German scientist. He was professor at the University of Göttingen. He won the Nobel Prize in 1925. After Hitler's rise to power, he went to the US and taught at Johns Hopkins University and the University of Chicago. During World War II he worked on the atom bomb project.

Franco-Mendes, David (1713–92) Dutch Hebrew writer. He was born in Amsterdam and became a leading Hebrew poet there. He engaged in trade and served as honorary secretary of the Amsterdam Spanish and Portuguese community. Besides poetry, he wrote plays, articles, biographies of famous Sephardi Jews, and responsa.

Frank, Anne (1929–45) Dutch diarist. Her family fled from Germany to Amsterdam in 1933. When deportations of Jews from Holland began in 1942, she and her family went into hiding. In December 1944 she was deported to Bergen-Belsen where she died. Her diary about her experiences while hiding from the Nazis was published in 1947.

Frank, Jacob (1726–91) Polish communal leader, founder of the Frankist movement. He was born in Podolia. He was regarded as the successor to **Shabbetai Tzevi.** His mystical festivities were alleged to be accompanied by sexual orgies. He and his followers were excommunicated in 1756. The Frankists later renounced the Talmud, and debates were held between Frankists and rabbis, which concluded with the baptism of members of the Frankist sect. When the Polish authorities discovered that the Frankists revered Frank as their lord, he was tried and secluded in a monastery. He was released by the Russians in 1772 and settled at Offenbach, which became the centre of his movement.

Frankau, Julia (1859–1916) English novelist and critic. She used the pseudonym Frank Danby for her fiction. Her novel *Dr Philips: A Maida Vale Idyll* is a story of London Jewish life. She edited a weekly publication, *Jewish Society*, from 1889–1901.

Frankel, David ben Naphtali Hirsch (1707–62) German rabbi and scholar. He served as a rabbi at Dessau and Berlin, and wrote a commentary on the Palestinian Talmud.

Frankel, Zacharias (1801–75) German rabbi and scholar. He was born in Prague. He served as rabbi at Litomerice and Teplice and became chief rabbi of Dresden in 1836. In 1854 he became director of the Breslau Rabbinical Seminary. He founded the positivist-historical school which later influenced Conservative Judaism in the US. At the second Reform rabbinical conference at Frankfurt am Main in 1845 he protested against the gradual abolition of Hebrew in the liturgy and withdrew from the conference. He published studies of halakhic issues, the history of the oral tradition, and the methodolgy of the Mishnah and the Talmud. He also founded and edited the *Monatsschrift für Geschichte und Wissenschaft des Judentums.*

Frankenthaler, Helen (b. 1928) American painter. She was born in New York. Her work includes ark curtains for the Temple of Aaron Congregation in St Paul, Minnesota.

Frankfurter, Felix (1882–1965) American jurist. He was born in Vienna and was taken to New York at the age of 12. He served as professor at Harvard Law School (1914–39), and associate justice of the US Supreme Court (1939–62). In 1919 he was the legal adviser to the Zionist delegation at the Paris Peace Conference, and later maintained an interest in the establishment of a Jewish national home in Palestine.

Frankl, Ludwig August [von Hochwart, Ritter] (1810–94) Austrian poet. He was born in Bohemia. He was appointed secretary and archivist of the Vienna Jewish community in 1838 and in 1842 he started to edit the literary periodical *Sonntagsblätter.* Half a million copies of his revolutonary poem *Die Universität* were circulated, and it was set to music 28 times. In 1856 he founded the Lamel school in Palestine, which offered a secular, as well as a religious, education for children. In 1876 he founded the Vienna Jewish Institute for the Blind and was ennobled.

Frankl, Victor E. (1905–97) Austrian psychiatrist. He was a prisoner at Auschwitz and other concentration camps. His experiences led to the formulation of his existential psychotherapeutic approach (known as logotherapy), which is described in *Man's Search for Meaning.*

Franklin, Arthur Ellis (1857–1938) English banker and art collector. He served as chairman of the Routledge publishing firm, president of the Jewish Religious Education Board, and vice-president of the board of Deputies of British Jews. His collection of Jewish ritual art is in the Jewish Museum in London.

Franklin, Jacob Abraham (1809–77) English editor and communal leader. He founded and edited the journal *Voice of Jacob* as a forum for anti-Reform opinion. He was active in communal organizations and left most of his fortune to endow educational projects, including the publication of Jewish textbooks.

Franklin, Rosalind (1920–58) British chemist. She studied at Cambridge University. In 1947 she was employed at the Laboratoire Central des Services Chimiques de l'État in Paris. Several years later she worked at Kings College, London and subsequently Birkbeck College, London. Her unpublished data and X-ray photographs arguably enabled Maurice Wilkins and Francis Crick to discover the structure of DNA.

Franklin, Selim (1814–81) British Columbia pioneer, of English origin. He emigrated to the US and took part in the California gold rush. Settling in Victoria, British Columbia, he was elected to the legislative assembly.

Franklin, Sidney [Frumkin, Sidney] (1903–76) American bullfighter. He grew up in Brooklyn and became the most famous bullfighter in Mexico. He was a friend of Ernst Hemingway.

Franks, Jacob (1688–1769) American merchant. He was born in London and settled in New York. In 1712 he married Abigail Bilhah Levy, the daughter of one of New York's richest Jews. He was active in the congregational affairs of Shearith Israel in New York. He served as president of the congregation in

1729, and was a founder of the congregation's Mill Street synagogue.

Franzos, Karl Emil (1848–1904) Austrian novelist and journalist. He was born in Czortkow. He worked as a journalist for several newspapers and in 1873 he began publishing in the *Neue Freie Presse* tales about the life of eastern European Jewry. His writings include *Der Pojaz, Aus Halb-Asien* and *Die Juden von Barnow.*

Freed, Isadore (1900–60) American composer, organist, pianist and educator. He was born in Brest-Litovsk, Belorussia, and went to the US as a child. He taught at music schools in Philadelphia and New York, and at the Hart School of Music in Hartford, Connecticut. He also served as an organist and choir director in several temples. His work includes the book *Harmonizing the Jewish Modes.*

Freehof, Solomon (1892–1990) American Reform rabbi and scholar. He was born in London and was taken to the US. He served as professor of liturgy at the Hebrew Union College, and was later a rabbi in Chicago and at Congregation Rodeph Shalom in Pittsburgh. In 1955 he was appointed head of the Responsa Committee of the Central Conference of American Rabbis. He published numerous collections of responsa.

Freidus, Abraham Solomon (1867–1923) American librarian and bibliographer. He was born in Riga, Latvia and lived in Paris, Palestine and London, before settling in New York in 1889. In 1897 he was appointed first chief of the Jewish Division of the New York Public Library. He developed a classification scheme used for Judaica.

Freier, Recha (1892–1984) German youth leader. She was born in Norderney. In 1932 in Berlin she founded the Youth Aliyah movement to aid Jewish young people to prepare for agricultural life. After 1933 she organized agricultural training outside Germany and directed pupils to Palestine, where she settled in 1941.

Freiman, Archibald Jacob (1880–1944) Canadian Zionist. He was the head of the Ottawa Jewish Community and the founder of a large department store. He became president of the Federation of Zionist Societies in 1920.

Freiman, Lillian (1885–1940) Canadian Zionist, the wife of **Archibald Jacob Freiman**. She headed the Canadian Hadassah (1919–40).

Freimann, Aron (1871–1944) German scholar, son of **Israel Meir Freimann**. He was born in Filehne, in the province of Posen. He worked at the municipal library in Frankfurt am Main, where he assembled a large collection of Judaica and Hebraica. After the Nazis came to power, he emigrated to the US. Between 1939 and 1945 he served as consultant to the New York Public Library. He was the author and editor of books and articles about Jewish history, culture and bibliography.

Freimann, Avraham Ḥayyim (1889–1948) Jurist and rabbinic scholar of Moravian origin. He served as magistrate at Köningsberg and county judge at Braunsberg. In 1944 he began lecturing on Jewish law at the Hebrew University in Jerusalem. In 1947 he was appointed head of an advisory committee for Jewish law on personal status in the proposed Jewish state. He published studies of medieval rabbinics and Jewish law in modern Israel, and also wrote a work which deals with changes in Jewish marriage laws after the talmudic period.

Freimann, Israel Meir (1830–84) Polish rabbi. He served communities in the province of Posen and published a critical edition of the *Ve-Hizhir* midrashic work.

Freimann, Jacob (1866–1937) German rabbi, scholar and editor. He was born in Kraków. He served as a rabbi at Kanitz in Moravia and Holleschau (1890–1913). In 1913 he became chief rabbi of Posen. In 1928 he joined the rabbinate of the Berlin Jewish community and later lectured on rabbinics and Jewish history at the Berlin Rabbinical Seminary. He published studies in medieval rabbinical literature.

Frenk, Azriel Nathan (1863–1924) Polish journalist and historian. He was born in Wodzislaw. He began to write for the Jewish press in Warsaw in 1884, publishing articles about current events, stories about Ḥasidic life, and studies of Jewry in Poland.

Freud, Anna (1895–1982) Psychoanalyst of Austrian origin. The daughter of **Sigmund Freud**, she was an elementary school teacher and later gravitated to the Vienna Psychoanalystic Society. She founded and edited the journal, *The Psychoanalytic Study of the Child*. Her most noted work was *The Ego and the Mechanism of Defence*. In 1943 she founded the Hampstead Clinics in Great Britain.

Freud, Lucien (b. 1922) British artist. The grandson of **Sigmund Freud**, his work aroused considerable interest and has been purchased for many national collections of 20th-century art.

Freud, Sigmund (1856–1939) Austrian psychologist, founder of psychoanalysis. He was born in Freiberg. He worked as a neuropathologist and clinical neurologist in Vienna and as a result of his work and research formulated a new approach to understanding the human mind. In addition to numerous psychoanalytical studies, he published *Moses and Monotheism*. He was a member of the Jewish community in Vienna and was a loyal member of the local B'nai B'rith.

Fried, Erich (1921–88) Austrian writer. In 1938 his parents were arrested and he fled the Nazis, settling in England. After the war he worked on periodicals and then was a political commentator for the BBC. From 1946 he worked on a novel *Ein Soldat und ein Mädchen* which was published in 1960. His poetry includes: *Poems of Warning, 100 Poems Without a Country, Fear and Consolation: Stories and Poems About Jews and Nazis.*

Friedan, Betty (b. 1921) American feminist. Born in Peoria, Illinois, her book, *The Feminine Mystique*, was considered to have stimulated the second wave of 20th-century feminism.

Friedberg, Abraham Shalom [Har-Shalom] (1838–1902) Polish Hebrew writer, editor and translator. He was born in Grodno, Belorussia, and after wandering from town to town in southern Russia returned to his native city in 1858. After the pogroms of 1881 he joined the Ḥibbat Zion movement. In 1886 he went to Warsaw, where he was an editor of the first Hebrew encyclopaedia, *Ha-Eshkol*. His *Memoirs of the House of David* is a series of stories embracing Jewish history from the destruction of the Temple to the beginning of the Haskalah period in Germany.

Freidberg, Bernhard (1876–1961) Israeli scholar and bibliographer. He was born in Kraków and moved to Frankfurt am Main in 1900. In 1904 he set up his own publishing firm. He later entered the diamond trade and moved to Antwerp. In 1946 he settled in Tel Aviv. He published Jewish biographies, family histories, and a series of works on the history of Hebrew printing. His *Beit Eked Sepharim* is a bibliographical lexicon.

Fried, Alfred Herman (1864–1921) Austrian pacifist. He received the Nobel Peace Prize in 1911. During World War I his actions were viewed as treasonable, and he escaped to Switzerland.

Friedell, Egon (1878–1938) Austrian writer. Born in Vienna, he studied there and in Heidelberg. He converted to Protestantism and believed that Jews should overcome their Jewishness. He was a cabaret performer, and later became an opponent of the Nazis. He committed suicide when the Gestapo came to his apartment in Munich. He published *A Cultural History of the Modern Age.*

Friedenwald, Aaron (1836–1902) American ophthalmologist. He was born in Baltimore. He was a professor at the College of Physicians and Surgeons in Baltimore. He was active in the Baltimore Hebrew Orphan Asylum, the Jewish Theological Seminary of America, the Federation of American Zionists, and the American Jewish Historical Society.

Freidenwald, Harry (1864–1950) American ophthamologist, son of **Aaron Friedenwald**. He was born in Baltimore and taught at the Baltimore College of Physicians and Surgeons. He was president of the Federation of American Zionists from 1904 to 1918. In 1911 and 1914 he went to Palestine, where he was a consultant for eye diseases in several hospitals. His writings include *The Jews and Medicine* and *Jewish Luminaries in Medical History.*

Friedlaender, Israel (1876–1920) American scholar and communal leader. He was born in Kovel, Poland, and grew up in Warsaw. He became lecturer in Semitics at the University of Strasbourg, then in

1904 was appointed professor of Bible at the Jewish Theological Seminary of America. He also taught at Dropsie College in Philadelphia and was active in Jewish communal life. He published studies of Islamic sects, Judeo-Arabic literature, and Jewish influences on Arabic folklore, and translated Simon Dubnow's *History of the Jews in Russia and Poland.*

Friedland, Abraham Hyman (1891–1939) American writer and educator. He was born in Hordok, near Vilna, and emigrated to the US in 1906. In 1911 he founded the National Hebrew School in New York. He later served as superintendent of the Cleveland Hebrew Schools, and in 1924 became director of the Cleveland Bureau of Jewish Education. He wrote poems, short stories and articles, and edited educational texts.

Friedlander, Albert (1927–2004) British rabbi. He was born in Berlin. He served as senior lecturer and dean of the Leo Baeck College in London and rabbi of Westminster Synagogue. His writings include *Out of the Whirlwind* and *Leo Baeck.*

Friedländer, David (1750–1834) German communal leader and author. He was born in Königsberg and settled in Berlin in 1770, where he established a silk factory. He was a founder and director of the Jewish Free School in Berlin and led the fight for equal rights for Prussian Jewry. After the death of **Moses Mendelssohn**, he was the leader of the German Jewish Enlightenment movement. He championed extreme religious reform.

Friedländer, Michael (1833–1910) British educator and writer. He was born in Jutrosin in the province of Posen. He served as the head of the Talmud Torah school in Berlin from 1862, and was principal of Jews College in London from 1865 to 1910. He took an active part in the communal and cultural life of Anglo-Jewry. His writings include *Jewish Religion, Textbook of the Jewish Religion* and *Jewish Family Bible.*

Friedlander, Moritz (1844–1919) Hungarian educator and writer. He became secretary of the Israelitische Allianz and worked in Galicia assisting the emigration of Russian Jews to the US. With the help of Baron **Maurice de Hirsch** and his wife, he established and supervised more than 50 schools for boys and girls in Galicia. He wrote studies of the relationship of Hellenism and Christianity in Judaism.

Friedländer, Saul (b. 1932) Israeli historian. He was born in Prague, lived in France from 1939 to 1948, and then emigrated to Israel. He later taught at the Institut des Hautes Études Internationales in Geneva, and he was appointed professor of history and international relations at the Hebrew University in 1969. His writings include *Hitler et les États-Unis, 1939–41*, *Prelude to Downfall: Hitler and the United States*, and *Pius XII and the Third Reich.*

Friedman, Bruce Jay (b. 1930) American novelist. He was born in the Bronx and in his novels satirized middle-class American Jewish life. His works include *Stern*, *A Mother's Kisses* and *The Dick.*

Friedman, Elisha Michael (1889–1951) American economist. He acted as economic consultant to several US governmental agencies. He was an active Zionist and a supporter of the Hebrew University. His *Survival or Extinction* is a discussion of the Jewish problem.

Friedman, Lee Max (1871–1957) American lawyer and historian. He was professor of law at Portia Law School in Boston and vice-president of the school. He served as president and later honorary president of the American Jewish Historical Society. He published studies on various aspects of Jewish history.

Friedmann, David Aryeh (1889–1957) Israeli critic and editor. After studying medicine at Moscow University, he emigrated to Palestine in 1925, where he practised ophthalmology. He published studies on Hebrew and world literature, art criticism, and the history of Jewish medicine.

Friedmann, David ben Samuel [David of Karlin] (1828–1917) Lithuanian rabbi and halakhic authority. He was born in Biala, and served as rabbi of Karlino near Pinsk from 1868. His *Piskei Halakhot* is an exposition and summary of matrimonial law. In his *Emek Berakhah* he discussed the conditions under which a religious ban should be imposed. Although he initially was active in the Ḥibbat Zion movement, he later became an opponent of Zionism.

Frigeis, Lazaro de (fl. 16th century) Italian physician. He was a friend of the anatomist Andrea Vesalius in Padua and supplied the Hebrew names for some of the anatomical structures described in Vesalius' work, *De humani corporis fabrica*. These terms were taken from the Hebrew translation of the *Canon* of Avicenna and from the Talmud.

Frischmann, David (1859–1922) Polish Hebrew and Yiddish writer. He was born in Zgierz, near Lódź. His first works were written in the spirit of the Haskalah; later writings include satires, stories, critical essays and poems. He also published translations of European literature and worked in journalism. He served as editor of several periodicals and anthologies and contributed to the Hebrew press.

Fromm, Erich (1900–80) American psychoanalyst and social philosopher. He was born in Frankfurt am Main and worked at the Institute for Social Research there from 1929 to 1932. After the Nazis came to power, he emigrated to the US and taught at Bennington College, the National University of Mexico, Michigan State University, and New York University. Much of his writing was influenced by Jewish sources. His publications include *The Art of Loving* and *You Shall Be as Gods.*

Frug, Simon Samuel (1860–1916) Ukrainian Yiddish poet. He was born in Kherson province. He published three volumes of Russian poetry and was the first poet to treat Jewish themes in Russian verse. Later he published Yiddish songs and ballads. In his Zionist lyrics he pleaded for a return of the Jews to productive labour in their ancestral homeland.

Frumkin, Aryeh Leib (1845–1916) Palestinian rabbinic scholar and writer, of Lithuanian origin. He visited Palestine in 1867 and 1871 and began research for a history of the rabbis and scholars of Jerusalem. He returned to Europe and served as a rabbi at Ilukste in Latvia. Later he became a farmer-scholar in Ptaḥ Tikvah, Palestine, where he established a yeshivah. In 1894 he settled in London, but he eventually emigrated to Palestine. His *Seder Rav Amran* is a siddur with notes and a commentary.

Frumkin, Israel Dov (1850–1914) Palestinian journalist. He was born in Belorussia and was taken to Jerusalem when he was nine. He edited the Jerusalem periodical *Ḥavatzelet* from 1870 to 1910. From the mid-1880s his journalistic writings attacked the Ḥibbat Zion movement.

Fuchs, Daniel (1909–93) American novelist, short-story writer and screenwriter. He was born in New York. He taught elementary school in Brooklyn and wrote several novels during summer vacations. His *Summer in Williamsburg* depicts the lives and fantasies of several poor Jewish families.

Fuchs, Ernst (b. 1930) Austrian painter. He was born in Vienna and became a member of the Viennese school of Fantastic Realism. Some of his paintings include allusions to the kabbalah, Hebrew script and biblical themes.

Fuchs, Eugen (1856–1923) German jurist. He was an executive member of the German Barristers' Association and wrote legal studies. He led the anti-Zionist Central-Verein Deutscher Staatsbürger Jüdischen Galubens.

Funk, Casimir (1884–1967) American biochemist. Born in Warsaw, he worked at the Pasteur Institute in Paris where he concentrated on protein chemistry and metabolism. From 1906–10 he was in Berlin, and then went to the Lister Institute in London. He later went to the US and worked at the Harriman Research Laboratory.

Fünn, Samuel Joseph (1818–90) Lithuanian Hebrew writer. He was born in Vilna and was a founder of the first Jewish school in the city. He taught the Bible and Hebrew there, and later taught at the local rabbinical school. In 1856 he was appointed inspector of the government Jewish schools in the Vilna district. In 1863 he opened a printing press in Vilna, which enabled him to publish *Ha-Karmel*, a journal which he edited and to which he contributed studies of Russian Jewry. He wrote a biographical lexicon of notable Jews and a Hebrew dictionary.

Fürst, Julius (1805–73) Polish Hebraist, bibliographer and historian. He settled in Leipzig, where he taught at the university. His publications include a bibliography of Jewish books and books on Judaism, a history of Karaism, a Bible concordance, a Hebrew and Aramaic lexicon, and a history of Jewish literature.

Furstenthal, Raphael Jacob (1781–1855) German author and translator. He wrote poetry and translated **Maimonides**' *Guide for the Perplexed*, **Baḥya ibn Pakuda**'s *Hovot ha-Levanot*, and **Issac Aboab**'s *Menorat ha-Maor* from Hebrew into German. He also translated Jewish liturgical works.

Furtado, Abraham (1756–1817) French politician and communal leader. Of Portuguese descent, he lived in Bordeaux. He was elected president of the Assembly of Jewish Notables convened by Napoleon, and acted as secretary of the Paris Sanhedrin. He published *Mémoire d'Abraham Furtado sur l'état des Juifs en France jusqu' à la Revolution.*

Füst, Milán (1888–1967) Hungarian poet. He was from a lower middle-class family in Budapest. He studied law and taught in a commercial school there; subsequently he travelled abroad extensively. During the 1950s he taught at the University of Budapest. His works include: *You Cannot Change It, Selected Poems, Vision and Impulse in Art, The Story of My Wife.*

G

Gabor, Dennis (1900–79) Hungarian physicist. Born in Hungary, he was educated in Budapest and Berlin. He taught at the University of Berlin-Charlottenburg. He left Germany in 1934 for Britain, and later settled in the US. He received the Nobel Prize for Physics in 1971.

Gad (i) (fl. 19th–16th cent. BCE) Israelite, son of **Jacob** and **Zilpah** (Genesis 30:10–11). His tribal territory lay to the east of the Jordan. The tribe of Gad flourished during the rule of **Saul** and **David**.

Gad (ii) (fl. 11th–10th cent. BCE) Israelite prophet. He was one of the three prophets during the days of King **David**. He joined **David** when he fled from **Saul** to Adullam, and persuaded him to return to Judah (I Samuel 22:5). He remained at the court of **David** in Jerusalem (II Samuel 24:11–14; I Chronicles 21:9–30), and was one of the organizers of the Levitical service in the Temple (II Chronicles 29:25).

Galante, Abraham (1873–1961) Turkish scholar. He was born in Bodrum. He was first a teacher and inspector in the Jewish and Turkish schools of Rhodes and Smyrna. Later he lived in Egypt, where he edited the Ladino newspaper *La vara*. He encouraged the acculturation of Turkish Jewry to its homeland, and fought for Jewish rights. Eventually he returned to Istanbul where he became a professor at the university. He wrote studies of Jewish history in Turkey.

Galante, Abraham ben Mordecai (fl. 16th cent.) Palestinian kabbalist. He was born in Rome and settled in Safed. He wrote a commentary on the Zohar.

Galante, Moses ben Jonathan (1620–89) Palestinian rabbi. He studied in Safed and later moved to Jerusalem, where he was a leading rabbi and head of a yeshivah. Influenced by the Shabbetaians, he and other rabbis went to Gaza to seek purification of the soul from **Nathan of Gaza**. He accompanied **Shabbetai Tzevi** to Smyrna and Constantinople. He wrote responsa and commentaries on the Torah.

Galante, Moses ben Mordecai (fl. 16th cent.) Palestinian talmudist and kabbalist. He was born in Rome. He became a disciple of **Joseph Caro** and his teacher in the field of kabbalah was **Moses ben Jacob Cordovero**. From 1580 he served as av bet din in Safed. He wrote responsa, an index of biblical passages interpreted in the Zohar, and a homiletic and kabbalistic commentary on Ecclesiastes.

Galich, Alexander (1919–77) Ukrainian poet, songwriter and dramatist. He was born in Yekaterinoslav. In the 1960s he was baptized into the Russian Orthodox Church, and was later expelled from the Writers' Union. In 1974 he left the USSR and settled in Munich and Paris. His works include comic ballads, and songs and poems on the Holocaust and the Stalinist camps.

Galili, Israel (1910–86) Israeli Labour and Haganah leader. He was born in the Ukraine and was taken to Palestine at the age of four. In 1924 he was among the founders of the youth wing of the Histadrut. He joined the central command of the Haganah in 1941 and from 1945 to 1947 he was one of the principal organizers of underground armed activities in Palestine. In 1947 he was appointed head of Haganah's territorial command. He served as deputy minister of defence in the provisional government in 1948. From 1966 to 1970 he was minister without portfolio in the Israeli government, responsible for the information services.

Gallico, Abraham Jagel ben Hananiah [Jagel, Abraham] (fl. 16th cent.) Italian writer on ethics. He served as mint-master to the Prince of Correggio. His *Valley of Vision* is an imitation of Dante's *Divine Comedy*. He also wrote *Lekaḥ Tov*, the first Jewish catechism.

Gama, Gaspar da (c. 1440–1510) Portuguese navigator. After journeying to Jerusalem and Alexandria, he was sold into slavery in India. When he was granted his freedom, he served the ruler of Goa. When the Portuguese explorer Vasco da Gama landed on the shores of Goa, he was sent to meet him. He then served with the Portuguese. He was forced to be baptized and took his master's name.

Gamaliel the Elder (fl. 1st cent.) Palestinian elder, grandson of **Hillel**. He was president of the Sanhedrin and, according to Acts, **Paul** was one of his pupils. He maintained close contact with Jews in Palestine and the diaspora. He was responsible for many takkanot.

Gamaliel II (fl. 1st–2nd cent.) Palestinian elder. He was president of the Sanhedrin at Jabneh, and strengthened the new centre there. He consolidated Jewish law and sought to unite the Jewish people around the Torah. He provoked a revolt against his authority and **Eleazar ben Azariah** was appointed nasi in his place. Later he was reinstated.

Gamaliel III (fl. 3rd cent.) Palestinian elder, son of **Judah ha-Nasi**. He was appointed nasi in the first half of the 3rd century.

Gamoran, Emanuel (1895–1962) American educator. He was born in Russia and was taken to the US in 1907. In 1923 he became the education director of the Commission of Jewish Education of the Union of American Hebrew Congregations. He also served as president of the National Council for Jewish Education (1927–8). His writings include *Changing Concepts in Jewish Education.*

Gance, Abel (1889–1981) French film director. Born in Paris, he was initially a stage actor and dramatist. His films include *La folie du Docteur Tube, Mater Dolorosa, J'accuse, La roue, Un grand amour de Beethoven* and *Bonaparte et la Révolution.*

Gans, David ben Solomon (1541–1613) Bohemian chronicler, astronomer and mathematician. He was born in Lippstadt, Westphalia. He studied with **Moses Isserles** in Kraków and later settled in Prague, where he was in contact with Johann Kepler and Tycho Brahe. He wrote works on astronomical and mathematical problems, Jewish and general history, the calendar, and the geography of Israel.

Gans, Eduard (1798–1839) German jurist and historian. Together with **Leopold Zunz** and Moses Mosher, he founded in 1819 the Society for Jewish Culture and Learning. In 1820 he was appointed a lecturer at the University of Berlin. He converted to Christianity in 1825 and became a professor at the university. He wrote studies of law, edited Hegel's lectures on the philosophy of history, and founded the journal *Jahrbücher für Wissenschaftliche Kritik.*

Ganzfried, Solomon (1804–86) Hungarian rabbi and author. He was born in Ungvar. He served as rabbi of Brezewicz and later head of the bet din of Ungvar. His *Kitzur Shulḥan Arukh* is an abridgement of the Shulḥan Arukh.

Gardner, Herb (b. 1934) American playwright. He was born in Brooklyn. His plays deal with Jewish characters and include *The Goodbye People, I'm Not Rappoport* and *Who is Harry Kellerman and Why Is He Saying those Terrible Things About Me?*

Gardosh, Kariel [Dosh] (1921–2000) Israeli cartoonist. He was born in Budapest. He emigrated to Israel in 1948, and joined the staff of the paper *Maariv* as editorial cartoonist. Signing himself 'Dosh', he created the figure of Little Israel, a young boy who became the popular symbol of the State and its people. He also illustrated books and wrote short stories and plays. He has exhibited in Israel and other countries.

Gary, Romain (1914–80) French novelist. Born in Vilna, he moved to Poland when he was seven, and in 1926 settled in Nice. He served in the French diplomatic service and was consul-general in Los Angeles from 1956 to 1960. His *A European*

Education includes elements of Jewish interest. In *The Dance of Genghis Cohn*, he tells the story of a Jewish comedian shot by the Nazis who haunts his executioner. Jewish characters frequently appear in his novels.

Gasser, Herbert (1888–1963) American physiologist. He taught at Cornell University Medical School, and later was the director of the Rockefeller Institute. He received the Nobel Prize in 1944.

Gaster, Moses (1856–1939) British rabbi and scholar. He was born in Bucharest and taught Romanian language and literature in the university there. Later he settled in England. He taught Slavonic literature at Oxford University. In 1887 he was appointed Ḥaham of the English Sephardi community. From 1891 to 1896 he was principal of Judith Montefiore College in Ramsgate. He was active in Ḥibbat Zion and later in the Zionist movement. He published studies of Romanian literature, comparative and Jewish folklore, Samaritan history and literature, rabbinic scholarship, liturgy, Anglo-Jewish history, and biblical studies.

Gaster, Theodor Herzl (1906–92) American educator and scholar, son of **Moses Gaster**. He was born in London. He taught comparative religion at Dropsie College in Philadelphia and at other universities in the US. His writings include: *Passover: Its History and Traditions, Purim and Hanukkah in Custom and Tradition, Thespis: Ritual, Myth, and Drama in the Ancient Near East, Festivals of the Jewish Year, Holy and Profane* and *New Year: Its History, Customs and Superstitions.*

Gavsie, Charles (1906–67) Canadian public official. He was a lawyer in Montreal and became deputy minister of national revenue and taxation. He became vice-president of St Lawrence Seaway Authority.

Geber, Hana (1910–90) American sculptor. She was born in Prague and eventually settled in New York. Her sculptures deal with Jewish themes. She has also produced mezuzot, spice holders, kiddush cups and Ḥanukkah lamps.

Gebirtig, Mordecai (1877–1942) Polish Yiddish poet. He was born in Kraków and worked as a carpenter. Regarded as a Yiddish bard, he composed the works and melodies for his songs, which were collected in 1936 in a volume edited by **Menachem Kipnis**. His most famous song, *Our Town Is Burning*, was written in 1938 under the impact of the pogrom in Przytyk.

Gedaliah (fl. 6th cent BCE) Babylonian governor of Judah. He was appointed after the destruction of the First Temple in 586 BCE, and resided at Mizpah. He was murdered by **Ishmael ben Nethaniah**, who hoped to overthrow Babylonian rule.

Gehazi (fl. 9th cent. BCE) Israelite, servant of **Elisha**. In the story of the wealthy Shunammite woman (II Kings 4:8–37), he acted as **Elisha**'s faithful messenger and loyal protector. However, he is depicted as greedy and cunning in the story of **Naaman**; after trying to deceive **Elisha**, he was cursed with the leprosy of which Naaman was cured (II Kings 5). In the story of the woman from Shunem and the King of Israel (II Kings 8:1–6), he told the king about the great deeds which **Elisha** had performed.

Geiger, Abraham (1810–74) German Reform leader and scholar. In 1832 he became rabbi in Wiesbaden, where he reformed the synagogue services and published the *Wissenschaftliche Zeitschrift für jüdische Theologie.* In 1837 he convened the first meeting of Reform rabbis. He later became rabbi in Breslau, where he established a school for religious studies and led a group that worked on Hebrew philology. He participated in subsequent Reform synods and from 1863 served as rabbi in Frankfurt am Main. In 1870 he became rabbi of the Berlin congregation, and helped to establish the Hochschule für Wissenschaft des Judentums in the city. His works include studies of the Bible, the Sadducees and Pharisees, Jewish history, mishnaic Hebrew, and **Maimonides**.

Geiger, Lazarus (1829–70) German philosopher and philologist, nephew of **Abraham Geiger**. He was born in Frankfurt am Main and later taught at the Jewish educational institute Philanthropin there. His writings include *Ursprung und Entweicklung der menschlichen Sprache und Vernunft* and *Der Ursprung der Sprache.*

Geiger, Ludwig (1848–1919) German literary historian, son of **Abraham Geiger**. He studied at his father's Hochschule in Berlin, and 1880 was appointed professor of German literature and cultural history at Berlin University. He made contributions to Renaissance and Reformation studies, German-Jewish history, and research on Goethe. From 1909 he edited the Jewish newspaper *Allgemeine Zeitung des Judentums.*

Gelber, Nathan Mikhael (1891–1966) Austrian historian and Zionist leader. He was born in Lemberg. He was general secretary of the eastern Galician delegation of the Vaad Leumi in Vienna (1918–21), and later became secretary of the Austrian Zionist Organization. In 1934 he emigrated to Palestine where he worked in the head office of Keren ha-Yesod in Jerusalem. He published books and articles on Jewish history and contemporary Jewish life.

Gell-Mann, Murray (b. 1929) American physicist. He taught at the California Institute of Technology. He received the Nobel Prize in 1969.

Gélleri, Andor Endre (1907–45) Hungarian novelist. He was born in Budapest and worked as a dyer and locksmith. His writings include *The Laundry*, *Thirsty Apprentices*, *Hold Street*, *The Harbor* and *Lightning and Evening Fire*. Jewish figures appear in many of his works.

Gelman, Aryeh Leon (b. 1887) American journalist and Zionist leader. He was born in Russia and went to the US at the age of 23. He was the principal of various Hebrew schools in St Louis, and later served as editor and publisher of the Yiddish *St Louis Jewish Record*. He was president of the American Mizraḥi movement from 1935 to 1939 and subsequently was editor of various Mizraḥi publications in New York.

Gentili, Gershom ben Moses (1683–1700) Italian rabbinic scholar, son of **Moses ben Gershom Gentili**. He was the author of *Yad Ḥaruzim*, a Hebrew rhyme lexicon; it contains an introduction, 12 rules for Hebrew usage in poetry, and an appendix containing a poetical formulation of the 613 commandments.

Gentili, Moses ben Gershom (1663–1711) Italian scholar. He was born in Trieste. He served as rabbi in Venice and was the author of *Melekhet Maḥashevet*, a philosophical commentary on the Torah. His *Ḥanukkat ha-Bayit* deals with the construction of the Second Temple.

George, Manfred (1893–1965) American journalist and editor. He was born in Berlin. He worked as a newspaper editor and writer in Germany until the Nazis came to power. He then moved to Prague and later emigrated to the US. In New York he took over the newsletter (*Aufbau*) of the German-Jewish New World Club

Gerchunoff, Alberto (1884–1950) Argentine journalist and writer. He was born in Russia and was taken to Argentina as a child. In 1908 he joined the staff of the daily *La nación* with which he was associated for over 40 years. His *The Jewish Gauchos of the Pampas* contains a collection of articles describing the life of Jewish colonists in Entre Rios at the beginning of the 20th century. Following the rise of Hitler, he became an ardent Zionist.

Gerondi, Isaac ben Zerachiah (fl. 13th cent.) Spanish Hebrew poet. About 20 of his liturgical poems survive.

Gerondi, Jacob ben Sheshet (fl. 13th cent.) Spanish kabbalist. He lived in Gerona. He wrote *Meshiv Devarim Nekoḥim*, in which he formulated kabbalistic meanings of the essence of the Torah, the creation of the world, divine providence and retribution.

Gerondi, Jonah ben Abraham (fl. 13th cent.) Spanish talmudist. While living in Montpellier, he signed the ban that led to the burning of the works of **Moses Maimonides**. He subsequently vowed to go on a pilgrimage to Palestine to seek forgiveness, but was induced to remain in Toledo to direct a yeshivah. He wrote novellae on talmudic tractates as well as ethical treatises.

Gerondi, Nissim ben Reuben [Nissim, Rabbenu Gerondi; Ran] (fl. 14th cent.) Spanish talmudist, physician and astronomer. He lived in Barcelona, where he played an important role in communal life. He wrote commentaries on the writings of **Isaac ben Jacob Alfasi** and on numerous talmudic tractates.

Gerondi, Samuel ben Meshullam (fl. ?12th–13th cent.) Spanish scholar. He lived in Gerona. He wrote a code of laws, *Ohel Moed*, which have practical applications.

Gerondi, Zerachiah ben Isaac (fl. 12th cent.) Italian rabbinic scholar and poet. He was born in Gerona and settled in Lunel. His *Sepher ha-Maor* is a critical examination of the writings of **Isaac ben Jacob Alfasi**. In *Sepher ha-Tzava* he provided an introduction to talmudic methodology. He also composed liturgical poems.

Gershom ben Judah (c. 960–1028) German talmudic scholar and spiritual leader. He was born in Metz and lived in Mainz, where he conducted a yeshivah. He issued legal decisions and takkanot, laid the foundations for a commentary on the Talmud, transcribed and corrected the Mishnah and the *Masorah Gedolah* of the Bible, and composed seliḥot and piyyutim.

Gershom ben Solomon (fl. 13th cent.) Provençal scholar. He lived in Béziers. His *Shalman* gives the halakhic rulings of the Talmud according to the order of the halakhot of **Isaac ben Jacob Alfasi**, and approximating to the order of **Maimonides** in the *Mishneh Torah*.

Gershuni, Grigori (1870–1908) Russian revolutionary. Born in Shavli, Lithuania, he settled in Minsk where he was in charge of a bacteriological laboratory. He was part of the anti-czarist Social Revolutionary Party. Later he organized the undergound terrorist group of the movement. In 1903 he was captured and condemned to death. His sentence was commuted to exile in Siberia. He subsequently went to the US.

Gershwin, George (1898–1937) American composer. Born in Brooklyn, he was responsible for forming the jazz style into acceptable concert music. His *Rhapsody in Blue* was a landmark, as was *American in Paris*. He wrote successful musical comedies and film scores as well as an opera *Porgy and Bess*.

Gertler, Mark (1891–1939) Born in Spitalfields, his family returned to Austria but settled in England in 1896. He was a member of the Whitechapel School in painting. He was part of the intellectual, social and artistic elite in London; he was the inspiration for Loerke in D. H. Lawrence's novel, *Women in Love*.

Gestetner, Sigmund (1897–1956) British industrialist. His father settled in England from Hungary, and manufactured a duplicating process. He became chairman of the company and expanded it. He was an ardent Zionist and was active in resettling refugees from Germany.

Ghirondi, Mordecai Samuel (1799–1852) Italian scholar and biographer. He was born in Padua and taught theology at the rabbinical college there; he became the city's chief rabbi in 1831. His writings include a biographical dictionary of Jewish scholars and rabbis.

Gideon (fl. 12th cent. BCE) Judge of the tribe of Manasseh. He defeated the Midianites near En Harod. When offered the kingship of Israel he refused out of loyalty to the principle that God is the King of Israel (Judges 6–8). In Judges 6:32 he is referred to by the name Jerubaal.

Gideon, Miriam (1906–96) American composer and educator. She was born in Greely, Colorado, and grew up in Boston. She taught at Brooklyn College, City College of the City University of New York, the Cantors Institute of the Jewish Theological Seminary, and the Manhattan School. Her works on Jewish themes include *Friday Evening Service, Sabbath Morning Service, Adon Olam, Psalm 84, Biblical Masks* and *Aetet Hashahar*.

Gikatilla, Isaac (fl. 10th cent.) Spanish Hebrew poet and grammarian. A student of **Menaḥem ben Saruq**, he took part in the controversy on grammar between his teacher and **Dunash ben Labrat**. He lived at Lucena.

Gikatilla [Ibn Gikatilla], Moses ben Samuel (fl. 11th cent.) Spanish liturgical poet and grammarian. He was born in Cordoba and lived in Zaragoza. He wrote poetry as well as studies of Hebrew grammar and Bible exegesis.

Gilbert, Martin (b. 1936) English historian. He was born in London. He has been a fellow of Merton College, Oxford, and visiting professor at the Hebrew University and Tel Aviv University. His publications include *Exile and Return: A Study in the Emergence of Jewish Statehood, The Holocaust, Auschwitz and the Allies, The Jews of Hope, The Plight of Soviet Jewry Today, Jerusalem: Rebirth of a City* and *The Jewish History Atlas.*

Gilboa, Amir (1917–84) Israeli poet. He was born in Radzywilow, Volhynia, and went to Palestine in 1937, where he worked initially as a labourer. He began to publish poetry while serving in the Jewish Brigade during World War II. Some of his poems concern biblical characters.

Gimbel, Adam (1817–96) American trade pioneer, of Bavarian origin. He was an immigrant from Bavaria in 1835, settled in New Orleans, and worked as a peddler. He was joined by his six brothers and two sisters. He opened his first store in Vincennes, Indiana in 1842. This was the beginning of a commercial empire.

Ginsberg, Allen (1926–97) American poet. He was born in Newark, New Jersey. His work includes *Kaddish.*

Ginsberg, Harold Louis (1903–90) American biblical scholar and Semitist. He was born in Montreal. He became professor of Bible at the Jewish Theological Seminary of America in 1941. He wrote studies of biblical philology, history and religion. In addition, he contributed to Aramaic lingistics and was a pioneer in the interpretation of Ugaritic texts and their application to the Bible.

Ginsburg, Christian David (1831–1914) British biblical scholar. He was born in Warsaw. He converted to Christianity in 1846 and settled in England, where he wrote studies of the masoretic text of the Bible; his *The Massorah* contains the original text of the masorah as well as additional notes. He also published standard editions of the Hebrew Bible, contributed to a new critical Hebrew Bible text, wrote commentaries on several books of the Bible, and produced studies of the Karaites and kabbalistic literature.

Ginsburg [Günzburg], Jekuthiel (1889–1957) American mathematician and Hebrew writer. He was born in Russia and emigrated to the US in 1912. In 1930 he was appointed professor and head of the department of mathematics at Yeshiva College. His publications include studies of Jewish contribution to mathematics.

Ginsburg, Ruth (b. 1933) American lawyer. Born in Brooklyn, she studied at Cornell, Harvard and Columbia Universities. She taught at Rutgers and Columbia Law Schools and became a circuit judge in 1980. She was appointed to a Justice of the Supreme Court in 1993.

Ginsburg, Saul (1866–1940) Russian author and historian. He was born in Minsk. In 1903 he established the first Yiddish daily in Russia. Later he devoted himself to the study of the cultural history of the Jews in Russia. He left the USSR in 1930 and settled in Paris, later moving to New York. Together with Peretz Marek he published *Jewish Folk Songs.* His *Historical Works* contains material on 19th-century Russian Jewry.

Ginzburg, Louis (1873–1953) American talmudic scholar. He was born in Kovno, Lithuania, and emigrated to the US. He joined the staff of the *Jewish Encyclopedia* as editor of the rabbinic department. In 1903 he was appointed professor of Talmud at the Jewish Theological Seminary. His writings deal with the origins of aggadah, halakhah, and the literature of the geonim. In *The Legends of the Jews* he collected together legends, maxims and parables from midrashic literature.

Ginzburg, Natalia (1916–91) Italian novelist and playwright. She was born in Palermo and studied in Turin. The characters in her novels include many Jews. Her works include *Family Sayings,* a psychological novel based on the author's recollections of her own family and the events of her youth.

Gittelsohn, Roland (1910–95) American rabbi. He was born in Cleveland. He was rabbi at the Central Synagogue of Nassau Country in Long Island from 1936 to 1953, then served as rabbi of Temple Israel in Boston. In 1968 he became president of the Central Conference of American Rabbis. His writings include *Modern Jewish Problems, Little Lower than the Angels, Man's Best Hope, My Beloved Is Mine* and *Fire in My Bones.*

Glanz, Leib (1898–1964) American cantor and composer. He was born in Kiev and held cantorial positions at Kishinev and in Romania before emigrating to the US in 1926. He served as cantor of the Ohev Shalom Synagogue in Brooklyn and of Heikhal Sinai Synagogue and the Shaarei Tefillah Synagoguge in Los Angeles. In 1954 he settled in Israel and became chief cantor of the Tiferet Ẓevi Synagogue in Tel Aviv. He founded the Tel Aviv Institute of Religious Jewish Music.

Glaser, Donald (b. 1926) American scientist. He was professor of nuclear physics at the University of Michigan and later professor of molecular biology at the University of California. He was awarded the Nobel Prize in 1960 for his work on bubble chambers.

Glaser, Eduard (1855–1908) Bohemian explorer and Arabist. He was born in Deutsch-Rust. He made four journeys to Arabia between 1883 and 1894, discovering many geographical locations, numerous inscriptions, archaeological remains and Arabic manuscripts.

Glatstein, Jacob (1896–1971) American Yiddish poet, novelist and critic.He was born in Lublin and emigrated to the US in 1914. He helped to inaugurate Inzikhist, an introspective school of American Yiddish poetry. He later became one of the most important elegists of eastern European Jewish life. He was also a columnist for a New York Yiddish daily, and contributed to various periodicals.

Glatzer, Nahum Norbert (1903–90) American scholar, teacher and editor. He was born in Lemberg. He became professor of Jewish philosophy and ethics at the University of Frankfurt am Main in 1932. In the next year he left Germany and settled in Palestine, where he taught at Bet Sepher Reali in Haifa. From 1938 he lived in the US, and became professor of Near Eastern and Judaic Studies at Brandeis University in 1956. He was also a director of the Leo Baeck Institute. His writings include studies of talmudic history, the history of 19th-century Jewry, and the life and thought of **Franz Rosenzweig**.

Glicenstein, Enrico (1870–1942) American sculptor, painter and printmaker. He was born in Poland, lived in Munich, settled in Italy in 1897, and finally emigrated to New York in 1928. He produced 60 plates to illustrate an edition of the book of Samuel. A Glicenstein Museum containing his library was established in Safed, Israel.

Glick, Hirsch (1922–44) Lithuanian Yiddish poet. He was born in Vilna and was influenced in his writing by the Yiddish poets of the Yung Vilne group. He edited and published four issues of the poetry review *Yumgvald.* His *Lider un poemes* were published posthumously in 1953. His poem *Mir zaynen do* became the table song of the Vilna partisan fighters in World War II.

Glick, Srul Irving (1934–2003) Canadian composer, conductor and music producer. He was born in Toronto. He taught theory and composition at the Royal Conservatory of Music in Toronto and at York University. From 1962 to 1986 he was a music producer for the CBC.In 1969 he became the choir director of Beth Tickvah Synagogue in Toronto. His works include *Hashirim Asher l'Yisrael, Kedusha, Sing Unto the Lord a New Song, Deborah, Music for Passover, Yiddish Suite, Suite Hebraique, Sonata Hebraïque, Psalm for Orchestra* and *Sonata for Orchestra 'Devequt'.*

Glickson, Mosheh (1878–1939) Palestinian author and Zionist leader, of Lithuanian origin. He edited the weekly *Ha-Am* in Moscow, as well as the miscellanies *Olamenu* and *Massuot* published in Odessa during World War I. In 1919 he settled in Palestine and was the chief-editor of *Ha-Aretz* from 1922 to 1937. He wrote studies of **Aḥad ha-Am** and **Maimonides**.

Glückel of Hamelin (1646–1724) German Yiddish writer. She lived mainly in Hamburg. After her husband's death, she wrote her memoirs in Yiddish. They are an important source of information about German Jewish life, court Jews, the impact of **Shabbetai Tzevi**, and the history of Yiddish.

Glueck, Nelson (1900–71) American archaeologist. He was born in Cincinnati. He was director of the American School of Oriental Research at Jerusalem (1932–3, 1936–40, 1942–7), and at Baghdad (1933–4). In 1947 he was elected president of the Hebrew Union College. His writings include *Explorations in*

Eastern Palestine, The Other Side of the Jordan, The River Jordan, Rivers in the Desert and *Deities and Dolphins: The Story of the Nabateans.*

Gnessin, Uri Nisan (1881–1913) Ukrainian Hebrew author. He was born in Starodub, but lived an unsettled life, wandering from city to city and often enduring hardship. He published poems, literary criticism, stories, translations and sketches. He was among the first Hebrew writers to explore the alienation and uprootedness of Jews in modern society.

Gniessin, Michael Fabianovich (1883–1957) Russian composer. He was born in Rostov-na-Donu. He was professor of composition at the Moscow Conservatory (1923–35), taught composition at Leningrad Conservatory (1935–45), and later headed the composition department at the music school in Leningrad which bore his and his sister's name. He published books on composition, aesthetics, and Jewish music, and a study of Rimsky-Korsakov. In addition, he pioneered the new Russian symphonic style in his music, and the use of the folk music of the peoples of the USSR. Many of his works have Jewish titles.

Goehr, Alexander (b. 1932) British composer. He was born in Berlin, the son of a distinguished conductor. The family moved to England in 1933 and he studied at the Royal Manchester College of Music, and later in Paris. From 1968 he taught in the US, and later was a professor at Leeds and Cambridge Universities. His works include *Little Symphony, Naboth's Vineyard, Romanza, Konzertstuck,* and *Concerto for Piano and Orchestra.*

Goido, Issac (1868–1925) American Hebrew and Yiddish author. He published a number of popular Yiddish editions in Vilna. In 1894 he settled in New York, where he was active as a theatre critic and dramatist. Among his works is a history of Yiddish drama.

Goitein [Koitein], Shelomoh Dov (b. 1900) Israeli orientalist. He was born in Burgkunstadt, Germany, and emigrated to Palestine in 1923. In 1928 he became a member of the faculty of the Institute of Oriental Studies at the Hebrew University, where from 1947 he was professor. From 1957 to 1970 he was professor of Arabic at the University of Pennsylvania. He published works on the religious institutions of Islam, the culture of the Jews of Yemen, and texts from the Cairo Genizah.

Gold, Herbert (b. 1924) American novelist. He was born in Cleveland. He taught at the University of California at Berkeley. His novels deal with the search for love between men and women and children and parents. A number of his novels deal with American Jewish life.

Gold, Michael (1893–1967) American communist author and journalist. He worked as a copy-editor on the socialist *Call* and contributed articles and poetry to *Masses.* Later he was editor of the communist *Liberator* and of the *New Masses.* He also worked with the left-wing New Playwrights' Theatre. His novel *Jews Without Money* is an account of Jewish immigrant life in New York.

Gold, Ze'ev (1889–1956) American rabbi and leader of religious Zionism. He was born in Poland and became rabbi in Juteka. In 1907 he emigrated to the US, where he served several congregations and was in the forefront of Zionist workers. He was president of the American Mizraḥi from 1932 to 1935, when he settled in Palestine. He later became head of the country's Department for Torah Education and Culture.

Goldberg, Abraham (1883–1942) American journalist and Zionist leader. He was born in Russia and settled in New York in 1901. He was co-founder of Poale Zion in the US, and editor of its newspaper, *Freie shtimme.* He became editor of the New York Zionist journal *Dos yiddishe folk* in 1909. In 1920 he was appointed editor of the Hebrew monthly *Ha-Toren.*

Goldberg, Arthur (1908–90) American labour lawyer. Born in Chicago, he was a labour lawyer there. During World War II he was the head of the labour section of the office of strategic services. Subsequently he served as secretary of labour (1961–2) and was appointed to the Supreme Court in 1962. Eventually he served as ambassador to the United Nations.

Goldberg, Dov Ber (1801–84) French scholar of Polish origin. He devoted himself to the publication of editions of Jewish manuscripts in European libraries. He travelled widely, visiting libraries in Europe and England, and from 1852 lived in Paris. He wrote numerous articles in Hebrew periodicals.

Goldberg, Isaac Leib (1860–1935) Lithuanian Zionist leader and philanthropist. After studying at the Kovno yeshivah, he settled in Vilna. He was one of the first members of the Ḥibbat Zion movement, and founded the Ohavei Zion society in Vilna. In 1908 he established a farm at Hartuv and purchased the first plot of land on Mount Scopus for the future Hebrew University. In 1919 he settled in Palestine.

Goldberg, Leah (1911–70) Israeli Hebrew poet and critic. She was born in Königsberg and lived in Russia until after the Revolution, when she settled in Kovno, Lithuania. In 1935 she emigrated to Tel Aviv. In 1952 she was invited to organize the Department of Comparative Literature at the Hebrew University, where she became a professor. She published poetry, literary criticism, translations, children's works, a novel and a play.

Goldberg, Rube (1883–1970) American cartoonist. The Reuben is the annual award of the American National Cartoonist Society named after him.

Goldemberg, Isaac (b. 1945) Peruvian novelist. He went to Israel at the age of 17 and later settled in New York. His works include a Spanish-American novel, *The Fragmented Life of Jacobo Lerner.*

Golden, Harry Lewis (1902–81) American author, editor and publisher. He was born in New York. He was sentenced to five years' imprisonment for running a Wall Street gambling house. Later he became the editor of the *Carolina Israelite.* His publications include *Only in America, For 2 Cents Plain* and *Enjoy.*

Goldenberg, Eliezer (1846–1916) Russian socialist. He was arrested while a student in St Petersburg, but escaped to London. Together with **Aaron Samuel Liebermann** he was a founder of the Society of Hebrew Socialists.

Goldenthal, Jacob (1815–68) Austrian orientalist. He was born in Brody. He was principal of the Jewish school in Kishinev. Then in 1846 he settled in Vienna and taught oriental languages, rabbinics and literature at the University of Vienna. He published studies of medieval Jewish literature and philosophy, as well as the first Hebrew textbook for the study of Arabic.

Goldfaden, Abraham (1840–1908) Ukrainian Yiddish poet. He established the first modern Yiddish theatrical company in Romania in 1876. By 1880 his troupe was giving performances throughout Russia. When in 1883 the Russian government banned performances in Yiddish, Yiddish theatres were established in Paris, London and New York. In 1887 Goldenfaden moved to New York, but he returned to Europe to produce and direct performances. He wrote 60 plays, many of which are in the form of operas and operettas.

Goldhar, Pinchas (1901–47) Australian Yiddish writer. He was born in Łódź and in 1928 settled in Melbourne, where he operated a dye-shop. He edited the first Yiddish weekly in Australia. His stories describe the integration of Polish-Jewish immigrants into Australian life.

Goldin, Judah (b. 1914) American scholar. Born in New York City, he was ordained at the Jewish Theological Seminary. He taught at Yale University. His works include *The Fathers According to Rabbi Nathan* and *Living Talmud.*

Golding, Louis (1895–1958) English novelist. He was born in Manchester. He joined an ambulance unit during World War I and served in Macedonia and France. During the 1920s he travelled widely and his novels reflect his experiences. His *Magnolia Street* is the first of a cycle of novels about Anglo-Jewish life. In *The Glory of Elsie Silver* he depicted his response to Nazism and his sympathy for Zionism. He also wrote *The Jewish Problem* and *Hitler through the Ages.*

Goldman, Emma (1869–1940) American anarchist. She was born in Kovno, Lithuania, and emigrated to the US in 1885. Her lectures and journal (*Mother Earth*) aimed to illustrate the injustice of American society. In 1919 she was deported to the USSR. She eventually fled Russia, disillusioned with the suppression of the individual. Her writings include *Anarchism and Other Essays, My Disillusionment in*

Russia, My Further Disillusionment in Russia and *Living My Life.*

Goldman, Solomon (1893–1953) American Conservative rabbi. He was born in Volhynia and was taken to the US as a child. He was rabbi of the Anshe Emet Synagogue of Chicago from 1929. He was known as an orator, scholar, communal leader and Zionist. His publications include *A Rabbi Takes Stock, The Jew and the Universe, Crisis and Decision, Undefeated, The Book of Books, In the Beginning* and *From Slavery to Freedom.*

Goldman, William (b. 1911) English novelist. He was born in London. His publications include *East End My Cradle, Light in the Dust, A Tent of Blue, A Start in Life* and *A Saint in the Making.*

Goldmann, Nahum (1895–1982) American statesman and Zionist leader. He was born in Lithuania and was taken to Germany as a child. In 1925 he helped to found the Eshkol publishing house in order to produce the *Encyclopaedia Judaica.* Together with **Stephen Samuel Wise**, he organized the World Jewish Congress in 1936; he became chairman of its executive board and later its president. He was also president of the Zionist Organization. He played an important role in negotiating the reparations agreement with Germany after World War II. In 1962 he left the US and became an Israeli citizen.

Goldmark, Karl (1830–1915) Hungarian composer. His father was the cantor of a synagogue. He studied the violin and began to compose in 1842. In 1844 he went to Vienna and later studied at the Vienna Conservatory. In 1858 he organized a concert of his own compositions. His works include: *String Quartet, Overture Sakuntala, Die Königin von Saba, Das Heimchen am Herd,* and *Ein Wintermärchen.*

Goldschmidt, Lazarus (1871–1950) German orientalist and bibliophile. He was born in Lithuania and lived in Berlin, later emigrating to London. His early studies dealt with the Ethiopian language and literature. He published an edition of the Sepher Yetzirah, a Hebrew translation of the Koran, and a translation of the Babylonian Talmud into German.

Goldschmidt, Meir Aaron (1819–87) Danish novelist and journalist. He was born in Vordingborg, Zealand, and settled in Copenhagen, where he founded *Corsaren*, a satirical weekly. From 1847 to 1859 he published the periodical *Nord og syd.* He wrote novels and plays dealing with Jewish subjects.

Goldschmidt, Victor Moritz (1888–1947) Norwegian mineralogist. Born in Zurich, he studied at Heidelberg and at the University of Christiania. He was an instructor at the University of Christiania, and became a professor at the Mineralogical Institute. Later he taught at the University of Göttingen, but resigned his chair as a result of Nazi policy. During World War II he escaped to Sweden and then to England where he joined the staff at the Macaulay Institute of Soil Research in Aberdeen.

Goldsmid, Albert Edward Williamson (1846–1904) English communal leader, nephew of **Isaac Goldsmid**. A soldier by profession, he adopted Judaism later in life. He was a leading member of Ḥovevei Zion and administered the Jewish colonies in Argentina in 1892–4. He may have been the model for the protagonist in George Eliot's *Daniel Deronda.*

Goldsmid, Benjamin (1755–1808) English bill broker. He and his brother Abraham became rich by helping raise loans for the English government.

Goldsmid, Isaac Lyon (1778–1859) English communal leader. In his business life he financed railway construction. Prominent in the struggle for Jewish emancipation in England, he was one of the founders of University College, London. He also played a role in the establishment of the Reform synagogue. He was made a baronet in 1841 and in 1846 he was created Baron de Palmeira by the King of Portugal.

Goldstein, Israel (1896–1986) American Conservative rabbi and Zionist leader. He was born in Philadelphia and served as a rabbi of Congregation B'nai Jeshurun in New York. He was president of the Jewish National Fund of America and the Zionist Organization of America. He also served as a member and officer of various Jewish, interfaith and public organizations. In 1961 he settled in Israel, where he was world chairman of the Keren ha-Yesod-United Israel Appeal. He wrote a history of his congregation in New York and also published collections of sermons and essays.

Goldwyn, Samuel (1882–1973) American film producer. He emigrated at the age of 13 from Warsaw to the US. In 1918 he formed the Goldwyn Pictures Corporation. Later he established Metro-Goldwyn-Mayer.

Goldziher, Ignaz (1850–1921) Hungarian scholar. He was born in Székesfehérvár. He became lecturer at the University of Budapest in 1872. He served as secretary of the Budapest Neolog Jewish community for 30 years, becoming professor of religious philosophy at the Budapest Rabbinical Seminary in 1900. Four years later he was appointed professor at the university. He published studies of pre-Islamic and Islamic culture, the religious and legal history of the Arabs, and their ancient and modern poetry.

Goll, Iwan (1891–1950) Franco-German poet and author. He was born in Saint-Dié, Vosges. He was initially active in German expressionist circles, but during World War I he moved to Switzerland. Later he settled in Paris, where he established the magazine *Surréalisme*. After living for a period in the US, he returned to Paris in 1947. Jewish themes frequently appear in his poetry.

Gollancz, Hermann (1852–1930) British rabbi and teacher, brother of **Israel Gollancz**. He was born in Bremen and settled in London. He officiated at the Bayswater Synagogue (1892–1923) and taught Hebrew at University College, London (1902–24). He published critical editions and translations of Hebrew, Aramaic, and Syriac texts. He was the first British rabbi to receive a knighthood.

Gollancz, Israel (1864–1930) English literary scholar, brother of **Hermann Gollancz**. He was a lecturer in English at University College, London (1892–5), and then at Cambridge University. In 1903 he became professor of English at King's College, London. He published studies of Shakespeare and early English literature and philology. He served on the council of Jews College for several years.

Gollancz, Victor (1893–1967) English publisher and writer. He founded his own publishing house in 1928 and later helped to establish the Left Book Club, whose aim was to expose Nazism. During World War II he campaigned for the National Committee for Rescue from Nazi Terror. From 1945 he endeavoured to secure the admission of Jewish refugees to Palestine. His writings include *The Brown Book of the Hitler Terror, My Dear Timothy, More for Timothy* and *The Case of Adolf Eichmann.*

Golomb, Eliyahu (1893–1945) Palestinian Zionist. He was born in Belorussia and settled in Palestine in 1909. At the outbreak of World War I he helped to form an independent Jewish defence force. From 1921 he was a member of the Haganah Committee of the Histadrut and the following year he was sent abroad to purchase arms. Beginning in 1931, he attempted to establish a broad popular basis for the Haganah. He was one of the founders of the Palmaḥ.

Gompers, Samuel (1850–1924) American trade unionist. He emigrated in 1863 to the US from England. He was the founder and president of the American Federation of Labour.

Gomperz, Heinrich (1873–1942) Austrian philosopher. Born in Vienna, he was the son of **Theodor Gomperz**. He studied in Vienna, Freiburg and Berlin. From 1905 he lectured at Vienna, and later became professor of philosophy. In 1935 he went to the US. He wrote various works of philosophy.

Gomperz, Theodor (1832–1912) Austrian scholar. Born in Brünn, Moravia, he studied at Vienna, and later became professor there. His works include *Griechische Denker.*

Goodhart, Arthur (1891–1978) American jurist. He studied at Oxford where he became professor of jurisprudence and master of University College. He received an honorary knighthood in 1948.

Goodman, Arnold (b. 1913) British lawyer. He served as chairman of the Arts Council of Great Britain and chairman of the Newspaper Publishers Association. From 1972–84 he was president of the National Book League. In 1968 he became president of the English National Opera and later served as Master of University College, Oxford.

Goodman, Benny (1909–86) American musician. Born in Chicago, he studied at the Lewis Institute in Chicago. In 1933 he formed his own band. He played a blend of jazz and contemporary popular music. His band featured in various movies.

Goodman, Paul (1875–1949) British Zionist leader. He was born in Estonia and went to England in 1891. He served as secretary of the Spanish and Portuguese Congregation, and held various positions in the Zionist movement in London. His publications include *The Synagogue and the Church*, *History of the Jews*, *Moses Montefiore*, *Zionism in England* and *The Jewish National Home*.

Goodman, Percival (1904–89) American architect. He was born in New York and became professor of architecture at Columbia University. He designed numerous synagogues in the US.

Goor, Yehudah (1862–1950) Israeli educator and lexicographer. He was born in Belorussia and emigrated to Palestine in 1887. He was a co-founder of the first Hebrew Teachers' Assocation in Palestine, and was one of the pioneers of the Ivrit be-Ivrit method of teaching Hebrew. He wrote manuals on the study of Hebrew, Jewish history, natural sciences, and the geography of Palestine, and translated classical literature into Hebrew. He also published several dictionaries, including the *Dictionary of the Hebrew Language*.

Gordin, Jacob (1853–1909) American Yiddish playwright and journalist. He was born in the Ukraine. He taught at a russified Jewish school in Yelizavetgradka, and in 1880 he founded the Spiritual Biblical Brotherhood. In 1891 he emigrated to the US, where he worked as a Yiddish journalist and wrote more than 100 Yiddish plays.

Gordis, Robert (1908–92) American rabbi and biblical scholar. He was born in New York. He served as rabbi of Temple Beth El in Rockaway Park, New York, from 1931 until his retirement in 1968. From 1940 he was professor of Bible at the Jewish Theological Seminary. He served as editor of the journal *Judaism* and president of the Rabbinical Assembly and Synagogue Council of America. He has published studies of wisdom literature, biblical poetry and the masorah.

Gordon, Aaron David (1856–1922) Palestinian Hebrew writer. He was born in Troyanov, Russia. He held a post in the financial management of Baron Horace Günzburg's estate for 23 years. In 1904 he emigrated to Palestine, where he worked as an agricultural labourer. In his writings he emphasized that self-realization can be attained only through settlement on the land.

Gordon, David (1831–86) Hebrew journalist and editor. He was born in Podmerecz and settled in Sergei, where he worked as a teacher. In the mid-1850s he emigrated to England, where he taught Hebrew and German. In 1858 he moved to Lyck, where he was assistant editor and later editor of the Hebrew weekly *Ha-Maggid*. He became one of the leading members of Ḥibbat Zion in the 1880s. He published several books and contributed to Hebrew and Yiddish journals.

Gordon, George (1751–93) English convert to Judaism. He was president of the United Protestant League and was implicated in the serious anti-Catholic riots of 1780. As a result he was tried for high treason, but was acquitted. In 1787 he was circumcised and assumed the name Israel ben Abraham. He was later tried for libel and was imprisoned in Newgate, London, where he surrounded himself with foreign Jews.

Gordon, Judah Löb (1831–92) Lithuanian Hebrew poet and writer. He was born in Vilna, and taught in various government schools in the Kovno province. Later he became critical of Jewish religious life. In 1872 he went to St Petersburg as secretary to the Jewish community and director of the Society for the Promotion of Culture Among the Jews in Russia. Although his early poetry was romantic in character, his later work was full of disillusionment and despair. He is regarded as the creator of Hebrew realist poetry.

Gordon, Michel (1823–90) Lithuanian Hebrew and Yiddish poet. He was born in Vilna. He was influenced by the Haskalah circle of **Abraham Dov Lebensohn**. He wrote Hebrew books and articles as well as Yiddish songs. His later poetry is pessimistic in character.

Gordon, Samuel Löb (1865–1933) Palestinian writer and biblical scholar. He was born in Lithuania and emigrated to Palestine in 1898, where he taught at the boys' school in Jaffa. In 1924 he returned to Palestine. He composed a commentary on the Bible, contributed poems, articles and translations to Hebrew periodicals, and wrote for chidren.

Goren, Charles (1901–91) American bridge player. Born in Philadelphia, he studied at McGill University and became a lawyer. He eventually became a teacher of contract bridge and won numerous titles. He published several books dealing with bridge.

Goren, Shelomo (1917–94) Israeli rabbi of Polish origin. After settling in Palestine he joined the Haganah and fought in the War of Independence. He became chief chaplain of Haganah and was later responsible for the organization of the military chaplaincy and regulations for religious observance in the army. In 1961 he received the Israel Prize for the first volume of his comprehensive commentary on the Jerusalem Talmud. He was elected Ashkenazi chief rabbi of Tel Aviv-Jaffa in 1968 and of Israel in 1972.

Gottheil, Gustav (1827–1903) American Reform rabbi, liturgist and Zionist leader. He was born in Pinne, in the Posen district. He was a teacher to the Reform congregation in Berlin from 1855 to 1860, and served as rabbi of the progressive Congregation of British Jews in Manchester, England, from 1869 to 1873. He then emigrated to New York, where he became co-rabbi at Temple Emanu-El. He published a hymnal and a devotional compilation.

Gottheil, Richard James Horatio (1862–1936) American orientalist, son of **Gustav Gottheil**. He was born in Manchester, England, and was taken to New York in 1873. From 1886 he taught Semitic languages at Columbia University; he also served as director of the Oriental Department of the New York Public Library from 1896. He was an active Zionist, and served as president of the American Federation of Zionists from 1898 to 1904. He published studies of Zionism and of Semitic languages.

Gottlieb, Adolf (1903–74) American painter. He lived in New York and Tucson, Arizona, and created works of art for various synagogues.

Gottlieb, Jack (b. 1930) American composer and conductor. He taught at Loyola University and the Institute of Judaic Arts at Warwick, New York. He was appointed music director of Congregation Temple Israel in St Louis in 1970, then in 1973 became composer-in-residence at the Hebrew Union College in New York. His compositions include *Love Songs for Sabbath*, *New Year's Service for Young People* and *Verses from Psalm 118*.

Gottlieb, Maurycy (1856–79) Polish painter. He was born in Galicia and lived in Lemberg, Vienna, Munich and Kraków. Many of his paintings are based on Jewish themes.

Gottlober, Abraham bär (1810–99) Hebrew and Yiddish writer and poet. He was born in Starokonstantinov and was taken to Tarnopol, Galicia, at the age of 17. Influenced by the Haskalah, he developed a hostility toward orthodoxy and Ḥasidism. During a period when he was living in Podolia, he wrote in Yiddish and Hebrew. From 1830 to 1850 he lived in Bessarabia, Berdichev and Kremenetz. Later he became an instructor in Talmud at the rabbinical seminary in Zhitomir. He published poems, dramas, stories, memoirs, translations and studies of the history of the Karaites, kabbalah and Ḥasidism.

Gottschalk, Alfred (b. 1930) American communal leader. Born in Oberwessel, Germany, he served as president of the Hebrew Union College-Jewish Institute of Religion and professor of Bible and Jewish thought.

Gottschalk, Max (1889–1976) Belgian social scientist. He was born in Liège. He joined the Institute of Sociology of the Free University of Brussels as research professor in 1923. During World War II he taught at the New School for Social Research in New York but when the war was over he returned to the institute in Brussels. He served as president of the International Association of Social Progress and of the Brussels National Centre of Jewish Studies.

Goudchaux, Michel (1797–1862) French banker and politician. He was born in Nancy. He worked as a banker and founded a working-class newspaper, *Le national*. After the revolution of 1848 he was mayor of his district of Paris, member of the general council of the department of the Seine, and paymaster general in Strasbourg. He later became minster of finance in the Second Republic, and was vice-president of the National Assembly in 1849.

Goudsmit, Samuel (1884–1954) Dutch author. He was born in Kampen. His publications include *Dievenschool*, *In de grote leerschool*, *Jankefs jongste*, *Jankefs oude sleutel*, *Simcha, de knaap uit Worms* and *De gouden kroon van Beieren*.

Grade, Ḥayyim (1910–82) Lithuanian Yiddish poet and novelist. He was born in Vilna and became leader of the Yung Vilne literary movement. During World War II he lived in Soviet Russia, later settling in Poland. He subsequently moved to Paris, where he was active in revivifying Yiddish cultural life. Eventually he emigrated to New York, where he was associated with the Yiddish daily *Jewish Morning Journal*. His poetry reflects Jewish life in eastern Europe.

Graetz, Heinrich (1817–91) German historian and biblical scholar. He was born in Xions, in the district of Posen. He lectured in Jewish history and the Bible at the Jewish Theological Seminary of Breslau; in 1869 he was made an honorary professor at the university there. His multi-volume *History of the Jews* influenced subsequent Jewish historians.

Granott, Avraham (1890–1962) Israeli economist of Bessarabian origin. He became secretary of the Jewish National Fund in 1919. After settling in Jerusalem in 1922 he became the fund's managing director, and later chairman of its board of directors and president. He was elected to the Knesset in 1949 and served as chairman of its finance committee. He published studies of agrarian reform.

Gratz, Rebecca (1781–1869) American philanthropist. She is reputed to have been the model for Rebecca in Walter Scott's novel *Ivanhoe*. She lived in Philadelphia, where she aided in founding the Female Hebrew Benevolent Society, the Hebrew Sunday School Society, and the Philadelphia Jewish Foster Home and Orphan Asylum.

Grayzel, Solomon (1896–1980) American historian and editor. He was born in Minsk, Belorussia. He taught Jewish history at Gratz College from 1929. In 1939 he became editor-in-chief of the Jewish Publication Society of America. From 1966 he taught Jewish history at Dropsie College. He published studies of the relationship of Christians and Jews during the Middle Ages.

Green, Gerald (b. 1922) American novelist. He was born in Brooklyn. His publications include *To Brooklyn with Love*, *An American Prophet*, *The Legion of Noble Christians* and *Holocaust*.

Greenberg, Ḥayyim (1889–1953) American Zionist leader, essayist and editor. He was born in Todoristi in Russia. He edited the Russian Jewish weekly *The Dawn*, before moving in 1921 to Berlin, where he edited *Haolam*, the official weekly of the World Zionist Organization. He settled in the US by 1924, when he became editor of the Yiddish Zionist publication *Farn Folk*. In 1934 he was appointed editor of the labour Zionist monthly *The Jewish Frontier*. During World War II he served as head of the American Zionist Emergency Council and after the war he was director of the Department of Education and Culture of the Jewish Agency in America. He published studies espousing Zionism.

Greenberg, Henry [Hank] (1911–86) American baseball player. Born in New York City, he played for the Detroit Tigers which won the American league championship several times.

Greenberg, Irving (b. 1933) American scholar. Born in New York, he studied at Bais Yosef Yeshivah and was influenced by **Joseph Soloveichik**. As an Orthodox Jew, he wrestled with the religions implications of the Holocaust as well as the meaningfulness of the halakhah in modern Jewish life.

Greenberg, Joanne (b. 1932) American novelist. She was born in Brooklyn. She served as adjunct professor at the Colorado School of Mines. Her novels include *The King's Persons*, *I Never Promised You a Rose Garden*, *The Monday Voices*, *In this Sign*, *Founders Praise* and *A Season of Delight*.

Greenberg, Leopold Jacob (1861–1931) English editor and Zionist. He was born in Birmingham. He served as **Theodor Herzl**'s representative in his dealings with the British government. In 1907 he and a group of his friends acquired the *Jewish Chronicle*, and he was appointed its editor-in-chief. He was a founder of a number of publications, including the *Jewish Year Book*.

Greenberg, Uri Tzevi (1894–1981) Israeli poet. He was born in Galicia and was taken as a child to Lemberg. After World War I he became a leader of a group of Yiddish expressionist poets. In 1924 he emigrated to Palestine, where he became a spokesman for the Revisionist movement. His *Book of Incitement and Faith* is an attack on the Jewish Agency's policy of self-restraint, and a defence of his conception of fighting Jewish youth; he supported underground movements that struggled against the British. He was a Ḥerut member in the first Knesset (1949–51). After World War II he published poems about the destruction of European Jewry.

Greenstone, Julius Hillel (1873–1955) American educator and author. He was born in Lithuania, and emigrated to the US in 1894. In 1905 he joined the faculty of Gratz College, where he taught Jewish education and religion, and from 1933 to 1948 he was principal of the college. His writings include *The Jewish Religion* and *The Messiah Idea in Jewish History*. For 20 years he contributed a popular column to the Philadelphia weekly *Jewish Exponent*.

Greidiker, Ephraim (fl. 18th cent.) Polish jester. Influenced by German and Italian motifs, his jokes resembled those of the German folk hero Till Eulenspiegel.

Greiner, Leo (1876–1928) Austrian author. He wrote poems and plays, edited literary journals, and compiled anthologies.

Grodzinski, Ḥayyim Ozer (1863–1940) Lithuanian talmudic scholar. In 1887 he was appointed one of the dayyanim of the bet din of Vilna. He was one of the initiators of the Vilna Conference of 1909, which resulted in the formation of the Orthodox Keneset Israel organizaton. He was also a sponsor of the conference of rabbis at Grodno in 1924, which founded the Council of the Yeshivot. He was an opponent of Zionism and secular education for Jews. His responsa were published in three volumes.

Gronemann, Sammy (1875–1952) German author and Zionist leader. He was born in Strasburg, West Prussia. He settled in Tel Aviv in 1936. An active Zionist, he was a member of the Zionist Action Committee in Germany and president of the Zionist Congress court. His novels depict the eastern European Jewish milieu; he also wrote comedies, which were adapted for the Hebrew stage.

Gropper, William (1897–1979) Amercian cartoonist. Born in New York City, he studied at the Ferrer School and the New York School of Fine and Applied Art. He became a cartoonist for the *New York Tribune*, and later worked for *The Rebel Worker*, *New Masses* and the *Sunday Worker*, and the Yiddish paper, the *Freiheit*. During the 1920s and 1930s he contributed to the *New Yorker* and *Vanity Fair*. He also painted subjects dealing with American folklore and religional lifestyles as well as Jewish themes.

Gross, Charles (1857–1909) American historian. He was born in Troy, New York. He became professor of history at Harvard University. He published studies on medieval English administrative and economic history, and on the Exchequer of the Jews in England in the Middle Ages.

Gross, Ḥaim (1904–91) American sculptor and graphic artist. He was born in Galicia, studied in Budapest, and went to Vienna in 1920. In 1921 he emigrated to the US. His work is dominated by Judaic and biblical themes.

Gross, Heinrich (1835–1910) Bavarian rabbi and scholar. He was born in Szenicze, Hungary. He served as a rabbi in Gross-Strelitz, then from 1870 in Augsburg, Bavaria. He wrote studies of the lives of French rabbis and their communities in the Middle Ages. His *Gallia Judaica* is a geographic dictionary of France according to rabbinic sources.

Grossbard, Batia (b. 1910) Israeli artist. Born in Ostrow, Poland, she emigrated to Palestine in 1938 and served with the British Army. She eventually settled in Haifa and married the painter Yehoshua Grossbard. Her work includes mountainscape drawings of the post-Six Day War period through to the 1970s. Her later work is highly abstract.

Grossman, David (b. 1954) Israeli novelist. He was born in Jerusalem and worked as an editor and broadcaster on Israeli radio. His publications include *The Smile of a Lamb*, *See Under Love* and *The Yellow Wind*.

Grossman, Elias Mandel (1898–1947) American artist. He was born in Poland and emigrated to the US in 1911. His works are based on Jewish life.

Grossman, Meir (1888–1964) Israeli Zionist leader. He was born in Russia. He lived in Copenhagen during World War I, where he began the publication of a Yiddish daily. At the suggestion of **Vladimir Jabotinsky**, he published a periodical, *Di Tribune*, which promoted the cause of a Jewish legion. After the Russian Revolution, he helped to establish the Jewish Correspondence Bureau. In 1934 he settled in Palestine. Initially a leader of the Revisionist and Jewish State parties, he joined the General Zionists in 1953. From 1948 to 1961 he was a member of the executive of the Jewish Agency.

Grossman, Vasily Semyonovich (1905–64) Russian writer. He was born in Berdichev and moved to Moscow as a young man. He later worked as a chemical engineer in the coal mines of Donbas. His trilogy *Stephan Kolchugin* includes Jewish themes. His *Cartea Neagră* provides documentary evidence of Nazi crimes committed against Jews in Soviet territory.

Gruening, Ernst (1887–1974) American journalist and politician. Born in New York City, he studied medicine at Harvard University. He was a journalist eventually becoming editor of various newspapers including the New York *Evening Post.* In 1939 he became govenor of Alaska, and eventually US Senator.

Grumberg, Jean-Claude (b. 1939) French dramatist. He was born in Paris and first worked in a tailor's shop. His plays include *Dreyfus*.

Grünbaum, Max (1817–98) German folklorist and philologist. He was born in Seligenstadt. He became director of the Hebrew Orphan Asylum in New York in 1858, but in 1870 he returned to Europe and settled in Munich, where he engaged in research about Jewish folklore. He wrote studies of Jewish folklore and the structure and evolution of the Yiddish language and a chrestomathy of Judeo-Spanish. He is regarded as one of the founders of Yiddish philology.

Grünbaum, Yitzḥak (1879–1970) Israeli Zionist leader and author of Polish origin. He was born in Warsaw, where he later edited several newspapers. During World War I he lived in St Petersburg, but he returned to Warsaw, where he became the leader of Polish Zionism. In 1919 he was elected to the Sejm. In 1933 he became a member of the executive of the Jewish Agency and settled in Palestine. As a representative of the General Zionist Party, he was minister of the interior in 1948–9. He published studies on Polish and Zionist history.

Grünberg, Carlos (1903–68) Argentine writer. Born in Buenos Aires, he studied at the University of Buenos Aires and later taught Spanish literature. His work includes *Mester de Juderia* and *Junto a un rio de Babel.*

Grunwald, Max (1871–1953) Israeli rabbi and folklorist of German origin. He was born in Hindenburg. He served as a rabbi in Hamburg (1895–1903) and Vienna (1905–35), then in 1938 settled in Jerusalem. He wrote studies of the communities he served and of Jewish folklore.

Grusenberg, Oscar (1866–1940) Russian lawyer. He was a St Petersburg trial lawyer and championed political and civil liberties. He acted for the defence in the Beilis blood libel case of 1913.

Grynszpan, Herschel (b. 1921) German Jewish activist. He was born in Hanover and moved to Paris in 1938. He killed Ernst vom Rath, a German embassy official in Paris, in order to arouse public opinion in the West about Nazi persecution. This event served as a pretext for the pogroms of 9–10 November 1938 against the Jews.

Güdemann, Moritz (1835–1918) Austrian rabbi and historian. He was born in Hildesheim, Prussia.

He served as rabbi in Magdeburg (from 1862) and Vienna. In 1869 he became head of the Vienna bet din, and subsequently chief rabbi. He wrote a study of trends and institutions in medieval Jewish life from the viewpoint of the non-Jewish environment. He was a leader of the opposition to **Theodor Herzl**'s Zionism.

Guedalla, Philip (1899–1944) English historian. He lectured on the history and personalities of 19th-century England. He served as the president of the English Zionist Federation from 1924–8.

Guggenheim, Meyer (1828–1905) American industrialist. When his father emigrated from Lengnau, Switzerland to the US, he worked with him as a travelling salesman. Meyer became a manufacturer of polish, a shop owner, and a spice merchant as well as an importer of fine lace and embroidery. In 1877 he created the firm of M. Guggenheim's Sons in Philadelphia. Later he established the Guggenheim Exploration Company. In 1901 the Guggenheims bought the American Smelting and Refining Company.

Guggenheim, Peggy (1898–1979) American art patron. The daughter of **Meyer Guggenheim**'s son Benjamin, she had an important influence on modern art in Europe and the US. During the 1920s and 1930s she lived in Europe and opened the Guggenheim Jeune Gallery in London. When the Nazis invaded France, she shipped her collection to New York. Later she returned to Europe.

Guglielmo, Ebreo [William the Jew; Guglielmo da Pesaro] (fl. 15th cent.) Italian dancer. He studied with Domenico da Piacenza. They collaborated in organizing the wedding festivities of Costanzo Sforza and Camilla d'Aragona in Pesaro in 1475. He arranged festive dances in Milan, Mantua, Urbino, Bologna, Naples and Venice. His work includes *Trattato del'arte de ballo.*

Gumplowicz, Ludwig (1838–1909) Austrian sociologist. He was born in Kraków. He taught at the University of Graz from 1862. He converted to Christianity, but maintained an interest in Jewish affairs. He exercised an important influence on the development of sociology as a science.

Günzburg, David (1857–1910) Russian scholar and orientalist, son of **Horace Günzburg**. He was born in Kamenets-Podolskiy. He published studies on oriental subjects and linguistics and medieval Arabic poetry. He was active in the St Petersburg Jewish community and the Society for the Promotion of Culture Among the Jews in Russia. In 1908 he established the Jewish Academy, where he taught rabbinics and Arabic literature.

Günzburg, Horace (1833–1909) Russian communal leader, son of **Joseph Yozel Günzburg**. He was born in Zvenigorodka in the province of Kiev, and became active as a banker in St Petersburg. During the blood libel case in Kutais in 1878 he encouraged Daniel Chwolson to write a book about the history of blood libel. In 1881–2 he attempted to establish an organization of Russian Jews. Later he headed the Jewish community in St Petersburg and the Society for the Promotion of Culture Among the Jews in Russia.

Günzburg, Joseph Yozel (1812–78) Russian banker and communal leader. He was born in Vitebsk and settled in Paris in 1857. In 1859 he founded the Joseph Yozel Günzburg Bank in St Petersburg. He was active in attempts to improve the situation of Russian Jewry. As a founder of the Society for the Promotion of Culture Among the Jews in Russia, he provided scholarships for Jewish youth to encourage higher education.

Günzburg, Mordecai Aaron (1795–1846) Lithuanian Hebrew author and educationalist. He was born in Salantai and settled in Vilna in 1835. Together with Solomon Salkind, in 1841 he founded the first modern Jewish school in Lithuania, where he served as headmaster. As a spokesman for the Vilna Haskalah, he published studies of French and Russian history, translations, and an autobiography (*Aviezer*).

Günzburg, Pesaḥ (1894–1947) Palestinian writer and journalist. He was born in Volhynia and lived in the US (1912–14). Scandinavia (1914–17), and London (1917–22), before settling in Palestine. He published poems and stories, as well as translations from English and the Scandinavian languages into Hebrew.

Günzburg, Shimon (1890–1944) Palestinian poet and critic. He was born in Volhynia and lived in the US from 1912 and in Palestine from 1933. He wrote poetry and edited the plays and letters of **Moses Ḥayyim Luzzatto**.

Günzburg, Yevsel (1812–78) Russian banker. The grandson of Naphtali-Herz Günzburg, he became a spokesman of the Jews in the commercial concessions offered by the government of Nicholas I. In 1859 he founded the Günzburg Banking House.

Günzig, Azriel (1868–1931) Polish rabbi and scholar. He was born in Kraków and served as a rabbi in Czechoslovakia and Antwerp. He edited and published the literary journal *Ha-Eshkol* from 1899 to 1913. He wrote about the history of the Haskalah and Galicia.

Guri, Ḥayyim (b. 1922) Israeli poet, novelist and journalist. He was born in Tel Aviv and spent his early ears in the Palmaḥ In 1947 he went to Europe as an aliyah official. His writings include volumes of poetry and novels, dealing with Holocaust survivors and memories of his Tel Aviv childhood. He has also made a documentary about the Holocaust.

Guston, Philip (1913–80) American painter. His work was mainly abstract and was strongly affected by the horrors of the Holocaust.

Gutmacher, Elijah (1796–1874) Polish Zionist. He was born in Borek. He served as a rabbi in Pleschenitsy and Grodzisk Wielkopolski. His studies of the kabbalah led him to the view that the Jewish return to Palestine was necessary to purify Jewry from the pollution of exile. He took part in the Thron conference in 1860, which discussed the problems of Palestinian colonization, and worked with **Tzevi Hirsch Kalischer** to encourage Jewish settlement in Palestine.

Gutman, Naḥum (1898–1980) Israeli artist. He was born in Romania and was taken to Palestine at the age of seven. He designed scenery for the Ohel Theatre in 1935, and created a mosaic for the chief rabbinate building in Tel Aviv in 1961. He also wrote chidren's stories.

Guttmann, Jacob (1845–1919) German rabbi and historian. He was born in Beuthen, Silesia. He served as rabbi in Hildesheim from 1874 to 1892 and in Breslau from 1892. From 1910 he was president of the German Rabbinical Assembly. He published studies of medieval Jewish philosophers and the relation between Christian scholasticism and medieval Jewish philosophy.

Guttmann, Julius (1880–1950) Israeli philosopher and historian of German origin. He lectured in philosophy at the University of Breslau (from 1910) and in Jewish philosophy at the Hochschule für die Wissenschaft des Judentums in Berlin (from 1919). In 1934 he settled in Jerusalem, where he became professor of Jewish philosophy at the Hebrew University. He published sociological studies of Jewry, philosophical investigations, and explorations of the history of Jewish philosophy.

Guttmann, Michael (1872–1942) Hungarian talmudic scholar. He lectured on Jewish law at the Budapest Rabbinical Seminary from 1907 to 1921. He was then rabbi and professor of Talmud and halakhah at the Breslau Jewish theological seminary (1921–33), of which he became head in 1933. He published studies of rabbinic literature and began work on a talmudic encyclopaedia.

H

Haan, Jacob Israel de (1881–1924) Dutch poet and Orthodox leader. Born in Smilde, he initially rejected his Jewish background, but later reverted to an Orthodox lifestyle. In 1919 he left Holland for Palestine, abandoning his non-Jewish wife. He became a member of the Orthodox Agudat-Israel party and wrote articles for the Dutch and British Press. He was later murdered by opponents.

Haas, Jacob de (1872–1937) Zionist publicist. A London journalist, he corresponded with **Theodor Herzl** and acted as his secretary in England and at early Zionist congresses. He went to Boston in 1902 and edited Jewish journals. In 1910 he introduced **Louis D. Brandeis** to Zionism. He was later drawn to the Revisionist movement.

Haber, Fritz (1868–1934) German physical chemist. Born in Breslau, he became director of the Kaiser Wilhelm Research Institute for Chemistry in 1911. He gained the Nobel Prize in Chemistry in 1918.

Habermann, Avraham Meir (1901–80) Israeli bibliographer and scholar of medieval Hebrew literature. He was born in Galicia. After serving as librarian at the Schocken library in Berlin, he emigrated to Palestine in 1934, where he was director of the Schocken library in Jerusalem until 1967. From 1957 he taught medieval literature at Tel Aviv University and at the Graduate Library School of the Hebrew University. He wrote studies of Jewish bibliography, the history of Hebrew poetry, and medieval Hebrew poetry.

Habshush, Chaim (d. 1899) Yemenite writer. When the oreintalist **Joseph Halévy** arrived in Yemen in about 1870 to trace ancient Sabean inscriptions, he acted as his guide. Later he wrote an account of these explorations, *Masot Habshush.*

Ha-Cohen, Mordecai ben Hillel (1856–1936) Hebrew author of Russian origin. He was born in Belorussia. He began publishing articles in Hebrew periodicals when he was 18. In 1875 he moved to St Petersburg, where he wrote a comprehensive survey of Jewish agriculturalists in modern Russia. In 1881 he joined the Ḥibbat Zion movement, and he later formed two societies for promoting settlement in Palestine. He moved to Palestine himself in 1907 and was one of the founders of Tel Aviv. He played an active role in the economic and cultural life of the yishuv.

Hadamard, Jacques (1865–1963) French mathematician. Born in Versailles, he studied at the École Normale Superieure and the University of Paris. He taught at the University of Paris, and became a professor at the College de France as well as at the École Polytechnique and the École Centrale des Arts et Manufactures. He was a brother-in-law of **Alfred Dreyfus** and helped with his defence. In 1941 he fled to the US and later settled in England. His works include: *Lessons on the Calculus of Variations*, and *Essay on the Psychology of Invention in the Mathematical Field.*

Hadassi, Judah ben Elijah (fl. 12th cent.) Turkish Karaite scholar. He lived in Constantinople. He wrote *Eshkol ha-Kopher*, an encyclopaedic survey of Karaite belief and knowledge. It explains the mitzvot and the halakhot, and the reasons for their observance in accordance with specific commandments.

Haffkine, Waldemar (1860–1930) Russian bacteriologist. Born in Odessa, he studied at the University of Novorossik, worked at the Zoological Museum of Odessa and later moved to Switzerland where he worked at the Pasteur Institute in Geneva. He subsequently tested cholera inoculation in India.

Haggai (fl. 6th cent. BCE) Biblical prophet. The prohecies of Haggai date from the second year of the reign of Darius I, King of Persia (c. 520 BCE). They deal with the construction of the Temple, the restoration of the nation, and the greatness of **Zerubbabel**.

Ḥagiz, Jacob (1620–74) Palestinian scholar. He lived in various communities in Italy as a youth. In 1658 he emigrated to Jerusalem, where he became head of the Bet Yaakov yeshivah. He was an opponent of **Shabbetai Tzevi**. His writings include a commentary on the Mishnah, a study of talmudic methodology, and responsa.

Ḥagiz, Moses (1672–?1751) Palestinian scholar and kabbalist. He was born in Jerusalem. He left Palestine in 1694 to collect money to found a yeshivah. He travelled to Egypt, Italy, Prague, and Amsterdam, where together with **Tzevi Ashkenazi** he struggled against Shabbetaianism. Later he lived in Altona, and eventually settled in Safed. His writings include novellae on the Shulḥan Arukh, ethical works and responsa.

Hai Gaon (939–1038) Babylonian gaon, son of **Sherira Gaon**. Initially he assisted his father in administering and teaching in the academy at Pumbedita. He was appointed head of the bet din in 986 and gaon in 998. Under his leadership the Pumbedita academy became a centre of Jewish learning; he was the last gaon of Pumbedita. He issued thousands of responsa covering numerous areas of halakhic literature. In addition, he wrote a commentary on several tractates of the Talmud, poetry, and a treatise on commercial transactions.

Haim, Victor (b. 1935) French playwright. He was born in Asnières. In 1954 he went to Paris, where he supported himself as a journalist. Some of his work integrates Jewish and universal themes.

Halberstamm, Ḥayyim (1793–1876) Polish rabbinic scholar. He was born in Tarnogrod, and was appointed rabbi of Nowy Sadz in Galicia in 1830. He became drawn to Ḥasidism and founded the Sanzer dynasty of Hasidic rabbis. He was the head of a yeshivah in Zanz which attracted both Ḥasidim and mitnaggedim. In 1869 he was involved in a dispute with the Sadagora Ḥasidim. He published works on talmudic subjects as well as responsa.

Halberstamm, Solomon Zalman Ḥayyim (1832–1900) Polish Hebrew scholar and bibliophile. He was born in Kraków and became a successful merchant in Bielsko-Biala, Poland, where he collected rare books and manuscripts. In 1890 he published a catalogue of his manuscripts.

Halévy, Élie (1760–1826) French Hebrew writer and poet. He was born in Fürth, Bavaria, and moved to Paris, where he served as cantor, secretary of the Jewish community, and teacher. From 1817 to 1819 he edited and published a weekly journal, *L'Israélite français*. His *Teachings of Religion and Ethics* is a textbook for Jewish religious instruction. His poem *Ha-Shalom* commemorates the ceasefire between France and England in 1802.

Halévy, Isaac (1847–1914) Polish rabbinic scholar. Born in Ivenets, he lived in various cities including Pressburg, Homburg and Hamburg, where he served as Klausrabbiner. His *Dorot ha-Rishonim* is a history of the oral law from biblical times to the period of the geonim.

Halévy, Jacques François Fromental (1799–1862) French composer, son of **Élie Halévy**. He was born in Paris, and taught at the Paris Conservatoire from 1816, becoming professor of counterpoint and fugue in 1833, and professor of composition in 1840. He composed operas, cantatas and ballets. His opera *La Juive* is the story of a Renaissance prince in love with a Jewess.

Halévy, Joseph (1827–1917) French orientalist and Hebrew writer. He was born in Turkey and later taught in Bucharest. In 1868 he visited Ethiopia to study the Falashas. Later he explored southern Arabia and discovered numerous Sabean inscriptions. In 1879 he taught Ethiopic at the École Pratique des Hautes Études in Paris and became the librarian of the Société Asiatique. In 1893 he founded the *Revue semitique d'épigraphique et d'historie ancienne*, to which he contributed articles on epigraphy and biblical studies. He was an ardent Hebraist and Zionist.

Halévy, Léon (1802–83) French writer and dramatist, son of **Élie Halévy**. He was born and lived in Paris. He became assistant professor of French literature at the École Polytechnique in 1831 and head of the antiquities department of the ministry of education in 1837. His writings include *Résumé de l'histoire des juifs anciens* and *Résumé de l'histoire de juifs modernes.*

Halévy, Ludovic (1834–1908) French writer. The son of **Léon Halévy**, he provided the libretto for various musical compositions by Offenbach.

Halkin, Abraham (b. 1903) American orientalist and educator, brother of **Simon Halkin**. He was born in Russia and was taken to the US in 1914. From 1928 to 1950 he was a lecturer in Semitic languages at the City College of New York, and latterly professor of Hebrew. He also taught at the Jewish Theological Seminary from 1929 to 1970. He edited **Maimonides**' *Epistle to Yemen*, and published studies of Judeo-Arabic literature and history.

Halkin, Shemuel (1897–1960) Russian Yiddish poet. He was born in Belorussia. He published a book of lyrics in 1922 and later Yiddish translations of English, American and Russian classics, as well as poetry and plays about Jewish history. Initially he supported Zionism and was criticized for his advocacy of Jewish nationalism.

Halkin, Simon (1898–1987) American Hebrew poet, novelist and educator, brother of **Abraham Halkin**. He was born in Russia and emigrated to the US in 1914. He taught at the Hebrew Union College School for Teachers in New York from 1925 to 1932, when he settled in Palestine. He returned to the US in 1939 and became professor of Hebrew literature at the Jewish Institute of Religion in New York. In 1949 he was appointed professor of modern Hebrew literature at the Hebrew University. He wrote novels and works of literary criticism, and made translations.

Halper, Ben Zion (1884–1924) American Hebraist, Arabist and editor. He was born in Lithuania and emigrated to Germany, from there to England, and finally to the US. From 1913 he taught at Dropsie College in Philadelphia, becoming professor of cognate languages in 1923. He served as editor of the Jewish Publication Society of America from 1916 to 1924. He published studies of Hebrew and Arabic, an anthology of post-biblical Hebrew literature, and a catalogue of documents from the Cairo Genizah.

Halprin, Rose Luria (1896–1978) American Zionist leader. She was born in New York. She served as president of the women's Zionist organization Hadassah from 1932 to 1934 and 1947 to 1951. From 1934 to 1939 she was Hadassah's correspondent in Palestine. In 1947 she was elected to the executive of the Jewish Agency for Israel, on which she served for over 20 years; in 1968 she became chairman of the American section of the Jewish Agency.

Halter, Marek (b. 1932) French artist and writer. Born in Warsaw, he escaped from the the Warsaw Ghetto and lived in Soviet Uzbekistan. In 1945 he returned to Poland, but later moved to Paris, where he was appointed director of the Centre du Judaisme. His artistic works include *Croquis de mai*, and his literary works include *Le Fou et les rois* and *Le Mémoire d'Abraham.*

Ḥama bar Ḥanina (fl. 3rd cent.) Palestinian scholar. He lived in Sepphoris where his father **Ḥanina Bar Ḥama** headed an academy. He is known for his aggadic interpretations.

Hambro, Joseph (1780–1848) Danish financier. Born in Copenhagen, he became court banker to the king of Denmark and negotiated financial and trade agreements on behalf of the Danish government with Britain and Norway. He later settled in London where he founded a bank which was named after him.

Hamburger, Jacob (1826–1911) German rabbi and scholar. He was born in Poland and served as a rabbi in Neustadt and Mecklenburg-Strelitz. His *Real-Encyklopaedie für Bibel und Talmud* was later expanded into a three volume *Real-Encyklopaedie des Judentums.*

Hamburger, Michael (b. 1924) British poet. He went to England in childhood as a refugee from Nazi Germany. His works include *Treblinka.*

Ha-Meiri [Feuerstein], Avigdor (1890–1970) Israeli poet, novelist and translator. He was born in the Carpathian region of Russia and settled in Palestine in 1921. He published poems, stories, translations and critical articles. His writings include *The Great Madness* and *Hell Below.*

Hammerstein, Oscar II (1895–1960) American librettist. He was the grandson of Oscar Hammerstein who built theatres and opera houses in New York City. He collaborated with **Richard Rodgers** and produced musicals including *Oklahoma, South Pacific, The King and I* and *The Sound of Music.*

Hamnuna (fl. 4th cent.) Babylonian amora. He was born in Harpania in Babylonia and lived in Harta of Argiz near Baghdad. He was a pupil and colleague of **Ḥisda.**

Hamnuna Saba (fl. 3rd cent.) Babylonian amora. He was a pupil of **Rav** and succeeded him as head of the academy at Sura.

Hamnuna Zuta (fl. 4th cent.) Babylonian amora. His confession of sin, which he recited on the Day of Atonement, is included in the liturgy for this holy day.

Hanamel (fl. 1st cent. BCE) Israelite high priest (37–36 BCE, and again in 34 BCE). He was born in Egypt. He was appointed high priest by **Herod** who passed over **Aristobulus III**, the brother of **Mariamne**. Owning to the protests of **Alexandra** and **Mariamne, Herod** deposed Hanamel and appointed **Aristobulus III**. But after **Aristobulus** was murdered, Hanamel was restored to office.

Hananel ben Ḥushiel (d. 1055) Babylonian rabbinic scholar. He was born in Kairovan. He was given the title 'chief among the rabbis' by the Babylonian academies. He wrote commentaries on the Babylonian Talmud and the Pentateuch.

Hananiah (fl. 2nd cent.) Babylonian tanna. In his youth he lived in Palestine, but later he settled in Babylonia, where he remained until his death. He was the greatest scholar in Palestine at the time of the Hadrianic persecutions. He established the calendar in exile, which was followed by the Jews of Babylonia. After Hadrian's death, the Sanhedrin was reconstituted and called on him to recognize its authority. He agreed and exhorted all Babylonian congregations to recognize the Palestinian Sanhedrin.

Hananiah ben Ḥakhinai (fl. 2nd cent.) Babylonian tanna. He lived in Palestine and was one of those who debated before the sages in Jabneh. He studied with **Akiva** in Bene-Berak for 12 years. Later he resided in Sidon. According to tradition, he was one of the Ten Martyrs under the Hadrianic persecutions.

Hananiah ben Teradyon (fl. 2nd cent.) Babylonian tanna. He was head of the yeshivah of Siknin in Galilee. He was sentenced to death for teaching the Torah in defiance of Hadrian's decree forbidding religious instruction. He was burned at the stake wrapped in a Torah scroll.

Ḥanina bar Ḥama (fl. 3rd cent.) Palestinian scholar. He was born in Babylonia and emigrated to Palestine, settling in Sepphoris, where he was a pupil of **Judah ha-Nasi**. He earned a living by trading in honey, and also practised medicine. He was a noted aggadist.

Ḥanina ben Dosa (fl. 1st cent.) Palestinian tanna. He lived in extreme poverty and was noted for his piety and his ability to perform miracles; his prayers for the sick had great efficacy.

Ḥankin, Yehoshua (1864–1945) Palestinian Zionist pioneer. He was born in the Ukraine and went to Palestine in 1882. In 1897 he negotiated for the purchase of land in the Jezreel Valley, but not until 1909 was the sale completed. In 1915 he was exiled in Anatolia by the Turkish authorities, but he returned to Palestine three years later. In 1920 he purchased a second tract of land in the Jezreel Valley, on which many agricultural settlements were established. From 1932 he served as director of the Palestine Land Development Corporation. He wrote *Jewish Colonization in Palestine.*

Hannah (fl. 11th cent. BCE) Israelite woman; she was the wife of **Elkanah** and mother of **Samuel**. She was barren and in praying for a child she vowed to dedicate any son she had to the Temple. When her son **Samuel** was born, she left him with **Eli** the priest to serve in the Temple (I Samuel 1–2).

Hannover, Nathan Nata (fl. 17th cent.) Polish preacher, kabbalist, lexicographer, and chronicler. During the Chmielnicki massacres, he left his birthplace in Volhynia and wandered through Poland, Germany and the Netherlands. In 1653 he went to Italy. In 1662 he was appointed president of the bet din and head of the yeshivah in Jassy, Walachia. Later he moved to Moravia. He published sermons, a Hebrew-German-Latin-Italian lexicon, a kabbalistic prayerbook, and an account of the Chmielnicki persecutions.

Ḥaphetz Ḥayyim [Cahan [Kahan], Israel Meir] (1835–1933) Lithuanian talmudist and communal leader. He was born in Poland and became one of the leaders of Eastern European Orthodox Jewry. He founded and was the head of a yeshivah in Radin, Lithuania, and was active in Agudat Israel. The name by which he is commonly known derives from his ethical and religious treatise *Ḥaphetz Ḥayyim*.

Harby, Isaac (1788–1828) American writer, teacher and Reform leader. He was born in Charleston, South Carolina, and worked on various newspapers there. He helped to establish the Reformed Society of the Israelites, of which he became president in 1827.

Ha-Reuveni, Ephraim (1881–1953) Israeli botanist. He was born in the Ukraine and settled in Palestine in 1906. He founded the Museum of Biblical and Talmudic Flora in 1912 which was later transferred to the Hebrew University. He was appointed lecturer in biblical botany at the Hebrew University in 1935. He published studies of the flora of Palestine.

Harkavy, Albert (1835–1919) Russian orientalist. He was born in Belorussia. He became head of the department of Jewish literature and oriental manuscripts at the Imperial Library in St Petersburg in 1877. He published studies of the Khazars, the Karaites, and the history and languages of Russian Jewry. His writings on the ancient Jewish tombstones in the Crimea exposed the fabrications of **Abraham Firkovich**.

Harkavy, Alexander (1863–1939) American Yiddish lexicographer and writer. He was born in Belorussia and emigrated to the US in 1881. He first joined a collective agricultural colony, but after it failed he lived in numerous cities, including Paris, New York, Montreal and Baltimore. He published textbooks and dictionaries for immigrants, including the *Yiddish-English-Hebrew Dictionary*.

Hart, Aaron (1670–1756) British rabbi. He was born in Breslau. He emigrated to England and was appointed rabbi of the Ashkenazi community in London in 1705. He is regarded as the first chief rabbi of Great Britain. His *Urim ve-Tummim* (1707) was the first book printed entirely in Hebrew in London.

Hart, Abraham (1810–85) American publisher. He was the founder of the Jewish Publication Society and its first president. He was also the president of Maimonides College.

Hart, Moss (1904–61) American playwright. Born in New York City, he wrote a number of successful plays either by himself or in collaboration with **George S. Kaufman**. His work includes *You Can't Take it with You*, *The Man who Came to Dinner*, *George Washington Slept Here* and *Act One*.

Hart, Solomon (1806–81) English painter. He studied at the Royal Academy and painted miniatures. Later he painted in oils and developed a formal academic style; his subjects deal with Jewish topics as well as English historical events.

Hartog, Numa Edward (1846–71) English mathematician. He studied mathematics at Cambridge University. His inability to graduate because of his Jewish origin occasioned the abolition of religious tests imposed on university students in England.

Hassan, Joshua (1915–97) Chief minister of Gibraltar. He was born in Gibraltar and worked as a lawyer. He was mayor of the colony, leader of its legislative council and chief minister.

Hatvani, Lajos (1880–1961) Hungarian writer, literary critic and journalist. He was born in Budapest. He was a founder of the literary periodical *Nyugat* and served as the editor of the journal *Pesti Napló* before and during World War I. At the outbreak of the communist revolution in 1919 he went to Vienna, but later returned to Budapest. He spent World War II in England and returned to Hungary in 1947. In his writings he dealt with the problem of the Hungarian attitude towards the Jews, as well as Jewish assimilation and nationalism.

Hays, Arthur (1881–1954) American lawyer. He served as general counsel for the American Civll Liberties Union. He was the defence in a number of important cases including the Dayton, Ohio prosecution of Scopes for teaching evolution, and the Sacco and Vanzetti trial. After the Reichstag fire in 1933, he went to Germany to defend the communist who was accused as responsible for this act. After World War II he worked with the Allied Occupation authorities to establish democratic institutions in Germany. He published a number of books dealing with the struggle for civil rights as well as an autobiography.

Ḥayyon, Nehemiah (c.1655–c.1730) Kabbalist. He was born in Safed and became a rabbi at Uskub. Later he wandered from place to place and eventually joined the Shabbetaian movement. He then lived in Italy, Prague and Berlin. He published kabbalistic studies, and advocated a new form of Shabbetaianism, based on the doctrine of the Trinity, comprising the First Cause, the Infinite, and the Holy Father (who was identified with **Shabbetai Tzevi**). He was involved in a controversy in Amsterdam, and his works were criticized and banned by European rabbis. He finally settled in North Africa.

Ḥayyuj, Judah ben David (c.945–c.1000) Spanish Hebrew grammarian. He was born in Fez but arrived in Cordoba in 960 and lived most of his life in Spain. He wrote a study of Hebrew pronunciation, a philological commentary on the biblical books from Johsua to Ezekiel, and two treatises on Hebrew verbs. A translation of his grammatical works from Arabic into Hebrew by **Moses Gikatilla** was the first of its kind.

Hazaz, Ḥayyim (1898–1973) Israeli writer. He was born in Zidorovichi and in his youth moved from one Russian city to another. During and after the Russian Revolution, he worked on the Hebrew daily *Ha-Am* in Moscow. In 1921 he went to Constantinople, and then lived in Paris and Berlin. He emigrated to Palestine in 1931 and settled in Jerusalem. In his novels he depicted Jewish life in various countries.

Hecht, Anthony (b. 1923) American poet. Born in New York City, he studied at Bard College. He taught at Kenyon College and published poems in *Kenyon Review*. Later he taught at New York University and studied at Columbia. His work includes *A Summoning of Stones*, *The Seven Deadly Sins: Poems* and *The Hard Hours*.

Hecht, Ben (1893–1964) American novelist and playwright. He was born in New York and grew up in Racine, Wisconsin. He wrote plays and novels, including *Jew in Love*. In the 1940s he became an advocate of the Palestinian underground organizaton Irgun Tzevai Leumi. His *A Guide for the Bedeviled* is an analysis of anti-Semitism.

Heidenheim, Wolf Benjamin (1757–1832) German Hebrew grammarian, masoretic scholar, exegete and commentator on the liturgy. He was born in Heidenheim. In 1800 he published the first volume of a nine-volume edition of the maḥzor. He also published other works in the field of liturgy.

Heifetz, Jascha (1901–87) American violinist, of Lithuanian origin. Born in Vilna, he performed in public from the age of seven. He studied at the St Petersburg Conservatory, and at 11 began performing throughout Europe. The family escaped from Russia during the 1917 revolution, and he settled in California. He embarked on American tours as well as tours throughout the world.

Heijermans, Hermann (1864–1924) Dutch playwright and novelist. He was born in Rotterdam. He published short stories, novels and plays. In his play *Ahasuerus* he expressed concern for the fate of Jewry. His novels

Sabbath and *Diamanstad* and the play *Ghetto* contrast the narrow-mindedness of the inhabitants of the Amsterdam ghetto with the liberal attitudes of Dutch Christians.

Heilprin, Jehiel ben Solomon (1660–1746) Lithuanian talmudic scholar and historian. He served as a rabbi in Glussk, and in 1711 was appointed head of the yeshivah in Minsk. His *Seder ha-Dorot* contains a chronology of events and personages to 1696, an alphabetical list of tannaim and amoraim, and a catalogue of post-talmudic Hebrew authors and books.

Heine, Heinrich (1797–1856) German poet and essayist. He was born in Düsseldorf and settled in Berlin, where he published his first book of poetry. Influenced by **Moses Mendelssohn** and **Leopold Zunz**, he joined the Society for the Culture and Science of Judaism. In 1825 he embraced Christianity, but later expressed regret for leaving the Jewish faith. In many of his works, such as *The Rabbi of Bacherach* and *Hebrew Melodies*, he exhibited an interest in Judaism. He later lived in Paris, where he worked as a journalist and poet. He influenced the development of the Haskalah movement as well as Hebrew and Yiddish poetry.

Heinemann, Yitzḥak (1876–1957) Israeli humanist and philosopher. He was born in Frankfurt am Main. From 1919 to 1938 he lectured in Jewish philosophy and literature at the Jewish Theological Seminary in Breslau. In 1939 he settled in Jerusalem. His writings deal with Hellenistic and medieval Jewish philosophy.

Helena (fl. 1st cent.) Parthian queen, wife of Monobaz I, King of Adiabene. She and her sons Izates II and Monobaz II converted to Judaism through the inflence of Ananias, a Jewish merchant. She spent the latter part of her life in Jerusalem, where she built herself a palace. When a famine raged in Israel she bought food for the people. She also made gifts to the Temple, and was fastidious in the observance of Jewish law.

Heller, Bernhart (1871–1943) Hungarian Arabist and literary scholar. He was born in Nagybicse. He taught languages at high schools in Budapest and became director of the Jewish High School; in 1922 he was appointed professor of Bible at the Rabbinical Seminary. He published studies of ancient Jewish literature, Jewish folk literature, and Muslim legends.

Heller, Chaim (1878–1960) American rabbinic and biblical scholar. He was born in Bialystok, Poland, and served as rabbi in Lomża. In 1917 he settled in Berlin, where he established a new type of yeshivah for research on the Bible and Talmud. In 1929 he joined the faculty of the Isaac Elchanan Theological Seminary in New York. He wrote studies of Syriac and Samaritan translations of the Bible and halakhic issues. He also published and edition of **Maimonides**' *Book of the Commandments*.

Heller, James (1892–1971) American Zionist and communal leader, son of **Maximilian Heller**. He was rabbi of Isaac Mayer Wise Temple in Cincinnati and president of the Labour Zionist Organization of America.

Heller, Joseph (1923–99) American novelist. Born in Brooklyn, he served in the American Air Force in World War II. He then studied at the Universities of New York, Columbia, and Oxford. He worked for various magazines and published *Catch–22* in 1961. Other works include *Something Happened*, *Good as Gold* and *God Knows*.

Heller, Joseph Elijah (1888–1957) British Hebrew writer. He was born in Lithuania and lived in Russia and Germany. In 1938 he moved to London, where he edited the Zionist organization's journal, *Tarbut*, and taught. He published studies of Jewish and general philosophy, and translated several of Plato's dialogues into Hebrew.

Heller, Maximilian (1860–1929) American rabbi and Zionist. He was rabbi of Temple Sinai in New Orleans, and a prominent Zionist in the American Reform movement.

Heller, Yom Tov Lipmann (1579–1660) Bavarian talmudist. He became dayyan in Prague at the age of 18. In 1629 he was fined for libelling the state and Christianity, and was forbidden to act as a rabbi in Prague. Later he served several communities. During the Chmielnicki massacres of 1648–9 he lived in Kraków, where he composed penitential psalms and commemorative prayers for those who died. His *Tosaphot Yom Tov* is a commentary on the Mishnah. He also wrote studies of religious subjects as well as works on mathematics and natural science.

Hellman, Lillian (1906–84) American playwright. Born in New Orleans, she worked as a manuscript reader; she then was a theatrical play reader and film scenario reader. In the 1930s she began to write her own plays, some of which were adapted for the screen. She also wrote three books of memoirs.

Heltai, Jeno (1871–1957) Hungarian writer. Born in Budapest, he was a cousin of **Theodor Herzl**. He studied law at Budapest University, and became a journalist. He lived in Vienna, Paris, London, Berlin and Constantinople and translated plays and novels from English, French and German. From 1900 he became involved with the theatre. His work includes: *Jaguar*, *The Last of the Bohemians* and *House of Dreams*. He converted to Christianity, but later returned to Judaism.

Heman (fl. 11th–10th cent. BCE) Levite musician. He and his sons were among those who performed at the dedication of the Temple (II Chronicles 5:12).

Heman the Ezrahite (fl. 13th cent. BCE) Sage. He is named in the Bible as one of the great sages who was surpassed in wisdom only by **Solomon** (I Kings 5:11). Psalm 88 is attributed to him.

Henriques, Basil Lucas Quixano (1890–1961) English social reformer, son of **Henry Straus Quixano Henriques**. He was born in London. With the help of his wife, he established the St George's Jewish Settlement in London after World War I. He served as magistrate and later as chairman of the East London Juvenile Court. He visited boys' homes and prisons, suggested reforms, and took an interest in Jewish offenders. After World War II he headed the anti-Zionist Jewish Fellowship. He wrote *The Indiscretions of a Warden*, *The Indiscretions of a Magistrate* and *The Home Menders*.

Henriques, Henry Straus Quixano (1864–1924) English lawyer, communal worker and historian. He served as president of the Board of Deputies of British Jews from 1922 to 1925. He wrote *The Jews and the English Law* and *Jewish Marriages and the English Law*.

Ḥephetz ben Yatzliaḥ (fl. 10th cent.) Persian scholar. He was active in Mosul. His *Sepher ha-Mitzvot* interprets the 613 commandments according to talmudic sources.

Herberg, Will (1906–77) American writer. He was active in the Young Communist League and edited communist party publications. In the 1940s he renounced communism and developed Jewish interests. His writings include *Judaism and Modern Man* and *Protestant, Catholic and Jew*.

Herman, Joseph (b. 1911) British painter. He was born in Warsaw, and moved to Brussels, France and Glasgow; in 1944 he settled in Wales. His work of 1938–43 depicts the world of his Jewish childhood.

Herod I [the Great] (fl. 1st cent. BCE) King of Judea (37–4 BCE), son of **Antipater II**. He was appointed governor of Galilee by his father in 47 BCE. When he successfully crushed a Galilean revolt, he was censured by the Great Sanhedrin. Later he was appointed tetrarch of Judea and subsequently king. As ruler he constructed a Greek theatre and amphitheatre in Jerusalem, transformed Samaria into a Greco-Samarian city, built the port of Caesarea, and rebuilt the Temple in Jerusalem. During his reign he dealt harshly with anyone whom he believed to constitute a threat to his powers; he put many people to death, including his wife **Mariamne** and her sons.

Herod Agrippa I (10 BCE–44 CE) King of Judea (41–4), son of **Aristobulus** and **Berenice I** and grandson of **Herod** the Great. Educated in Rome, he served as market overseer in Tiberius and later returned to Rome, where he became a friend of Caligula. After being imprisoned for treachery, he was freed by Caligula, who appointed him King of Judea. He was sympathetic to the Pharisees and observant of Jewish law.

Herod Agrippa II (28–92) King of Judea (50–92), son of **Herod Agrippa I**. He was the last king of the house of **Herod**. During the Jewish revolt against Rome, he sided with the Romans. When Titus became emperor, he served under him. According to the New Testament, he was indifferent to the spread of Christianity.

Herod Antipas (20 BCE–c. 40 CE) Tetrarch of Galilee and of the Judean Transjordan, son of **Herod** the Great. He founded Tiberias in honour of the emperor. His forbidden marriage to **Herodias** (wife of his half-brother **Philip**) evoked the hostility of the population; **John the Baptist** was put to death when he denounced the marriage. During the reign of Caligula, Herod Antipas was accused of plotting against Rome and was exiled to Gaul.

Herod Archelaus (fl. 1st cent. BCE–1st cent CE) Israelite, ruler of Judea (4 BCE–6 CE). He was a son of **Herod** the Great and under **Herod**'s will he was appointed king. When he went to Rome to ratify this appointment, the Jewish community protested. The emperor, Augustus, abolished the title of king, but confirmed him as ruler of Judea, Idumea and Sumeria. He was later removed from office and exiled to Gaul.

Herodias (fl. 1st cent.) Judean queen, wife of **Philip**, the son of **Herod** the Great and **Mariamne II**. She bore **Philip** a daughter, **Salome**. In 31 she was divorced from her husband and married his half-brother **Herod Antipas**. This marriage violated Jewish law and angered the Jewish population; **John the Baptist**, who led the opposition, was imprisoned and, according to the New Testament, was killed at the request of **Salome**.

Herod of Chalcis (d. 48) King of Chalcis (41–8), son of **Aristobulus** and grandson of **Herod** the Great and **Mariamne**. He was granted the kingdom of Chalcis in 41. After the death of **Herod Agrippa I** in 44, he was given charge of the Temple administration and treasury and invested with the ability to appoint high priests.

Herschell [Hirschel], Solomon (1762–1842) English rabbi. He was born in London. He served as a rabbi in Prussia, then in 1802 became rabbi of the Great Synagogue in London. He was recognized as chief rabbi by the Ashkenazi communities throughout Britain.

Herschmann, Mordechai (1888–1940) American cantor. Born in the Ukraine, he served as a cantor in Zhitomir, and in 1913 became chief cantor of Vilna. In 1920 he emigrated to the US, where he became cantor of Beth El Temple in Brooklyn. Later he made concert tours in Europe, Palestine and the US.

Hertz, Gustav (1887–1950) German scientist. He was a professor at Halle and Berlin. In 1925 he shared the Nobel Prize in Physics for work on electrons. He was forced to resign his post after Hitler came to power. From 1945 he worked in the Soviet Union and East Germany.

Hertz, Henri (1878–1966) French poet, novelist and critic. He was born in Norgent-sur-Seine. As a journalist, he discussed Jewish problems. In 1925 he became General Secretary of the French Zionist organization, France-Palestine. His story *Ceux de Job* explores the aspirations and despair of the Jewish nation, and his poetry pursues themes of revolt against the Jewish condition.

Hertz, Joseph Herman (1872–1946) British rabbi. He was born in Slovakia and in 1884 was taken to New York. He served as a rabbi in Syracuse, New York, and Johannesburg, South Africa. In 1911 he returned to the US and became rabbi of Congregation Oraḥ Ḥayyim in New York. In 1913 he was appointed chief rabbi of Great Britain. He was critical of Russian anti-Jewish policies and liberal Judaism. He supported Zionism and later struggled against Nazism. His writings include the *Book of Jewish Thoughts* and commentaries on the Pentateuch and the Prayer Book.

Hertzberg, Abel (1893–1989) Dutch author and lawyer. He was born in Amsterdam. He became the editor of *De joodsche wachter*, the journal of the Dutch Zionist Federation. His publications include *Amor fati* and *Brieven ann mijn kleinzoon.*

Herz, Henriette (1764–1847) German society leader, wife of **Marcus Herz**. She held a salon in her home in Berlin which attracted many of the leading figures in society; both **Moses Mendelssohn** and **Solomon Maimon** were frequent guests. She belonged to the Tugenbund, a youth group dedicated to encouraging ethical ideals. In 1817 she was baptized through the influence of Friedrich Schleiermacher.

Herz, Marcus (1747–1803) German physician and philosopher. He was born in Berlin, and became a doctor at the Jewish Hospital there. He published philosophical works and corresponded with Immanuel Kant. As a friend of **Moses Mendelssohn** he promoted the welfare of Prussian Jewry.

Herzfeld, Levi (1810–84) German Reform rabbi and historian. He was born in Ellrich. A spokesman for moderate Reform, he was one of the conveners of the first Reform Rabbinical Conference in Braunschweig, and particpated in the two following conferences. He and **Ludwig Philippson**, headed the Institut zur Förderung der Israelitischen Literatur from 1860 to 1873. He wrote studies of the history of the Second Temple and the Jews in antiquity.

Herzl, Theodor (1869–1904) Austrian writer and journalist, founder of political Zionism. He was born in Budapest. From 1891 to 1895 he was the Paris correspondent for the Vienna *Neue Freie Presse*. In his play *Das neue Ghetto* he criticized Jewish assimilation, and after the Dreyfus case, he wrote *Der Judenstaat* (The Jewish State), in which he advocated the establishment of a Jewish homeland. He convened the First Zionist Congress in Basle in 1897, at which the World Zionist Organization was established. Herzl was elected its president. He subsequently began negotiations with world leaders to create a Jewish state.

Herzog, Yitzḥak ha-Levi (1888–1959) Israeli rabbinic scholar. He was born in Poland and was taken by his family to Leeds, England, when he was nine. He served as a rabbi in Belfast (1916–19), and Dublin (1919–36), where he was chief rabbi of the Irish Free State. He became chief rabbi of Palestine in 1937. During World War II he attempted to rescue Jews from persecution in Europe, and after the war he travelled throughout Europe to find orphaned Jewish children. He published studies of the institutions of Jewish law and the Talmud as well as responsa.

Heschel, Abraham Joshua (1907–72) American theologian. He was educated in Berlin, then in 1938 deported by the Nazis to Poland; he later emigrated to England. From 1940 he taught philosophy and rabbinics at the Hebrew Union College in Cincinnati; in 1945 he was appointed professor of Jewish ethics and mysticism at the Jewish Theological Seminary of America. He wrote studies of medieval Jewish philosophy, the Bible, kabbalah, Ḥasidism, and the philosophy of religion.

Hess, Moses (1812–75) German socialist. He was born in Bonn. In 1841 he helped found the socialist daily *Rheinische Zeitung*, of which **Karl Marx** became editor. Subsequently he lived in Belgium, Switzerland and Paris. In 1862 he published *Rome and Jerusalem* which espoused Zionist ideals. Later he engaged in the work of the Alliance Israélite Universelle. His other publications include *The History of Humanity* and *The European Triarchy*.

Hess, Myra (1890–1965) British pianist. She studied at the Guildhall School of Music and at the Royal Academy of Music. She converted to Christianity but remained proud of her background. She devoted herself to teaching and performing and made tours of the US and Canada. During the war she appeared at the Myra Hess midday concerts held in the National Gallery in London.

Hessen, Julius (1871–1939) Russian historian. He was born in Odessa. His scholarly and communal activities were concerned with the emancipation of Russian Jewry. He served as the secretary of the Union for Full Equality of the Jewish People in Russia in 1905–6. Later he initiated the publication of the *Russian Jewish Encyclopedia* and served as its general secretary. His publications include studies of the history of the Jewish people in Russia.

Hevesi [Handler], Simon (1868–1943) Hungarian scholar and rabbi. In 1894 he was appointed rabbi of Kassa, and later became chief rabbi of Budapest. From 1905 he was lecturer in homiletics and Jewish philosophy at the Budapest Rabbinical Seminary. His publications include a Hungarian translation of the liturgy.

Hevesy, George (1885–1966) British chemist, of Hungarian origin. Born in Budapest, he became a professor at Freiburg University. He was compelled by the Nazis to resign and he fled to Sweden. In 1943 he was awarded a Nobel Prize in Chemistry for the use of radioactive isotopes.

Heymann, Isaac (1818–1906) Russian cantor and composer. He served as cantor in Filehne, Graudenz, and Gnesen. He was later appointed chief cantor of the Great Synagogue of the Amsterdam Ashkenazi congregation.

Heyse, Paul (1830–1914) German author. He wrote elegant novels and novellas, but towards the end of the century they were attacked by the German naturalist school. He was awarded the Nobel Prize for Literature in 1910.

Hezekiah (i) (fl. 8th–7th cent. BCE) King of Judah (715–687 BCE). Unlike his father **Ahaz**, he attempted to free Judah from Assyrian influence. He removed pagan images and altars from the Temple and renewed the religion of ancient Israel. These reforms were supported by **Isaiah**. When Hezekiah led a league of states against Assyria, Sennacherib invaded Judah, but did not occupy Jerusalem. As a consequence, Hezekiah was forced to pay tribute to the Assyrians.

Hezekiah (ii) (d. c. 1058) Babylonian exilarch and gaon. He served as exilarch from 1021. When **Hai Gaon** died in 1038 Hezekiah succeeded him as gaon and head of the academy at Pumbedita.

Higger, Michael (1898–1952) American talmudic scholar. He was born in Lithuania and emigated to the US in 1915. He served as consultant to the law committee of the Rabbinical Assembly of America. He edited minor treatises of the Talmud and compiled all of the baraitot and the non-Mishnaic tannaitic statements found in the Babylonian and the Palestinian Talmuds.

Hildesheimer, Azriel (1820–99) German rabbi, scholar and leader of Orthodox Jewry. Born in Halberstadt, he served as secretary to the community there. In 1851 he became rabbi of the Austro-Hungarian community of Eisenstadt, where he set up a yeshivah. In 1869 he became a rabbi in Berlin and he later established a rabbinical seminary there. Together with **Samson Raphael Hirsch**, he was a leader of the Orthodox Jewish community of Germany. He assisted the victims of Russian pogroms from 1882, and was a supporter of the Jews in Palestine. His publications include an edition of the Halakhot Gedolot.

Hildescheimer, Meier (1864–1934) German rabbi, son of **Azriel Hildesheimer**. From 1899 he was a preacher at the Adass Jisroel Synagogue in Berlin. Subsequently he became executive director of the rabbinical seminary founded in Berlin by his father. He represented Orthodox German Jewry in numerous Jewish organizations. He published several studies on Jewish subjects and edited a collection of some of his father's writings.

Hillel (fl. 1st cent. BCE) Palestinian rabbinic scholar. He was born in Babylonia and settled in Palestine, where he studied with **Shemaiah** and **Avtalyon**. He was later appointed president of the Sanhedrin. Together with **Shammai**, he was the last of the pairs (zugot) of scholars. He formulated seven hermeneutical rules for scriptural interpretation. He was the founder of the school known as Bet Hillel.

Hillel II (fl. 4th cent) Palestinian patriarch (nasi) (330–65). After the revolt of the Jews against the emperor Gallus in 351–2, the Roman government attempted to restrict the privileges of the nasi. Hillel II agreed to limit his authority. In 358 he published a system of intercalation to equalize the solar and lunar years.

Hillel ben Samuel (fl. 13th cent) Italian physician, talmudic scholar and philosopher. He lived in Rome, Naples and finally Capua, where he practised medicine. He played a major role in the controversies of 1289–90 concerning the philosophical writings of **Maimonides** whom he defended. His *Tagmule ha-Nephesh* explores the nature of the soul and the concept of reward and punishment in the hereafter.

Hiller, Ferdinand (1811–85) German composer. From 1828 to 1835 he was active as a music teacher and pianist in Paris. He subsequently converted to Christianity and held various positions in Germany and Italy. He founded the Conservatory of Cologne in 1850 which he directed. His compositions include the oratorios *The Destruction of Jerusalem*, *Saul and Rebecca*, and settings of the Psalms.

Hillesum, Etty (1914–43) Dutch writer. She was born in Middelburg. She was active in the left-wing, anti-Facist movement and in 1942 she began work at an office of the Jewish Council in Amsterdam. Later she was transferred to the Dutch transit camp, where she was assigned to care for people who were to go to extermination camps. She herself was killed in Auschwitz. Her letters describe life in the transit camp.

Hillman, Sidney (1887–1904) American labour leader, of Lithuanian origin. Born in Zagare, Lithuania, he studied at a yeshivah in Kovno. Later he was involved in revolutionary politics and imprisoned. He emigrated to England, and then New York and Chicago. He worked for a clothing factory and helped organize a strike. Later he became active as a union organizer. Eventually he became president of the Amalgamated Clothing Workers of America.

Hillquit, Morris (1869–1933) American socialist, of Latvian origin. Born in Riga, Latvia, he went to New York City in 1886. He helped organize the United Hebrew Trades, and later entered the Socialist Labour Party. He played an important role in the affairs of the Socialist Party of America. He wrote *Socialism in Theory and Practice.*

Himmelstein, Lena [Malsin, Lane Bryant] (1881–1951) American dress merchant. She was the daughter of an immmigrant family from Lithuania. She pioneered the design and sale of dresses first for pregnant women and then for outsize women. She developed the Lane Bryant chain throughout the US.

Hirsch, Emil Gustav (1851–1923) American rabbi and scholar. He was born in Luxembourg, and went to the US in 1866. He served as a rabbi in Baltimore and Louisville, and to the Chicago Sinai Congregation. He taught rabbinic literature and philosophy at the University of Chicago, and served as editor of the section on the Bible in the *Jewish Encyclopedia.* He was a spokesman for the radical wing of Reform Judaism.

Hirsch, Maurice de (1831–96) German financier and philanthropist. He was born in Munich, moved to Brussels in 1851, and later settled in Paris. In 1873 he made contributions to the Alliance Israélite Universelle to establish Jewish schools in Turkey, and in 1891 he set up the Jewish Colonization Association (ICA) to establish agricultural colonies in Argentina and elsewhere. He also founded the Hirsch Fund, the purpose of which was to open agricultural and crafts schools in Galicia, and the Baron de Hirsch Fund in New York for the technical and agricultural training of immigrants.

Hirsch, Samson Raphael (1808–88) German rabbi and writer. He was born in Hamburg. He served as a rabbi at Oldenburg and Emden, and as chief rabbi of Moravia (from 1846); from 1851 he was a rabbi in Frankfurt am Main. He was the founder of neo-Orthodoxy, which attempted to combine European culture with loyalty to traditional Judaism. His writings include *Nineteen Letters on Judaism* and *Horeb: Essays on Israel's Duties in the Diaspora.* He was the leader and a foremost exponent of Orthodoxy in Germany in the 19th century.

Hirsch, Samuel (1815–89) American Reform rabbi. He was born in Prussia. He served as a rabbi in Dessau and as chief rabbi of Luxembourg before emigrating to the US; there he became rabbi of the Reform congregation Keneseth Israel in Philadelphia. In his *Die Religionsphilosophie der Juden* he depicted Judaism as an evolving religious system.

Hirschbein, Peretz (1880–1948) American Yiddish dramatist and novelist. He was born in Poland and lived in Warsaw from 1904. His first drama *Miriam* is the story of a prostitute. In 1908 he organized a dramatic group in Odessa to produce Yiddish plays. From 1912 to 1917 he wrote a series of folk dramas, which were later staged at the New York Yiddish Art Theatre. He eventually settled in the US, where he wrote numerous works, including the Yiddish novel *Babylon,* describing Jewish life in America.

Hirschfeld, Georg (1873–1942) German playwright and novelist. Dissatisfied with a career in his father's factory in Berlin, he began to write plays. His *Die Mütter* depicts life among the Jewish bourgeoisie. A later play, *Agnes Jordan,* deals with Berlin Jewish society.

Hirschfeld, Hartwig (1854–1934) British orientalist. He was born in Thron, Prussia, and went to England in 1889. He first taught at Montefiore College in Ramsgate, then in 1901 became librarian and later professor of Semitic languages at Jews College, London. His publications include an edition of the *Kuzari* by **Judah ha-Levi**, a Hebrew translation of the *Book of Definitions* by **Isaac ben**

Solomon Israeli, studies of the Koran, and works on Arabic and Hebrew philology and bibliography.

Hirszenbeg, Samuel (1865–1908) Polish artist. He taught at the Bezalel School of Arts and Crafts in Jerusalem in his later years. His paintings were influenced by Jewish sentiment.

Ḥisda (c.217–309) Babylonian amora. He was born in Kafri. He became wealthy as a brewer in 294 and rebuilt the academy of Sura at his own expense. During the last ten years of his life he was the academy's head. Numerous aggadic sayings are attributed to him, many on the topic of health and hygiene. He and **Huna** were known as the pious men of Babylonia.

Ḥiyya (fl. 2nd cent.) Palestinian tanna. He was born in Babylonia. He studied with **Judah ha-Nasi** and became an important halakhist. He and his pupil **Hoshaiah** were responsible for a collection of baraitot.

Ḥiyya bar Abba (fl. 3rd–4th cent.) Palestinian amora. He was born in Babylonia and settled in Palestine, where he was the outstanding pupil of **Johanan**. He was appointed by Judah ha-Nasi II as his emissary to the diaspora.

Hobson, Laura (1900–1986) American novelist. She grew up in Long Island and studied at Cornell University. Her novels include *The Trespassers, Gentleman's Agreement, First Papers* and *Consenting Adult.*

Hod, Mordekhai (b. 1926) Israeli military leader. He was born in Deganyah. He became commander of the Isreli Air Force in 1966. He was in charge of the air strike at the beginning of the Six Day War in 1967 which destroyed the Egyptian, Jordanian and Syrian air forces.

Hoffmann, David (1843–1921) German biblical and talmudic scholar. He was born in Verbo. He taught at the Hildesheimer Rabbinical Seminary in Berlin, where he later became rector. He was regarded as the supreme halakhic authority of German Orthodox Jewry. In 1918 he was awarded the title 'professor' by the German government. He opposed the Reform movement and attacked the Wellhausen school of biblical criticism. His publications include commentaries on parts of the Pentateuch and an introduction to tannaitic midrashim.

Hofstadter, Robert (1915–90) American physicist. He was professor of physics at Stanford University. He studied the effects of bombarding atomic nuclei with electrons. He shared the Nobel Prize in Physics in 1961.

Hofsteyn, David (1889–1952) Ukrainian Yiddish poet. He wrote poems that acclaimed the achievements of the Communist Revolution of 1917. Later he protested against the banning of Hebrew and the persecution of Hebrew writers. He left the USSR but returned in 1926. When Israel became a state in 1948, he was an enthusiastic supporter; as a consequence he was arrested, transported to Siberia, and executed.

Holdheim, Samuel (1806–60) German Reform leader. He was born in Kempno near Posen. He served as a rabbi in Frankfurt an der Oder, Mecklenburg-Schwerin, and Berlin. He advocated radical reform at rabbinical conferences in Braunschweig (1844), Frankfurt am Main (1845), and Breslau (1846).

Homberg, Herz (1749–1841) Bohemian educationalist and leading figure of the Haskalah. He was born in Lieben near Prague. He served as tutor to **Moses Mendelssohn**'s son in 1779. In 1782 he moved to Vienna, and later in the 1780s taught at the Jewish school in Trieste. In 1787 he became superintendent of German-language schools in Galicia and assistant censor of Jewish books. He subsequently was censor of Hebrew books in Vienna. From 1814 he was government inspector of Jewish schools in Bohemia. He advocated the reform of Jewish education, the teaching of Hebrew grammar and German, and the purging of Jewish literature of superstition and hatred of the gentiles.

Hond, Meyer de (1882–1943) Dutch rabbi and author. He studied at the Rabbinical Seminary in Amsterdam and at the University of Amsterdam. Later he studied at the Rabbinical Seminary in Berlin and at the University of Würzburg. He worked as a religious teacher for young pupils and adults. In 1908 he founded the drama circle for the

Jewish working-class society 'Betsalel'. He wrote short stories about life in the Amsterdam Jewish quarter.

Ḥoni ha-Meaggel [Honi the Circle-Drawer]. (fl. 1st cent. BCE) Palestinian miracle worker. His name originated from his habit of drawing a circle around himself, which he refused to leave until hs prayer was granted. According to the Talmud, his prayers for rain were efficacious. During the war between **Aristobulus II** and **Hyrcanus II**, he was seized by the supporters of **Hyrcanus** and told to curse **Aristobulus** and his army; when Ḥoni ha-Meaggel refused to comply, he was stoned to death.

Hook, Sidney (1902–89) American philosopher. Born in Brooklyn, he studied at City College and at Columbia University. He taught at New York University and later at the New School for Social Research. His works include: *Pragmatism and the Tragic Sense of Life*, *John Dewey, an Intellectual*, *Common Sense and the Fifth Amendment* and *Out of Step*.

Hophni (fl. 11th cent. BCE) Israelite priest, son of **Eli**. The Bible describes Hophni and his brother **Phinehas** as following an evil way and they died in battle against the Philistines (I Samuel 2–4).

Hore-Belisha, Leslie (1898–1957) British politican. Of Spanish origin, he studied at Oxford and at the Sorbonne and Heidelburg. During World War I he served in the army in France and Greece. Later he was called to the bar and was elected to the House of Commons in 1923. He served as minister of transport from 1934. In 1937 he became minister of war. He was made a peer in 1954.

Ḥorin [Chorin], Aaron ben Kalman (1766–1844) Hungarian Reform leader. He was born in Hranice and became rabbi of Arad in 1789. In 1803 he published *Emek ha-Saveh*, which attacked those customs he believed had no basis in Judaism. He subsequently put his reforms into practice, and also endeavoured to improve the social and cultural status of Hungarian Jewry.

Horkheimer, Max (1895–1973) German sociologist. He was born in Stuttgart. He became professor of social philosophy at the University of Frankfurt am Main in 1930. He emigrated to Paris in 1933 and the following year went to the US. From 1945 to 1947 he served as chief research consultant to the American Jewish Committee. In 1948 he returned to Germany and re-established the Institut für Sozialforschung in Frankfurt, which had been closed under Nazi rule. After 1954 he taught at the University of Chicago.

Horodetzky, Shemuel Abba (1871–1957) Israeli scholar of Ḥasidism and Jewish mysticism. He was born in Malin. After going as a delegate to the eighth Zionist Congress in 1907, he remained in the West, living from 1908 to 1938 in Switzerland and Germany. In 1938 he settled in Tel Aviv. He published studies of mysticism, Ḥasidism, and the history of Polish Jewry, as well as biographies of medieval rabbis.

Horovitz, Bela (1898–1955) British publisher. He was born in Budapest. He set up the Phaidon Verlag in Vienna in 1923, then in 1938 transferred his publishing activities to London. In 1944 he founded the East and West Library, which published books of Jewish interest.

Horovitz, Israel (b. 1939) American playwright. He was born in Wakefield, Massachusetts. His plays include *Today, I am a Fountain Pen*, *A Rosen by Any Other Name* and *The Chopin Playoffs*.

Horovitz, Joseph (b. 1926) British composer, of Austrian origin. The son of **Bela Horovitz**, he was born in Vienna. He came to England with his family in 1938. He studied at New College, Oxford and the Royal College of Music. He began his career as a composer in London, and later was associate conductor of the Glyndebourne Opera. He taught composition at the Royal College of Music.

Horovitz, Leopold (?1837–1917) Hungarian painter. Born in Rozgony, Hungary, he specialized in portraiture. From the 1870s he started to produce scenes of Jewish life.

Horovitz, Marcus (1844–1910) German Orthodox rabbi, historian and halakhist. He was born in Hungary. He served as an Orthodox rabbi to the Frankfurt am Main general community after Reform had eliminated all Orthodox institutions.

His publications include *Frankfurter Rabbinen*, a study of the rabbis who served the Frankfurt community.

Horovitz, Saul (1859–1921) German talmudic scholar. He was born in Hungary. He became lecturer in religious philosophy and homiletics at the Breslau Rabbinical Seminary in 1896; later he served as religious tutor at the seminary. He wrote studies of Jewish and Islamic philosophy, and began to publish critical editions of the halakhic midrashim.

Horovitz, Vladimir (1904–89) Born in Kiev, he studied at the Kiev Conservatory. He made his debut at Kharkov, and gave a series of performances in various Russian cities. He settled in the US at the age of 24. He was one of the most distinguished pianists of his age, celebrated for his technical virtuosity. He was influenced by Toscanini whose daughter he married.

Horowitz, David (1899–1979) Israeli economist. He was born in Galicia and settled in Palestine in 1920. From 1935 to 1948 he was director of the Economic Department of the Jewish Agency. From 1948 to 1952 he served as director general of the ministry of finance. After he left his ministry post he worked to establish the Bank of Israel, of which he became the first governor in 1954. He published studies of economics and finance.

Horowitz, Eleazar (1803–68) Austrian rabbi. He was born in Bavaria. He officiated as rabbi in Vienna from 1828. He engaged in disputes with anti-Semites and successfully advocated the abolition of the Jewish Oath. He contributed to Hebrew periodicals.

Horowitz, Isaiah (c. 1565–1630) Scholar and kabbalist. He was born in Prague. He became av bet din of Dubno in 1600, and av bet din and head of the yeshivah of Ostraha in 1602. He later served as av bet din of Frankfurt am Main and rabbi of Prague. After the death of his wife, he settled in Jerusalem, where he became the rabbi of the Ashkenazi community. His *Two Tablets of the Convenant* is a study of Jewish laws and customs influenced by the kabbalah. He was known as 'Sheloah' a name derived from the title of this work (*Shene Luḥot ha-Berit*).

Horowitz, Jacob Isaac [Rabbi of Lublin] (fl. 18th–19th cent.) Polish Ḥasidic rabbi. Originally from Galicia, he moved to Lublin at the turn of the century. He was believed by the Ḥasidim to be possessed of the Holy Spirit and was referred to as 'Ha-Hozeh' (the seer). He published studies of the Bible, stressing the importance of the tzaddik.

Horowitz, Leopold (1839–1917) Slavokian painter. He lived in Warsaw from 1869 to 1893, and then in Vienna. He painted the Austrian royal family as well as scenes from Jewish life.

Horowitz, Moses ha-Levi (1844–1910) American Yiddish playwright. He organized a Yiddish company in 1878, which performed plays throughout Europe. In 1886 he settled in New York, where he wrote for the Yiddish stage. He introduced operetta into the repertory of the American Yiddish theatre.

Horowitz, Phinehas (1730–1805) German rabbi. He was born in Czortkow, Poland, and served as a rabbi in Witkowo and Lachowicze. In 1771 he became a rabbi in Frankfurt am Main. He was an opponent of the Haskalah movement and criticized **Moses Mendelssohn**'s German translation of the Pentateuch and its commentary. His *Haphlaah* consists of novellae on parts of the Talmud.

Hos, Dov (1894–1940) Labour leader in Palestine. He was born in Belorussia and emigrated to Palestine in 1906. At the beginning of World War I he was a founder of the Jaffa Group, which promoted military training. In 1919 he joined the Aḥdut ha-Avodah Party and became a member of its executive committee. He was also active in the Histadrut and the Haganah. From 1935 to 1940 he served as deputy mayor of Tel Aviv.

Hosea (fl. 8th cent. BCE) Israelite prophet. He exhorted the Israelite nation to concentrate on religious and moral reform rather than dabble in international politics. Nonetheless he adopted a compassionate stance, using his own matrimonial difficulties as a symbol for God's love for his wayward people.

Hoshaiah (fl. c. 200) Palestinian amora. He was the head of an academy at Sepphoris. He was a noted halakhist and aggadist.

Hoshea (fl. 8th cent. BCE) King of Israel (732–724). He was the last king of Israel. He secured the throne after his revolt against Pekah (II Kings 15:30). He later rebelled against Assyria and was imprisoned by Shalmaneser IV, who then captured Samaria (II Kings 17:1–6).

Houdini, Harry [Weiss, Ehrich] (1874–1926) American magician. He was the son of a religious leader from Budapest. He began his career as a trapeze artist and magician. He later attained fame as an escapologist.

Howard, Leslie (1893–1943) British actor. The son of a Hungarian father, he was born in London. He initially worked as a bank clerk. Obtaining a commission in the Twentieth Hussars, he was sent to France. In 1917 he was invalided out of the army. He then embarked on a stage career, and founded Minerva Films with Adrian Brunel. In the 1930s he appeared in numerous films including *Of Human Bondage*, *Intermezzo*, *The Petrified Forest* and *Gone with the Wind.*

Howard, Michael (b. 1941) Born in Wales, he studied at Cambridge University. He served as an MP for Folkestone and Hythe, later becoming a cabinet minister, and leader of the Tory party.

Howe, Irving (1920–2000) American literary and social critic. He was born in New York and taught English literature at Brandeis University and Hunter College. He wrote studies of English and American novelists and Yiddish literature. His works include *A Treasury of Yiddish Stories* and *A Treasury of Yiddish Poetry.*

Huberman, Bronislaw (1882–1947) Israeli violinist, of Polish origin, he began performing at the age of ten. After World War I, he became active in the Pan-European movement. With the rise of Facism in Europe, he turned his energy to Palestine: he conceived of a comprehensive institute of music, at the centre of which would be a symphony orchestra, a professional school of music, and additional ensembles. In the 1930s he concentrated on founding the Palestine Philharmonic Orchestra.

Hübsch, Adolph (1830–84) American rabbi and orientalist. He was born in Liptó-Szentmiklós in Hungary and served as a rabbi in Miawa and Prague. In 1886 he was appointed head of Congregation Ahawath Chesed in New York. He published an edition of the Syriac Peshitta on the Five Scrolls.

Huldah (fl. 7th cent. BCE) Israelite prophetess. She is the only prophetess mentioned in the biblical account of the period of the monarchy (II Kings 22:14–20). She prophesied God's judgement on the nation after **Josiah**'s death.

Huna (d. c. 297) Babylonian amora. He became a leading authority in his time and served as the head of the academy at Sura from 256.

Hurok, Sol (1888–1974) American impresario, of Russian origin. He arrived in New York at the age of 16. He became the leading American impresario for foreign cultural productions, particularly in the field of ballet.

Hurst, Fannie (1889–1968) American author. Born in Hamilton, Ohio, she became widely acclaimed as a short-story writer and then as a novelist. Her works include *A President Is Born*, *Back Street*, *Any Woman.*

Hurwitz, Henry (1886–1961) American editor and Jewish educationalist. Born in Lithuania, he went to the US at the age of five. In 1906, he organized the Harvard Menorah Society, and in 1913 established the Intercollegiate Menorah Association of which he was president and chancellor. In 1915 he founded the *Menorah Journal*, a magazine of Jewish opinion.

Hurwitz, Saul Israel (1860–1922) Russian Hebrew author. He was born in Uvarovichi and became a merchant and banker. He moved to Berlin after the 1905 revolution, but having returned to Russia in 1914 he lost his fortune in the Communist Revolution of 1917. Eventually he moved back to Berlin, where he became a prominent figure among emigré Hebrew writers. With **Ḥayyim Naḥum Bialik**, he directed the Kelal Publishing House. He contributed stories and articles to Hebrew journals and established his own periodical, *He-Atid.*

Ḥushi, Abba (1898–1969) Israeli labour leader. He was born in Galicia and emigrated to Palestine in

1920. He served as secretary of the Haifa Labour Council (1938–51), as Mapai member of the Knesset (1949–51), and as Mayor of Haifa (1951–69).

Ḥushiel ben Elhanan (fl. 10th–11th cent.) North African talmudist. He was head of the academy of Kairouan. According to tradition, he was one of the four shipwrecked scholars from Bari who were ransomed in various communities. He developed new methods of study, stressing the importance of the Palestinian Talmud and the halakhic midrashim.

Husik, Isaac (1876–1939) American historian of Jewish philosophy. He was born in Russia and moved to Philadelphia in 1888. From 1898 to 1916 he taught at Gratz College in Philadelphia, later becoming professor of philosophy at the University of Pennsylvania. His publications include *A History of Medieval Jewish Philosophy.*

Husserl, Edmund (1859–1938) German philosopher. Born in Prossnitz, Moravia, he studied at the universities of Leipzig, Berlin and Vienna. He converted to Protestantism. He taught at the University of Halle, and then at the universities of Göttingen and Freiburg. His writings have been published in 11 volumes.

Hyamson, Albert Montefiore (1875–1954) English administrator. From 1917 to 1919 he edited the *Zionist Review.* He served as chief immigration officer in Palestine under the British Mandate, returning to England in 1934. He was president of the Jewish Historical Society of England from 1945 to 1947. He published studies of Palestine and Zionism as well as a history of the Jews of England.

Hyamson, Moses (1862–1949) American rabbi and scholar. Born in Lithuania, he was taken to England at the age of five. He served as a rabbi in England, Wales and the US. He taught the codes of Jewish law at the Jewish Theological Seminary of America from 1915 to 1940. His writings include translations of **Maimonides**' *Mishneh Torah* and **Bahya ibn Pakuda**'s *Duties of the Heart.*

Hyrcanus II (fl. 1st cent. BCE) Judean high priest and ethnarch, elder son of **Alexander Yannai** and **Salome Alexandra**. He succeeded his mother to the Judean throne but was driven out and had the high priesthood wrested from him by his brother **Aristobulus II**. With the help of **Antipater**, he resolved to overcome **Aristobulus**. The brothers appealed for arbitration to Pompey, who preferred Hyrcanus. After conquering **Aristobulus** and his supporters, Pompey apointed Hyrcanus high priest with limited political authority. Following Pompey's death Hyrcanus supported Julius Caesar, who elevated him to the position of ethnarch. When Judea was invaded by the Parthians, he was taken captive. He subsequently returned to Judea, where he was accused of treason by **Herod** the Great and executed.

Apparition of the angels to Abraham, fresco, TIEPOLO, Giambattista: 1696–1770

Abraham

Westminster Psalter English Manuscript c.1175

King David

Maimonides

Benedict Spinoza

Benjamin Disraeli

Sarah Bernhardt

Karl Marx

Henri-Louis Bergson

Sigmund Freud

Theodor Herzl

Niels Bohr

Martin Buber

Leo Baeck

© David Rubinger/CORBIS

David Ben-Gurion

© Bettmann/CORBIS

Marc Chagall

© Bettmann/CORBIS

Irving Berlin

© The Art Archive / Culver Pictures

Anne Frank

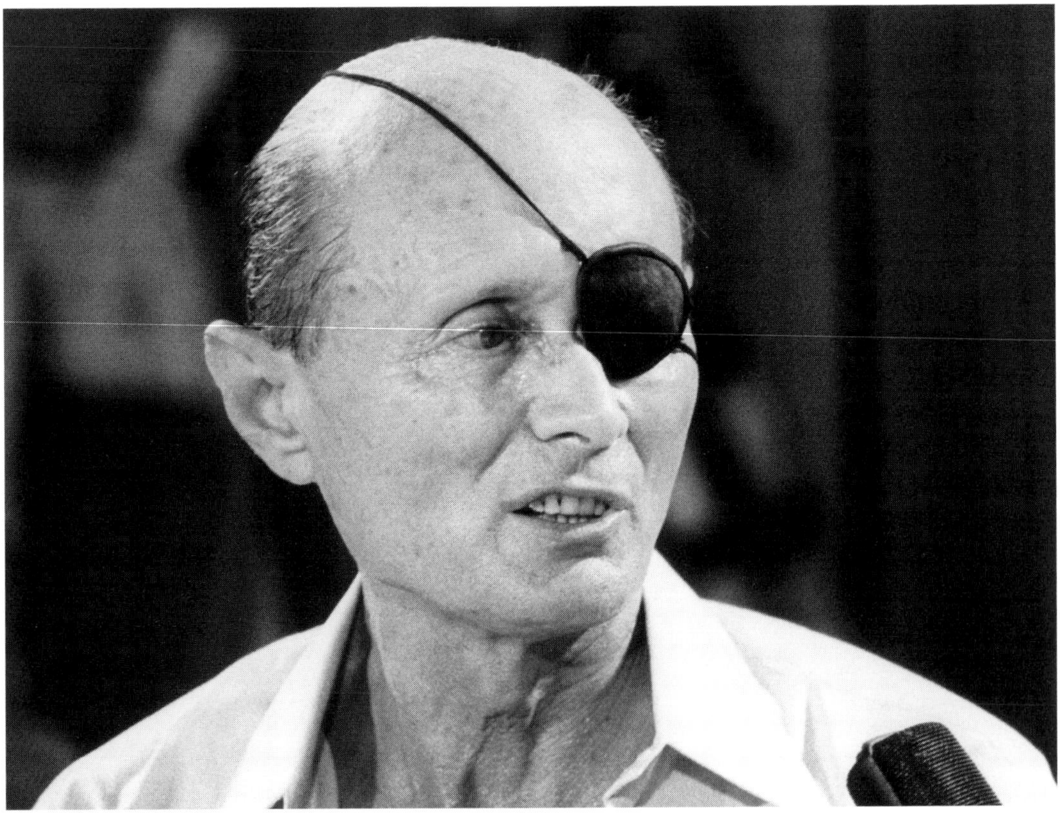

Moshe Dayan

Leonard Bernstein

I

Ibn Abitur, Joseph ben Isaac (fl. 10th–11th cent.) Spanish scholar. After **Moses ben Enoch**'s death in Córdoba, his place as rabbi and head of the yeshivah there was taken by his son Enoch. Ibn Arbitur attempted to displace Enoch, causing a split in the community. He was forced into exile and travelled to North Africa, Pumbedita and Damascus. He wrote an Arabic commentary on the Talmud, a Hebrew commentary on the Psalms, and liturgical poetry.

Ibn Aknin, Joseph ben Judah (1150–1220) North African philosopher and poet. He was born in Barcelona and moved to North Africa, where he lived as a crypto-Jew. He wrote studies of Jewish law and philosophy. He should not be confused with **Maimonides**' disciple Joseph ben Judah ibn Shimon who is also referred to as Ibn Aknin.

Ibn Balam, Judah ben Samuel [Judah ibn Balam] (fl. 11th cent.) Spanish biblical commentator and Hebrew grammarian. He was born in Toledo and lived in Seville. He wrote biblical commentaries, a study of the stylistic devices in the Bible, and works on Hebrew verbs and particles.

Ibn Barun, Isaac ben Joseph (fl. 11th–12th cent.) Spanish Hebrew grammarian and lexicographer. He lived in Zaragosa and Malaga. He wrote Hebrew poetry, and developed the comparative lingusitic studies begun by **Judah ibn Kuraish**, **Dunash ben Tamim** and **Jonah ibn Janaḥ**.

Ibn Daud, Abraham (c. 1110–80) Spanish historian, philosopher, physician and astronomer. He was born in Cordoba and settled in Toledo. His *Emunah Ramah* (Sublime Faith) is a philosophical treatise based on Aristotelian principles. In this work he explores central problems connected with God, the soul, prophecy and creation, and free will. His *Sepher ha-Kabbalah* (Book of Tradition) relates the history of talmudic scholarship to his own day.

Ibn Ezra, Abraham (1089–1164) Spanish poet, grammarian, biblical commentator, philosopher, astronomer and physician. Born in Toledo, he lived in Spain and later journeyed to Italy, France, England and Palestine. He wrote poetry, Bible commentaries, grammatical works, philosophy and astronomical studies.

Ibn Ezra, Moses (b.c. 1055–after 1135) Spanish Hebrew poet and philosopher. He was born in Granada and became a friend of **Judah ha-Levi**. After the Almoravides captured Granada in 1090, he led a wandering life. He wrote poetry, an examination of the methodology and meter of Hebrew and Arabic poetry, an Arabic philosophical work based on Neoplatonism, and penitential prayers.

Ibn Gabirol, Solomon [Gabirol] (c. 1021–c. 1056) Spanish poet and philosopher. He was born in Zaragoza. He wrote secular and religious poetry and philosophical studies. His poem *Keter Malkhut* (Crown of Divine Kingship) has been incorporated into the liturgy. Two of his philosophical works have survived: *Mekor Ḥayyim* (Source of Life) and *Tikkun Middot ha-Nephesh* (Improvement of the Moral Qualities). His philosophical investigations are based on Neoplatonic principles.

Ibn Ḥasan, Jekuthiel ben Isaac (d. 1039) Spanish statesman and philanthropist. He served as vizier in the Muslim state of Zaragoza. He was a patron of **Solomon ibn Gabirol**, who wrote three dirges in his memory after he had been deposed and executed.

Ibn Ḥasdai, Abraham ben Samuel ha-Levi [Abraham ben Samuel Ḥasdai; Abraham ben Ḥasdai ha-Levi; Abraham ibn Ḥasdai; Ḥasdai] (fl. 13th cent.) Spanish translator and Hebrew poet. He lived in Barcelona. He translated numberous Arabic works into Hebrew, and was an ardent defender of **Maimonides**.

Ibn Ḥaviv, Jacob [Ḥabib] (?1445–1515/16) Spanish rabbinic scholar. He was born in Zamora in Castile, and became head of a yeshivah in Salamanca. When the Jews were expelled from Spain in 1492, he went to Portugal and later settled in Salonica, where he was one of the leading scholars. His *En Yaakov* is a compilation of aggadic sections of the Palestinian and Babylonian Talmuds.

Ibn Ḥaviv, Levi (c. 1480–1545) Palestinian rabbinic scholar, son of **Jacob ibn Ḥaviv**. He lived in Salonica. He completed his father's talmudic compilation, *En Yaakov*. Later he moved to Palestine, where he became chief rabbi in Jerusalem. He was an opponent of **Jacob Berab**'s plan to revive rabbinic ordination.

Ibn Janaḥ, Jonah (fl. 11th cent.) Spanish Hebrew grammarian and lexicographer. Born in Córdoba, he settled in Zaragoza where he was a physician. He wrote studies of biblical exegesis and Hebrew philology. His *Sepher ha-Dikduk* includes a list of roots of Hebrew words, interpreted in the light of biblical and rabbinic literature and compared with other Semitic languages. It was translated from Arabic into Hebrew by **Judah ibn Tibbon**.

Ibn Killis, Yakub ben Yusuf (930–91) Egyptian statesman. He was born in Baghdad and first settled in Palestine. Later he went to Egypt and converted to Islam. He served several caliphs, and as vizier reorganized the administrative system of the Fatimid caliphate.

Ibn Kuraish, Judah (fl. 10th cent.) North African philologist. He was born in Morocco and became a physician. He wrote an Arabic letter to the Jewish community in Fez, protesting against the elimination of the recitation of the Aramaic Targum. In this letter he laid the foundation for a method which was later of considerable help in solving problems of biblical vocabulary.

Ibn Latif, Isaac ben Abraham (c. 1220–90) Spanish philosopher, kabbalist and physician. He spent the latter part of his life in Palestine. He established a new method of kabbalah based on Aristotelian philosophy and natural science. He also used a kabbalistic terminology derived from philosophy and mathematics.

Ibn Migas, Joseph ben Meir ha-Levi (1077–1141) Spanish talmudic scholar. He served as the head of a yeshivah in Lucena, as a successor to **Isaac Alfasi**. He wrote novellae to the Talmud and numerous responsa.

Ibn Polegar, Isaac ben Joseph [Ibn Pulgar; Ibn Pulkar] (fl. 14th cent.) Spanish theologian. He wrote a polemical reply to the anti-Jewish tract, *Minḥat Kenaot*, written by the convert **Abner of Burgos**. This work, *Ezer ha-Dat*, attempts to reconcile faith and philosophical reason.

Ibn Sahulah, Isaac ben Solomon (fl. 13th cent.) Spanish Hebrew writer. He worked as a physician at Guadalajara. He wrote a kabbalistic commentary on the Song of Songs, and a book of fables, *Meshal ha-Kadmoni* (Easterner's Parable).

Ibn Shaprut, Ḥasdai [Shaprut] (c. 915–c. 970) Spanish statesman and physician. He served at the courts of the caliphs Abder-Raḥman III and Ḥakam II at Córdoba, and was employed on various foreign missions. He supported Jewish scholars and scholarship and defended Jewish communities. He wrote a well-known letter to the king of the Khazars expressing his joy at their independent Jewish kingdom. His scholarly activities included collaboration in translating a work of Dioscorides into Arabic.

Ibn Shaprut, Shemtov ben Isaac [Shaprut] (fl. 14th–15th cent.) Spanish scholar and physician. In 1375 he conducted a disputation in Pamplona with the future Pope Benedict XIII. He wrote a polemical work to combat apostasy (*Even Boḥan*), a commentary on Avicenna, a supercommentary to **Abraham ibn Ezra**'s Bible commentary, and a philosophical explanation of talmudic aggadah.

Ibn Shemtov, Joseph ben Shemtov (c. 1400–c. 1460) Spanish philosopher. He served in the Castilian court of King John II and his successor Henry IV. In 1452 he was sent to Segovia to suppress an anti-Semitic movement. Later he wandered around the country giving lectures. His *Kevod Elohim* is a theological study which seeks to find a compromise between **Maimonides** and the anti-philosophical views of contemporary Jewish scholars.

Ibn Shemtov, Shemtov (c. 1380–c. 1441) Spanish kabbalist. In *Sepher ha-Emunot* he criticized rationalists from **Abraham ibn Ezra** through **Levi ben Gershom** and **Isaac Albalag**. He was sharply opposed to the views of **Maimonides** and was particularly incensed by his *Guide for the Perplexed*.

Ibn Tibbon, Jacob [Don Profiat] (c. 1230–1312) French astronomer, physician, writer and translator. He was born in Marseilles and lived at Montpellier, where he taught medicine at the university. He translated Euclid, Averroes and Al Ghazzali from Arabic into Hebrew. In addition he produced astronomical tables, which were translated into Latin and used by Dante for his *Divine Comedy*. He was a defender of **Maimonides**.

Ibn Tibbon, Judah ben Saul [Tibbon] (c. 1120–after 1190) Spanish physician and translator. Born in Granada, he settled in Lunel, France. He translated such Jewish works as **Saadyah Gaon**'s *Beliefs and Opinions*, **Baḥya ibn Pakuda**'s *Duties of the Heart*, and **Judah ha-Levi**'s *Kuzari* from Arabic into Hebrew.

Ibn Tibbon, Moses ben Samuel [Tibbon] (d. c. 1283) French writer and translator. He lived in Marseilles, where he practised medicine. He translated philosophical and scientific works from Arabic into Hebrew, and also wrote commentaries on the Bible and rabbinical studies.

Ibn Tibbon, Samuel ben Judah [Tibbon] (c. 1150–c. 1230) French translator, scholar and physician. After travelling widely, he settled in Marseilles. He translated **Maimonides**' *Guide for the Perplexed* from Arabic into Hebrew in collaboration with the author. He also translated other writings of **Maimonides** and wrote philosophical commentaries on the Bible.

Ibn Tzaddik, Joseph ben Jacob (c. 1075–c. 1149) Spanish philosopher and poet. From 1138 he served as a dayyan at Córdoba. His philosophical study *Olam Katon* explores cosmology, the nature of man, and his relation to the external world. This work was influenced by Neoplatonism and Aristotelian concepts.

Ibn Verga, Joseph (d. c. 1559) Turkish scholar, son of **Solomon ibn Verga**. When the Jews were expelled from Spain in 1492, he fled to Lisbon with his father. Later he emigrated to Turkey, where he served as a rabbi and dayyan in Adrianople. He published his father's *Shevet Yehudah*, a collection of narratives describing persecutions and disputations, together with supplementary material. He also wrote a study of talmudic principles.

Ibn Verga, Solomon (fl. 15th–16th cent.) Spanish historiographer. After the conquest of Malaga in 1487, he was sent by Spanish Jewish communities to raise funds for ransoming Jews captured there. When the Jews were expelled from Spain in 1492, he settled in Lisbon. From 1497 he was compelled to live as a Converso, but he later emigrated to Italy. His *Shevet Yehudah* is a narrative describing the persecution of the Jews from the destruction of the Second Temple until his own time. It was published with additions by his son **Joseph ibn Verga**.

Ibn Yaḥia, David ben Joseph [Yaḥia] (1465–1543) Portuguese rabbi, grammarian and philosopher. Born in Lisbon, he became a leader of Portuguese Jewry, and an adviser to the kings of Portugal. In 1525 he was appointed rabbi of Naples. After the Jews were expelled from Naples in 1540 he settled in Imola. He wrote studies of grammar and philosophy as well as poetry.

Ibn Yaḥia, David ben Solomon (c. 1440–1524) Portuguese biblical commentator and grammarian. He was born in Lisbon and served as a rabbi there. Later he lived in Naples and Constantinople. He wrote biblical commentaries, grammatical and legal studies, and a commentary on **Maimonides**' *Guide for the Perplexed.*

Ibn Yaḥia, Gedaliah ben Joseph (1515–87) Italian historiographer and talmudist. He was born in Imola and lived in various cities in Italy before settling in Alexandria. His *Shalshelet ha-Kabbalah* consists of a history of the Jewish people, scientific tractates and a chronicle of events from creation to the 16th century.

Ibn Yaḥia, Jacob Tam (d. 1542) Portuguese scholar and physician, son of **David ben Solomon ibn Yaḥia**. He served as a rabbi and as court physician in Constantinople. He was the author of numerous responsa and completed *Tehillah le-David,* a study of the principles of Judaism begun by his father.

Ibn Yaḥia, Joseph (1494–1534) Italian biblical commentator and philosopher. He was born in Florence and moved with his family to Imola. He wrote biblical commentaries, a commentary on talmudic sayings, and studies of eschatology and the commandments.

Ibn Yaish, Solomon [Abenaes] (d. 1603) Turkish statesman and merchant. Born a Portuguese marrano, he reverted to Judaism in Turkey. He later became Duke of Mytilene and was the organizer of the Anglo-Turkish alliance against Spain.

Ibn Zabara [Zabara], Joseph (c. 1140–c .1200) Spanish Hebrew poet. He was born in Barcelona and worked as a physician there. His *Sepher Shaashuim* (Book of Amusements) contains a literary account of his journey to several countries, together with stories and proverbs.

Ibn Zeraḥ, Menaḥem (d. 1385) Spanish codifier. He was injured in the attack on the Jews of Navarre in 1328, and afterwards settled in Toledo. His *Tzedah la-Derekh* is a handbook of essential Jewish laws for the use of Jews at the royal court.

Ichabod (fl. 11th cent. BCE) Israelite, son of **Phinehas** and grandson of **Eli. Phinehas**' wife was in labour when news reached her of the capture of the Ark by the Philistines and the death of **Phinehas**, his brother **Hophni** and **Eli**. She died in childbirth after naming her son Ichabod, which means 'there is no glory' (I Samuel 4:10–22).

Idel, Moshe (b. 1944) Israeli scholar of Romanian origin. Born in Targu Neamt, Romania, he emigrated to Israel in 1963. He served as professor of Jewish Thought at the Hebrew University and as a visiting professor at Yale, Harvard and Princeton. His works include *Kabbalah: New Perspectives and Messianic Mystics, Hassidism: Between Ecstasy and Magic* and *From Midrash to Kabalah.*

Idelsohn, Abraham Zvi (1882–1938) American musicologist, of Lithuanian origin. He served as cantor in Leipzig, Regensburg and Johannesburg, and later settled in Jerusalem. There he worked as a cantor and music teacher at the Hebrew Teachers' College. He later became professor of Jewish music at the Hebrew Union College in Cincinnati. He was the founder of modern Jewish musicology and one of the pioneers of ethnomusicology. His publications include a *Thesaurus of Hebrew Oriental Melodies, Jewish Music in its Historical Development* and *Jewish Liturgy.*

Ignatov, David (1885–1954) American Yiddish author. He was born in the Ukraine and was active in the revolutionary movement in Kiev in 1903–6 before he emigrated to the US. He was one of the founders of the eastern European literary group Di Yunge, and edited various literary journals. He was one of the creators of the modern Yiddish novel and also reworked Ḥasidic tales and medieval Jewish fables. His stories describe the lives of Jewish workers in the US.

Ikor, Roger (1912–86) French novelist. He was born in Paris and became a teacher there. His novel *The Sons of Avrom* is a depiction of Jewish immigrant life in Paris during the early decades of the 20th century.

Ikriti, Shemariah (1275–1355) Italian philosopher and biblical commentator. He was brought up in Crete and spent most of his life in Italy. In 1352 he went to Spain on an unsuccessful mission to reconcile Karaites and Rabbinites; he was accused of messianic pretentions and died in prison. His works include a philosophical commentary on the Bible, a cosmological polemic, and a study of talmudic legends.

Imber, Naphtali Herz (1856–1909) American Hebrew poet. He was born in Galicia and went to Palestine in 1882, where he served as secretary and adviser on Jewish affairs to Laurence Oliphant (1882–8). He then returned to Europe and wandered as far as India, where he was wooed by missionaries; he was later accused of converting to Christianity. In 1892 he went to the US. His first volume of poems contained *Tekvatenu* which as *Ha-Tikvah* became the anthem of the Zionist movement and ultimately the Israeli national anthem.

Imber, Shmuel-Yankev (1889–1942) Yiddish poet, of Galician origin. He studied in Lemberg, and in 1912 emigrated to Palestine. In 1918 he went to Vienna, visited the US, but returned to live in Lemberg and Kraków. He was murdered in 1942. He was an innovator in Yiddish poetry. He wrote poems of longing for Palestine, and was also a polemicist against anti-Semitism.

Immanuel ben Solomon of Rome (c. 1261–after 1328) Italian poet and rabbinic commentator. He was born in Rome and lived in various cities in Italy. He wrote philosophical commentaries on the Bible, poetry and hymns; he introduced Spanish metrical forms into Italy and the sonnet form into Hebrew. His *Maḥberot Immanuel* contains poems on love, wine and friendship, riddles, epigrams, epistles, elegies, religious poems, and an account of a journey through Hell and Paradise. The piyyut *Yigdal*, which is included in the daily prayerbook, is an adaptation of one of his poems in this work.

Imma Shalom (fl. 1st–2nd cent.) Palestinian woman, wife of **Eliezer ben Hyrcanus** and sister of Rabban **Gamaliel II**. She was praised for her learning and religious devotion. She is one of the few women mentioned in talmudic literature.

Ionesco, Eugène (1912–94) Romanian-French playwright. He achieved fame with a series of plays which mocked bourgeois life and the fascist tendencies of his background. He was influenced by **Franz Kafka** and is viewed as the father of the Theatre of the Absurd.

Isaac (i) (fl.? 19th–16th cent. BCE) Israelite, son of **Abraham** and **Sarah**. He was born when **Abraham** was 100 years old (Genesis 21:5). He was the heir of the Abrahamic tradition and covenant (Genesis 17:19; 21:12). In order to test him, God ordered **Abraham** to sacrifice Isaac, but the boy was saved at the final moment (Genesis 22). Isaac married **Rebekah**, who bore him two sons, **Esau** and **Jacob**.

Isaac (ii) (fl. 8th–9th cent.) Jewish merchant of Aachen. In 797 he was appointed by Charlemagne as guide and interpreter to an official delegation to Harun al-Rashid. When Charlemagne's ambassadors died on the way, Isaac completed the journey and was received by Charlemagne in audience when he returned after four years.

Isaac, Jules (1877–1963) French historian. He was born in Rennes. His *Cours d'histoire* served as a textbook in French schools and colleges. In 1936 he was appointed inspector-general of education for France. After his family was killed by the Nazis, he wrote about the Christian roots of anti-Semitism in *Jésus et Israel* and *Genèse de l'antisémitisme.*

Isaac ben Abba Mari (?1120–?1190) Franco-Spanish rabbinic scholar. Active in Provence and Spain, he corresponded with the important scholars of his generation. His *Sepher ha-Ittur* is a compilation of the main halakhic laws that have practical application. It was regarded as the authoritative code until the appearance of **Jacob ben Asher**'s *Tur*, which superseded it.

Issac ben Joseph of Corbeil [Baal ha-Ḥotem] (fl. 13th cent.) French codifier. His *Sepher Mitzvot Katan* contains a compendium of halakhah, together with ethical homilies, parables and aggadot. This work, known from its initials as *Semak*, received recognition from scholars in France and Germany.

Isaac ben Meir of Düren (fl. 14th cent.) German codifier. His *Sepher Shearim* (also known as *Sharre Dura* or *Issur ve-Hetter*) served as the authoritative code for dietary laws until the publication of the Shulḥan Arukh.

Isaac ben Moses of Vienna [Isaac Or Zarua] (c. 1180–c.1250) Bohemian halakhic authority. He became known as Isaac Or Zarua from the title of his halakhic work *Or Zarua*. This study is arranged on the basis of the Talmud, and contains commentaries on talmudic subjects, together with earlier codifications and responsa. It also includes material about medieval Jewish life in Germany, France and Italy.

Isaac ben Samuel of Acre (fl. 13th–14th cent.) Spanish kabbalist. In 1291 he left Acre for Italy, and then went to Spain, where he met **Moses de Leon**. His publications include a commentary on **Nahmanides**' mysticism, a mystical diary, a commentary on the Sepher Yetzirah, and a study of the composition of the Zohar.

Isaac ben Samuel of Dampierre (d. c. 1185) French tosaphist. He lived in Ramerupt, assisting his teacher and uncle, **Jacob Tam**. Later he settled in Dampierre. Together with **Jacob Tam**, he was a central figure in the activity of the tosaphists.

Isaac ben Sheshet Perfet [Ribash] (1326–1408) Spanish rabbi and halakhic authority. He was born in Barcelona. After the persecution of the Jews in 1391, he left Spain and settled in Algiers, where he served as a rabbi. He wrote numerous responsa, which exercised considerable influence on later halakhah and contain information about popular customs in Spain and North Africa. He also wrote commentaries on talmudic tractates and the Pentateuch, as well as poetry.

Isaacs, Abraham Samuel (1852–1920) American rabbi, writer and educator. He taught Hebrew and German at New York University between 1885 and 1906. He served as a preacher at the East 86th Street Synagogue in New York and rabbi of the B'nai Jeshurun Congregation in Patterson, New Jersey. In 1878 he became editor of the *Jewish Messenger* and continued in that post until the journal merged with the *American Hebrew* in 1903. His publications include *A Modern Hebrew Poet: The Life and Writings of Moses Chaim Luzzatto* and *What is Judaism?*

Isaacs, Isaac (1855–1948) Australian governor-general. Born in Melbourne, he worked as a teacher in local schools, and later studied law at Melbourne University. He initially worked as a lawyer, later serving as a member of the Victorian leglislative assembly. He was solicitor-general and attorney-general. Subsequently he was a justice of the federal high court, becoming chief justice. In 1931 he was appointed governor-general of Australia.

Isaacs, Nathaniel (1808–c. 1860) South African explorer, of English origin. Born in England, he went to St Helena at the age of 14 to work for his uncle. He later spent several years among the Zulu tribes in Natal, exporing, trading and teaching the Africans basic agricultural techniques. His works include *Travels and Adventures in Eastern Africa.*

Isaacs, Rufus (1860–1935) British lawyer. He was the son of a London fruit merchant. He went into the stock market, but later studied law and became a barrister. In 1904 he was elected to parliament; in 1910 he became attorney-general and was knighted and subsequently made a peer. During World War I he secured a war loan from the US and served as a link between the prime minister and President Wilson. He served as special ambassador to Washington. He later became viceroy of India.

Isaacs, Samuel Myer (1804–78) Preacher and communal leader. He was born in the Netherlands and first settled in London, where he served as principal of an orphan asylum. He emigrated to the US in 1839. He was the first cantor and preacher of Congregation B'nai Jeshurun in New York. Later he became rabbi of Congregation Shaarei Tefila. He founded the first English-language Jewish weekly in the US, *The Jewish Messenger*, which supported the abolition of slavery and opposed Reform Judaism. In 1859 he was one of the organizers of the Board of Delegates of American Israelites, which advocated Jewish civil and religious rights.

Isaac the Blind (fl. 12th–13th cent.) Franco-Spanish kabbalist, son of **Abraham ben David of Posquières**. He was one of the earliest kabbalists in Provence and Spain. He transmitted his teachings orally and wrote a commentary on the Sepher Yetzirah. He has been referred to as the 'father of kabbalah'.

Isaiah (fl. 8th cent. BCE) Israelite prophet. He prophesied in Jerusalem from the death of **Uzziah** until the middle of **Hezekiah**'s reign (740–701 BCE). He protested against unrighteousness and demanded justice for the poor and downtrodden. He opposed all treaties with neighbouring states and insisted that the people should put their trust in God. He proclaimed that the nation would be punished through Assyrian conquest and domination, but that a remnant of the people would return and continue the covenant. Most scholars believe the book of Isaiah should be divided into two sections (1–39; 40–66); they are believed to have been written by different authors: Isaiah and Second Isaiah.

Isak, Aron (1730–1816) Founder of the Swedish Jewish community. Born in Germany, he was a peddler but taught himself seal-engraving. He went to Sweden, and brought his brother and partner to Stockholm there. Later other Jews began to settle in Sweden, and he served as head of the Jewish community.

Ish-bosheth [Eshbaal] (fl. 11th cent. BCE) Israelite prince, son of **Saul**. After **Saul** and his other sons died in battle, Ish-bosheth was proclaimed king by **Saul**'s general, **Abner** (II Samuel 2:8–9). Abner led the war against **David** (II Samuel 2:12–17; 3:6), but eventually abandoned Ish-bosheth. According to II Samuel 4, Ish-bosheth was murdered by Rechab and Baanah.

Ishmael (fl.? 19th–16th cent. BCE) Israelite, son of **Abraham** and Hagar. After Hagar conceived, she was treated harshly by **Sarah**; she fled to the wilderness, but eventually returned. After the birth of **Isaac**, she and her son, Ishmael, were expelled by **Abraham** at **Sarah**'s request (Genesis 21).

Ishmael ben Elisha (fl. 2nd cent.) Palestinian tanna. He lived at Kephar Aziz. He disputed with **Akiva** about halakhic and aggadic matters, and expanded to 13 the seven hermeneutical rules laid down by **Hillel**. He was also one of the leading aggadists of the period. According to legend, he was one of the martyrs who was killed in the persecutions that followed the Bar Kokhba revolt. Many mystical statements and literary works were ascribed to him.

Ishmael ben Nethaniah (fl. 6th cent. BCE) Israelite soldier. After the destruction of Jerusalem by the Babylonians, he fled to Baalis, King of the Ammonites. When the Babylonians made the Israelite **Gedaliah** King of Judah, he gathered the scattered remnants of the people together and prepared to govern them. Ishamel murdered him and endeavoured to take the remaining Jewish community to Ammon, but was thwarted by **Johanan ben Kareaḥ** (Jeremiah 40–41).

Ishmael of Akbara (fl. 9th cent.) Babylonian sectarian. He was the founder of the Akbaraites who seceded form the Karaite community. He did not recognize the masoretic emendations in the text of the Bible. He permitted the consumption on the Sabbath of food cooked or gathered on that day by non-Jews, and the use of the income of a business which operated seven days a week.

Ish-Shalom [Friedmann], Meir (1831–1908) Austrian scholar. He was born in Slovakia. He taught midrash at the Vienna Rabbinical Seminary and published editions of midrashic and aggadic literature.

Isidor, Lazare (1814–81) French rabbi. He was born in Lixheim, Lorraine. He served as rabbi of Pfalzburg and Paris, and later as chief rabbi of France. During his time at Pfalzburg he refused to allow a member of the congregation of Saverne to pronounce the Jewish oath, *more judaico*. He was subsequently prosecuted, defended by Adolphe Crémieux, and acquitted.

Israel ben Samuel Ashkenazi of Shklov (d. 1839) Palestinian talmudic scholar of Lithuanian origin. He was born in Shklov, and during his years in Lithuania was entrusted with the publication of the Vilna Gaon's [**Elijah ben Solomon Zalman**] commentaries. He later settled in Safed. In 1816 he was chosen to succeed Menaḥem Mendel of Shklov, the leader of the Kolel ha- Perushim, in Safed. After an earthquake in 1837, he moved to Jerusalem. His *Peat ha-Shulḥan* supplements the Shulḥan Arukh with a codification of laws relating to life in Palestine, which had been omitted by **Joseph Caro**.

Israel ben Shabbetai of Kozienice [Maggid Kozienicer] (c. 1737–1814) Polish Ḥasidic leader and scholar. He lived in Kozienice in central Poland. He was known for his ability to perform miraculous cures by means of prayers and the use of amulets. According to tradition, the failure of Napoleon's Russian expedition of 1811 was due to Israel ben Shabbetai's prayers.

Israeli, Isaac ben Joseph (fl. 14th cent.) Spanish astronomer. He lived in Toledo and is known for his *Yesod Olam*, which deals with the geometrical problems of the earth in the Ptolemaic system of the universe.

Israeli, Isaac ben Solomon [Isaac Judaeus] (c. 855–c. 955) Physician and philosopher. He was born in Egypt. At about the age of 50 he moved to Kairouan, where he served as court physician. He wrote eight medical works, including treatises on pharmacology, fevers and ophthalmology, as well as studies of logic and psychology. He was one of the first Jewish medieval philosophers, and attempted to reconcile Jewish theology with Neoplatonism.

Israeli, Isaac d' (1766–1848) English author. He was the son of an Italian-born merchant. His first essays were among the earliest Jewish contributions to English literature. His writings include *Curiosities of Literature* and *Commentary on the Life and Reign of Charles I.* In 1813 he was fined by the Sephardi synagogue in London for refusing to serve as warden. He resigned from the congregation and had his children baptized. **Benjamin Disraeli**, later prime minister and Earl of Beaconsfield, was his son.

Israels, Jozef (1824–1911) Dutch painter. He was born in Groningen, and earned his living in Amsterdam by painting portraits and historical subjects, including scenes from Jewish life and history. In 1855 he settled in Zandvoort, and later he moved to The Hague.

Issachar (fl? 19th–16th cent. BCE) Son of **Jacob** and **Leah**. His birth was considered by **Leah** to be a sign of divine favour after a long period of barrenness, as a reward for her having given her handmaid to **Jacob** (Genesis 30:18). Issachar was the ancestor of the tribe bearing his name.

Isserlein, Israel ben Pethahiah (1390–1460) German rabbi and talmudist. He was born in Regensburg and served as rabbi in Marburg and Wiener-Neustadt, where he was the leading halakhic authority of his time. His responsa were collected together in *Terumat ha-Deshen.*

Isserles, Moses [Rema] (c. 1525–72) Polish codifier. He was born in Kraków, where he later founded and maintained a yeshivah. When **Joseph Caro**'s code, *Bet Yoseph*, appeared, Isserles wrote the *Darkhe Mosheh*, which explained the views of Ashkenazi scholars. After the abridgement of **Caro**'s code, the Shulḥan Arukh, was published, Isserles wrote the *Mappah*, which incorporated Ashkenazi practice. It was through these additions to the Shulḥan Arukh that the code was eventually accepted as authoritative among the Ashkenazim. He also wrote studies of philosophy and kabbalah.

Italia, Salom (c. 1619–c. 1655) Italian engraver, etcher and draftsman. He was born in Mantua, but lived and worked in Amsterdam. He produced engraved portraits and book illustrations, as well as copperplate borders for the Ketubbah and Megillah.

Ithamar (fl. ?13th cent. BCE) Israelite, youngest son of **Aaron**. During the wanderings of the Israelites in the wilderness he was assigned special duties as leader over all the Levites (Exodus 31; 38:21). The house of Eli traced descent to him (I Samuel 14:3; I Chronicles 24:3).

Itzig, Daniel Jaffe [Jaffe, Daniel] (1723–99) German financier, leader of the Berlin Jewish community. He minted coins on behalf of the Prussian state during the Seven Years' War. In 1797 he was appointed court banker and inspector of road construction. He was also the chief representative of Prussian Jewry and responsible for the foundation of the Jewish Free School.

Izates II (fl. 1st cent.). King of Adiabene (c. 35–60) In his youth he was sent by his father to the court of Abnerigos, King of Mesene. There he was attracted to Judaism, as was his mother, Helena. His conversion to the Jewish faith aroused considerable opposition in Adiabene.

J

Jabès, Edmond (1912–91) French writer and poet. He was born in Cairo and settled in Paris in 1957. His works, most of which are theological, include *The Book of Questions* and *The Book of Resemblances.*

Jabotinsky, Vladimir (1880–1940) Russian Zionist leader, soldier and writer. Born in Odessa, he first worked as a foreign correspondent in Berne and Rome. After returning to Odessa, he formed a Jewish self-defence group there. During World War I he advocated the recruiting of Jewish regiments to fight on the Palestinian front, and after the war he supported the maintainance of a Jewish legion in Palestine to protect Jews from Arab hostility. In 1920 he organized a Jewish self-defence unit in Jerusalem, for which he was arrested, tried and punished by a British military tribunal. In 1925 he formed the World Union of Zionist Revisionists, and from 1936 he urged the evacuation of Eastern European Jewry to Palestine. He was the spiritual father and head of the Jewish underground movement Irgun Tzevai Leumi, founded in 1937. Besides his military activities, he was also a translator, writer and poet.

Jacob [Israel] (fl. ?19th–16th cent. BCE) Israelite, son of **Isaac** and **Rebekah**. He bought the birthright of his brother **Esau** in exchange for food when **Esau** was faint with hunger, and later succeeded in securing the blessing **Isaac** intended to bestow on **Esau**. Fearing his brother's anger, Jacob left home and went to Haran, where he married **Rachel** and **Leah**, the daughters of his uncle **Laban**; by them and their handmaids **Bilhah** and **Zilpah** he had 12 sons and a daughter. After many years he made his way back to Canaan; during the journey he wrestled with an angel at a ford on the river Jabbok. In his old age, during a time of famine in Canaan, he was reunited with his son **Joseph**, who had been sold into slavery by his brothers and had become Pharaoh's chief minister in Egypt (Genesis 25–50).

Jacob, Benno (1862–1945) German rabbi and biblical scholar. He was born in Breslau. He served as a rabbi in Göttingen and and Dortmund before settling in Hamburg and then (in 1939) in England. He published studies of the Pentateuch, defending it against the modern bibical criticism, and claimed that 'higher criticism' of the Bible was anti-Semitic. He was also opposed to Zionism, viewing it as a secularization of Judaism and a basis for Jewish atheism.

Jacob ben Asher [Baal ha-Turim] (c. 1270–c. 1343) Spanish codifier, son of **Asher ben Jehiel**. He was born in Germany and went with his father to Spain in 1303. He lived first in Barcelona and later in Toledo. His code, *Arbaah Turim*, contains the decisions found in both versions of the Talmud, and those of the geonim, as well as those given in earlier commentaries and codes. The work is divided into four parts: 'Oraḥ Ḥayyim' deals with daily conduct, including prayers, Sabbaths and holidays; 'Yoreh Deah' lays down dietary laws; 'Even ha-Ezer' covers personal and family matters; and 'Ḥoshen Mishpat' describes civil law and adminstration.

Jacob ben Jacob Moses of Lissa (d. 1832) Polish talmudist. He served as a rabbi at Kalisz, Lissa and Stryy. He was opposed to the Reform movment and to Ḥasidism. His *Derekh ha-Ḥayyim* is a compendium of Jewish practice.

Jacob ben Meir Tam [Rabbenu Tam] (c. 1100–71) French tosaphist, grandson of **Rashi** and brother of **Samuel ben Meir**. He lived at Ramerupt, and later settled at Troyes, where the first conference of French rabbis met under his leadership. His *Sepher ha-Yashar* contains many of his tosaphot and novellae. He wrote studies of grammar and biblical interpretation, and composed liturgical poetry.

Jacob, François (b. 1920) French biologist. He worked at the Pasteur Institute in Paris. In 1965 he shared the Nobel Prize in Medicine and Physics for work on cellular genetic function and the influence of viruses.

Jacob ben Moses ha-Levi Mölln [Mölln, Jacob ben Moses] (c. 1360–1427) German codifier. He served as a rabbi in Mainz and later in Worms. He was a leading authority on Jewish customs and liturgy. His religious practices were recorded by his disciple Zalman of St Goar in *Sepher Maharil*.

Jacob ben Reuben (fl. 12th cent.) Turkish Karaite biblical commentator. A native of Constantinople, he travelled to various countries to spread Karaism. His biblical commentary, *Sepher ha-Osher*, contains excerpts from Karaite authors.

Jacob ben Samson (fl. 12th cent.) French historian and scholar, pupil of **Rashi**. According to the tosaphists, he was the author of *Seder Olam*, a chronology of the tannaim and amoraim.

Jacob ben Wolf Kranz [Jacob of Dubno; Maggid of Dubno] (c. 1740–1804) Polish preacher and scholar. He was active in Poland and Galicia, and at Dubno in the Ukraine. His writings were published posthumously.

Jacob ben Yakar (d. 1064) German rabbi. He was a teacher of **Rashi** and the head of a yeshivah at Worms. He was known for his humility. He wrote glosses on several talmudic tractates.

Jacobi, Frederick (1891–1952) Amercian composer. He was assistant conductor at the Metropolitan Opera House in New York and taught composition at the Juilliard School of Music from 1936 to 1951. Many of his works are based on Jewish themes.

Jacobi, Karl (1804–51) German mathematician. The son of a banker in Postsdam, he converted to Christianity. He was professor at the University of Königsberg, and later taught at the University of Berlin. He made fundamental contributions to the fields of mathematical analysis, number theory, geometry and mechanics.

Jacob Isaac of Przysucha (1766–1814) Polish tzaddik. He inaugurated a Ḥasidic approach to Judaism based on the speculative study of the Torah and Ḥasidism. He was, however, opposed to the more popular form of Ḥasidism, with its belief in miracles.

Jacob Joseph of Polonnoye (d. 1782) Ukrainian Ḥasidic scholar. He was a rabbi at Sharagrod, but left his position after he became a follower of the **Baal Shem Tov**. Later he served as a rabbi at Rashkov, Nemirov and Polonnoye. His *Toledot Yaakov Yoseph* is a primary source for the teachings of the **Baal Shem Tov**; it led the Vilna Gaon, **Elijah ben Soloman Zalmon**, to issue a ban against the Ḥasidim. His other works include the biblical commentaries *Ben Porat Yoseph*, *Tzaphenat Paneaḥ*, and *Ketonet Passim*.

Jacob Joshua ben Tzevi Hirsch Falk (1680–1756) Polish talmudist. He served as a rabbi in several Polish and German cities; his yeshivah at Lwów became the centre of rabbinic learning in Poland. In 1730 he became a rabbi in Berlin and later in Frankfurt am Main, though he resigned the latter post because of his support for the rabbinical scholar **Jacob Emden**. His *Pene Yehoshua* contains novellae on the Talmud.

Jacobowski, Ludwig (1868–1900) German poet and author. He was born in Strelno, in the Posen district, and lived in Berlin. He edited a newspaper, wrote several volumes of poetry, and published a number of novels. He was a significant Jewish figure in the last decade of 19th-century German literature; his writings sought to create a synthesis of Judaism with German culture.

Jacobs, Joseph (1854–1916) British historian, folklorist and scholar. Born in Australia, he settled in England, where he became active as an author and journalist. He was the founder (in 1896) and editor of the *Jewish Year Book*. His studies of medieval Anglo-Jewish history include *Jews of Angevin England*. In 1900 he settled in the US, where he was an editor of the *Jewish Encyclopedia* and taught at the Jewish Theological Seminary.

Jacobs, Louis (b. 1920) English rabbi and scholar. He was born in Manchester and served as a rabbi there, and later in London. From 1959 to 1962 he was a tutor at Jews College, but he was disqualified by Chief Rabbi Brodie as a candidate for the post of principal of the college because of his views. He subsequently founded the New London Synagogue, where he served as a rabbi. He wrote on halakhic issues, Jewish theology and philosophy, and Jewish mysticism. His publications include *We Have Reason to Believe*, *Principles of the Jewish Faith* and *A Jewish Theology*.

Jacobson, Dan (b. 1929) British novelist. He was born in Johannesburg, lived in Israel, and later settled in London. His novels deal with the problems of apartheid in South Africa and of Jewish identity in the modern world.

Jacobson, Howard (b. 1942) English novelist. Born in Manchester, he was a lecturer in English literature at Sydney University. He returned to Britain, and in 1975 became a lecturer in English at Wolverhampton Polytechnic. His novels deal with Jewish characters.

Jacobson, Israel (1768–1828) German Reform leader. He was born in Halberstadt. He was president of the Jewish consistory in Westphalia, where he worked for the reform of Jewish education and the synagogue liturgy. In 1801 he founded the Jacobson School for Jewish and Christian pupils in Seesen, Braunschweig. He set up a Reform synagogue in Seesen in 1810. Later he moved to Berlin, where he held Reform services in his home.

Jacobson, Victor (1869–1935) Russian Zionist leader and diplomat. He was born in Simferopol in the Crimea. From 1899 he was a member of the Zionist General Council. In 1903 he opposed the Uganda Scheme, and was one of the organizers of the Kharkov Conference in opposition to **Theodor Herzl**. He served as head of the Beirut office of the Anglo-Palestine Company from 1906, and later directed its branch in Constantinople. During World War I he ran the Zionist office in Copenhagen and subsequently he represented the Zionist organization and the Jewish Agency in Paris and at the League of Nations.

Jacoby, Johann (1805–77) Prussian politician. He was born in Königsberg. He advocated Jewish religious reform and emancipation. In 1848 he was elected to the Prussian Landtag, and in the following year to the German Nationalversammelung in Frankfurt am Main. From 1863 he served in the Prussian House of Representatives.

Jaffe, Joseph (1865–1938) American Yiddish poet. Born in Lithuania, he settled in New York in 1892. His poetry deals primarily with the theme of love.

Jaffe, Leib (1876–1948) Russian Zionist leader and writer. He was born in Grodno in Belorussia. He participated in the First Zionist Congress in 1897 and those following it. He edited Zionist periodicals in Russia, and later was called to Moscow to edit the monthly journal of the Zionist Organization. He subsequently moved to Lithuania, where he was elected president of the Zionist Organization and edited its newspaper. In 1920 he emigrated to Palestine, and became editor of the daily paper *Haaretz*. As a writer he published Zionist literature in Russian, Russian anthologies of Hebrew poetry, and a selection of world poetry on Jewish nationalist topics.

Jaffe, Meir ben Israel (fl. 15th cent.) German copyist and book binder. He wrote a Haggadah at the end of the 15th century.

Jaffe, Mordecai ben Abraham (c. 1535–1612) Talmudist, kabbalist and communal leader. He was born in Prague. He studied in Poland under **Solomon Luria** and **Moses Isserles**, then returned to Prague, where he became head of a yeshivah. Later he settled in Venice but he eventually moved back to Eastern Europe and was appointed av bet din and head of the yeshivah of Grodno. He subsequently lived in Lublin, Kremenets, Prague and Posen. He was the author of *Levush Malkhut*, a comprehensive code of Jewish law which provoked widespread criticism.

Jaffe, Tzevi Hirsch (1853–1929) Russian mathematician. He wrote studies of mathematical theory and invented a calculating machine. He was also a talmudic scholar and an authority on the Jewish calendar.

Jair (i) (fl.?13th–12th cent. BCE) Israelite hero. During the Israelites' wanderings in the wilderness he captured a group of villages from the Amorites (Numbers 32:41).

Jair (ii) (fl.12th cent. BCE) Israelite judge. He flourished in the generation preceding **Jephthah** and judged Israel for 22 years (Judges 10:3–5).

Jakobovits, Immanuel (1921–99) British rabbi. He was born in Königsberg. He served as a minister in several London synagogues and became chief rabbi of Dublin in 1949. From 1958 he was a rabbi at the Fifth Avenue Synagogue in New York; in 1966 he was appointed chief rabbi of the United Hebrew Congregations of the British Commonwealth. He was subsequently knighted and created a peer. His publications include *Jewish Medical Ethics.*

Jakobson, Roman (1896–1982) Russian philologist. Born in Moscow, he studied at Moscow University and Prague University. He helped establish the Moscow Linguistic Circle to study linguistics, poetics, metrics and folklore. In Prague he was a founder of the Cercle Linguistique de Prague. He taught at Masaryk University in Brno, Czechoslovakia from 1933. In 1939 he fled the Nazis and worked in Copenhagen and Uppsala. He later emigrated to the US and was a professor at Columbia University, Harvard University and the Massachusetts Institute of Technology.

James, Harry (1916–83) American musician. He played with various bands, and eventually joined **Benny Goodman**'s group. In 1939 he formed his own band. He was most popular for his skill as a jazz trumpet player.

Janco, Marcel (1895–1984) Israeli painter. He was born in Bucharest. Early in his career he was involved in Dadism in Paris, but he left the movement and returned to Romania, where he worked as an architect. In 1941 he settled in Palestine and began to paint works that reflect the colours of the landscape and its picturesque aspects. In 1947 he was a founder member of the New Horizons group. Later he established Ein Hod, an artists' village outside Haifa.

Janner, Barnett (1892–1982) Welsh politician and communal leader. He served as a member of parliament – as a Liberal from 1931 to 1935 and as a Labour member from 1945 to 1970. He was also president of the Zionist Federation of Great Britain and Ireland, and of the Board of Deputies of British Jews. He was knighted and then created a life peer.

Janner, Greville (b. 1928) Welsh politician and communal leader, son of **Barnett Janner**. He was born in Cardiff. He became a barrister and served as a Labour member of parliament. He worked in various Jewish comunal bodies and has written and contributed to a number of books.

Janowsky, Oscar (b. 1900) American historian. He was born in Poland and was taken to the US in 1910. In 1948 he became professor of history at New York City College. His writings include: *The Jews and Minority Rights (1898–1919), The American Jew: A Composite Portrait, The American Jew: A Reappraisal, The Education of American Jewish Teachers* and *Foundations of Israel.*

Japheth ben Ali ha-Levi (fl.10th cent.) Palestinian Karaite scholar. He lived in Jerusalem. He wrote biblical commentaries, a translation of the Bible into Arabic, and polemical tracts against **Saadyah Gaon**.

Jaques, Heinrich (1831–94) Austrian lawyer and politician. He was born in Vienna, and worked as a lawyer and banker. In 1879 he entered the Reichstat as a German Liberal. He published a tract on Jewish emancipation.

Jason (fl.2nd cent. BCE) Israelite high priest. He bribed Antiochus IV to depose his brother, **Onias III**, so that he could become high priest. But later he was dismissed from the high priesthood by the king, and **Menelaus**, who offered Antiochus IV a large sum of money, was appointed instead. Jason's Hellenizing policy contributed to the Hasmonean revolt (166–164 BCE), which freed Judea from the rule of the Seleucids.

Jastrow, Marcus (1829–1903) American rabbi and philologist. He was born in Rogasen, in the Posen district. After serving as preacher to the progressive German congregation in Warsaw, he became a rabbi in Worms. In 1866 he emigrated to the US and was appointed rabbi at Rodeph Shalom in Philadelphia. His publications include *Dictionary of the Targumim, the Talmud Babli and Yerushalmi, and the Midrashic Literature.*

Jastrow, Morris (1861–1922) American orientalist, son of **Marcus Jastrow**. Born in Poland, he was brought up in the US. He taught Semitics at the University of Pennsylvania, where he became research professor of Assyriology. He wrote studies of biblical and Assyriological topics.

Javits, Jacob (1904–86) American politician. Born in New York City, he studied at Columbia University and New York University. He worked as a trial lawyer and became a US senator in 1956. From 1969 he was a member of the Senate Foreign Relations Committee.

Jawitz, Ze'ev (1847–1924) Polish historian. He settled in Palestine in 1888, and worked as a teacher and writer. He left Palestine in 1894 and moved in succession to Vilna, Germany and London. His *Toledot Yisrael* is a 14-volume history of the Jews.

Jeduthun (fl. 11th cent. BCE) Israelite seer and singer of **David**'s household (II Chronicles 35:15). He was head of a family of singers whom **David** singled out from the Levites (I Chronicles 25:1). Psalms 39, 62 and 77 are attributed to him.

Jehiel ben Joseph of Paris (d. c.1265) French talmudist and tosaphist. He was the leading Jewish protagonist in the Disputation of Paris (1240) held at the court of Louis IX, which originated from the charges of the apostate **Nicholas Donin**. As a result of this disputation, copies of the Talmud were burned in Paris in 1242. Jehiel ben Joseph continued to lead the Jewish academy in Paris, but in 1260 he moved to Palestine and settled in Acre, where he opened a yeshivah.

Jehiel Michal of Zloczov [Maggid of Zloczov] (c.1731–86) Galician Ḥasidic leader. He was born in Brody and served as a preacher there and, later, in Zloczov. He was one of the early propagators of Ḥasidism in Galicia; he was strongly opposed by the mitnaggedim. Towards the end of his life he settled in Yampol, Podolia. Miraculous tales are told of his asceticism and saintliness.

Jehoahaz (i) [Joahaz] (fl. 9th cent. BCE) King of Israel (c.814–800 BCE), son of **Jehu**. During his reign, Aram turned Israel into a tributary nation, reduced its army, and controlled large parts of its territory (II Kings 13:1–9).

Jehoahaz (ii) [Shallum] (fl. 7th cent. BCE) King of Judah (609 BCE), son of **Josiah**. His name was originally Shallum (Jeremiah 22:11), but it was changed to Jehoahaz when he was made king after his father had been killed in the battle against Pharaoh Necho II at Megiddo. Three months later Necho II deposed Jehoahaz and put his elder brother **Jehoiakim** in his place (II Kings 23:33–34; II Chronicles 36:3–4). Jehoahaz died in captivity in Egypt (II Kings 23:29–34).

Jehoiachin [Coniah; Jeconiah] (fl. 6th cent. BCE) King of Judah (597 BCE), son of **Jehoiakim**. He ascended the throne at the age of 18 during the rebellion against Babylon. He was exiled to Babylon by Nebuchadnezzar, together with his family and 10,000 captives (II Kings 24:12ff). He was released during the reign of Evil-Merodach (II Kings 24–25; II Chronicles 36:8–10).

Jehoiada [Joiada] (fl. 9th cent. BCE) High priest. After **Athaliah** assumed the throne and killed the royal family (II Kings 11:1), it was feared that the entire house of **David** would be eliminated. But Jehoiada's wife, Jehosheba, hid **Joash**, the baby son of King **Ahaziah**, in the Temple. Jehoiada later proclaimed **Joash** king, had **Athaliah** slain, and acted as regent until **Joash** was seven. Under Jehoiada's influence, the cult of Baal was prohibited and the Temple at Jerusalem restored (II Kings 12).

Jehoiakim [Eliakim; Joiakim] (fl. 7th–6th cent. BCE) King of Judah (608–598 BCE), son of **Josiah**. He was made king by Pharaoh Necho II in succession to his brother **Jehoahaz (ii)**. During the first three years of his reign Judah was subject to Egypt. After Necho II was defeated in the battle of Carchemish in 605 BCE, Judah came under the Babylonian yoke; according to II Chronicles, Nebuchadnezzar bound him in fetters to take him to Babylon (II Chronicles 36:6ff). Jehoiakim was a vassal of Babylon for three years before he rebelled (II Kings 24:1), which brought about his downfall and death.

Jehoram (i) [Joram] (fl. 9th cent. BCE) King of Israel (853–842 BCE), son of **Ahab**. He joined **Jehoshaphat** of Judah in the war against Mesha of Moab. He was engaged in battle with Aram and was wounded in the battle of Ramoth-Gilead; while he was recuperating in Jezreel, **Jehu** assassinated him (II Kings 8–9).

Jehoram (ii) [Joram] (fl. 9th cent. BCE) King of Judah (851–843 BCE), son of **Jehoshaphat** of Judah. He was married to **Athaliah** who introduced the cult of Baal into Judah. During his reign, Edom rebelled against Judah and Judah was ravaged by the Philistines (II Kings 8; II Chronicles 21).

Jehoshaphat (fl. 9th cent. BCE) King of Judah (874–850 BCE), son of **Asa**. He was the first king of Judah to make a treaty with Israel. He married his son **Jehoram (ii)** to **Athaliah**, the daughter of King Omri of Israel (II Kings 8:26). Together with **Ahab**, he waged war unsuccessfully against Aram. With **Ahab**'s son **Jehoram (i)**, he engaged in battle with Mesha of Moab.

Jehu (fl. 9th cent. BCE) King of Israel (c. 842–814 BCE). He was commander-in-chief to **Jehoram (i)** but conspired with the army against the king. With the assistance of **Elisha**, he eliminated the royal family (including **Jehoram**, **Ahaziah** of Judah and **Jezebel**), as well as the priests of Baal, whose worship had flourished under **Jehoram**'s reign. He fought unsuccessfully against Aram and paid tribute to Shalmaneser III of Assyria for protection from the Arameans. His dynasty continued for 100 years (II Kings 9–11).

Jeiteles [Jeitteles], Alois (1794–1858) Bohemian physician and poet, nephew of **Baruch** and **Judah Jeiteles**. Born in Brünn, he served as a physician there. In 1819 he published, with **Ignaz Jeiteles**, the short-lived Jewish periodical *Siona*. A cycle of his poetry was set to music by Beethoven.

Jeiteles [Jeitteles], Baruch (1762–1813) Bohemian Hebrew writer and physician, brother of **Judah Jeiteles**. He maintained a yeshivah in Prague, but later became a supporter of the Haskalah movement. He wrote halakhic novellae as well as Hebrew poems and translations. In 1813 he persuaded leading individuals in the Prague community to open a hospital for wounded soldiers of all nationalities in the Jewish quarter.

Jeiteles [Jeitteles], Ignaz (1783–1843) Bohemian writer, son of **Baruch Jeiteles**. He studied law at Prague University before moving to Vienna, where he worked as a merchant. With his cousin **Alois Jeiteles** he published the short-lived Jewish periodical *Siona* in 1819. He wrote studies of literature, philosophy, history and statistics as well as poetry.

Jeiteles [Jeitteles], Judah (1773–1838) Bohemian orientalist, brother of **Baruch Jeiteles**. He was one of the four chairmen of the Jewish community in Prague, where he supervised the German-language school. He was the first to use the word 'Haskalah' for the Jewish Enlightenment movement. In 1830 he settled in Vienna. He contributed to Hebrew periodicals, and was the author of an Aramaic grammar in Hebrew.

Jellinek, Adolf (c. 1820–93) Austrian preacher and scholar. He was born in Moravia and moved to Prague in 1838. He was a rabbi in Leipzig from 1845, and in Vienna from 1856, where he became a famous preacher. He published studies of the history of the kabbalah and medieval Jewish philosophy, editions of smaller midrashim in his Bet ha-Midrash, and bibliographical booklets on medieval Jewish history and literature.

Jephthah (fl. c. 12th cent. BCE) Israelite judge. When Gilead was threatened by the Ammonites, he went to war against them. Before he engaged in battle, he vowed to sacrifice to God whatever came first from his house should he return safely. To his grief he was met by his daughter whom he subsequently sacrificed (Judges 11). Later he was victorious over the Ephramites.

Jeremiah (i) (fl. 7th–6th cent. BCE) Israelite prophet. When he first emerged as a prophet he rebuked the nation for idolatry. After the religious revival that marked the reign of **Josiah**,

Jeremiah warned the people to keep the newly made covenant with God. When Nebuchadnezzar became king in Babylonia, Jeremiah prophesied that he would conquer Judah. Later he foretold the defeat of **Zedekiah** and his anti-Babylonian alliance, and advocated surrender. After the fall of Jerusalem, he went to Egypt, where he condemned Egyptian Jewry for idol-worship.

Jeremiah (ii) (fl. 4th cent.) Palestinian amora. He was born in Babylonia and became head of the academy at Tiberias. He engaged in halakhic discussions with most contemporary sages.

Jeroboam I (fl. 10th cent. BCE) King of Israel (c. 928–907 BCE). During **Solomon**'s reign, he was a superintendent of forced labour, and led a revolt against the monarchy. After **Solomon**'s death, he led a delegation representing the northern tribes, which met **Rehoboam** at Shechem. The delegation demanded changes in the system of labour; when its request was refused, the northern tribes declared their independence and appointed Jeroboam king. He first made his captial at Shechem, but later moved it to Penuel. He set up new shrines at Bethel and Dan, centred round the worship of golden calves (I Kings 11–15; II Chronicles 10, 13).

Jeroboam II (fl. 8th cent. BCE) King of Israel (789–748 BCE), son of **Joash**. He was the greatest ruler of the dynasty of **Jehu**. During his reign the Northern Kingdom attained the height of its economic, military and political power. His rule was marred by corruption, which was denounced by the prophets **Amos** and **Hosea** (II Kings 14).

Jerusalem, Wilhelm (1854–1923) Austrian philosopher. He was born in Drenic, Bohemia. He became a schoolmaster and later taught philosophy and pedagogics at the University of Vienna; between 1894 and 1902 he also taught at the Jüdisch-Theologische Lehranstalt in Vienna. He wrote studies of the psychology of language and thought, the theory of consciousness, and problems of logic.

Jeshua ben Damna (fl. 1st century) Israelite, high priest (c. 61–3). He was apponted by **Herod Agrippa II** but after a short period of office was displaced by **Joshua ben Gamla**. At the end of the Roman siege of Jerusalem (70 CE) he fled for refuge to the Romans, together with other members of priestly families.

Jeshua ben Judah (fl. 11th cent.) Palestinian Karaite scholar. He lived in Jeruslaem. His principal works are an Arabic translation of the Pentateuch with a philosophical commentary, a study of the law of incest, and philosophical tracts.

Jesofowicz, Michael (d. 1531) Lithuanian financier and communal leader. In 1514 Sigismund I appointed him 'elder and judge' of Lithuanian Jewry, chief collector of dues, and the Jewish representative at court. In 1525 he was ennobled.

Jesse (fl. 11th–10th cent. BCE) Israelite, father of **David**. He lived in Bethelehem, but later settled in Moab for fear of **Saul**. The royal house of **David** is referred to in the Bible as growing from the root of Jesse (Isaiah 11:1, 10).

Jessel, George (1824–83) British jurist. Born in London, he studied at the University of London and began to practise law at Lincoln's Inn in 1847. In 1868 he entered parliament as a Liberal, and in 1871 became solicitor-general. In 1873 he was appointed master of the rolls. Later he became president of the chancery division of the court of appeal. From 1873 to 1883 he was head of the patent office. He was knighted in 1872.

Jesurun, Isaac (fl. 17th cent.) Dalmatian merchant. He was a merchant at Ragusa, where he was accused in 1622 of the ritual murder of a Christian girl. His suffering is described in Hebrew and Spanish accounts. Banished for his supposed crime, he died in Palestine.

Jesurun, Reuel (fl. c. 1575–1634) Portuguese marrano. He was born in Lisbon. In 1599 he travelled to Rome, intending to join a Christian monastic order. On the journey he was persuaded to return to Judaism, and went back to Lisbon. In 1604 he settled in Amsterdam, where he worked as the administrator of the Talmud Torah rabbinical school. His *Diálogo dos montes* is a dramatic poem in praise of Judaism.

Jesus (fl. 1st cent. BCE–1st cent. CE) Palestinian religious leader. According to the New Testament, he grew up in Galilee and was baptized by **John the Baptist**. He performed various miracles and announced the coming of the kingdom of God. He was arrested and crucified by order of the Roman procurator, Pontius Pilate, at the instigation of the Jewish authorities. His followers believed that he rose from the dead and ascended to heaven. They formed the core of the earliest Christian Church, and actively spread the good news about Jesus, whom they believed to be the Messiah (hence the addition to his name of 'Christ': the anointed one). According to Christian belief, Jesus was God incarnate and is restored to the Godhead in the form of the Trinity.

Jezebel (fl. 9th cent. BCE) Israelite woman of Sidonite origin, wife of **Ahab**, and daughter of Ethbaal, King of Sidon. She introduced her native cult of Baal worship into Israel, thereby arousing the anger of **Elijah**. In I and II Kings she is portrayed as a callous woman who unjustly brought about the death of **Naboth** and persecuted the prophets (I Kings 16–II Kings 9). She was killed in **Jehu**'s revolt against the monarchy.

Joab (fl. 10th cent. BCE) Israelite commander-in-chief, nephew of **David**. When **David** became king, Joab was appointed head of the army. He defeated the Ammonites and led the campaign against **Absalom**. During the revolt of Sheba, son of Bichri, he was replaced as commander-in- chief by **Amasa**, whom he later murdered. He supported **Adonijah**'s claim to succeed **David**, and was put to death by **Solomon** in accordance with **David**'s wishes (II Samuel 2–3, 10–11, 14, 17–21; I Kings 1–2; II Chronicles 11:18–21, 27).

Joachim, Joseph (1831–1907) German violinist of Hungarian origin. He was born in Köpcsény and moved with his family to Budapest. He studied under **Felix Mendelssohn**, and later led Liszt's orchestra at Weimar. From 1854 to 1864 he was concertmaster and conductor of the Royal Hanoverian Orchestra. During this period he converted to Christianity. In 1866 he settled in Berlin, where he was director of the Hochschule für Musik, and founded the Joachim Quartet. His compositions, mainly for violin, include *Hebrew Melodies.*

Joash (i) [Jehoash] (fl. 9th cent. BCE) King of Judah (835–798 BCE). His grandmother **Athaliah** seized the throne and murdered all members of the house of **David** when Joash was a year old. He was rescued by his aunt Jehosheba, wife of the high priest **Jehoiada**. **Jehoiada** later crowned him king, had **Athaliah** put to death, and acted as regent until Joash became king when he was seven. Joash restored the Temple, but he later deviated from following Jewish law. During his reign, Judah was invaded by Hazael of Aram. Joash was killed by conspirators (II Kings 11–14).

Joash (ii) [Jehoash] (fl. 9th cent. BCE) King of Israel (801–785 BCE). After Aram was defeated by the Assyrians, he recaptured several towns ceded by his father **Jehoahaz**. When **Amaziah** of Judah attempted to free his country from Israelite domination, Joash captured Jerusalem, plundered the Temple and royal treasures, and reduced the country to vassaldom (II Kings 13:10–13).

Job (?) A righteous man who questioned God's justice in allowing him to suffer. His friends argued that his suffering was a result of wickedness, but Job refused to accept this explanation. God eventually spoke from a whirlwind and stressed Job's finite knowledge compared with his designs for the universe.

Jocehbed (fl.? 13th cent. BCE) Israelite woman, wife of **Amram** and mother of **Moses**, **Aaron** and **Miriam** (Exodus 6:20).

Joel (?) Israelite prophet. The book of Joel depicts a plague of locusts (chapters 1–2) and describes the Day of the Lord, when God will rescue the Jewish people from captivity and punish their enemies in the Valley of Jehoshaphat (chapters 3–4).

Joel, Manuel (1826–90) German rabbi and scholar. He was born in Birnbaum, Poznania. In 1854 he joined the faculty of the Breslau Rabbinical Seminary, and ten years later became rabbi of the Breslau community. In the rabbinical assemblies of Kassel and Leipzig, he advocated moderation in Reform practice. He published studies of **Ibn Gabirol**, **Maimonides**, **Ḥasdai Crescas** and **Levi ben Gershom**; he also wrote a two-volume work on comparative religion.

Joel, Solomon Barnato (1865–1931) South African industrialist. Born in London, he and his brothers left London to work for their uncle Barney Barnato who was a partner in the control of the Kimberly diamond mines in South Africa. After the suicide of Bernato and the shooting of one of his brothers, he became the head of the mining empire that centred on the Johannesburg Consolidated Investment Company and the family stake in De Beers.

Joezer (fl. 1st cent. BCE-1st cent. CE) High priest, son of Boethus. He was a brother of **Herod**'s wife, **Mariamne**, and of Eleazar, who also served as high priest. He played a role in pacifying the people when they resisted the attempts of Quirinius (governor of Syria) to conduct a census in Judea.

Joffe, Abraham (1880–1960) Russian physicist. Born in Romny, Ukraine, he was appointed professor of physics at the Polytechnic Institute. He created the Physical-Technical Institute of Leningrad where he was director. He won the Stalin Prize in 1942, and was named hero of Socialist Labour in 1955.

Joffe, Adolf Abramovich (1883–1927) Russian diplomat. Born in Simferopol, he joined the Mensheviks. He became a friend of **Leon Trotsky** and helped him edit the Viennese *Pravda*. He was arrested and imprisoned in 1912. He was released following the 1917 revolution and joined the Bolsheviks. He led the peace talks with Germany in Brest-Litovsk and later became Soviet ambassador in Berlin. In 1920 he led the Russian delegation to the peace talks with Poland. Allied with **Trotsky**, he was part of the opposition to Stalin. He served as ambassador in Vienna and Tokyo.

Joffe, Eliezer (1882–1944) Israeli agriculturalist. Born in Bessarabia, he went to the US to study agriculture and later founded an experimental farm in Palestine. He was a founder-member of the first moshav ovdim, Nahalal in 1928. He wrote various works on agricultural subjects.

Johanan [Gadi] (fl. 2nd cent. BCE) Israelite fighter, son of **Mattathias** the Hasmonean. He and his brothers fought in the uprising against the Syrians. He was killed while on a mission to the Nabateans.

Johanan bar Nappaḥa (c. 180–c. 279) Palestinian amora. He was born in Sepphoris. He studied with **Judah ha-Nasi**, and was the brother-in-law of **Simeon ben Lakish**. He founded his own academy in Tiberias. His teachings constitute a major part of the Jerusalem Talmud.

Johanan ben Kareaḥ (fl. 6th cent. BCE) Israelite military commander, active in Judah at the time of the destruction of the First Temple (Jeremiah 40–43). He supported **Gedaliah** and warned him of **Ishmael ben Nethaniah**'s treachery; after **Gedaliah**'s murder, he prevented **Ishmael** from carrying away prisoners. Out of fear of Babylonian reprisals, he went to Egypt along with other exiles including **Jeremiah**.

Johanan ben Nuri (fl. 2nd cent.) Palestinian tanna. Living in poverty, he influenced the formulation of laws and customs of the Jews in Galilee. He is often mentioned in the Mishnah as taking part in debates with **Akiva**.

Johanan ben Zakkai (fl. 1st cent.) Palestinian tanna. He was the leading sage at the end of the Second Temple period and in the years following the destruction of the Temple. During the rebellion against Rome (66–70), he was among the peace party in Jerusalem. According to legend, he was carried out of the city in a coffin, approached Vespasian, and predicted his accession to the imperial throne. As a reward, he was allowed to continue his teaching. He founded an academy at Jabneh, which became the seat of the Sanhedrin after the fall of Jerusalem.

Johanan ha-Sandelar (fl. 2nd cent.) Palestinian tanna. He was born in Alexandria and became a pupil of **Akiva**. After Hadrian's reign (117–38), which saw widespread persecution of the Jews, and the death of **Akiva** at Caesarea, Johanan transmitted **Akiva**'s teaching.

Johlson, Joseph (1773–1851) German scholar and teacher. He taught at the Philanthropin school in Frankfurt am Main from 1813 to 1830. He based the teaching of Hebrew on the mastery of grammar and established a systematic plan for teaching Judaism. He published textbooks about Jewish history in biblical times, a biblical dictionary, and a German translation of the Bible.

John Hyrcanus (fl. 2nd cent. BCE) High priest and ethnarch (135–104 BCE), son of Simon the Hasmonean.

After the murder of his father and his two brothers by Ptolemy, he escaped to Jerusalem. In 135–134 BCE Antiochus Sidetes captured Jerusalem, and John Hyrcanus was confirmed as high priest. Later he threw off Syrian domination, attacked the Samaritans, destroying their temple on Mount Gerizim, and forced the Idumeans to convert to Judaism. Although initially allied with the Pharisees, he subsequently drew closer to the Sadducees.

John of Giscala (fl. 1st cent.) Palestinian fighter, leader of the revolt against Rome (66–70). He was born in Giscala. He conducted retaliatory raids against the Syrians after they had destroyed his native city. In 66 when **Josephus** arrived as commander in Galilee, a controversy arose between the two military leaders: John suspected **Josephus** of disloyalty and advocated his removal. After Galilee was conquered by Vespasian, John fled to Jerusalem. He took control of the Temple from the Zealots, who subsequently fought under his command during Titus' siege. He was later captured by the Romans, sentenced to life imprisonment, and died in a Roman prison.

John the Baptist (fl. 1st cent.) Palestinian religious leader, forerunner of **Jesus**. He preached repentance, proclaimed the coming of the messianic age, and practised baptism of those who accepted his preaching; **Jesus** was among those whom he baptized. He was put to death by **Herod Antipas** at the behest of **Herodias**, his wife, whose marriage to **Herod** John the Baptist condemned.

Jolowicz, Heymann (1816–75) German Reform leader and writer. He was a preacher in various German towns. Belonging to the radical element of the Reform movement, he wrote on Jewish theology and, together with **David Cassel**, translated **Judah ha-Levi**'s *Kuzari* into German.

Jolson, Al [Yelson, Asa] (1886–1950) American entertainer, of Lithuanian origin. Born in Srednik, Luthiania, he went to the US with his family. The son of a cantor, he was drawn to the theatre, and began his career performing in Washington, DC. Later he went on the vaudeville circuit, and adopted the black face minstrel act. In 1927 he appeared in *The Jazz Singer.*

Jonah (i) Israelite prophet. The book of Jonah relates God's command to Jonah, son of Amittai, to go to Nineveh and proclaim judgement upon its inhabitants for their wickedness. On a sea voyage Jonah was swallowed by a great fish and eventually spewed out on dry land. As a result of his prophecy, the inhabitants of Nineveh repented of their evil ways.

Jonah (ii) (fl. 4th cent.) Palestinian amora. He and Yose were heads of the academy in Tiberias. Discussions between these sages are contained in the Palestinian Talmud.

Jonathan (i) (fl. 11th cent. BCE) Israelite prince, eldest son of **Saul**. He was a devoted friend of **David**. Together with **Saul**, he was killed in a battle against the Philistines on Mount Gilboa. The news of their deaths caused **David** to compose his famous lament (II Samuel 1:17–27).

Jonathan (ii) (fl. 2nd cent. BCE) Israelite head of state (160–143 BCE), youngest son of **Mattathias**. Together with his brother **Judah Maccabee**, he fought in the battles at the beginning of the Hasmonean revolt (166–164 BCE). On the death of his brother, he took over the leadership of the anti-Syrian campaign. Alexander Balas (a contender with Demetrius I for the Syrian throne) conceded to him the title of high priest and recognized him as governor of Judah. He was captured by the Syrian leader Tryphon at Acre and killed.

Jonathan ben Amram (fl. 2nd–3rd cent.) Palestinian sage. A pupil of **Judah ha-Nasi**, he lived during the period between the tannaim and the amoraim. The halakhot quoted by him concern laws of levitical cleanness.

Jonathan ben David ha-Cohen of Lunel (c. 1135–after 1210) French talmudic scholar. He was active in Provence. He defended **Maimonides** in the controversy about him encouraged by **Meir Abulafia**. He wrote commentaries on the Mishnah, the Talmud and **Alfasi**'s Code.

Jonathan ben Eleazar (fl. 3rd cent.) Palestinian amora. He is the Jonathan ben Eleazar mentioned in the Talmud and midrash. Of Babylonian origin, he went to Palestine in his youth and became a pupil of Simeon ben Yose ben Lakunya. He lived in Sepphoris and was one of the great aggadists of his time.

Jonathan ben Uzziel (fl. 1st cent. BCE–1st cent. CE) Palestinian translator. He was an outstanding pupil of **Hillel** and was responsible for the first translation of the biblical books of the prophets into Aramaic.

Jong, Erica (b. 1942) American feminist. Born in New York, she studied at Barnard College and Columbia University. Her works include *Fear of Flying, How to Save Your Own Life, Parachutes and Kisses, Any Woman's Blues* and *Fear of Fifty.*

Joselewicz, Berek (c. 1768–1809) Polish patriot. Born in Kretinga, Lithuania, he worked in commerce and entered the service of Vilna's prince-bishop. He was later attracted to the ideals of the French Revolution, and he became an ally of Polish liberals who favoured Jewish emancipation. He later organized a separate Jewish cavalry in the Polish uprising against the Russians. He later joined Napoleon's Polish Legion and became a French dragoon officer.

Joselman [Josel] of Rosheim [Loanz, Yoseph ben Gershom] (1480–1544) German writer and communal leader. In 1510 he was elected warden and leader by the Alsatian Jewish communities. He represented German Jewry before secular authorities and interceded for the Jewish community in times of danger. In 1532 he attempted to curb the activities of the pseudo-messiah **Solomon Molcho**. Later he defended the Jews against the charges made by Martin Luther.

Joseph (fl. ?19th–16th cent. BCE) Israelite, 11th son of **Jacob** and first-born of **Rachel**. As his father's favourite son, he aroused the anger of his brothers, who sold him into slavery in Egypt. He was bought as a slave by Potiphar, a high official. Later he was imprisoned on a false charge made by Potiphar's wife. After interpreting Pharaoh's dreams, he achieved high office in Egypt. Eventually he was reconciled with his brothers and reunited with his father, after which his family settled in the Goshen region.

Joseph, Keith (1918–94) British politician. Born in London, he studied at Oxford University and was a fellow of All Souls. He was elected to parliament as a Conservative in 1956 and later established the Centre for Policy Studies. He was one of the architects of Thatcherism.

Joseph, Morris (1848–1930) English Reform rabbi. He served as minister at the West London Synagogue for nearly 20 years. He also taught homiletics at Jews College in 1891–2. His writings include *Judaism as Creed and Life, The Ideal in Judaism, The Message of Judaism* and *The Spirit of Judaism.*

Joseph bar Ḥiyya (fl. 9th cent.) Babylonian gaon. He was gaon of Pumbedita (828–33). During the controversy between the exilarch David ben Judah and his brother Daniel, Joseph bar Ḥiyya and Abraham ben Sherira presided over the academy at Pumbedita. When peace was restored, Joseph renounced the office of gaon and temporarily resumed the position of av bet din at Pumbedita.

Joseph ben Abraham ha-Cohen [Joseph abu Jacob; Abu Yakub al-Basir] (fl. 11th cent.) Babylonian or Persian Karaite scholar. He travelled widely, seeking converts to Karaism. Despite his blindness, he wrote religio-legal and philosophical works.

Joseph ben Gorion (fl. 1st cent.) Palestinian military leader. He participated in the revolt against Rome. His name was associated with the authorship of the Hebrew historical narrative, *Josippon.*

Joseph ben Isaac ha-Levi (fl. 17th cent.) Bohemian philosopher of Lithuanian origin. He lived in Prague, where he taught medieval religious philosophy. He wrote a commentary on **Maimonides**' *Guide for the Perplexed*, which was published by **Yom Tov Lipmann Heller** with his own introduction and annotations. Joseph ben Isaac's *Ketonet Passim* treats the basic ideas of the *Guide.*

Joseph ben Jacob bar Satya (fl. 10th cent.) Babylonian gaon. In 930 he was appointed gaon of Sura by the exilarch **David ben Zakkai** after the exilarch had become embroiled in a dispute with **Saadyah Gaon**. **Saadyah** was later reinstated but Joseph ben Jacob resumed the post after **Saadyah**'s death. Some time after 943 he left Sura and settled in Basra.

Joseph ben Joshua ha-Cohen (1496–c. 1575) Italian historian. He was brought up in Italy and practised medicine in Genoa. His *History of the Kings of France and Turkey* describes the struggle between Christians and Muslims from the time of the crusades. In *Valley of Weeping* he recounts the trials of the Jews in the Middle Ages.

Joseph ben Nathan [Official, Joseph] (fl. 13th cent.) French writer, son of **Nathan ben Joseph Official**. He was born of a family who had close relations with the local nobility, and he himself was in the service of the archbishop of Sens as a financial agent. His *Sepher ha-Mekanne* recounts the religious arguments he and his circle had with the Christian community.

Joseph ben Tanḥum Yerushalmi (b. 1262) Egyptian Hebrew poet. At the age of 15 he composed a collection of poems in imitation of **Moses ibn Ezra**. On his father's death in 1291 he composed a lamentation in which he mentions the conquest of Acre by the crusaders. He was the most representative Hebrew poet of Egypt in the 13th century.

Josephs, Wilfred (b. 1927) English composer. He was born in Newcastle upon Tyne. He composed operas, ballets, vocal and choral works, and chamber and instrumental music. His compositions on Jewish themes include the *Jewish Requiem.*

Josephus, Flavius [Flavius Josephus; Joseph ben Mattathias] (c. 38–after 100) Palestinian historian and soldier. He was born in Jerusalem. In 64 he went to Rome on a mission to secure the release of several priests. At the outbreak of the Jewish rebellion against the Romans in 66, he was appointed commander of Galilee, and when the Romans attacked the province in 67, he directed the resistance. He surrendered to the Romans after Jotapata was captured; he accompanied Vespasian and Titus during the siege of Jerusalem. After the Roman victory he lived in Rome. His writings include *The Jewish War, The Antiquities of the Jews, Against Apion* and an *Autobiography.*

Joshua (fl. ?13th cent. BCE) Israelite leader. As **Moses**' successor, he was assigned the task of leading the people in the conquest of Canaan. He commanded the Israelites in the war with the Amalekites (Exodus 17:14–16). Later he was one of the 12 spies sent to reconnoitre the land of Canaan. After the Israelites had crossed the Jordan, Joshua led them to victory over the alliance of southern kings, and then the northern kings. He subsequently brought the Tabernacle to Shiloh and divided the newly won territory among the 12 tribes.

Joshua ben Gamla (d. 69/70) High priest. He married one of the wealthiest women in Jerusalem (Martha, daughter of Boethus). He established a universal system of education throughout Palestine. An opponent of the Zealots at the time of the Jewish rebellion against Rome, he was put to death by the Idumeans.

Joshua ben Hananiah (fl. 1st–2nd cent.) Palestinian tanna. During the siege of Jerusalem (70), he helped his teacher **Johanan ben Zakkai**, to escape. Favoured by the Romans, he travelled repeatedly to Rome on national missions to aid the Jewish cause. After the death of **Gamaliel II** he became av bet din at the Jabneh academy. His polemical debates with Christians are recorded in rabbinic literature. For some time he had a school in Pekiin.

Joshua ben Jehozadak (fl. 6th cent. BCE) High priest. He went to Jerusalem with **Zerubabel**. Encouraged by **Zechariah** and **Haggai**, he set up the altar as the first step in the restoration of the Temple. His descendants remained in office until the time of the Hasmoneans.

Joshua ben Korḥa (fl. 2nd cent.) Palestinian tanna. He studied under **Johanan ben Nuri** and **Eleazar ben Azariah**. He laid down the rule that where there is a difference of opinion the stricter view should be adopted with regard to a biblical injunction, but the more lenient view where the injunction is of rabbinic provenance. He engaged in disputations with sectarians and non-Jews.

Joshua ben Levi (fl. 3rd cent.) Palestinian amora. He was born in Lydda and later taught there, also concerning himself closely with communal needs. He was involved in affairs affecting the community in its relations with the Roman authorities, and travelled on various missions to Caesarea and Rome. He was a master of the aggadah, and some of his sayings are recorded in the Mishnah.

Joshua ben Peraḥyah (fl. 2nd cent. BCE) Palestinian leader, head of the Sanhedrin. Together with **Nittai the Arbelite**, he formed the second of the pairs ('zugot') of sages. The Babylonian Talmud records that he was a teacher of **Jesus**.

Joshua Heshel ben Jacob of Lublin (1595–1663) Polish rabbi. Born in Lublin, he succeeded his father as a rabbi of the community in 1650. Later he succeeded **Yom Tov Lipmann Heller** as rabbi of Kraków. Subsequently he moved to Vienna and sought to exert pressure on the government in the interests of Jewry. He eventually returned to Poland, where he continued his educational activities. He was a noted hahakhic authority.

Josiah (fl. 7th cent. BCE) King of Judah (640–609 BCE), son of **Amnon**. He was proclaimed king while still a child after his father was assassinated. His reign was marked by a great religious revival; he removed foreign cults and re-established monotheism. During the restoration of the Temple, Hilkiah, the high priest, announced the discovery of a book of the law. This prompted Josiah to convene an assembly of the people, during which he made a covenant with God. He also discontinued worship in the high places and centralized it in the Temple at Jerusalem.

Josiah ben Zakkai (fl. 10th cent.) Babylonian exilarch. He was appointed exilarch after his brother **David ben Zakkai** was deposed from office by **Saadyah Gaon**. The caliph intervened in **David**'s favour; Josiah was then banished to Chorassan, where he died.

Jost, Isaac Marcus (1793–1860) German historian. He was born in Bernburg. He served as head of a private high school in Frankfurt am Main; from 1835 he taught at the Philanthropin high school in Frankfurt, and in 1853 he founded an orphanage for Jewish girls there. He published a Pentateuch for young people, a vocalized Mishnah text with translations and notes, a textbook of English, a dictionary of Shakespeare, and a manual of German style. He was a pioneer in modern Jewish historiography and a supporter of the Reform movement.

Jotham (i) (fl. c. 12th cent. BCE) Israelite, youngest son of **Gideon**. He was the sole survivor of **Abimelech**'s massacre in which all his brothers died (Judges 9). He escaped to Mount Gerizim where he denounced the Shechemites for accepting **Abimelech** as king (Judges 9:8–15).

Jotham (ii) (fl. 8th cent. BCE) King of Judah (c. 742–735 BCE), son of **Uzziah**. He defeated the Ammonites in battle (II Chronicles 27:5), and during his reign the country enjoyed considerable prosperity. He made repairs and additions to buildings in the Temple area in Jerusalem (II Chronicles 27:3; II Kings 15:35).

Judah (fl. ?19th–16th cent. BCE) Israelite, fourth son of **Jacob** and **Leah**. When the sons of **Jacob** turned against **Joseph**, the 11th son Judah convinced them to sell **Joseph** to travelling Ishmaelites rather than leave him to die in a pit (Genesis 37). Judah later received **Jacob**'s patriarchal blessing (Genesis 49:8). David belonged to the tribe of Judah and his accession to the throne assured its supremacy. When the Israelite kingdom split after **Solomon**'s death, the tribe of Judah supported **Rehoboam** and became predominant in the south.

Judah bar Ezekiel (d. 299) Babylonian amora. He was the founder of the academy at Pumbedita, and was an authority on halakhah. His teachings are extensively quoted in the Babylonian and Jerusalem Talmuds.

Judah ben Asher (1270–1349) Spanish rabbi and talmudist, of German origin. He was born in Cologne, but left Germany with his family as a consequence of anti-Jewish outbreaks in 1283, and settled in Toledo. In 1321 he was appointed to his father's successor as rabbi of the Toledo community and later became the head of the bet din and the Toledo yeshivah. His *Zikhron Yehudah* comprises 83 responsa. In *Iggeret Tokheḥah* he offered a testament to his children containing ethical sayings, an account of his family history, and instruction in the method of learning.

Judah ben Barzillai al-Bargeloni (fl. 11th–12th cent.) Spanish rabbi. He was rabbi of the community of Barcelona. He wrote numerous halakhic studies, incorporating summaries of talmudic discussions and gaonic material, as well as a commentary on the Sepher Yetzirah.

Judah ben Bathyra I (fl. 1st cent.) Babylonian tanna. He lived in Jerusalem in his youth, but left Palestine before the destruction of the Temple and settled in Nisibis in Babylon.

Judah ben Bathyra II (fl. 2nd cent.) Babylonian tanna, possibly the grandson of **Judah ben Bathyra I**. He was born in Rome and studied in Palestine. Subsequently he went to Babylon and settled in Nisibis. At the time of the Hadrianic persecutions, he was regarded as an authority of equal rank with **Akiva**.

Judah ben Bava (fl. 1st–2nd cent.) Palestinian tanna. He was a leading sage in Jabneh, renowned for his piety. During the Hadrianic persecutions he was put to death by the Romans for ordaining five scholars, in transgression of the law forbidding ordination.

Judah ben Ilai (fl. 2nd cent.) Palestinian tanna. Born in Usha, he was a pupil of his father and of **Tarphon** and **Akiva**. His account of their teachings was used by **Judah ha-Nasi** in compiling the Mishnah. He was the original author of the *Siphra* and was a renowned aggadist. After the Hadrianic persecutions, he helped to establish the academy at Usha.

Judah ben Isaac [Sir Léon of Paris] (1166–1224) French tosaphist, grandson of **Rashi**. He became the head of the Paris bet midrash, which was reopened when the Jews returned to France following their expulsion in 1182. He composed tosaphot to nearly all the Talmud, based on the teachings of **Isaac ben Samuel of Dampierre**.

Judah ben Kalonymos (d. 1196/1199) German scholar. He lived in Speyer. His *Yiḥuse Tannaim va-Amoraim* provides biographical details of talmudic rabbis and outlines their views.

Judah ben Samuel he-Ḥasid of Regensburg (c. 1150–1217) German rabbi and mystic. He lived in Speyer and later settled in Regensburg. He was one of the most important scholars of the Middle Ages in the fields of ethics and theology, and was the main teacher of the Ḥaside Ashkenaz movement. His writings include magical treatises and the *Book of Divine Glory*, a commentary on the prayers of the Jewish liturgy. He was also the principal author of the *Sepher Ḥasidim*. His teachings were popularized by **Eleazar ben Judah of Worms**.

Judah ben Simon (fl. 4th cent.) Palestinian amora. He was a leading aggadist. **Judah ben Tabbai** (fl. 1st cent. BCE). Palestinian sage. With his colleague **Simeon ben Setaḥ**, he formed the third of the pairs ('zugot') of sages during the time of **Alexander Yannai**.

Judah ha-Levi [Zionides] (before 1075–1141) Spanish Hebrew poet and philosopher. Born in Toledo, he lived in various towns in Christian and Muslim Spain, where he was active as physician. Eventually he left Spain for Palestine. He wrote about 800 poems, including eulogies and laments, covering such topics as love, Jewish festivals, personal religious experience, and longing for Zion. His philosophical work *The Kuzari* describes a disputation conducted before the King of the Khazars by a rabbi, a Christian, a Muslim and an Aristotelian philosopher.

Judah ha-Nasi (fl. c. 2nd–3rd cent.) Palestinian communal leader, son of **Simeon ben Gamaliel II**. He lived most of his life in Galilee, first at Bet Shearim and then at Sepphoris. He was known as 'Rabbenu ha-Kadosh' (our holy teacher), and is referred to in rabbinic literature as 'Rabbi'. He served as the political and religious head of the Jewish community in Palestine. His major contribution was to the redaction of the Mishnah.

Judah Ḥasid ha-Levi (?1660–1700) Lithuanian Shabbetaian preacher. He was born in Dubno. He was maggid in Szydlowiec, and was active in preparing the people for the second appearance of **Shabbetai Tzevi** in 1706. He travelled throughout the communities and urged total repentance, mortifications and fasts. He and hundreds of followers set out for Palestine to await the Messiah. He died a few days after arriving in Jerusalem in 1700.

Judah Löw ben Bezalel [Maharal] (c. 1525–1609) Bohemian rabbi, talmudist, moralist and mathematician. He served as chief rabbi of Moravia from 1553 to 1573, and later settled in Prague. There he founded a yeshivah, organized circles for the study of the Mishnah, and regulated the statutes of the ḥevra kaddisha. Revered for his piety and asceticism, he was active in all aspects of communal life, particularly education. He wrote studies of halakhah, aggadah, ethics, philosophy and homiletics, as well as rabbinic commentaries. According to legend, he was the creator of the Prague golem.

Judas Maccabee (fl. 2nd cent BCE) Palestinian rebel leader, third son of **Mattathias** the Hasmonean. He succeeded his father as leader of the revolt against Antiochus IV Epiphanes. After occupying Jerusalem in 164 BCE, he purified the Temple and assisted Jewish communities in Transjordan and Galilee. He was later killed in battle at Elasa. He is celebrated as the prototype of Jewish heroism.

Judah Nesiah (fl. 3rd cent.) Palestinian nasi, son of **Gamaliel III**. He was the first nasi to settle in Tiberias. He was assisted by **Johanan bar Nappaḥa** and **Resh Lakish**.

Judah the Galilean (d. c. 6) Palestinian Zealot leader. He was born in Gamala in the Golan. He participated in the disturbances in the country following the death of **Herod** the Great. He was the head of a band of rebels active around Sepphoris, who had seized control of the armoury in **Herod**'s palace there. Though the rebels were defeated, Judah escaped. Together with Zadok the Pharisee he founded the Zealots, and opposed the census conducted in Judea by Quirinius.

Judith (fl. 7th–6th cent. BCE) A Simeonite woman living in Bethulia in northern Samaria. During the siege of the city by the Assyrians she succeeded in beheading their general Holophernes, as a result of which the besieging army took flight.

Jung, Leo (1892–1987) US Orthodox rabbi, of Moravian origin. He became rabbi of Congregation Kenesseth Israel in Cleveland in 1920, and later of the Jewish Centre in New York. He was professor of ethics at Yeshiva University from 1931 and later at Stern College for Women. In 1935 he was appointed chairman of the New York State Adivsory Board for Kashrut Law Enforcement. He was also a member of the supreme council of the Agudath Israel organization. He started the series known as the *Jewish Library* in 1928 and edited eight of its volumes.

Juster, Jean (c. 1886–1916) French lawyer and historian, of Romanian origin. He became an advocate at the Paris Court of Appeal. His major work was *Les juifs dans l'empire romain: leur condition juridique, économique et sociale.*

Justus of Tiberias (fl. 1st cent.) Historian. He was a contemporary of **Josephus** and opposed his actions in Galilee during the Jewish rebellion against Rome (66–70). With his father and others Justus was arrested and taken to Tarichaea. Later he fled to Beirut, where he became the private secretary of **Herod Agrippa II**.

K

Kabak, Ahron Avraham (1880–1944) Lithuanian writer. Born in Smorgon in the province of Vilna, he lived in Turkey, Palestine, Germany, France and Switzerland. In 1921 he settled in Palestine, where he taught at the Jerusalem Reḥavyah Gymnasium. His novel *By Herself* was regarded as the first Zionist novel in Hebrew literature. His other novels include *Daniel Shafranov, Victory, Shelomo Molkho, Between the Sea and the Desert, The Narrow Path, History of One Family, The Empty Space, In the Shadow of the Gallows* and *Story Without Heroes.*

Ka'b Al-Aḥbār (fl. 7th cent.) Yemenite scholar. Though born a Jew, he converted to Islam. He was one of the followers of the caliph Omar when he entered Jerusalem. At Omar's request, Ka'b Al-Aḥbār pointed out the site where the Temple had stood. Many teachings of the rabbis and words of the aggadah are attributed to him in Muslim literature.

Kadoorie, Ellis (1865–1922) Hong Kong philanthropist. He was born in Baghdad and settled in Hong Kong. He bequeathed funds for the building of two agricultural schools for Jews and Arabs, one at Tulkarm and one near Mount Tabor. He also contributed to the Anglo-Jewish Association for Education.

Kadoorie, Elly Silas (1867–1944) Hong Kong businessman, brother of **Ellis Kadoorie**. He was born in Baghdad and settled in Hong Kong, developing business interests in Shanghai and other cities. He was an active Zionist and served as president of the Palestine Foundation fund in Shanghai, established agricultural schools in Palestine, and contributed to the construction of the Hebrew University.

Kafka, Franz (1883–1924) German novelist of Czech origin. He was born in Prague and worked in a law office and then an insurance company, pursuing his writing in his spare time. His short stories (including *Metamorphosis*) were published in his lifetime. At his death he instructed his friend **Max Brod** to burn his remaining manuscripts; but Brod succeeded in publishing three novels, *The Trial, The Castle* and *America.* Some commentators interpret Kafka's works as reflecting the Jew's isolation in society.

Kaganovich, Lazar Moiseyevich (1893–1991) Soviet politician. Born in Kiev, he joined the Bolsheviks in 1911. From 1914 he was a member of the communist party's Kiev committee. He played an active role in the period leading up to the October Revolution of 1917. In 1930 he became a member of the committee which controlled the communist party in the Soviet Union. He remained in the Politburo until 1957 when he was accused of belonging to the anti-Party group of Molotov, Malenkov and Shepilov and dismissed from all government posts.

Kahan, Ya'akov (1881–1960) Hebrew poet and playwright of Russian origin. Born in Slutsk, Russia, he moved to Lodz, Poland. His first collection of poetry appeared after he moved to Berne, Switzerland. There he founded Ivriyyah, an international organization for Hebrew language and culture and edited the journal *Ha'ivri hehadash.*

Kahana (i) (fl. 2nd–3rd cent.) Babylonian amora. He and **Assi** were prominent scholars when **Rav** returned from Palestine to Babylonia. Later Kahana emigrated to Palestine, where he joined some of the last tannaim.

Kahana (ii) [Kahana, pupil of Rav] (fl. 3rd cent.) Babylonian amora. It is recorded that he read the weekly Bible portion at **Rav**'s academy. After executing a person who had threatened to denounce a fellow Jew to the Persian authorities, he fled from Babylonia to Palestine. There he joined the academy of **Johanan**.

Kahana (iii) [Kahana, pupil of Rava] (fl. 4th cent.) Babylonian amora. He taught at the academy of Pum Nahara; among his pupils was **Ashi**, the redactor of the Babylonian Talmud.

Kahana (iv) (d. 414) Babylonian amora. He succeeded Rafram ben Papa as head of the academy of Pumbedita from 396.

Kahana, Aharon (1904–67) Israeli painter and ceramic artist. He was born in Stuttgart and lived in Berlin and Paris before settling in Palestine in 1934. In 1947–8 he was a founder member of the New Horizons group of artists. Initially his work was influenced by biblical themes, but later his painting became more abstract. Subsequently he returned to figurative painting.

Kahana, Avraham (1874–1946) Russian biblical scholar and historian. He emigrated to Palestine in 1923, where he served as librarian at the Sha'ar Zion Library in Tel Aviv. From 1903 he worked on an edition of the Hebrew Bible, which was published with a critical commentary and introduction. He also edited the Apocrypha, wrote historical studies, published biographical works, and contributed to Hebrew linguistics.

Kahane, Meir (d. 1990) Israeli rabbi and politician, of American origin. He was ordained at the Mirrer Yeshiva, and received a law degree at the New York Law School. He was the founder of the Jewish Defense League, the Jewish Identity Center, and the organization Shuva. His publications include *Never Again*, *Time to Go Home*, *The Story of the Jewish Defense League* and *Why Be Jewish?*

Kahanovitz, Phinehas [Der Nister] (1884–1952) Russian Yiddish author. He is chiefly known for his realistic historical novel of Ukrainian Jewish life, *House of Crisis*, the first volume of which appeared in 1939.

Kahn, Bernhard (1876–1955) German American community leader. He was born in Sweden, but spent much of his life in Germany, where he became involved in Jewish affairs. He was appointed secretary-general of the Hilfsverein der Deutschen Juden in 1904. In 1921 he became director of the refugee department of the American Jewish Joint Distribution Committee (JDC), and later the JDC's European director, as well as managing director of the American Joint Reconstruction Foundation. In 1939 he emigrated to the US, where he served as honorary chairman of the JDC European Council.

Kahn, Gustave (1859–1936) French writer. Born in Metz, his parents moved to Paris in 1870. He studied at the École des Chartes. He was the editor of *Vogue* and *La Revue Indépendante* and contributed to various literary reviews. He also wrote weekly columns for daily newspapers including *Le Quotidien*. From 1932 he edited the French–Jewish review *Menorah*.

Kahn, Louis (1901–74) American architect, of Estonian origin. Born in Osel, Estonia, he came to the US at the age of four. He studied at the University of Pennsylvania, and worked in various architectural offices. He later taught architecture at Yale University. From 1957 to 1974 he taught at the University of Pennsylvania. He designed a range of buildings as well as synagogues and community centres.

Kahn, Zadok (1839–1905) French rabbi. He was born in Mommenheim, Alsace. He became director of the Talmud torah of the École Rabbinique in Metz. In 1866 he became assitant to chief rabbi Isidore Lazare of Paris, whom he succeeded in 1868, and in 1889 he became chief rabbi of France. He was active in the Ḥibbat Zion movement, and served as president of the Société des Études Juives. He served as editor of the French translation of the Hebrew Bible, and assisted **Isidore Singer** in preparing the American *Jewish Encyclopedia*.

Kaidanover, Aaron Samuel [Aaron Samuel ben Israel Kaidanover; Maharshak] (1614–76) Polish talmudist. He was active as a religious leader in Polish and German Jewish communities. His publications include talmudic novellae, sermons and responsa.

Kaidanover, Tzevi Hirsch (d. 1712) Lithuanian writer son of **Aaron Samuel Kaidanover**. He was imprisoned for four years in Vilna on a false charge. After his release he published his father's writngs in Frankfurt am Main. He was himself the author of an ethical treatise, *Kav ha-Yashar*, which he also translated into Yiddish.

Kalich, Bertha Rachel (1875–1939) American actress. She was born in Poland and settled in New York in 1895. In her youth she appeared at the Bucharest National Theatre. After emigrating to the US she became the first Yiddish speaking actress to be recognized in the English-language theatre; she also appeared in Yiddish repertory.

Kalinsky, René (1936–81) Belgian writer. Born in Brussels, he was in hiding during the war. He then worked as a journalist until 1972 when he settled in Paris. His essays include *L'Origine et L'Essor du Monde Arabe* and *Sionism ou Dispersion*. His plays include *Jim Le Téméraire* and *Dave au bord de la Mer*.

Kalischer, Tzevi Hirsch (1795–1874) German rabbi and Zionist pioneer. He was born in Lissa, in the Posen district, and settled in Thorn in 1824. An opponent of Reform Judaism, he advocated Jewish settlement in Palestine, and in *Derishat Zion* argued for the establishment of a Jewish agricultural society there. In 1864 he was responsible for the founding in Berlin of the Central Committee for Palestine Colonization. He believed that Jewish redemption would come about through human endeavour before the coming of the Messiah. His publications deal with rabbinic topics and Zionism.

Kallen, Horace Meyer (1882–1974) American philosopher. He was born in Berenstadt, Silesia, and was taken to the US in 1887. He taught at the New School for Social Research from 1919 to 1952, and was an active member of the Jewish community. His publications include *The Book of Job as a Greek Tragedy*, *Zionism and World Politics* and *Judaism at Bay*.

Kallir, Eleazar (fl. ?7th cent.) Hebrew poet. He lived in Tiberias. He was the greatest and most prolific of the early composers of piyyutim, writing examples for all the main festivals, special Sabbaths, weekdays of festive character and fasts.

Kalmanovitch, Zelig (1881–1944) Lithuanian Yiddish writer, philologist and translator. He was born in Latvia and settled in Vilna in 1929, where he joined the YIVO Institute and served as editor of its journal. In 1943 he was deported to a concentration camp in Estonia, where he was killed the following year. He published studies on Yiddish philology, the influence of Hebrew on Yiddish syntax, and Yiddish dialects. He also translated various works into Yiddish.

Kalonymous ben Kalonymous [Maestro Calo] (1286–after 1328) French Hebrew author and translator. He lived in various French cities and also in Rome. He translated philosophical and scientific works from Arabic into Hebrew and Latin for King Robert of Naples. His *Even Boḥan* is an ethical study in rhymed prose. In *Masekhet Purim* he presented a satirical parody of a talmudic tractate.

Kaminer, Isaac (1834–1910) Ukrainian Hebrew writer. He was born in Lewkiow in the Ukraine and from 1854 to 1859 taught at the government school for Jews in Zhitomir. Later he served as a physician in Kiev. He wrote verse satires for the Hebrew socialist papers, criticizing supporters of the Haskalah, the Ḥasidim, and rich communal leaders. After the pogroms of the 1880s he joined the Ḥibbat Zion movement.

Kaminka, Armand Aharon (1866–1950) Austrian scholar. He was born in Berdichev in the Ukraine. He served as rabbi at Frankfurt an der Oder, and then as preacher at the Reform temple in Prague. After a period as rabbi to the Jewish community in Esseg, Slavonia, he moved to Vienna, where he became secretary of the Israelitische Allianz. In 1924 he founded Maimonides College, and from 1924 lectured on the Talmud and Jewish philosophy at the University of Vienna. After the annexation of Austria by Hitler in 1938, Kaminka settled in Palestine. His works include biblical and rabbinic studies, translations of Greek and Latin classics into Hebrew, and poetry.

Kaminski, Esther Rachel (1870–1925) Polish Yiddish actress, wife of Abraham Isaac Kaminski. She toured Poland acting in her husband's theatre company. In 1909–11 she appeared in the US, and in 1913 played in London and Paris.

Kaminski, Ida Kaminska (1899–1980) Polish Yiddish actress, daughter of **Esther Rachel Kaminski** and Abraham Isaac Kaminski. As a child she acted in her father's company, and later became the outstanding actress on the Yiddish stage in Poland. She left Poland in 1968 after anti-Semitic disturbances.

Kaniuk, Yoram (b. 1930) Israeli author. He was born in Tel Aviv. His publications include *The Acrophile, The Last Jew* and *Confessions of a Good Arab.*

Kann, Jacobus Henricus (1872–1945) Dutch banker and Zionist. He was born in The Hague and became the owner and manager of his family's bank (Lissa and Kahn) from 1891. As an aide to **Theodor Herzl**, he was one of the founders of the Jewish Colonial Trust in 1899. He was an active participant in the Zionist Congresses and was elected to the Zionist Organization's executive in 1905. Later he worked on various projects in Palestine.

Kaplan, Eliezer (1891–1952) Russian Labour Zionist. He was born in Minsk. He was one of the founders of the Tzeire Zion in Russia in the early years of the 20th century. He became active in the Labour Zionist movement in Europe, and from 1923 in Palestine. He was a member of the executive of the Jewish Agency from 1933, and served as head of its finance department until the establishment of the State of Israel in 1948. He then became Israeli minister of finance, and later was appointed deputy prime minister.

Kaplan, Jacob (b. 1895) French rabbi and author. He was born in Paris. He held rabbinical positions in Mulhouse, Alsace and Paris. During the German occupation of France he worked with the Resistance movement. In 1950 he became chief rabbi of Paris, and in 1955 was appointed chief rabbi of France. He was a lecturer at the Institut d'Études Politiques and a member of the Académie des Sciences Morales et Politiques in Paris. His writings include *Le Judaïsme et la justice sociale, Racisme et Judaïsme, French Jewry Under the Occupation, Le Judaïsme dans la société contemporaine* and *Témoignages sur Israël.*

Kaplan, Mordecai Menaḥem (1881–1983) American rabbi and founder of the Reconstructionist movement. He was born in Lithuania and at the age of nine emigrated with his family to the US. After his ordination he became rabbi of Kehillath Jeshurun synagogue in New York. In 1909 he became dean of the Teachers Institute of the Jewish Theological Seminary of America in New York. Later he taught homiletics, midrash and philosophy of religion at the seminary's rabbinical school. He developed a concept of Judaism known as Reconstructionism, and in accordance with his ideas in 1922 set up a congregation known as the Society for the Advancement of Judaism. He also established the Jewish Reconstructionist Foundation. His writings include *Judaism as a Civilization, The Meaning of God in Modern Jewish Religion* and *The Future of the American Jew.*

Kaplansky, Shelomoh (1884–1950) Israeli Zionist labour leader, of Polish origin. He was born in Bialystok and lived in Vienna from 1903 to 1912. After moving to London, he was chairman of the finance and economics committee of the Zionist Executive (1919–21). From 1927 to 1929 he was a member of the Zionist Executive in Jerusalem and the director of its Settlement Department. He then served as an emissary of the Zionist labour movement to the British Labour Party. In 1932 he was appointed director of the Haifa Technion.

Kara, Abigdor ben Issac (d. 1439) Bohemian rabbi, kabbalist and poet. He lived in Prague. There he witnessed the massacre of the Jewish community in 1389 as a result of the accusation that they had desecrated the host; he wrote an elegy to commemorate their sufferings. His other writings include rabbinic studies and kabbalistic works. He also engaged in polemical debates with Christians. According to legend, he was a favourite of Wenceslaus IV, King of Bohemia, and played an important role in his court.

Kara, Joseph ben Simeon (c. 1060–c. 1130) French Bible commentator. He lived in Troyes and Worms. He took part in theological discussions with

Christians, wrote commentaries on most of the books of the Bible, and commented extensively on the piyyutim.

Karavan, Dani (b. 1930) Israeli sculptor. He was born in Tel Aviv. He produced abstract forms for decorative walls including the Assembly Hall of the Knesset. His large-scale sculptures include *The Monument to the Negev Brigade.*

Kardos, Gyorgy (b. 1925) Hungarian writer. He settled in Palestine but later returned to Budapest, where he was active as a freelance writer. He wrote three novels about his postwar experiences in the Middle East.

Karkasani [Qirqisani], Abu Yusuf Yakub [Jacob; Kirkisani, Jacob] (fl. 10th cent.) Babylonian Karaite scholar. He came from Karkasan near Baghdad. He was the most important proponent of Karaism of his age. His *Book of Lights and Watch-Towers* is a systematic code of Karaite law. In *Book of Gardens and Parks* he commented on the non-legal parts of the Torah.

Karlitz, Avraham Yeshayahu [Ḥazon Ish] (1878–1953) Israeli rabbi and codifier, of Russian origin. He was born in the province of Grodno and lived in Vilna. Later he settled at Bene Berak in Palestine, where he founded a yeshivah. Writing under the name Ḥazon Ish, he became one of the most important modern codifiers.

Karman, Theodore Von (1881–1963) American aerodynamics expert, of Hungarian origin. He left Hungary and took up a teaching and research post at the California Institute of Technology. His work had a major impact on the development of supersonic aircraft and rockets. During World War II he was in charge of American jet-propulsion research. In 1951 he became chairman of the Aeronautical Research and Development Committee of NATO.

Karni, Yehuda (1884–1949) Hebrew poet of Russian origin. He was born in Pinsk. After settling in Palestine, he served on the editorial board of the daily *Ha-Aretz* from 1921. In his *Shirei Yerushalayim*, Jerusalem is presented as the eternal symbol of the people and their destiny. In later writings he lamented the victims of the Holocaust.

Karpleles, Gustav (1848–1909) German literary historian. He was born in Einwanowitz, Moravia. He edited the *Allgemeine Zeitung des Judentums* in Berlin from 1890 and also played an important role in establishing and running the Association of Societies for Jewish History and Literature. He wrote various literary studies including a history of Jewish literature.

Kasher, Menaḥem (1895–1983) American rabbi and halakhist. He was born in Warsaw. In 1925 he went to Palestine, and founded the yeshivah Sefat Emet in Jerusalem. From 1939 he lived in the US. His *Torah Shelemah* is an encyclopaedia of the Talmud and midrash, in which all relevant material in the oral law is collected according to the scriptural verse to which it applies.

Kassovsky [Kossovsky], Ḥayyim Yehoshua (1873–1960) Israeli rabbinic scholar. His writings include concordances of the Bible, Targum Onkelos, the Mishnah, the Tosephta and the Babylonian Talmud.

Kastein, Joseph [Katzenstein, Julius] (1890–1946) German writer and biographer. Born in Bremen, he lived in Switzerland and in 1933 settled in Palestine. He wrote poems, plays, tales, novels and studies of Jewish figures.

Kasztner, Rezso (1906–57) Hungarian Zionist. During World War II, he served as a lawyer in the Zionist office in Budapest. In 1944 the Germans took over Hungary and Adolph Eichmann proposed to Kasztner that Hungarian Jews be allowed to leave for Palestine in exchange for military trucks and equipment. This transaction was referred to as Blut für Ware. Kasztner went on various trips to Germany and Geneva where he met officials of the Jewish Agency and the American Joint Distribution Committee urging them to comply. After the war he settled in Palestine. Later he was accused of collaborating with the Nazis and was assassinated. He was subsequently exonerated by the Israeli Supreme Court.

Katsch, Abraham (b. 1908) American educator. He was born in Poland and emigrated to the US in 1925. He joined the staff of New York University in 1933 and taught Hebrew education and culture. From 1957 he served as director of the university's Hebrew language and literature section, and from 1962 was director of its Institute of Hebrew Studies. In 1967 he became president of Dropsie College. His writings include *Judaism in Islam*.

Katz, Ben-Tziyyon (1875–1958) Israeli journalist and author, of Russian origin. In 1903 he founded and edited the Hebrew periodical *Ha-Zeman*, which appeared first at St Petersburg and later at Vilna. In 1916 he established a Hebrew weekly *Ha-Am*, in Moscow. After World War I he settled in Berlin, and in 1931 moved to Palestine, where he continued his work in Hebrew journalism. He published studies of Russian Jewish history.

Katz, Bernard (1911–2003) British physiologist, of German origin. Born in Germany, he emigrated to England and became professor of biophysics at University College, London. In 1970 he was awarded the Nobel Prize in Medicine and Physiology for his research on the nerve impulse and nerve–muscle connections.

Katz, Jacob (b. 1904) Israeli scholar of Hungarian origin. Born in Hungary, he studied at the University of Frankfurt. With the rise of Nazism, he went to England and then to Israel where he became a professor at the Hebrew University. His work concerns Jewish–Gentile relations, and modern Jewish society and includes *Tradition and Crisis*, *Exclusiveness and Tolerance* and *Out of the Ghetto*.

Katz, Menke (1906–91) American Yiddish poet. He was born in Tsvintsyan, Lithuania, and emigrated to the US in 1920. His publications include *Three Sisters*, *Burning Village*, *My Grandmother Moyne Speaks*, *Safed* and *Aspects of Modern Poetry: A Symposium*.

Katzenelson, Isaac (1886–1944) Polish Hebrew poet and playwright. He was born in Korelichi and later lived and taught in Łódź. He was one of the pioneers of the modern Hebrew theatre. During World War II he was active in Warsaw and other cities. His works of this period describe the catastrophe that befell European Jewry.

Katzenelson, Judah Löb Benjamin (1864–1917) Russian physician, writer and scholar. He was born in Chernigov in the Ukraine. He practised medicine in St Petersburg and his medical writings contributed to the formulation of a Hebrew terminology in medicine. A supporter of the Haskalah, he was a lecturer at the Institute of Jewish Studies in St Petersburg and later its head. He was one of the editors of the Russian Jewish encyclopaedia, and also wrote articles, stories and fables.

Katzir, Aharon (1914–72) Israeli scientist, of Polish origin. He emigrated from Poland to Palestine in 1925. He studied at the Hebrew University and specialized on polymers and membranes, becoming professor of physical chemistry at the Hebrew University from 1952. He joined the Haganah in 1936 and in 1947 helped found Hemed. In May 1972 he was one of those massacred at Lod airport by a group of Japanese terrorists.

Katzir, Ephraim (b. 1916) The brother of **Aharon Katzir**, he went to Palestine as a child. He graduated from the Hebrew University and from 1951 was professor and head of the biophysics department at the Weizmann Institute of Science. He received the Israel Prize, the Rothschild Prize, and the Linderstrom-Lang gold medal. In 1966 he was the first Israeli elected to the United States National Academy of Sciences. In 1973 he became President of Israel.

Katznelson, Berl (1887–1944) Palestinian labour leader. He was born in Belorussia and emigrated to Palestine in 1909. He became an ideologist of the labour movement. He was one of the founders of the Aḥdut ha-Avodah party in 1919, and of the Histradrut in 1920. He served in various positions in the Zionist Organization and edited various labour journals, including the Histadrut daily *Davar*. He was a founder of Mapai in 1930.

Kaufman, Bel (b. 1911) American author and educator, of German origin. Born in Berlin, she grew up in Russia. Her grandfather was **Sholem Aleichem**. She studied at Hunter College and Columbia University, and taught in New York high schools. From 1964 she taught in several New York colleges. Her works include *Up the Down Staircase*.

Kaufman, George S. (1889–1961) American playwright. Born in Pittsburg, he collaborated with **Moss Hart** and **Edna Ferber**.

Kaufman, Shirley (b. 1923) American poet and translator. She was born in Seattle. Her poetry deals with Jewish themes, and her publications include *The Floor Keeps Turning*, *Gold Country* and *From One Family to Another*.

Kaufmann, David (1852–99) Hungarian scholar. He was born in Kojetein, Moravia. He taught Jewish history, religious philosophy and homiletics at the new rabbinical seminary in Budapest. He published studies of Jewish history, medieval Jewish philosophy, history of religion, and the history of Jewish art.

Kaufmann, Isidor (1854–1921) Hungarian painter. He was born in Arad. He travelled throughout Galicia, Poland and the Ukraine, making sketches of shtetl life. He was a pioneer in the depiction of Eastern European Jewish life.

Kaufmann, Yeḥezkel (1889–1963) Israeli biblical scholar and philosopher. He was born in Russia and settled in Palestine in 1920, where he later became professor of Bible studies at the Hebrew University. In *A History of the Israelite Faith* he challenged numerous theories of biblical criticism.

Kaye, Danny [Kaminsky, David Daniel] (1913–87) American actor. Born in Brooklyn, he worked as an entertainer in the Catskill Mountains. He appeared in various films and plays including *The Secret Life of Walter Mitty*, and *Hans Christian Anderson*. Later he toured on behalf of the United Nations International Children's Emergency Fund and subsequently began to host his own musical variety show on television.

Kayserling, Meyer (1829–1905) German rabbi and historian. He was born in Hanover. He served as a rabbi in Switzerland and later in Budapest. He published studies of Jewish history, literature and religion, and a seminal study of marrano history.

Kayyara, Simeon [Simeon ha-Darshan; Simeon Kahira] (fl. 9th cent.) Babylonian scholar. He was the compiler of the *Halakhot Gedolot*.

Kazin, Alfred (1915–98) American critic. Born in Brooklyn, he studied at City College of New York and Columbia University. He taught at the State University of New York at Stony Brook. His works include a multi-volume autobiography: *A Walker in the City*, *Starting Out in the Thirties* and *New York Jew*.

Keesing [Hertzberg], Nancy (b. 1923) Australian writer. Born in Sydney, her works include: *Australian Bush Ballads*, *Old Bush Songs*, *Lily on the Dustbin*, *The White Chrysanthemum* and *According to My Memory*.

Kellner, Leon (1859–1928) Austrian scholar and Zionist. He was a specialist in English literature and, after teaching in high schools, became a lecturer in literature at the University of Vienna. From 1904 to 1914 he was a professor at the University of Czernowitz. When World War I broke out, he returned to Vienna, and he later served as an English expert in the office of the Austrian president. He was one of **Theodor Herzl**'s advisers and published a selection of **Herzl**'s writings as well as the first part of a biography of **Herzl**.

Kemelman, Harry (1908–96) Amercian novelist. His novels deal with an amateur detective, Rabbi Small, who solves murders by using talmudic logic. His publications include *Friday the Rabbi Slept Late*, *Saturday the Rabbi Went Hungry* and *Someday the Rabbi Will Leave*.

Kemph, Franz (b. 1928) Australian artist and printmaker. He was born in Melbourne. He became president of the Contemporary Art Society of the South Australian School of Art, and later head of the graphic art department at the school. Influenced by the Ḥabad movement, he became a pratising Jew. His work contains biblical and Ḥasidic themes.

Kern, Jerome (1885–1945) American composer. Born in New York, he published his first song in 1902. Later he wrote his first hit song: *How'd You Like to Spoon with Me?* Until the outbreak of World War I, many of his songs were written for New York productions of London shows. During the 1920s he collaborated with **Oscar Hammerstein II** and Otto Harbach. Later he and **Hammerstein** won an Oscar for *The Last Time I Saw Paris*.

Kessel, Joseph (1898–1979) French author, Born to Russian parents in Argentina, he went to Russia as an infant and later settled in Paris. He was a student at the Conservatoire Dramatique, and embarked on a career of journalism. During World War I he served as a pilot in the air force. After the war he wrote his first novel, *L'équipage*. He published numerous other novels; some of his books were adapted for the movie screen. From 1939 to 1940 he was a war correspondent, and escaped to London where he was an aide to General Charles de Gaulle. Among his best known works was *Belle de jour*. He wrote several books on Zionism and Jewish topics including *Terre d'amour* and *Terre de feu*.

Kesten, Hermann (1900–96) German novelist. He was appointed literary adviser to the Berlin publishing house of Kiepenheuer in 1927. In 1933 he left Germany and became active in European refugee circles; he later settled in the US. After the collapse of Fascism in Italy, he went to Rome. In *Spanish Fire* he re-created the period of the Jewish expulsion from Spain in the late 15th century. His *Die fremden Götter* portrays the return to Judaism of a father and daughter under the Nazis.

Kestenberg, Leo (1882–1962) Israeli pianist and music educator, of Hungarian origin. He served as music counsellor at the ministry of culture in Berlin, and from 1933 directed the Czech Society for Musical Education. He arrived in Palestine in 1938, where he became the general manager of the Palestine Orchestra. In 1945 he founded the Music Teachers' Training College in Tel Aviv, of which he became the director.

Kimḥi, David [Redak] (?1160–?1235) French grammarian and exegete, son of **Joseph Kimḥi**. He was a teacher in Narbonne, Provence, where he was also active in public life. During the Maimonidean controversy of 1232, he undertook a journey to Toledo to gain the support of Judah ibn Alfakhar for the adherents of **Maimonides**. His *Mikhlol*, which assembled the researches of Spanish Jewish grammarians and philologists, consists of a Hebrew grammar and biblical dictionary. He also wrote biblical commentaries, which combine Spanish speculative, philological, and philosophical traditions with the rabbinic midrashic method of exegesis and the interpretations of **Rashi**.

Kimḥi, Dov (1889–1961) Israeli author, translator and editor, of Galician origin. He was born in Jaslo, Galicia, and emigrated to Palestine in 1908. He settled in Jerusalem, where he taught at Reḥaviah Gymnasium. He wrote novels, short stories and essays, and produced numerous translations.

Kimḥi, Joseph [Joseph ben Isaac Kimḥi] (c.1105–c.1170) Spanish grammarian exegete, translator and polemicist. As a refugee from the Almohad persecutions in Spain, he settled in Narbonne, Provence. His writings include grammars, commentaries on biblical books, religious poems, and translations from Arabic. His *Sepher ha-Berit* was one of the first anti-Christian polemical works written in Europe.

Kimḥi, Moses (d. c.1190) French grammarian and exegete, son of **Joseph Kimḥi**. He was active in Narbonne, Provence. His *Mahalakh Shevile ha-Daat* was the first printed Hebrew grammar (1489); translated into Latin, it was used by Christian scholars during the period of the Reformation. He was also the author of commentaries on Proverbs, Ezra and Nehemiah as well as liturgical poems.

Kingsly, Sidney (1906–95) American playwright. Born in New York, he studied at Cornell University. He acted in a stock company in the Bronx and then served as a play reader for Columbia Pictures. His works include: *Men in White*, *Dead End*, *The Patriots*, *Darkness at Noon*, *Lunatics and Lovers* and *Night Life*.

Kipnis, Menachem (1878–1942) Polish singer, folklorist and writer. He was born in Ushomir, in the Ukraine, and moved to Warsaw in 1901. From 1912 to 1932 he toured Poland, Germany and France, appearing with his wife Zimra Seligsfeld, in lecture-recitals of Jewish folk songs. These he published in numerous collections; he also published articles on various aspects of Jewish music.

Kirchheim, Raphael (1804–89) German scholar. He was born in Frankfürt am Main and became a partner in a banking house. Initially he was an opponent of Reform Judaism, but under the influence of **Abraham Geiger** he became a supporter. His publications include editions of various medieval Hebrew works.

Kirsch, Olga (b. 1924) South African Jewish Afrikaans poet. She grew up in the Orange Free State and studied at the University of Witwatersrand. He work includes: *Die Soeklig, Mure van die Hart* and *Negentien Gedigte.* She settled in Jerusalem in 1948.

Kirschen, Ya'akov (b. 1938) Israeli cartoonist. He was born in Washington DC and grew up in Brooklyn. In 1968 he settled in Israel. He created 'Dry Bones', a daily political comic strip which appeared in the *Jerusalem Post.*

Kisch, Alexander (1848–1917) Austrian rabbi and scholar. He was born in Prague. He served as a rabbi in Brüx, Bohemia (1874–7), Zurich (1877–81), Jungbunzlau, Bohemia (1881–6), and Prague (1886–1917). In Zurich he founded the first Swiss-Jewish weekly. In 1899 Franz Joseph I awarded him a gold medal for 25 years' service as a military chaplain. He was the first rabbi in Austria to be appointed a government professor of religion and inspector of religious education. His writings include studies of Bohemian Jewish history.

Kisch, Egon (1885–1948) Czech journalist. Born in Prague, he studied at the University of Prague. From 1906 to 1913 he was the crime reporter of the Prague journal *Bohemia.* Later he was a political journalist for the Berliner *Tageblatt.* He was a co-founder of the International Federation of Socialist Revolutionaries and led the communist Red Guards in Vienna. He later travelled extensively to Europe, Africa, the Soviet Union and the US. After the 1933 Reichstag fire he was arrested and deported to Czechoslovakia. He then moved to Paris and made his way to Australia. From 1937 to 1938 he fought in the Spanish Civil War. Subsequently he moved to Prague.

Kisch, Frederick Hermann (1888–1943) British soldier and Zionist. He was born in India. He joined the Indian Army and was posted to Baluchistan in World War I. Later he was appointed to the directorate of military intelligence at the war office, working in the section covering Russia, Persia, China and Japan. He was a member of the British delegation to the Paris Peace Conference (1919–21). In 1923 he became a member of the Zionist Executive in Jerusalem and head of its political department. Later he advised the Jewish community on security matters. During World War II he returned to active sevice in the British Army.

Kisch, Guido (1889–1986) American legal historian. He was born in Prague. He taught the theory and history of law at the universities of Leipzig, Königsberg, Halle and Prague. After emigrating to the US in 1935 he taught history at the Jewish Institute of Religion in New York. In 1962 he moved to Basle, where he taught at the university. He published studies on medieval law and German Jewry. He was also the founder and editor of the periodical *Historia Judaica.*

Kishon, Ephraim (b. 1924) Israeli humourist. He was born in Hungary and moved to Israel in 1949. From 1952 he wrote a column in the newspaper *Maariv*, which dealt with political and social issues. He published books, plays, film scripts, stories and articles reflecting Israeli life.

Kisling, Moïse (1891–1953) French painter, of Polish origin. Born in Kraków, Poland, he studied at the Academy of Fine Art there and later went to Paris. He exhibited at the Salon d'Automne, Salon des Indépendents and the Salon des Tuileries. He was on the list of painters condemned by the Nazis. He fled to Portugal and then to New York. He worked for the Four Arts Association, collecting art supplies for families of artists living in France. After the war he returned to France.

Kiss, Joseph (1843–1921) Hungarian poet. He was born in Mezocsat. After the publication of several volumes of his poetry, he became acknowledged as a leading figure in Hungarian literature. In his writings he described social change, moral degeneration and the breakdown of traditional Jewish family life. The theme of anti- Semitism is a prevailing motif throughout his work.

Kissinger, Henry (b. 1923) American politician and scholar, of Bavarian origin. He lived in Fürth, Bavaria as a child but went with his family to the US in 1938. He was drafted in 1943 and served in Germany as an interpreter, then as administratior of a civilian district. He studied at Harvard, later becoming a professor. He was a consultant to Presidents Eisenhower, Kennedy and Johnson before accepting a full-time White House position in 1968 in the Nixon administration. He helped negotiate a peace settlement in the Middle East after the Yom Kippur War. He won the Nobel Peace Prize in 1973.

Kitaj, R. B. (b. 1932) Amercian painter. He was born in Cleveland and later lived in England. From the 1970s he became concerned with Jewish identity as a conscious and subconscious impulse. His paintings include *The Murder of Rosa Luxemburg*, *The Jew Etc.*, and *If Not, Not.*

Klaczko, Julian (1825–1906) Polish author, critic and historian. Raised in the atmosphere of the Lithuanian Haskalah, he wrote poetry in Hebrew and Polish. In 1840 he moved to Germany and then settled in Paris. After converting to Catholicism, he continued to live in France from 1849 to 1869. Subsequently he served in the Galician and imperial Austrian parliaments. From 1888 he lived in Kraków.

Klatzkin, Jacob (1882–1948) German Hebrew editor and philosopher. He was born in Bereza Kartuskaya, Russia. He worked in Germany as a writer for Hebrew periodicals. After World War I, he and Nahum Goldmann founded the publishing house Eshkol, which produced the *Encyclopaedia Judaica* under Klatzkin's editorship. With the rise of the Nazis to power in Germany, Klatzkin moved to Switzerland. He published studies of **Hermann Cohen** and **Baruch Spinoza**, as well as his own philosophical works.

Klausner, Yoseph Gedaliah (1874–1958) Israeli literary critic, historian and Zionist. Born in Olkienik, near Vilna, he was raised in Odessa. At the age of 28 he moved to Warsaw, where he became editor of the literary monthly *Ha-Shiloaḥ* In 1919 he emigrated to Palestine, where he was active in the Academy of the Hebrew Langauge. Appointed to the chair of Hebrew literature at the Hebrew University, he subsequently became professor of the history of the Second Temple. His publications include histories of modern Hebrew literature, the Second Temple period, and the idea of the Messiah, studies of Jesus and Paul, philological works, monographs on Hebrew authors, and philosophical works. From 1950 he served as editor-in-chief of the *Encyclopaedia Hebraica.*

Klein, Abraham M. (1909–72) Canadian poet and author. He was born in Montreal, and became a partner in a law firm. He is regarded as the first outstanding Jewish contributor to Canadian literature. In addition to writing his own poetry, he made numerous translations of Hebrew and Yiddish poems. His publications include *Hath not a Jew*, *The Hitleriad*, *Poems* and *The Rocking Chair.* His work was influenced by Jewish themes, talmudic erudition and Yiddish folklore.

Klein, Melanie (1882–1960) Austrian psychoanalyst. Born in Vienna, she studied at the University of Vienna. After moving to Budapest she was drawn to the works of **Sigmund Freud** and was analysed by **Sandor Ferenczi**. She went to Berlin and later settled in London. She was the founder of the object relations school of psychoanalysis.

Klein, Shemuel (1886–1940) Hungarian historian and geographer of Palestine. He served as a rabbi in Dolnja Tuzla, Bosnia (1909–13), and Ersekujvar (1913–28). In 1929 he became professor of historical topography of Palestine at the Hebrew University. In his writings he used the Talmud and midrash as primary sources of information on the country's topography and the history of its settlement.

Klemperer, Otto (1885–1973) German musician. Born in Breslau, he studied in Frankfurt and Berlin. He was chorus master and then conductor at the German theatre in Prague. In 1917 he became music director of the Cologne Opera. Later he led several German opera companies. When the Nazis came to power, he emigrated to the US. He directed the Los Angeles Philharmonic Orchestra and the Pittsburgh Symphony Orchestra. From 1947 to 1950 he was director of the Budapest Opera. In 1954 he began conducting and recording with the Philharmonia Orchestra of London, becoming its principal conductor.

Kluger, Solomon ben Judah Aaron (1785–1869) Austrian rabbinic scholar. He was also known as the Maggid of Brody. He initially lived in Rava, where he worked as a shopkeeper. He then became rabbi at Kolki. From there he went to Josefov, and in 1820 to Brody. An opponent of the maskilim, he wrote hundreds of responsa and numerous books.

Klutznick, Philip Morris (1907–99) American communal leader and diplomat. He was born in Kansas City, Missouri. He held a succession of appointments connected with community planning: in 1935–6 he was a special assistant on housing to the US attorney general; in 1938–41 general counsel for the Omaha Housing Authority; and in 1944–6 federal housing commissioner. From 1961 to 1963 he served as ambassador to the United Nations Economic and Social Council. He held several positions in Jewish organizations, including international president of B'nai B'rith, general chairman of the United Jewish Appeal, and vice-president of the Jewish Welfare Board.

Kobrin, Leon (1873–1946) American Yiddish dramatist and novelist. He was born in Russia, and emigrated to the US in 1892, where he worked in a sweatshop. His stories and plays describe Jewish life in the US during the period of immigration, depicting the problems of nationalism, assimilation and relations between parents and children.

Koenig, Leo (1889–1970) British Yiddish author, critic and journalist. He was born in Odessa. He wrote art criticism for leading Yiddish periodicals in Paris, before moving to London in 1914; he then worked for the Yiddish press in England and abroad. In 1952 he settled in Haifa.

Koestler, Arthur (1905–1983) English author. Born in Budapest, he travelled widely, settling in England in 1940. Initially a communist in the 1930s, he later repudiated communism. His works include novels, essays and reminiscences. *Thieves in the Night* portrays kibbutz life in Palestine, and *Promise and Fulfilment* deals with Zionism.

Kogan [Kahana], David (1838–1915) Ukrainian scholar. He was born in Odessa. He wrote numerous studies of Jewish history and literature, including *History of the Kabbalists, Sabbataians and Ḥasidim.*

Kohen, Gershom ben-Solomon (d. 1544) Bohemian printer. He produced four prayerbooks, an edition of the Pentateuch, and an illustrated edition of the Passover Haggadah. He received a royal patent which authorized him to be the only Hebrew printer in Bohemia.

Kohen, Tzedek ben Joseph (fl. 10th cent.) Babylonian gaon. He was gaon of Pumbedita from 917 to 936. He was appointed gaon by the exilarch **David ben Zakkai I**, but the scholars of the academy refused to recognize him and elected Mevasser Kahana instead. As a result both men served simultaneously as geonim, but after Mevasser's death in 926 Kohen Tzedek ben Joseph assumed the post alone.

Kohler, Kaufmann (1843–1926) American Reform leader. He was born in Fürth in Bavaria and emigrated to the US in 1869. He served as rabbi of the Congregation of Beth El in Detroit, Sinai Congregation in Chicago, and Temple Beth El in New York. He was a leading figure at the Pittsburgh Conference of Reform Jewish in 1885, at which the Pittsburgh Platform (a statement of the tenets of American Reform Judaism) was adopted. In 1903 he became president of the Hebrew Union College. His publications include *Jewish Theology.*

Kohler, Max James (1871–1934) American attorney and communal leader. He was born in Detroit. He served as assistant US district attorney in the southern district of New York from 1894 to 1898, and then entered private law as a defender of the legal and public rights of immigrants, naturalized citizens and aliens. His writings include *Immigration and Aliens in the United States: Studies of American Immigration Laws and the Legal Status of Aliens in the United States.*

Kohler, Rose (1873–1947) American sculptor and painter, daughter of **Kaufmann Kohler**. Her works include busts and portraits of Jewish leaders, as well as a medallion entitled *The Spirit of the Synagogue.*

Kohn, Abraham (1807–48) Ukrainian rabbi. He was born in Bohemia, and served as a rabbi in Hohenems. In 1844 he became a preacher in Lemberg, where his reforms aroused the opposition of Orthodox Jews. When he and his son died from food poisoning, Orthodox leaders were arrested, but they were later released for lack of evidence.

Kohn, Hans (1891–1971) American historian, of Czech origin. Born in Prague, he studied at the University of Prague. He joined the Czech regiment of the Austro-Hungarian army and was captured by Russian forces. He later returned to Prague, and in 1921 went to London where he joined the Independent Labour party. In 1928 he published *A History of Nationalism in the East.* He later lived in Jerusalem where he wrote books on the Middle East. Subsequently he moved to the US and taught at Smith College, and later at City College of New York. His works include *The Idea of Nationalism.*

Kohn, Samuel (1841–1920) Hungarian rabbi and scholar. He was born in Baja, Hungary. He served as a rabbi in Budapest from 1866 to 1905, when he was appointed chief rabbi of Hungary. He was one of those responsible for the establishment of the Jewish Theological Seminary in Budapest. He published works on the Samaritans, and the history of the Jews in Hungary.

Kohut, Adolph (1848–1917) German journalist and writer, of Hungarian origin. He was the editor of several German papers. He published studies of history, culture and Jewish affairs, as well as a history of the Jews in Germany.

Kohut, Alexander (1842–94) American rabbi and scholar, of Hungarian origin. He served as a rabbi in Stuhlweissenburg, and later became chief rabbi of Fünfkirchen. In 1885 he left for the US, where he served as rabbi of Congregation Ahavath Chesed in New York. He helped to establish the Jewish Theological Seminary, where he taught midrash and talmudic methodology. His *Arukh ha-Shalem* is a lexicon of talmudic terms based on the talmudic dictionary of **Nathan ben Jehiel**.

Kohut, Rebekah (1864–1951) American educator and community leader, wife of **Alexander Kohut**. She was born in Kaschau. From 1897 to 1901 she was president of the New York Council of Jewish Women, and in 1914 was appointed head of the employment bureau of the Young Women's Hebrew Association. In 1942 she became president of the World Congress of Jewish Women. Her writings include *My Portion, More Yesterdays* and *George Alexander Kohut: His Memoir.*

Koigen, David (1879–1933) Ukrainian philosopher and sociologist. He lived in Germany until 1912, when he returned to Russia. In 1921 he was appointed professor of philosophy and sociology at the Ukrainian University of Kiev. His writings include studies of the Jewish experience in history and culture.

Kollek, Theodor (b. 1911) Israeli politician. He was born in Vienna. In 1934 he emigrated to Palestine, where he became a member of kibbutz En Gev. From 1940 to 1947 he served in the political department of the Jewish Agency. He then (1947–8) represented the Haganah in the US and in 1951–2 served as Israel's minister plenipotentiary in Washington. He was director of the Israeli prime minister's office from 1952 to 1964, and chairman of the Israel Government Tourist Corporation from 1956 to 1964. In 1965 he was elected Mayor of Jeruslaem.

Kompert, Leopold (1822–1886) Austrian novelist. He was born in Bohemia. In 1840 he moved to Hungary, where he became editor of the German-language literary periodical *Pannonia* published in Pressburg. Later he settled in Vienna, where he worked as a journalist. His writings deal with Eastern European Jewish life, mixed marriages and anti-Semitism. He was active in Jewish affairs and Viennese civic life, taking a special interest in education and the welfare of orphans.

Konrád, György (b. 1933) Hungarian author. He was born in Berettyóújfalu in eastern Hungary. His writings include *The Loser.*

Kook, Avraham Yitzḥak (1865–1935) Palestinian rabbinic scholar of Latvian origin. He was born in Greiva, Latvia, and served as rabbi of Zaumel and Bauska, before emigrating to Palestine in 1904. An ardent Zionist, he became chief rabbi of the Ashkenazi community in Palestine in 1921. He believed that the return to Palestine marked the beginning of divine redemption. His writings include *Orot* (on holiness in the newborn nationalism), *Orot ha-Teshuvah* (on repentance), and *Halakhah Berurah* (on halakhic issues).

Kops, Bernard (b. 1926) English playwright and novelist. He was born in the East End of London, which became the subject of his work. His writings include *The World Is a Wedding, Yes from No-Man's Land, By the Waters of Whitechapel* and *The Hamlet of Stepney Green.*

Kopytman, Marc (b. 1929) Israeli composer, of Russian origin. He went to Israel in 1972, and became professor of composition at the Rubin Academy of Music in Jerusalem. Some of his work is influenced by traditional Jewish cantillation.

Korah (fl. 13th cent. BCE) Levite, kinsman of **Moses**. Together with **Dathan**, **Abiram** of the tribe of Reuben, and 250 Israelite leaders, he rebelled against **Moses** and **Aaron** (Numbers 16). As a punishment, the earth opened and swallowed them (Numbers 26:11).

Korczak, Janos (1879–1942) Polish author, educator and communal leader. He was born in Warsaw, where he worked as a physician and became concerned with the plight of the poor; his early writings depict the condition of homeless orphans in the cities. In 1911 he became head of a Jewish orphanage in Warsaw. He published theoretical studies about pedagogical method, as well as children's books. With the rise of Hitler, he became Poland's non-Zionist representative on the Jewish Agency. In 1942 he was deported to a concentration camp, where he was killed.

Korda, Alexander [Korda, Sandor Laszlo] (1893–1956) British film producer and director, of Hungarian origin. Born in Hungary, he studied at the Royal University in Budapest. He initially worked as a journalist, but later turned to film production. He founded the trade journals *Pest Movie*, *The Movie* and *Film Week*. He produced a number of Hungarian films. He eventually went to Hollywood, and later he settled in London where he founded London Films Limited. He was knighted in 1942.

Kornberg, Arthur (b. 1918) American biochemist. He worked in the public health service, later becoming professor of microbiology at Washington University; subsequently he became professor of biochemistry at Standford University. He shared the Nobel Prize in Medicine and Physiology in 1959.

Kornfeld, Joseph Saul (1876–1943) American rabbi and diplomat, of Austro-Hungarian origin. He went to the US as a child. He served congregations in Pine Bluff, Arkansas; Montreal; and Columbus, Ohio, where he became active in civic affairs. He was appointed American ambassador to Persia in 1921. In 1925 he became rabbi of the Collingwood Avenue Temple in Toledo, Ohio.

Kornfeld, Paul (1889–1942) German playwright. He was born in Prague. He wrote tragedies, comedies and an historical drama, *Jud Süss*. He was deported by the Nazis and died in the Lódź Ghetto.

Korngold, Erich (1897–1957) American composer, of Czech origin. Born in Brünn, Moravia, he was the son of the music critic Julian Korngold. He took composition lessons and at the age of 11 composed *Der Schneemann*. In the 1920s he taught opera and composition at the Vienna State Academy. In 1934 he went to Hollywood and wrote a number of film scores as well as concertos and symphonies.

Koufax, Sanford [Sandy] (b. 1935) American baseball player. He was the pitcher for the Brooklyn Dodgers. His club won three National League pennants and two World Series.

Koussevitzky, Serge (1874–1951) American conductor, of Russian origin. Born in Tver, Russia, he moved to Moscow at the age of 14 where he was baptized. He studied double bass at the Musico-Dramatic Institute in Moscow and later joined the Bolshoi Opera. He subsequently settled in Germany where he continued to perform on the double bass and began conducting with the Berlin Philharmonic. He organized his own symphony orchestra in Moscow and went on various tours. After the 1917 revolution he became director of the State Symphony Orchestra. In 1920 he went to Berlin and Rome, finally residing in Paris. In 1924 he became conductor of the Boston Symphony.

Kovner, Abba (1918–87) Lithuanian resistance fighter and Hebrew poet. Born in Sevastopol, he grew up in Vilna. He was a commander of the Vilna Ghetto and fought the Germans as leader of the partisan groups in the surrounding forests. In 1945 he settled in Palestine, but he was imprisoned in Egypt by the British when he attempted to return to Europe to continue Jewish rescue work. His poems and novels deal with Jewish partisans during the Nazi period and Israel's War of Independence.

Kovner, Abraham Uri (1842–1909) Russian Hebrew author. He was born in Vilna. He published a collection of essays, *Ḥeker Davar*, in 1865, which condemned Haskalah literature, and in *Tzeror Peraḥim* he attacked Hebrew as a dead language. In 1870 he settled in St Petersburg, where he contributed weekly articles to the Russian journal *Golos*. Condemned to exile in Siberia for a criminal offence, he later adopted Christianity. His last years were spent in Lomża, Poland, where he worked as a government official.

Kozakov, Mikhail (1897–1954) Russian author. He was born in the Ukraine. His novel *The Fall of the Empire* deals with the last years of imperial Russia and the revolution. Some of his early stories describe life in a Jewish shtetl in the Pale of Settlement. His novella *The Person Kissing the Ground* deals with Russian anti-Semitism.

Krakauer, Leopold (1896–1954) Israeli architect and designer of Austrian origin. He was born in Vienna. He helped to design the parliament building in Belgrade. In 1924 he emigrated to Palestine, settling in Jerusalem. He designed public buildings and private houses, and later concentrated on town planning. He also produced drawings of the countryside around Jerusalem.

Kramer, Jacob (1892–1962) British painter. He was born in the Ukraine; his family emigrated to England in 1900 and settled in Leeds. His paintings include *The Day of Atonement*, and *Hear Our Voice, O Lord Our God.*

Kraus, Karl (1874–1936) Austrian satirist and poet. He was born in a provincial Bohemian town; when he was three his family moved to Vienna. He studied law at the University of Vienna and began writing at the age of 18. He founded a satirical magazine *Die Fackel.* In 1921 he converted to Roman Catholicism. He wrote plays and lyric poetry which was collected in nine volumes.

Krauskopf, Joseph (1858–1923) American Reform rabbi. He was born in Prussia and settled in the US in 1872. He served congregations in Kansas City and Philadelphia. A leader of radical reform, he was an important figure in the national organizations of Reform Judaism. He established the National Farm School in Doylestown, Pennsylvania, and in 1917 was appointed to direct food conservation among Jews for the US Food Administration.

Krauss, Samuel (1866–1948) Austrian historian, philologist, talmudic scholar, of Hungarian origin. He taught Bible and Hebrew at the Jewish teachers' seminary in Budapest. In 1906 he was appointed to teach the Bible, history and liturgy at the Vienna Rabbinical Seminary (the Israelitische-Theologische Lehranstalt); later he became head of the seminary and rector. When the Nazis came to power, he fled to England. He published studies in the fields of philology, history, the Bible, the Talmud, Christianity, and medieval literature.

Krebs, Hans (1900–81) German biochemist. Born in Hildesheim, Germany, he studied at Hamburg University. From 1926 to 1930 he was assistant to Otto Warburg at the Kaiser Wilhelm Institute. With the rise of Nazism, he fled to England and worked at Cambridge, and later at Sheffield University where he became professor. In 1953 he was awarded the Nobel Prize for Medicine and Physiology. Later he became professor at Oxford University.

Krein, Alexander (1883–1951) Russian composer, brother of **Grigori Krein**. He studied at the Moscow Conservatory, where he served as professor (1912–17). He was then secretary of the Russian Board of Education (1918–20), and a member of the board of the State Publishing Department (1918–27). He was one of the leaders of the Jewish musical movement and an active member of the Society for Jewish Folk Music. His music contains Jewish traditional folk motifs.

Krein, Grigori (1885–1955) Russian composer and violinist, brother of **Alexander Krein**. He studied in Moscow and later in Leipzig. From 1926 to 1934 he lived in Paris and later in Tashkent. A number of his compositions have a Jewish content.

Kreiser, Jacob (1905–69) Soviet general. He was the son of a Cantonist in the military service, who was coerced to convert to Christianity. He became a general at 31. During World War II, he was commander of the Moscow Proletarian Infantry Division. Later he became commander of the Third Army. He was moved to the Second Army and then to the Fifty-First.

Kreisky, Bruno (1911–90) Austrian politician. Born in Vienna, he was active in the socialist party and studied at the University of Vienna. He moved to Sweden where he worked as a foreign correspondent. In 1951 he returned to Austria and became deputy chief of cabinet in the office of the federal president. Later he was undersecretary of state in the foreign ministry. In 1956 he was elected to the Austrian parliament and served as foreign minister. He was elected chancellor in 1970.

Kreitman, Esther (1891–1954) Polish Yiddish author, sister of **Israel Joshua Singer** and **Isaac Bashevis Singer**. She was born in Bilgoraj, Poland. Her publications include *Der sheydem-tants*, *Brilyantn* and *Yikhes.*

Krementzky, Johann (1850–1934) Austrian Zionist leader. He was born in Odessa; he settled in Vienna in 1880 and built several factories. An ardent Zionist, he became an adherent of **Theodor Herzl**; he served as a member of the Zionist Executive and the Zionist General Council and was appointed director of the Jewish National Fund.

Krochmal, Abraham (d. 1888) Galician-born writer and scholar. He lived in Lemberg, Brody, Odessa and Frankfurt am Main. In Galicia and Odessa he moved in Haskalah circles. He wrote studies of the Talmud and the Bible, philosophical works on Judaism, and articles advocating religious reform.

Krochmal, Naḥman (1785–1840) Galician philosopher and historian. He was born in Brody, and lived in Zolkiew in Galicia. Later he returned to Brody, and eventually moved to Tarnopol. He was a leading figure in the Haskalah movement and the founder (in the 1830s) of Wissenschaft des Judentums. His *Guide to the Perplexed of the Time* is a philosophical investigation of the course of Jewish history.

Kronenberger, Louis (1904–80) American critic and writer. Born in Cincinnati, Ohio, he studied at the University of Cincinnati. He initially worked for the *New York Times*, and subsequently was an editor with Boni and Liveright. From 1933 to 1938 he was an editor for Alfred A. Knopf. From 1938 to 1961 he was the drama critic for *Time.* His works include *The Thread of Laughter: Chapters on English Stage Comedy from Jonson to Maugham, The Grand Manner, Grand Right and Left, A Month of Sundays, Marlborough's Duchess: A Study in Worldliness* and *Oscar Wilde.*

Kuhn, Walt (1877–1949) American painter. Born in Brooklyn, he was a newspaper cartoonist and illustrator. Later he studied in Europe, returning to New York in 1903. He was allied with the Ashcan group of painters. He was the organizer of the Armory Show in 1913 which introduced European modernists to the American public. He painted portraits of show people.

Kulisher, Michael (1847–1919) Russian historian, ethnographer and communal worker. He studied at the rabbinical seminary in Zhitomir in the Ukraine, and at the law faculty of the University of St Petersburg. From 1869 to 1871 he was on the editorial board of the Russian Jewish newspaper *Den.* He published a life of **Jesus** as well as studies of gentile attitudes to the Jews.

Kumin, Maxine (b. 1925) American poet and writer. She was born in Philadelphia. She taught at Tufts, Columbia and Princeton universities. Some of her poetry deals with her Jewish identity.

Kun, Bela (1886–1939) Hungarian communist leader. Born in a small Translyvanian town, he was educated at Kolozsvar. He joined the Hungarian Social Democratic party in 1902 and later the army. From 1918 he led the Hungarian group in the Russian Communist party. During the same year he returned to Hungary and founded the Hungarian Communist party and its organ *Voeroes Ujsag.* He was arrested but liberated the next year and became commissar for foreign and military affairs. He later emigrated to Austria, and then to the Soviet Union where he became a member of the Third Congress of the Communist International. He was subsequently arrested during the Stalinist purges, and executed.

Kunitz, Stanley (b. 1905) American poet. Born in Worcester, Massachusetts, he studied at Harvard. He edited literary reference works and held a number of academic posts. His work includes *Intellectual Things, Passport to the War, Selected Poems 1928–1958* and *The Testing Tree.*

Kurzweil, Baruch (1907–72) Israeli literary critic. He was born in Moravia, and emigrated to Palestine in 1939. He was appointed professor of modern Hebrew literature at Bar-Ilan University in 1955. His writings include *On the Novel*, *Our New Literature: Continuation or Revolution?*, *Bialik ve-Tchernichovsky*, *Massot al Sippurei S.Y. Agnon* and *Between the Vision and the Absurd.*

Kusevitsky, Mosheh (1899–1966) Polish cantor. He served as chief cantor at the main synagogue in Warsaw. From 1947 he lived in the US and made concert tours abroad.

Kushner, Harold (b. 1935) American rabbi. He has served congregations in New York and Massachusetts. His publications include *When Bad Things Happen to Good People.*

Kutscher, Edward Yechezkel (1909–71) Israeli linguist. He was born in Topoltshani, Slovakia, and went to Israel in 1941. He taught at the Hebrew University and later at Bar-Ilan University, specializing in Hebrew and Semitic languages. His publications include *The Language and Linguistic Background of the Isaiah Scroll*, and *History of the Hebrew Language.*

Kuznets, Simon (1905–85) American economist, of Russian origin. Born in Pinsk, he went with his family to Kharkov. He studied at the University of Kharkov and worked in the Division of Statistics of the Central Soviet of Trade. In 1922 he settled in the US and studied at Columbia University. From 1930 to 1954 he was professor at the University of Pennsylvania. Later he taught at Johns Hopkin's University and Harvard. He received the Nobel Prize in 1971.

Kvitko, Leib (1890–1952) Russian Yiddish writer. He worked in various cities in the Ukraine as a dyer, shoemaker, porter and stevedore. In 1920 he settled in Germany, but he later returned to the USSR. He was arrested in the Stalinist purges in 1949, and executed with other Yiddish writers in 1952. He wrote novels and poetry, as well as stories for children.

Kwartin, Zavel (1874–1953) American cantor and composer. He was born in the Ukraine. He served as a cantor in synagogues in Vienna, St Petersburg and Budapest, before emigrating to the US in 1919. He became cantor at Temple Emanuel in Borough Park, Brooklyn. He moved to Palestine in 1926, but later returned to the US.

L

Laban (fl?19th–16th cent. BCE) Israelite herdsman, brother of **Rebekah** and father of **Leah** and **Rachel**. He was a breeder of sheep and goats. He gave his sister **Rebekah** in marriage to **Isaac** (Genesis 24). Later he consented to the marriage of his daughter **Rachel** to **Jacob**, but deceived **Jacob** by substituting her sister **Leah**; he finally gave **Rachel** to **Jacob** as a wife in exchange for a further seven years of labour (Genesis 29).

Lachover, Yeruḥam Fishel (1883–1947) Israeli literary scholar. He was born in Chorzele, Poland. He began his literary career as a critic in 1904, and in 1908 moved to Warsaw, where he edited several journals and miscellanies. He settled in Palestine in 1927. His publications include a history of modern Hebrew literature and a biography of **Bialik**.

Laemel, Simon von (1766–1845) Austrian financier. He was a wealthy wool trader. He helped end the Jewish poll tax and reduce Jewish tax in Bohemia. He was ennobled for his financial service to Austria during the Napoleonic wars.

Laemmle, Carl (1867–1939) American film executive, of German origin. Born in Laupheim, Germany, he went to the US at the age of 17. He worked as a bookkeeper. In 1909 he opened a nickelodeon and became a partner of the Motion Picture Patents Company. In 1912 the Universal Film Company was formed as a result of a merger between his Independent Motion Picture Company and other firms. In 1915 he opened Universal City Studio in Hollywood.

Lafer, Horacio (1893–1965) Brazilian politician. Born in São Paulo, he studied economics, philosophy and law before entering industry and politics. He worked with the Klabin firm which developed the cellulose and paper industry in Brazil. He founded the Brazilian National Economic Development Bank and served as governor of the World Bank. In 1928 he was the Brazilian delegate to the League of Nations, and was elected to the federal chamber of deputies. In 1951 he was appointed minister of finance in Brazil; subsequently he became foreign minister.

La Guardia, Fiorello (1882–1947) American politician. Born in New York City, he was educated in Prescott, Arizona. Later his family went to Budapest where he obtained employment in the US consulate. On his return to the US, he opened a law office. He later became New York State deputy attorney general, and was elected to Congress in 1916. In 1932 he became mayor of New York. Subsequently he became director general of the United Nations Relief and Rehabilitation Administration.

Laguna, Daniel Israel Lopez (1653–1723) Jamaican marrano poet. As a child he was taken to Peyrehorade in the south of France. Later he was arrested by the Inquisition in Spain. He settled in Jamaica, where he practised Judaism. In about 1720 he moved to London but he eventually returned to Jamaica. During his time in London he published a paraphrase of the Psalms in Spanish verse forms.

Lambert, Mayer (1863–1930) French scholar. He was born in Metz. He lectured on Arabic, Syriac and Hebrew at the École Rabbinique and taught Hebrew at the École Normale Orientale of the

Alliance Israélite Universelle. In 1903 he began teaching Hebrew and Syriac at the École Pratique des Hautes Études. His publications include studies of Hebrew grammar and the writings of **Saadyah Gaon**.

Lamdan, Yitzḥak (1899–1954) Hebrew poet. He was born in Milnov, in the Ukraine, and witnessed the Ukrainian pogroms after World War I. In 1920 he emigrated to Palestine, where he initially worked as a labourer. From 1934 he published and edited the literary monthly *Gilyonot.* His poem *Masadah* reflects the spirit of the pioneers of the 1920s.

Lämel, Simon von (1776–1845) Bohemian merchant. He established a wool factory in Prague and was ennobled in 1812 for his services to Austria during the Napoleonic Wars. He was a benefactor of various Jewish causes.

Lamm, Norman (b. 1927) American scholar. He was born in Brooklyn. He became professor of philosophy and president of Yeshiva University. His publications include *A Hedge of Roses, The Royal Reach, Faith and Doubt, Torah Lishmah* and *The Good Society*. He has also served as the editor of the Library of Jewish Law and Ethics.

Lampronti, Isaac ben Samuel (1679–1756) Italian humanist. Born in Ferrara, he taught in the Talmud Torah of the Italian and Sephardi community in the city. Later he became head of the yeshivah there. His *Paḥad Yitzḥak* is a talmudic encyclopaedia.

Land, Edwin (1909–91) American inventor. Born in Bridgeport, Connecticut, he studied at Harvard and in 1937 founded the Polaroid Corporation. In 1941 he developed a three-dimensional motion-picture process based on polarized light and worked on the possiblity of instant photography; in 1948 the Polaroid system was launched.

Landa, Myer (1874–1947) English writer. Born in Leeds, he embarked on provincial journalism but later moved to the London *Daily Mail* and subsequently the *Daily News*. In 1919 he became editor of the Zionist Organization's daily bulletin. His works include *The Jew in Drama, Palestine as it Was* and *The Shylock Myth.*

Landau, Adolph (1842–1902) Russian journalist, educator and publisher. He was born in Lithuania. He contributed to the Russian liberal press, and in 1871 began to publish a literary-historical anthology, the *Jewish Library*. In 1881 he founded the monthly journal *Voskhod,* later adding a weekly supplement in which he attacked Ḥibbat Zion, Zionists and those who hated Jews.

Landau, Ezekiel ben Judah (1713–93) Bohemian halakhic authority. He was born in Opatów, Poland, and served as dayyan of Brody and rabbi of Yampol. In 1754 he became rabbi of Prague and the whole of Bohemia. He attempted to mitigate the conflict between **Jadob Emden** and **Jonathan Eibeschütz**, fought against the Shabbeteains, and opposed Ḥasidism. He objected to **Moses Mendelssohn**'s German translation of the Bible. His *Noda bi-Yhudah* contains over 800 responsa.

Landau, Jacob (1892–1952) Austrian journalist and publisher. He was born in Vienna. In 1914 he established the Jewish Correspondence Bureau, a news agency, in The Hague. He later moved his offices to London and renamed the organization the Jewish Telegraphic Agency. Branch offices were opened in Berlin, Warsaw, Prague, Paris, New York and Jerusalem, and headquarters were subsequently established in New York. In 1940 he helped to found the Overseas News Agency.

Landau, Judah Leo (1866–1942) South African rabbi, scholar, poet and playwright, of Galician origin. He served as minister of the North Manchester Hebrew Congregation (1900–4) before moving to Johannesburg to become rabbi of the Johannesburg Hebrew Congregation. In 1915 he became chief rabbi there and professor of Hebrew at Witwatersrand University. He wrote Hebrew poems and plays, as well as studies of modern Hebrew literature.

Landau, Lev Davidovich (1908–68) Russian physicist. Born in Baku, he studied at the University of Baku and the University of Leningrad. In 1929 he went to Copenhagen to study with **Niels Bohr**. From 1932 he was employed at the Ukrainian Physico-Technical Institute at Kharkov. In 1937 he became the head of the theoretical division of the Institute of Physical Problems in Moscow. In 1962 he was awarded the Nobel Prize for theories dealing with condensed matter.

Landau, Zisho (1889–1937) American Yiddish poet, of Polish origin. He settled in New York, where he published an *Anthology of Yiddish Poetry in America Until 1919*. Deeply affected by Jewish suffering during World War I, he reverted to Jewish themes in his later poetry.

Landauer, Gustav (1870–1919) German philosopher and writer. The son of a wealthy Karlsruhe merchant, he was attracted to anarchism in his youth and was twice imprisoned for political agitation. In 1918 he became editor of the theatrical periodical *Masken* published in Düsseldorf. When the Bavarian Soviet Republic was proclaimed in 1919, he accepted an invitation to become minister of public instruction. Following the overthrow of the government, he was murdered by counter-revolutionary soldiers in Munich. He published novels and philosophical and literary essays, and translated foreign literature into German.

Landauer, Samuel (1846–1937) German orientalist. He was born in Hürben. He taught oriental languages at the University of Strasbourg from 1875, and in 1905 became director of the state and university library. Later he settled in Augsburg. He published the Arabic original of **Saadyah Gaon**'s *Emunot ve-Deot*, as well as a standard edition of the works of the Persian poet Firdausi.

Landesmann, Heinrich [Lorm, Hieronymus] (1821–1902) German author. Born in Nikolsburg, he lived in Leipzig, Berlin, Vienna, Dresden and Brünn. Although he was both deaf and blind, he published fiction, works of philosophy and poetry. His novel *Gabriel Solmar* depicts a Jew's disillusionment with emancipation and his return to the Jewish community.

Landman, Isaac (1880–1946) American rabbi, of Russian origin. He emigrated to the US in 1890 and served as a Reform rabbi in New York. He edited the *American Hebrew* as well as the *Universal Jewish Encyclopedia*. From 1906 to 1916 he served as executive secretary of the National Farm School.

Landowska,Wanda(1879–1959) Polishmusician.She studied with the Chopin interpreter, Michalowski, at the Warsaw Conservatory. In 1895 she went to Berlin to study counterpoint and composition. In 1900 she eloped with the musician Henry Lew to Paris. From 1909 she devoted herself to the revival of the harpsichord. She began playing the harpsichord in public in 1903 and taught harpsichord at the Berlin Hochschule für Musik. Later she went to Switzerland and settled in Paris. She began recording and embarked on a series of tours. In 1925 she founded the School for Ancient Music at Saint-Leu-la-Forêt. She eventually settled in the US.

Landshath, Eliezer (1817–87) German liturgical scholar and historian. He was born in Lissa. He worked as a bookseller and later was superintendent of the cemetery of the Berlin Jewish community. His *Ammude ha-Avodah* is a history of Jewish liturgical poets and their works.

Landsteiner, Karl (1868–1943) Austrian scientist. Born in Vienna, he studied at the University of Vienna and later in Würzburg, Munich and Zurich. He worked in laboratories and hospitals in Vienna and Berlin, and later at the University of Vienna and subsequently the Wilhelmina Hospital in Vienna. After World War I he moved to Holland, eventually settling in the US where he worked at the Rockefeller Institute of Medical Research in New York. In 1930 he received the Nobel Prize.

Landstone, Charles (1891–1978) British dramatist and novelist. He was taken to London from Vienna at the age of four. He was a founding member of the Jewish Drama League and later its secretary. He reviewed fiction for the *Jewish Chronicle* and subsequently became its theatre critic. His publications include *The Kerrels of Hill End* and *I Gatecrashed.*

Lang, Fritz (1890–1976) Austrian film director. He initially was a painter in Paris, but returned to Austria at the outbreak of World War I. In 1919 he began directing and produced a number of films. He was offered the directorship of the film industry of the Third Reich, but he feared his Jewish origin would be discovered and fled to France. Later he went to Hollywood. During the war he made a number of anti-Nazi films. He eventually returned to Germany.

Langer, František (1888–1965) Czech writer. He served as head of the Czechoslovak Army Medical Corps, and was a playwright. His plays include *Outskirt* and *The Camel through the Needle's Eye.*

Langer, Jiři (1894–1943) Czech poet and author, the brother of **František Langer**. After a visit to Palestine in 1913, he stayed for some time at the court of the Rokeaḥ dynasty of Ḥasidic rabbis in Galicia. Returning to Prague, he led a religiously observant life, became a teacher at a Jewish school, and wrote Hebrew poetry. In various studies he applied Freudian theories to the appreciation of certain aspects of Jewish literature and ritual. His *Nine Gates* is a volume of Ḥasidic tales.

Lansky, Meyer (1902–83) American gangster. He was associated with American gambling syndicates. He moved to Israel in 1970 when he faced criminal charges in the US, but his application to remain in Israel was rejected. He then went to South America, but later returned to Miami where he was arrested.

Lanzmann, Claude (b. 1925) French writer and film-maker. He was born in Paris. He produced the film *Shoah* dealing with the Holocaust.

Laqueur, Walter (b. 1921) American author. Born in Breslau, he served as Director of the Wiener Library, and at the Centre for Strategic and International Studies in Washington, DC. His works include *Communism and Nationalism in the Middle East, Young Germany, Russia and Germany, The Road to War – 1967, Europe since Hitler, A History of Zionism* and *Holocaust Encyclopedia.*

Lara, David Cohen de (1602–74) German philologist, lexicographer, writer and translator. He was born in Lisbon, and became ḥakham of the Spanish–Portuguese community in Hamburg. He later lived in Amsterdam and then returned to Hamburg. His *Keter Kehunnah* deals with talmudic words which do not appear in the *Arukh* of **Nathan ben Jehiel** of Rome. He also translated ethical works from Hebrew into Spanish.

Lasker, Albert (1880–1952) American advertiser. He was a member of a Texan family prominent in Jewish affairs. He worked as a journalist and later as an advertising executive with the Chicago agency of Lord and Thomas. He pioneered the techniques of successful copywriting. He was chairman of the US Shipping Board (1921–3), and reorganized the merchant marine.

Lasker, Eduard (1829–84) German Liberal politician. He was born in Posen. He took part in the Revolution of 1848. During 1853 he went to England to study the system of British parliamentary government. He was elected to the Prussian parliament in 1865, and later led the Liberal Party in the Reichstag. He was a champion of Jewish rights.

Lasker, Emanuel (1868–1941) German chess-master. Born in Berlin, he studied mathematics at university. He became a chess-master and played in various tournaments. He won the world title in 1894. Later he settled in New York and published *Lasker's Chess Magazine.* His writings include *Lasker's Manual of Chess.*

Lasker-Schüler, Else (1869–1945) German poet. She first emigrated to Switzerland, then later settled in Palestine. Her writings express affection for Eastern European Jews and their rabbis; her poems include *Hebraïsche Balladen.*

Laski, Harold (1893–1950) British political scientist. Born in Manchester, he studied at University College, London and at Oxford. He worked as a journalist on the Labour newspaper *Daily Herald.* He taught at McGill University and then at Harvard. Eventually he returned to Britain and became a professor at the London School of Economics. He was invited to become president of Brandeis University, but refused since he believed it was important for him to remain in Britain. His works include *The Problem of Sovereignty, Authority in the Modern State, The Foundations of Sovereignty, A Grammar of Politics, The State in Theory and Practice, Parliamentary Government in England.*

Laski, Neville Jonas (1890–1969) English barrister and communal worker. He served as president of the Board of Deputies of British Jews from 1933 to 1939. He was also chairman of the administrative committee of the Jewish Agency for Palestine, and vice-president of the Anglo-Jewish Association. His publications include *Jewish Rights and Jewish*

Wrongs and *The Laws and Charities of the Spanish and Portuguese Jews Congregation of London.*

Laskin, Bora (1912–84) Canadian scholar and jurist. Born in Fort Willam Onatrio, he studied at the University of Toronto and Harvard University. Later he taught at the University of Toronto. In 1965 he became a justice of the Ontario Court of Appeals; later he was a judge of the Supreme Court of Canada. In 1973 he was appointed chief justice.

Laskov, Ḥayyim (1919–82) Israeli military commander. He was born in Borisov, Belorussia, and moved to Palestine in 1925. In 1944 he served with the Jewish Brigade Group in Italy. He joined the permanent staff of the Haganah in 1947, later becoming commander of the Israeli Air Force. After the Sinai Campaign against Egypt in 1956 he was appointed commanding officer of the southern command of the Israeli forces, and in 1958 fifth chief of general staff. In 1961 he became director-general of the ports authority.

Lasky, Jesse (1880–1958) American film producer. Born in San Francisco, he appeared in vaudeville and later formed the Jesse L. Lasky Feature Play Company which merged with the firm of Adolph Zukor in 1916. The Famous Players-Lasky Corporation became known as Paramount. He was in charge of the West Coast operations until the early 1930s.

Lassalle, Ferdinand (1825–64) German socialist. Born in Breslau, he attended trade school in Leipzig, and later studied at the University of Breslau. He participated in the revolution of 1848. In 1863 he became the president of the General German Workers' Association, the first workers' political party in Germany. The next year he was engaged to Helene von Donniges in Switzerland, and was killed in a duel.

Latteiner, Joseph (1853–1935) American Yiddish dramatist. He was born in Romania, and emigrated to New York in 1884. Initially he chose biblical subjects for his plays, but later turned to contemporary sources. He produced more than 80 plays, comedies and musicals.

Lattes, Bonet (fl. 15th–16th cent.) Italian rabbi, astronomer and physician. He was born in southern France, and later settled in Rome, where he served as rabbi and dayyan of the community. He foretold the coming of the Messiah in 1505. In 1513 Johannes von Reuchlin asked Lattes to use his influence with Pope Leo X to support him in his controversy with the Dominicans.

Lattes, Dante (1876–1965) Italian writer, journalist and educator. From 1896 he worked for the paper *Corriere Israelitico* in Trieste. Subsequently he helped to found the weekly *Israel* in Florence and *La rassegna mensile di Israel.* He also taught Hebrew language and literature at the Institute for Oriental Languages in Rome. He translated the work of writers of the Jewish national revival movement into Italian, and also produced commentaries on the Torah, the Prophets and the Psalms.

Lattes, Isaac ben Jacob (fl. 14th cent.) French rabbi and physician. He was active in Provence. His *Kiryat Sepher* explains passages in the oral law, the process of transmission of the oral traditon, and the basis of the Mishnah and Tosephta. This work also lists the 613 commandments in the order of their appearance in the Torah and interprets them according to **Maimonides**.

Lattes, Isaac Joshua ben Immanuel (d. c. 1570) Italian rabbi. He was born in Provence, and emigated to Italy, where he became a rabbi. He lived in Rome, Bologna, Mantua, Venice and Ferrara. He wrote responsa and poetry, and was associated with the printing of the Mantua edition of the Zohar.

Lattes, Judah ben Jacob (fl. 13th cent.) French scholar. He was educated at Béziers. His *Baal Asuphot* is a collection of rabbinical decisions and responsa.

Lattes, Moses (1846–83) Italian scholar. He wrote works on Italian Jewish history, talmudic lexicography, and the historical writings of **Elijah Capsali**.

Latzky-Berthold, Jacob Wolf (1881–1940) Ukrainian socialist leader. He was born in Kiev. He became involved in socialist activities and became minister for Jewish affairs in the government of the independent Ukraine in 1918. In 1920 he settled in Berlin, but he later returned to Riga, where he edited the Yiddish daily newspapers *Dos folk* and *Frimorgen.* In 1935 he moved to Palestine.

Lauterbach, Jacob Zallel (1873–1942) American rabbinic scholar. He was born in Galicia, and went to New York in 1903. After working on the staff of the *Jewish Encyclopedia*, he served as a rabbi in Peoria, Illinois; Rochester, New York; and Huntsville, Alabama. In 1911 he became professor of Talmud at the Hebrew Union College. His publications included an edition of the *Mekhilta de-Rabbi Ishmael* with an English translation.

Lauterpacht, Hersch (1897–1960) British jurist. He was an immigrant from Galicia. He served as professor of international law at Cambridge University (1938–55) and was a member of the International Court of Justice at The Hague (1955–60). He was knighted in 1956.

Lavi, Shlomo (1882–1963) Israeli pioneer. He arrived from Eastern Europe with the Second Aliyah. He played a key role in the development of the labour movement and of agricultural settlement. He was a founder of Ein Harod, the first large kibbutz. He served as a member of the Knesset.

Lavon, Pinḥas (1904–76) Israeli labour leader. He was born in eastern Galicia, and was one of the organizers of Gordonia in Galicia and Poland. In 1929 he settled in Palestine, where he was secretary of Mapai in 1938–9, and later general-secretary of the Histadrut. He served in the government as minister without portfolio (1950–2) and minister of defence (1953–4). He was involved in the dispute within Mapai which led to a split in the party.

Lavry, Marc (1903–67) Israeli composer and conductor. He was born in Riga, and was active as a conductor in Riga, Saarbrücken, and Berlin. In 1935 he settled in Palestine, where he conducted at the Opera Amamit and for the Palestine Broadcasting Service. In 1949 he became director of the music section of the Kol Zion la-Golah broadcasting service. Later he settled in Haifa. His compositions include an opera, a Sabbath morning service, symphonic poems, oratorios and music for the stage.

Layton, Irving (b. 1912) Canadian poet. He was born in Romania, and was taken to Montreal as a child. He later worked in a library and taught in Jewish parochial schools. In some of his poetry he used biblical imagery to illustrate contemporary issues.

Lazare, Bernard (1865–1903) French writer. He was born in Nîmes. He lived in Paris, where he was involved in Jewish affairs and worked on a number of Jewish periodicals. In *Anti-Semitism, its History and Causes* he argued that anti-Semitism could help to bring about the advent of socialism by teaching hatred of Jewish capitalism. After the Dreyfus affair he changed his views.

Lazaron, Morris Samuel (b. 1888) American Reform rabbi. He was born in Savannah, Georgia. He served as a rabbi in Wheeling, West Virginia, and later to the Baltimore Hebrew Congregation. He was a founder and vice-president of the American Council for Judaism.

Lazarus, Emma (1849–87) American poet. She was born into a New York Sephardi family. She wrote poetry, tragedies and numerous essays, as well as translated the works of medieval Spanish Jewish poets. Her sonnet *The New Colossus* was inscribed on the Statue of Liberty in New York. Her writings include *Songs of a Semite* and *By the Waters of Babylon.*

Lazarus, Moritz (1824–1903) German philosopher and psychologist. He was born in Filehne, in the district of Posen. He became professor of philosophy at the University of Berne, and later rector of the university. In 1868 he moved to Berlin, where he lectured in psychology, political science and education at the military academy, and then became professor at the University of Berlin. Later he taught at the Hochschule für die Wissenschaft des Judentums in Berlin. His writings include *Ethik des Judentums.*

Leah (fl.?16th cent. BCE) Israelite woman, elder daughter of **Laban** and wife of **Jacob**. She was married to **Jacob** as a result of **Laban**'s trickery in substituting her for her sister **Rachel** (Genesis 29:23–25). She gave birth to **Reuben**, **Simeon**, **Levi**, **Judah**, **Issachar**, **Zebulun** and **Dinah** (Genesis 29:32–35; 30:14–21).

Lebensohn, Abraham Dov [Adam ha-Cohen] (1794–1878) Lithuanian Hebrew poet. He was born in

Vilna where he became a successful broker. He was a central figure in the Haskalah movement in Lithuania, and an outstanding poet; his poetry was collected in *Shire Sephat Kodesh.* With **Isaac Benjacob** he published a Bible edition – *Mikrae Kodesh* – with **Moses Mendelssohn**'s German translation – *Biur* – and his own notes. In 1847 he became a teacher of Hebrew, Aramaic and biblical exegesis at the government rabbinical school of Vilna.

Lebensohn, Micah Joseph [Michal] (1828–52) Lithuanian Hebrew poet of the Haskalah. He was born in Vilna. His publications include a Hebrew translation of part of Virgil's *Aeneid,* but later he turned to subjects from Hebrew literature. His poems were published in *Songs of the Daughter of Zion* and the posthumous collection *Lyre of the Daughter of Zion.*

Lederberg, Joshua (b. 1925) American scientist. In 1947 he was appointed professor of genetics at the Universty of Wisconsin, and later at Stanford University. In 1961 he became director of the Kennedy Laboratories for Molecular Biology and Medicine. He and a colleague at Yale University discovered that certain bacteria were capable of sexual reproduction and thus of genetic intermingling. In 1958 he won the Nobel Prize for Medicine and Physiology.

Lee, Sidney [Lazarus, Sidney] (1859–1926) English literary historian. From 1913 to 1924 he was professor of English literature and language at London University. He was editor of the *Dictionary of National Biography* and published a study of Jews and crypto-Jews in Shakespearean England.

Lehman, Herbert Henry (1878–1963) American banker, politician and statesman. He worked for his father's banking and investment firm, Lehman Bros. During his political career he served as lieutenant governor of New York State (1928–32), governor of New York State (1932–42), and director-general of the United Nations Relief and Rehabilitation Agency (1943–6). From 1949 to 1957 he was US Senator for New York.

Lehman, Irving (1876–1945) American jurist. He was born in New York. He served as state justice in the Supreme Court until 1924 and then as judge on the New York State Court of Appeals (1924–45). He was president of the Jewish Welfare Board (1921–40), honorary vice-president of the American Jewish Committee (1942), and a supporter of development projects in Palestine.

Lehmann, Behrend (1661–1730) German court Jew. He was born in Essen. He was a financial adviser to Augustus II of Saxony, who became King of Poland. He used his influence to improve the position of the Jewish community.

Lehmann, Marcus (1831–90) German rabbi, scholar and writer. He was born in Verden. From 1854 he served as a rabbi in Mainz, where he founded the weekly *Israelit,* the principal voice of German Orthodoxy. Lehmann became one of the leaders and spokesmen of modern German Orthodox Jewry. He wrote historical novels, short stories and Sabbath lectures, and made a German edition of the Haggadah.

Lehrer, Leibush (1887–1965) American Yiddish writer and educator. He was born in Poland. After living in Belgium from 1906 to 1909 he emigrated to the US. He helped to develop the Shalom Aleichem schools and founded and directed the Yiddish-speaking Camp Boiberik. He taught in the Teachers Seminary of the Shalom Aleichem Folk Institute in New York, and from 1921 to 1947 was director of the Shalom Aleichem Secondary School. He wrote studies of literature, psychology, education and Judaism.

Leibowitz, Samuel (1893–1978) American lawyer, of Romanian origin. Born in Jassy, Romania, he went to the US in 1897. He studied at Cornell University and worked in a civil law frim. Later he practised criminal law. In 1940 he became judge in Kings County Court in Brooklyn, and later as New York supreme court justice.

Leibowitz, Yeshayahu (1903–94) Israeli scientist and writer. He was born in Riga. He emigrated to Palestine in 1935 and became professor of organic chemistry, biochemistry and neurophysiology at the Hebrew University. He has written studies of **Maimonides**, Jewish Orthodoxy and Israeli politics.

Leivick, Halpern [Leyvik, Halpern] (1886–1962) American Yiddish poet and dramatist. He was born in Igumen, Belorussia. He was active in revolutionary politics and was exiled to Siberia as a result. He escaped to the US in 1913, where he worked in a sweatshop and as a paper-hanger. His writings include *Der goylem, Shmates, In Treblinka bin ich ni geven* and *Di chasene in fernvald.*

Lekert, Hirsh (1879–1902) Russian revolutionary. A bootmaker by trade, he was a member of the Jewish socialist party, the Bund, in Dvinsk, Kovno, Yekaterinoslav and Vilna. He was executed for shooting the governor of Vilna because he had ordered the flogging of 26 demonstrators on 1 May 1902.

Lelyveld, Arthur (1913–96) American Reform rabbi and community leader. He was born in New York. He served as national director of the B'nai B'rith Hillel Foundations from 1947 to 1956, and later as rabbi of Fairmount Temple in Cleveland. From 1966 he was president of the American Jewish Congress, and he was also appointed general chairman of the Jewish Welfare Fund campaign of Cleveland. He wrote *Atheism is Dead,* a response to radical theology.

Lemon, Hartog (c. 1750–1823) Dutch physician and protagonist of Jewish rights. Living in Amsterdam, he was a central figure in the Felix Libertate society, which struggled for Jewish rights. He served as a deputy in the second national assembly of the Batavian Commonwealth, and was a delegate to the Napoleonic Sanhedrin in Paris in 1807.

Lempkin, Raphael (1901–1959) Polish lawyer. Most of his family was killed by the Nazis. He escaped and reached the US where he campaigned for an internatonal convention on genocide.

Lensky, Ḥayyim (1905–42) Russian Hebrew poet. He was born in Slonim, a district of Grodno in Russia, and lived in Moscow and Leningrad. In Moscow he wrote poems which he sent to literary periodicals in Palestine. Later he was sentenced to imprisonment in Siberia for writing in Hebrew, but in 1937 he was transferred to a forced-labour camp near the Soviet-Mongolian border. Although he returned to Leningrad on his release, he was again arrested; he is assumed to have died in captivity. His poetry describes his childhood and Siberian exile as well as his faith in the Jewish people.

Leon, Judah Messer [Judah ben Jehiel; Messer Leon] (fl. 15th cent.) Italian rabbi and author. He was the head of a yeshivah in Mantua. He engaged in a controversy with **Joseph Colon** which split the Jewish community there. Subsequently he lived in Venice, Bologna, Ancona and Naples, where he was the head of the yeshivah. His writings include *Nophet Tzuphim,* a Hebrew work based on the rhetorical rules of Aristotle, Cicero and Quintilian.

Leon Templo, Jacob Judah Aryeh [Temple, Judah] (1603–75) Dutch rabbi and scholar. He was born in Hamburg. He officiated at Middelburg in the Netherlands, and taught in Amsterdam from 1643. He constructed a model of Solomon's Temple and published an accompanying exposition in Spanish, which was translated into several langauges. He also produced a model and exposition of the Tabernacle.

Leonard, Benny [Leiner, Benjamin] (1896–1947) American boxer. Born in New York City, he became the world champion lightweight boxer in 1917 and remained so until his retirement in 1925.

Leopold, Nathan (b. 1904) American criminal. He and **Richard Loeb** were university graduates from wealthy Jewish families. They abducted and killed a 14-year-old boy in 1924. **Loeb** was murdered in jail, while Leopold was parolled in 1958.

Lerner, Max (1902–92) American writer, of Russian origin. Born in Minsk, Russia, he went to the US at the age of five. He taught at Sarah Lawrence College, Harvard University, Williams College and Brandeis University. His works include *It Is Later than You Think, Ideas Are Weapons, Ideas for the Ice Age, America as a Civilization* and *The Age of Overkill.*

Leroy, Mervyn (1900–87) American film producer. Born in San Francisco, he was a vaudeville performer. In 1919 he asked his cousin **Jesse Lasky** for a job. From most of the 1930s he was one of Warner Brothers directors. Later he moved to Metro-Goldyn-Mayer. His films included *The Wizard of Oz.*

Lesser, Isaac (1806–68) American rabbi and author. He was born in Westphalia, and went to America in 1824. From 1829 he officiated as ḥazzan to the Mikveh Israel Congregation in Philadelphia. He was editor of a monthly newspaper *The Occident*, and founded the first Jewish Publication Society of America. He published the first American translation of the Bible and edited various prayerbooks.

Lessing, Theodor (1872–1933) German philosopher. He was born in Hanover. He converted to Lutheranism in 1908 and was appointed instructor at the Technische Hochschule in Hanover. He published studies of Schopenhauer, Wagner and Nietzsche. Later he returned to Judaism, and expressed his views in *Jewish Self-Hate*. Towards the end of his life he lived in Marienbad, where he was murdered by the Nazis.

Lestchinsky, Jacob (1876–1966) German scholar. He was born in Horodicz in the Ukraine, and left the USSR in 1921 for Berlin. In the 1920s he helped to establish the Institute for Research into Contemporary Jewry and Judaism. He was a pioneer in the study of the sociology, economics and demography of Jewish life and published studies of Eastern European Jewry.

Letteris, Meir ha-Levi (?1800–71) Galician Hebrew poet, writer and editor. He was born in Zolkiew. He worked as a copy-reader in Vienna, Pressburg and Prague. He published books of Hebrew poetry, translations, and collections of Hebrew literature. Among his editions of Hebrew texts was the Bible, which he prepared for the British and Foreign Bible Society.

Levanda, Lev [Leib, Yehudah] (1835–88) Russian author. He was born in Minsk, where from 1854 to 1860 he taught at a government Jewish school. In 1860 he became the Jewish adviser to the governor-general of Vilna. After the pogroms of 1881 Levanda became a supporter of the Ḥovevei Zion. His writings include Russian stories depicting Jewish life in the Pale of Settlement.

Levanon, Mordekhai (1901–68) Israeli painter of Transylvanian origin. He went to Palestine in 1921 and he worked as an agricultural labourer. From 1922 he studied painting in Jerusalem and Tel Aviv. His works include paintings of Jerusalem, the Sea of Galilee and Safed.

Leven, Narcisse (1833–1915) French public figure. He was born in Germany, and moved to Paris as a child. He was secretary to **Isaac-Adolphe Crémieux** during the Franco-Prussian War, and later practised law. One of the founders of the Alliance Israélite Universelle, he served successively as its secretary, vice-president and president. He was also president of the Jewish Colonization Association. His writings include *Cinquante ans d'histoire: l'Alliance Israélite Universelle*.

Levertin, Oscar Ivar (1862–1906) Swedish poet and literary citic. He was born in Gryt. He became a professor of literature at the Academy of Stockholm. Some of his poems and stories deal with Jewish themes.

Levi (fl. 19th–16th cent. BCE) Israelite, third son of **Jacob** and **Leah**. He was the founder of the tribe of Levites. He and **Simeon**, his brother, killed the men of Shechem who raped their sister, **Dinah** (Genesis 34); because of this act they were rebuked by **Jacob**, who foretold that their descendents would be scattered throughout Israel (Genesis 49:7).

Levi, Carlo (1902–75) Italian writer and painter. Born in Turin, he studied to be a doctor, but embarked on a career as a painter. He exhibited at the Venice biennial festival in 1924 and 1926. In 1934 he was arrested for his political activities and sent to Basilicata. His works include *Cristo si è fermato a Eboli* and *Corragio dei miti: scritti contemporanei, 1922–1974*.

Levi, David (1742–1801) English Hebraist and polemicist. He was born in London, and worked as a hatter. He published translations of the Pentateuch for use in the synagogue, a Hebrew grammar and dictionary, and polemics in defence of Jews and Judaism.

Levi, Hermann (1839–1900) German conductor. Born in Giessen in Upper Hesse, he studied music at Mannheim and at the Leipzig Conservatory. He held various conducting posts including Hofkapellmeister at the Court Theatre of Munich.

He was regarded as one of the most accomplished conductors of his time.

Lévi, Israel (1856–1939) French rabbi. He was born in Paris. He began teaching Jewish history at the École Rabbinique in 1892, and the Talmud and rabbinic literature at the École Pratique des Hautes Études in 1896. In 1886 he became editor of the *Revue des Études Juives*. From 1919 to 1938 he was the chief rabbi of the French Central Consistoire. He published studies of the Bible, Apocrypha, Talmud, midrash and Jewish history.

Levi, Primo (1919–87) Italian author. He was born in Turin, and trained as a chemist. His works, many of which describe his experiences in Auschwitz, include *If this Is a Man* and *The Truce*.

Lévi, Sylvain (1863–1935) French Indologist. He was born in Paris. He taught at the Sorbonne, the École des Hautes Études, and the Collège de France. He also served as president of the Alliance Israélite Universelle and the Société des Études Juives. His publications include studies of Buddhism.

Levias, Caspar (1860–1934) American orientalist and lexicographer, of Lithuanian origin. He was an instructor in Semitic languages at the Hebrew Union College (1895–1905), and then (1910–20) principal of the Plaut Memorial Hebrew Free School in Newark, New Jersey. His writings include *A Grammar of the Aramaic Idiom Contained in the Babylonian Talmud.*

Levi bar Sisi (fl. 2nd–3rd cent.) Palestinian and Babylonian amora. A pupil of **Judah ha-Nasi**, he settled in Nehardea in Babylonia. His baraitot are mentioned in the Talmud.

Levi ben Abraham ben Ḥayyim (c. 1245–c. 1315) French talmudist and philosopher. He was born in Villefrance-de-Conflent, and lived in various towns in southern France, earning his living as a teacher. His book *Livyat Ḥen* deals with various branches of science, and includes his theological and philosophical views. He was persecuted by opponents of **Maimonides** because of his rational interpretation of miracles as well as his allegorical biblical exegesis.

Levi ben Gershon [Gersonides; Ralbag] (1288–1344) French philosopher, mathematician, astronomer, biblical commentator and talmudist. He was born at Bagnols-sur-Cèze, and lived in Orange and Avignon. His *Milḥamot Adonai* deals with the imortality of the soul, prophecy, omnipotence, providence, astronomy, creation and miracles. He also wrote a study of the 13 hermeneutical rules of Rabbi **Ishmael**, and works on arithmetic, geometry, harmonic numbers and trigonometry. In addition he produced commentaries on Aristotle, Averroes and the Bible.

Levi ben Japheth (fl. 10th–11th cent.) Palestinian Karaite scholar. He lived in Jerusalem. His *Book of the Precepts* deals with Karaite law.

Levi-Bianchini, Angelo (1887–1920) Italian naval officer and member of the Zionist Commission. He was born in Venice. He lectured at the naval academy and the military school in Turin. He was appointed to the Zionist Commission and travelled to Palestine in 1918. In 1920 he helped to obtain the approval of the Italian Foreign Office for the British Balfour Declaration and the Mandate on Palestine.

Levi-Civita, Tullio (1873–1941) Italian mathematician and mathematical physicist. Born in Padua, he studied at the University of Padua where he later became a professor. Later he became professor of mathematics at the University of Rome.

Levi Isaac of Berdichev (c. 1740–1810) Polish Ḥasidic leader. A pupil of **Dov Ber of Mezhirich**, he was a rabbi in Zhelikhov, Pinsk and Berdichev. He founded Ḥasidism in central Poland, consolidated the movement in Lithuania, and expanded it in the Ukraine. His *Kedushat Levi* contains his teaching.

Levin, Hanoch (b. 1943) Israeli playwright. He was born in Tel Aviv. His plays include *You and I and the Next War*, *Ketchup*, *Queen of the Bathtub*, *Solomon Grip* and *Yaacobi and Leidental.* In 1988 he became house playwright at Israel's Cameri Theatre.

Levin [Loebel], Hirschel [Hirschel Levin; Lyon, Hart] (1721–1800) German rabbi and author. He was born in Galicia. He served as rabbi at the Great Synagogue in London from 1756 to 1763, then officiated in Halberstadt, Mannheim and Berlin.

He opposed **Naphtali Herz Wesseley**'s reforms in Jewish education, and was an advocate of **Moses Mendelssohn**'s German translation of the Hebrew Bible, *Biur*.

Levin, Judah Leib [Yehalel] (1844–1925) Russian Hebrew socialist poet and writer. In 1870 he became a tutor and secretry to the Brodskis, Jewish sugar magnates of Kiev. Between 1874 and 1880 he contributed poetry to the literary monthly *Ha-Shaḥar*, which introduced socialist themes into Hebrew literature. After the pogroms of 1881 he joined Ḥibbat Zion as one of its founding members in Kiev. Later he settled in Tomashpol, where he continued his literary work. He published his memoirs in 1910. He eventually returned to Kiev.

Levin, Mayer (1905–81) American novelist. He was born in Chicago, and became a reporter for the *Chicago Daily News*. In his writings he retold stories of the Ḥasidim and depicted his own generaton of Chicago Jews. He also wrote various histories of Israel for young people and published books on the synagogue and the Jewish way of life. In 1958 he settled in Israel.

Levin [Lefin; Satanower], Mendel (1749–1826) Russian author, translator and educator, and a leading figure in the Haskalah movement. He was born in Satanev, Podolia. From 1780 to 1784 he lived in Berlin, where he met **Moses Mendelssohn**, through whom he came into contact with the leaders of the Haskalah. Later he lived in various Russian centres and became one of the chief advocates of the Haskalah in Galicia. His publications include studies of natural sciences, translations of classics, and a Yiddish translation of various books of the Bible.

Levin [Varnhagen von Ense], Rachel (1771–1833) German socialite. She was born in Berlin. Her home there was a meeting-place for literary, intellectual and social leaders. She married Karl August Vernhagen von Ense, and converted to Protestantism.

Levin, Shemaryahu (1867–1935) Russian Zionist leader and author. He was born in Svisloch, Belorussia. He served as a rabbi in Grodno (1896–7) and Yekaterinoslav (1898–1904) and a preacher in Vilna (1904–6). At the Sixth Zionist Congress he was one of the leaders of the opposition to the project to found a Jewish homeland in Uganda. Later he represented Vilna in the Russian Duma. He left the USSR and lived first in Berlin, then, during World War I, in the US, where he promoted Zionism. From 1922 he worked in Berlin for the Devir Publishing Company. He finally moved to Palestine, and was one of the founders of the Haifa-Technion.

Levin, Yitzḥak Meir (1894–1971) Israeli activist and politician, leader of the Agudat Israel movement. He was born in Gora, Poland. He served in various offices in Agudat Israel. In 1940 he settled in Palestine, where he was active in rescue operations to help Jews escape from Nazi-controlled Europe. He was appointed minister of social welfare in the first Knesset. In 1954 he became president of the World Actions Committee and chairman of the World Executive of Agudat Israel.

Levinas, Emmanuel (1905–95) French philosopher, of Lithuanian origin. He became head of the École Normale Orientale of the Alliance Israélite Universelle in Paris, and taught at the University of Paris at Nanterre. His writings include *De l'existence à l'existant*, *En découvrant l'existence ave Husserl et Heidegger*, *Totalité et infini*, *Difficile liberté* and *Quatres lectures talmudiques*.

Levine, Jack (b. 1915) American painter. Born in Boston, he studied under Harold Zimmerman and Denman Ross. He was part of the Boston School of Figurative Expressionism.

Levine, Phillip (b. 1928) American poet. Born in Detroit, he taught at California State University and later moved to Barcelona. His poetry includes *On the Edge* and *Sweet Will*.

Levinsohn, Isaac Ber (1788–1860) Russian Hebrew author. He was born in Kremenetz in Volhynia, and lived in Radzivilov and later in various towns in eastern Galilcia. He was one of the founders of the Haskalah movement in Russia, and from 1820 to 1823 spread its ideas as a private tutor. His writings extol the virtues of the Enlightenment and manual labour, and seek to combat anti-Semitism. His publications include *Teudah be-Yisrael*, *Bet Yehudah* and *Zerubbabel*.

Levinthal, Bernard (1865–1952) American Orthodox rabbi, of Lithuanian origin. He emigrated to the US in 1891 and became rabbi of Congregation B'nai Abraham in Philadelphia. He served as head of the United Orthodox Rabbis of the United States and Canada. In addition he helped to establish the Mizraḥi Organization of America.

Levinthal, Israel Herbert (1888–1978) American rabbi. He served as rabbi of the Brooklyn Jewish Center from 1919. Active in the Zionist movement, he was president of the Rabbinical Association of America. His writings include *Judaism: An Analysis and an Interpretation*, *Point of View: An Analysis of American Judaism* and *Judaism Speaks to the Modern World*.

Levinthal, Louis (b. 1892) American communal leader. He practised law in Philadelphia, eventually becoming judge in the Philadelphia Court of Common Pleas. He served as president of the Zionist Organization of America, chairman of the Board of Governors of the Hebrew University, and president of the Jewish Publication Society of America.

Levi-Strauss, Claude (b. 1908) French anthropologist. Born in Brussels, he studied at the Sorbonne and became professor in Sao Paulo, Brazil, and later Director of Studies, École Pratique des Hautes Études in Paris and professor at the Collège de France. His works include *A World on the Wane*, *Structural Anthropology*, *The Savage Mind*, *Totémisme* and *Elementary Structures of Kinship*.

Levita, Elijah [Baḥur, Elijah] (1468–1549) Italian Hebrew philologist, grammarian and lexicographer. He was born in Neustadt but spent most of his life in Italy, where he taught Hebrew. Numerous Christian humanists, such as Cadinal Egidio da Viterbo, were his students. He also served as proofreader for the Protestant Hebraist Paul Fagius in Isny. He wrote studies of Hebrew grammar, lexicographical works, and a Yiddish-Hebrew dictionary. In addition he composed Hebrew and Yiddish poetry and produced various Yiddish translations.

Levontin, Zalman David (1856–1940) Russian banker and pioneer of Jewish settlement in Palestine. He was born in Belorussia. In 1882 he went to Palestine, where he purchased land and founded the town of Rishon-le-Zion in the Judean coastal plain. He subsequently served as branch bank manager in various towns in the Pale of Settlement. In 1901 he was summoned by **Theodor Herzl** to become one of the directors of the Jewish Colonial Trust in London. Two years later he returned to Palestine to establish the Anglo-Palestine Bank which he directed.

Levy, Amy (1861–89) British writer. Born in Clapham, she studied at Cambridge University. Her works include *Xanthippe and Other Verse*, *A Minor Poet and Other Verse* as well as *Reuben Sachs: A Sketch*.

Levy, Asser (d. 1681) Dutch merchant and landowner. He was among the first Jews to arrive in New Amsterdam in 1654, and became the most prominent member of the Jewish community there, defending the rights of the Jews in the New World.

Levy, Benjamin (c.1650–1704) British merchant, founder of the Ashekanzi community in London. The son of Levy Moses of Hamburg, he arrived in London in about 1670. In 1697, in the course of the reorganization of the Royal Exchange, he became one of the 12 original Jewish brokers of the City of London. In 1696 he purchased a cemetery for the Ashkenazi community.

Lévy, Bernard-Henri (b. 1947) French philosopher. Born in Béni-Sof, Algeria, he went to Paris as a child. He studied at the Lycée Pasteur and the Lycée Louis-le-Grand. His works include La *Barbarie à visage humain*, *Le Testament de Dieu* and *L'idéologie Française* as well as *Le Diable en Tête*.

Levy, Emmanuel (1900–85) English painter. Born in Manchester, he studied at the Manchester School of Art. Later he studied at the St Martin's School of Art and subsequently in Paris. He taught at the Manchester School of Architecture, and the Stockport School of Art. Later he lived in London.

Levy, Jacob (1819–92) German rabbi and lexicographer. He was born near Poznán in Poland. He served as rabbi of Rosenberg, Upper Silesia, but then for a period devoted himself to scientific work. In 1857 he became assistant rabbi in Breslau, and later was appointed to the Breslau court to administer the Jewish oath. In 1878 he was appointed lecturer at the Mora-Salomon Leipziger Foundation. He compiled dictionaries of the Targum and of the Talmud and midrash.

Levy, Louis Edward (1846–1919) American chemist, inventor and newspaper editor. He was born in Pilsen, Bohemia, and was taken to the US at the age of eight. He published and edited the *Philadelphia Evening Herald*, the *Mercury* and the *Jewish Year*. He was a leader of the Philadelphia Jewish community and served as president of the Association for Relief and Protection of Jewish Immigrants. His writings include *The Russian Jewish Refugees in America*.

Levy, Moritz Abraham (1817–72) German scholar. He taught Semitic palaeography and epigraphy at the Breslau Synagogen-Gemeinde. He wrote textbooks on Jewish history and religion, and a history of Jewish coins.

Levy, Moses Elias (1782–1854) American settler. Born in Mogador, Morocco, his father converted to Islam and settled in England. He worked on a sailing ship travelling to the West Indies. He disembarked at St Thomas in the Caribbean and engaged in the lumber business. He purchased land in Florida. In 1821 he went to Saint Augustine as a colonizer.

Levy, Reuben (1891–1966) English orientalist. He was born in Manchester. He was a lecturer in Persian language and literature at Oxford University (1920–3), then (1923–6) taught biblical literature at the Jewish Institute of Religion in New York. He later became professor of Persian at Cambridge University. He edited and translated classical Persian and Arabic texts, wrote textbooks about Persian language and literature, and published studies of Islam.

Levy, Uriah (1792–1862) American naval officer. Born in Philadelphia, he served as a cabin boy at an early age. He purchased a share in a schooner, and in 1811 became the first Jewish sea captain. During the war of 1812 he volunteered for service but was captured by the British. He became the first Jewish officer in the US Navy in 1817. In 1860 he became a commodore of the Mediterranean fleet.

Levy-Bruhl, Lucien (1857–1939) French philosopher. Born in Paris, he taught at Potiers and Amiens. Subsequently he became professor of higher rhetoric at the Lycée Louis-Le-Grand and a lecturer at the École Normale Supérieure. He then moved to the Sorbonne and lectured at the École Libre des Sciences politiques. In 1925 he established the Institut d'Ethnologie. His works include *Ethics and Oral Science*.

Lewandowski, Louis (1821–94) German choral director and composer. He was born in Wreschen, near Posen. After moving to Berlin he served as conductor of the choir at the Old Synagogue in the Heidereutergasse, and later at the New Synagogue. He also served as a singing teacher at the Jewish Free School and the Jewish Teachers Seminary. His compositions had a profound influence on Western Ashkenazi synagogue music, and his style was transferred to numerous Conservative and Reform congregations in the US.

Lewin, Benjamin Manasseh (1879–1944) Israeli rabbinic scholar, educator and authority on gaonic literature. He was born in Gorodets, Russia. In 1912 he went to Palestine, where he was a teacher and later head of the religious schools network, Netzaḥ Yisrael. His *Otzar ha-Geonim* is a collection of the teachings of the geonim of Sura and Pumbedita.

Lewin, Judah Leib (1894–1971) Russian rabbi. Born in Yekaterinoslav, he became the rabbi of Grishino, and later at Yekaterinoslav. He then returned to Grishino where he worked as a religious scribe. In 1957 he was appointed principal of the yeshivah of the Moscow Great Synagogue; after the death of Solomon Schliefer he became the rabbi there.

Lewin, Kurt Zadek (1890–1947) German psychologist. Born in Mogilno, Germany, he studied at the University of Freiburg. the University of Milan and the University of Berlin. In 1933 he went to the US and taught at Cornell University. He later became professor of psychology. His works include *A Dynamic Theory of Personality* and *Principles of Topological Psychology*.

Lewinski, Elhanan Löb (1857–1910) Russian Hebrew writer and Zionist leader. He was born in Podberezye, Russia. He travelled to Palestine after the pogroms of 1881 and returned an ardent Zionist. He settled in Odessa and in 1896 became the representative in Russia of the Palestinian Carmel wine company. He was a founder of the Moriah publishing house and supported literary enterprises. He also served as a treasurer and preacher in the Zionist synagogue in Odessa. His writings were published in various journals.

Lewis, Bernard (b. 1916) English orientalist. He was born in London. He was appointed assistant lecturer at the University of London in 1938. During World War II he served in the army and was seconded to the Foreign Office. In 1949 he became professor of Near and Middle Eastern history at the School of Oriental and African Studies at London University. He published studies of Arab and Turkish history and translated Hebrew prose and poetry into English.

Lewis [Los], David (b. 1909) Canadian political leader, of Polish origin. His parents immigrated to Canada from Poland when he was 12. He was a Rhodes Scholar and studied at Oxford University. He practised law in Toronto and later became secretary of the Cooperative Commonwealth Federation. He subsequently was a member of parliament, becoming leader of the New Democratic Party.

Lewis, Ted [Mendeloff, Gershon] (1893–1970) British boxer. He was the British featherweight champion and later European champion. He was also middleweight champion of Britain, the Empire and Europe.

Lewisohn, Ludwig (1883–1955) American author and translator. Born in Berlin, he was taken to Charleston, South Carolina, in 1890. He was professor of German at Ohio State University (1911–19), and from 1948 professor of comparative literature at Brandeis University. Between 1924 and 1940 he lived in Paris. His writings include novels on Jewish subjects: *The Island Within* and *The Last Days of Shylock.* He also wrote books dealing with Judaism and Zionism, including *Israel, Theodor Herzl: A Portrait for this Age, The American Jew: Character and Destiny* and *What Is the Jewish Heritage?*

Lewy, Israel (1841–1917) German rabbi and scholar. He was born in Inowroclaw, Poland. He became a lecturer in Talmud at the Hochschule für die Wissenschaft des Judentum in Berlin, then in 1883 took up an appointment at the Breslau Rabbinical Seminary. He published studies of Talmudic literature.

Liberman, Serge (b. 1942) Australian novelist and editor. He was born in Fergana in Uzbekistan, and went to Australia in 1951. He became the editor of the *Melbourne Chronicle.* His publications include *Ethnic Australia, Jewish Writing from Down Under, Joseph's Coat: An Anthology of Multicultural Writing* and *Bibliography of Australian Judaica.*

Liberman, Yevesey Grigoryevich (1897–1983) Soviet economist. Born in Volyn in the Ukraine, he studied at Kiev University and the Kharkov Engineering Economics Institute. He initially worked in factories and later became professor of economic and organization of machine building industry at the Kharkov Institute. He suggested a programme for economic reform in the Soviet Union which included using profit as a means of measuring success.

Libin, Solomon (1872–1955) American Yiddish writer. He was born in Russia, and emigrated to London in 1891, later moving to New York. He wrote hundreds of stories about early immigrant life and the suffering of sweatshop workers. In addition, he wrote about 50 plays.

Lichine, David (1910–72) Russian dancer and choreographer. Born in Rostov-on-Don, he went to Paris as a boy. In 1932 he joined Colonel de Basil's Ballets Russes de Monte Carlo and began choreographing. In 1941 he and his wife the ballerina Tatiana Riabouchinska went to the US where they joined the American Ballet Theatre as guest artists. Eventually they moved to South America, but returned to the US in 1952 where they opened a school.

Lichtenstein, Hillel (1815–91) Hungarian rabbi. He served as rabbi in Margarethen, Kolozsvar, Szikszó

(1865–7), and Kolomyya in Galicia. He was an ardent critic of religious reform.

Lichtenstein, Morris (1889–1938) American rabbi. He emigrated from Eastern Europe to the US in 1907. He inaugurated the Jewish Science movement in opposition to Christian science.

Lichtheim, Richard (1885–1963) German Zionist. He was born into an assimilated Berlin family and studied economics. Before World War I he worked on the staff of the Zionist headquarters in Berlin, editing *Die Welt.* From 1913 to 1917 he worked in Constantinople. After the war, he returned to Germany and was a member of the Zionist executive. He eventually settled in Palestine.

Lidzbarski, Mark (1868–1928) German Semitic philologist. He was born in Plock in the Russian part of Poland, and in adulthood converted to Protestantism. In 1896 he began lecturing in oriental languages at the University of Kiel. In 1907 he took up an appointment at the University of Greifswald, and in 1917 one at the University of Göttingen. He was the founder of Semitic epigraphy, and also published various studies and texts of the gnostic Mandeans.

Lieberman, Saul (1898–1983) American scholar. He was born in Motol, near Pinsk, Belorussia, and settled in Jerusalem in 1928. In 1931 he was appointed lecturer in Talmud at the Hebrew University. He also taught at the Mizraḥi Teachers Seminary, and was dean of the Harry Fischel Institute for Talmudic Research. In 1940 he became professor of Palestinian literature and institutions at the Jewish Theological Seminary where he later served as dean and rector of the rabbinical school. He published studies of Jewish Hellenism, editions of the Tosephta, and works on the Palestinian Talmud.

Liebermann, Aaron Samuel (1845–80) Lithuanian socialist and Hebrew writer. He was born in Lunna, Lithuania, and became secretary of the Jewish community of Suwalki. Later he lived in Vilna, where he worked with an insurance company and as a draftsman. From 1872 he was a leader of a local revolutionary group. He subsequently joined socialist circles in Berlin and became a pioneer of Jewish socialism. He lived successively in London (where he worked as a typesetter), Vienna (from where he was expelled to Germany), London again, and eventually the US. He published various works about socialism.

Liebermann, Max (1847–1935) German painter. He was born in Berlin, and lived in various cities including Paris. His work includes *Judengasse*, a series of paintings of street scenes in the Jewish quarter of Amsterdam.

Liebman, Joshua Loth (1907–48) American Reform rabbi. He was born in Hamilton, Ohio. He served as a rabbi in Lafayette, Indiana, and as an instructor at the Hebrew Union College. Later he was rabbi to congregations in Chicago and Boston, where he also taught at Boston University and at Andover-Newton Theological Seminary. He published *Peace of Mind.*

Liebmann, Jost (c. 1640–1702) Prussian court Jew. He was court jeweller and mint-master to Friedrich Wilhelm and Friedrich III of Brandenburg. Towards the end of the 17th century he was one of the richest Jews in Prussia. The owner of the only synagogue in Berlin, he played an important role in the Jewish community.

Lieme, Nehemiah de (1882–1940) Dutch economist and Zionist leader. He was involved in life insurance and education for Dutch workers. In 1913 he became chairman of the Dutch Zionist Federation, and from 1919 to 1921 he served as president of the Jewish National Fund.

Liessin, Abraham (1882–1938) American Yiddish poet and editor. He was born in Minsk, and went to the US in 1897, where he became an active socialist. From 1913 he was editor of *Zukunft*, a Yiddish literary and cultural monthly. In his writings he described the heroes and martyrs of the Jewish past.

Lifschitz, Joshua Mordecai (1829–1878) Russian Yiddish lexicographer and author. He propounded the idea of a secular Jewish culture based on Yiddish. His writings include a Yiddish–Russian dictionary.

Lifshitz, Nehama (b. 1927) Israeli Yiddish and Hebrew singer. Born in Kaunas, Lithuania, she went to Uzbekistan during World War II. In 1946 she returned to Soviet Lithuania and studied at the Vilna conservatoire. She later travelled throughout the USSR giving concerts of Yiddish songs. In 1969 she emigrated to Israel.

Lilien, Ephraim Moses (1874–1925) German artist. He was born in Drohobycz, Galicia. He first worked in Munich as a cartoonist, later in Berlin as a book illustrator. An active Zionist, he was a founder and editor of the Berlin publishing house Jüdischer Verlag. In 1902 he published *Juda*, a volume of ballads on scriptural themes with his illustrations. He was a member of the committee formed to establish the Bezalel School of Arts and Crafts in Jerusalem. Among his works are a group of etchings that include impressions of Palestine.

Lilienblum, Moses Leib (1843–1910) Russian Hebrew writer, critic and political journalist. He was born in Kedainiai, near Kovno. He was initially attracted to the Haskalah and encouraged religious reform, but in his autobiography *Ḥattot Neurim* (1876), he criticized the impracticality of the Haskalah movement and expressed his socialist ideas. After the pogroms of 1881 he became an advocate of Zionism and a leader and ideologist of Ḥibbat Zion; he published articles in Hebrew, Yiddish and Russian.

Lilienthal, David (1899–1981) American lawyer and civil servant. Born in Morton, Illinois, he became a lawyer in 1923. Until 1931 he served as a utilities lawyer in Chicago. In 1931 he was appointed to the Wisconsin Public Service Commission; later he became director of the Tennessee Valley Authority, and in 1946 chairman of the Atomic Energy Commission.

Lilienthal, Max (1813–82) American educator and rabbi, of Russian origin. He was born in Munich, Bavaria. He served as director of the Jewish school of Riga. In 1841 the czarist government invited him to initiate the creation of state schools for Jews. Encountering opposition from the Jewish community, he eventually realized that this proposal was aimed at the conversion of Jewry. He left Russia and settled in the US, becoming rabbi of the Bene Israel Congregation in Cincinnati.

Lind, Jacob (b. 1927) Austrian writer. Born in Vienna, he went to the Netherlands in 1938. During the Nazi period he worked as a gardener, and escaped deporation by acquiring false papers and finding employment in Germany. He lived in Palestine after the war, and later settled in London. His publications include *Soul of Wood* and *Counting My Steps.*

Linder, Max [Leuvielle, Gabriel] (1882–1925) French comedian. Born in Bordeaux he initially spent three years with a Bordeaux repertory company. Later he acted on the stage in Paris. From 1905 he worked at the Pathé studios where he stared in his own series of comedies. Subsequently he worked in the US, but later returned to Paris.

Linetzki, Isaac Joel (1839–1935) Ukrainian Yiddish author. He was born in Podolia. Living in Odessa, he became a spokesman for the radical wing of the Haskalah. He published various works including *Dos poylische yingel*, which criticized Jewish life and satirized the Ḥasidim.

Lipchitz, Jacques (1891-1973) American sculptor. He was born in Lithuania and in 1925 became a French citizen. He left Paris in 1940 and settled in the US. In his work he often utilized biblical episodes and themes taken from Jewish life and history.

Lipiner, Siegfried [Salomon] (1856–1911) Austrian writer. Born in Jaroslaw, near Lemberg in Galicia, he studied in Vienna. His work includes *Der Entfesselte Prometheus* and *Adam.* From 1881 he served as librarian of the Austrian Reichsrat. In 1891 he converted to Protestantism.

Lipman, Maureen (b. 1946) British actress. Born in Hull, she appeared in the films *Solomon and Gaenor, The Pianist* and various television programmes.

Lipmann, Fritz (1899–1986) American biochemist, of German origin. With the rise of Nazism, he left Germany for the US, later moving to Denmark. Subsequently he became professor at the Rockefeller Institute for Medical Research in 1957. He shared the Nobel Prize in Medicine and Physiology in 1953 for work on a compound he called coenzyme A, connected with the way carbohydrates, fats and proteins are broken down in the body for energy purposes.

Lipmann, Gabriel (1845–1921) French physicist. In 1883 he became professor of probability and mathematical physics at the Sorbonne. Due to his work on electro-capillarity and colour photography, he was awarded the Nobel Prize in Physics in 1908.

Lippe, Karpel (1830–1915) Romanian Zionist, of Galician origin. He was born in Stanislav, Galicia. He became a physician in Jassy, Romania. Active in Ḥibbat Zion, he was one of the initiators of the Zionist idea. In 1911 he returned to Galicia. He published scientific studies, Jewish apologetics, works on the rights of Romanian Jews and poetry.

Lippmann, Walter (1889–1974) American journalist. Born in New York, he studied at Harvard. He became editor of Lincoln Steffen's *Everybody's Magazine* in 1911, and published *A Preface to Politics* in 1913. The next year he was a founder of the New Republic. In 1917 he served as assistant to the secretary of war. In 1929 he became editor of the *New York World*. Later he became a columnist for the *New York Herald Tribune*.

Lipschütz, Israel ben Gedaliah (1782–1860) German rabbinic scholar. He was a rabbi in Wronki, Dessau and Colmer, and Danzig. His *Tiferet Israel* is a commentary on the Mishnah.

Lipschütz, Jacob (1838–1922) Russian author. He was born in Vilkomir. He became the secretary and chief assistant of **Isaac Elhanan Spektor**, the rabbi at Kovno, and opposed the Haskalah and Zionism. His *Zikhron Yaakov* is a book of reminiscences which casts light on Russian Jewish history.

Lipsky, Louis (1870–1963) American Zionist leader, journalist and author. He was born in Rochester, New York. He founded the Zionist periodical *The Maccabean* in 1901, and also edited the *American Hebrew*. From 1922 to 1930 he was president of the Zionist Organization of America. He was a founder of Keren ha-Yesod, the Jewish Agency, and the American and World Jewish Congresses. His writings include *Thirty Years of American Zionism*.

Lipton, Seymour (b. 1903) American sculptor. He trained as a dentist and practised in New York before devoting himself to sculpture. Some of his works are based on Jewish motifs.

Liptzin, Solomon (b. 1901) Israeli literary scholar. He was born in Satanov, Russia, and taken to the US at an early age. He was professor of German at City College, New York. Later he settled in Israel. His writings include *Peretz, Eliakum Zunser, The Flower of Yiddish Literature, The Maturing of Yiddish Literature* and *The Jew in American Literature.*

Lisitzky, Ephraim E. (1885–1962) American Hebrew poet and educator, of Russian origin. He was born in Minsk. He emigrated to the US and settled in New Orleans, where he became the principal of the city's Hebrew school. He wrote Hebrew poetry about American Indians as well as Jewish themes.

Litakov, Moses (1875–?1938) Russian Yiddish writer. He was born in Cherkassy in the Ukraine. He wrote in Russian, Hebrew and Yiddish on social and literary issues. After the revolution of 1905 he became a member of the central committee of the territorialist Socialist-Zionist Party. He edited periodicals in Vilna, and after 1917 he contributed to Yiddish journals in Kiev. In 1919 he joined the communist party and became a leader of Moscow's Yevsektzia. From 1924 he edited *Emes*, the Yiddish organ of the Communist party. He was arrested in the Stalinist purges of 1937 and died in prison.

Litvinoff, Emanuel (b. 1915) English poet. He was born in London. He wrote poetry and novels, including *The Last Europeans*, which deals with the position of Jews in the diaspora.

Litvinov, Maxim [Wallach, Meir Moiseevich] (1876–1951) Russian revolutionary and Soviet diplomat. He joined the Russian social democratic party in 1898. In 1901 he was arrested and exiled. He escaped to Switzerland where he met Lenin. The next year he returned to Russia and took part in the 1905 revolution. He spent the next 12 years in exile in France and Britain. After the revolution, he was appointed the Soviet agent in Britain. In 1921 he became deputy foreign minister of the Soviet Union. From 1928–30 he was acting foreign minister; later he became foreign minister. Subsequenty he was appointed ambassador to the US.

Litvinovksy, Pinḥas (1894–1985) Israeli painter. He was born in the Ukraine. He settled in Palestine and studied at the Bezalel School of Arts and Crafts in Jerusalem. Later he studied at the St Petersburg Academy. After returning to Jerusalem in 1919 he participated in the first group exhibitions of Palestinian artists there from 1923, and in Tel Aviv from 1926. In his paintings he utilized various styles to depict traditional themes.

Locker, Berl (1887–1972) Israeli Labour Zionist leader. He was born in Galicia and became the editor of the Lemberg Labour Zionist newspaper. Before World War I he organized the Poale Zion party in the Austrian empire, and from 1916 he ran the world office of Poale Zion at The Hague. From 1931 to 1936 he was a member of the executives of the Zionist Organization and the Jewish Agency in London. He settled in Palestine in 1936 and served as a member of the executive of Histadrut. From 1948 to 1956 he was chairman of the Jewish Agency in Jerusalem. He wrote articles in Yiddish, German, Hebrew and English.

Loeb, Isidore (1839–92) French rabbi and scholar. He was a tutor in Bayonne and Paris, and later served as a rabbi at St Étienne. In 1869 he was appointed secretary of the Alliance Israélite Universelle. From 1878 he taught Jewish history at the École Rabbinique. He wrote studies of biblical and talmudic literature, medieval historiography, and Jewish history in Spain and France.

Loeb, Richard (1905–36) American criminal. He and **Nathan Freutenthal Leopold** were university graduates from wealthy Jewish families. They abducted and killed a 14-year-old boy in 1924. They were sentenced to life imprisonment. He was murdered in prison.

Loewe, Heinrich (1867–1950) German Zionist and scholar of Jewish folklore. He was born in Wanzleben. He founded Jung Israel, the first Zionist group in Germany, in 1892, and edited various Zionist publications. From 1899 he worked as a librarian in the University of Berlin, where he became a professor in 1915. In 1933 he settled in Palestine and worked as a librarian in Tel Aviv. He published studies in the field of Jewish folklore.

Loewe, Herbert Martin James (1882–1940) English orientalist. He was born in London. He taught rabbinic Hebrew at Oxford, rabbinics at Cambridge (1931), and Hebrew at the University of London. He published studies of rabbinics and Jewish history. With C.G. Montefiore, he edited the *Rabbinic Anthology*.

Loewe, Joel ben Judah Loeb [Brill, Joel ben Judah Loeb] (1762–1802) German Hebrew writer, grammarian and exegete. He was born in Berlin, and joined **Moses Mendelssohn**'s Haskalah movement. In 1791 he was appointed principal of the Wilhelms-Schule in Breslau. He published an introduction and commentary to **Mendelssohn**'s German translation of the Psalms, a scientific grammar of biblical Hebrew, and epigrams in the style of the book of Proverbs. He also translated the Passover Haggadah into German.

Loewe, Louis (1809–88) British orientalist. He was born in Zülz, Germany, and settled in England. In 1837 he visited Egypt (where he deciphered various inscriptions) and Palestine. From 1839 he was Sir **Moses Montefiore**'s secretary, as well as the director of the oriental department of the Duke of Sussex's library. He was principal of Jews College in 1856–8, and later served as principal of Ohel Moseh vi-Yhudit, the theological seminary founded by Montefiore. He published works on the life of **Montefiore** and on oriental languages.

Loewe, Raphael (b. 1919) British scholar. Born in Calcutta, he studied at Cambridge University and served as professor at Hebrew at University College, London. His works include *Women in Judaism*, *Omar Kayyam*, *The Rylands Sephardi Haggadah*, *Ibn Gabirol* and *The North French Hebrew Miscellany*.

Loewi, Otto (1873–1961) German physician and pharmacologist. Born in Frankfurt, he studied at Strasbourg University. From 1906 to 1909 he taught in Vienna, later becoming professor of pharmacology in Graz. He won the Nobel Prize for Physiology and Medicine in 1936. With the rise of Nazism, he fled to Britain and later settled in the

US and was professor at the New York College of Medicine.

Loewisohn, Solomon (1788–1821) Austrian Hebrew poet and scholar. He was born in Hungary, and settled in Vienna, where he worked as a proofreader. He was one of the outstanding Hebrew authors of the Haskalah movement. His *Melitzat Yeshurun* is an exposition of biblical poetry, and his *Meḥkere Aretz* is the first modern lexicon of biblical geography.

Lomborso, Cesare (1836–1909) Italian criminologist. Born in Verona to a distinguished Jewish family, he studied at the Universty of Turin as well as in Padua, Paris and Vienna. During the 1859 war he was a physician in the army. He became professor of psychiatry and medical jurisprudence at Turin. His works include *The Criminal Man* and *The Man of Genius.*

London, Meyer (1871–1926) American lawyer and socialist leader. He was born in Poland, and went to the US in 1891. In 1914 he was elected to the House of Representatives as a socialist for the immigrant district on the Lower East Side in New York. He opposed the US entry into World War I, and had little sympathy with Zionism.

Lonzano, Menaḥem di (1550–before 1624) Palestinian linguist, poet and kabbalist. Born in Constantinople, he emigrated to Jerusalem and later moved to Safed. Forty years later he went to Turkey and Italy, returning to Jerusalem in 1618. He wrote studies of the masoretic text of the Bible, Hebrew grammar, prosody and lexicography. His *Shete Yadot* contains original writings and midrashic literature.

Lookstein, Joseph Hyman (1902–79) American rabbi, of Russian origin. He went to the US as a child. He served as rabbi of Kehilath Jeshurun Congregation in New York and professor of homiletics and sociology at Yeshiva University. In 1958 he became president of Bar-Ilan University in Tel Aviv.

Lopez, Aaron (1731–82) American merchant shipper. He was born in Portugal, and settled in Newport, Rhode Island, in 1752. There he became a leader of the Yeshuat Israel Congregation. He built up an extensive transatlantic mercantile empire and became Newport's leading merchant. A supporter of the rebel cause, he moved to Leicester, Massachusetts, when the British captured Newport.

Lopez, Roderigo (1525–94) British marrano physician. Originally from Portugal, he settled in London during the reign of Queen Elizabeth. He was appointed physician to the Earl of Leicester and to Queen Elizabeth. In 1594 he was arrested, found guilty of plotting to poison the Queen, and executed.

Lorki [de Lorca], Joshua [Geronimo de Santa Fé] (d. c.1419) Spanish physician and writer. He was born in Lorca, Spain. He converted to Christianity in 1412 and assumed the name Geronimo de Santa Fé. He became a physician to anti-Pope Benedict XIII. He initiated the Disputation of Tortosa (1413–14) in which he was a participant; subsequently he travelled widely, attempting to convert Jews to Christianity.

Lorre, Peter [Lowenstein, Ladislav] (1904–64) American actor, of Hungarian origin. Born in Rozsahegy, Hungary, he moved to Austria as a child. He acted on the Berlin stage and in flims until the rise of Nazism. He went to England and later worked in Hollywood. He appeared in such films as *M*, *The Man who Knew too Much*, *Mad Love*, *The Maltese Falcon*, *Casablanca*, *Arsenic and Old Lace* and *The Beast with Five Fingers.*

Lot (fl. ?19th–16th cent. BCE) Israelite, nephew of **Abraham**. The Bible depicts his sojourn in Sodom, escape from the city, and the disaster that befell his wife who looked back at the destruction of Sodom and became a pillar of salt. After the devastation of the city, Lot lived in a cave with his two daughters, who plied him with wine and, when he was drunk, committed incest with him. Each daughter bore him a son, Ammon and Moab (Genesis 19).

Lothar, Ernst (1890–1974) Austrian writer and stage director. He was born in Brünn, Moravia, and became a civil servant. He was later active as a theatre critic and director. Although he converted to Catholicism, he had to leave Austria in 1938. He lived in the US, but later returned to Vienna. His publications include *The Angel and the Trumpet*, which discusses intermarriage.

Louvish, Simon (b. 1947) Israeli author. He was born in Glasgow, and moved to Israel in 1949. His publications include *A Moment of Silence, The Therapy of Avram Blok* and *The Death of Moishe Ganef.*

Löw, Eleazar (1758–1837) Polish rabbi. He was born in Wodzislaw, and became dayyan there. Later he was rabbi of Pilica, Třešt, Pilsen, Liptovsky, Mikuláš, Slovakia and Santo. An opponent of religious reform, he published studies of the halakhah.

Löw, Immanuel (1854–1944) Hungarian rabbi and scholar, son of **Leopold Löw**. He was rabbi of Szeged. From 1927 he represented non-Orthodox communities in the upper chamber of the Hungarian parliament. He published works in the field of Hebrew and Aramaic philology as well as *The Flora of the Jews.*

Löw, Leopold (1811–75) Hungarian scholar. He served as a rabbi in several Hungarian communities. From 1850 he officiated at Szeged. He was an extreme reformer and engaged in controversy with the Orthodox. He wrote studies of the history of Hungarian Jewry. In addition he was the publisher of a journal of Jewish studies (*Ben Ḥananiah*) from 1858 to 1867.

Löwenberg, Jacob (1856–1929) German poet. He was a teacher in Hamburg. By stressing Jewish themes in his writing, he reacted against German anti-Semitism. His *Vom goldnen Überfluss* is an anthology of modern German poets.

Lowenthal, Marvin (1890–1969) American author. He was born in Bradford, Pennsylvania. He organized the Zionist movement on the West Coast. From 1924 to 1929 he was the European editor of the *Menorah Journal*, and during this period wrote about literature, politics and Zionism. He served on the Zionist Advisory Commission (1946–9), and was editor of the *American Zionist* (1952–4). He translated and edited *Memoirs of Glueckel of Hameln*, and edited *Henrietta Szold: Life and Letters.*

Lozowick, Louis (1892–1973) American painter, graphic artist and art critic. He was born in Ludovinka, a small village in the Kiev district, and went to the US in 1906. He published articles in the *Menorah Journal* on the works of Jewish artists. His *Hundred American-Jewish Painters and Sculptors* is a comprehensive study of modern American Jewish art.

Lubetkin, Zivia (1914–76) Polish underground member. Born in Beten, Poland, she was active in the Zionist youth movement. At the outbreak of World War II, she was in eastern Poland but fled to Warsaw. She helped found the Jewish Fighting Organization. She participated in the 1943 uprising in the Warsaw Ghetto and again in the revolt on 19 April 1943. On 10 May she escaped in the sewers and remained in hiding. After the war she became active in survivor circles and the Beriha, an organization devoted to bringing Jews from Europe to Palestine. In 1946 she emigrated to Palestine.

Lubitsch, Ernst (1892–1947) American film director, of German origin. Born in Berlin, he initially worked as a bookkeeper for his father. He appeared in various films, and began directing his own comedies. Later he went to the US and worked at Paramount.

Lublin, Meir ben Gedaliah of [Maharam Lublin] (1558–1616) Polish talmudist. He was born in Lublin, and became head of the yeshivah there (1582–7). He later served as dayyan and head of the yeshivah at Kraków. From 1595 to 1613 he was a rabbi in Lemberg, and he was then appointed rabbi and head of the yeshivah in Lublin. His *Meir Ene Ḥakhamim* contains novellae on the entire Talmud. His responsa were published in *Manhir Ene Ḥakhamim.*

Lublinski, Samuel (1868–1910) German playwright, literary historian and philosopher of religion. He was born in East Prussia. As a young man he was apprenticed to a bookseller in Italy, and he eventually devoted himself to literature. He lived in Berlin, Dresden and Weimar. His writings include *Jüdische Charaktere bei Grillparzer, Hebbel und Otto Ludwig, Die Enstehung des Judentums* and *Der urchristliche Erdkreis und sein Mythos.*

Ludwig, Emil [Cohn, Emil] (1881–1948) German author. Born in Breslau, he was baptized as a

Catholic. Later he renounced Christianity. In 1907 he left Germany and subsequently became a Swiss citizen, living in Ascona. He wrote plays, poems and biographies.

Lukács, Gyôrgy (1885–1971) Hungarian philosopher and literary critic. He was born in Budapest, where he later became commissar of education. When Hitler came to power he fled to the USSR. After World War II he returned to Hungary, was elected to parliament, and was appointed a professor of aesthetics and cultural philosophy at the University of Budapest. He published Marxist interpretations of literature and was influenced by the socialist views of **Moses Hess**.

Lunchitz, Solomon Ephraim (d. 1619) Czech talmudist. He was the head of the yeshivah in Lwów. From 1604 he served as chief rabbi in Prague. He contributed to talmudic study and composed liturgical poems.

Luncz, Abraham Moses (1854–1918) Palestinian author, publisher and editor. He was born in Kovno, and emigrated to Jerusalem in 1869. Although he became blind, he published 12 volumes of a yearbook about Palestine, as well as a literary alamanc, which appeared from 1895 to 1915; he also edited geographical works on Palestine.

Lunel, Armand (1892–1977) French novelist. He was born in Aix-en-Provence and taught philosophy in Monaco. He wrote novels about Provençal life, including portrayals of the region's Jewish inhabitants. He also wrote the librettos for **Darius Milhaud**'s *Esther de Carpentras*, and the oratorio *David*.

Luria, Isaac ben Solomon [Ari; Ashkenazi] (1534–72) Palestinian kabbalist. He was born in Jerusalem and educated in Egypt. From 1570 he lived in Safed. His kabbalistic teachings were received by his disciples orally; they were later recorded by his pupil **Ḥayyim Vital** in *Etz Ḥayyim*, *Peri Etz Ḥayyim* and *Sepher ha-Gilgulim*. His kabbalistic theories profoundly influenced the development of Jewish mysticism. In his teaching he propounded doctrines about divine contraction (tzimtzum), the shattering of the vessels (shevirat ha-kelim), and cosmic repair (tikkun).

Luria, Solomon ben Jehiel [Maharshal] (?1510–74) Polish codifier. He officiated in communities in Lithuania and Poland. His *Yam shel Shelomoh* was critical of the Shulḥan Arukh, which according to Luria relied on the codifiers instead of being based on the Talmud.

Lustig, Arnošt (b. 1926) Czech author. Born in Prague, he was deported to Auschwitz and Buchenwald. He studied at the College of Political and Social Sciences in Prague and worked as a journalist. In 1968 he emigrated to Israel, and later settled in the US where he was professor of literature and creative writing at the American University in Washington. His writings include *Night and Hope*, *Diamonds of the Night*, *A Prayer for Katerina Horovitzova*, *Darkness Casts No Shadow* and *Children of the Holocaust*.

Luxemburg, Rosa (1871–1919) German revolutionary, of Polish origin. Born in Zamość, eastern Poland, she studied at the University of Zurich. She was a leader of the Polish and Lithuanian Social Democratic Party, and sought to overthrow the czar. She became a German citizen and was one of the leaders of the militant left wing of the German party. In 1914 she helped form the Spartacus League. She was imprisoned for most of the war, and freed in 1918. She helped transform the Spartacus League into the German Communist Party. She and a fellow leader of the left, Karl Liebknecht, were arrested, and murdered by army officers when they were being taken to prison.

Luz, Kadish (1895–1972) Israeli labour leader. He was born in Bobruisk, Belorussia, and served in the Russian army during World War I. He was a founder of the organization of Jewish soldiers in Russia and of the Zionist pioneer movement. He settled in Palestine in 1920. From 1951 to 1969 he was a Mapai member of the Knesset. He was minister of agriculture (1955–9) and speaker of the Knesset (1959–69).

Luzki, Joseph Solomon ben Moses (d. 1844) Crimean Karaite scholar. He was born in Kukizow, near Lemberg, and lived at Lutsk, Volhynia. In 1802 he moved to Yevpatoriya in the Crimea, where he became rabbi of the Karaites. He went with Simḥah Babovich to St Petersburg to obtain exemption for the Karaites from military service. In 1831 he settled in Palestine, but he later returned to Yevpatoriya. He wrote religious poems, studies of Hebrew grammar and Bible commentary.

Luzki, Simhah Isaac ben Moses (d. 1766) Crimean Karaite writer and bibliographer. He was born in Lutsk, and lived in Chufut-Kale in the Crimea, where he became head of a bet midrash. He was a copyist of early Karaite manuscripts, and wrote various studies of theology, philosophy, halakhah and kabbalah. His *Oraḥ Tzaddikim* is a history of the Karaites and Karaite literature.

Luzzatti, Luigi (1841–1927) Italian statesman and economist. He was born in Venice, where he founded a mutual aid society for the gondoliers. Expelled from the city as a revolutionary, he went to Milan, where he became professor of economics at the Instituto Tecnico; he was later appointed professor of constitutional law at the University of Padua. In 1869 he became general-secretary to the ministry of agriculture, industry and commerce, and from 1871 he served in parliament in various posts, becoming prime minister in 1910. He acted on behalf of oppressed European Jews, and supported Zionist activities in Palestine.

Luzzatto, Moses Ḥayyim [Ramḥal] (1707–46) Italian kabbalist. Hebrew poet and writer. He was born in Padua. He engaged in mystical practices and gathered around himself a group of disciples. He believed he was in communion with a maggid who dictated secret doctrines to him. His messianic claims provoked the hostility of the rabbis. Forced to leave Italy, he settled in Amsterdam and subsequently went to Palestine. He wrote kabbalistic studies, ethical works, theological investigations, poetry and verse drama. He is regarded as the father of modern Hebrew literature.

Luzzatto, Samuel David [Shadal] (1800–65) Italian scholar, philosopher, biblical commentator and translator. From 1829 he was professor at the Padua Rabbinical College. He wrote studies of the Bible, Hebrew grammar and philology, Jewish liturgy, Hebrew poetry, and philosophy. In addition he edited the poems of **Judah ha-Levi**, translated parts of the Bible into Italian, and composed poetry in Hebrew in traditional Italian style. He was opposed to the kabbalah and criticized several Jewish philosophers including **Maimonides**, **Ibn Ezra** and **Spinoza**. His correspondence with other Jewish scholars is of historical importance.

Luzzatto, Simone (1583–1663) Italian rabbi. Born in Venice, he served as rabbi there for 57 years. His *Socrate* espouses the view that human reason is impotent unless aided by revelation. In another work he argued for Jewish toleration largely on economic grounds. He also wrote a treatise defending the authority of tradition and the oral law.

Lvovich, David (1882–1950) American communal worker. He was born in southern Russia, and was a founder of the Jewish socialist party SS. From 1921 he lived in Berlin, and later settled in Paris (1932–9). He then went to the US where he worked for ORT. He had already served as the vice-chairman of its World Federation since 1921. After World War II he organized occupational training in displaced persons' camps in Europe.

Lwoff, André (1902–94) French biologist. He was head of the microbial physiology laboratory of the Pasteur Institute in Paris. During World War II he was active in the French Resistance. He shared the 1965 Nobel Prize in Medicine and Physiology for work on the cellular genetic function of bacteria and its influence on viruses.

M

Maccoby, Hyam (1924–2003) English historian. He was born in Sunderland. He served as librarian and lecturer at Leo Baeck College in London, and visiting professor at the University of Leeds. His publications include *Revolution in Judaea*, *Judaism on Trial*, *The Sacred Executioner*, *The Mythmaker* and *Early Rabbinic Writings*.

Mack, Julian William (1866–1943) American judge and Zionist leader. He was born in San Francisco. He began his career as a professor of law at Northwestern University (1895–1902). He served as a judge in the circuit court of Cook County, Illinois, in the Chicago juvenile court, and in the US commerce court. In 1913 he was appointed to the US circuit court of appeals. He was president of the Zionist Organization of America (1918–21) and was the first president of the American Jewish Congress. He was also the first chairman of the Comité de Délégations Juives at Versailles (1919).

Maggid of Kelm (1828–99) Lithuanian preacher. He studied under **Israel Salanter** at Kovno, and later became the envoy and preacher of the Musar movement. He travelled throughout the Pale of Settlement and also lived in London.

Magnes, Judah Leon (1877–1948) American rabbi and educator. He was born in San Francisco. He was the rabbi of Temple Israel in Brooklyn, and later assistant rabbi of Temple Emanu-El in New York. He was also president of the kehillah in New York. In 1922 he emigrated to Palestine, where he helped build up the Hebrew University; when the university opened in 1925 he became its chancellor, and he was its president from 1935. He inspired the founding of the peace movement Berit Shalom and its successor, Iḥud.

Magnus, Katie (1844–1924) English author, wife of **Sir Philip Magnus**. She published traditional and historical tales for young readers. Her works include *Outlines of Jewish History* and *Jewish Portraits*.

Magnus, Laurie (1872–1933) English writer, son of **Sir Philip Magnus** and Lady **Katie Magnus**. He wrote various studies of Judaism including: *Aspects of the Jewish Question*, *Religio laici Judaici* and *The Jews in the Christian Era and their Contribution to its Civilization*. From 1917 he served as editor of the anti-Zionist *Jewish Guardian*. He was active in Jewish communal life.

Magnus, Philip (1842–1933) English Reform minister. He was born in London. He served as minister of the West London Synagogue of British Reform Jews from 1866 to 1880. He lectured in applied mathematics at University College, London, and in 1880 he became the organizing secretary and director of the City and Guilds of London Institute. From 1906 to 1922 he served as London University's member of parliament. He was knighted in 1886 and created a baronet in 1917. He played an important role in Anglo-Jewish affairs.

Mahler, Eduard (1857–1945) Hungarian orientalist, mathematician and astronomer. He was born in Cziffer. He taught oriental history and languages at Budapest University, becoming professor there in 1914. In 1912 he was appointed director of the Egyptological Institute in Budapest and in 1922 director of the Oriental Institute. His *Handbuch* *der jüdischen Chronologie* established the systems of the different Jewish calendars and chronologies in the light of ancient Near Eastern and medieval calculations.

Mahler, Gustav (1860–1911) Austrian musician. Born in Kalischt, Bohemia, he studied at the Vienna Conservatory and worked in several operatic companies in Kassel, Prague and Leipzig. He later became musical director of the Budapest Opera and at the Hamburg Municipal Theatre. He converted to Catholicism and became Kapellmeister at the Vienna Court Opera, and later artistic director. Subsequently he became guest conductor of the Metropolitan Opera, and later the New York Philharmonic.His reputation is based largely on ten symphonies and song cycles.

Mahler, Raphel (1899–1977) Galician historian. He was born in Nowy Sadz in eastern Galicia. He served as a teacher in Jewish secondary schools in Poland. In 1937 he went to the US and taught in various educational institutions in New York. In 1950 he went to Israel, where he lectured on the history of Israel at Tel Aviv University. He was appointed professor there in 1961. He wrote various works about Jewish history from a Marxist perspective, including a history of the Jews in modern times, and studies of the Jews in Poland, the Karaites, and Gallician Jewry.

Maid of Ludomir (1805–92) Ukrainian Ḥasidic leader. Her real name was Hannah Rachel and she was the daughter of Monesh Werbermacher. After an illness, she followed Ḥasidic customs, built her own synagogue, and observed the religious duties of men (putting on tallit and tefillin when she prayed). She later emigrated to Palestine where she continued her mystical studies and practised rituals designed to hasten the coming of the Messiah.

Mailer, Norman (b. 1923) American novelist. He was raised in Brooklyn and studied at Harvard. He published *The Naked and the Dead*, a novel about war in the Pacific.This was followed by *Barbary Shore* and *The Deer Park*. Other works include *Armies in the Night*, *Miami and the Siege of Chicago*, *A Fire on the Moon*, *The Executioner's Song* and *Ancient Evenings*.

Maimon, Solomon (1754–1800) Polish philosopher. Born in Sukoviboeg, Poland, he was a child prodigy in the study of rabbinical literature. He initially supported his family by working as a tutor. In his spare time he studied Jewish philosophy and kabbalah, adopting the name Maimon in honour of **Maimonides**. He later left his home and went to Berlin, where he was a member of **Moses Mendelssohn**'s circle. He subsequently lived in various cities, returning to Berlin in 1786. His work was praised by Immanuel Kant and he published various studies of philosophical subjects.

Maimon [Fishman], Yehudah Leib (1876–1962) Israeli rabbi and leader of Mizraḥi. He was born in Bessarabia, where he served as a rabbi and became active in the Zionist movement. In 1913 he moved to Palestine. After World War I he arranged for the executive of the World Centre of Mizraḥi to be based in Palestine and became its head. He was a member of the executive of the Jewish Agency from 1935 to 1948, and Israeli minister for religious affairs from 1948 to 1951; concurrently he was a Mizraḥi delegate to the Knesset (1949–51). He wrote on folklore, and talmudic and Zionist subjects. He was also the director of the Mosad ha-Rav Kook which he initiated.

Maimon ben Joseph (d. 1165/70) Spanish rabbi and dayyan, father of **Maimonides**. He served as dayyan in Córdoba, and wrote an Arabic commentary on the Bible. In 1148 he left Spain with his family because of persecution by the Almohades after their conquest of the city. For about ten years he wandered through Spain and possibly also Provence. In about 1160 he emigrated to Fez, Morocco; he later moved to Palestine, where he died. His writings include *Iggeret ha-Neḥamah*, a guide for forced converts to Islam.

Maimonides [Moses ben Maimon; Rambam] (1135–1204) North African philosopher and halakhist. He is commonly referred to by the name Maimonides, though his given Hebrew name was Moses ben Maimon; the name Rambam is derived from the title Rabbi Moses ben Maimon. He was born in Córdoba, but left the city with his family in 1148 when it was captured by the Almohades. After years of wandering, they settled in Fez. During this perid he wrote treatises on the Jewish calendar, logic and halakhah. In 1168 he completed his commentary on the Mishnah; from 1170 to 1180 he worked on the *Mishneh Torah* (also known as *Yad Ḥazakah*), a compilation of the halakah. In 1190 he completed his philosophical study, the *Guide for the Perplexed* which evoked a controversy that lasted for a century; the work was accused by some of excessive rationalism, which might lead to heresy, while others supported Maimonides' views. He also wrote medical studies and became physician to the Sultan of Egypt. Maimonides exercised a profound influence on Jewish scholarship: his codification of Jewish law remained a standard guide to halakhah and he is perceived as the principal Jewish philosopher of the Middle Ages.

Maisel-Shohat, Hana (b. 1890) Israeli educator. Born in Belorussia, she studied in Odessa and Switzerland. In 1909 she settled in Palestine, and was the founder and principal of the Girls' Agricultural School at Nahalal.

Makhir, ben Abba Mari (fl.?14th cent.) French exegete. His *Yalkut ha-Makhiri* is a collection of aggadot on the books of the prophets and the hagiographa.

Malachi (fl. 5th cent. BCE) Israelite prophet. He protested against the transgression of ritual laws concerning sacrifice and tithes, and also condemned mixed marriages and divorce. His eschatology embraced a vision of the Day of the Lord preceded by the coming of **Elijah**. According to rabbinic tradition, he was the last of the prophets.

Malamud, Bernard (1914–86) Amerian novelist. He was born in New York. He taught at Oregon State University and Bennington College. A number of his novels deal with Jewish themes, including *Idiots First, The Assistant* and *The Fixer.*

Malbim, Meir Leibush (1809–79) Rabbinic scholar. He was born in Volochisk, and lived in Warsaw and Łęczyca. In 1839 he became rabbi of Wreschen, and then moved to Kempen. In 1858 he became chief rabbi of Romania. He attacked the Reform movement, was forced to leave the country, and subsequently wandered throughout Europe. He wrote a commentary on the Bible.

Malter, Henry (1864–1925) American rabbi and scholar. He was born in Bonze, Galicia. He became the librarian of the Jewish community in Berlin. In 1900 he went to the US, where he taught medieval Jewish philosophy, the Bible, and rabbinic law and literature at the Hebrew Union College, and served as the rabbi of Shearith Israel Congregation in Cincinnai. In 1909 he became a professor of talmudic literature at Dropsie College. His writings include *Saadia Gaon: His Life and Works.*

Mamet, David (b. 1947) American playwright. Born in Chicago, his works include *Duck Variations, Sexual Perversity in Chicago, American Buffalo* and *Glengarry Glen Ross.*

Manasseh (i) (fl. ?19th–16th cent. BCE) Israelite, first son of **Joseph** and **Asenath** (Genesis 41:50–51). One of the 12 tribes was named after him.

Manasseh (ii) (fl. 7th cent. BCE) King of Judah (698–643 BCE), son of **Hezekiah**. He ascended to the throne at the age of 12 (II Kings 21:1). He revoked his father's reforms and reintroduced pagan practices. According to II Kings 21:11–17, the destruction of the Temple was due to his unrighteousness. He paid tribute to Esarhaddon and Assurbanipal of Assyria. According to II Chronicles 33:11–19 he was taken captive to Babylon.

Manasseh ben Israel (1604–57) Dutch rabbi. Born a marrano in Madeira, he was taken to Amsterdam as a child. He succeeded **Isaac Uziel** as preacher to the Neveh Shalom congregation in 1622. In 1626 he founded the earliest Hebrew printing press in Amsterdam and proceeded to publish numerous works in Hebrew, Spanish and Latin. He represented Jewish scholarship in the Christian world, corresponded with various gentile scholars, and was a friend of Grotius and Rembrandt. In 1655 he presented a petition to Oliver Cromwell to allow the Jews to return to England.

Manasseh ben Joseph of Ilye (1767–1831) Lithuanian talmudic scholar. He was born in Smorgon, and became a disciple of the Vilna Gaon, **Elijah ben Solomon Zalman**. He was versed in both rabbinic and secular studies. In his writings he challenged the Talmud as well as **Rashi**'s understanding of the Mishnah. An advocate of halakhic change, he was persecuted by the Orthodox. He later worked as a private teacher in Russia and Galicia, where he became acquainted with the maskilim.

Mandelkern, Solomon (1846–1902) German Hebrew poet and scholar of Polish origin. He was born in Mlynow. He served as assistant to the government-appointed rabbi of Odessa from 1873 to 1880, then settled in Leipzig, where he devoted himself to research. A supporter of Ḥibbat Zion, he attended the First Zionist Congress at Basle in 1897. His publications include *Hekhal ha-Kodesh* (a Bible concordance), a history of Russia, a history of Russian literature, and a German–Russian dictionary.

Mandelstam, Osip (1891–?1938) Russian poet. He was born in Warsaw, and lived in Leningrad. In 1934 he was arrested and exiled to the eastern USSR, where he died in a prison camp. His writing is filled with Jewish self-hatred.

Mandelstamm, Benjamin (1805–86) Lithuanian Hebrew author, brother of **Leon Mandelstamm**. He was born in Zagare. In the 1840s he settled in Vilnius, where he adopted an extremist stance in Haskalah circles in which he moved. Critical of Russian Jewish life, he advocated governmental intervention to forbid the printing of the Talmud, removed kabbalistic and Ḥasidic works from circulation, and dissolved the traditional ḥeder system.

Mandelstamm, Leon (1819–89) Russian writer, of Lithuanian origin, brother of **Benjamin Mandelstamm**. He was born in Zagare. He studied at St Petersburg University and was the first Jew to enrol in a Russian university. In 1846 he was appointed to take charge of Jewish affairs in the ministry of education and to establish a network of governmental schools for Jews; he also supervised the Jewish ḥeder and Talmud Torah schools, and prepared Jewish textbooks. His work obliged him to travel throughout the Pale of Settlement. Dismissed from his post in 1857, he lived in Germany, where he engaged in trade and contracting. He eventually returned to Russia and lived in St Petersburg.

Mandelstamm, Max Emanuel (1839–1912) Russian opthalmologist and Zionist of Lithuanian origin, nephew of **Benjamin** and **Leon Mandelstamm**. He was born in Zagare. He opened a clinic in Kiev, where his practice flourished, and lectured in ophthalmology at Kiev University. A founder of the H.ibbat Zion movement in Russia, he became an associate of **Theodor Herzl**. At the Seventh Zionist Congress, he participated in the Founding Conference of the Jewish Territorial Organization. He was the head of the emigration offfice established by the Territorialists in Kiev to organize the emigration of Jews to Galeveston, Texas.

Mané-Katz (1894–1962) French artist. He was born in Russia, moved to France in 1921, and later lived in the US. His early subjects included biblical scenes and figures from the ghetto. There is a museum dedicated to his paintings in Haifa.

Manger, Itzik (1901–69) Yiddish poet, dramatist and novelist. He was born in Czernowitz, and lived in Germany as a child. He learned Yiddish in Romania and published ballads and plays, which were influenced by German lyricists and such writers as **Eliakum Zunser**. During and after World War II he lived in London, later moving to the US. He finally settled in Israel.

Mani Leib [Brahinski, Mani Leib] (1883–1953) American Yiddish poet and journalist. He was born in Russia and emigated to the US in 1905. He served on the editorial staff of *Forverts* from 1916 to 1953 and edited a number of journals of the Yiddish literary movement Di Yunge. He translated several Russian novels into Yiddish and published poems in Di Yunge's periodicals and anthologies. His ballads and tales for children were sung and recited in Yiddish schools.

Mankowitz, Wolf (b. 1924) English author. He was born in London, where he became an antique dealer. He wrote various books inspired by his childhood in the East End of London. His publications include *A Kid for Two Farthings*, *Make Me an Offer*, *The Boychick* and *The Mendelman Fire*.

Mann, Jacob (1888–1940) American scholar. He was born in Galicia. He studied in London, and subsequently taught history at the Hebrew Union College in Cincinnati. He utilized genizah material in a series of studies on the history and literature of the gaonic period. His publications include *The*

Jews of Palestine and Egypt Under the Fatimids, Texts and Studies in Jewish History and Literature and *The Bible as Read and Preached in the Old Synagogue.*

Manne, Mordecai Tzevi (1859–86) Lithuanian Hebrew lyric poet and artist. He was born near Vilna, and studied art there. In 1880 he became a student at the Academy of Arts in St Petersburg, and began to write poems and articles. He later went to Warsaw, where he designed the covers for anthologies of works by **Naḥum Sokolow** and **Saul Phinehas Rabinowitz**. His poem *Masat Nafshi* expresses his longing for Palestine.

Mannheim, Karl (1893–1947) Hungarian sociologist. Born in Budapest, he studied at the University of Budapest. He initially taught high school in Budapest, then at a teacher's training college of the University of Budapest and later at Heidelberg. In 1930 he was appointed professor of sociology and economy at the University of Frankfurt. With the rise of the Nazis, he emigrated to England and became professor at the LSE. His works include *Ideology and Utopia, Man and Society in an Age of Reconstruction* and *Diagnosis of Our Time.*

Mannheimer, Isaac Noah (1793–1865) Austrian preacher and liturgist. He was born in Copenhagen, where he taught religion and held services for adherents of Reform Judaism. In 1824 he became a preacher at the new Seitenstetten Synagogue in Vienna. He later adopted a more Conservative approach to Reform Judaism, and translated the prayerbook and the festival prayers into German. In 1848 he was elected to the Reichstag where he advocated Jewish rights.

Mantino, Jacob (d. 1549) Italian physician and translator, of Spanish origin. He practised medicine in Bologna, Verona and Venice. During the debate on the annulment of the marriage of Henry VIII of England and Catherine of Aragon, he opposed Henry's supporters. He thus earned the gratitude of Pope Clement VII, by whose influence he was appointed lecturer in medicine at Bologna University. In 1533 he was invited by the pope to Rome, where he took a stand against the messianic claims of **Solomon Molcho**. The following year he was appointed personal physician to Pope Paul III, and became professor of practical medicine at the Sapienza in Rome. His scholarly work included translations of philosophical works from Hebrew into Latin.

Mapu, Abraham (1808–67) Lithuanian Hebrew novelist. He worked as a children's tutor and lived in various towns, including Slobodka, Georgenberg, Kovno, Rossyieny and Vilna. His *Ahavat Tziyyon* is a historical romance set in the period of **Hezekiah**. In *Alyit Tzavua* he satirized contemporary Lithuanian Jews. His other novels include *Ashmat Shomron* and *Ḥozeh Ḥezyonot.*

Marceau, Marcel (b. 1923) French mime. As a young man, he worked in the underground and helped smuggle Jewish children into Switzerland. He was regarded as the greatest exponent of mime.

Marcus, David [Stone, Mickey] (1902–48) American soldier. He was born in New York. He served in the US attorney-general's office, and later as commissioner of correction in New York. He joined the army, and was appointed head of its war crimes branch. In 1948 he was one of **David Ben-Gurion**'s military advisors, taking the name Mickey Stone. In the same year he became commander of the Jerusalem front. He was killed during the Israeli War of Independence.

Marcus, Jacob Rader (1896–1995) American rabbi and historian. He was born in Connellsville, Pennsylvania. He taught history from 1920 at the Hebrew Union College, where he founded the American Jewish Archives. He published numerous studies of American Jewry.

Marcus, Ralph (1900–56) American scholar of Hellenistic Judaism. He was born in San Francisco. He taught at Columbia University and at the University of Chicago. He edited, translated and annotated four volumes of the works of **Josephus** and two of those of **Philo** in the Loeb Classical Library series.

Marcuse, Herbert (1898–1979) German philospher. Born in Berlin, he studied in Berlin and Freiburg. He initially worked at the Frankfurt Institute for Social Research, but from the early 1940s he was an intelligence analyst in various US agencies. He was a fellow of Russian research centres at Columbia and

Harvard, and became professor of philosophy and politics at Brandeis University in 1954, and later at the University of California at San Diego. His works include *Reason and Revolution*, *Eros and Civilization* and *One-Dimensional Man*.

Margolin, Eliezer (1874–1944) Australian military commander. He was born in Belgorod, Russia. He moved to Palestine in 1892 and settled in Rehovot. In 1900 he went to Australia and he served in the Australian army during World War I, later commanding the Second Battalion of the Jewish Regiment. In 1919 he became commander of the Jewish Legion. When the legion was dismantled, he became commander of the Jewish unit of the Palestine Defence Force. Subsequently he returned to Australia.

Margoliouth, David Samuel (1858–1940) English classical scholar and orientalist. He was born in London, and became a professor of Arabic at Oxford University. He published studies in the fields of Islamic history and literature, and edited medieval Arabic texts. His writings include *The Origin of the 'Hebrew Original' of Ecclesiasticus* and *Relations Between Arabs and Israelites Prior to the Rise of Islam*.

Margoliouth, George (1853–1952) English bibliographer. He converted to Christianity and became a priest. He was in charge of the Hebrew, Syriac and Ethiopic manuscripts in the British Museum from 1891 to 1914. His publications include *The Liturgy of the Nile*, *The Palestine Syriac Version of the Holy Scriptures* and *Catalogue of the Hebrew and Samaritan Manuscripts in the British Museum*.

Margolis, Max Leopold (1886–1932) American biblical and Semitic scholar. He was born in Russia, and went to the US in 1889. He taught at the Hebrew Union College, and in 1897 went to the University of California at Berkeley to teach Semitic languages. He then returned to the Hebrew Union College, but resigned in 1910, to become professor of biblical philology at Dropsie College. He supervised the translation of the Bible published by the Jewish Publication Society of America, and collaborated with **Alexander Marx** on the *History of the Jewish People*.

Margoshes, Samuel (1887–1968) American Yiddish journalist. He was born in Galicia, and went to the US in 1905. He engaged in communal, educational and relief activities before, during and after World War I. Later he served as editor of the New York Yiddish daily, *Dertog* (1926–42). He supported Zionism in the US and took an active role in the American Congress and Zionist activities.

Mariamne (?60–29 BCE) Israelite queen, daughter of **Alexander** (son of **Aristobulus II**) and granddaughter of **John Hyrcanus**. She was the second wife of **Herod** the Great, though she hated him because he had killed nearly all the members of her family, and had replaced her own dynasty (the Hasmoneans) with his own. Herod eventually put her to death.

Mariamne II (d. c.20 BCE) Israelite queen, daughter of the high priest Simeon ben Boethus. She was the third wife of **Herod** the Great. Her son, also Herod, was designated to succeed to the throne after **Antipater III** (**Herod** the Great's son by his first wife, Doris). Although Mariamne knew of **Antipater**'s intentions to kill his father, she held her peace because of the succession. When **Antipater**'s plot was discovered, **Herod** divorced her and expunged her son's name from his will.

Marinoff, Jacob (1869–1964) American Yiddish poet and editor. He was born in Russia. He moved to London, where he worked in a tailor's shop (1891–93), then emigrated to the US and settled in Denver. From 1895 he contributed poems to Yiddish periodicals. He was a co-founder of the journal *Der groyser kundas* in 1909 and served as its editor.

Markfield, Wallace (b. 1926) American novelist. He was born in Brooklyn. His publications include *To an Early Grave*, *Teitelbaum's Window* and *You Could Live if They Let You*.

Markish, David (b. 1938) Israeli novelist, of Russian origin. He settled in Israel in 1972 and has worked as a novelist and journalist. His publications include *The World of Simon Ashkenazy*, *The Jewters*, *The Dog*, *In the Shade of the Great Rock* and *The Crimson Well*.

Markish, Peretz (1895–1952) Ukrainian Yiddish poet, novelist and playwright. Born in Volhynia, he left Russia in 1921 and lived in Poland and France. From 1921 to 1926 he wrote poetry about the anti-Jewish pogroms in the Ukraine. In 1926 he returned to the USSR, where he published epic poems and novels. He was accused of Jewish natonalism and executed.

Markon, Isaac Dov Ber (1875–1949) Russian scholar and librarian. Born in Rybinsk on the Volga, he was a professor of Jewish studies at the University of St Petersburg, and later professor at the Belorussian University at Minsk. In 1926 he settled in Berlin. Expelled from Germany in 1938, he went to Holland and then England, where he joined the Montefiore College in Ramsgate. His publications deal with Karaite history and literature and associated topics.

Markova, Alicia [Marks, Lilian Alicia] (1910–2004) English prima ballerina. Born in London, she appeared with the Diaghilev company, and in 1933 founded her own together with Anton Dolin. She was made a Dame of the British Empire in 1963. The same year she became director of the Metropolitan Ballet in New York. In 1970 she became professor of ballet at the University of Cincinnati.

Marks, Simon (1888–1964) English industrialist and philanthropist. He was born in Manchester. He became chairman of the board of Marks and Spencer Ltd chainstores in 1917. He was an active Zionist and served as secretary of the Zionist delegation to the Versailles Peace Conference. Later he became chairman of the Keren ha-Yesod Committee, vice-president of the Zionist Federation, and a member of the executive of the Zionist Organization.

Marmorek, Alexander (1865–1923) French bacteriologist and Zionist leader. He was born in Mielnice, Galicia. He became assistant and later senior researcher at the Pasteur Institute in Paris. He was an associate of **Theodor Herzl** and served as a member of the Zionist General Council at the first 11 Zionist Congresses. He was a co-founder of the Paris Zionist monthly *L'écho Sioniste.*

Marmorek, Oscar (1863–1909) Austrian architect and Zionist leader. He was born in Skala, Galicia. He built important buildings in Vienna and Austria, and designed synagogues based on old Jewish architecture. After the publication of **Theodor Herzl**'s *Der Judenstaat,* Marmorek joined **Herzl** and was elected to the executive of the Zionist Organization at the first six Zionist Congresses. He was a co-founder of the Zionist weekly *Die Welt.*

Marmorstein, Arthur (1882–1946) British rabbi, scholar and teacher. He was born in Miskolc, Hungary, and served as a rabbi at Jamnitz, Czechoslovakia. From 1912 he taught at Jews College in London. His publications embrace a wide range of Jewish topics and include *Doctrine of Merits in Old Rabbinic Literature* and *Old Rabbinic Doctrine of God.*

Marshall, Louis (1856–1929) American lawyer and communal leader. He was born in Syracuse, New York, and became a partner in a New York legal firm. He was the chief spokesman for the German-Jewish elite in Jewish affairs. In 1912 he became president of the American Jewish Committee. He also served as president of Temple Emanu-El in New York, and chairman of the board of directors of the Jewish Theological Seminary. During World War I he was president of the American Jewish Relief Committee.

Martin, David (b. 1915) Australian poet and novelist. He was born in Hungary. He fought in the Spanish Civil War, then lived in London from 1938. In 1949 he moved to Sydney, where he became editor of the Sydney *Jewish News.* His novel *The Shepherd and the Hunter* deals with the Palestine problem in the 1940s, and *Where a Man Belongs* discusses various aspects of modern Jewish life.

Martov, Julius (1873–1923) Russian revolutionary. He was a student in St Petersburg and joined the Russian Social Democratic Party. In 1901 he helped publish the revolutionary journal, *Iskra.* He was exiled in Paris where he continued to work for the party. After the revolution he returned to Russia; in 1920 he went to Berlin, and was the leader of the Mensheviks outside Russia. His works include a four-volume history of the social democratic movement in Russia.

Marx, Alexander (1878–1953) German historian, bibliographer and librarian. He was born in Elberfeld, Germany, and emigrated to the US in 1903. He served as librarian and taught history at the Jewish Theological Seminary. He published studies of bibliography and history, and collaborated with **Max Margolis** on the *History of the Jewish People.*

Marx, Groucho (1895–1977) American comedian. He and his brothers were children of German immigrants. Together they were a vaudeville act. Later they became Broadway stars and appeared in several films. Groucho had his own quiz show, *You Bet Your Life*, and published several books.

Marx, Karl (1818–1883) German social philosopher, founder of modern communism. He was born in Trier, and converted to Protestantism at the age of six. He was the editor of the Cologne daily, *Rheinische Zeitung.* He moved to Paris in 1843, and then went to Brussels. In 1848 he and Friedrich Engels published *The Communist Manifesto.* In 1849 he settled in London, where he wrote *Das Kapital.* In his writings he expressed hostility towards Jews and Judaism.

Masliansky, Tzevi Hirsch (1856–1943) Polish-American preacher. He was born in Slutsk, Belorussia, and taught at the Polish Talmud Torah and at the yeshivah of Pinsk. Active in Ḥibbat Zion, he left the country in 1894, and undertook a lecture tour of central and Western Europe. In 1895 he settled in New York where he helped to popularize Zionism through Friday evening sermons at the Educational Alliance on East Broadway.

Matsa, Joseph (1919–86) Greek scholar and Hebrew folklorist. He was born in Ioannina and taught Greek literature at a high school there. His publications include *The Hebrew Songs of the Jannina Jews* and *The Names of the Jews of Ioannina.*

Matsas, Nestoras (b. 1932) Greek author, painter and film director. Born in Athens, he was baptized into the Greek Orthodox Church during the Nazi occupation. Some of his stories and novels deal with Jewish themes.

Mattathias (fl. 2nd cent. BCE) Israelite priest and rebel leader. He was priest of Modiin and led the uprising of the Hasmoneans against Antiochus IV in 166–164 BCE. He led the revolt in the Judean hills, waging war on the Syrians. He was succeeded by his son **Judah Maccabee.**

Mattathias ha-Yitzhari (fl. 14th–15th cent.) Spanish scholar. A pupil of **Ḥasdai Crescas**, he wrote a commentary on Psalm 119, a commentary on Avot, and homiletical explanations of the Pentateuch. He played a role in the Disputation of Tortosa in 1413–15, representing the Zaragoza community.

Mattuck, Israel Isidor (1883–1954) British liberal rabbi, of Lithuanian origin. He went to the US as a child and served as a rabbi in Far Rockaway, New York and Lincoln, Nebraska. In 1911 he became the leader of the Liberal Jewish Synagogue in London. He served as chairman of the World Union of Progressive Judaism. His writings include *What Are the Jews?, Essentials of Liberal Judiasm, Jewish Ethics* and *Thoughts of the Prophets.*

Matyah ben Harash (fl. 2nd cent.) Palestinian tanna. He left Palestine after the Hadrianic persecutions of 135–8 and settled in Rome, where he founded a rabbinical academy.

Maurois, André [Herzog, Emile] (1885–1967) French novelist. Born in Elbeuf, Normandy he studied in Rouen and Caen. He worked in the family business, but began to publish novels and short stories. Fleeing from France during the war, he went to the US and taught at Princeton University. He subsequently returned to France. A 16-volume collection of his collected works appeared in 1950–5.

Mauss, Marcel (1872–1950) French ethnologist. Born in Alsace, he was a nephew of **Emile Durkheim.** He taught at the University of Paris and at the Collège de France. In 1925 he founded the Ethnological Institute of the University of Paris. His works include *Essai sur le Don.*

Maybaum, Ignaz (1897–1976) British Reform rabbi and theologian. Born in Vienna, he was a rabbi in Bingen, Frankfurt an der Oder, and Berlin. In 1939 he settled in England and served as a rabbi in London. He also lectured on theology and homiletics at the Leo Baeck College. His writings include *The Face of God After Auschwitz.*

Mayer, Carl (1894–1944) German screenwriter. His works include *Das Kabinett des Dr Caligrai, Genuine, Scherben, Erdgeist, Der letze Mann* and *Sunrise.*

Mayer, Daniel (b. 1909) French politician. After World War II, he became secretary-general of the socialist party. He was elected to the Chamber of Deputies and held several cabinet posts. After 1958 he became involved in European human rights and was president of the League for the Rights of Man.

Mayer, Leo Ari (1895–1959) Israeli orientalist. He was born in Stanislav in the Ukraine. He moved to Palestine in 1921 and became inspector of antiquities, and librarian and keeper of records for the Department of Antiquities. From 1923 to 1958 he was professor of Near Eastern art and archaeology at the Hebrew University. He published works on Islamic art, costume, epigraphy and numismatics.

Mayer, Louis [Mayer, Lazar] (1885–1957) American film producer, of Russian origin. Born in Minsk, Russia, he went to Canada with his parents. In 1904 he worked in the scrap-metal business in Boston. Several years later he invested in a small theatre in Haverhill, Massachusetts. This was followed by several other theatres and he branched out into film distribution. In 1918 he established his own studio in Los Angeles; subsequently he became head of Metro-Goldwyn-Mayer studios.

Mayer, René (1895–1972) French politician. Born in Paris, he studied at the Sorbonne. He served as the Conseil d'État in 1919 and was lecturer at the École Libre des Sciences Politiques (1922–32). Later he became administrator of Air France and the French railroad system. During the war he joined the Resistance and fled to Algeria. He served twice as minister of finance and economic affairs, and in 1953 headed the French government.

Mayer, Sigmund (1831–1920) Austrian merchant and writer. He was born in Pressburg, Hungary. He became active in efforts to defend Jewish interests in Austria. His publications include *A Jewish Merchant* and *The Viennese Jews: Commerce, Culture and Politics.*

Mayzel [Meisel], Naḥman (1887–1966) Polish Yiddish writer. From 1921 he edited Yiddish periodicals in Warsaw. He emigrated to New York in 1937 and became the central figure of the Yiddish culture society Yiddisher Kultur Farband, and editor of its monthly journal, *Yiddisher kultur.* He wrote studies of Jewish life in Poland and Russia. In 1964 he settled in Israel.

Mazar [Maisler], Binyamin (1906–95) Israeli archaeologist and historian. He was born in Ciechanowiec in Poland, and settled in Palestine in 1929. In 1951 he became professor of the history of the Jewish people in the biblical period and the archaeology of Palestine at the Hebrew University. In 1952 he became rector of the university, and the following year, president. He directed various archaeological excavations. His publications include numerous archaeological studies, a historical atlas of the country, and a history of Palestine up to the period of the monarchy.

Medini, Ḥayyim Hezekiah (1832–1904) Palestinian rabbi. He was born in Jerusalem. From 1867 to 1899 he was a rabbi in Karasubazar in the Crimean peninsula. He subsequently moved to Palestine and settled in Hebron, where he founded a yeshivah. His *Sede Ḥemed* is a halakhic encyclopaedia.

Megged, Aharon (b. 1920) Israeli writer and editor. He was born in Wloclawek, Poland, and went to Palestine in 1926 with his family. In 1950 he settled in Tel Aviv, where he edited the journal *Ba-Sha'ar* and was a founder of the literary magazine *Massa.* From 1960 to 1971 he was Israel's cultural attaché in London. His stories and novels depict modern life in Israel.

Meijer, Jacob (1912–93) Dutch historian, author and poet. He was born in Winschoten, and taught history at the Jewish Lyceum in Amsterdam in 1941–3. He was deported to Bergen-Belsen in 1944. After the war he taught history in Amsterdam, and later in Haarlem. He published studies of the pre-war history of the Jews of the Netherlands.

Meir (fl. 2nd cent.) Palestinian tanna. A pupil of **Akiva**, he was a member of the Sanhedrin at Usha after the Hadrianic persecutions. He was sometimes known as Rabbi Meir Baal ha-Nes. His Mishnah was one of the main sources of the Mishnah of **Judah ha-Nasi**. His wife, **Beruryah**, was also an outstanding scholar.

Meir [Meyerson], Golda (1898–1978) Israeli politician. She was born in Kiev, and emigrated to the US in 1906. In 1921 she settled in Palestine. Active in Labour Zionism, she held important positions in the Histadrut and the Jewish Agency. After the establishment of the State of Israel in 1948, she was appointed minister to Moscow. In 1949 she was elected to the Knesset as a member of Mapai. Later she was minister of labour in successive governments, and from 1956 to 1966 she served as foreign minister. She was prime minister from 1969 to 1974.

Meir, Yaakov (1856–1939) Palestinian rabbi. Born in Jerusalem, he was a Zionist and advocated the revival of spoken Hebrew. In 1906 he was elected Ḥakham Bashi. From 1908 to 1919 he served as chief rabbi of Salonica, and in 1921 he became Sephardi chief rabbi in Palestine.

Meir ben Isaac Nehorai (fl. 11th cent.) German religious poet. He lived in Worms and wrote hymns, including the acrostic poem *Akdamut*. According to tradition he was killed by the crusaders in in 1096.

Meir ben Samuel (c. 1060–c. 1135) French Tosaphist, son-in-law of **Rashi**. He lived with **Rashi** in Troyes, but later moved to Remerupt where he founded a bet midrash. He wrote commentaries to the Talmud. Halakhic statements by him were quoted by his son **Jacob Tam** in his writings.

Meiri, Menaḥem ben Solomon, of Perpignan (1249–1316) French talmudist. He was born in Perpignan. He was a participant in **Solomon Adret**'s polemic against **Maimonides**, which led to **Adret**'s excommunicating any person who read philosophical works in his youth. Later Meiri disassociated himself from **Adret**, and supported freedom of thought for the scholars of every country. He wrote studies of halakhah, customs, ethics and philosophy. His *Bet ha-Behirah* is a commentary on the Talmud.

Meir of Przemyslany (1780–1850) Polish Ḥasidic leader. He was a miracle worker. Thousands of Ḥasidim went to receive his blessing and hear his teaching.

Meir of Rothenberg (c. 1215–93) German teacher, scholar, tosaphist and communal leader. He was born in Worms. He became the outstanding rabbinic authority of his generation. He was imprisoned by Emperor Rudolf I at Ensisheim in 1286 for attempting to settle in Palestine; refusing to be ransomed lest European rulers begin to blackmail other communities in a similar way, he died a prisoner. His body was ransomed 14 years later. He wrote numerous responsa, as well as tosaphot and novellae to 18 tractates of the Talmud.

Meisel, Mordecai Marcus (1528–1601) Bohemian financier, philanthropist and communal leader. He was a court banker to the Austrian imperial house, and built the Meisel Synagogue in Prague in 1597; he also financed the building of a hospital, a bet midrash and a mikveh. In addition he sent money to Jerusalem and granted loans to the Jewish communities in Kraków and Poznán.

Meisels, Dov Berush (1798–1870) Polish rabbi and patriot. He settled in Kraków, where he opened a bank, and was later elected rabbi of the city; rabbi Saul Landa and his followers did not, however, recognize this election and established their own bet din. Opposed to the Haskalah, Meisels played a major role in the life of the Kraków Jewish community. In 1846 he was elected to the senate of the Kraków Republic and two years later to the Austrian parliament. In 1856 he became chief rabbi of Warsaw. He participated in the events leading to the Polish rebellion of 1863. His writings include a commentary on **Maimonides**' *Sepher ha-Mitzvot*.

Meitner, Lise (1878–1968) Austrian scientist. She studied at the University of Vienna and later worked in Berlin. In 1918 she discovered protactinium. During World War I she served as an X-ray nurse for the Austrian army. Later she returned to Germany. In 1938 she fled to Sweden. She was the first to calculate the energy released by splitting the uranium atom.

Melamed, Samuel Max (1885–1938) American writer and journalist. He was born in Lithuania, and in 1914 settled in the US, where he edited periodicals including the *American Jewish Chronicle*. His writings include *Der Staat in Wandel der Jahrtausende*, *Psychologie des Jüdischen Geistes* and *Spinoza und Buddha*.

Melchoir, Marcus (1897–1969) Chief rabbi of Denmark. During the Nazi occupation in World War II, the Danish people made heroic efforts to save their Jewish population. In October 1940 the Danish undergound secretly transported most of the Jews to safety in Sweden. Melchoir who was a Danish rabbi, served them there. After the war he became the chief rabbi of Denmark.

Meldola, David (1797–1853) English rabbi, son of **Raphael Meldola**. He succeeded his father as presiding rabbi of the Sephardi community in London. He was a founder of the *Jewish Chronicle* and opposed the Reform movement.

Meldola, Raphael (1754–1828) British rabbi. He was born in Livorno. In 1804 or 1805 he became Ḥaham of the Sephardi community in London. In this capacity he reformed Jewish educational institutions, introduced a choir into the synagogue, and co-operated with Solomon Hirscher, the Ashkenazi chief rabbi. He published a handbook of marital life, as well as sermons, memorial poems and a catechism.

Melnikoff, Avraham (1892–1960) Israeli sculptor. He was born in Russia, studied sculpture in Chicago, and in 1918 emigrated to Palestine. His work includes a monument to the soldier and pioneer **Joseph Trumpeldor** and his comrades.

Meltzer, Shimshon (b. 1909) Israeli poet. He was born in Tluste, and settled in Palestine in 1933. Initially he taught in a school in Tel Aviv, and later he engaged in editorial work. From 1959 he was on the editorial staff of the Zionist Library publications produced by the Jewish Agency. He published poems and ballads combining Ḥasidic tales and motifs. He also translated Yiddish literature into Hebrew.

Memmi, Albert (b. 1920) French author and sociologist. He was born in Tunis. He fought with the Free French during World War II, and later became head of a psychology institute in Tunis. In 1966 he became professor at the École Pratique des Hautes Études. His writings, which concern north African Jewry, include *Pillar of Salt, Agar: Portrait of a Jew* and *The Liberation of the Jew.*

Menaḥem (fl. 8th cent. BCE) King of Israel (c. 746/7–737 BCE). He siezed the throne after assassinating **Shallum**, son of Jabesh. When the Assyrian king Tiglath-Pileser III invaded Israel, Menaḥem was forced to pay him tribute (II Kings 15:19).

Menaḥem ben Judah (fl. 1st cent.) Israelite rebel leader, son of **Judah the Galilean**. He led the group known as the Sicarii in the war against Rome (66–70), successfully attacking the stronghold of Masada, and gaining victory over the Romans in **Herod**'s palace. Later he antagonized **Eleazar ben Hananiah** and his followers, who killed him.

Menaḥem ben Saruk (c. 910–c. 970) Spanish Hebrew lexicographer. He was born in Tortosa. He served as the secretary of **Ḥasdai ibn Shaprut**, but was dismissed and persecuted for his heretical views. His *Maḥberet*, the first Hebrew dictionary, was attacked by **Dunash ben Labrat**.

Menaḥem Mendel of Chernobyl (1730–89) Ukrainian Ḥasidic rabbi. Initially he engaged in ascetic practices and fasting. After studying with the **Baal Shem Tov**, he became a maggid, spreading Ḥasidism in Russia and the Ukraine. He collected money for ransoming Jewish captives and for other charitable ends. He emphasized the importance of the spiritual state known as 'devekut' and upheld the position of the tzaddik.

Menaḥem Mendel of Przemyslany (fl. 18th cent.) Palestinian Ḥasidic leader. A pupil of the **Baal Shem Tov**, he went to Palestine in 1764 and settled in Tiberias. He was an extreme enthusiast among the first generation of Ḥasidic leaders, and emphasized the importance of prayer.

Menahem Mendel of Rymanov (fl. 18th–19th cent.) Galician Ḥasidic rabbi. His preaching attracted thousands of Ḥasidim to visit him in Rymanov, Galicia. During the Napoleonic Wars, he predicted the coming of the Messiah.

Menaḥem Mendel of Vitebsk (1730–88) Polish Ḥasidic leader. A disciple of **Dov Ber of Mezhirich**, he became the head of a congregation in Minsk. In 1772 he went with **Shneour Zalman** to defend the Ḥasidic movement to the Vilna Gaon, **Elijah ben Solomon Zalman**, but the Vilna Gaon refused to meet them. In 1773 he settled in Gorodok in Belorussia and later moved to Palestine, where he became the leader of the Ḥasidic community. He subsequently settled in Tiberias. He taught that God is present through the process of contraction (tzimtzum), whereby he makes a space in which creation can take place. His writings include *Peri ha-Aretz*, *Peri ha-Etz*, *Etz Peri* and *Likkutei Amarim*.

Menaḥem the Essene (fl. 1st cent. BCE) Israelite seer. He prophesied that **Herod** would become king but that he would act unjustly and be punished. Later **Herod** questioned Menaḥem about how long he would reign.

Mendelssohn, Erich (1887–1953) Israeli architect. He was born in Allenstein, Germany. From the 1920s he was a member of the revivalist movement in European architecture. He left Germany in 1933 and worked in Britain and Palestine. Between 1934 and 1939 he designed various buildings in Palestine, including the Anglo-Palestine Bank in Jerusalem, the Hadassah hospital on Mount Scopus, and the government hospital in Haifa. He subsequently built a number of synagogues in American cities.

Mendelssohn [Mendelssohn-Bartholdy], Felix (1809–47) German composer, grandson of **Moses Mendelssohn**. He was baptized, and later converted to Christianity. His compositions include the oratorio *Elijah*; he was also responsible for the revival of Bach's *St Matthew Passion*.

Mendelssohn, Moses (1729–1986) German philosopher. He was born in Dessau. He lived in Berlin, where he studied philosophy, mathematics, Latin, French and English, and became a partner in a silk factory. In 1754 with the help of Gotthold Ephraim Lessing, he began to publish philosophical studies and in 1763 was awarded the first prize of the Prussian Royal Academy of Sciences for his philosophical works. He became embroiled in a dispute about Judaism, and from 1769 devoted his literary work to issues dealing with the Jewish faith. He published a German translation of the Pentateuch with a Hebrew commentary (*Biur*). His *Jerusalem* is an analysis of Judaism and a defence of toleration.

Mendes, Henry Pereira (1852–1937) American Sephardi rabbi. He was born in Birmingham, England, and served as a rabbi to the new Sephardi congregation of Manchester from 1874 to 1877. He then emigrated to New York, where he served as a rabbi to the Shearith Israel congregation. He was a founder of the Union of Orthodox Congregations of America, the Jewish Theological Seminary, and the New York Board of Jewish Ministers. He wrote about Jewish and general topics for the weekly paper *American Hebrew*. His works include *Looking Ahead*, *Bar Mitzvah*, *Esther and Harbonah*, *Jewish Religion Ethically Presented*, *Jewish History Ethically Presented*, *Mekor Ḥayyim: Mourners' Handbook* and *Derekh Ḥayyim: Way of Life*.

Mendes-France, Pierre (1907–82) French politician. Born in Paris, he joined the radical socialist party and later became a member of the national assembly. He held a junior post in the Popular Front government from 1936–8. After the Nazi occupation, he became a member of the Resistance. He was imprisoned but escaped to Britain and joined the Free French under General de Gaulle. Later he served as finance commissioner in Algeria. He was minister for economic affairs and then French governor of the Bank for Reconstruction and Development. In 1954 he became prime minister.

Mendoza, Daniel (1764–1836) British boxer. Born in London, he was the first boxer to be granted royal patronage. He opened his own academy and wrote *The Art of Boxing* and *Memoirs*.

Menelaus (fl. 2nd cent. BCE) High priest. He obtained the priesthood in 171 BCE by means of bribery. An extreme Hellenizer, he supported the persecution of the Jews by Antiochus IV Epiphanes. At the beginning of his tenure of office, he plundered the Temple. Later he lost favour in the Seleucid court and was put to death on the advice of Lysias.

Menes, Abraham (1897–1969) American Jewish historian. He was born in Grodno, Poland, and founded a branch of the socialist party the Bund there; he later became vice-chairman of the Grodno Jewish community. In 1920 he moved to Berlin, and he subsequently settled in Paris, where he contributed to the *Yiddish Encyclopedia*. In 1940 he moved to the US. He published studies of the economic and social aspects of Jewish history.

Menken, Adah Isaacs (1835–68) American actress. Born in New Orleans, Louisiana, she achieved notoriety for her role in *Mazeppa*, a dramatization of Byron's poem.

Menuhin, Yehudi (1916–99) American musician. Born in New York, he made his debut at the age of eight. He became a world famous violinist and served as president of the International Musical Council of UNESCO. He was knighted for his services to music in 1965 and received the Order of Merit in 1987.

Metchnikoff, Elie (1845–1916) Russian scientist. He was a professor at the University of Odessa, but left Russia due to the pogroms of the 1880s. He settled in Messina, Italy where he studied marine life. In 1888 he went to Paris to work with Louis Pasteur. Later he succeeded him as director of the Institute. In 1908 he received the Nobel Prize in Medicine and Physiology.

Meyer, Ernst H. (1905–88) German composer. He was a refugee from Nazism and settled in Britain in 1933. He worked in the GPO Film Unit as an expert on sound. Later he composed music for the cartoons of Halas-Batchelor. Subsequently he became professor and director of the Institute for Musicology at Humbolt University in Berlin and played an important role in East German music.

Meyer, Eugene (1875–1959) American banker, newspaper editor and publisher. Born in Los Angeles, he studied at Yale University. In 1901 he founded the banking firm of Eugene Meyer, Jr and Company. In 1917 he was appointed adviser to the War Industries Board and later became managing director of the War Finance Corporation. In 1946 he became president of the International Bank for Reconstruction and Development. In 1947 he became chairman of the Board of the *Washington Post* and *Times-Herald.*

Meyerbeer, Giacomo [Beer, Jakob Liebmann] (1791–1864) German composer. Born in Vogelsdorf, he was the son of a wealthy Berlin banker. He composed operas in Italy in the style of Rossini, and then moved to Paris where he produced *Robert le Diable*. Other works include *Les Huguenots*. In 1842 the King of Prussia appointed him General Music Director in Berlin.

Meyerhof, Otto (1884–1951) German scientist. He was professor of physiological chemistry at the University of Kiel. In 1923 he shared the Nobel Prize for Medicine and Physiology. He fled Germany in 1938 and became research professor of physiological chemistry at the University of Pennsylvania.

Meyerson, Émile (1859–1933) French philosopher. Born in Lublin, he studied chemistry at Heidelberg, and settled in Paris in 1882. He served as director-general of the Jewish Colonization Association. He conducted the first study into the situation of the Jews in Russia. His works include *Identité et Realité.*

Micah (fl. 8th cent. BCE) Israelite prophet. He lived in Judah, where he defended the people against the oppression of the ruling classes. He prophesied the destruction of the country and exile to Babylon, and also predicted the coming of a king of the House of David who would bring peace to the world.

Michal (fl. 10th cent. BCE) Israelite princess and queen, daughter of **Saul** and wife of **David**. She helped her husband to escape from **Saul**'s messengers, who had been sent to kill him. Subsequently she was given in marriage to Paltiel son of Laish, but was eventually restored to **David**. When **David** danced in front of the Ark, she rebuked him. She died childless (I Samuel 18–19; II Samuel 16; I Chronicles 15).

Michaelis, Max (1860–1932) South African art patron, of German origin. He went to South Africa from Germany at the age of 16 and became a diamond buyer in Kimberley. Later he settled in Capetown and became a benefactor of art. He endowed the Michaelis School of Fine Art at the University of Capetown.

Michelson, Albert (1852–1931) American physicist, of East Prussian origin. Born in Strelno, Germany, he went to the US at the age of three. His family moved to Nevada, and he studied at the US Naval Academy. He became an instructor in science there and later professor of physics at Case School of Applied Science in Cleveland, and later at Clark University in Worcester, Massachusetts. Subsequently he was professor of physics at the University of Chicago. In 1907 he received the Nobel Prize in Physics.

Mielziner, Moses (1828–1903) American Reform rabbi and scholar. He was born in Czerniejewo, and served as a preacher and teacher in Waren. From 1857 to 1865 he was head of the Jewish school in Copenhagen. He emigrated to the US, where he served as a rabbi in New York and later became a professor of Talmud and rabbinic literature at the Hebrew Union College. His writings include *Introduction to the Talmud, The Jewish Law of Marriage and Divorce in its Relation to the Law of the State* and *The Introduction of Slavery Among the Ancient Hebrews.*

Miesas, Matisyohu (1885–1945) Galician Yiddish semiologist. He was born in Pshemeshl, Galicia. At a language conference held at Czernowitz in 1908 he gave a paper on the scientific analysis of Yiddish; this was the first such study to be written in the language itself. His publications include *Enstehungsursache der jüdischen Dialekte, Die jiddische Sprache* and *Die Gesetze der Schriftgeschichte.*

Mikhoels, Solomon (1890–1948) Russian Yiddish actor. He was born in Dvinsk. He became the chief actor in Alexander Granovsky's drama group, and later succeeded him to the directorship of the Jewish State Theatre in Moscow. During World War II he visited western countries on behalf of the Jewish Anti-Fascist Committee. He was assassinated by the Soviet secret police.

Milhaud, Darius (1892–1974) French composer. He was born in Aix-en-Provence. He served as secretary to the French minister in Brazil in 1917–18. After returning to Paris, he wrote a wide variety of musical compositions including *David, Service sacré, Poèmes Juifs, Chants populaires Hébraïques, La création du monde* and *Le candelabre á sept branches.* In 1940 he settled in he US, where he was appointed professor at Mills College in California. Later he was a professor of composition at the Paris Conservatory.

Miller, Arthur (b. 1915) American novelist and playwright. He was born in New York. His early works included *Focus*, a novel about anti-Semitism. He later wrote *Incident at Vichy*, which concerns the arrest of Frenchmen, including Jews, during the Nazi occupation of France.

Millin, Sarah (1889–1968) South African author, of Lithuanian origin. Born in Zagar, Lithuania, she settled in South Africa. Her writings include *God's Stepchildren, The South Africans, The Night Is Long* and *The Coming of the Lord.*

Minkowski, Hermann (1864–1909) German mathematician. Born in Lithuania, his parents went to Germany when he was eight. He studied at the University of Königsberg and taught at the University of Bonn, later becoming a professor at the University of Göttingen.

Minkowski, Maurice (1881–1930) Polish artist. Although he was deaf and dumb, he was an important chronicler of traditional Jewish life during the czarist period.

Minkowksy, Phinehas (1859–1924) Ukrainian cantor. He was born in Belaya Tserkov. He officiated at Kishinev, Kherson and New York, and later became the chief cantor of the Brody Synagogue in Odessa. He introduced a modern form of service, which utilized an organ and a choir. He taught at the Jewish Conservatory in Odessa and published studies of Jewish music. In 1923 he settled in the US.

Miriam (fl? 13th cent. BCE) Israelite woman, sister of **Moses**. According to Exodus 2:2–8, she advised Pharaoh's daughter, who had discovered the hiding place of the baby **Moses**, to call a Hebrew nurse for **Moses** and succeeded in having his mother engaged to care for him. Later, when she and **Aaron** challenged **Moses**' exclusive right to speak in the name of the Lord (Numbers 12), she was stricken with leprosy, but she was healed by **Moses**, who interceded with God on her behalf.

Mises, Ludwig von (1881–1973) Austrian economist. Born in Lemberg, Galicia he studied in Vienna where he became an assistant professor. In 1940 he settled in the US. His works include *The Theory of Money and Credit, Socialism* and *Human Action.*

Mishkovsky, Zelda (1914–84) Israeli poet. She was born in Chernigov in the Ukraine. She emigrated to Jeruslaem at the age of 11, and taught in a religious school for girls. Her poetry contains ultra-Orthodox and modern sensibilities. She became known by her forename alone.

Mittwoch, Eugen (1876–1942) German orientalist. He was born in Schrimm. He helped **Paul Nathan** to set up a school system in Palestine under the auspices of the Hilfsverein der deutschen Juden. He taught at the universities of Berlin and Greifswald, and in 1919 became a professor at the Seminary for Oriental Languages in Berlin, where he was eventually appointed director. In 1933 he directed the office of the Joint Distribution Committee in Berlin and in 1939 moved to England. He published studies of the influence of Jewish prayer on the liturgy of Islam, Hebrew epigraphy, and Islamic art and politics.

Mizraḥi, Elijah (c.1450–1526) Ottoman rabbinic authority. He was born in Constantinople, and became the foremost rabbinic authority in the Ottoman empire. He adopted a more tolerant attitude to the Karaites than other rabbinic scholars. He wrote various responsa, a super-commentary on **Rashi**'s commentary to the Pentateuch, and a mathematical treatise.

Mocatta, Frederick David (1828–1905) English philanthropist, scholar and communal leader. He was active in the Charity Organization Society and the Jewish Board of Guardians. An observant Jew, he was a member of Orthodox as well as Reform synagogues. He donated his library to University College, London, and the Jewish Historical Society of England. His writings include *The Jews and the Inquisition.*

Modena, Aaron Berechiah (fl.17th cent.) Italian kabbalist. He composed collections of material for liturgical use. His *Maavar Yabbok* contains prayers for the sick and the dead in addition to regulations concerning mourning.

Modena, Leone [Leon of Modena] (1571–1648) Italian rabbi, scholar and writer. Born in Venice, he initially became an elementary teacher and preacher there. In his autobiography, *Ḥayyei Yehudah*, he listed the various occupations he resorted to throughout his life. He was regarded by Christian scholars as the most distinguished Jewish scholar of his day. His writings include sermons, as well as polemics against the oral law, the kabbalah and Christianity.

Modiano, Patric (b. 1947) French novelist. Born in Paris, his works include *La Place de l'Étoile, Les Boulevards de ceinture* and *Rue des boutiques obscures.*

Modigliani, Amedeo (1884–1920) Italian painter and sculpture. Born in Livorno, he studied at a local art school and later in Florence and Venice. In 1906 he went to Paris where he mixed with fellow emigrés. In the early 1920s he was stricken with tubercular meningitis, and died in a charity hospital. His sculptures were influenced by primitive art.

Mohilever, Samuel (1824–98) Polish rabbi and religious Zionist. He was born in Glebokie, in the district of Vilna, and became a rabbi there in 1848. Later he served in Szaki, Suwalki and Radom. From 1874 he actively supported Jewish settlement in Palestine, and his views on this influenced **Baron de Hirsch**. He formed the first society of Ḥovevei Zion in Warsaw, and later supported **Theodor Herzl**. In 1884 he was the honorary president of the Kattowitz Conference.

Mohr, Abraham Menaḥem Mendel (1815–68) Galician Hebrew scholar and maskil. He was born in Lemberg. His writings, in Hebrew and Yiddish, include a geography of Palestine and its Jewish inhabitants, Purim plays, and editions of *Mikveh Yisrael* by **Manasseh ben Israel** and *La-Yesharim Tehillah* by **Moses Ḥayyim Luzzatto**. He also published a Yiddish newspaper.

Moïse, Penina (1797–1880) American poet, hymn-writer and teacher. She was born in Charleston, South Carolina, and became the superintendent of the Beth Elohim Congregation's Sunday school there. She was the author of the first American Jewish hymnal. Her hymns and poetry were published in *Secular and Religious Works* in 1911.

Moissan, Henri (1852–1907) French chemist. He was professor of inorganic chemistry at the Sorbonne. In 1906 he was awarded the Nobel Prize in Chemistry.

Moissis, Asher (1899–1975) Greek author, translator and communal leader. He was born in Trikkala. He became a lawyer and participated in Jewish communal and Zionist affairs. In 1917 he founded the Zionist monthly *Israel*, which he also edited. In the 1930s he published books on Jewish subjects, particularly Greco-Jewish relations through the ages. He served as president of the Jewish National Fund (1930–8), the Salonika Jewish community (1934–6), and the Greek Zionist Federation (1936–8). Later he was president of the Central Council of Jewish Communities in Greece (1944–9), and from 1948 served as honorary consul of Israel in Athens.

Molcho, Solomon (c.1500–32) Italian kabbalist and pseudo-messiah. He was born in Lisbon of marrano parents, and his given name was Diogo Pires. He became secretary to the King of Portugal's council and recorder at the Court of Appeals. After meeting **David Reuveni** he circumcised himself and took his Hebrew name. He lived for a time in Salonika, where he studied kabbalah, then returned to Italy. Believing himself to be the Messiah, he preached about the coming of messianic redemption. Although he obtained the protection of Pope Clement VII against the Inquisition, he was accused by an inquisitional court of Judaizing (trying to persuade converts to Chritianity to return to Judaism) and was condemned to be burned at the stake. He was reprieved on this occasion, but was condemned again after refusing to convert to Christianity and was burned in 1532. Many Jews and marranos in Italy refused to believe that he had died, and thought he had been saved once more.

Moldova, György (b. 1934) Hungarian writer. He was born in Budapest. He began his career by writing film scripts, but was obliged to do manual work. Some of his writings deal with the situation of Hungarian Jews during World War II and in the post-war years.

Molnár, Ferenc [Neumann] (1878–1952) Hungarian writer. Born in Budapest, he studied at the universities of Budapest and Geneva. In 1896 he joined the daily *Budapesti Napló*. His articles were collected in *Memoirs of a War Correspondent*. His plays include *The Lawyer*, *The Devil*, *Liliom*, *The Guardsman*, *The Wolf*, *The Swan* and *The Red Mill*. His novels include *The Pal Street Boys*. In the 1930s he emigrated to Switzerland, and later to the US.

Molodowski-Lew, Kadia (1894–1975) American Yiddish poet and novelist. She was born in Lithuania. She participated in the publications of the Kiev Yiddish Group after 1917, but soon moved to Warsaw to teach in Yiddish schools. In 1935 she settled in New York. Her verse reflects her experiences in Europe, America and Israel. After the establishment of the State of Israel, she wrote lyrics expressing joy at the restoration of Zion. She also wrote novels, short stories and plays, depicting Jewish life in Poland as well as biblical and historical themes.

Momigliano, Arnaldo (1908–87) Italian historian. He was born in Caraglio. He taught in Rome, Turin, Pisa, London and Chicago. He wrote studies about ancient history, the Maccabees and Judaica, and the history of the Second Temple period. His publications include *Alien Wisdom: The Limits of Hellenisation*.

Monash, John (1865–1931) Australian engineer and soldier. He was born in Melbourne and studied at the University of Melbourne. In 1894 he became a consulting engineer and patent attorney. During World War I he led the Australian Fourth Infantry Brigade, becoming major general in 1916. In 1918 he was commander of the Australian Army Corps. Later he became director-general of the repatriation and demobilization programme, and subsequently general manager and chairman of the Victoria State Electricity Commission.

Mond, Alfred Moritz (1868–1930) English industrialist and statesman. He entered his father's firm, which later became Imperial Chemical Industries. He was elected to parliament as a liberal in 1906, and was appointed commissioner of works, and later minister of health. He subsequently became a member of the conservative party. He was made a baron in 1928. A dedicated Zionist and contributor to Zionist causes, he helped found the Jewish Agency in 1929 and became the chairman of its council.

Mond, Henry (1898–1949) English Zionist and communal leader, son of **Alfred Moritz Mond.** He was brought up in the Christian faith but converted to Judaism after the rise of Hitler. An ardent Zionist, he succeeded his father as chairman of the council of the Jewish Agency. He also served as the president of the World Union of Maccabi.

Monis, Judah (1683–1764) American Hebraist. He is believed to have been born in Algiers or Italy. He was educated in Livorno and Amsterdam, and later settled in the US, where he was admitted as a freeman of New York in 1715. In 1722 he was baptized in the hall of Harvard College in Cambridge, Massachusetts. In the same year he was appointed instructor of Hebrew at the college. His essays are an apology for, and a defence of, his new faith.

Monsky, Henry (1890–1947) American communal leader, of Russian origin. He lived in Omaha, Nebraska, where he was active in Jewish and communal organizations. An ardent Zionist, he was the principal organizer of the American Jewish Conference of 1943. In 1945 he served as a consultant to the US delegation to the United Nations Organizing Conference in San Francisco. He was president of the Supreme Lodge of B'nai B'rith from 1943 until his death.

Montagu, Edwin Samuel (1879–1924) English politician, son of **Samuel Montagu**. He was elected to parliament in 1906, and served as parliamentary undersecretary of state for India from 1910 to 1914. In that year he became financial secretary to the Treasury, and in 1916 chancellor of the Duchy of Lancaster and minister of munitions. From 1917 to 1922 he was secretary of state for India. He was an opponent of Zionism and the Balfour Declaration.

Montagu, Ewen Edward Samuel (1901–85) English lawyer and communal leader, grandson of **Samuel Montagu**. He was judge-advocate of the fleet and chairman of the Middlesex Quarter Sessions. He served as president of the United Synagogues from 1954 to 1962.

Montagu, Lilian Helen (1873–1963) English social worker and magistrate, daughter of **Samuel Montagu**. She founded the West Central Girls' Club in London in 1893. Together with **Claude Goldsmid Montefiore**, she established the Jewish Religious Union in 1902, and the World Union for Progressive Judaism in 1926.

Montagu, Samuel (1832–1911) English banker and communal leader. He was born in Liverpool. In 1853 he founded the merchant bankers Samuel Montagu and Company. He served as the liberal member of parliament for Whitechapel from 1885 to 1900. In 1894 he was made a baronet, and in 1907 a baron. He was the leader in Britain of Orthodox Russian Jewish immigrants, and in 1887 founded the Federation of Synagogues. He travelled to Palestine, Russia and the US on behalf of Jewry, but was an opponent of Zionism.

Montefiore, Claude Joseph Goldsmid (1858–1938) English theologian and leader of Liberal Judaism. He studied at Balliol College, Oxford, and the Hochschule für Wissenschaft des Judentums in Berlin. In 1888 he founded the scholarly journal the *Jewish Quarterly Review*. He was a founder of the Jewish Religious Union in 1902 which led to the establishment in 1926 of the Liberal Jewish Synagogue in London. In 1926 he was elected president of the World Union for Progressive Judaism. With Baron von Hugel, he founded the London Society for the Study of Religion. An opponent of Zionism, he served as president of the Anglo-Jewish Association. His writings include *Aspects of Judaism*, *The Synoptic Gospels*, *Liberal Judaism*, *Outlines of Liberal Judaism* and *Rabbinic Literature and Gospel Teaching*. With **Herbert Loewe** he edited *A Rabbinic Anthology*.

Montefiore, Francis Abraham (1860–1935) English Sephardi leader. A supporter of **Theodor Herzl** he was active in Ḥibbat Zion and served as chairman of the English Zionist Federation.

Montefiore, Moses (1784–1855) British communal leader. He was born in Livorno, but grew up in London, where he worked as a broker. An observant Jew, he maintained his own synagogue in Ramsgate from 1833; he was an opponent of Reform Judaism. In 1837 he was sheriff of the City of London, and he was the first Jew to be knighted in Britain. He went on a mission to the Levant with **Isaac-Adolphe Crémieux** in 1840 at the time of the Damascus Affair, and he intervened with their governments on behalf of the Jews of Russia, Morocco and

Romania. He visited Palestine on several occasions and worked to improve the conditions under which the Jewish community lived there. From 1838 to 1874 he was president of the Board of Deputies of British Jews.

Montor, Henry (1905–82) American Zionist, of Canadian origin. He was assistant editor of the journal *New Palestine* from 1926 to 1930. He served with the United Palestine Appeal (1930–9), and was then executive vice-president and chief executive of the American Financial and Development Corporation for Israel.

Mor (Friedmann-Yellin], Nathan (b. 1913) Israeli public figure. He was born in Poland, and settled in Palestine in 1941. He joined the underground terrorist movement Loḥame Ḥerut Yisrael, which he headed from 1943. After the assassination of Count Bernadotte in 1948, he was sentenced to prison, but he was freed under the terms of the general amnesty of February 1949. He represented the Fighters' Party in the first Knesset. Later he was active in Semitic Action, which supported the idea of a Jewish–Arab federation.

Morais, Sabato (1823–97) American rabbi. He was born in Livorno. At the age of 22 he became assistant ḥazzan to the Spanish and Portuguese congregation in London. In 1851 he became ḥazzan to the Mikveh Israel Congregation in Philadelphia. A leading opponent of Reform, he was an Abolitionist during the Civil War. In 1856 he helped to establish the Jewish Theological Seminary and he then served as president of its faculty.

Moravia, Alberto (1907–90) Italian novelist. Born in Rome to a Jewish father, he was baptized by his Catholic mother. In the 1930s he worked as a journalist in various parts of the world. After the war, he was regarded as one of the outstanding writers in Europe. His writings include *The Age of Indifference*, *The Conformist*, *The Woman of Rome* and *The Two of Us*. He was married to Elsa Morante, a well-known Italian writer.

Mordecai (fl. 5th cent. BCE) Persian palace official at Shushan during the reign of Ahasuerus. His niece **Esther** was part of the king's harem. Through her Mordecai informed the king of an assassination plot against him. Later, when Mordecai refused to bow to the vizier Haman, the vizier resolved to avenge himself on the Jewish population; his plan was frustrated by **Esther**; Haman was hanged; and Mordecai assumed Haman's position as chief minister. These events are recorded in the book of Esther.

Mordecai ben Hillel (fl. 13th cent.) German codifier. He lived in Nuremberg, where he died a martyr's death in the Rindfleisch massacres along with his wife and five children. His *Sepher Mordekhai* is a compendium in the style of the tosaphot, dealing with talmudic problems. He also wrote responsa and liturgical poetry.

Morgenstern, Julian (1881–1976) American biblical scholar. He was born in St Francisville, Illinois. He served as a rabbi in Lafayette, Indiana, and later taught at the Hebrew Union College, where he became president in 1922. He published studies of a wide range of biblical topics.

Morgenstern, Lina [Breslau, Lina Bauerlin] (1830–1909) German writer. She founded a society for the welfare of poor youth at the age of 18. She later moved to Berlin where she continued with her work; subsequently she wrote a textbook concerning kindergartens, and served as president of a society that supported kindergartens. In 1896 she convened the first International Women's Congress in Berlin. She wrote books on varying topics including children's stories and novels.

Morgenthau, Hans (1904–80) German political scientist. Born in Cogburg, he studied at the university of Frankfurt and Munich where he practised law. In 1932 he went to Geneva to study at the Graduate Institute for International Studies and became an instructor there. Subsequently he taught at the Madrid Institute of International and Economic Studies; later he taught at Brooklyn College, the University of Kansas City, and the University of Chicago. His works include *Politics Among Nations*, *In Defense of the National Interest*, *Dilemmas of Politics*, *The Purpose of American Politics*, *Policies in the Twentieth Century* and *Truth and Power*.

Morgenthau, Henry (1856–1946) American financier and diplomat. He was born in Mannheim, Germany, and settled in the US in 1865. Initially he practised law, but then became active in real estate and banking. From 1913 to 1916 he was US ambassador to Turkey. Later he led a commission to investigate the condition of Jews in Poland. He was active in secular as well as Jewish religious and philanthropic work.

Morgenthau, Henry Jr (1891–1967) American agriculturalist and politician, son of **Henry Morgenthau**. He was born in New York. He became chairman of the Agricultural Advisory Commission in 1928, and in 1934 was appointed secretary to the Treasury. He was active in a wide range of Jewish organizations.

Morpurgo, Rachel (1790–1871) Italian Hebrew poet. She was born in Trieste. Her poetry, which shows the influence of **Samuel David Luzzatto**, describes autobiographical and family incidents. Written in the style of Spanish and Italian Hebrew religious poetry, it depicts Jewish historical values and traditions.

Morpurgo, Salomone (1860–1942) Italian philologist and librarian. From 1884 to 1942 he was director of the Biblioteca Riccardiana in Rome. He also served as head of the Biblioteca Marciana in Venice, which he transferred to the Palazzo della Zecca, and of the National Library in Florence (1905–23). His studies included an investigation of the medieval Italian version of the legend of the Wandering Jew.

Morpurgo, Samson (1681–1740) Italian rabbi and physician. He was born in Gradisca d'Isonzo, in Friuli. He became a member of the bet din of the kabbalist Joseph Fiametta in 1709, and he later served as a rabbi in Ancona. He had contacts with all the great scholars of his generation, and his skills as a doctor were widely recognized. In 1713 he was involved in the polemics of the rabbis against **Nehemiah Ḥayyon**. He published a polemic against the priest Luigi Maria Benetelli, who wrote an anti-Semitic work. He also wrote numerous responsa and a philosophical commentary on **Jedaiah Bedersi**'s *Beḥinat Olam.*

Mortara, Marco (1815–94) Italian rabbi and scholar. From 1842 he served as rabbi of Mantua. An advocate of reform, he published books on the principles of Judaism and a new edition of the prayerbook. He produced a catalogue of the manuscripts in the library of the Mantua community, and a list of Jewish scholars who lived in Italy from the 1st to the 19th centuries.

Morteira, Saul Levi (c.1596–1660) Dutch rabbi and scholar, of Venetian origin. He became Ḥakham of the Beit Ya'akov community in Amsterdam, and founded the Keter Torah Yeshivah there. He was a member of the bet din that excommunicated **Benedict Spinoza**. His *Givat Shaul* is a collection of sermons. He also wrote responsa and Jewish apologetics.

Moscheles, Ignaz (1794–1870) German-Czech pianist. Born in Prague, he performed in major musical centres in Europe, and later taught at the Royal Academy of Music.He became conductor of the Philharmonic Society and in 1846 became Professor of Pianoforte at the Leipzig Conservatory.

Mosenthal, Solomon Hermann von (1821–1877) German author. He was born in Kassel. He wrote poems, stories, melodramas and opera libretti. His works include the play *Deborah* and a volume of stories about Jewish life.

Moses (fl. ?13th cent. BCE) Lawgiver, leader of the Israelites. He was born in Egypt to **Amram** and **Jochebed**, who hid him in a basket among the reeds of the Nile to escape Pharaoh's decree to slaughter all newborn Jewish males. He was found by Pharaoh's daughter, who raised him in the royal household. In early manhood he killed an Egyptian whom he discovered beating a Hebrew. He fled to Midian and became a shepherd to the local priest Jethro, whose daughter, **Zipporah**, he married; she bore him two sons. While keeping Jethro's sheep on Mount Horeb he encountered God, who spoke to him from the burning bush and commanded him to free the Hebrew slaves. He interceded with Pharaoh who eventually released the Hebrews after ten plagues had afflicted Egypt. Moses led the people across the Red Sea, which miraculously parted to let them pass, and guided them for 40 years in the desert. On Mount Sinai he received God's revelation of the law, embodied in the ten commandments written on tablets of stone. Before his death he appointed **Joshua** his successor.

Moses, Adolph (1840–1902) American rabbi, of Polish origin. He emigrated to the US in 1870, and served as rabbi to the Reform congregation in Louisville from 1881 until his death. With Isaac S. Moses and **Emil G. Hirsch**, he edited the German-language weekly *Zeitgeist.* A collection of his writings appeared posthumously as *Yahvism and Other Discourses.*

Moses ben Enoch (fl. 10th cent.) Spanish scholar. In the story of the Four Captives in *The Book of Tradition*, **Abraham ibn Daud** relates that four rabbis including Moses ben Enoch were captured by Saracen pirates after they sailed from Bari in southern Italy in 972. Moses ben Enoch was ransomed in Córdoba, and was appointed rabbi of the community.

Moses ben Isaac di Rieti [Rieti, Moses of] (1388–c. 1460) Italian physician, philosopher and poet. He worked as a physician at Rieti until 1422, and then lived in Perugia, Narni, Fabriano, and Rome, where he was a rabbi and physician to Pope Pius II. His *Mikdash Me'at* is a moral and philosophical poem in *terza rima*; in contains a vision of Paradise, and an account of Jewish scholars down to his own time. He also wrote medical and other philosophical studies.

Moses ben Jacob of Coucy (fl. 13th cent.) French scholar. An itinerant preacher, he began his ministry in Spain in 1236, where he preached sermons that attracted a huge audience. Later he visited other countries, and participated in the Disputation of Paris in 1240. His *Sepher Mitzvot Gadol* (also known as *Semag*) contains the oral law presented as groups of positive and negative commandments. His other writings include the *Tosaphot Yeshanim* and a commentary on the Torah.

Moses ben Jacob of Russia (1449–1520) Ukrainian talmudic scholar. He was born in Seduva, Lithuania. He lived in Kiev, where he pursued his studies as a biblical exegete, talmudist, poet, linguist and kabbalist. When the Tartars attacked the city in 1482 he escaped, but his children were taken captive to the Crimea; after ransoming them, he returned to Kiev. In 1495 the Jews of Lithuania and the Ukraine were expelled, and he was forced to wander. In 1506 he was himself taken captive by the Tartars and was ransomed by the Jews of Salkhat. He then settled in Kaffa, where he became rabbi and head of the community. His writings include a liturgy according to the Crimean rite.

Moses ben Shem Tov de León (1250–1305) Spanish kabbalist. He lived in Guadalajara and, from 1290 in Avila. He wrote some 20 kabbalstic works and is known for his revelation of the Zohar: according to kabbalistic tradition, the book (attributed to **Simeon ben Yoḥai**) was sent by **Naḥmanides** from Palestine to Spain, where it reached Moses ben Shem Tov, who made it known.

Moses ha-Darshan [Narboni, Moses] (fl. 11th cent.) French scholar. He lived in Narbonne. His writings, notably commentaries on the Bible, influenced **Rashi.**

Moses of London (fl. 13th cent.) English grammarian, halakhist and Jewish scholar. His *Darkhe ha-Nikkud veha-Neginah* is a treatise on Hebrew punctuation and accentuation.

Moses of Narbonne [Maestro Vidal Blasom] (fl. 14th cent.) French philosopher, translator, and physician. His commentary on **Maimonides**' *Guide for the Perplexed* is based on an Aristotelian-Averroistic perspective.

Moses of Sodilkov [Ephraim Moses Ḥayyim of Sodilkov] (c. 1737–c. 1800) Ukrainian Ḥasidic leader, grandson of the **Baal Shem Tov**. He studied under **Dov Ber Mezhirich**, and lived as a rabbi and preacher in Sodlikov in Volhynia. His *Degel Maḥaneh Ephraim* is based on the doctrines of the **Baal Shem Tov** and teaches that the goal of Ḥasidism is humility and self-evaluation. The role of the tzaddikim is to reprove and reform those who are negligent, and to elevate the people through prayer and religious teaching.

Moss, Celia (1819–73) English writer. Together with her sister Marian Moss (1821–1907), she wrote *The Romance of Jewish History* and *Tales of Jewish History.*

Mosse, Rudolf (1843–1920) German publisher and philanthropist. He was born in Oraetz. He founded an advertising business in 1867, and several years later established the *Berliner Tageblatt*, one of Germany's leading newspapers. In 1880 he acquired the *Allgemeine Zeitung des Judentums*. His activities on behalf of the community included the setting up of a hospital in Graetz and the founding of an educational institute in Wilhelmsdorf.

Motke Ḥabad [Rakover, Mordecai] (fl. 18th cent.) Lithuanian jester. He was a famous figure among Lithuanian Jewry.

Motta, Jacob de la (1789–1845) American physician and communal leader. He was born in Savannah, Georgia. He served as an army surgeon in the war of 1812. He was prominent in Jewish communal life in Savannah and later in Charleston, South Carolina.

Motzkin, Leo (1867–1933) Ukrainian Zionist leader. He was born in Brovary, near Kiev. In 1887 he helped to found the Russian Jewish Scientific Society in Berlin, which included Jewish students from Russia and Galicia who supported the Ḥibbat Zion movement. A follower of **Theodor Herzl**, he was active in the Zionist movement; in 1901 he joined the Democratic Fraction, formed at the Fifth Zionist Congress. During World War I he directed the Zionist bureau in Copenhagen, and in 1919 he acted as secretary and president of the Comité des Délégations Juives at the Paris Peace Conference. In 1925 he was appointed chairman of the Zionist Executive. He served in this capacity and as head of the organization of European National Minorities until his death in 1933. His publications include a history of Russian pogroms.

Mühlhausen, Yomtov Lipmann [Lipmann, Yomtov ben Solomon; Yomtov Lipmann] (fl. 14th–15th cent.) Bohemian scholar, philosopher, kabbalist and polemicist. He lived in Prague, where he participated in a disputation with the apostate Peter (Pesaḥ) who alleged that the Jews blasphemed Christian beliefs. Eighty Jews were martyred as a consequence, but Mühlhausen was saved. His *Sepher Nitzaḥon* contains a depiction of this disputation.

Mukdoni [Kappel], Alexander (1877–1958) American Yiddish essayist and theatre critic. He was born in Lyakhovichi in Belorussia. After World War I he edited the Yiddish daily *Nayes* produced in Kovno. In 1922 he settled in the US, where he wrote for the Yiddish daily *Jewish Morning Journal*.

Muller, Hermann Joseph (1890–1967) American scientist. He was professor at the University of Indiana and established that biological mutations were the result of chemical changes that could be induced artificially. He was awarded the Nobel Prize in Medicine and Physiology in 1946.

Müller, Joel (1827–95) Moravian rabbinic scholar. He was born at Mährisch Ostrau and served as a rabbi there, and later in Leipa, Bohemia. After teaching religion in Vienna, he took up a post at the Berlin Hochschule für die Wissenschaft des Judentums. He published studies of gaonic and French responsa.

Müller-Cohen, Anita (1890–1962) Austrian social worker. She was born in Vienna. She served as a relief worker in Galicia and Bukovina during World War I. She established hospitals for mothers, day nurseries, medical services for children, and institutions for the care of the aged. After the war she helped returning soldiers to readjust to civilian life and established milk stations for undernourished children in Austria. She also directed the placement of orphans in Jewish homes. In 1936 she settled in Tel Aviv.

Muni, Paul [Weissenfreund, Muni] (1895–1967) American actor. He began acting at the age of 12 in Chicago and in 1918 joined the Yiddish Art Theatre in New York. He appeared in numerous plays on Broadway as well as in films.

Muñiz, Angelina (b. 1936) Mexican novelist, of French origin. She was a lecturer in literature at the Colegio de México and the Universidad Autónoma de México. Her publications include *Morada interior*, *Tierra adentro*, *La guerra del unicornio* and *Huerto cerrado, huerto sellado*. Her works deal with Jewish cultural and religious themes.

Munk, Solomon (1803–67) French orientalist. He was born in Glogau, Silesia. He settled in Paris in 1828, where he took charge of Semitic manuscripts at the Bibliothéque Nationale. In 1840 he joined the delegation to Egypt led by Sir **Moses Montefiore** and **Isaac-Adolphe Crémieux**, and intervened in the Damascus Affair. He became blind in 1850, but was nevertheless appointed professor of Hebrew and Syriac literature at the Collège de France in 1864. His writings include studies of Hebrew and Arabic literature of the Golden Age of Spain, as well as an edition of the Arabic text of **Maimonides**' *Guide for the Perplexed.*

Münz [Minz], Judah (c. 1409–1509) German rabbi. After the Jews were expelled from Mainz in 1461, he settled in Padua, where he founded a yeshivah and taught philosophy at the university; he remained in Italy for the rest of his life. He wrote numerous responsa and engaged in a polemic with **Elijah Delmedigo**.

Münz [Minz], Moses (c. 1750–1831) Hungarian rabbi. He was born either in Podolia or in Galicia. He served as a rabbi in Vishravitz and Brody, then in 1789 was appointed rabbi of Alt-Ofen, where he represented the Jewish community at royal ceremonies. In 1793 he became chief rabbi of the entire Pest region. Initially tolerant of reformers, he later became anatagonistic towards them. He wrote responsa and published (with annotations) the *Peri Ya'akov* of **Jacob ben Moses**.

Myers, Michael (1837–1950) Chief justice of New Zealand. Born in Motueka, he went to Wellington and became a barrister and solicitor. In 1922 he became king's counsel, and in 1929 chief justice.

N

Nabal (fl. 11th–10th cent. BCE) Israelite landowner, husband of **Abigail**. He was wealthy man, the owner of thousands of sheep and goats in Carmel. When ten followers of **David** visited him he received them inhospitably. **David** gathered a band of 400 together to take revenge on Nabal, but was appeased by **Abigail**. However, Nabal did not escape. He was killed by God a few days later, and **David** married **Abigail** (I Samuel 25).

Naboth (fl. 9th cent. BCE) Israelite landowner. He possessed a vineyard, which **Ahab** coveted. When Naboth refused to give it up, **Ahab**'s queen **Jezebel** plotted to bring about his downfall. She persuaded the local elders to honour Naboth and then to bring false evidence of blasphemy against him. Eventually he was stoned to death. This act led **Elijah** to predict the downfall of **Ahab** (I Kings 21; II Kings 9).

Nadab (i) (fl. ?13th cent. BCE) Israelite priest, eldest son of **Aaron**. With his brother **Abihu**, he ascended Mount Sinai to behold God's revelation (Exodus 24:1–11). Later they made a fire sacrifice on the altar against God's will and were struck dead by fire as punishment (Leviticus 10:1–3).

Nadab (ii) (fl. 10th cent. BCE) King of Israel (907–906 BCE), son and successor of **Jeroboam I**. He and the House of Jeroboam were assassinated by **Baasha** (I Kings 15:25–31).

Nadel, Arno (1878–1943) German poet and musicologist. He was born in Vilna. He became conductor of the choir at the synagogue in Pestalozzistrasse in Berlin, and later was the musical supervisor of the Berlin synagogues. He published poetry, collected synagogue music and Eastern European Jewish folk songs, painted portraits and landscapes, and composed music.

Nadir, Moshe [Reiss, Isaac] (1885–1943) American Yiddish writer. He was born in eastern Galicia, and emigrated to New York in 1898. He contributed to numerous literary publications, and wrote poetry, drama and essays.

Naḥman bar Jacob (fl. 3rd–4th cent.) Babylonian amora. He was born in Nehardea, and married into the family of the exilarch. When Nehardea was destroyed by the Palmyrenes in 259, he went to Shekanzib, but after it was rebuilt he returned to Nehardea, where he taught and served as a dayyan. The Talmud contains may of his halakhic and aggadic statements.

Naḥmanides [Bonastruc de Porta; Moses ben Naḥman; Ramban] (1194–1270) Spanish talmudist, kabbalist and biblical commentator. He is commonly known by the name Naḥmanides, though his Hebrew name was **Moses ben Naḥman** and his Spanish name Bonastruc de Porta; the name Ramban is derived from the title Rabbi Moses ben Naḥman. He served as rabbi of Gerona. In 1263 he was challenged by **Pablo Christiani** to a religious disputation, which took place in Barcelona in the presence of King James I (1213–76). Later he was tried for blasphemy and forced to leave Spain. From 1267 he lived in Palestine, settling in Acre. Naḥmanides was regarded as the foremost Spanish talmudist of his day. Among his works are *Torat ha-Adam* which deals with the rites of mourning, and popular Bible commentary.

Naḥman of Bratzlav (1772–1811) Ukrainian Ḥasidic leader, great-grandson of the **Baal Shem Tov**. He was born in Medzhibozh and lived in Medvedevka in the province of Kiev, where he attracted numerous disciples. In 1798 he went to Palestine, but he later settled in Zlatopol in the province of Kiev, where he engaged in controversy with **Aryeh Leib of Shpola**. In 1802 he moved to Bratslav. His various journeys are described in works by his disciple Nathan Sternhartz. In 1810 he settled in Ukrainian city of Uman. In his teachings he emphasized simple faith and prayer, and developed the theory of the tzaddik as the intermediary between God and humans.

Nahoum, Haim (1873–1960) Turkish rabbi and scholar. He went to Abyssinia in 1907 to investigate the Falashas. From 1908 to 1920 he served as Ḥakham Bashi of Turkey, and from 1923 he was chief rabbi of Cairo; he was later appointed chief rabbi of Egypt. He also served as a member of the Egyptian Senate (1930–4).

Nahshon (fl. ?13th cent. BCE) Israelite, chief of the tribe of Judah during the Exodus and the wanderings in the desert. He was the brother-in-law of **Aaron**. According to rabbinic tradition, he was the first Israelite to embark on the crossing of the Red Sea during the flight from Egypt.

Nahum of Gimzo (fl. 1st–2nd cent.) Palestinian tanna. His system of exegesis was based on the view that in the Torah the untranslated Hebrew particle 'et' signfies that the word it precedes should be given a wide rather than a narrow connotation. This method was developed by his pupil **Akiva**.

Naidistsch, Isaac (1868–1949) Russian philanthropist and Zionist. He was born in Pinsk, and lived in Moscow, where he was an alcohol industrialist. An ardent Zionist, he contributed to Hebrew periodicals. At the beginning of the World War I, he was a founder and director of the Central Committee for the Relief of Jewish War Sufferers. After the Russian Revolution, he became a strong supporter of Hebrew culture. Later he emigrated to France, but he fled to the US during the Nazi occupation. He returned to Paris in 1941. He was a friend and advisor of **Chaim Weizmann**.

Najara, Israel ben Moses (c. 1555–c. 1625) Syrian Hebrew poet. Born in Damascus, he was secretary to the Jewish community there. In 1587 he published two collections of hymns, *Zemirot Yisrael* and *Mesaḥ eket ba-Tevel* in Safed. Later he served as a rabbi in Gaza.

Namier, Lewis Bernstein (1888–1960) British historian and Zionist. He was born in eastern Galicia. He was professor of modern history at Manchester University from 1931. An ardent Zionist, he served as political secretary of the Jewish Agency from 1929 to 1931. He wrote studies of the social-political structure of England in the 18th century, the 1848 revolutions, and the events leading up to World War II.

Namir, Mordekhai (1897–1975) Israeli politician. Born in Bratolinbovka, Ukraine, he settled in Palestine in 1924. From 1929 to 1935 he was director of the statistical section of the Histadrut, and in 1936–43 he served as secretary-general of the Tel Aviv Workers' Council. After the establishment of the State of Israel in 1948 he held diplomatic posts in Bulgaria, Czechoslovakia, Romania and the USSR. From 1951 he served in the Knesset, and became minister of labour; he was also the first mayor of Tel Aviv.

Naomi (fl. 12th–11th cent. BCE) Israelite woman, wife of **Elimelech**. With her husband and sons (Mahlon and Chilion), she left Bethlehem for Moab during a famine. After several years, during which time **Elimelech** and her sons died, she returned with **Ruth**, her daughter-in-law, whom she helped to marry the Israelite landowner **Boaz**.

Naphtali (fl. ?16th cent. BCE) Israelite, sixth son of **Jacob**, and second son of **Bilhah**, **Rachel**'s maid (Genesis 30:7). The tribe of Naphtali was named after him.

Naphthali, Peretz (1888–1961) Israeli economist. He was born in Germany. He served as economic editor of the *Frankfurter Zeitung* (1921–6) and manager of the Labour Movement's Economic Research Bureau in Berlin (1926–33). He settled in Palestine in 1933 and directed the Workers' Bank from 1938 to 1949. He was then elected a Mapai member of the Knesset; during his ten years in parliament (1949–59) he was minister without portfolio (1951–2; 1955–9), and minister of agriculture (1952–5).

Nardi, Naḥum (1901–77) Israeli composer. He was born in Kiev. After studying the piano and composition at the Kiev, Warsaw and Vienna Conservatories, he emigrated to Palestine in 1923 where he gave piano recitals and began composing. His work was inspired by Arab bedouin and peasant songs as well as Sephardi and Yemenite melodies.

Nasi [Mendes], Gracia (c.1510–69) Portuguese marrano stateswoman and patroness. She was born in Portugal (as Beatrice de Luna), and married the banker Francisco Mendes. On his death she went to Antwerp in 1537. Fearing religious persecution, she escaped to Venice in 1545, but she was denounced and imprisoned there. Released in 1549, she moved to Ferrara, where she was known as a Jewess and became a patron of writers. She also controlled an underground organization which rescued marranos from Portugal. In 1553 she went to Constantinople, where she became known as Gracia Nasi. Joined by her nephew **Joseph Nasi**, she became the leader of Turkish Jewry. She built synagogues, helped fugitive marranos, and began a project for the colonization of Tiberias.

Nasi, Joseph (c.1524–79) Portuguese statesman, active in Turkey. He was born a marrano in Portugual under the name Joao Micas. He accompanied his aunt **Gracia Nasi** when she went from Lisbon to Antwerp in 1537, but when in 1545 she fled to Italy, he remained behind to settle her affairs. In 1554 he joined her in Constantinople, where he embraced Judaism publicly and married her daughter, Reyna. He became an intimate of Selim, the heir to the Turkish throne. In 1561 he obtained from the sultan the lease of Tiberias and control of an adjacent area, which he developed as a Jewish centre. He was eventually created Duke of Naxos and the Cyclades.

Nassy, David (fl.18th cent.) Caribbean physician and communal leader. He was born in Surinam, and became president of the Jewish community there. His *Essai historique sur la colonie de Surinam* is a record of the Jewish role in the colony's history. Eventually he settled in Philadelphia and became the first Jewish physician to practise in the city. In 1795 he returned to Surinam, where he went into business. Later he published a tract supporting the emancipation of Dutch Jewry.

Nathan (i) (fl.11th–10th cent. BCE) Israelite prophet. He prophesied during **David**'s reign and declared to **David** that his royal dynasty would be established perpetually. Yet he prevented **David** from building a Temple in Jerusalem and accused him of plotting the death of Uriah the Hittite. Subsequently he was instrumental in securing **Solomon**'s succession. According to I Chronicles 29:29, he wrote an account of **David**'s reign.

Nathan (ii) (fl.2nd cent.) Palestinian tanna and son of the exilarch. He went to Palestine to study, but was forced to leave during the Hadrianic persecutions. Later he returned and became president of the court at Usha. An expert judge in civil suits, he was opposed to the fixing of the calendar outside Palestine. The *Avot de-Rabbi Natan* is attributed to him.

Nathan, Ernesto (1845–1921) Italian politician. Born in England, he went to Italy in 1859. He lived in Pisa, Florence, Milan and eventually moved to Genoa. He later went to Rome after the city was liberated from papal control. Subsequently he became mayor of Rome.

Nathan, Frederick Lewis (1861–1933) English soldier and chemist. He became an explosives expert and during World War I organized munitions manufacture. He was president of the Institute of Chemical Engineers from 1925 to 1927. From 1905 to 1926 he served as commandant of the Jewish Lads' Brigade.

Nathan, George (1882–1958) American drama critic. Born in Fort Wayne, Indiana, he studied at Cornell University and the University of Bologne. He was initially a reporter on the *New York Herald.* From 1914–23 he co-edited the *Smart Set* and in 1924 helped found the *American Mercury.*

Nathan, Isaac (?1790–1864) Australian composer, singer and writer. He was born in Canterbury, England, and began a career as a singer, composer and music teacher in London in 1810. He was a friend of Lord Byron who at his request wrote *Hebrew Melodies*, which Nathan set to music. In 1841 he emigrated to Australia and settled in Sydney. He was Australia's first resident professional composer.

Nathan, Paul (1857–1927) German philanthropist and public figure. He was the editor of the Berlin liberal publication *Die Nation* and the founder of the Hilfsverein der Deutschen Juden. He was active in international Jewish conferences on emigration and the relief of Jewish victims of persecution and war. During the trial of **Menaḥem Mendel Beilis** in 1913 on a blood libel charge Nathan helped to organize **Beilis**'s defence outside Russia. Opposed to the Zionist movement, he advocated assimilation as a solution to anti-Semitism. After World War I, he fostered agricultural settlement among Russian Jewry.

Nathan, Robert (1894–1985) American novelist. He was born in New York. He wrote a number of novels which deal with Jewish themes, such as *Jonah*, *Road of Ages* and *A Star in the Wind*.

Nathan ben Isaac of Baghdad [Nathan the Babylonian] (fl. 10th cent.) Babylonian chronicler. He lived in Baghdad and his *Akhbar Baghdad* is a book on the Jews of the city. This work is an important source for the history of Babylonian Jewry in the 10th century. It contains an account of the organization of the gaonic academies in Mesopotamia as well as the disputes that occurred during this period.

Nathan ben Jehiel of Rome [Arukh] (1035–c. 1110) Italian lexicographer. He was also called 'Baal he-Arukh' after the title of his lexicon. He was taught by his father, the head of the yeshivah in Rome; when his father died, he and his two brothers in turn succeeded him in that office. Nathan's *Baal he-Arukh* (by which he was sometimes known) is a lexicon of the Talmud and the midrashim.

Nathan ben Joseph Official (fl. 13th cent.) French talmudist. He engaged in religious controverises with Christians. These disputes were recorded by his son Joseph in his *Yosef ha-Mekanne*.

Nathan of Gaza [Ghazzati, Nathan Benjamin] (1643–80) Palestinian religious leader, disciple of **Shabbetai Tzevi**. He was born in Jerusalem, and lived in Gaza, where he engaged in kabbalistic study and practices. He met **Shabbetai Tzevi** in Gaza and proclaimed him to be the Messiah. After **Shabbetai Tzevi** converted to Islam, Nathan travelled throughout the Balkans and Italy, developing and preaching the theology of Shabbetainism which was based on Lurianic kabbalah. He was expelled by the rabbis of Venice, and returned to the Balkans. He died at Uskub near Salonica.

Nathansen, Henri (1868–1944) Dutch playwright. He was born in Hjørring, Jutland, and trained as a lawyer. In 1909 he became the stage director of Copenhagen's Royal Theatre. Many of his plays deal with Jewish issues. In 1919 he protested against the persecution of Polish Jewry and later he called for the Copenhagen Jewish community to counteract Nazi anti-Semitism. In 1943 he fled to Sweden.

Nathanson, Mendel Levin (1780–1868) Danish merchant and journalist. He was born in Altona, and moved to Copenhagen at the age of 12. From 1798 he was a wholesale draper. In 1838 he became editor of the newspaper *Berlingske Tidende*. He worked for the emancipation of the Jews and helped to establish the Jewish Free School for boys in Copenhagen in 1805 and later a similar school for girls. He wrote a history of the Jews of Denmark.

Natronai bar Hilai (fl. 9th cent.) Babylonian gaon of the academy at Sura (853–6). He was one of the most prolific writers of responsa among the geonim in the 9th century. His responsum to a query from the Lucena Jewish community as to how to fulfil the rabbinic dictum to recite 100 benedictions daily became the basis of the prayerbook.

Natronai bar Nehemiah (fl. 8th cent.) Babylonian gaon of the academy at Pumbedita (719–30). He married into the family of the exilarch. He was known for his severity with scholars in the academy, some of whom left for Sura, returning to Pumbedita only after his death.

Naumbourg, Samuel (1815–80) German musicologist. He was born in Dennelohe, near Ansbach. He became the first ḥazzan at the synagogue in the rue Notre-Dame-de-Nazareth in Paris in 1845. Two years later he published two volumes of *Zemirot Yisrael*, which contain musical settings of the entire liturgical cycle. His *Agudas Shirim* is a collection of traditional synagogue melodies.

Navon, Joseph (1852–1934) Palestinian philantropist. He was born in Jerusalem and became a merchant banker. He helped settlers in Palestine and supported popular housing schemes in Jerusalem. In 1888 he received a concession to construct a railway from Jaffa to Jerusalem. He settled in Paris in 1894.

Neander, Johann August Wilhelm [Mendel, David] (1789–1850) German church historian. Of Jewish birth, he was a convert to Christianity. He became a professor of church history at Berlin University, and in 1847 opposed the admission of Jews to the university. During the Damascus Affair, he argued that the murder charge against members of the Jewish community was a falsehood.

Nehemiah (fl. 5th cent. BCE) Israelite, governor of Judah. He was a cupbearer to the Persian king Artaxerxes I, of whom he asked permission to go to Jerusalem. The king agreed, and appointed him governor of Judah. Nehemiah organized the repair of the walls of Jerusalem, and initiated various social and religous reforms. Later he returned to Susa, but subsequently settled in Jerusalem. He and **Ezra** took steps to discourage the Israelites from contracting mixed marriages.

Neher, André (1913–88) French scholar. He was born in Alsace, and became professor of Jewish studies at the University of Strasbourg. He wrote works dealing with prophecy and with the teachings of **Judah Löw ben Bezalel**.

Neḥunyah ben ha-Kanah (fl. 1st cent.) Palestinian tanna. He was born in Emmaus in Judea. His students included **Ishmael ben Elisha**, who was influenced by his method of interpreting Scripture. He adopted the interpretive principle of 'kelal u-pherat' (general followed by a particular), in opposition to the system of **Naḥum of Gimzo**. A number of mystical works are ascribed to him, including the Bahir and the acrostic prayer *Anna be-koaḥ*

Nemerov, Howard (b. 1920) American writer. He was a student at Harvard, and later taught at Bennington College, Hollins College, Brandeis University and Washington University in St Louis. He also served as consultant in poetry to the Library of Congress. Some of his work deals with Jewish subjects.

Németh, Andor (1891–1953) Hungarian writer. He studied at the University of Budapest, and became the press attaché of the Hungarian Soviet Republic in Austria. From 1919 to 1926 he lived in Vienna, but then returned to Budapest. He settled in France in 1939, but in 1947 he finally returned to Hungary. His writings include *Kafka ou le mystère juif.*

Nemoy, Leon (b. 1901) American scholar and librarian. He was born in Buta, Russia. He was the librarian successively at the Society for the Propagation of Knowledge in Odessa, at the Academic Library in Odessa, and at the University Library of Lwów. In 1923 he settled in the US and was appointed curator of Hebrew and Arabic literature at Yale University library. He published numerous studies of the Karaites.

Netanyahu, Benjamin (b. 1949) Born in Tel-Aviv, he served as deputy chief of mission at the Israeli embassy in Washington, deputy minister, and prime minister of Israel. His works include *Terror: Challenge and Reaction, Terrorism: How the West Can Win, International Terrorism: Challenge and Response, A Place Among the Nations: Israel and the World, Fighting Terrorism: How Democracies Can Defeat Domestic and International Terrorism* and *A Durable Peace.*

Netter, Charles (1826–82) French philanthropist. He was born in Strasbourg. He went into business in Lille, Moscow and London, and in 1851 settled in Paris, where he engaged in various public activities. One of the founders of the Alliance Israélite Universelle, he served as its treasurer. He established the Mikveh Israel Agricultural School near Jaffa, and was its first director (1870–3). He was also active in Jewish philanthropic work in Europe.

Neubauer, Adolf (1831–1907) British bibliographer, of Hungarian origin. He went to Oxford in 1868 to complete the catalogue of Hebrew manuscripts in the Bodleian Library, which had been begun by **Moritz Steinschneider**; he later became a sublibrarian. His writings include a series of medieval Hebrew chronicles, as well as studies of the geography of the Talmud.

Neuberger, Julia (b. 1950) British rabbi. Born in London, she studied at Cambridge University and at the Leo Baeck College. She was chief-executive of the King's Fund and has been a broadcaster and author. She became a dame and life peer.

Neugeboren, Jay (b. 1938) American author. He was born in Brooklyn, and taught in the New York public schools and at Stanford University and SUNY. He later became writer-in-residence at the University of Massachusetts. His publications include the novels *The Stolen Jew* and *Before My Life Began.*

Neuman, Abraham Aaron (1890–1970) American rabbi, historian and educator. He was born in Brezan, Austria, and emigrated to the US in 1898. He taught history and later became president of Dropsie College. He was active in the Zionist movement. His writings include *The Jews of Spain, Cyrus Adler, A Biography* and *Landmarks and Goals.*

Neumann, Alfred (1895–1952) German author. Born in Lautenburg, West Prussia, he studied at the universities of Berlin and Geneva. He later became a writer and settled in Italy, and subsequently France. In 1940 he went to the US and worked in Hollywood. After the war he went on extensive European tours. His works include *Der Teufel* and *Der patriot.*

Neumann, Emanuel (1893–1980) American Zionist leader. He was born in Libau, Latvia, and was taken to the US as an infant. He founded the youth movement Young Judea in 1909, and served as education director of the Zionist Organization of America. He subsequently was director of the Keren ha-Yesod in the US (1921–5) and chairman of the executive committee of the United Palestine Appeal (1925–8). In 1929–30 he was president of the Jewish National Fund in the US; he then moved to Palestine, where he worked for the Jewish Agency in Jerusalem (1931–41). He was also president of the Zionist Organization of America (1947–8, 1956–8). In 1954 he founded the Herzl Foundation and served as its president. He was elected president of the World Union of General Zionists in 1963.

Neumann, John (1903–57) American mathematician, of Hungarian origin. He studied at the University of Budapest and later at the University of Zurich. He was assistant professor at the University of Berlin, and later at the University of Hamburg. Subsequently he was professor at the Institute of Advanced Study at Princeton.

Neumann, Robert (1897–1975) Austrian author. He was born in Vienna. After working as a chocolate manufacturer he went to sea. He wrote poetry, parodies and anti-Nazi novels. After the war he settled in Switzerland, where he wrote documentary works dealing with the Nazi period.

Neumann, Solomon (1819–1908) German physician and public worker. He engaged in work on medical statistics and public hygiene. His refusal in 1845 to take the special form of medical oath for Jews led to its abolition in Prussia. Besides his professional work he was active in Jewish communal activities and was a patron of scholarship.

Neumark, David (1866–1924) American Reform scholar, of Galician birth. He was a rabbi in Rakonitz, Bohemia, and later professor of Jewish philosophy at the Veitel-Heine-Ephraimschen Lehrenstalt in Berlin. In 1907 he became professor of philosophy at the Hebrew Union College. His writings include a *History of Jewish Philosophy* and *Essays in Jewish Philosophy.*

Neurath, Otto (1882–1945) Austrian philosopher and sociologist. Born in Vienna, he studied in Vienna and Berlin. He taught at the Handelsakademie, and later was in charge of planning of the Bavarian Republic. He then returned to Vienna and founded the Social and Economic Museum. He was also part of the Vienna Circle of philosophers. In 1934 he went to Holland, and later settled in England.

Neurath, Wilhelm (1840–1901) Hungarian scholar. Born in Miklos, near Pressburg, he studied in Vienna and later taught economics at Vienna's Technical High School. Subsequently he became a professor at the Agricultural College. He regarded economic planning and social control as necessary for social justice. In 1881 he converted to Catholicism.

Neusner, Jacob (b. 1932) American scholar. He was born in Hartford, Connecticut; he taught at Columbia University, the University of Wisconsin, Dartmouth College, Brown University and the University of Southern Florida. An expert in rabbinics, he published numerous books and received various scholarly awards. In 1968–9 he served as president of the American Academy of Religion.

Neutra, Richard (1891–1970) American architect, of Austrian origin. He studied at the Technische Hochschule in Vienna. Subsequently he went to Switzerland and worked as a landscape architect. In 1921 he went to Berlin where he worked in the Municipal Building Office. In 1923 he emigrated to the US and was an architect in Detroit and Chicago. Later he moved to Los Angeles. He believed that buildings should fit into their natural surroundings.

Nevelson, Louise (1899–1998) American sculptor. She was born in Kiev, and emigrated to the US in 1905. Her work includes *Six Million*, composed in memory of the victims of the Holocaust.

Newhouse, Samuel (1895–1979) American publisher. Born in New York City, he entered the newspaper business at the age of 16. He purchased a variety of newspapers, and by 1959 he obtained a controlling interest in the Condé-Nast magazines.

Newman, Barnett (1905–70) American painter. Born in New York, he studied at the Art Students League and later worked as an art teacher. He held a number of one-man shows, and subsequently taught at the University of Saskatchewan, and the University of Pennsylvania. He was noted for abstract expressionist paintings in which large areas of flat colour were divided into sections by narrow stripes of a second or third colour.

Newman, Louis Israel (b. 1893) American rabbi and writer. He was rabbi of Temple Rodeph Shalom in New York, and taught at the Jewish Institute of Religion. He published *Jewish Influence on Christian Reform Movements*, *The Jewish People, Faith and Life* and *The Ḥasidic Anthology*.

Niemirover, Jacob Israel (1872–1939) Romanian chief rabbi. He was born in Lemberg, and served as rabbi of Jassy. He became rabbi of the Sephardi community of Bucharest in 1911 and later chief rabbi of Romania. In 1926 he was elected to the Romanian senate, where he served as the representative of Romanian Jewry. Active in educational and Zionist circles, he also served as president of the order of B'nai B'rith in Romania. He wrote studies of various Jewish topics.

Nieto, David (1654–1728) British rabbi and philosopher. He was born in Venice. He served as a rabbi in Livorno, and in 1702 became Ḥaham of the Sephardi community in London. He wrote about the Inquisition and also produced anti-Shabbetaian polemics. His *Matteh Dan* is a philosophical defence of Judaism.

Niger, Samuel [Charney, Samuel] (1883–1955) American Yiddish literary critic. He was born in Russia, and began his career contributing to various Russian literary magazines. In 1909 he went to Berlin; several months later he edited a Yiddish monthly, *Di yidishe velt*, in Vilna. In 1919 he emigrated to the US, where he became literary editor of *Der tog*. His studies of Yiddish literature appeared in various volumes.

Nikel, Lea (b. 1916) Israeli painter, of Ukrainian origin. Born in the Ukraine, she went to Palestine at the age of two. She was a member of 'The Group of Ten' which dominated Israeli art until the mid-1950s.

Nirenberg, Marshall (b. 1927) American biochemist. He worked in the National Institute of Health in Bethesda, Maryland. He was awarded the Nobel Prize for Medicine and Physiology in 1968.

Nissenbaum, Isaac (1868–1942) Polish rabbi, author and Zionist. He was born in Bobruysk, Belorussia, and lived in Minsk, where he was an active Zionist. Later he became head of a secret nationalistic association formed by members of the yeshivah of Volozhin after it was closed. In 1894 he moved to Bialystok, where he became secretary to **Samuel Mohilever**. After **Mohilever**'s death, he preached about Zionism throughout Russia, Poland, Latvia and Lithuania. In 1900 he settled in Warsaw, where he was active in the Mizraḥi organization. He wrote numerous works about Zionism.

Nissenson, Hugh (b. 1933) American novelist and short-story writer. He was born in New York. His work explores the difficulties of sustaining religious belief in modern socieity. His fictional publications include *My Own Ground* and *Tree of Life*. In 1961 he reported on the trial of Eichmann for the magazine *Commentary*. His *Notes from the Frontier* is a memoir of visits to a kibbutz before and during the Six Day War.

Nissim, Yitzḥak Raḥamim (1896–1981) Israeli rabbi. He was born in Baghdad, and settled in Jerusalem in 1925. In 1955 he was elected Rishon le-Zion, Sephardi chief rabbi of Israel. He published and edited volumes of responsa.

Nissim ben Jacob ben Nissim [Ibn Shahin] (c.990–1062) North African talmudist. Born in Kairouan, he became head of the academy there after the death of **Hananel**. He had close contacts with **Samuel ibn Nagrela**, and corresponded with **Hai Gaon**. His *Kitab Miftah Maghalik al-Talmud* (Key to the Locks of the Talmud) is a commentary on the Talmud and its methodology.

Nittai the Arbelite (fl. 2nd cent. BCE) Palestinian sage, one of the zugot. He served as president of the Sanhedrin when **Joshua ben Peraḥyah** was patriarch.

Noah, Mordecai Manuel (1785–1851) American newspaper editor, politician and playwright. He was born in Philadelphia and started his career as a clerk to the US Treasury. In 1809 he went to Charleston, South Carolina, where he edited the *City Gazette*. Later he became the editor of the *National Advocate* in New York and established the *New York Enquirer*. In 1841 he became a judge of the Court of Sessions. He was active in the congregations of Mikveh Israel in Philadelphia and Shearith Israel in New York. In 1825 he helped to purchase land on Grand Island near Buffalo, New York, which he planned to develop as a Jewish colony. After the failure of this project, he became an advocate of Palestine as a national home for the Jews.

Nomberg, Hirsch David (1876–1927) Polish writer. He was born in Mszczonów, near Warsaw, and from 1903 to 1905 he wrote for the Warsaw Hebrew paper *Ha-Tzopheh*. He published a collection of Hebrew stories in 1905. This was followed by five collections in Yiddish. A disciple of **Isaac Leib Peretz**, he helped resolve the struggle between Hebraists and Yiddishists at the Czernowitz Yiddish conference in 1908. After 1910 he engaged in politics and journalism. In 1916 he was a founder of the Polish People's Party, and later was a member of the Polish Sejm. He was also president of the Society for Jewish Writers and Journalists.

Nordau, Max [Zidfeld, Simeon] (1849–1923) Hungarian author and Zionist leader. He was born in Budapest. In 1880 he settled in Paris, where he practised as a doctor. In 1883 he published *Conventional Lies of Our Civilization*; this was followed by *Paradoxes*, *The Malady of the Century* and *Degeneration*. An associate of **Theodor Herzl**, he participated in all the Zionist congresses until 1911. Later he was a political counsellor to the president of the Zionist Organization, **David Wolffsohn**. After **Wolffsohn**'s policy was rejected by the practical Zionists, Nordau joined the opposition circles within the Zionist movement, which worked against cultural Zionism advocated by, among others, **Aḥad ha-Am**.

Norell, Norman (1900–72) American fashion designer. Born in Noblesville, Indiana, his father ran a clothing store. He became a designer for Hollywood stars during the silent movie era.

Norman, Edward Albert (1900–55) American financier and philanthropist. He was born in Chicago, and entered his family's financial business. He served as president of the American Fund for Israel Institutions, president of the American Economic Commission for Palestine, national secretary for the American Jewish Committee, and director of the Joint Distribution Committee. In addition he was president of the Group Farming Research Institute.

Norsa [Norzi], Jedidiah Solomon ben Abraham (1560–1616) Italian rabbi and biblical scholar. He was born in Mantua. He wrote a critical masoretic commentary on the Bible.

Norsa [Norzi], Raphael ben Gabriel (1520–?1583) Italian rabbi. He served as rabbi at Ferrara and Mantua, and wrote various studies of ethical issues connnected with religious questions.

Nossig, Alfred (1864–1943) Polish author, sculptor and musician. He was born in Lemberg. He initially belonged to the circle of assimilationist Polish Jews, but later he became a supporter of Zionism and advocated the establishment of a Jewish state in Palestine. In 1908 he founded a Jewish colonization organization. He published studies about Jewish national problems, and his work on Jewish statistics served as the basis for the Jewish Statistical and Demographic Institute. He also produced sculptures with Jewish themes. He lived in Berlin, but was expelled to Poland when the Nazis rose to power; suspected of collaborating with the Nazis, he was sentenced to death by the Jewish underground.

Novomeysky, Moshe (1873–1961) Russian mining engineer. He worked on the Siberian gold mines, and in 1911 visited Palestine and analysed samples of Dead Sea water, which contained potash and bromide magnesium as well as other chemical salts. Later he returned to Palestine and established the Palestine Potash Company.

Nuñez, Hector (1521–91) Portuguese physician and merchant. He became leader of the marrano community in England. His overseas trading activities enabled him to supply valuable information to the English government.

Nuñez, Maria (fl. 16th cent.) Portuguese marrano communal leader. With other marranos she escaped from Portugual on a ship bound for the Netherlands. Captured by a British vessel, they were diverted to London. According to one account, Nuñez was presented to Queen Elizabeth, who took her on a tour of London. She eventually settled in Amsterdam, where she founded a community that became a haven for other marranos.

O

Obadiah (i) (fl. 9th cent. BCE) Israelite official, governor of the house of King **Ahab**. He hid 100 prophets of God to save them from **Jezebel**'s persecution (I Kings 18).

Obadiah (ii) (fl. 6th cent. BCE) Israelite prophet. His life spanned the Babylonian conquest of Judah, and he spoke out against the Edomites for having refused to assist Jerusalem in its time of need.

Obermann, Julian (1888–1956) American orientalist. He was born in Warsaw. He taught Semitic languages at the University of Hamburg from 1919 to 1922. After emigrating to the US he became professor of Semitic philology at the Jewish Institute of Religion in New York, and later professor of Semitic languages at Yale University. In 1944 he was appointed director of Judaic research and editor of the Yale Judaica Series. He wrote works on Semitic philology and epigraphy, biblical and Ugaritic studies, Islamic culture, and Arabic philosophy.

Ochs, Adolf (1858–1935) American publisher. Born in Cincinnati, his family moved to Knoxville, Tennessee. He began working on the *Knoxville Chronicle*, and later at the *Knoxville Tribune* and then at the *Louisville Courier-Journal*. Later he became editor of the *Chattanooga Dispatch*, and subsequently the *Chattanooga Times*. In 1896 he purchased the *New York Times*.

Odel (fl. 18th cent.) Polish matriarch, daughter of the **Baal Shem Tov**. She was the mother of several tzaddikim. In Ḥasidic literature she is presented as the ideal type of womanhood.

Odets, Clifford (1906–63) American playwright. Born in Philadelphia, his family moved to the Bronx. In 1925 he began to present radio programmes that he wrote himself. In 1935 his play *Waiting for Lefty* was produced; this was followed by *Till the Day I Die*, *Awake and Sing* and *Paradise Lost*, *Golden Boy*, *Rocket for the Moon*, *Night Music* and *Clash by Night*. He also wrote screenplays including *The General Died at Dawn*, *None But the Lonely Heart* and *The Sweet Smell of Success*.

Ofek, Abraham (b. 1935) Israeli painter. He was born in Burgus, Bulgaria, and emigrated to Israel in 1949. He has taught at the Bezael School of Arts and Crafts and at the University of Haifa. His paintings cover the walls of Kfar Uriah, the Jerusalem Central Post Office, the Agron and Stone schools in Jerusalem, the Tel Aviv University Library, and the entrance to the main building of the University of Haifa.

Offenbach, Jacques (1819–80) French composer, of German origin. He was the son of a Cologne cantor. He became the conductor of the Theatre Français in Paris. He composed over a hundred operettas including *The Tales of Hoffman*.

Oistrakh, David (1908–74) Russian violinist. Born in Odessa, he studied at the Odessa Music School and later taught at the Moscow Conservatory. During the 1930s he won various competitions including the Ysaye competition in Brussels. During World War II he performed at the front, in hospitals and in factories. In 1953 he played in Paris and London, and later in New York.

Olgin, Moses Joseph [Novomski, Moissaye) (1876–1939) American journalist and translator. He was born near Kiev, and began his career as a teacher. In 1913 he moved to Vienna, where he was co-editor of the Bundist Yiddish weekly *Di tsayt*. He emigrated to the US and settled in New York in 1914. He was a staff member of the Yiddish daily paper *Forverts*, and later edited the communist Yiddish daily *Freiheit* and the monthly *Der hamer*. He wrote about political affairs, literature and the theatre.

Olivetti, Adriano (1901–60) Italian industrialist. The son of an Italian inventor, **Camillo Olivetti**, he studied in Turin and became an apprentice at the Olivetti Company. He later became director of the firm and company president.

Olivetti, Camillo (1868–1943) Italian inventor, he opened a small factory in Ivrea, Italy that manufactured electrical measurement instruments; this was followed by typewriters including the Olivetti typewriter.

Olman, Israel (1883–1968) Dutch composer and choirmaster. He studied music in Amsterdam and became choirmaster of the Santo Servicio choir of the Sephardi synagogue there. His compositions include *Jigdal*, *Populus Sion*, *Jerusalem* for performance in the synagogue, as well as liturgical works for Jewish choirs.

Olsen, Tillie (b. 1913) American writer. Born in Omaha, Nebraska to Russian immigrant parents, she was a political activist and union organizer during the Depression. Her works include *Silences*, a collection of short stories.

Omri (fl. 9th cent. BCE) King of Israel (c. 882–871 BCE) During his reign he transferred the capital of Israel from Tirzah to Samaria (I Kings 16:21–28). According to the Moabite Stone, he conquered Moab.

Onan (fl. ?19th–16th cent. BCE) Second son of **Judah** and Shua (Genesis 38:2–4; 46:12; Numbers 26:19). After the death of his brother Er, his father instructed him to marry his childless sister-in-law, **Tamar**. He refused to fulfil his duty, and would not consummate the marriage. His conduct was viewed as abhorrent, and God took his life (Genesis 38:8– 10).

Onias I (fl. 4th cent. BCE) High priest. According to I Maccabees 12:20–23, Areios I, King of Sparta, sent a letter to Onias I claiming that the Spartans and the Jews were both descended from Abraham.

Onias II (fl. 3rd cent. BCE) High priest, grandson of **Onias I**. He wished to free the Jewish people from the yoke of Ptolemaic Egypt; in pursuit of this aim he conspired with the enemies of Ptolemy III and withheld payment of taxes. Ptolemy responded by threatening to expel the Jews from Judea, but was pacified through the intervention of Onias' nephew, Joseph son of Tobias.

Onias III (fl. 2nd cent. BCE) High priest, grandson of **Onias II**. Simeon, an official in the Temple, demanded from Onias the post of market commissioner, which was in his gift. When his petition was refused, Simeon revealed to Appollonius, the commander of the Syrian army, that the treasures of King Seleucus of Syria were being held in the Temple vaults. Seleucus then sent his chancellor Heliodorus to remove them. When his mission failed, Onias fell out of favour with his Syrian overlords. After Antiochus IV Epiphanes ascended the throne, Onias was summoned to Antioch and his brother **Jason** became high priest in his place. Later **Jason** was replaced by **Menelaus**, who was an extreme Hellenizer.

Onias IV (fl. 2nd cent. BCE) Son of **Onias III**. After he was ousted as high priest by Akimus, he went from Judea to Egypt. In 145 BCE Ptolemy VI Philometer granted him authority to build a temple in Leontopolis.

Onkelos (fl. 2nd cent.) Palestinian proselyte. He was a contemporary of Rabban **Gamaliel II** of Jabneh. He translated the Pentateuch into Aramaic.

Opatoshu, Joshua [Opatovsky, Joseph] (1886–1954) American Yiddish novelist, of Polish origin. He settled in the US in 1907. From 1910 he contributed stories to periodicals and anthologies. Later he joined the staff of the New York Yiddish daily paper *Der tog*. His novels deal largely with Jewish life in Poland and America.

Ophüls, Max [Oppenheimer Maximilian] (1902–57) French film director, of German origin. Born in Saarbrücken, He went on the stage at the age of 17. Later he was a theatre director. His first film work was as a dialogue director for the German UFA company; later he became a film director. In 1932 he settled in France. He fled to Hollywood during the Nazi occupation. In 1950 he resumed film-making in France with *La Ronde.*

Oppen, George (1908–84) America poet. Born in New Rochelle, New York, to a German-Jewish family, he moved to San Francisco at the age of five. He studied at Oregon State University, and from 1929 to 1933 he and his wife, Mary Corby, published poetry in France. In 1969 he won the Pulitzer Prize. His work includes *Collected Poems.*

Oppenheim [Oppenheimer], David (1664–1736) German rabbi. He was born in Worms, and served as a rabbi in Nikolsburg and Prague. His library contained 7000 volumes, including 1000 manuscripts; they became the basis of the Hebrew section of the Bodleian Library in Oxford.

Oppenheim, Moritz Daniel (1799–1882) German painter. He was born in Hanau. In 1821 he went to Rome, where he was influenced by a Christian group known as the Nazarenes, who painted pictures based on the New Testament. Later he returned to Germany and setted in Frankfurt am Main. He painted biblical scenes and pictures on Jewish themes, including confrontations between Jews and Christians.

Oppenheimer, Ernest (1880–1957) South African financier, of German origin. Born in Friedberg, Germany, he became a junior clerk in a London diamond firm. In 1902 he went to Kimberley, South Africa where he became mayor. In 1917 he founded a gold mining enterprise, and later the Diamond Consolidated Mines of South West Africa. In 1929 he became chairman of De Beers. He was knighted in 1921 and from 1924 to 1938 he was a member of the Union Parliament. He converted to Christianity.

Oppenheimer, Franz (1864–1943) German economist and sociologist. He was born in Berlin. From 1919 to 1929 he was a professor of sociology at the University of Frankfurt am Main. After Hitler's rise to power, he taught at the Hochschule für die Wissenschaft des Judentums in Berlin. In 1938 he settled in the US. He was associated with the Zionist movement, and the Merḥavyah co-operative settlement in Palestine was founded in accordance with his theories.

Oppenheimer, Joseph (c. 1698–1738) German financier. His father was a merchant in Heidelberg and collector of taxes from the Jews of the Palatinate. In 1732 Oppenheimer became the finance minister of Karl Alexander of Württemberg. After the duke's death in 1737 he was accused of stealing state finances and was hanged at Stuttgart; he refused to save his life by accepting baptism. His life was the subject of the novel *Jud Süss* by **Lion Feuchtwanger**.

Oppenheimer [Oppenheim], Samuel (1630–1703) Austrian financier and philanthropist. He was Leopold I's agent and financier, and was the first Jew to be allowed to settle in Vienna. He helped to finance Leopold's wars with the Turks and the War of the Spanish Succession. In 1697 he was accused of conspiring to murder **Samson Wertheimer**, but was acquitted. Among his benefactions were support for the poor, Jewish scholars and **Judah Ḥasid ha-Levi**'s movement for a Jewish settlement in Palestine.

Oppert, Jules (1825–1905) French philologist, orientalist and archaeologist. Born in Hamburg, he settled in France early in his life. He became an authority on Old Persian and Assyrian, and in 1851 he went on an expedition to explore Mesopotamia, where he identified the site of ancient Babylon. In 1874 he became professor of Assyrian philology and archaeology at the Collège de France. He wrote studies on various aspects of oriental scholarship. He was an active member of Jewish communal and scholarly bodies.

Orgad, Ben-Zion (b. 1926) Israeli composer and educator. He was born in Germany, and in 1933 settled in Palestine, where he later became a superintendent of music education. His works are motivated by national ideology.

Orlinsky, Harry (1908–92) American biblical scholar. He was born in Toronto, and went to the US in 1931. He was professor of Bible at the Hebrew Union College from 1943, and served as president of the Society for Biblical Literature 1969–70. He was also editor-in-chief of the Jewish Publication Society's translation of the Torah. His writings include *Understanding the Bible through History and Archaeology.*

Orloff, Chana (1888–1968) French sculptor, of Ukrainian origin. Born in the Ukraine, her family emigrated to Palestine in 1905. She later settled in Paris. She studied at the École Nationale des Arts Decoratifs and the Académie Russe, and became a member of a group of artists known as École de Paris. In 1942 she fled to Switzerland and returned to Paris in 1945. In addition to drawings and sculpture, she produced public monuments in Ramat Gan and Ein Gev in Israel.

Ormandy, Eugene [Blau, Jean] (1899–1985) American musician, of Hungarian origin. Born in Budapest, he studied at the Budapest Royal Academy where he became professor of violin. In 1921 he went to New York and eventually played with the Philadelphia Orchestra; later he became music director of the Minneapolis Symphony Orchestra. In 1938 he became music director of the Philadelphia Orchestra.

Ornitz, Samuel (1890–1957) American author. He was born in New York, where he worked as a social worker from 1908 to 1920. An advocate of Jewish assimilation, he saw no virtue in Jewish immigrant life. His novels chiefly concern the Jewish immigrant generation of the 1880–1914 period and portray Jewish types in an unsympathetic light.

Ornstein, Leo (1892–2002) American musician, of Russian origin. Born in Kremetchug, Russia, he studied at the St Petersburg Conservatory. His family emigrated to the US in 1907 and he studied at the New England Conservatory and the Institute of Musical Art in New York. From 1911 to 1933 he gave concerts throughout the US as well as in other countries. In 1935 he became head of the piano department of the Zeckwen Hahn School in Philadelphia, and later established the Ornstein School of Music.

Osiris, Daniel (1825–1908) French financier and philanthropist. He was born in Bordeaux. His beneficiaries included the French state, the Institut de France, and the Jewish community.

Ostropoler, Hirsch (fl. 18th cent.) Polish Yiddish jester. He was born in Balta, Podolia, and lived at Medzibozh. He derived his name from Ostropol in Poland, where he was the shoḥet. He later wandered throughout Podolia. Booklets recording his tales and anecdotes were published posthumously.

Othniel (fl. ?13th cent. BCE) First judge of Israel. He was a hero of the tribe of Judah during the period of conquest. After capturing Debir for his brother **Caleb**, he received **Caleb**'s daughter Achsah in marriage. Later he led the army which vanquished Cushan Rishathaim, King of Aram-Naharaim, who had enslaved Israel for eight years (Judges 3:8–11).

Oz, Amos (b. 1939) Israeli novelist. He was born in Jerusalem. His works include *Where the Jackals Howl, Elsewhere Perhaps, My Michael, Unto Death, Touch the Water, Touch the Wind, A Perfect Peace, In the Land of Israel* and *The Black Box.*

Ozick, Cynthia (b. 1928) American novelist. She was born in New York. Her writings include *The Pagan Rabbi and Other Stories* and *The Messiah of Stockholm.*

P

Pacifico, David (1784–1854) Anglo-Portuguese merchant and diplomat. Born in Gibraltar, he was a British subject. He served as Portuguese consul in Morocco (1835–7) and Greece (1837–42). In a riot against the Jewish community of Athens, he was attacked and his house was destroyed. When his claim for compensation was refused the British blockaded the port of Piraeus and captured 200 Greek ships. The Greek government then made financial reparations to Pacifico.

Pagis, Dan (1930–86) Israeli scholar and poet. He was born in Bukovina, Romania. In his youth he was imprisoned by the Nazis. He settled in Israel in 1947 and later became professor of medieval Hebrew literature at the Hebrew University. He published studies of Hebrew literature; an annotated anthology of Hebrew love poetry of the 10th to 18th centuries from Spain, Italy, Turkey and the Yemen; and his own poetry.

Palache, Juda Lion (1886–1944) Dutch orientalist and teacher. He was born in Amsterdam, and in 1925 became professor of the Bible and Semitic languages at the University of Amsterdam. He also served as parnas (or head) of the Spanish and Portuguese congregation in the city. He published studies of Judaism, Islam and comparative Semitic philology.

Palache, Samuel (d. 1616) Community leader. He was the first person to settle in Amsterdam as a declared Jew, and he obtained authorization for other Jews to settle there. In 1596 he gathered the first minyan in Amsterdam at his home for prayers on the Day of Atonement. He also built the first synagogue in the Netherlands. In 1608 he was appointed ambassador to The Hague by the Moroccan sultan Mulay Zidan, and in 1610 he negotiated an alliance between Morocco and the Netherlands – the first treaty of alliance between Christian and Muslim states. Later he assumed command of a small Moroccan fleet which seized some ships belonging to the King of Spain; he was charged with piracy, but was acquitted.

Paley, Grace (b. 1922) American writer. Born in New York City of Russian immigrants, she married Jess Paley and later began to write short stories. She taught at Columbia University and Syracuse University. Her work includes *The Little Disturbances of Man: Stories of Women and Men at Love* and *Later the Same Day*.

Paley, William (1901–90) American media executive. Born in Chicago to immigrants from the Ukraine, he studied at the University of Pennsylvania and joined his father's cigar manufacturing company. Later he became president of the Columbia Broadcasting System.

Pann [Pfefferman], Abel (1883–1963) Israeli artist, of Russian origin. He trained in Vienna and Paris. In 1913 he moved to Palestine, where he was a teacher at the Bezalel School of Arts and Crafts. His paintings depict Bible stories and scenes of Israeli settlement life.

Panofsky, Erwin (1892–1968) American art historian, of German origin. Born in Hanover, he studied at the University of Freiburg and became professor at Hamburg. After the Nazi rise to power, he went to the US and became a professor at New York University, and later at Princeton University; subsequently he was professor at Harvard.

Pap, Karoly (1897–1945) Hungarian writer, son of the chief rabbi of Sopron. He served in the Hungarian Red Army, and later settled in Budapest. Some of his writings deal with the issue of Jewish identity and assimilation.

Pappa (c. 300–75) Babylonian amora. He studied under **Rava** and **Abbaye**. He founded an academy at Neresh, near Sura, which he directed. He frequently participated in halakhic disputes. Besides his scholarly activities, he engaged in the sale of poppy seeds and the brewing of date beer.

Pappenheim, Bertha (1859–1936) German communal leader. She was born in Vienna, where she was treated by the neurologist **Joseph Breuer**, who viewed her case as important in the development of psychoanalysis. Later she settled in Frankfurt am Main, where she became the headmistress of an orphanage. In 1904 she founded the relief organizaton Jüdischer Frauenbund and visited Galicia, Romania and Russia to carry out its work. In 1914 she established and directed an institute near Frankfurt for unmarried mothers, prostitutes and delinquent women. She translated Yiddish works into German and wrote under the name of Paul Berthold.

Pappus and Julianus (fl. 2nd century) Judean patriots. They were brothers. According to rabbinic legend, they set up banks to assist wayfarers in Jerusalem. They were probably the leaders of the Jewish revolt against Trajan (115–17), since they were captured by the Romans at Laodicea in Syria and executed.

Pardo, David (1718–90) Palestinian rabbinical author and poet. He was born in Venice, and served as a rabbi in Spalato in Dalmatia and in Sarajevo. Between 1776 and 1782 he travelled widely, making his way to Palestine; he settled in Jerusalem, where he became head of a yeshivah. He wrote commentaries and novellae on tannaitic literautre, as well as liturgical poetry.

Pardo [Brown], Saul (d. 1708) American ḥazzan, also known as Saul Brown. He was the first ḥazzan of the Jewish community of New York, the Congregation Shearith Israel.

Parḥon, Solomon (fl. 12th cent.) Italian lexicographer. He was born in Qal'a, Spain, and became a pupil of **Judah ha-Levi**, and **Abraham ibn Ezra**. He settled in Italy, where he wrote a biblical lexicon (*Maḥberet he-Arukh*) in 1160 at Salerno.

Parker, Dorothy (1893–1967) American author. Born in West End, New Jersey, she initially wrote drama reviews for *Vogue* and *Vanity Fair*. Later she reviewed books and theatre for the *New Yorker*. Her works include *Not So Deep as a Well*, *Laments for Living*, *After Such Pleasures* and *Here Lies*.

Partos, Ödön (1909–77) Israeli composer and violinist. He was born in Budapest. He became first violinist of the Lucerne Orchestra in 1924, and from 1936 to 1938 taught violin and composition at the conservatory in Baku. In 1938 he went to Palestine and joined the Palestine Orchestra as a viola player. He was appointed director of the Israel Conservatory and Academy of Music in Tel Aviv in 1953. His compositions include *Song of Praise* for viola and orchestra and the symphonic fantasy *En Gev*.

Pascin, Jules (1885–1930) Artist. Born in Vivin, Bulgaria, his family moved to Bucharest and he worked in his father's business. He later went to Vienna where he studied art. He then went to Berlin where he sold caricatures and satirical drawings. In 1905 he settled in Paris and sent his drawings to the magazine *Simplicissimus* and exhibited his work in Berlin. After extensive travels, he returned to Paris in 1920.

Pasten, Linda (b. 1932) American poet. She was born in New York. A number of her poems deal with Jewish themes.

Pasternak, Boris (1890–1960) Russian author. Born in Moscow, he wrote pastoral and romantic poems and translated classical poetry and drama. During the 1930s he began working on *Doctor Zhivago*. He was denounced by the Soviet literary establishment and expelled from the Union of Soviet Writers. In 1958 he was awarded the Nobel Prize for Literature.

Patai, Joseph (1882–1953) Hungarian poet and editor. He was born in Gyöngyöspata, and taught at a Budapest high school. He published a Hebrew verse collection, anthologies of Hungarian poetry, Hungarian versions of Hebrew poetry and memoirs. He was also the editor of a Zionist monthly. In 1938 he settled in Palestine.

Patai, Raphael (b. 1910) American anthropologist and biblical scholar, son of **Joseph Patai**. He was born in Budapest, and in 1933 moved to Palestine, where he became an instructor in Hebrew at the Hebrew University. In 1944 he founded the Palestine Institute of Folklore and Ethnology in Jerusalem and served as its director of research. In 1947 he settled in the US, where he taught anthropology at Dropsie College and later at Fairleigh Dickinson University. He published studies dealing with the culture of the ancient Hebrews and the modern Middle East.

Patterson, David (b. 1922) British scholar. Born in Liverpool, he taught at Oxford University and was later president of the Oxford Centre for Postgraduate Hebrew Studies. His works include *Abraham Mapu* and *The Hebrew Novel in Czarist Russia.*

Pauker, Ana (1890–1960) Romanian communist leader. Born Hannah Rabinsohn, she was the daughter of a kosher butcher. She taught Hebrew in a Bucharest Jewish primary school. Later she went to Paris where she married a communist, Marcel Pauker. She organized an underground communist cell and was eventually arrested. Following the Soviet occupation of Bessarabia, she was exchanged for Romanian political detainees and welcomed by Stalin. After World War II, she became a communist leader in Romania. In 1947 she became minister of foreign affairs and first deputy prime minister.

Paul [Saul of Tarsus] (fl. 1st cent.) Early Christian evangelist. He was born in Tarsus in Asia Minor, and was a Roman citizen. He studied under **Gamaliel the Elder**. As a result of a vison he was converted to Christianity, changed his name from Saul to Paul, and travelled throughout the Mediterranean and Middle East as an 'aspotle to the gentiles'. His epistles form a central part of the New Testament.

Pearlstein, Philip (b. 1924) American artist. Born in Pittsburgh, he studied at the Carnegie Institute of Technology. He moved to New York and worked as a typographer and mechanical draftsman. He initially painted landscapes but later displayed a preference for realism.

Peerce, Jan (1904–84) American singer. He was born in New York. He sang at Radio City Music Hall from 1932 and later performed in numerous operas. He also gave recitals of cantorial music and recorded cantorial works and Jewish folksongs.

Peixotto, Benjamin Franklin (1834–90) American lawyer, diplomat and communal leader, grandson of **Moses Levy Maduro Peixotto**. He was born in New York, and became a clothing merchant in Cleveland, Ohio. He was Grand Sar (president) of B'nai B'rith in 1863–4. In 1866 he moved to New York to practise law. In 1870 he was appointed the first US consul in Bucharest, where he argued for Jews to be allowed to emigrate to the US. He was US consul in Lyons from 1877 to 1885.

Peixotto, Moses Levy Maduro (1767–1828) American merchant. From 1820 he was ḥazzan of New York's Congregation Shearith Israel.

Pekah (fl. 8th cent. BCE) King of Israel (735–732 BCE). He gained the throne by killing **Pekahiah**. He formed an alliance with Rezin of Aram-Dammesek and together they attacked Judah. King **Ahaz** of Judah appealed to the Assyrian king Tiglath-Pileser III who invaded the allied kingdom, abolished Aram-Dammesek as a state, and stripped Israel of Galilee and Gilead. Pekah was later killed by **Hoshea**.

Pekahiah (fl. 8th cent. BCE) King of Israel (737–735 BCE). He reigned at the same time as **Uzziah**, King of Judah. According to II Kings 15:24, he did what was evil in the sight of the Lord. He was killed by **Pekah** who took his place on the throne.

Peli, Meir (b. 1894) Israeli publisher of Russian origin. He and his brother Berakhah (b. 1897) emigrated to Palestine in 1921. They founded the Massadah Publishing Company which produced the *Encyclopedia Hebraica.*

Perec, Georges (1936–82) French writer. Born in Paris, he was sent away to escape deportation by the Nazis. In the 1960s he joined an experimental literary workshop, Oulipo. His first novel, *Les Choses*, describes the daily life of a young French couple and criticizes consumerist society. Other works include *La vie mode d'emploi* and *Woule souvenir d'enfance*.

Pereira, Abraham Israel [Rodrigues, Tómas] (d. 1699) Spanish religious leader and writer. He escaped from the Spanish Inquisition to the Netherlands, where he founded a Talmud Torah in Amsterdam. He also established the Ḥesed Abraham yeshivah at Hebron. A member of the Shabbetaian movement, he wrote *La certeza del camino* to encourage marranos to repent in preparation for the messianic age. He set out for Palestine to meet **Shabbetai Tzevi** but stopped in Italy.

Péreire, Jacob Rodriguez (1715–80) French educator and communal leader. He was born into a marrano family in Berlangua, Spain, and went to France, where he embraced Judaism. He was a teacher of deaf mutes, and his work was recognized by Louis XV. He was also an inventor. Active in Jewish spheres, he was a counsellor of the Sephardi community in Paris from 1749.

Perelman, Sidney Joseph (1904–79) American author. Born in Brooklyn, he grew up in Providence, Rhode Island. He studied at Brown University, and later lived in Greenwich Village where he drew cartoons for the weekly *Judge*. From 1934 he contributed to the *New Yorker*. His works include *Dawn Ginsbergh's Revenge, Acres and Pains, Westward Ha!, Swiss Family Perelman, The Rising Gorge, Baby, It's Cold Inside* and *Vinegar Pass*. He wrote movie scripts and collaborated with the Marx Brothers for *Monkey Business* and *Horsefeathers*. His screenplay for *Around the World in Eighty Days* won an Academy Award.

Peres, Shimon (b. 1923) Israeli politician, of Polish origin. He went to Palestine in 1934. He served as chairman of the labour party from 1977. He was acting prime minister in 1987 and prime minister of Israel in 1984–6. His publications include *From these Men, Tomorrow Is Now* and *The Next Phase*.

Peretz, Isaac Leib (1852–1915) Polish Yiddish and Hebrew poet and author. He was born in Zamość. Educated in the Eastern European religious tradition he also came into contact with modern learning. He practised law and lived in Warsaw, where he was an employee in the Jewish Communal Bureau. He began writing at an early age, and eventually decided to use Yiddish as a means of making literary material available to the Jewish masses. He was a master of the Yiddish short story, in which he depicted the misery and virtues of Polish Jewry. He also wrote romantic and symbolic stories based on Jewish legend and mysticism, mystic dramas and poetry, and edited a number of literary compilations.

Pereutz, Max (b. 1914) British biochemist. Born in Vienna, he emigrated to England in 1936. After World War II he worked at the molecular biology laboratory at Cambridge University. He shared the Nobel Prize for Chemistry. In 1962 he became chairman of the British Medical Research Council Laboratory of Molecular Biology.

Perl, Joseph (1773–1839) Galician Hebrew author and maskil. He was born in Tarnopol. He was initially attracted to Ḥasidism, but later embraced the Haskalah. In 1813 he established the first modern Jewish school in Galicia (in Tarnopol), which he directed. He encouraged the creation of Jewish agricultural colonies, and opposed the Ḥasidism in his satirical writings.

Perles, Felix (1874–1933) Austrian rabbi and scholar, son of **Joseph Perles**. He was active in the Zionist movement in Vienna. In 1899 he became a rabbi at Königsberg and taught at the university there. He wrote studies of Bible criticism, Hebrew and Aramaic lexicography, apocryphal and pseudepigraphical literature, medieval Hebrew poetry, liturgy and Jewish dialectics.

Perles, Joseph (1835–94) German rabbi and scholar. He was born in Baja, Hungary. He served as rabbi in Posen, and later in Munich. He wrote studies of Syriac, medieval literature, biblical exegesis and Hebrew and Aramaic lexicography and philology.

Persky, Daniel (1887–1962) American Hebraist, educator and journalist. He was born in Minsk, and in 1906 moved to the US, where he worked for the Hebraist movement, which aimed to foster the Hebrew language and literature. From 1921 he taught at the Herzliah Hebrew Teachers' College in New York. He contributed articles to the Hebrew weekly *Hadoar*. A number of his books were based on these contributions. He also edited several children's magazines.

Pevsner, Nikolaus (1902–83) British art historian, of German origin. Born in Leipzig, he became keeper of the Dresden Art Gallery, and later taught at the University of Göttingen. In 1934 he fled to England. He was professor of fine art at Cambridge, and later professor of the history of art at Birkebeck College, London. His works include *Outline of European Architecture*, *Pioneers of Modern Design: From William Morris to Walter Gropius*, *Mannerism to Romanticism* and *Sources of Modern Art*. He also edited the *Buildings of England*.

Pfefferkorn, Johann Joseph (1469–after 1521) Moravian apostate and anti-Jewish agitator. He was a butcher by trade. He was baptized at Cologne in 1504 and published a number of anti-Jewish tracts. In 1509 he was authorized by Emperor Maximilian to examine Jewish books in Germany and destroy any which blasphemed the Christian faith. As a result of various protests, the matter was referred to a group of scholars, including Johannes Reuchlin. Reuchlin's defence of the Talmud gave rise to a polemical dispute with Pfefferkorn. In 1520 the pope decided against Reuchlin, but the censorship of Jewish books was not revived and the Talmud was printed by **David Bomberg**.

Phasael (fl. 1st cent. BCE) Judean prince, son of **Antipater II** and brother of **Herod** the Great. He was appointed governor of Jerusalem by **Antipater** when **Herod** became governor of Galilee. Accompanied by **Hyrcanus II**, Phasael went to negotiate peace in the Parthian camp, but was imprisoned by the Parthians. According to tradition, he committed suicide. **Herod** called one of the towers on the wall of Jerusalem after him.

Philip (d. 34) Judean tetrarch, son of **Herod** the Great. He was educated in Rome. He was appointed tetrarch by the provisions of his father's will, and received the territories of Gaulanitis, Trachonitis, Bashan and the city of Paneas. He married **Salome**.

Phillips, Lionel (1885–1936) South African industrialist. He was one of the London Jews who went to South Africa after the discovery of the Kimberley diamond mine. He helped organize the diamond industry. He was a member of the first South African parliament.

Philippson, Franz (1851–1925) Belgian financier and communal leader, son of **Ludwig Philippson**. He was born in Magdeburg. He established a bank in Belgium in 1871. Later he was president of the Belgian Congo railway company and a founder of the Belgian Congo Bank. He served as president of the Jewish community in Brussels and contributed to Jewish colonization in Argentina and Brazil.

Philippson, Ludwig (1811–89) German rabbi and newspaper editor. He served as preacher to the Jewish community of Magdeburg and was instrumental in initiating Reform rabbinical synods in Germany. In 1837 he founded the *Allgemeine Zeitung des Judentums*, which he edited. He published a translation of the Bible, and helped found the Institut zur Förderung der Israelitischen Literatur.

Philippson, Martin (1846–1916) German historian and communal leader, son of **Ludwig Philippson**. He was born at Magdeburg. He taught at the University of Bonn, and later at the University of Brussels, where he became rector. Owing to anti-German attitudes in Brussels, he was forced to resign and settled in Berlin, where he became involved in Jewish affairs and served as head of the Lehranstalt für die Wissenschaft des Judentums. He published studies of modern history.

Philipson, David (1862–1949) American Reform rabbi. He was born in Wabash, Indiana and served as a rabbi in Baltimore and Cincinnati. He was president of the Central Conference of American Rabbis, and taught at the Hebrew Union College. His writings include *The Reform Movement in Judaism*, *The Jew in English Fiction* and *My Life as an American Jew*.

Philo (c. 25 BCE–40 CE) Hellenistic philosopher. He lived in Alexandria. He combined Hellenistic thought with Jewish belief in Holy Scripture; his writings include a legal exposition, philosophical interpretation, and a commentary on the Pentateuch.

In 40 CE he was a member of the Jewish deputation which travelled to Rome to make representations to the Emperor Caligula concerning anti-Jewish activities in Alexandria.

Phinehas (i) (fl. ?13th cent. BCE) Israelite priest, grandson of **Aaron**. He slew **Zimri** and as a reward he and his descendants were granted the priesthood (Numbers 25). He was also given a holding on Mount Ephraim. Phinehas continued to officiate and was still in office at the time of the campaign against **Benjamin** (Judges 20:28). The Zadokites traced their ancestry to him.

Phinehas (ii) (fl. 11 cent. BCE) Israelite priest, second son of **Eli**. He and **Hophni** his brother, officiated at Shiloh but were guilty of conduct unworthy of priests. While accompanying the Ark of the Covenant into battle against the Philistines, they were killed (1 Samuel 4).

Phinehas ben Abraham of Koretz (1726–91) Lithuanian Ḥasidic rabbi. He lived in Volhynia, where he came under the influence of the **Baal Shem Tov**. An opponent of the tradition of legal interpretation known as 'pilpul', he preached simplicity and humility.

Phinehas ben Jair (fl. 2nd cent.) Palestinian tanna, son-in-law of **Simeon ben Yoḥai**. He was a prominent halakhist.

Piatigorsky, Gregor (1903–76) Ukrainian cellist. Born in Ekaterinoslav, Ukraine, he received his first music lessons from his father. He studied at the Moscow Conservatory and in 1919 became a member of the Lenin Quartet and principal cellist of the Bolshoi Theatre Orchestra. In 1921 he went to Warsaw, Leipzig and later Berlin. He subsequently became first cellist of the Berlin Philharmonic, but left to become a soloist and performed in major capitals throughout the world.

Picon, Molly (b. 1898) American actress. She was born in New York. She played Yiddish roles on Second Avenue, acted at Kessler's Theatre, and went on tour with her husband, Jacob Kalich. From 1942 she managed the Molly Picon Theatre in New York. After World War II she visited displaced persons' camps and toured widely. Subsequently she appeared in plays and films and on television. Her *So Laugh a Little* is a family biography.

Pijade, Mosa (1890–1957) Yugoslavian politician. A native of Belgrade, he studied painting and worked as an art teacher. In 1921 he was jailed after joining the Yugoslav communist party. He translated **Karl Marx**'s *Das Kapital* into Serbian. He became an organizer of the communist partisans and a Jewish resistance fighter. When Tito became premier, he became an associate and helped to draft Yugoslavia's constitution. He served as president of the Serbian republic and chairman of Yugoslavia's National Assembly.

Pike, Lipman (1845–93) American baseball player. Born in New York City, he joined the Atlantics and later the Cincinnati Reds.

Pilichowski, Leopold (1869–1933) Polish painter. Born in Zadzin, he lived in Lódź, Paris and London. He painted work scenes of wool-dyers at Lódź, and shopkeepers and artisans in London's Whitechapel. He also executed portraits of **Ḥayyim Naḥman Bialik**, **Albert Einstein**, **Aḥad ha-Am**, **Max Nordau** and **Chaim Weizmann**. His other works include *The Opening of the Hebrew University in Jerusalem.*

Pincus, Louis Arieh (1912–73) Israeli lawyer and Zionist, of South African Origin. In 1948 he moved to Israel where he became a legal adviser and general secretary to the ministry of transportation. Later he was appointed managing director of El Al. In 1961 he became a member of the executive of the Jewish Agency. He was acting chairman of the 27th Zionist Congress, and served as chairman of the board of governors of Tel Aviv University.

Pines, Jehiel Michal (1843–1913) Russian author, Zionist and yishuv leader. He was born in Ruzhany, Belorussia. He contributed to the Hebrew press, arguing against assimilation, and made plans to establish an agricultural school. He represented the Mazkeret Mosheh society in Palestine from 1878, and played an important role in the early stages of Jewish settlement. One of the founders of the Hebrew-speaking movement in Jerusalem, he opposed Ḥalukkah and fanaticism; his attitudes gave rise to conflict with rabbis in Jerusalem.

Pines, Shlomo (1908–90) Israeli scholar. He was professor of General and Jewish Philosophy at the Hebrew University from 1952 to 1977.

Pinsker, Judah Loeb [Leon] (1821–91) Russian Zionist. He was born in Tomaszów, Poland, and was one of the first Jews to enrol at Odessa University, where he studied law. Later he studied medicine at the University of Moscow, and returned to Odessa to set up practice in 1849. He was a founder of the first Russian Jewish weekly to which he contributed. Initially he was an advocate of the Haskalah movement, but after the wave of pogroms in 1881 he argued that only national territorial rebirth could solve the Jewish problem. In his pamphlet *Auto-Emancipation* he called for the creation of a Jewish territory, where the Jews could support and govern themselves. In 1884 he convened the Kattowitz Conference of Ḥovevei Zion where he was elected president of Ḥibbat Zion's presidium.

Pinsker, Simḥah (1801–64) Galician scholar. He was born in Tarnów. He was the founder of the first successful modern Jewish school in Russia, in Odessa in 1826. He accumulated a collection of ancient Hebrew manuscripts, several of which were examined and described by the Karaite scholar, **Abraham Firkovich** on a visit to Osessa. Eventually Pinsker moved to Vienna, where he published a history of Karaism and Karaite literature. He later returned to Odessa.

Pinski, David (1872–1959) American Yiddish dramatist and novelist. He was born in Mohilev on the Dnieper, and lived in Warsaw. In 1899 he emigrated to the US, where he wrote for the Yiddish stage. His early works deal with Jewish suffering in Russia, but later he wrote poetic and symbolic treatments of Jewish historic themes. His plays include *The Treasure*, *The Eternal Jew* and *Shabbetai Tzevi*. He also composed novels and short stories. Active in Jewish affairs, he served as president of the Jewish Workers' Alliance; later he settled in Israel.

Pinter, Harold (b. 1930) British dramatist. Born in London, he studied at the Royal Academy of Dramatic Art. From 1949 to 1960 he was a professional actor. His works include *The Room*, *The Birthday Party*, *The Caretaker*, *The Homecoming*, *A Night Out*, *A Slight Ache*, *The Collection*, *Landscape*, *Silence*, *Old Times* and *Betrayal*.

Pirbright, Lord [Worms, Henry de] (1840–1903) British statesman. He was active in London Jewish communal life, serving as president of the Anglo-Jewish Association from 1874 to 1886. He was then undersecretary of state for the colonies (1888–92).

Pissaro, Camille (1830–1903) French painter. Born in St Thomas, Virgin Islands, he studied in Paris and returned to St Thomas to work in his family's store. He left to paint in Venezuela; in 1855 he moved to Paris. He became an important figure in the French Impressionist group.

Plisetskaya, Maya (b. 1925) Russian dancer. She achieved fame as the prima ballerina of the Bolshoi Ballet and was awarded the Lenin Prize in 1964.

Podhoretz, Norman (b. 1930) American writer and editor. He was born in Brooklyn. In 1960 he became editor of the monthly *Commentary* published by the American Jewish Committee. His writings include *Doings and Undoings: The Fifties and After in American Writing*, *The Commentary Reader* and *Making it*.

Polanyi, Michael (1891–1976) Hungarian chemist and philosopher. He studied at the University of Budapest and worked on the chemisty of liquids and thermodynamics. He later emigrated to Germany and worked at Karlsruhe University and subsequently the Kaiser Wilhelm Institute. When Hitler came to power, he went to Manchester, England and became a professor of chemistry at the University of Manchester. Later he became professor of social studies there. His works include *The Concept of Freedom: The Russian Experiment and After*, *Full Employment and Free Trade*, *Science, Faith and Society*, *Personal Knowledge*, *Beyond Nihilism* and *Knowing and Being*.

Poliakov, Léon (b. 1910) French historian. He was born in St Petersburg, and moved to France in 1920. He was on the staff of *Pariser Tageblatt* until 1939, then served in the French army during World War II. After the war he became head of the research department of the Centre de Documentation Juive

Contemporaine, and in 1952 research fellow at the Centre National de la Recherche Scientifique. He was appointed to a post at the École Pratique des Hautes Études in 1954. His writings include *History of Anti-Semitism.*

Pollak, Jacob (1460/1470–after 1522) Polish rabbi and halakhic authority. He was born in Bavaria, and became a rabbi in Prague, where he was a member of the bet din. Later he went to Kraków, where he opened the first yeshivah in Poland, and instituted the intepretive method known as pilpul (fine distinctions). In 1503 he was appointed by King Alexander as the rabbi of the whole of Poland.

Pomi, David de (1525–88) Italian physician, linguist and philosopher. He was born in Spoleto. He was a rabbi and physician at Magliano, and later settled in Venice, where he published most of his works. Pope Pius IV gave him permission to attend Christians, but this concession was revoked by Pius V, though it was later restored by Pope Sixtus V. He published a treatise on gynaecology, a historical defence of Jewish physicians, and a Hebrew–Latin–Italian dictionary (*Tzemaḥ David*) containing scientific and historical information.

Pommer, Erich (1889–1966) American film producer. He came from Hildesheim and worked in Germany, France, England and the US. His films include *Die Spinnen, Der Müde Tod, Dr Mabuse, der Spieler, Der Letze Mann* and *Faust.* He was head of production for the film company UFA in Germany; with the rise of the Nazi party, he went to Hollywood. By 1936 he was in England and in 1937 he helped create Mayflower Pictures.

Pool, David de Sola (1885–1970) American rabbi, communal leader and historian. He was born in London. After moving to the US he became minister of Congregation Shearith Israel in New York in 1907. He wrote studies in the fields of American Jewish history, religion, education and Zionism, and edited and translated liturgical works.

Popper, Julius (1857–93) Romanian explorer. He arrived in Buenos Aires in 1885 and made an expedition to Tierra del Fuego in 1886. He obtained permission to lead explorations to the northern part of the area and discovered gold at Bahia San Sebastian. He later established the Gold Washers Company of the South and founded a mining establishment in San Sebastian Bay.

Popper-Lynkeus, Josef (1838–1921) Austrian philosopher and social reformer. Born in Kolin, he studied at the Polytechnikum in Prague. In 1858 he studied at the Imperial Polytechnikum in Vienna. He became a clerk in Hungary, but later returned to Vienna and became a private tutor. He invented a device to eliminate deposits from collecting in engine boilers. He continued with his scientific work as well as philosophical reflection.

Portaleone, Abraham ben David (1542–1612) Italian physician and author. He graduated from the University of Pavia in 1563, and later served as physician to the ducal house there. In 1591 he was given papal authorization to attend Christian patients. He wrote a Latin work containing guidance for physicians, and a study of the applications of gold in medicine. His *Shields of the Mighty* is a study of the Temple and its service.

Potocki, Valentin (d. 1749) While studying in Paris, he became a friend of Zaremba, another Polish aristocrat; both men converted to Judaism. Zaremba settled in Palestine and Potocki lived in Ilya near Vilna. Eventually he was put on trial as a proselyte, condemned and burned to death. His grave became a place of pilgrimage for Jews and his life has been celebrated in various literary studies.

Potok, Chaim (b. 1929) American novelist. He was born in New York. He taught at the University of Judaism in Los Angeles and the Jewish Theological Seminary. In 1965 he became editor of the Jewish Publication Society. His novels include *The Chosen, The Promise, My Name Is Asher Lev, In the Beginning, The Book of Lights* and *Davita's Harp.*

Poznanski, Samuel Abraham (1864–1921) Polish scholar. He served as a rabbi in Warsaw from 1897. He wrote studies of gaonic and Karaite history, edited medieval commentaries and produced a biographical lexicon of Karaite literature.

Praag, Siegfried van (1899–2002) Dutch novelist. He was born in Amsterdam. He became a schoolteacher and settled in Brussels; later he lived in

London, where he worked for the BBC. A number of his novels deal with Jewish topics and his later writings recall the Jewish life of Amsterdam that was destroyed by the Nazi invasion.

Prawer, Siegbert Salomon (b. 1925) British scholar. He was born in Cologne, and went to England in 1939. He taught at the University of Birmingham, and later became a professor of German at London University. In 1969 he was appointed professor of German at the University of Oxford. His publications include *Heine's Jewish Comedy: A Study of His Portraits of Jews and Judaism.*

Preil, Gabriel (b. 1911) American Hebrew poet. He was born in Dorpat, Estonia, and went to the US in 1922. He published essays, translated Hebrew texts into English, and wrote Hebrew poetry.

Preminger, Otto (1905–86) American film director, of Austrian origin. Born in Austria, he succeeded Max Reinhardt at a Vienna theatre. In 1935 he left Europe from the US. He directed the film *Laura* in 1944. His films include *The Moon Is Blue, The Man with a Golden Arm, Anatomy of a Murder, Exodus, Carmen Jones* and *Porgy and Bess.*

Pressburger, Emeric (1902–88) British film producer and novelist. Born in Hungary, he was a journalist and later worked in the film industry. With the rise of the Nazis, he left for France and settled in England in 1935. His films include *The Life and Death of Colonel Blimp, I Know where I'm Going, A Matter of Life and Death, Black Narcissus, The Red Shoes* and *The Tales of Hoffmann.* He also wrote a novel, *The Glass Pearls,* about a Nazi concentration camp doctor.

Presser, Jacob (1890–1970) Dutch writer and historian. He was born in Amsterdam, and became professor of modern history at the university there. His writing includes *The Destruction of Dutch Jewry.*

Preuss, Joseph (1861–1913) German physician and medical historian. Born in Gross-Schoenebeck, he studied at Berlin University and practised medicine. His works include *Biblisch-talmudische Medizin.*

Priesand, Sally (b. 1946) American rabbi. A graduate of the University of Cincinnati, and the Hebrew Union College, she was the first woman to be ordained as a rabbi in the US.

Prilutski, Noyakh [Prylucki, Noah] (1882–1941) Polish Yiddish scholar and political leader. He was born in Berdichev, and grew up in Kremenetz. He was an activist in the campaign for Jewish access to higher education. In 1909 he set up a private law practice in Warsaw and founded a Yiddish daily newspaper. The following year he was elected to the Warsaw city council, and later he served as a member of the Polish parliament. He helped establish Yiddish-speaking schools in Poland, organized the country's first Yiddish cultural conference, and helped to set up schools and libraries in rural areas. He published various works on Yiddish scholarship. He later became professor of Yiddish at the University of Vilna.

Prinz, Joachim (1902–88) American rabbi and communal leader. He was born in Burchartsdorf, Germany, and became the rabbi of the Berlin Jewish community in 1926. He attacked Nazism from the pulpit and was expelled from Germany. In 1939 he became rabbi at Temple B'nai Abraham in Newark, New Jersey. Active in Jewish affairs, he served as president of the American Jewish Congress from 1958 to 1966. His writings include *Wir Juden, Das Leben im Ghetto* and *The Dilemma of the Modern Jew.*

Proskauer, Joseph Meyer (1877–1971) American lawyer and communal leader. He was born in Mobile, Alabama, and became a lawyer and later a judge. An associate of Alfred E. Smith, he worked with him in his 1928 presidential campaign. In 1935 he was a member of the New York Charter Revision Commission. He also served as president of the American Jewish Committee.

Prossnitz, Löbele (c.1670–1730) Moravian preacher and miracle worker. Born in Uherský Brod, he settled in Prossnitz. He underwent a spiritual transformation, and studied the Mishnah, the Zohar and kabbalistic writings. He claimed that in his study of kabbalah he was accompanied by the souls of **Isaac Luria** and **Shabbetai Tzevi**, and predicted the return of **Shabbetai Tzevi** in 1706. He was criticized by the Moravian rabbis, but continued to preach in Austria and Germany. Later he claimed to be the Messiah ben Joseph. He subsequently lived in Hungary.

Proust, Marcel (1871–1922) French novelist. He was born in Paris. Although he was raised as a Catholic, he retained Jewish sympathies. His *A la recherche du temps perdu* contains three Jewish characters: the actress Rachel, the intellectual Albert Bloch and Charles Swann. The work also alludes to the Dreyfus Affair.

Pulitzer, Joseph (1847–1911) American newspaper publisher, of Hungarian origin. Born in Mako, Hungary, of a Jewish father and a Roman Catholic mother, he studied in Budapest. At the age of 17 he went to the US. He served with Lincoln's Calvary. He became a reporter for the *St Louis Westliche Post* and was elected to the Missouri state legislature. In 1874 he purchased the *St Louis Staats-Zeitung*; in 1878 he bought the *St Louis Dispatch* and merged it with the *St Louis Evening Post*. In 1883 he purchased the *New York World*. Later he founded the *New York Evening World*.

Q

Querido, Israel (1872–1932) Dutch novelist. He was born in Amsterdam, and in his novels portrayed Jewish diamond workers and the life of poor Jews of his native city. He also wrote plays with biblical backgrounds.

Querido, Jacob (c. 1650–90) Greek religious leader. His sister became the last wife of **Shabbetai Tzevi**. After **Shabbetai**'s death in 1676 she returned to Salonica and claimed that her brother was the recipient of her husband's soul. In 1683 there was a mass apostasy to Islam of a large group of Salonica families, who nevertheless continued to observe Shabbetaian and Jewish rites in secret. This group formed the nucleus of the Dönmeh sect. Taking the Turkish name Abdullah Yacoub, Querido became the most important leader of these sectarians.

R

Rabb, Maxwell Milton (b. 1910) American lawyer, government official, and communal leader. He was born in Boston. He served as associate counsel to President Eisenhower in 1953–4, and later as secretary to the cabinet. Active in Jewish affairs, he became chairman of the government division of the United Jewish Appeal.

Rabbah bar Ḥanah (fl. 3rd cent.) Babylonian amora. He studied at the academy of **Johanan ben Zakkai** in Palestine. Later he returned to Babylonia, where he transmitted **Johanan**'s teachings. Legends about his journeys are recorded in the tractate Bava Batra.

Rabbah bar Naḥmani [Rabbah] (c. 270–330) Babylonian amora. He studied under **Huna** at Sura and **Judah bar Ezekiel** at Pumbedita. Known for his interpretation of the Mishnah, he was knowledgeable about ritual purity. He was nicknamed Oker Harim ('uprooter of mountains') because of his dialectical ability.

Rabbi Binyamin [Ha-Talmi, Yehosua; Radler-Feldman, Yehoshua] (1880–1957) Israeli journalist. He was born in Zborov, Galicia, and went to London in 1906. The following year he travelled to Palestine, where he worked as a labourer, and later served as secretary of Herzila high school in Tel Aviv. In 1910 he moved to Jerusalem, where he taught high school. After World War I he was active in the Mizraḥi party, and edited the national monthly *Ha-Hed* (1926–53). He was a founder (in 1926) of Berit Shalom, a society that advocated a binational state for Jews and Arabs. He published numerous books, articles and essays.

Rabbinovitz, Raphael Nathan (1835–88) Galician talmudic scholar. He was born in Novo-Zhagory, in the Kovno district. He lived in Lemberg and Pressburg, and travelled widely. His *Dikduke Sopherim* consists of 16 volumes of variant readings from Talmud manuscripts. He also wrote a study of the printed editions of the Talmud.

Rabbinowitz, Israel Michael (1818–93) French writer and scholar. He was born in Gorodets, Lithuania. He became a physician and settled in Paris, where he devoted himself to scholarship. He participated in the Kattowitz Conference of Ḥibbat Zion in 1884, and was head of the Benei Zion of Paris. In 1889 he went to Russia, and he eventually lived in London. His publications include *Législation civile du Talmud*, *Législation criminelle du Talmud*, *La medicine du Talmud* and *Le traité des poisons de Maimonide*.

Rabi, Isidore (1898–1988) American scientist. Born in Austria-Hungary, he went to the US as a child. He studied at Cornell University and later at Columbia University where he became a lecturer in the physics department. He subsequently was associate director of the radiation laboratory at Massachusetts Institute of Technology, and in 1940 became a professor at Columbia University. In 1944 he received the Nobel Prize for Physics.

Rabikovitch, Dalia (b. 1936) Israeli poet. Born in Ramat Gan, she studied at the Hebrew University in Jerusalem. Her works include *The Love of an Orange*, *A Rough Winter*, *The Third Book* and *True Love*.

Rabin Chaim (1915–96) Israeli scholar. He taught at the University of Oxford and later was professor of Hebrew language at the Hebrew University. His major contribution is in the field of linguistics.

Rabin, Yitzḥak (1922–95) Israeli soldier and diplomat. He was born in Jerusalem. He joined the Palmaḥ in 1940 and participated in underground activities against the British mandatory government. In 1947 he became deputy commander of the Palmaḥ, and later chief of operations of the Southern Command. From 1956 to 1959 he was chief of operations of the Northern Command. He subsequently became head of the General Staff Branch, deputy chief of staff, and eventually chief of staff. In 1968 he was Israeli ambassador to the US, and subsequently prime minister.

Rabinovich, Joseph (1837–1899) Bessarabian missionary. He was active in Kishinev. Initially attracted by the Haskalah, he joined Ḥibbat Zion in the 1880s and visited Palestine. In 1883 he founded a sect known as the Children of Israel of the New Testament, which accepted the tenets of Christianity while retaining Jewish nationalism and traditions. Two years later he converted to Protestantism. His writings include *Prayers and Principles of Faith of the Children of Israel of the New Testament* and *Words of Comfort.*

Rabinovich, Ossip (1817–69) Ukrainian journalist. He was born in Kobelyaki. In 1845 he settled in Odessa, where he was an adviser and pleader of the commercial court, and later a notary. He founded the first Russian weekly, *Rasviet*, in Odessa in 1860. He advocated reforms in Jewish life, the acceptance of Jews as Russian citizens, and the integration of Jewry into Russian society.

Rabinowitz, Alexander Süsskind (1854–1945) Palestinian Hebrew scholar, also known as Azar. He was born in Lyady, Belorussia. He taught in Poltava in the Ukraine, and became active in the Ḥibbat Zion movement. In 1906 he moved to Palestine, where he became a teacher and a librarian. He wrote stories, monographs, translations of world literature and Judaica into Hebrew, and textbooks.

Rabinowitz, Louis M. (1887–1957) American manufacturer and philanthropist. He was born in Rosanne, Lithuania, and moved to the US in 1901, where he established a corset-manufacturing company. He was active in Jewish community affairs.

Rabinowitz, Saul Phinehas [Sepher] (1845–90) Polish Hebrew writer and Zionist leader, of Lithuanian origin. He lived in Warsaw where he was initially attracted to Jewish nationalism and later to Zionism. After the pogroms of 1881, he helped to organize the emigration of Jewish refugees. He was secretary of the Kattowitz Conference of Ḥibbat Zion in 1884, and subsequently secretary of the movement's Warsaw office. He contributed to Hebrew journalism, edited the annual *Keneset Yisrael* in 1886–8, translated **Heinrich Graetz**'s *History of the Jews* into Hebrew, and wrote studies of the Jews exiled from Spain in the 1490s.

Rachel (i) (fl. ?19th–16th cent. BCE) Israelite woman, daughter of **Laban** and wife of **Jacob**. Her father was a herdsman in Haran, for whom **Jacob** worked. **Jacob** wished to marry Rachel but was tricked into marrying her elder sister **Leah**. Subsquently Rachel also became his wife and bore him two sons, **Joseph** and **Benjamin** (Genesis 29–35).

Rachel (ii) [Blovstein, Rachel] (1890–1931) Palestinian Hebrew poet, of Russian origin. In 1909 she emigrated to Palestine, where she worked as a labourer. Her poetry is imbued with love for the countryside of Palestine and the Jewish pioneers.

Rachel (iii) [Felix, Eliza Rachel] (1821–58) French actress. Born in Switzerland, she was the daughter of a peddlar. She made her debut at the Théâtre du Gymnase. She acted in the revival of French classical tragedies.

Radek [Sobelsohn], Karl (1885–?1939) Russian revolutionary. Born in Lwów, he joined the Polish social democratic party prior to World War I. He later settled in Switzerland where he was a friend of Lenin. At the outbreak of the Russian Revolution, he went to Sweden and subsequently returned to Russia. He became head of the central European section of the Foreign Affairs Commissariat. He later joined the Trotskyite opposition to Stalin, but was expelled from the party and exiled to the Urals.

After his recantation he was readmitted to the party and served as editor of *Pravda* and *Izvestia*.

Radnóti, Miklós (1909–44) Hungarian poet. Born in Budapest, he studied at the University of Szeged in Hungary. His works include *Pagan Greeting, Keep Walking, You, the Death-Condemned!* and *Foaming Sky*.

Ragoler, Elijah ben Jacob (1794–1850) Lithuanian talmudist. He was born in Sogindat in the Zamut region, and became known throughout Lithuania for his talmudic knowledge; he was also an expert on kabbalah. He served as rabbi of Slobodka in the Ukraine (1824–40) and later Kalisz in Poland. He was a fierce opponent of religious reform. He produced manuscript studies in all spheres of Torah study.

Rahv, Philip [Greenberg, Ivan] (1908–73) Literary critic. Born in Galicia, he went to the US at the age of 14. In 1932 he joined the communist party. He was a co-founder of *Partisan Review*. In 1957 he began teaching at Brandeis University.

Raisin, Max (1881–1957) American rabbi and author, of Polish origin. He served as rabbi of Congregation B'nai Jeshurun in Paterson, New Jersey, from 1921 to 1953. His writings include *Mordecai Manuel Noah: Zionist, Author and Statesman, Israel in America, A History of the Jews in Modern Times* and *Great Jews I Have Known*.

Rakoski, Matyas (1892–1971) Hungarian politician. Born in Ada, he went to Budapest where he worked as a bank clerk. He was active in the socialist movement, and later arrested. Released from prison in 1940 he went to Moscow where he organized the Hungarian communist propaganda campaign. After the Soviet occupation of Hungary, he reorganized the workers' party. He was deputy head of a coalition government and subsequently served as prime minister of Hungary.

Rambert, Marie (1888–1982) British dance teacher, of Polish origin. Born in Poland, she went to Paris to study medicine, but settled in Geneva where she studied at the Jacques Dalcroze School of Eurhythmics. She later taught at the school and later joined the Diaghilev Company. She subsequently established a school in London, and later the Ballet Rambert.

Rank, Otto (1884–1939) Austrian psychoanalyst. Born in Vienna, he met **Sigmund Freud** and studied at the University of Vienna. His works include *The Trauma of Birth*. He subsequently went to the US and developed the theory and technique of 'will therapy'.

Raphael, Frederic (b. 1931) British novelist and screenwriter. He was born in Chicago, and moved to England at the age of seven. Some of his novels deal with Jewish themes. His publications include *The Limits of Love, Lindmann, A Wild Surmise, Orchestra and Beginners, The Glittering Prizes* and *Heaven and Earth*.

Raphael ben Jekuthiel Cohen [Cohen, Raphael] (1722–1803) Polish talmudist. He served as rabbi at Minsk (1757–63), Pinsk (1763–76), Posen (1772–6), and Altona (1776–99). An opponent of **Moses Mendelssohn**, he was critical of modernism. His *Torat Yekutiel* is a commentary on the first part of the Shulḥan Arukh.

Rapoport, Solomon Judah [Shir] (1790–1867) Galician rabbi. He was born in Lemberg. He was a rabbi in Tarnopol from 1837 to 1840, when he was appointed chief rabbi of Prague. He was attacked by the Ḥasidim and the ultra-Orthodox for his enlightened approach to Jewish study, which laid the foundation for modern Jewish scholarship. He wrote studies of Jewish scholars of the gaonic period, began a talmudic encyclopaedia, and translated European poetry into Hebrew. He was also known as Shir, a name derived from his initials.

Rappoport, (O.) Yehoshua (1895–1971) Australian Yiddish essayist, translator and editor of Polish origin. He was born in Bialystok, and emigrated to Australia in 1947. He wrote about the Bible and the Talmud and translated works from Russian, German, French and Hebrew into Yiddish. In Australia he was the editor of the newspaper *Yidishe neies*.

Rashi [Solomon ben Isaac; Solomon [Salomon] Yitzḥak ben Isaac] (1040–1105) French rabbinic scholar. He was born in Troyes. After studying in the

Rhineland he returned to Troyes, where he established a school. He published responsa, composed penitential hymns and wrote commentaries on the Bible and the Talmud. His commentary on the Talmud established the correct text, defined numerous terms, and explained unusual words and phrases. His Bible commentary served as the basis for later interpretations of Scripture. Both works include numerous examples of textual gloss known as 'laaz' – an explanatory word in French (or another language) transliterated into Hebrew script.

Raskin, Saul (1886–1966) American artist. He was born in Nogaisk, Russia, and went to the US in 1904. He painted scenes of Jewish life on the East Side of New York and later in Palestine. He also illustrated various Hebrew texts.

Rasminsky, Louis (1908–98) Canadian banker. Born in Montreal, he served with the League of Nations Secretariat in Geneva and later returned to Ottawa. In 1945 he was chairman of the Bretton Woods Conference that created the International Monetary Fund (IMF). He represented Canada on the World Bank and the IMF. In 1961 he became governor of the Bank of Canada.

Rathenau, Walter (1867–1922) German statesman. His father, Emil Rathenau, was a co-founder of the German Edison company. He succeeded his father as head of the AEG electricty trust and during World War I was in charge of Germany's war economy. In 1922 he became minister of foreign affairs, but was assassinated by nationalists the same year.

Rathaus, Karol [Bruno, Leonhard] (1895–1954) American composer of Austrian orign. After 1933 he went to Paris, and then England; eventually he settled in the US. He composed symphonies, ballets, orchestral suites and chamber works as well as film scores.

Ratosh, Yonatan (1909–81) Israeli poet, of Russian origin. He emigrated to Palestine in 1921. His poetry portrays Hebrew youth as strong and heroic, in contrast to the downtrodden Jews of the diaspora. He is best known for his championship of the anti-Zionist nationalist ideology known as 'Canaanism' and for his 'Manifesto to Hebrew Youth'.

Rav [Abba Arikha] (fl. 3rd cent.) Babylonian amora, also known as Abba Arikha. He was born at Kafri in southern Babylonia. He went to Palestine, where he studied under **Ḥiyya** and joined the academy of **Judah ha-Nasi**. Later he returned to Babylonia; he declined the position of head of the Nehardea academy at Sura, which flourished for eight centuries. He and **Samuel** are the two sages whose teachings figure most prominently in the Talmud. According to tradition, he was the author of the Alenu prayer.

Rava (fl. 4th cent.) Babylonian amora. He was born in Maḥoza, and established an academy there when **Abbaye** became head of the academy at Pumbedita. After **Abbaye**'s death, Rava succeeded him at Pumbedita, which he amalgamated with Maḥoza. His controversies with **Abbaye** were famous; with six exceptions the ordinances of halakhah were determined in accordance with his views.

Ravitsh, Melekh (1893–1976) Canadian Yiddish poet and essayist, of Galician origin. He was born in Radymno, eastern Galicia. He travelled widely, and in Warsaw during the 1920s he was a member of the poetic group known as Khalyastre. In 1941 he settled in Montreal, though he spent 1953–6 in Israel. In addition to poetry, he published a three-volume biographical work on Yiddish literary figures.

Ravnitzky, Yehoshua Ḥana (1859–1944) Palestinian Hebrew and Yiddish author and editor. He was born in Odessa. He became a member of a group of Ḥovevei Zion and was one of the founders of Bene Mosheh. In 1899 he was appointed editor of the Yiddish periodical *Der Yid*, and later was a co-founder of the publishing house Moriah. In 1922 he emigrated to Palestine, where he helped to establish the Devir publishing house. Together with **Ḥayyim Naḥman Bialik**, he published the *Sepher Aggadah.*

Rawidowicz, Simon (1897–1957) American philosopher, of Polish origin. He taught at Leeds University (1941–7), the Chicago College of Jewish Studies (1948–51) and Brandeis University (1951–7). He published studies of philosophical thinkers and subjects, as well as works on contemporary Jewish topics. From 1927 to 1930 he was co-editor of the scholarly journal *Ha-Tekuphah*; he was also editor of the scholarly and literary journal *Metzudah*, and a founder of Berit Ivrit Olamit.

Ray, Man [Radnitsky, Emanuel] (1890–1976) American photographer. Born in Philadelphia, he studied at the Francisco Ferrer Centre and the Art Students League. In 1921 he went to Paris and became involved with the Dada movement. He worked as a photographer and also produced short films. In 1940 he went to Los Angeles, but returned to France in 1951.

Raziel, David (1910–41) Palestinian underground fighter. He was born in Smorgon, near Vilna, and went to Palestine with his parents at an early age. During the 1929 Arab riots he joined the Haganah. He was a founder (in 1937) and commander of the underground organization Irgun Tzevai Leumi. Captured by the British in 1939, he was later released. In 1941 he was killed in a German air-raid while on a mission for the British to Iraq.

Rebekah (fl. ?19th–16th cent. BCE) Israelite woman, wife of **Isaac**. When **Abraham** sent his servant **Eliezer** to Aram Naharaim to seek a wife for his son **Isaac**, **Eliezer** chose Rebekah. She bore **Isaac** twin sons, **Esau** and **Jacob** (Genesis 24–28).

Recanti, Menaḥem ben Benjamin (fl. 13th–14th cent.) Italian kabbalist and halakhic authority. He lived in Recanati. He introduced German mysticism and the study of the Zohar into Italy.

Reggio, Isaac Samuel [Yashar] (1784–1855) Italian scholar and mathematician. He was born in Gorizia. His inspiration led to the founding of the Collegio Rabbinico Italiano in Padua in 1829. He published an Italian translation of the Pentateuch with a commentary in Hebrew. In 1846 he became the rabbi of Gorizia. His writings include *Torah and Philosophy*.

Rehoboam (fl. 10th cent. BCE) King of Judah (930–908 BCE). He was the son of **Solomon** by his wife Naamah. When he refused to moderate his policy of taxation, the country split into the kingdoms of Israel and Judah; only the tribes of Judah, Simeon and most of Benjamin remained loyal to Rehoboam. Subsequently Shishak of Egypt invaded Judah and plundered the Temple (I Kings 11ff).

Reich, Steve (b. 1936) American composer, conductor and percussionist. He was born in New York, and lived in San Francisco, where he wrote music for the San Francisco Mime Troupe and presented concerts at the San Francisco Tape Music Centre. His compositions include *Tehilim*, based on pseudo-biblical cantillation.

Reich, Wilhelm (1897–1957) Austrian psychoanalyst. Born in Galicia, he studied at the University of Vienna and joined the Vienna Psychoanalytic Society. He emphasized sexual repression as a source of pathology. An avid communist, he moved to Berlin in 1930 and founded Sexpol which promoted communism and sexual liberation. In 1939 he went to the US.

Reichstein, Tadeus (b. 1897) Swiss chemist. Born in Poland, he grew up in Switzerland. In 1938 he became head of the Institute of Pharmacy at Basle University. In 1950 he shared the Nobel Prize in Medicine and Physiology.

Reifmann, Jacob (1818–95) Polish Hebrew scholar. He engaged in historical and philological research and corresponded with the major scholars of his time. His publications include studies of the Talmud and other areas of Judaica.

Reik, Ḥavivah (1914–44) Palestinian resistance fighter of Slovak birth. She settled in Palestine in 1939. In 1944 she volunteered to join the allied forces as a parachutist. She was dropped into Poland, where she organized radio communications with the allies and Jewish partisan groups, and aided the escape of refugees. She was eventually captured and shot.

Reik, Theodor (1888–1969) Austrian psychoanalyst. Born in Vienna, he practised in Vienna, Berlin and the Hague. In 1938 he went to the US and became president of the National Association for Psychoanalytic Psychology in 1946. His works include *Listening with the Third Ear*.

Reilly, Sidney [Rosenblum, Sigmund Georgeievich] (1874–?1925) British spy. Born in Odessa, he worked in St Petersburg as an arms dealer. During World War I he was a British agent. At the beginning of the Russian Revolution he was stationed in St Petersburg. He was involved in an attempt to assassinate Lenin and fled to England in 1918, but returned to Russia in 1925 to meet with anti-Boshevik groups.

Reina, Joseph della (fl. 15th cent.) Palestinian kabbalist. According to tradition, he attempted to hasten the coming of redemption by breaking the power of the angel Samael, but his failure postponed the event. According to one legend he failed because he took pity on Samael. Another tradition holds that he was too preoccupied with the mystical combination of divine names to carry out the instruction to slay Samael.

Reinach, Joseph (1856–1921) French politician, brother of **Salomon** and **Theodore Reinach**. In 1881–2 he served as head of Léon Gambetta's cabinet, and he later served as a deputy (1893–8; 1906–14). He attempted to establish the innocence of **Alfred Dreyfus**, to which end he published a seven-volume history of the affair. He also wrote works on politics and history, including several on Gambetta.

Reinach, Salomon (1858–1932) French archaeologist and historian, brother of **Joseph** and **Theodore Reinach**. He directed the excavations at Carthage in 1883, and three years later was appointed curator of the French national museums. He lectured at the Louvre School, and from 1902 directed the Musée des Antiquités Nationales de Saint-Germain-en-Laye. He was the author of authoritative works on ancient Greece and the history of religions. He served on the council of the Jewish Colonization Association and on the central committee of the Alliance Israélite Universelle.

Reinach, Theodore (1860–1928) French historian and numismatist, brother of **Joseph** and **Solomon Reinach**. After working as a lawyer, he edited the scholarly journals *La revue des études grecques* (1888–1907) and *La gazette des beaux arts* (1906–28). He taught at the Sorbonne (1894–1901), the *École des Hautes Études* (director of studies from 1903), and the Collège de France (professor of numismatics from 1924). He was a member of the Chamber of Deputies from 1906 to 1914. He was active in the Société des Études Juives, and some of his work deals with Hellenism and Judaism. He also edited the French translation of the works of **Josephus**.

Reines, Isaac Jacob (1839–1915) Lithuanian rabbi and Zionist. He officiated as a rabbi in various Lithuanian centres, evolving a method of talmudic study based on abstract rules of logic. In 1882 at a rabbinical conference in St Petersburg, he advocated the introducton of secular studies into the syllabus of yeshivah training. He was one of the first rabbis to join the Zionist movement, and helped to found the religious Zionist Mizraḥi movement in 1902.

Reinhardt, Max (1873–1943) German producer and director. Born in Baden, Austria, he was an actor and assistant director at the Salzburg State Theatre. In 1894 he went to Berlin to the Deutsches Theatre. In 1903 he began directing, and in 1905 he became director of the Deutsches Theater. When the Nazis came to power, he left Germany and toured Europe; in 1933 he went to US.

Reisen, Abraham [Reyzen, Avrom] (1876–1953) American Yiddish poet and story writer, brother of **Zalman Reisen**. He was born in Koydenev, Belorussia. Initially he wrote tales and simple lyrics. He advocated the recognition of Yiddish as the Jewish national language, and helped to convene the Yiddish Language Conference at Czernowitz in 1908. He travelled throughout Europe and America supporting Yiddish cultural activities. In 1914 he settled in New York, where he contributed to Yiddish papers and magazines.

Reisen, Zalman [Reyzen, Zalman] (1888–1941) Lithuanian Yiddish editor and scholar, brother of **Abraham Reisen**. He was born in Koydenev, Belorussia. In 1915 he moved to Vilna, where he became a leader of the new Yiddish cultural movement. He edited the Yiddish daily *Vilner tog* (1919–39) and was a lecturer in Yiddish and Yiddish grammar at the Folk University and the Vilna Yiddish Teachers' Seminary. His writings include a grammar of Yiddish, a study of the origins of modern Yiddish literature, and a biographical and bibliographical encyclopaedia of Yiddish literature.

Remez [Drabkin], Moshe David (1886–1951) Israeli labour leader, of Russian origin. He settled in Turkey in 1911, and later in Palestine. He was active in the labour movement, serving as secretary-general of Histadrut (1926–36), chairman of the Vaad Leumi (1944–8), and a Mapai member of the Knesset. He served as minister of communications in 1948–50, and minister of education in 1950–1.

Resnick, Judith (1949–86) American astronaut. Born in Cleveland, she grew up in Akron, Ohio. She studied at Carnegie-Mellon University and the University of Maryland. She was a design engineer for RCA, biomedical engineer at the National Institutes of Health, and senior systems engineer for the Xerox Corporation. In 1978 she was selected to become an astronaut. In 1989 she died aboard the US space shuttle *Challenger* when it exploded in space.

Reuben (fl.?19th–16th cent. BCE) Eldest son of **Jacob** and **Leah**. He opposed his brothers' plot to kill **Joseph** (Genesis 37). When **Jacob** learned of Reuben's incestuous relations with **Bilhah**, he transferred his rights as firstborn to Joseph (Genesis 48–49).

Reuter, Paul [Israel Beer Josaphat] (1816–99) German founder of Reuter's Telegraph Company. Born in Kassel, Germany, he was a clerk in his uncle's bank in Göttingen. Later he joined a publishing firm in Berlin; in 1949 he began a carrier pigeon service. In 1851 he went to London and opened a telegraph office. He converted to Christianity and in 1871 was made a baron by the duke of Saxe-Coburg-Gotha.

Reuveni [Reubeni], David (fl. 16th cent.) Italian adventurer. He claimed to be the son of a King Solomon and brother of a King Joseph, who ruled the lost tribes of Reuben, Gad, and half Manasseh in the desert of Habor. After travelling through Palestine and Egypt, he appeared in Venice in 1523. Later he settled in Rome, and Pope Clement VII gave him letters of recommendation. In 1525–7 he lived in Portugal, where he was greeted by marranos (including **Solomon Molcho**) who believed him to be the herald of the Messiah. In 1532 he and **Molcho** appeared before Charles V. **Molcho** was burned at the stake, and Reuveni was taken to Spain where he died. He left a diary which records these events.

Revel, Bernard (1885–1940) American educator and scholar. He was born in Kovno, Lithuania, and settled in the US in 1906. Initially he ran an oil-refining business in Oklahoma. In 1915, as rosh yeshivah, he reorganized the Isaac Elhanan Yeshiva, and in the folowing year founded the Talmudic Academy in New York. In 1928 he founded Yeshiva College which he directed as president. He wrote studies of Targum Jonathan, **Josephus**, Jubilees, the development of ancient exegesis and Karaism.

Reznikoff, Charles (1894–1976) American poet and lawyer. He was born in Brooklyn. He wrote several books on legal and social history, as well as poetry influenced by Jewish literary and liturgical traditions. Some of his work deals with the plight of urban Jews in the US.

Ribalow, Menaḥem (1895–1953) American Hebrew critic and editor. He was born in Chudnov, Volhynia. He studied in Odessa and began to publish poems and essays at an early age. In 1921 he emigrated to the US, where he became editor of the Hebrew weekly *Ha-Doar*, and edited anthologies of American Hebrew literature.

Ribicoff, Abraham (b. 1910) American politician. The son of a Polish immigrant, he established a law practice in Hartford, Connecticut, and later became a member of the House of Representatives, governor of Connecticut, secretary of health, education and welfare, and US senator.

Ricardo, David (1772–1823) English economist. He was born in London. He was a member of the stock exchange until 1814, when he retired to devote his energies to economics. Although he left Judaism when he married a Quaker, he advocated the removal of Jewish disabilities.

Ricchi, Imanuel Ḥai (1668–1743) Italian rabbi, kabbalist and poet. He was born in Ferrara and raised in Rovigo. At the age of 20 he travelled to various Italian cities. He was ordained a rabbi in 1717; the following year he emigrated to Palestine and settled in Safed, where he studied kabbalah. Because of a plague, he left the country and moved to Livorno. He later travelled to Smyrna, Salonica, Constantinople and London, before returning to

Palestine (1737) and finally Livorno. He wrote various kabbalistic works.

Rice, Elmer [Reisenstein, Elmer Leopold] (1892–1967) American writer. Born in New York City, he began to write plays in 1913. He wrote over 50 plays, most of which appeared on Broadway.

Rich, Adrienne (b. 1929) American poet. Her first book of verse, *A Change of World*, was chosen by W. H. Auden for the Yale Younger Poets Award. Later she was Phi Beta Kappa poet at William and Mary College, Swathmore College, and Harvard. Her work includes *Leaflets*, *Diving Into the Wreck*, *Poems: Selected and New* and *A Wild Patience Has Taken Me This Far.*

Richler, Mordecai (b. 1931) Canadian novelist and journalist. He was born in Montreal, and moved to London in the 1950s. His *Son of a Smaller Hero* and *The Apprenticeship of Duddy Kravitz* depict Jewish life in Montreal. In later novels he contrasted Jewish and gentile culture. *Joshua Then and Now* tells the story of a Canadian Jew obsessed with the desire to avenge his defeat in an enounter with an ex-Nazi.

Rickover, Hyman (1900–86) American naval engineer, of Russian origin. Born in Makov, Russia, he was the son of a tailor. He went to the US with his family when he was six. He was commissioned in the US navy; later he studied electrical engineering. During World War II he was in charge of the electrical side of naval shipbuiding. After the war, he conceived the idea of nuclear-powered submarines. He became a vice-admiral.

Ridbaz, Yaakov ([Slutzker Rav] (1845–1913) Russian rabbi. After serving as a rabbi in Russia, he lived in the US from 1900 to 1905. He subsequently emigrated to Palestine, where he founded and directed a yeshivah in Safed.

Riesser, Gabriel (1806–63) German lawyer and politician. He was born in Hamburg. After he was refused permission to practise as a notary in his native city because of his faith, he published a series of memoranda and articles demanding civil equality for Jewry. He became an important advocate of emancipation for German Jews. From 1832 to 1837 he edited *Der Jude*. He was elected to the parliament at Frankfurt am Main in 1848 and was a member of the 1850 'Union' parliament at Erfurt. In 1859 he became the first Jewish judge in Germany.

Rifkind, Malcolm (b. 1946) British politician. Born in Edinburgh, he served as MP for Edinburgh from 1974–97. He was foreign secretary from 1995 to 1997.

Ringelbaum, Emanuel (1900–44) Galician historian. He was born in Buchach, in eastern Galicia, and became a high-school history teacher. Active in the Poale Zion movement, he was sent by the American Jewish Joint Distribution Committee to Zbaszyń in 1938 to direct relief work and collect testimonies from Jews who had been deported there. During World War II he assembled a secret archive of events in the Warsaw Ghetto; it later came to light and constitutes an important source of information on what took place there.

Rivers, Larry [Grossberg, Yitzroch Loiza] (b. 1923) American painter and sculptor. Born in the Bronx, he studied at New York University, and was a figurative artist. In 1951 he began producing sculptures.

Robbins, Jerome (1918–98) American choreographer. He was born in New York. He began his career as a dancer, appearing with the New York City Ballet. His choreography for Broadway shows includes *Fiddler on the Roof.*

Robinson, Edward G. [Goldenberg, Emanual] (1893–1973) American film actor. Born in Bucharest, Romania, he went to the US in 1902. He was a student at the American Academy of Dramatic Art. He appeared in *Little Caesar*, *Five Star Final*, *Dr Ehrlich's Magic Bullet*, *Double Indemnity*, *The Woman in the Window*, *Scarlet Street* and *Key Largo*.

Rodgers, Bernard (1893–1968) American composer and educator. He was born in New York. He taught at the Hart School of Music and at the Eastman School of Music. Some of his work was influenced by biblical themes.

Rodgers, Richard (1902–79) American composer of musicals. He began writing songs at an early age.

He studied at Columbia University, and collaborated with Lorenz Milton Hart on a varsity show. Later they produced a variety of musicals. When Hart died, he collaborated with **Oscar Hammerstein II** on musicals including *Oklahoma!*, *South Pacific*, *The King and I* and *The Sound of Music*.

Rodkinson [Frumkin], Michael (1845–1904) American Hebrew writer and editor. He was born in Dubrovno, Belorussia, and initially wrote tales of the Ḥasidim. He later moved to Königsberg, where he published Hebrew periodicals from 1876 to 1880. In 1889 he settled in the US and devoted himself to translating the Talmud into English.

Rojas, Fernando de (fl. 16th cent.) Spanish marrano author. He was born in Puebla de Montalbán near Toledo. He was the author of one of the earliest Spanish tragedies, *La Celestina*. Members of his family suffered under the Inquistion.

Rokaḥ, Yisrael (1896–1959) Israeli communal leader and politician. He was born in Jaffa. He was a member of the Tel Aviv city council from 1922, the city's deputy mayor from 1929, and major from 1937 to 1953. He was elected to the Knesset in 1949 as a General Zionist member, and later served as minister of the interior (1953–5), and deputy speaker of the Knesset (1957–9).

Romberg, Sigmund (1887–1951) Hungarian composer. Born in Nagy Kaniza, he studied engineering in Vienna. In 1909 he went to the US and became a pianist in a café in New York. Later he became the staff composer for theatrical producers, J. J. and Lee Shubert. Subsequently he formed his own production company with Max R. Wilner. In the 1930s he went to Hollywood where he wrote screen scores. From 1942 he toured the US with his own orchestra; in 1945 he returned to New York.

Rosales, Jacob [Jacob Hebraeus] (c. 1588–c. 1668) Marrano physician and author. He was born in Lisbon, and became a physician there. Later he settled in Rome, where he came under the influence of Galileo. During the 1630s he went to Hamburg. Emperor Ferdinand III bestowed the title of Count Palatine on him in recognition of his scientific achievements. Later he lived as a Jew in Lovorno, assuming the name Jacob Hebraeus. He published works on medicine and astronomy.

Rosanes, Solomon Abraham (1862–1938) Bulgarian historian. He was born in Ruschuk. He was a businessman, but devoted himself to Jewish studies, and during World War I settled in Sofia, where he became librarian of the Jewish community. He published studies of Jewish history, including *A History of the Jews in Turkey and in the Orient.*

Rose, Billy [Rosenberg, William Samuel] (1899–1966) American impresario. Born in New York City, he became a shorthand stenographer. Determined to become a songwriter, he began to write songs. In 1924 he became a nightclub owner. During the 1940s he produced shows. After World War II he wrote a syndicated column and began investing in art and real estate. In 1965 he donated his sculpture collection to Israel.

Rose, Ernestine [Povtovsky, Louise Siismondi] (1810–92) American women's rights activist, of Polish origin. Born in Piotrkow, Poland, her father was an Orthodox rabbi. She renounced Judaism and left Poland. She travelled throughout Europe championing human rights. She later settled in England and was an associate of Robert Owen. Eventually she married William E. Rose and went to the US. She lectured on women's rights, abolition of slavery, temperance and freedom of thought.

Rosen, Joseph (1877–1949) American agronomist. He was born in Moscow, and emigrated to the US in 1903. In 1921 he returned to Russia for the American Jewish Joint Distribution Committee on a relief mission to the Jews. In 1924 he initiated a land-settlement project in the Ukraine and Crimea for Jews who had been deprived of Soviet citizenship. In 1940 he directed Jewish colonization in the Dominican Republic.

Rosen [Rosenblüth], Pinḥas (1887–1978) Israeli and Zionist leader, of German origin. He was born in Berlin. He served as chairman of the Zionist Organization of Germany (1920–3), and, after living in Palestine (1923–5), joined the Zionist Executive in London. In 1931 he returned to Palestine, where he practised law. He was active in the Aliyah Ḥadashah party, and in 1948 he became president of the Progressive Party. From 1949 to 1968 he was a member of the Knesset, serving as minister of justice in successive coalition cabinets (1948–61).

Rosenbach, Abraham Simon Wolf (1876–1952) American bibliophile. He was born in Philadelphia, where later he founded the Rosenbach Company, a rare-book business. He wrote an *American Jewish Bibliography* and a historical study of Congregation Mikveh Israel in Philadelphia. He served as president of the American Jewish Historical society, and was a benefactor of Gratz College.

Rosenbaum, Simon (1860–1934) Polish jurist and Zionist. He was born in Pinsk, and practised law there and in Minsk. Active in the Ḥibbat Zion movement, he was a delegate to the Zionist Congresses until World War I; he was an opponent of the Uganda plan. During World War I, he worked for an independent Lithuania, and later became the country's deputy foreign minister; subsequently he served as minister of Jewish affairs. In 1924 he settled in Palestine, where he was chairman of the Supreme Jewish Peace Court.

Rosenberg, Anna (b. 1902) American public official. Born in Hungary, she went to the US at the age of ten. She was a consultant on labour relations. Later she served as the New York State director for the War Manpower Commission. In 1950 she became US assistant secretary of defence.

Rosenberg, Isaac (1890–1918) English poet and painter. He was born in Bristol. Some of his poetry (such as *Chagrin*) expresses the rootless condition of the diaspora Jew.

Rosenberg, Julius (1918–53) American spy. Born in New York, he and his wife, Ethel Rosenberg, were convicted and executed as spies on the charge of obtaining atomic secrets for the Russians.

Rosenblatt, Joseph (1882–1933) American cantor and composer. He was born in Belaya Tserkov in the Ukraine, and in his youth toured Eastern Europe as a child prodigy. He was initially cantor in Mukachevo, then moved to Bratislava in 1901, and to Hamburg five years later. In 1912 he emigrated to the US where he became ḥazzan of the Ohab Zedek Congregation in New York. He was the most popular cantor of his time. His collection of sacred songs, *Zemirot Yosef*, contains many of his best-known works.

Rosenfeld, Isaac (1918–56) American writer. He was born in Chicago. Some of his essays deal with Jews, Judaism and Jewish life in America and Europe.

Rosenfeld, Morris (1862–1923) American Yiddish poet. He was born in Bolikshein in the Russian part of Poland, and grew up in Warsaw. After learning tailoring in London, he went to New York in 1886, where he worked in a sweatshop. Initially he published socialist poems. In 1894 he began editing a satirical weekly, and in 1905 the daily *New Yorker Morgenblat*. By this time he was recognized as a pioneer of Yiddish poetry and in 1908 he went on a tour of Galicia and Western Europe. He wrote poems on proletarian, national and romantic themes; he also published studies on **Heinrich Heine** and **Judah Ha-Levi**.

Rosenheim, Jacob (1870–1965) Orthodox leader, of German origin. He was born in Frankfurt am Main. He first worked in a bank, and later founded the Hermon Publishing House. In 1906 he transferred publication of the weekly *Israelit* from Mainz to Frankfurt where it became an influential organ of German Orthodoxy. He was a founder and leader of Agudat Israel, of which he was president from 1929. From 1940 he lived in the US and Israel; he helped to secure permission for Agudat Israel to participate in the Israeli government and Knesset. He wrote on various religious themes.

Rosenman, Samuel Irving (1896–1973) American judge. Born in San Antonio, Texas, his family moved to New York City. He studied at Columbia University and became an assemblyman for the 11th district of Manhattan. He later became governor's counsel and subsequently a judge in the state supreme court. He edited the *The Public Papers and Addresses of Franklin D. Roosevelt.*

Rosenthal, Herman (1843–1917) American writer and pioneer of Jewish settlement in the US. He was born in Friedrichstadt, near Kiel, and initially worked as a printer in the Ukraine. During the Russo-Turkish War, he served with the Red Cross. After the pogroms of 1881, he organized a group of 79 people and set out for the US, where he attempted to establish an agricultural settlement for Russian Jews on Sicily Island, near New Orleans. In 1891 he participated in the establishment of an ICA colony in Woodbine, New Jersey. From 1898 he was the head of the Slavonic department of the New York Public Library.

Rosenthal, Leser (1794–1868) German bibliophile and bibliographer. He was born in Nasnelsk, Plock, Russia. He taught at Paderborn, Germany, and later was Klausrabbiner at Hanover. His library contained 32 manuscripts and 6000 printed volumes, including incunabula and rare books.

Rosenwald, Julius (1862–1932) American merchant and philanthropist. He was born in Springfield, Illinois. He first worked in his uncle's clothing store in New York but later opened his own store. He began to manufacture summer clothing and in 1885 moved his business to Chicago. He became president of Sears, Roebuck and Company, and subsequently chairman of the board. He was president of the Associated Jewish Charities of Chicago, and contributed to Jewish war relief during World War I and in the post-war period. He also supported the Hebrew Union College and the Jewish Theological Seminary.

Rosenwald, Lessing Julius (1891–1979) American merchant, bibliophile and philanthropist, son of **Julius Rosenwald**. He was born in Chicago, where he later worked for Sears, Roebuck and Company. In 1943 he helped to found the American Council for Judaism, and served as its president. Opposed to Zionism, he campaigned against the establishment of Israel.

Rosenwald, William (b. 1903) American philantropist and financier, son of **Julius Rosenwald**. He was a director of Sears, Roebuck and company, but later concentrated on his own investments. He was chairman of the national United Jewish Appeal campaign and vice-chairman of the Joint Distribution Committee, and played an important role in the American Jewish Committee and United HIAS service.

Rosenzweig, Franz (1886–1929) German theologian. He was born in Kassel. He studied at various universities, and eventually considered converting to Christianity. After attending an Orthodox high holy day service in Berlin, he embraced Judaism. Later he served in the German army, and he wrote *Star of Redemption* while confined to military hospitals in Leipzig and Belgrade. After returning home he established an institute for Jewish studies, the Freies Jüdisches Lehrhaus, in Frankfurt am Main. In 1921 he became partially paralysed, but he continued to write. Together with **Martin Buber** he translated the Hebrew Scriptures into German.

Rosowsky, Shlomo (1878–1962) Israeli composer. In St Petersburg he was an active member of the Society for Jewish Folk Music. In 1925 he emigrated to Palestine, where he composed music for the Hebrew theatre. Besides composing, he studied Jewish music and published a work on the cantillation of the Bible. He later lived in the US and taught at the Jewish Theological Seminary.

Ross, Barney (1909–67) American boxer. Born in New York City, he grew up in Chicago. He became a professional boxer in 1929, and was world lightweight and welterweight champion.

Rossi, Azariah ben Moses dei [Adummim; Azariah dei Rossi] (c. 1511–c. 1578) Italian scholar. He was born in Mantua, and lived in Bologna, Ferrara, and Mantua. His *Meor Enayim* shows how classical sources cast light on Jewish history and literature in the classical period. In the third part of this work ('Imrei Binah'), he examined ancient Jewish history by comparing Hebrew texts with classical Jewish and non-Jewish sources. He also wrote poetry in Italian, Hebrew and Aramaic. His writings provoked the hostility of a number of rabbis.

Rossi, Salomone de' (fl. 17th cent.) Italian composer. He came from Mantua. He was the leading Jewish composer of the late Italian Renaissance, and a court musician of the Gonzaga rulers of Mantua. In 1587 he entered the service of Duke Vincenzo I as a singer and viola player. Later he became the leader of the duke's musical establishment and directed an instrumental ensemble. He published secular, instrumental and vocal music, including a collection of Hebrew religious songs (*Ha-Shirim Asher li-Shelomoh*).

Rosten, Leo Calvin (1908–97) American humorist. He was born in Lódź in Poland, and went to the US as a child. He later served in the US government. Under his pen name Leonard Q. Ross he wrote *The Education of H*y*m*a*n K*a*p*l*a*n* and *The Return of H*y*m*a*n K*a*p*l*a*n*. He also wrote the *Joys of Yiddish*.

Rotblat, Joseph (b. 1908) British scientist. Born in Warsaw, he was professor of physics at the University of London. He received the Nobel Peace Prize and a knighthood.

Rotenstreich, Natan (1913–93) Israeli philosopher. He was born in Sambor, Poland, and emigrated to Palestine in 1932. In 1955 he became professor of philosophy at the Hebrew University, and later dean of the faculty of humanities and rector. He wrote studies of Jewish thinkers and a survey of modern Jewish thought.

Roth, Cecil (1899–1970) English historian. He was born in London. He was a reader in Jewish studies at Oxford from 1939 to 1964, when he settled in Jerusalem and became visiting professor at Bar Ilan University. His publications include histories of the Jews in England and Italy, Jewish biographies, a history of the marranos, a study of Jews in the Renaissance, and studies of Jewish art. He served as editor-in-chief of the *Encyclopaedia Judaica* from 1966.

Roth, Henry (1906–95) American novelist. He was born in Austria, and went to the US as a child. He worked as a high-school teacher, precision metal grinder and farmer. His *Call it Sleep* deals with Jewish immigrant life in New York's East Side.

Roth, Joseph (1894–1939) Austrian novelist. He was born near Brody in eastern Galicia. He worked from 1923 for the *Frankfurter Zeitung*. Later he lived in Paris. His novel *Job* describes Eastern European Jewish life, and in *Juden auf Wanderschaft* he deals with the social position of Jews in Eastern Europe.

Roth, Leon (1896–1963) English philosopher. He was a lecturer in philosophy at Manchester University from 1923 to 1927. He settled in Palestine and became professor of philosophy at the Hebrew University, rector of the university, and dean of the faculty of humanities. He returned to England in 1951. He wrote philosophical studies, translated philosophical classics into Hebrew, and published a study of the Jewish religion (*Judaism: A Portrait*).

Roth, Philip (b. 1933) American novelist. He was born in New Jersey. Many of his novels and short stories depict the struggle of American Jewish men, especially the conflict between their Jewish background and the attractions of American Christian culture. His writings include *Goodbye Columbus*, *Letting Go*, *Portnoy's Complaint*, *The Anatomy Lesson*, *The Breast*, *My Life as a Man*, *The Ghost Writer*, *Zukerman Unbound*, *The Counterlife*, *The Professor of Desire*, *The Great American Novel* and *Reading Myself and Others*.

Rothenberg, Morris (1885–1950) American Zionist leader. He was born in Dorpat, Estonia, and was taken to the US in 1893. During World War I he was a member of a federal commission charged with fixing the price of bread. In 1937 he became city magistrate of New York. He was a founder and executive committee member of the Jewish Welfare Board, a founder of the Joint Distribution Committee, and an executive committee member of the Council for German Jewry. He also served as president of the Zionist Organization of America.

Rothenstein, William (1872–1945) English artist. He was born in Bradford. He studied in London, Paris and Oxford. During World War I he served as a war artist, and then became professor of civic art at the University of Sheffield. From 1920 to 1935 he was principal of the Royal College of Art. He painted portraits, still-lifes and landscapes, as well as Jewish subjects and synagogue interiors.

Rothstein, Arnold (1882–1928) American gambler. Born in New York, he allegedly fixed the 1919 baseball World Series. He masterminded a gambling empire in the US. With access to unlimited cash, he financied bootlegging, narcotic deals, and bought judges and public officials. He was the inspiration for Meyer Wolfsheim in F. Scott Fitzgerald's *The Great Gatsby*. He was shot over a gambling debt in Park Central Hotel.

Rothko, Mark (1903–70) American artist. Born in Dvinsk, Russia, he went to the US at the age of seven. He studied at Yale and later at the Arts Student League. He taught art to children at a school in Brooklyn and later at Brooklyn College. He painted huge spaces of colour in which floated soft-edged rectangles.

Rothschild, Amschel Mayer (1773–1855) Born in Germany, he took over the running of the parent bank in Frankfurt. In 1816 he and **Salomon Mayer Rothschild** were granted a hereditary title of nobility.

Rothschild, Anthony (1810–76) English communal leader, brother of **Lionel Rothschild**. He lived as a country gentleman and was active in the Jewish community. He served as the first president of the United Synagogue from 1870.

Rothschild, Edmond de (1845–1934) French philanthropist and art collector, son of **James de Rothschild**. He and his wife, Adelaide, were interested in Jewish affairs. When the first Zionist pioneers in Palestine appealed to Rothschild for assistance, he supported the colonization of Palestine. He sent agricultural experts and officials there to help in the settlement process, visited Palestine himself five times (1887, 1893, 1899, 1914, 1925), and purchased 125,000 acres of land in the country. In 1900 he transferred the management of the colonies to the ICA. Later he served as the honorary president of the Jewish Agency.

Rothschild, James de (1792–1868) French banker and communal leader. He settled in Paris in 1812, where he founded the firm Rothschild Frères. A financier to the Bourbon and Orleans kings of France, he later served Napoleon II. From 1840 the Rothschild family was active in the Jewish Consistory of Paris, the Central Consistory of the Jews of France, and the Jewish Charity Committee of Paris. They also played a role in the Damascus Affair.

Rothschild, Karl (1788–1855) Italian banker. In 1821 he founded the Italian branch of the Rothschild family in Naples. He was instrumental in establishing a Jewish community there.

Rothschild, Lionel (1808–79) English banker, brother of **Anthony Rothschild**. He was head of the family banking house at New Court in London. He was elected to parliament as a Liberal in 1847 but took his seat only in 1858, after the passing of the Jews' Disabilities Bill. The character Sidonia in *Coningsby* by **Benjamin Disraeli** is based on him.

Rothschild, Mayer Amschel (1744–1812) German banker. He studied at a rabbinical school in Fürth. He set up in business as a general trader and money-changer. In 1792 he attempted to establish a Jewish school with a modern curriculum. He served as intermediary for Prince William and other members of the royalty. In 1800 he became imperial crown agent. In 1796 he took his two older sons **Amschel Mayer** and **Salomon Mayer** into partnership and later his other boys, **Nathan Mayer**, Carl Mayer and James Mayer also became partners. They subsequently created an international banking syndicate.

Rothschild, Nathan Mayer (1777–1836) Born in England, in 1798 he set up a textile business in Manchester and served as agent for the Frankfurt bank. He expanded his business and established himself as a financier. Later he founded an office in London. In 1815 he became the principal financier to the British government, and eventually he became Austrian consul general in London.

Rothschild, Salomon Mayer (1774–1855) He opened the Rothschild bank in Vienna. He financed the construction of railroads to carry coal from Galicia to Vienna. In 1822 he and his brothers were granted the hereditary title of baron.

Rovina, Hanna (1892–1980) Israeli actress, of Russian origin. She was born in Berezino, Minsk, and first worked as head of an institute for refugee children at Saratov. In 1917 she joined a Hebrew theatrical studio in Moscow and became one of the founding members of the Ha-Bimah Theatre Company. In 1928 she went to Palestine with the company and became the country's leading actress.

Rozin, Joseph [Rogochover Gaon] (1858–1936) Latvian talmudist. He was born in Rogochover, and became rabbi of the Ḥasidic community of Dvinsk in 1889. During World War I he fled to St Petersburg, where he was the rabbi of a Ḥasidic community for ten years. He subsequently returned to Dvinsk. He wrote responsa and a commentary on **Maimonides'** *Mishneh Torah.* His collected works appeared under the title *Tzaphenat Paaneaḥ*

Roziner, Felix (b. 1936) Israeli writer of Russian origin. He was born in Moscow, and lived there until his emigration to Israel in 1978. He worked initially as an engineer, but gave up his job in 1969 to write. His *A Certain Finkelmayer* deals with the Jew as a Russian intellectual. In *The Silver Cord* he depicts seven generations of a Jewish family who migrate from the shtetl to Israel.

Rubens, Bernice (b. 1927) British novelist. She was born in Cardiff. She was first a schoolteacher, and later a writer and director of documentary films. Her early novels (*Set on Edge, Madame Sousatzka, Mate in Three* and *The Elected Member*) deal with middle-class Jewish life.

Rubenstein, Richard L. (b. 1924) American theologian. He was born in New York. He served as chaplain to Jewish students at the University of Pittsburgh, and in 1970 became professor of religion at Florida State University. His writings include *After Auschwitz* and *Approaches to Auschwitz.*

Rubin, Reuven (1893–1974) Israeli artist. Born in Romania, he studied at the Bezalel School of Arts and Crafts. Later he studied at the École des Beaux Arts in Paris. After World War I he lived in Italy, Romania and the US. In 1922 he returned to Palestine. His work is concerned with the landscape in Palestine.

Rubin, Solomon (1823–1910) Galician Hebrew writer. He was born in Dolnia. He became one of the most prolific writers of the Haskalah period, publishing studies of Jewish folklore, customs and superstitions and works about **Spinoza**.

Rubinstein, Anton Grigoryevich (1829–94) Russian pianist and composer. Born in Vykhvatinetz, Podolia, his family moved to Moscow. In 1844 the family moved to Berlin; when his father died the family went to Russia, but Anton spent two years in Vienna giving piano lessons. In 1848 he went to Moscow and with Elena Pavlovna helped found the Russian Musical Society, later the St Petersburg Conservatory. Subsequently he resumed his solo career.

Rubinstein, Artur (1886–1982) Polish pianist. Born in Poland, he gave his first solo performance in Berlin at the age of 11. He moved to the US in 1937. He was a virtuoso and composed works for the piano and chamber music.

Rubinstein, Helena (1871–1965) American cosmetics manufacturer. Born in Poland, she went to Australia at the age of 20 and began marketing cold cream. Later she went to London where she opened her own beauty salon. In 1914 she went to the US. Her innovations included a waterproof mascara, medicated face cream, and the selling technique of home demonstration.

Rubinstein, Ida (1885–1960) Russian dancer. An orphan, she inherited a large fortune. She studied dance with Fokine and also attended a drama school. She was a leading member of the Diaghilev Company. She later formed her own company.

Rubinstein, Isaac (1880–1945) Polish communal leader. He was born in Dotnuva, Lithuania. He was a rabbi in Genichesk, Urkaine, from 1906, and later became the government-appointed rabbi of Vilna. In 1920 he was minister of Jewish affairs in Vilna, and from 1922 to 1939 was a member of the Polish senate. He was also a leader of the Mizraḥi and active in the World Zionist Organization. In 1941 he emigrated to the US and taught at Yeshivah University.

Rukeyser, Muriel (1914–80) American poet, writer and translator. She was born in New York, and taught at Sarah Lawrence College. Her poetry includes works about Rabbi **Akiva**.

Rumkowski, Mordechai (1877–1944) Polish ghetto organizer. He became chairman of the Lodz Jewish Council and was responsible for the ghetto there. In 1944 he and his family were deported to Auschwitz.

Ruppin, Arthur (1876–1943) Palestinian Zionist, economist and sociologist. He was born in Rawicz, in the Posen district, and initially worked in the grain trade. From 1903 to 1907 he directed the Bureau for Jewish Statistics and Demography in Berlin. In 1907 he went to Palestine as a representative of the Zionist Organization. Later he founded various settlement companies and helped to establish labour colonization in the country. He was deported by the Turks in 1916, but returned in 1920. Subsequently he became director of the Zionist Executive's colonization department in Jerusalem. From 1926 he taught sociology at the Hebrew University. His writings include sociological studies of Jewry.

Rutenberg, Pinḥas (1879–1942) Palestinian engineer and Zionist teacher, of Ukrainian origin. He was born in Romny, in the Ukraine. He participated in the 1905 Russian Revolution, and after living for a time in Italy and the US, returned to Russia in 1917. He was again involved in revolutionary activities, but he left Russia in 1919 and settled in Palestine, where he founded the Palestine Electric Company. He was elected chairman of the Vaad Leumi in 1929.

Ruth (fl. 12th cent. BCE) Moabite woman. After her husband, Mahlon, died she went with **Naomi** (her mother-in-law) to Bethlehem, where she married **Boaz**.

Rutherston, Albert Daniel [Rothenstein, Albert Daniel] (1881–1953) English artist and illustrator. He designed an important Haggadah.

Ruzhin, Israel of (1797–1851) Russian Ḥasidic rabbi. He established a Ḥasidic centre at Ruzhin, where he lived in luxury. In 1838 he was accused of giving the order to put to death two Jewish informers. Imprisoned for 22 months, he was later released and settled in Sadagora in Bukhovina, which also became a Ḥasidic centre.

Ryback, Issachar (1879–1935) Russian artist. He was born in Yelizavetgradka in the Ukraine. He helped to establish an art section of the Jewish Cultural League in Kiev. From 1921 to 1925 he lived in Berlin, where he illustrated children's books in Yiddish, and published *The Shtetl and the Jewish Types of the Ukraine*. Later he produced *On the Fields of the Ukraine*. In 1926 he moved to Paris.

Rybakov, Anatolii (b. 1911) Ukrainian writer. He was born in Chernigov, and moved to Moscow in 1919. He was arrested and sentenced to imprisonment in Siberia; after his release in 1935 he worked as a ballroom-dancing teacher, automobile mechanic and driver. Later he served in the army, and began writing. His novel *Heavy Sand* deals with the Russian Jewish past and the Holocaust in the USSR.

S

Saad al-Daula (fl. 13th cent) Persian physician and statesman. He served as a physician in government service in Baghdad, and later became governor of Baghdad and Iraq. In 1289 he was appointed vizier by Arghun, the Mongolian ruler.

Saadyah Gaon [Saadyah ben Joseph] (882–942) Babylonian gaon. He was born in Pithom in the Faiym district of Egypt, and settled in Babylonia in 921. In 928 he became gaon of Sura, but two years later he was deposed by the exilarch **David ben Zakkai**; he was reinstated in 936. His earliest work was a polemic against the Karaite scholar **Anan ben David**. *Beliefs and Opinions* is his main philosophical treatise. His other scholarly works include a translation of the Bible into Arabic, Arabic commentaries on most biblical books, a Hebrew lexicon and grammar, and a list of biblical *hapax legomena.* He also produced a systematic compilation of the prayerbook, and wrote liturgical poetry. His *Sepher ha-Galui* is an account of his personal tribulations.

Sachar, Abram Leon (b. 1899) American educator and historian. He was born in New York. He taught history at the University of Illinois, and later served as national director of the Hillel Foundation (1933–48). In 1948 he became the first president of Brandeis University, subsequently becoming its chancellor. His publications include *History of the Jews* and *A History of Jewish Life Between Two World Wars.*

Sachs, Curt (1881–1959) German musicologist. Born in Berlin, he studied at the University of Berlin. He worked initially as an art critic, but later embarked on musicological studies. He became director of a collection of musical instruments; subsequently he was professor at the Berlin National Academy of Music and the University of Berlin. After the Nazis came to power, he went to Paris, and then moved to the US.

Sachs, Michael Jehiel (1808–1970) German rabbi. Born in Glougau, Silesia. He was a preacher in Prague, and later in Berlin where he also served as dayyan of the bet din. He was an opponent of the Reforming influence of **Samuel Holdheim** and his Berlin congregation.

Sachs, Nelly (1891–1970) German poet. She was hardly known outside Germany before World War II; in 1940 she went to Sweden. Much of her poetry deals with the Holocaust. In 1966 she was awarded the Nobel Prize for Literature.

Sackler, Harry (b. 1883) American Hebrew and Yiddish author. He was born in Bohorodczany, Galicia, and went to the US in 1902. He worked as an attorney and served as an officer of various Jewish organizations. In his stories, novels, plays and essays he recreated Jewry throughout the ages; his novel *Festival at Meron* depicts the period of the **Bar Kokhba** revolt (132–5 CE).

Sacks, Jonathan (b. 1948) English rabbi. He was born in London. He served as principal of Jews College, and in 1991 became chief rabbi of the United Hebrew Congregations of the British Commonwealth. His publications include *Traditional Alternatives, Tradition in an Untraditional Age* and *The Dignity of Difference.*

Sadan, Dov (1902–96) Israeli Yiddish and Hebrew writer. He was born in Galicia, and emigrated to Israel in 1925. He first worked on the newspaper *Davar* and for the Am Oved publishing company. In 1952 he was appointed to teach Yiddish literature at the Hebrew University; he also taught Hebrew literature at Tel Aviv University. He was elected to the Knesset in 1965. He translated many works from Polish, German and Yiddish, and published several collections of literary criticism.

Sadeh, Pinḥas (b. 1929) Israeli writer. He was born in Tel Aviv. He has written a wide variety of genres, including children's books, poetry and literary articles; he has also published an autobiography and a novel.

Sadeh, Yitzḥak [Landsberg, Yitzhak] (1890–1952) Israeli labour and military leader. He was born in Lublin, Poland. He served in the Russian army, then in 1920 left for Palestine, where he became the head of **Joseph Trumpeldor**'s Labour Battalion. In 1941 he organized the Palmaḥ, which he commanded until 1945; later he served on the staff of the Haganah. After the creation of the State of Israel, he commanded the Eighth Armoured Brigade. He published stories, plays and memoirs.

Sahl ben Matzliah (fl. 11th cent.) Palestinian Karaite. He travelled extensively, spreading his teaching. His writings incorporate information on the Karaites and Palestinian Jewry; they include polemics against the rabbis and an Arabic commentary on the Torah.

Saint-Léon, Arthur (1815–70) French dancer and choreographer. Born in Paris, he made his debut at the age of 14. From 1843 he began to choreograph for the ballerina Fanny Cerrito whom he later married. From 1859 he worked at the St Petersburg Imperial Theatre. Later he returned to Paris and was choreographer and ballet-master for the Paris Opera.

Salaman, Nina (1877–1925) English poet, wife of **Redcliffe Salaman**. She translated medieval Hebrew poetry. Her own writings included the collection *Apples and Honey*.

Salaman, Redcliffe (1874–1955) English pathologist and geneticist. He was the director of the Pathological Institute of the London Hospital from 1901 to 1904. In 1926 he became director of the potato virus research station in Cambridge. His writings include *Jewish Achievements in Medicine* and *Racial Origins of Jewish Types*. During World War I he served in Palestine, and published *Palestine Reclaimed*.

Salant, Samuel (1816–1909) Palestinian rabbi, of Polish origin. He was born near Bialystok. He set out for Palestine in 1840, but was delayed in Constantinople, where he met Sir **Moses Montefiore**. In 1841 he reached Jerusalem, where he became rabbi of the Ashkenazi community. In 1878 he became Ashkenazi chief rabbi. He served various Jewish organizations and travelled widely in Europe to collect money for religious institutions in Jerusalem. A number of his novellae were published in talmudic journals.

Salanter, Israel [Lipkin, Israel] (1810–85) Lithuanian scholar. He was born in Zhagory. He founded the Musar movement in Lithuania and Russia from around 1830, and set up 'Musar houses' for the study of ethical literature. He also published a journal, *Tevunah*, to promote his views. His pupils helped to spread the Musar movement, particularly among the Torah students of Lithuania. Salanter also travelled to Western Europe to propagate his ideas. Isaac Belzer collected his ethical writings in *Or Israel*.

Salk, Jonas (1914–95) American scientist. He was a research professor at the University of Pittsburgh. He developed the anti-polio vaccine which is used worldwide. He served as an adviser on virus diseases to the World Health Organization, and founded the Salk Institute for Biological Studies in California.

Salmon, Alexander (1822–66) English settler in Tahiti. He was the son of a London banker, and ran away to sea, reaching Tahiti on a whaler. He married a local native princess. Their daughter was the last queen of the Island. He was a spokesman for the islanders, and went to Paris with a petition to the Emperor Napoleon III.

Salome (fl. 1st cent.) Palestinian princess, daughter of **Herod**'s son **Philip** and **Herodias**. She is identified with the daughter of **Herodias** who was responsible for **John the Baptist**'s death (Matthew 14:3–6; Mark 6:17–29). She married her uncle, the tetrarch **Philip**, and subsequently **Aristobulus**, King of Lesser Armenia.

Salome Alexandra (fl 1st cent BCE) Queen of Judea (76–67 BCE). She succeeded her husband **Alexander Yannai**. Reversing his policy towards the Pharisees, she gave them internal control of the country while retaining responsibility herself for the army and foreign policy. When she appointed her son **Hyrcanus** as high priest and heir, his younger brother **Aristobulus** denounced her action.

Salomon, Gotthold (1784–1862) German preacher and reformer. After an Orthodox education, he was sent to Dessau, where he was influenced by modern trends, such as new approaches to biblical criticims. He became a teacher and preacher in Dessau, and was later appointed rabbi of the Hamburg Reform temple. The publicaton of his new version of the liturgy in 1841 provoked considerable controversy.

Salomon, Haym (1740–85) American patriot, of Polish origin. During the American War of Independence, he was a merchant in New York and was imprisoned by the British authorities for providing supplies and finances to the revolutionary army.

Salomons, David (1797–1873) English banker and communal leader. He was a founder of the joint stock banking system in England. An advocate of the admission of Jews into English public affairs, he was the first Jewish sheriff, alderman and lord mayor of London. He was elected to parliament in 1851, and took his seat without taking the Christian oath; as a result he was ejected, which drew prominently to public attention the problem of Jewish parliamentary disabilities.

Salomons, Julian (1836–1909) New South Wales politician. He emigrated to Australia from Birmingham at the age of 17 and settled in Sydney. He was a lawyer and served on the legislative council and in the office of the solicitor-general. He became chief justice in 1886, but did not take up the appointment. In the 1890s he became agent-general of the colony in London. He was knighted in 1891.

Salten, Felix [Zalzmann, Felix] (1869–1945) Austrian novelist and critic. He was born in Budapest. He lived in Vienna, where he was a contributor to the *Neue Freie Presse.* He also wrote plays, essays and stories, including the famous children's story *Bambi.* His Jewish interests are reflected in his novel *Simson*, and in essays about his visit to Palestine. In 1938 he settled in Hollywood, but after World War II returned to Europe to live in Zurich.

Salvador, Joseph (1797–1873) French historian. He was born in Montpellier. He initially studied medicine, but after settling in Paris he began to work on the history of religions. In *Paris, Rome, Jérusalem, ou la question religieuse au 19e siècle* he propounded a universal creed of religion. He also wrote a history of Roman rule in Judea, a study of the institutions of **Moses** and the Jewish people, and a work about **Jesus**.

Saminsky, Lazare (1882–1959) American composer, of Russian origin. He studied at the University of St Petersburg and with Rimsky-Korsakov at the conservatory there. A founder of the Society for Jewish Folk Music, he went to the Caucasus in 1913 as a member of an ethnological expedition. In 1923 he settled in New York, where he became music director of Temple Emanu-El. He wrote symphonies, including *Jerusalem, City of Solomon and Christ*, liturgical choruses and Hebrew services. His writings include *Music of Our Day, Music of the Ghetto and the Bible* and *Living Music of the Americas.*

Sampter, Jessie (1883–1938) American poet and Zionist writer. She grew up in the US, but later settled in Palestine, where she established evening classes for Yemenite working girls in Jerusalem. In 1920 she helped to organize the country's first camp for Jewish scouts. Subsequently she moved to Reḥovot, where she did social work. In *The Emek* she portrayed kibbutz life in a series of prose poems. She also wrote books, articles and poems about Zionism and Jewish subjects.

Samson (fl. 12th–11th cent. BCE) Israelite judge, son of Manoah of the tribe of Dan (Judges 13–16). He was a Nazirite of enormous strength, but when his mistress Delilah, revealed the secret of his strength as lying in his hair, he fell into the hands of the

Philistines. His hair was cut, his eyes were put out, and he was forced to turn the prison mill. When he was taken to Gaza to be mocked for the entertainment of Philistines at a festival, his strength returned to him and he destroyed the palace, killing all those assembled there.

Samson ben Abraham of Sens (fl. 12th–13th cent.) French tosaphist. During the first Maimonidean controversy (1202), he spoke on behalf of the French rabbis. He opposed the teachings of **Maimonides**' *Mishneh Torah* and attacked his view of resurrection. The founder of the academy at Sens, he was one of the leaders of 300 rabbis who settled in Palestine at the beginning of the 13th century. He wrote talmudic commentaries (*Tosaphot Sens*) and liturgical poetry.

Samuel (i) (fl. 11th cent. BCE) Israelite prophet and judge. He was consecrated as a Nazirite by his mother before his birth, and served in the Sanctuary at Shiloh. There he foretold the destruction of the House of Eli. After the death of **Eli** and his sons, and the defeat of the Israelites by the Philistines, Samuel attempted to restore traditional religious worship. He lived at Ramah and judged the Israelites in Bethel, Gilgal and Mizpah. Later he acceded to the Israelites' demand for a king and selected **Saul**. When **Saul** lost favour with God, Samuel was sent to Bethlehem, where at God's behest he anointed **David** as **Saul**'s successor (I Samuel 1–16).

Samuel (ii) [Mar Samuel] (fl. 1st–2nd cent.) Babylonian amora. He was born at Nehardea, and became head of the academy there. He was acknowledged the outstanding authority on civil law; his debates with **Rav** about halakhic problems are recorded in the Talmud. He was also an expert astronomer, whose opinion on questions concerning the Hebrew calendar was often sought. He was on friendly terms with King Sapor I of Persia.

Samuel, Herbert Louis (1870–1963) British statesman and philosopher. He was born in Liverpool. He entered parliament in 1902, becoming a privy councillor six years later. He served as postmaster-general and later home secretary. From 1920 to 1925 he was the high commissioner for Palestine. He was leader of the liberal party in both the House of Commons (1931–5), and the House of Lords (1944–55). He was also president of the council for German Jewry from 1936 and in 1939 founded the Children's Movement to bring refugee children from Germany to Britain. He wrote various philosophical works.

Samuel, Maurice (1895–1972) American author and translator. He was born in Măcin, Romania, and was taken to England, where he grew up in Manchester. In 1914 he settled in the US. His writings include *You Gentiles*, *I, the Jew*, *Jews on Approval*, *The Great Hatred*, *The Gentleman and the Jew*, *Harvest in the Desert*, *The Second Crucifixion*, *On the Rim of the Wilderness*, *The World of Shalom Aleichem*, *Prince of the Ghetto*, *Certain People of the Book*, *Blood Accusation* and *In Praise of Yiddish*. He translated Hebrew and Yiddish works.

Samuel, Saul (1820–1900) New South Wales politician. His family emigrated from London to New South Wales when he was 12. He engaged in gold mining and cattle ranching. He was the first Jew to be appointed to the legislature of the colony. He served as agent-general in London from 1880 and was knighted in 1882.

Samuel ben Ali ha-Levi (fl. 12th cent.) Babylonian gaon. He was the head of the academy in Baghdad, and engaged in polemics with **Maimonides** about halakhic issues and about **Maimonides**' view of the resurrection of the dead.

Samuel ben Avigdor (1720–93) Lithuanian rabbi. Between 1719 and 1746 he served as rabbi of Pruzhany, Zelwa, Volkovysk and Ruzhany. In 1750 he became rabbi of Vilna, succeeding his father-in-law, Judah ben Eliezer. In 1777 the community decided to remove him from office because he was suspected of nepotism, but a compromise was reached. In 1782 the controversy broke out again, and the dispute was brought before Jewish and gentile courts. Samuel ben Avigdor was dismissed from his post and Vilna was left without a rabbi. He was an ardent opponent of Ḥasidism.

Samuel ben Hophni (fl. 10th–11th cent.) Babylonian gaon. He was appointed gaon of Sura in 997. One of the most prolific writers of the gaonic period, he wrote responsa, talmudic treatises, biblical exegesis, philosophy, theology and polemics.

Samuel ben Meir [Rashbam] (c. 1085–1175) French biblical and talmudic commentator, grandson of **Rashi**. He was born in Ramerupt in northern France, and was a disciple of his grandfather. He engaged in sheep-farming and viticulture. His commentaries expound the simple and natural meaning of the Bible and Talmud texts. He completed **Rashi**'s commentary on Bava Batra and Pesaḥim, and his works were quoted by the tosaphists.

Samuel ha-Katan (fl. 1st cent.) Palestinian tanna. His prayer *Birkat ha-Minim* expresses anathema against Judeo-Christians, sectarians and informers. It was written at the request of **Gamaliel II** and was incorporated into the Amidah.

Samuel ibn Adiya (fl. 6th cent.) Arabian poet. He lived in Tamya in Hejaz, northern Arabia. His poetry is similar to that of other pre-Islamic Arab poets.

Samuel ibn Nagrela [Ha-Nagid; Ibn Nagdela; Ibn Nagrela; Samuel ha-Nagid] (933–1055) Spanish statesman, scholar and military commander. Born in Córdoba, he was forced to flee the city in 1013 and opened a spice shop in Málaga. He joined the staff of King Habbus, the Berber ruler of Granada, and was later appointed vizier of Granada. In 1027 he became the nagid of Spanish Jewry. When Habbus died in 1037, Samuel ibn Nagrela supported his son Badis, taking on the administration of the kingdom and command of the armies. He composed poetry, wrote grammatical works, and completed an introduction to the Talmud. He was also a patron of numerous scholars.

Samuelson, Paul (b. 1915) American economist. Born in Gary, Indiana, he was professor at the Massachusetts Institute of Technology. He was awarded the Nobel Prize for Economics in 1970.

Sandmel, Samuel (1911–79) American biblical scholar. He was born in Dayton, Ohio. He served as a Hillel rabbi at Yale University and was professor of Jewish literature and thought at Vanderbilt University (1949–52). In 1952 he became professor of Bible and Hellenistic literature at the Hebrew Union College. He published studies of **Philo** and the relationship between Judaism and Christianity.

Santa Maria, Paul de [Paul of Burgos; Solomon ha-Levi of Burgos] (c. 1352–1435) Spanish churchman. As Solomon ha-Levi he served as a rabbi in Burgos. After converting to Christianity, he became bishop of Cartagena, and then of Burgos. He was partly responsible for the anti-Jewish legislation enacted in Castile in 1412. His writings include biblical commentaries.

Sapir, Edward (1884–1939) American anthropologist. Born in Lauenberg, Germany, he went to the US at the age of five. He studied at Columbia University and became chief of the Division of Anthropology in the Geological Survey of the Canadian National Museum in Ottawa. Later he became a professor at Yale University. He was a founder of formal descriptive linguistics.

Sapir, Pinḥas (1907–75) Israeli labour leader. He was born in Suwalki, Poland, and in 1924 went to Palestine, where he worked in the citrus groves. He later became head of the Negev settlements' Civil Defence. In 1953 he served as director-general of the ministry of finance and from 1955 he was minister of commerce and industry. He became minister of finance in 1963, and general secretary of the Israel Labour Party and minister without portfolio in 1965; the following year he was again appointed minister of finance.

Sapir [Saphir], Yaakov (1822–85) Palestinian writer and traveller. He was born in Oshmiany in the province of Vilna; he was taken to Palestine in 1832 by his parents, who settled in Safed. In 1836 he moved to Jerusalem, where he became a teacher and scribe. In 1857 he travelled to oriental countries as an emissary of the Perushim community to raise funds for the construction of a synagogue. After returning to Jerusalem he recorded his travels in *Even Sappir*, which contains important information about Yemenite Jews.

Sapir, Yoseph (i) (1869–1935) Moldavian Zionist leader. He was born in Kishinev, and became a doctor. A supporter of Ḥibbat Zion, he founded a publishing house, Di Kopeke Bibliotek, to publish Zionist literature. In 1903 he wrote a popular study of Zionism; he also edited a Russian-language Zionist weekly. After the 1917 Revolution, he became chairman of the South Russia Zionist Organization. Following the Bolsehvik Revolution, he moved to Bessarabia, then to Palestine, where he served as director of a department of the Bikkur Ḥolim hospital in Jerusalem.

Sapir, Yoseph (ii) (1902–72) Israeli communal worker. He was born in Jaffa. He was active in the Farmers' Federation of Israel and worked for the Pardes citrus fruit company. In 1940 he became mayor of Petaḥ-Tikvah, and later he served as a member of the Knesset; he was minister of transportation (1952–5), and minister of commerce and industry. In 1968 he was elected chairman of the Liberal Party.

Sarah (fl. 19th–16th cent. BCE) Israelite woman, wife of **Abraham** and mother of **Isaac**. After many years of barrenness, she gave **Abraham** her maidservant **Hagar**, who bore him a son, **Ishmael**. Later Sarah gave birth to **Isaac**. She is one of the four matriarchs of Judaism.

Sarasoh, Kasriel Hersch (1835–1905) American newspaper proprietor. He was born in Russia, and was active as a rabbi and merchant before settling in the US in 1871. He founded the weekly *Die New Yorker yiddishe zeitung* and *Die yiddishe gazetten*, which paved the way for the first Yiddish daily paper in the US, the *Yiddishes tageblatt*. He also published a Hebrew weekly (*Ha-Ivri*), and was a founder of HIAS.

Sarna, Nahum (b. 1923) American scholar. Born in London, he served as professor at Brandeis University. His works include *Understanding Genesis, Exploring Exodus, Commentary on the Book of Exodus, Commentary on the Book of Genesis, A New Translation of the Book of Psalms* and *A New Translation of the Book of Job*.

Sarnoff, David (1891–1971) American broadcasting executive, of Belorussian origin. Born in Minsk, Belorussia, he went to the US with his family in 1901. He worked as an office boy at Commercial Cable Company. Later he became commercial manager at the Marconi Wireless and Telegraph Company of America. Subsequently he became president of RCA, and eventually chairman and chief executive officer.

Saruk, Israel (fl. 16th–17th cent.) Egyptian kabbalist. He created his own version of **Isaac Luria**'s doctrines. From 1594 to 1600 he propounded his views in Italy and founded a school of kabbalists. Subsequently he lived in Ragusa and Salonica. He produced various kabbalistic works.

Sasportas, Jacob (1610–98) North African rabbi. He was born in Oran, North Africa. He became rabbi of the Tlemcen community, and subsequently wandered throughout Europe. In 1664 he became Ḥakham in London, and later in Amsterdam. He was a critic of **Shabbetai Tzevi**, and in his *Tzitzat Novel Tzevi* reprinted certain Shabbetaian letters and pamphlets with his responses to their teaching.

Sassoon, David Solomon (i) (1792–1864) Indian businessman and philantropist. He took over his family businesss in Baghdad. In 1828 he went to Bushehr on the Persian Gulf, and later settled in Bombay. There he built a synagogue, contributed to various cultural and welfare organizations, helped to publish a Judeo-Arabic newspaper, and supported Jewish scholarship. In 1863 he built a synagogue in Poona, where he had his summer residence.

Sassoon, David Solomon (ii) (1880–1942) English Hebraist and bibliophile, son of **Flora Sassoon**. His collection included 1000 Hebrew and Samaritan manuscripts. His writings include *History of the Jews of Baghdad*.

Sassoon, Edward (1856–1912) English communal leader, grandson of **David Solomon Sassoon (i)**. In 1899 he was elected to parliament as a member of the Conservative Party. He was involved in various aspects of English Jewish life.

Sassoon, Flora (1859–1936) English Hebrew scholar, daughter-in-law of **David Solomon Sassoon (i)**. Initially she managed her husband's firm in Bombay; later she settled in England. In 1924 she gave a discourse on the Talmud at Jews College, and subsequently she published an essay on Rashi in the Jewish Forum.

Sassoon, Siegfried (1886–1967) English poet. He entered the British army in 1914 and was wounded and sent back to Britain. When he recovered, he was sent back to serve in Palestine and France. After the war he became literary editor of the socialist newspaper, the *Daily Herald*. His poems reflect the ugliness of the war. His works include *Memoirs of a Fox-Hunting Man* which described the English countryside and country life.

Satanov, Isaac (1732–1804) German Hebrew writer. He was born in Satanov, Podolia, and in 1771 settled in Berlin, where he was the director of a printing press of the Society for the Education of the Young. He wrote a Hebrew–German dictionary and thesaurus, studies of the liturgy, a collection of proverbs, an encyclopaedia of arts and sciences, and commentaries on **Maimonides**' *Guide for the Perplexed* and **Judah ha-Levi**'s *Kuzari*.

Saul (fl. 11th cent. BCE) King of Israel. He was the first king of Israel, selected by **Samuel** in response to the request of the people for a king. He organized an army, and undertook expeditions against the Philistines, Moabites, Ammonites and Arameans. Eventually a rift developed between Saul and **Samuel** (I Samuel 13); Saul persecuted **David** after his triumph over Goliath and drove him from the country. Saul fell in battle against the Philistines on Mount Gilboa together with three of his sons (I Samuel 8–II Samuel 3).

Saville, Victor (1897–1979) British film director. Born in Birmingham, he worked as manager of a Coventry film theatre. Later he worked in the features and newsreels department of Pathé Frères. Subsequently he became a film distributor in Leeds and helped found Victory Motion Pictures. Later he formed a production company, Burlington Film Company. During the 1930s he was a director for Gaumont-British and also worked with the London Film Productions of **Alexander Korda**. From 1939 he was associated with MGM in Hollywood.

Schaeffer, Susan Fromberg (b. 1941) American novelist and poet. She was born in Brooklyn, and taught at Brooklyn College. Her novel *Falling* deals with a young Jewish woman who attempts suicide. In *Anya* she tells the story of a victim of the Holocaust.

Schalit, Heinrich (1886–1976) American composer and organist. He was born in Vienna, and lived in Munich, where he was organist at the Munich Liberal synagogue. In 1932 he wrote *Freitagabend Liturgie*, a complete Sabbath Eve Service. He emigrated to the US and served various Jewish congregations. In 1948 he moved to Evergreen, Colorado. His works on Jewish themes include *Chassidic Dances*, *Builders of Zion*, *Sabbath Morning Liturgy* and *Songs of Glory*.

Schapira, Hermann Tzevi (1840–98) Lithuanian Zionist. He was born in Erswilken, and was initially rabbi and rosh yeshivah in a Lithuanian townlet. He later lived in Kovno, Berlin and Heidelberg, where he taught mathematics at the university. After the pogroms in Russia in 1881 he joined the Ḥibbat Zion movement, and was a delegate to the First Zionist Congress in 1897. At the Congress he proposed the foundation of the Jewish National Fund and the Hebrew University.

Schapiro, Israel (1882–1957) American bibliographer, orientalist and librarian. He was born in Sejny, Poland. From 1907 to 1910 he taught at the Jerusalem Teachers Training College. He then emigrated to the US and in 1913 he was appointed head of the Semitic division of the Library of Congress in Washington; he also lectured on Semitics at George Washington University from 1916 to 1927. He left his post at the Library of Congress in 1944, and in 1950 he settled in Israel. He published studies of Jewish history and bibliography.

Scharfstein, Zevi (1884–1972) Amerian Hebrew educator and publisher, of Ukrainian origin. He devoted himself to educational work and was the head of a Hebrew school in Tarnów, Galicia, from 1900 to 1914. After settling in the US, in 1916 he became an instructor at the Teachers Institute of the Jewish Theological Seminary in New York, where subsequently he became a professor of Jewish education. He published educational texts dealing with Hebrew language and literature, Jewish education and the Bible.

Schary, Dore (1905–80) American film producer. Born in Newark, New Jersey, he worked as a newspaperman and stage actor, director and writer. Later he wrote screenplays. In 1938 he joined MGM, winning an Academy Award for *Boys Town*. Later, he was in charge of low-budget productions. Eventually he became head of RKO. Subsequently he wrote plays for the theatre. In 1970 he became New York's first commissioner of cultural affairs.

Schatz, Boris (1867–1932) Palestinian painter and sculptor, of Lithuanian origin. He was born in Varna, in the province of Kovno. He studied sculpture in Paris, and in 1895 became court sculptor to Prince Ferdinand of Bulgaria. At the Zionist Congress of 1905 he proposed the idea of an art school in Palestine. In 1906 he went to Jerusalem, where he established the Bezalel School of Arts and Crafts. He produced sculptures dealing with Jewish religious practices, biblical subjects and Jewish leaders.

Schechter, Solomon (1847–1915) British rabbinic scholar. He was born in Foscani, Romania. He became tutor in rabbinics to **Claude Montefiore** in London; in 1890 he became a lecturer in rabbinics at Cambridge University, and two years later reader. He was also professor of Hebrew at University College, London, from 1899. During this time he discovered the Cairo Genizah, the contents of which he took to Cambridge. In 1901 he was appointed president of the Jewish Theological Seminary of America. His writings include *Studies in Judaism* and *Some Aspects of Rabbinic Judaism.*

Scheftelowitz, Isidor (1876–1934) British orientalist, of German origin. He was born in Sandersleben, in the Duchy of Anhalt. He worked at the British Museum in London and at the Bodleian Library in Oxford. In 1908 he returned to Germany and until 1926 was a rabbi and teacher of religion in Cologne; in 1923 he became professor of Sanskrit and Iranian philology at Cologne University. He later settled in England and taught at Oxford University. He published studies of Sanskrit and Iranian philology and history, as well as comparative religion.

Scheiber, Alexander (1913–85) Hungarian rabbi and scholar. He was born in Budapest, and became a professor and director of the Budapest Jewish Theological Seminary. He wrote studies of Jewish history, Jewish literature, comparative folklore, Jewish liturgy, bibliography and Jewish art.

Schenck, Joseph (1878–1961) American film producer. Born in Rybinsk, Russia, he went to the US as a child. He worked as an errand boy, and later owned drugstores in partnership with his brother. Together they later founded Loewe's exhibition company with Marcus Loewe. He then was an independent producer. In 1924 he became chairman of the board of United Artists. In 1933 he helped found Twentieth Century Pictures with Darryl F. Zanuck.

Schenirer, Sarah (1883–1935) Polish educationalist. Born in Kraków, Poland, she worked as a seamstress and became concerned with the lack of education for Orthodox women. During World War I she went to Vienna, but returned to Kraków in 1917 and opened a school in her home. In 1918 Agudat Israel adopted the programme for schools for girls. Under the name Bais Yaakov, it developed a network of institutions. In 1923 Schenirer began to train teachers for these schools. She also founded the Bnos Youth Organization.

Schiff, David Tevele (fl. 18th cent.) German rabbi. He was born in Frankfurt am Main. He served as maggid in Vienna, head of the bet midrash in Worms, and dayyan in Frankfurt. In 1765 he became rabbi of the Great Synagogue in London. A volume of his responsa, *Leshon Zahav*, was published by his son.

Schiff, Jacob Henry (1847–1920) American financier and philanthropist. He was born in Germany, and went to the US in 1885, where he became head of the banking firm of Kuhn, Loeb and Co. He was a founder of the American Jewish Committee, and contributed to a wide range of secular and Jewish organizations.

Schiff, Meir [Maharam] (1605–41) German talmudist. He was born in Frankfurt am Main. He was rabbi of Fulda, where he also directed a yeshivah. His novellae on the Talmud are recorded in *Maharam Schiff.*

Schick, Bela (1877–1967) American paediatrician, of Austrian origin. He studied at the University of Vienna where he became assistant professor. From 1923 he was director of the Pediatric Department of Mount Sinai Hospital in New York and was also professor of diseases of children and Columbia University.

Schildkraut, Rudolph (1862–1930) German actor. He was born in Istanbul, and grew up in Romania. He was an actor in Vienna, Hamburg and Berlin. In 1911 he settled in America, where he appeared in the Yiddish theatre; later he acted in German and English productions in the US.

Schiller-Szinessy, Solomon Mayer (1820–90) British scholar, of German origin. He was born in Altofen. He had a faculty appointment in Hebrew at Eperjes, where he also served the local community as its rabbi. In 1845 he attacked the Reform resolutions brought before the Frankfurt Rabbinical Conference. He was appointed rabbi of Manchester in 1851 and later taught talmudic and rabbinic literature at Cambridge University. His publications include the *Catalogue of Hebrew Manuscripts Preserved in the Cambridge University Library.*

Schindler, Alexander (b. 1925) American Reform leader. He was born in Munich, but left Germany in 1932, eventually settling in the US. He served in various congregations and became president of the Union of American Hebrew Congregations. In 1976 he became chairman of the Conference of Presidents of Major American Jewish Organizations.

Schipper, Ignacy (1884–1943) Polish historian and communal worker. He was born in Tarnów, Galicia. He was a member of the General Zionists from 1922. From 1922 to 1927 he served as a deputy in the Polish Sejm. Later he lectured on the history of Jewish economy at the Institute of Jewish Sciences in Warsaw. His writings include *The Economic Conditions of Medieval Polish Jewry*, *The History of Jewish Economy* and *History of Jewish Theatrical Art and Drama.*

Schlesinger, John (b. 1926) British film director. He began as an actor. His films include *A Kind of Loving*, *Billy Liar*, *Darling*, *Far from the Madding Crowd*, *Midnight Cowboy*, *Sunday Bloody Sunday*, *Marathon Man*, *Madame Sousatka* and *Pacific Heights.*

Schlettstadt, Samuel ben Araon (fl. 14th cent.) Alsatian rabbi. He was born in Schlettstadt and became rabbi of Strasbourg. After sentencing an informer to death, he was forced to flee from Strasbourg because of a controversy surrounding the affair. He lived in a castle near Colmar, and later wandered to Babylonia and Jerusalem, before eventually returning to Strasbourg. He wrote an abridgement of *The Book of Mordecai* by **Mordecai ben Hillel**.

Schlossberg, Joseph (1875–1971) American journalist and trade union leader. He was born in Belorussia and emigrated to the US with his family when he was a child. He worked in the sweatshops of New York and was prominent in the Garment Workers' Union. In 1913 he was elected secretary of the Brotherhood of Tailors and in 1914 was a member of the group which seceded from the United Garment Workers of America to form the Amalgamated Clothing Workers of America. After his retirement in 1940 he devoted himself to community and Zionist affairs.

Schnabel, Artur (1882–1951) Austrian pianist. Born in Lipnik, Austria, he went to Vienna with his family at the age of seven. He taught music in Berlin. With the rise of Nazism, he went to Switzerland and later settled in the US. He achieved renown for his interpretation of Beethoven, Mozart and Schubert.

Schneersohn, Isaac (1879–1969) French communal leader. He was born in Kamenets-Podol'skiy in the Ukraine. He was a crown rabbi in Gorodnya from 1906. Later he settled in France, where he founded the Centre de Documentation Juive Contemporaines during World War II. He also encouraged the establishment of a memorial to the unknown Jewish martyr in Paris; this initiative came to fruition in 1956.

Schneersohn, Menaḥem (1902–94) American Ḥasidic leader, of Russian origin. Born in Nikolayev, Russia, he went to the US as a young man. He married the daughter of the sixth Lubavitcher rebbe, and in 1950 became the seventh Lubavitcher rebbe. His headquarters on Eastern Parkway, Brooklyn served as a centre of pilgrimage. Many of his followers regarded him as the Messiah.

Schneiderman, Harry (1885–1975) American administrator. He was born in Saven, Poland, and went to the US in 1890. From 1909 he was a member of the staff of the American Jewish Committee and from 1914 to

1928 he served as its chief administrator. He was also editor of the *American Jewish Year Book* (1920–48).

Schneiderman, Rose (1882–1972) American labour union organizer. Born in Saven, Russian Poland, she went to the US at the age of eight. She worked in stores and later in the garment industry. In 1906 she helped found the National Women's Trade Union League, and became general organizer of the International Ladies Garment Workers' Union. In 1937 she became secretary of the New York State department of labour.

Schnitzler, Arthur (1862–1931) Austrian playwright and author. Initially he practised medicine in Vienna, only later devoting himself to writing. His views about the position of Jews in modern society are found in the play *Professor Bernhardi* and the novel *Der Weg ins Freie.*

Schocken, Gustav Gershom (1912–90) Israeli publisher. He was the owner and chief editor of *Ha-Aretz* from 1939, and director of the family publishing house in Israel. He served in the Knesset from 1955 to 1959.

Schocken, Shelomoh Salman (1877–1959) German Zionist, publisher and bibliophile. He was born in Margonin, in the province of Posen. A collector of rare books and manuscripts, he established the Research Institute for Medieval Hebrew Poetry in 1929 in Berlin, which transferred to Jerusalem in 1936. He also founded a publishing house in Berlin, branches of which were later opened in Tel Aviv and New York. In 1934 he went to Jerusalem, but he eventually settled in the US.

Schoenberg, Arnold (1874–1951) Austrian composer. He was born in Vienna, and held teaching positions in Vienna, Berlin and Amsterdam. In 1924 he settled in Berlin. He left Germany in 1933, and lived in the US. His compositions include the opera *Moses and Aron*, the psalm *De profundis* to the original Hebrew words, and two works for chorus, speaker and orchestra – *Kol Nidre* and *A Survivor from Warsaw.*

Schoffman, Gerson (b. 1880) Israeli novelist. He was the editor of literary journals in Poland and Austria, before settling in Palestine in 1938. He published novels and short sketches.

Scholem, Gershom Gerhard (1897–1982) Israeli scholar. He was born in Berlin, and emigrated to Palestine in 1923, where he worked as a librarian in the Judaica collection at the Hebrew University. Subsequently he was appointed professor of Jewish mysticism at the university. His writings include *Major Trends in Jewish Mysticism, The Messianic Idea in Judaism and Other Essays in Jewish Spirituality* and *From Berlin to Jerusalem.*

Schor, Ilya (1904–61) American artist and silversmith, of Polish origin. He studied in Warsaw and Paris. In 1941 he settled in the US, where he worked as a silversmith, creating religious objects, and as a book illustrator. His art reflects Eastern European Jewish life.

Schorr, Joshua Heshel (1818–95) Galician scholar, editor and leader of the Haskalah. He was born in Brody, and worked as a merchant there. In 1852 he established the periodical *He-Ḥalutz*, which he edited until 1887. In numerous articles he espoused religious and social reform. He engaged in satirical diatribes against Orthodox Judaism, and scholarly polemics against talmudic and rabbinic law. To the Jewish masses of Eastern Europe he became a symbol of heresy.

Schorr, Moses (1874–1941) Polish rabbi and scholar. He was born in Przemýsl, Galicia. He was appointed a lecturer in Jewish religious studies at the Jewish Teachers Seminary in Lemberg in 1899. He eventually became professor of Semitic languages and ancient history at Lemberg University, and later taught at Warsaw University. In 1928 he was one of the founders of the Institute for Jewish Studies, which served as the rabbinical seminary of Poland; he taught there and became the institute's rector. In 1935–8 he was a member of the Polish Sejm. He wrote studies of Polish Jewish history, Semitic history and philology, and the history of Babylonian and Assyrian culture.

Schreiber, Abraham Samuel Benjamin [Ketav Sopher] (1815–75) Hungarian rabbi, son of **Moses Sopher**. He succeeded his father as head of the Pressburg yeshivah, and became a leading critic of religious reform. He was known as 'Ketav Sopher' after his collection of responsa, Bible commentaries, and talmudic glosses of that name.

Schreiner, Martin (1863–1926) Hungarian scholar. He was born in Nagyvárad. He was a rabbi in Csurgó (1887–92), and an instructor at the Jewish Teachers Training Institute in Budapest (1892–4). From 1894 to 1902 he was a professor at the Lehranstalt für die Wissenschaft des Judentums in Berlin. He spent the rest of his life in a sanatorium. He wrote studies of the Islamic influence on medieval Jewish thought, interfaith polemics, Jewish philosphy and Karaism.

Schulberg, B. P. (1892–1957) American film producer. Born in Bridgeport, Connecticut, he studied at City College of New York. He became an editor of *Film Reports*, and later worked as a script editor. He later worked for **Adolph Zukor**'s Famous Players company. By 1928 he was in charge of Paramount's coast production. Subsequently he was a producer for Columbia.

Schulman, Kalman (1819–99) Polish Hebrew writer. He was born in Stari Bichov, Belorussia, and in 1843 settled in Vilna, where he worked as a tutor. Later he taught Hebrew language and literature in the high school attached to the state rabbinic school. He eventually devoted himself to literary work. His writings, including translations, were intended to spread the Haskalah. He also published a history of Palestine and its environs.

Schulmann, Eleazar (1837–1904) Lithuanian Hebrew writer. He was born in Salantai, Lithuania, and lived in Odessa and Kiev. Financially independent, he devoted himself to research, publishing studies of Yiddish language and literature.

Schulz, Bruno (1892–1942) Polish writer. Born in Drohobycz, he studied at the Academy of Art in Vienna. He commenced writing in the early 1920s. His works include *Sklepy Cynamonowe* and *Sanatorium pod klepsydra.*

Schwab, Moise (1839–1918) French scholar. He was born in Paris. He served as secretary to **Salomon Munk** (1857–66), then from 1869 worked at the Bibliothèque Nationale. He translated the Palestinian Talmud into French, and described the Hebrew manuscripts and incunabula in the library of the Alliance Israélite Universelle and other libraries. His writings include *Abravanel et son époque* and *Historie des Israélites.*

Schwabe, Mosheh David (1889–1956) Israeli scholar, of German origin. He was born in Halle. After World War I he was head of the department of schools in the Lithuanian ministry of Jewish affairs. In 1925 he settled in Jerusalem, where he taught at the Hebrew University; he served there as dean of the faculty of humanities and rector. He was an authority on Greek and Greco-Jewish inscriptions.

Schwartz, Delmore (1913–66) American poet, author and critic. He was born in Brooklyn. He became a member of the literary-political group centred on the journals *Partisan Review* and *Commentary.* From 1940 to 1947 he taught at Harvard and Princeton universities. His writings include *Genesis*, which depicts the Jewish immigrant's experience of America.

Schwartz, Joseph J. (1899–1974) American communal leader and scholar. He was born in Russia, and went to the US in 1907. During World War II he negotiated the rescue of Jews from Germany and the occupied territories. After the war he directed the transfer of Jews to Israel from Europe, North Africa and the Middle East; he also helped Jewish refugees emigrate to the US, Canada and Latin America. He served as director-general of the American Jewish Joint Distribution Committee, vice-chairman of the United Jewish Appeal, and vice-president of the State of Israel Bond Organization.

Schwartz, Maurice (1860–1960) American Yiddish actor. He was born in the Ukraine, and went to the US in 1901. In 1918 he launched the Jewish Art Theatre in New York. He subsequently acted throughout the Yiddish-speaking diaspora. In 1960 he went to Israel to establish a Yiddish art centre.

Schwarz, Adolf (1846–1931) Hungarian rabbi and scholar. He served as a rabbi at Karlsruhe from 1875, then in 1893 he became head of the Israelitsch-Theologische Lehranstalt in Vienna. His writings include studies of talmudic hermeneutics.

Schwarz, David (1845–97) Hungarian inventor. Born in Hungary, he worked as a lumber merchant in Zagreb, Croatia. He invented the rigid airship. Later he went to Russia and became an engineer. He built his first airship in aluminum in 1892.

Schwarz, Joseph (1804–65) Palestinian rabbi and Palestinographer. He was born in Floss, Bavaria, and settled in Jerusalem in 1833. His publications include maps of Palestine and a descriptive geography of the country.

Schwarzbard, Shalom (1886–1938) Russian Yiddish poet. He was born in Izmail, Bessarabia. He was active in the revolutionary movement of 1905, and in 1906 fled from Russia to Paris, where he worked as a watchmaker. In World War I he served in the French Foreign Legion, but in 1917 he returned to Russia, where he joined the Red Guard. In 1920 he went on a mission to Paris to assassinate Simon Petlyura, who had carried out pogroms in the Ukraine. His autobiography *Inem Iloyf fun yoren* describes his experiences.

Schwarz-Bart, André (b. 1928) French author. He was born in Metz, and served in the Free French Army before the liberation. His novel *The Last of the Just* reinterprets the Jewish legend of the 36 righteous men (lamed vav) in terms of the martyrdom of European Jewry.

Schwarzbart, Isaac Ignacy (1888–1961) Polish Zionist leader. He was born in Chrzanów, Galicia. He was the founder in 1929 of the World Union of General Zionists and served as its chairman. In 1938 he helped to establish a committee to co-ordinate the activities of the Zionists in western Galicia and Silesia. In the same year he was elected to the Polish Sejm. During World War II he was a member of the Polish government-in-exile in Paris and London. From 1946 he lived in the US, where he was active in the World Jewish Congress. His memoir *Between the Two World Wars* describes Jewish life in Kraków.

Schwarzschild, Stephen (1924–89) American scholar. Born in Frankfurt, he studied at the Hebrew Union College in Cincinnati, Ohio. In 1948 he returned to Germany to serve as a rabbi and later was a rabbi in the US. He was a professor at Washington University in St Louis and served as editor of the journal *Judaism.*

Schweid, Eleazar (b. 1929) Israeli scholar. He was born in Jerusalem, and became a professor at the Hebrew University. He published studies in the field of Jewish philosophy and Hebrew literature.

Schwinger, Julian (b. 1918) American physicist. Born in New York, he studied at Columbia University. Later he became a professor at Harvard. In 1965 he was awarded the Nobel Prize for Physics for his work on quantum electrodynamics.

Sciaky, Leon (1893–1958) Greek-American writer. He was born in Salonica, and went to New York in 1915. His novel *Farewell to Salonika* deals with the Jewish community of his birthplace.

Segal, George (b. 1924) American sculptor. He was born in New York. He began as a painter, then integrated freestanding plaster sculptures with his paintings, and eventually worked in sculptural forms alone. Some of his works refer to his Jewish background, and others to biblical subjects. He has also produced sculpture based on the Holocaust.

Segal, Lore (b. 1928) American novelist. She was born in Vienna. She taught creative writing at the University of Illinois at Chicago Circle. Her novel *My First American* explores the experiences of Jews and blacks. She has also written a collection of Bible stories, *The Book of Adam to Moses.*

Segal, Mosheh Tzevi Hirsch (1876–1968) Israeli Hebraist and Bible scholar. He was born in Myshad, Lithuania. He was a journalist in London, then in 1901 moved to Oxford, where he was minister to the Jewish congregation. In 1918 he went to Palestine as a member of the Zionist Commission. He settled there and became professor of Bible and Semitic Languages at the Hebrew University. His writings include *Grammar of Mishnaic Hebrew, Introduction to the Hebrew Bible* and *The Pentateuch: Its Composition and Authorship.*

Segall, Lasar (1891–1957) Brazilian painter, of Lithuanian origin. He was born in Vilna, and settled in Brazil in 1923. His works on Jewish themes include *Pogrom*, *Ship of Emigrants* and *Concentration Camp*.

Segrè, Emilio (1905–89) Italian physicist. During the 1930s he helped Enrico Fermi with his research into the neutron bombardment of uranium atoms. Later he bombarded molybdenum with deuterons and located small quantities of element number 43. In 1938 he emigrated to the United States and worked at the University of California. In 1959 he shared the Nobel Prize for Physics for the discovery of antiprotons.

Segrè, Joshua ben Zion (c. 1705–c. 1797) Italian dayyan and rabbi. He was born in Casale Monferrato. He was engaged as a children's tutor in Scandiano, but pretended to be a fully qualified rabbi, claiming to have graduated from the Mantua yeshivah; this led to a dispute with the rabbis under whose authority he worked. His *Asham Talui* is a polemic against Christianity.

Seixas, Gershom Mendes (1746–1816) American communal leader. He was the first Jewish minister to have been born in the US. In 1768 he became ḥazzan of Congregation Shearith Israel in New York. During the American Revolution, he moved to Connecticut, and then to Philadelphia, but in 1784 he returned to New York. He was one of the 13 clergy to participate in George Washington's inauguration.

Seligman, Joseph (1819–80) American banker. He emigrated to the US from Bavaria at the age of 18. He created a clothing business together with his brothers. They set up a branch in San Francisco, and with the profits embarked on banking in New York. In 1864 the banking house of J. and W. Seligman and Company was established.

Seligmann, Caesar (1860–1950) German leader of Liberal Judaism. He was born in Landau, and became the preacher of the Liberal synagogue in Hamburg in 1889. He then officiated as a rabbi in Frankfurt am Main (1902–39). In 1910 he published a two-volume prayerbook, and from 1910 to 1922 he edited the periodical *Liberales Judentum*. In 1929 he helped to publish the unified prayerbook, which included traditional and newly composed Liberal prayers. Among his other publications are a collection of lectures and a history of the Reform movement. He moved to London in 1939.

Seligsberg, Alice (1873–1940) American social worker. Born in New York, she was in charge of the American Zionist unit that went to Palestine in 1918. From this beginnning, she helped to develop Hadassah's medical programme. She was national president of Hadassah (1920–1).

Seligson, Esther (b. 1942) Mexican novelist. She was editor of the bi-monthly review of Jewish culture *Aqui estamos* in Oaxaca. Some of her writings deal with Jewish subjects.

Sellers, Peter (1925–80) British actor. Born in Portsmouth, he worked at a seaside theatre in Devon. He then served in the Royal Air Force. After World War II, he began to work in comedy, and later on radio. With Spike Milligan and Harry Secombe he produced *The Goon Show*. He subsequently appeared on film in *The Ladykillers* and *I'm All Right Jack*. By 1960 he was in Hollywood and appeared in *Lolita*, *Dr Strangelove*, *The Pink Panther* and *What's New Pussycat?*.

Selznick, David O. (1902–65) American film producer. Born in Pittsburgh, he and his brother, Myron, became Hollywood agents. In 1926 he worked at MGM as a script-reader. He then moved to Paramount, later becoming RKO's vice president in charge of production. In 1933 he returned to MGM before forming his own company, Selznick International. His films include *Gone with the Wind*.

Senator, Ronald (b. 1926) English composer. He was born in London. He became professor of music at London University, the University of Europe, and the Guildhall School of Music. His works on Jewish themes include *Kaddish fur Terezin*.

Senior, Abraham (c. 1412–c. 1493) Spanish courtier. During the reign of Henry IV he was chief tax officer of Castile. From 1476 he was rabbi to the Jews of Castile and the assessor of Jewish taxes. He was appointed treasurer of the Hermandad, a military organization, in 1488. He eventually converted to Christianity.

Sereni, Enzo (1905–44) Italian pioneer of settlement in Palestine. He was born in Rome, and was one of the first in Italy to support settlement in Palestine. He went to Palestine in 1927, and worked on an orange grove. Initially a pacifist, he joined the British army during World War II. As a parachutist, he was dropped in occupied Italy, captured and killed. His writings include *Arabs and Jews in Palestine* and *The Holy Spring.*

Serkes, Joel ben Samuel [Baḥ] (1561–1640) Polish codifier. Her served as a rabbi in Polish and Lithuanian communities. His *Bayit Ḥadash* is a commentary on the *Arbaah Turim* of **Jacob ben Asher**. He also wrote responsa and talmudic glosses.

Serlin, Yoseph (b. 1906) Israeli politician of Polish origin. He emigrated to Palestine in 1933 and was a founder of the General Zionist Party there. Elected to the Knesset in 1946, he served as deputy speaker (1951–2), and minister of health (1952–5).

Seter [Starominsky], Mordekai (1916–94) Israeli composer. He was born in Novorossik, Russia. He went to Palestine in 1926 and taught at the Israel Academy of Music in Tel Aviv. His compositions include *Sabbath Cantata, Tikkun Hatzot* and *The Legend of Judith.*

Setzer, Samuel Hirsch (1882–1962) American Yiddish and Hebrew journalist, of Polish origin. He was the literary editor of **Naḥum Sokolov**'s Hebrew journal *Ha-Tzepihirah* in Warsaw. Later he served as editor-in-chief of the Warsaw daily newspaper *Der Telegraph.* He lived in New York from 1912 to 1960, when he settled in Israel. He wrote studies of the German socialist writer **Lassalle, Judah ha-Levi**, the **Baal Shem Tov** and **Naḥman of Bratzlav.**

Seymour, David [Chim] (1911–56) American news photographer. He was the son of a Warsaw publisher of Hebrew and Yiddish books. He studied in Leipzig, and covered the Spanish Civil War. He later joined Robert Capa and Cartier-Bresson to form Magnum Photos in Paris.

Sforno, Obadiah ben Jacob (c. 1470–c. 1550) Italian biblical commentator. He taught Hebrew to Johannes Reuchlin in Rome (1498–1500). After living in various cities, he settled in Bologna, where he helped to re-establish a Hebrew printing house and organize the Jewish community. He founded and ran a bet midrash there. He wrote commentaries on the Pentateuch, Song of Songs, Ecclesiastes, Psalms, Job, Jonah, Habakkuk and Zechariah. He also wrote a commentary on Avot, a number of grammatical works, and a philosophical treatise.

Shabbazi, Shalom (fl. 17th cent.) Yemenite Jewish poet. He lived in a period of persecution and messianic expectations among the Yemenite Jews. According to legend he was a tzaddik and miracle worker. His poetry deals with exile and redemption, the Jewish people and God, wisdom and ethics, the Torah, and the after-life.

Shabbetai ben Meir ha-Cohen [Cohen, Shabbetai; Shak] (1621–62) Lithuanian rabbi. He was born in Amstivov near Vilkaviškis, and became dayyan in the bet din of Moses Lima in Vilna. He published *Siphte Kohen*, a commentary on *Yoreh Deah.* The alternative name, Shak, by which he was known, is derived from the initials of the title *Siphte Kohen.*

Shabbetai Tzevi (1626–76) Turkish scholar and pseudo-messiah. He was born in Smyrna. He devoted himself to talmudic and kabbalistic studies. In 1665 he met **Nathan of Gaza**, who recognized him as the Messiah and became his prophet; in December of that year Shabbetai proclaimed himself the Messiah in the synagogue at Smyrna. The Jewish world was seized with enthusiasm. He went to Constantinople in 1666 to claim his kingdom from the sultan, but he was arrested and imprisoned at Abydos, which his followers regarded as the Migdal Oz (Tower of Strength) of the kabbalah. Eventually Shabbetai was summoned to appear before the sultan and adopted Islam to save his life. His apostasy caused great dismay, but a number of his followers (Shabbetaians) believed that his conversion was part of the divine plan.

Shabtai, Jacob (1934–81) Israeli novelist and short-story writer. His most famous work, *Zikron Devanim*, describes nine months in the protagonist's life, beginning and ending with a death; despite its somber theme it is notable for its wit and penetrating insight.

Shaffer, Peter (b. 1925) English dramatist. He was born in Liverpool, and first worked as a coalminer. He spent some time in the US, where he worked at the New York Public Library. Later he was active as a literary and music critic in London. His play *The Salt Land* is set in a kibbutz in Israel. In *Yonadah* he adapted *The Rape of Tamar* by **Dan Jacobson**.

Shaḥam, Natan (b. 1925) Israeli author. He was born in Tel Aviv. He served with the Palmaḥ during the War of Independence, and later joined kibbutz Bet Alpha. He wrote fiction, plays and stories for children.

Shahar, David (b. 1926) Israeli novelist. He was born in Jerusalem, and took part in the War of Independence. A number of his stories deal with the childhood recollections of a narrator who lived in Jerusalem under British Mandatory rule. Between 1969 and 1986 he published a series of five novels, *The Palace of Shattered Vessels.*

Shahin (fl. 14th cent.) Persian poet. He lived in Shiraz. He based his work on the Bible; his *Sepher Sharḥ Shahin al ha-Torah* is a poetical paraphrase of the Pentateuch.

Shahn, Ben (1898–1969) American painter and graphic artist. He was born in Kovno, Lithuania. He settled in the US, but later travelled to Europe and North Africa. He made an early series of paintings based on the Dreyfus Affair. His later works include *Concentration Camp* and *This Is Nazi Brutality*. He also published works based on Hebrew letter forms and commissions for the decoration of synagogues.

Shaikevitch [Shomer], Nahum Meir (1849–1905) Russian Yiddish novelist and dramatist. Born in Nesvizh, Belorussia, he settled in Pinsk. He wrote Hebrew short stories and longer narratives, as well as about 200 Hebrew lyrics. Later he moved to Vilna, where he wrote novels of suspense, and plays for the Yiddish stage. His plays were produced in the US, where he settled in 1889.

Shaked, Gershon (b. 1929) Israeli scholar. He was born in Vienna, and settled in Palestine with his family at an early age. From 1959 he taught Hebrew literature at the Hebrew University. He published various studies of Hebrew literature and drama.

Shallum (fl. 8th cent. BCE) King of Judah (747 BCE) He slew Zechariah, son of **Jeroboam II** and seized the throne (II Kings 23:29–34). He was subsequently killed and succeeded by **Menaḥem**.

Shaltiel, David (1903–69) Palestine Haganah commander. Born in Germany, he joined the Haganah in Palestine. He was a founder of Shai, and later served as Haganah's chief of intelligence. During the War of Independence, he was commander of the Etzioni brigade and Jewish area commander in Jerusalem. He later served as Israeli ambassador to the Netherlands.

Shamgar (fl. 13th cent. BCE) Israelite judge. He defeated the Philistines, killing 600 men with an ox-goad (Judges 3:31)

Shamir, Mosheh (b. 1921) Israeli author. He was born in Safed. He served in the Palmaḥ in 1944–5, and later was a member of the Knesset. He edited various Hebrew literary magazines. His works include novels describing Israel's struggle for independence and historical novels, which make indirect criticism of modern Israel.

Shamir, Yitzḥak (b. 1915) Israeli statesman. He was born in Ruzinoy, Polland. He emigrated to Palestine in 1935 and joined Irgun Tzevai Leumi. He later helped to reorganize the Central Committee of the Loḥame Ḥerut Yisrael. He was elected to the Knesset in 1973 and has served as foreign minister, vice-premier and prime minister.

Shammai (fl. 1st cent. BCE) Palestinian rabbi. He was a contemporary of **Hillel**, and together they were the last of the zugot. He adopted a rigorous standpoint in moral and religious matters. The School of Shammai later disputed legal issues with the School of Hillel.

Shapero, Harold (b. 1920) American composer. He was born in Lynn, Massachusetts, and became professor of composition at Brandeis University in 1952. Some of his works deal with Jewish themes.

Shapey, Ralph (b. 1921) American composer. Born in Philadelphia, he taught at the University of Chicago since 1964 and was conductor of the Contemporary Chamber Players.

Shapira, Abraham (1870–1965) Palestine shomer. He was head of the shomrim guarding Petaḥ Tikvah in 1890. In May 1921 he led the defence of Petaḥ Tikvah against Arab attack.

Shapira, Constantin Abba (1840–1900) Russian Hebrew poet. He lived in St Petersburg, where he worked as a photographer. He converted to Christianity, but wrote Hebrew poetry and intended to settle in Palestine and return to Judaism. He died before he was able to carry out these plans.

Shapira, Moses William (c.1830–84) Polish dealer in antiquities. He was born a Jew but converted to Christianity. He dealt in antiquities in Jerusalem. In 1882 he offered what he claimed to be ancient manuscripts of parts of Deuteronomy to the British Museum. When they were pronounced forgeries by C.S. Clermont-Ganneau, Shapira committed suicide.

Shapira, Mosheh Ḥayyim (1902–70) Israeli politician. He was born in Grodno, Belorussia. He was a founder of the Mizraḥi youth movement. He settled in Palestine in 1925 and served on the executive of the Jewish Agency. After the founding of the State of Israel he represented the Ha-Poel ha-Mizraḥi in the Knesset, serving as minister of immigration, the interior, religious affairs, social welfare and health.

Shapiro, Harry (1902–90) American anthropologist. Born in Boston, he became curator in the department of anthropology of the American Museum of Natural History; from 1942 served as curator and chairman of the department. He was also professor of anthropology at Columbia University from 1943. His book *The Jewish People* deals with the racial origins of the Jews.

Shapiro, Harvey (b. 1924) American poet and editor. He was born in Chicago. He was editor of the *New York Times Book Review* from 1975 to 1983. His poetry is influenced by Jewish and, in particular, Ḥasidic themes.

Shapiro, Karl Jay (1913–2000) American poet and novelist. Born in Baltimore, he taught at the University of California, Davis and wrote *The Place of Love, Person, Place and Thing, V-Letter and Other Poems, Poems of a Jew* and *Adult Bookstore.*

Shapiro, Lamed (1878–1948) Polish Yiddish short-story writer. He was born in Rzhischev, in the district of Kiev. He lived in Warsaw, where he came under the influence of **Isaac Leib Peretz**. In 1906 he went to the US, but he returned to Warsaw and worked for the Yiddish newspaper *Der fraynd.* Later he settled in Zurich, and finally in the US. He wrote stories about Eastern European pogroms and Jewish life in New York; he also published a study of Yiddish literature and language.

Shapiro, Phineḥas (fl. 18th cent.) Polish Ḥasidic writer He lived in Koretz. A pupil of the **Baal Shem Tov**, he wrote *Midrash Pinḥas.*

Sharansky, Natan [Shcharansky, Antaloy] (b. 1948) Israeli human rights activist, of Russian origin. He trained as a mathematician, but Israel's near defeat in the Yom Kippur War of 1973 provoked him into political activity. His ardent campaigns on behalf of Soviet refuseniks led to his imprisonment in 1978. After serving eight and a half years of a 13-year sentence, he was released. He emigrated to Israel to join his wife, Avital, a constant campaigner for the rights of Soviet Jews. Subsequently, he became involved in Israeli politics.

Sharef, Ze'ev (1906–84) Israeli politician. He was born in Izbor, Bukovina, and settled in Palestine in 1925. In 1948 he became secretary of the Emergency Committee and the National Administration which laid plans for Israel's civil service. From 1948 to 1957 he was first secretary of the government of Israel. Later he became director of the state revenues. As a member of the Knesset he served as minister of commerce and industry, minister of finance and minister of housing.

Sharett [Shertok], Moshe (1894–1965) Israeli statesman and Zionist leader, brother of **Yehudah Sharett**. He was born in Kherson, in the Ukraine, and settled in Palestine in 1906. Active in socialist circles, he became head of the Jewish Agency's political department in 1933. He was a leader of the campaign against the policy set out by the British in the White Paper of 1939. In 1946 he was interned at Latrun. Later he was appointed foreign minister of the provisional government of Israel, and led the Israeli delegation to the United Nations Assembly (1949–50). He subsequently served as foriegn minister, and from 1953 to 1955 was prime minister. He was appointed chairman of the executive of the Jewish Agency in 1961.

Sharett [Shertok], Yehudah (1901–79) Israeli composer, brother of **Moshe Sharett**. He was born in Kherson, in the Ukraine, and went to Palestine as a child. He composed music, including children's songs, for his kibbutz, and published the *Yagur Passover Seder Service.*

Sharon, Ariel (b. 1929) Israeli soldier and politician. He was born in Kephar Malal. He joined the Haganah, fought in the War of Independence, and later led a commando group. In the Six Day War his brigade broke through the Egyptian positions. In 1969 he was appointed GOC Southern Command, and in the Yom Kippur War he commanded a division. He was elected to the Knesset in 1973, and served as minister of agriculture, minister of defence and prime minister.

Shaw, Irwin (1913–84) American novelist. Born in New York, he studied at Brooklyn College. He worked as a journalist and later went to Europe where he wrote novels, short stories and plays. In the 1930s he wrote screenplays, radio scripts and stories for the *New Yorker*. His works include *The Young Lions.*

Shazar, Zalman (1899–1974) Born in Mir, Belorussia, he studied at the Academy of Jewish Studies in St Petersburg. In 1907 he joined the Poale Zion and edited its publications. He was arrested by tsarist authorities and imprisoned for his Zionist activities. During World War I he edited *Jüdische Rundschau* and organized the labour movement in Germany. He migrated in 1924, and was an editor of the labour daily, *Davar* and later its editor-in-chief. He was a member of the Palestinian Jewish delegation to the 1947 United Nations General Assembly. He was elected to the Knesset and served as minister of education and culture. In 1963 he became president of Israel.

Shemaiah (i) (fl. 5th cent. BCE) Israelite false prophet. During the rebuilding of the walls of Jerusalem, Shemaiah was hired by **Tobiah** and **Sanballat** to persuade **Nehemiah** to hide from his enemies in the Temple; their plan was to expose him as an irreligious coward (Nehemiah 6:10), but **Nehemiah** saw through Shemaiah and refused to follow his advice.

Shemaiah (ii) (fl. 1st cent. BCE) Palestinian rabbi. He was head of the Sanhedrin in Palestine. He and **Avtalyon** were the fourth of the zugot.

Shemi, Yechiel (b. 1922) Israeli artist. Born in Haifa, his early works utilized local materials: stone and wood. Later works take into account the environment where they are placed.

Shenhar [Shenberg], Yitzḥak (1905–57) Israeli author. He was born in Voltshisk, on the border of Galicia and the Ukraine, and settled in Palestine in 1921. From 1942 he was an editor for the publisher Schocken. His novels deal with Jewish life in Eastern Europe and Israel. He also translated works from European literature into Hebrew.

Shephatiah ben Amittai (fl. 9th cent.) Italian liturgical poet and religious leader. He lived in Oria in southern Italy. When **Aaron ben Samuel** came to Italy, he passed on to Shephatiah kabbalistic secrets which Shephatiah used in performing deeds, as recorded in the *Chronicle of Ahimaaz.* In about 873 Shephatiah travelled to Constantinople to plead for the annulment of anti-Jewish decrees. His poem *Yisrael Nosha* is included in the Neilah service on the Day of Atonement in the Ashkenazi liturgy.

Sherira Gaon (906–1006) Babylonian gaon. He was gaon of Pumbedita (968–98) in succession to his father, Ḥanina, and his grandfather, Judah. With his son **Hai Gaon**, Sherira maintained contact by means of responsa, with Jews in North Africa, Spain and elsewhere. In an important epistle in response to an inquiry from Kairouan, he described the origins of the Mishnah and the Talmud and the traditions of the sevoraim and the geonim. He also wrote commentaries on the Bible and talmudic tractates. During the last years of his life he was imprisoned by the caliph Kadir.

Sheshbazzar (fl. 6th cent. BCE) Israelite administrator. In 538 BCE he was appointed by Cyrus II, King of Persia, as governor over Judah. He was entrusted with the Temple vessels, which he took from Babylon to Jerusalem, and also laid the foundations for the construction of the Second Temple (Ezra 1:8, 11; 5:14–16)

Shestov, Lev [Schwarzman, Lev Isakavich] (1866–1938) French philosopher, of Ukrainian origin. He was born in Kiev. He lived in France after the Russian Revolution of 1917. In 1922 he became professor of Russian philosophy at the University of Paris. His writings include *Speculation and Revelation* and *Athens and Jerusalem.*

Shimoni [Shimonovitz], David (1886–1956) Israeli poet, of Russian origin. He was born in Bobruisk, in the district of Minsk. He settled in Palestine in 1909, but later went to Germany to study, and returned to Russia at the outbreak of World War I. In 1921 he moved permanently to Palestine and taught at the Herzliyyah secondary school. He wrote poetry, parables, satires, meditations and memoirs.

Shin Shalom [Shapira, Shalom (b. 1904) Israeli poet of Ukrainian origin. He was the son of the Ḥasidic rabbi of Drohobycz. From 1914 to 1922 he lived in Vienna, and then settled in Palestine. He wrote mystical religious poetry, an autobiographical novel, stories and plays. He also translated the sonnets of Shakespeare into Hebrew.

Shinwell, Emanuel (1884–1986) British politician. Born in London, he joined the Garment Workers' Union and later became a member of the Independent Labour Party. Subsequently he became president of the Glasgow Trades Union Congress. In 1922 he was elected to parliament. From 1950–1 he was minister of defence.

Shitreet, Bekhor Shalom (1895–1967) Israeli politician. He was born in Tiberias. He was commander of the police in Lower Galilee and between 1935 and 1948 served as a magistrate in several towns. After the establishment of the State of Israel, he served as minister of police and minister of minorities, as a representative of Sephardi and Oriental communities. Subsequently he was a member of the Knesset for Mapai.

Shlonsky, Avraham (1900–73) Israeli poet. He was born in Karyokov, in the Ukraine. He settled in Palestine in 1921, and in 1928 joined the staff of the newspaper *Ha-Aretz.* In 1943 he joined the editorial staff of the journal *Mishmar,* and subsequently edited the quarterly *Orlogin.* Associated with the Mapam party, he participated in the activities of the international world peace movement of the 1950s. From the 1950s he criticized the Soviet attitude to Israel and Jewish culture in the USSR. In addition to writing poetry, he translated classics from several languages into Hebrew.

Shmeruk, Chone (b. 1921) Israeli Yiddish scholar. He was born in Poland and emigrated to Palestine as a young man. From 1961 until his retirement he was professor of Yiddish literature at the Hebrew University. He was the chief editor with H. H. Paper of the complete edition of the works of **Sholem Aleichem**, and co-editor of *The Penguin Book of Modern Yiddish Verse.*

Shneersohn, Dov Ber of Liubavich (1773–1827) Russian Ḥasidic leader. He was the successor of Shneour Zalman of Lyady. He founded the Ḥabad settlement at Hebron in Palestine, and advocated the establishment of Jewish agricultural settlements in Kherson province, in the Ukraine.

Shneersohn, Joseph Isaac (d. 1952) Russian Ḥasidic leader. He was imprisoned for his religious activities, and after his release in 1927 moved to Otwock in Poland. Later he emigrated to the US and settled in New York, where he founded yeshivot and schools in the Ḥabad tradition.

Shneersohn, Menaḥem Mendel (1789–1866) Russian Ḥasidic leader. He was the successor of **Dov Ber Shneersohn** of Liubavich (who was his father- in-law). He composed the halakhic work *Tzemaḥ Tzedek.*

Shneour Zalman (1886–1959) Russian Hebrew author. He was born in Belorussia, and lived in Vilna, Berlin, Paris, the US and Israel. In his poetric cycle *Luḥot Genuzim* he criticized the moral development of Judaism as found in biblical literature. His collections of stories *Peoples of Shklov* and *Noah Pandre* deal with Jewish life in the Pale of Settlement.

Shneour Zalman (ben Baruch) of Lyady (1747–1813) Russian Ḥasidic leader, founder of the Ḥabad movement. The pupil of **Dov Ber of Mezhirich,**

he joined the Ḥasidim at the age of 20. In 1777 he succeeded Menaḥem Mendel of Vitebsk as the movement's leader, and became involved in controversy with the mitnaggedim. He was arrested by the Russian authorities and imprisoned in St Petersburg; although he was released, he was later rearrested. In 1804 he settled in Lyady. His teaching emphasized a rational approach and stressed the importance of study and contemplation. He wrote a liturgy, a code of laws, a mystic commentary on the Pentateuch, and a kabbalist work, *Likkute Amarim* (also known as the *Tanya*).

Shochat, Israel (1886–1961) Founder of Hashomer. Born in Belorussia, he went to Palestine in 1904. He created a group of Jewish guards who to protect the yishuv. In 1907 he was a founder of Bar-Giora which was superseded by Hashomer chaired by Shochat. During World War I he was exiled by Ottoman authorities. In 1920 Hashomer was replaced by the Haganah.

Shofman, Gershon (b. 1880) Russian Hebrew writer. Born in Russia, he lived in Galicia and Austria, and went to Palestine when he was nearly 60. He is known for short stories, sketches and essays.

Shoham [Polakevich], Mattathias (1893–1937) Polish author. He lived in Warsaw. He wrote plays based on the conflict between Judaism and idolatry, sensualism and spirituality, and war and peace.

Sholem Aleichem [Rabinovitz, Solomon] (1859–1916) Ukrainian Yiddish author. He was born in Pereyaslav, and began writing novels, poems and plays at an early age. In 1888–9 he published the literary annual *Die yidishe folksbiblyotek*. He subsequently created the character of Tevye the milkman, who exemplifies the experience of Jewish life in Eastern Europe. He supported himself entirely by writing between 1900 and 1906, when he went to New York. He returned to Europe the following year. Many of his stories are set in an imaginary place called Kasrilevke, which was modelled on Voronkov, where he spent his childhood.

Shtif, Nochum [Baal Dimyon] (1879–1933) Ukrainian Yiddish critic and philologist. He was born in Rovno, Volhynia, and settled in Berlin in 1922. He was one of the founders of the Yiddish Scientific Institute (YIVO) in Vilna in 1925. From 1926 he was in charge of the work of the linguistic section of the Institute for Yiddish Proletarian Culture in Kiev. Eventually he was appointed to the chair of Yiddish at the Kiev State Academy.

Sidgwick, Cecily Ullman (1855–1934) British novelist, of German origin. She wrote short stories and novels dealing with Jewish characters.

Sieff, Israel Moses (1889–1972) English industrialist and Zionist. He was born in Manchester. He was a collaborator of **Chaim Weizmann** and served as secretary of the Zionist Commission to Palestine in 1918. In 1934 he founded the Daniel Sieff Research Institute at Rehovot. He contributed to various Zionist organizations.

Sieff, Rebecca (1890–1966) English Zionist, wife of **Israel Moses Sieff**. She was born in Leeds. She was a founder of the Woman's International Zionist Organization (WIZO) in London in 1920 and served as its president until 1963.

Siegel, Benjamin [Bugsy] (1906–47) American gangster. Born in New York, he bossed his own criminal gang at the age of 14. He joined **Meyer Lansky** to form a gang which sold protection, engaged in robbery and hijacking, and handled killings for bootleg gangs. In the 1930s he went to California to operate the syndicate's West Coast operations. During the war years he borrowed syndicate money to build the Flamingo in Las Vegas.

Silbermann, Eliezer Lipmann (1819–82) Prussian Hebrew journalist and editor. He lived in Lyck in East Prussia, where he worked as a shoḥet and cantor. He started the first Hebrew newspaper, the weekly *Ha-Maggid*, in 1856, and in 1862 helped to found the periodical *Mekitze Nirdamim*.

Silberschlag, Eisig (1903–88) American Hebrew poet and critic.He grew up in Metri, Galicia. After emigrating to the US, he became professor in Hebrew literature at the Hebrew Teachers College in Boston. He published poetry, wrote critical studies in Hebrew and English, and translated Greek classics.

Silkin, Jon (b. 1930) English poet. In 1952 he founded the magazine *Stand*, and in 1958 he was appointed to a poetry fellowship at Leeds University. His works include *Peaceable Kingdom*, *Nature with Man*, *The Psalms with their Spoils* and *Footsteps on a Downcast Past.*

Silkiner, Benjamin Nahum (1882–1933) American Hebrew poet. He was born in Vikija, Lithuania. He went to the US in 1904 and later taught at the Teachers Institute of the Jewish Theological Seminary in New York. He published texts for Hebrew schools, helped to produce an English–Hebrew dictionary and wrote narrative poetry.

Silva, Antonio José da (1705–39) Portuguese playwright. He was born in Rio de Janeiro, Brazil, and was of Converso origin. He moved to Lisbon, and studied at the University of Coimbra. While he was a student he wrote a satire, which led to his arrest; he was charged with Judaizing, but was later released. He became an important Portuguese dramatist. He was arrested by the Inquisition in 1737 and killed two years later.

Silva, Francisco Maldonado da [Nazareno, Eli] (c. 1592–1639) Chilean marrano martyr. He worked as a physician in Chile, where he converted to Judaism, circumcised himself, and adopted the name Eli Nazareno. He was arrested by the Inquisition, but continued to practise Jewish rites even in prison. He was burned at an auto-da-fé in Lima.

Silva, Samuel da (fl. 16th–17th cent.) Portuguese marrano physician. He was born in Oporto, but settled in Hamburg, where he lived as a Jew. He translated the section on repentance from the Mishneh Torah of **Maimonides** into Spanish. Later he wrote a reply to **Uriel da Costa**'s criticism of the Jewish tradition entitled *Treatise on the Immortality of the Soul.*

Silver, Abba Hillel (1893–1963) American Reform rabbi. He was born in Sirvintos, Lithuania, and was taken to the US in 1902. He served as a rabbi in Wheeling, Virginia, and Cleveland, Ohio. In 1938 he became chairman of the United Palestine Appeal and joint chairman of the United Jewish Appeal. He led the meetings of the American Zionist Emergency Council in 1943, and later was appointed chairman of the American section of the Jewish Agency. His writings include *History of Messianic Speculation in Israel from the First Through the Seventeenth Centuries*, *The Democratic Impulse in Jewish History*, *Religion in a Changing World*, *Where Judaism Differed* and *Therefore Choose Life.*

Silverman, Morris (1894–1972) American Conservative rabbi. He was born in Newburgh, New York. He served as rabbi of Mount Sinai Temple in Brooklyn (1917–20) and Emanuel Synagogue in Hartford, Connecticut (1923–61). He was active in various spheres of Jewish life and edited a series of prayerbooks.

Silverman, Samuel (1895–1968) British politician. Born in Liverpool, he studied at Liverpool University. He was a lecturer in English at the University of Helsinki. Later he worked as a solicitor and entered local politics. In 1932 he became a city councillor in Liverpool. Subsequently he entered parliament. He campaigned for the abolition of capital punishment for nearly 30 years.

Simeon (i) (fl. ?19th–16th cent. BCE) Israelite, second son of **Jacob**. To avenge the rape of his sister **Dinah**, he and **Levi** tricked the citizens of Shechem, captured the town, killed the male inhabitants, and took the women and children captive (Genesis 34).

Simeon (ii) (fl. 1st cent.) Palestinian Zealot leader, known as Simeon son of Judah the Galilean. He and his brother Jacob led the Zealots after their father's death. They were captured and crucified by the procurator Tiberius Julius Alexander.

Simeon ben Eleazar (fl. 2nd cent.) Palestinian tanna. A contemporary of **Judah ha-Nasi**, he lived in Tiberias. He is mentioned only infrequently in the Mishnah, but plays an important role in the Tosephta. He was a noted halakhist, aggadist and polemicist.

Simeon ben Gamaliel I (fl. 1st cent.) Palestinian nasi. He was leader of the Sanhedrin at the time of the destruction of the Second Temple in 70 CE. When the revolt against Rome began, in 66, he was among its leaders, but he later adopted a moderate policy. He is listed among the Ten Martyrs.

Simeon ben Gamaliel II (fl. 2nd cent.) Palestinian nasi, son of Rabban **Gamaliel II** of Jabneh and father of **Judah ha-Nasi**. After the Romans destroyed the house of the nasi in revenge for the **Bar Kokhba** revolt (132–5), he was one of the few survivors. He was forced to go into hiding, but later became nasi of the Sanhedrin at Usha. Many of his decisions are quoted in the Mishnah and the Tosephta.

Simeon ben Isaac ben Abun [Simeon the Great] (d. c.1015) German liturgical poet. He lived in Mainz. Many of his hymns are included in the Ashkenazi liturgy, notably that for the New Year. According to legend, he was the father of the pope Elhanan.

Simeon ben Lakish [Resh Lakish] (fl. 3rd cent.) Palestinian amora. In his youth he sold himself to men who hired participants in gladitorial contests. According to legend, **Johanan bar Nappaḥa** persuaded him to study the Torah, and gave him his sister in marriage. Eventually Simeon became one of the most important sages in the Tiberias academy.

Simeon ben Setaḥ (fl. 1st cent. BCE) Palestinian scholar. He was active during the reign of **Alexander Yannai** and **Salome Alexandra** (who was his sister). He and **Judah ben Tabbai** together formed one of the zugot. He was largely responsible for ensuring that the Pharisees were dominant in public and private life during the Second Temple period; he managed to change the Sanhedrin into a Pharisaic body.

Simeon ben Yohai (fl. 2nd cent.) Palestinian tanna. He was among the five pupils of Akiva who survived the failure of the **Bar Kokhba** revolt (132–5). When he expressed politicial opinions which were regarded by the Romans as seditious, he was forced to flee for his life; he is said to have hidden in a cave for 13 years. He was noted as a miracle worker, and was sent on a mission to Rome, where he succeeded in obtaining the withdrawal of a persecutory decree against the Jews. The authorship of the Zohar has been attributed to him, and he is frequently quoted in the Mishnah by his pupil **Judah ha-Nasi**.

Simeon ha-Tzaddik (fl. ?4th–2nd cent.) High priest. He played an important role in the Keneset Gedolah, which formulated the liturgy, estabished the canon of Scripture, and formed the Sanhedrin. Scholars have suggested that he belonged to the Hasideans and supported the Seleucids. He has also been credited with ensuring the central role of study in the Jewish tradition and stemming the influence of Hellenization.

Simḥah ben Samuel of Vitry (d. 1105) French scholar. He was a pupil of **Rashi**. He compiled the *Maḥzor Vitry*, which is regarded as an authoritative source for the prayerbook, synagogue customs and the hymnology of medieval French Jewry.

Simon, Ernest Akiva (1899–1973) Israeli educator and writer, of German origin. He was born in Berlin, where he co-edited the monthly journal *Der Jude* with **Martin Buber**. He settled in Palestine in 1928, and became a teacher and co-director of secondary schools and seminaries. He later was appointed professor of philosophy and history of education, and director of the school of education at the Hebrew University. He was an editor of the *Educational Encyclopaedia* and wrote books on education and philosophy.

Simon, James (1851–1932) German merchant and philanthropist. He helped to found the Hilfsverein der Deutschen Juden in 1901 and served as its chairman. He was an art collector and patron, and also financed archaeological expeditions to Jericho and Tel el Amarna.

Simon, John (1818–97) British lawyer and politician. He was born in Jamaica, and went to England in 1833, where he studied law. He returned to Jamaica to practise as a lawyer, but eventually settled permanently in England, where he became a queen's counsel. From 1868 to 1888 he was a Liberal member of parliament and championed the cause of oppressed Jewry.

Simon, Julius (1875–1969) Zionist leader, of German origin. He was born in Switzerland and lived in Alsace during World War I. Later he was invited by **Chaim Weizmann** to direct the economic activities of the Zionist Organization. In 1920 he was sent to Palestine to reorganize the Zionist Organization, but his report was not accepted by the Zionist Congress and he resigned from the organization. Between the wars Simon lived in Palestine and the US, and headed the Palestine Economic Corporation.

Simon, Leon (1881–1965) English civil servant, brother of **Maurice Simon**. He was born in Southampton. He was director of telegraphs and telephones in the General Post Office and later director of the National Savings Bank. An ardent Zionist, he was active in the establishment of the Hebrew University. He lived in Jerusalem from 1946 to 1953 and worked in the Israel ministry of posts. He subsequently returned to England. His writings include *Studies in Jewish Nationalism*, *The Case of the Anti-Zionists: A Reply* and *Zionism and the Jewish Problem.* He also translated **Aḥad ha-Am**'s writings into English.

Simon, Maurice (1874–1955) South African Hebraist and translator, brother of **Leon Simon**. He was born in Manchester. He moved to South Africa and later was associated with the Soncino Press. He was the co-translator into English of the Zohar and Midrash Rabbah, and helped with the Soncino translation of the Talmud.

Simon, Neil (b. 1927) American playwright. Born in New York, he studied at New York University. He initially wrote for a number of television shows. Subsequently he wrote shows for the theatre including *Come Blow Your Horn*, *Plaza Suite*, *The Sunshine Boys*, *California Suite*, *The Odd Couple*, *Last of the Red Hot Lovers*, *The Prisoner of Second Avenue* and *I Ought to Be in Pictures.*

Simonsen, David Jacob (1853–1932) Danish rabbi. He was born in Copenhagen, and served as a rabbi there. During World War I he assisted war victims and took an interest in the Palestine Jewish community. His library of books about Judaism contained about 40,000 volumes. He published various works of oriental studies.

Simon the Hasmonean [Simeon ben Mattathias] (fl. 2nd cent. BCE) Palestinian ruler and high priest, second son of **Mattathias** the Hasmonean. In 142 BCE he succeeded his brother **Jonathan** as head of the Jewish state. He captured Gezer, secured the evacuation of Greek troops from the Jerusalem area, and gained from Demetrius II exemption from the tribute previously paid to the Seleucides. Elected high priest (an office which then became hereditary), ethnarch and general, he renewed the treaty with Rome and defeated Antiochus VII at Jabneh. He was killed by his son-in-law Ptolemy, and was succeeded by his son **John Hyrcanus**.

Simon the Just (fl. ?4th–2nd cent. BCE) High priest. According to **Josephus**, he is identifiable with Simeon I, the son of **Onias I** (4th– 3rd cent. BCE). However, the Talmud identifies him as the father of Onias, who built a temple at Leontopolis in Egypt; according to this account he was Simeon II, the father of **Onias III** (c. 200 BCE). In rabbinic literature he is described as one of the last members of the Great Assembly.

Simpson, David (1853–1932) Danish rabbi. Born in Copenhagen, he studied at the Jewish Theological Seminary in Breslau. In 1892 he became chief rabbi of Copenhagen.

Simpson, Louis [Marantz, Aston] (b. 1923) American poet of Jamaican origin. He went to the US at the age of 17. He studied at Columbia University and was professor of English at State University of New York at Stony Brook. His works include *The Arrivistes: Poems 1940–1949*, *Good News of Death and Other Poems*, *A Dream of Governors*, *At the End of the Open Road*, *Adventures of the Letter I* and *Caviar at the Funeral.*

Sinclair, Clive (b. 1948) English author. He was born in London. His novel *Blood Libels* combines an account of the Israeli invasion of Lebanon and its repurcussions in Israel with fantasies about the rise of anti-Semitism in England. His *Brothers Singer* is a biography of **Isaac Bashevis Singer**, **Israel Joshua Singer** and **Esther Kreitman**.

Sinclair, Jo [Said, Ruth] (b. 1913) American writer. Born in Brooklyn, she studied at Cleveland College. Her work includes *Wasteland*, *Sing at My Wake*, *The Changelings* and *Anna Teller.*

Singer, Isaac Bashevis (1904–91) American author, brother of **Israel Johua Singer** and **Esther Kreitman**. He was born in Leoncin, Poland, and moved to Warsaw in 1923. In 1935 he settled in New York, where he worked for the Yiddish daily newspaper *Forverts*. In 1978 he won the Nobel Prize for Literature.

Singer, Isidore (1859–1939) American writer and editor. He was born in Weisskirchen, Moravia. After working as an editor and as literary secretary to the French ambassador in Vienna, he settled in Paris in 1887, and took a post in the press bureau of the French foreign office. He was active in the defence of **Alfred Dreyfus** and founded and edited the periodical *La vraie parole* (1893–4). In 1895 he went to New York, where he became managing editor of the *Jewish Encyclopedia*.

Singer, Israel Joshua (1893–1944) Polish Yiddish novelist and playwright, brother of **Isaac Bashevis Singer** and **Esther Kreitman**. He was born in Bilgoraj, Poland, and lived in Warsaw and Kiev. He settled in the US in 1937. His writings include *Yoshe Kalb* and *The Brothers Ashkenazi*.

Singer, Simeon (1848–1906) English rabbi. He was headmaster of Jews College School, and later served as minister of the New East End Synagogue. He edited and translated the siddur as *The Authorizied Daily Prayer Book*.

Sinkó, Ervin (1898–1967) Yugoslav author. He initially wrote verse, fiction and drama. After engaging in revolutionary activities, he fled to Paris, where he wrote *The Optimists*. He returned to Yugoslavia in 1939, and wrote novels, short stories, essays and literary studies. His novel the *Law of Aaron* deals with a Jewish Revolutionary who fought in the Spanish Civil War. In 1959 he became professor of Hungarian language and literature at the University of Novu Sacz.

Sintzheim, Joseph David (1745–1812) French rabbi. He was born in Trier. He was head of the yeshivot in Bischheim and Strasbourg. During the Reign of Terror he fled from France, but later returned to Strasbourg, where he served as rabbi. In 1806 he was appointed to the French Assembly of Jewish Notables, and formulated the replies to the 12 questions put to the Assembly by Napoleon. In 1807 he became president of the Great Sanhedrin and in 1808 chief rabbi of the Central French Consistory. His *Yad David* consists of responsa on sections of the Talmud.

Sirota, Gershon (1874–1943) Lithuanian cantor. He was born in Podolia. He became ḥazzan in Odessa, and later served in Vilna and Warsaw. He undertook concert tours in Europe and the US.

Skoss, Solomon Leon (1884–1953) American Arabic and Hebrew scholar. He was born in Chusovoi, Siberia. He served in the Russian army, then in 1907 settled in the US. Later he taught at Dropsie College. His publications include a study of early Hebrew philology and an edition of the dictionary of the Karaite **David Alfasi**.

Slanskly, Rudolf (1901–52) Czechoslovakian communist. He joined the communist party but was criticized for his opportunistic policy. In 1939 he went into exile. Later he became secretary-general of the Czechoslovakian communist party and later president. He was arrested and removed from all party posts. He was tried for espionage, high treason and sabotage and executed.

Sliosberg, Henry (1863–1937) Russian jurist and communal leader. He was born in Mir, Belorussia, and settled with his family in Poltava, in eastern Ukraine. In 1889 he became legal counsel on Jewish affairs to Baron **Horace Günzburg**. He intervened with the Russian government in Jewish affairs and was involved in several Jewish legal disputes. He also served as chairman of the Jewish community of St Petersburg. In 1920 he moved to France, where he became head of the Russian Jewish community in Paris. His memoirs, *Bygone Days*, present an account of Jewish life in Russia before the Revolution.

Slonimksi, Antoni (1895–1976) Polish poet and author. Born in Warsaw, he was the son of an assimilated physician who converted to Christianity. Known as a liberal Roman Catholic, he was part of the Polish poetic revival that occurred with the re-emergence of a free and independent Poland. He was the founder of *Skamander*. After World War II, he returned to Poland from exile. From 1949 to 1951 he was head of the Polish Cultural Institute in London.

Slonimski, Ḥayyim Selig (1810–1904) Polish Hebrew writer and editor. He was born in Bialystok. During the Haskalah he wrote articles on popular science, and in 1834 he published the first part of a mathematics textbook; later he wrote a work on astronomy. He also invented a calculating machine and in 1862 founded a Hebrew newspaper, *Ha-tzephirah*, devoted to popular science.

Slouschz, Naḥum (1871–1966) Israeli scholar, archaeologist and historian, of Lithuanian origin. He was born in Smorgon, near Vilna, and as a child went to Odessa, where he later became involved in political and cultural activities. In 1904 he was appointed to the chair of Hebrew language and literature at the Sorbonne in Paris; he also taught at the École Normale Orientale of the Alliance Israélite Universelle. He wrote various studies of Jewry in North Africa. In 1919 he settled in Palestine, where he participated in archaeological explorations.

Smilansky, Moshe (1874–1953) Israeli writer. He was born in the Ukraine and in 1890 emigrated to Palestine, where he started a farm near Rehovot. He was a frequent contributor to the Zionist press. He also wrote a set of six autobiographical novels and several histories of the early days of agricultural settlement in Israel.

Smilansky, Yizhar [Yizhar, S.] (b. 1916) Israeli author. He was born in Reḥovot. He worked as a teacher and principal in various schools and served in the Knesset. His writings include the novel *The Days of Ziklag.*

Smolenskin, Peretz (1840–85) Russian Hebrew novelist and editor. He was born in Monastyrshchina, in the province of Mohilev, Belorussia. He wandered for several years before settling in Odessa and later Vienna. In 1868 he founded in Vienna the journal *Ha-Shaḥar,* which served as a central organ of Hebrew literary activities and Jewish national thought. Ten years later he established the weekly *Ha-Mabbit.* He wrote numerous stories and romances about Eastern European Jewish life. His articles promoted a Jewish national theory opposed to religious Orthodoxy and the Haskalah. After the pogroms in Russia in 1881, he supported the Ḥibbat Zion movement.

Sneh, Mosheh [Kleinbaum, Mosheh] (1909–72) Israeli politician. He was born in Radzyn, Poland. He joined the General Zionists in 1935. After the outbreak of World War II, he fled from Warsaw to Vilna, and then to Palestine. From 1941 he served as chief of the national command of the Haganah. He became a member of the executive of the Jewish Agency in 1945, but later resigned and joined the Mapam party. Eventually he established the Socialist Left Party (1953), which later joined the Israeli communist party (Maki). He was editor of the communist newspaper *Kol ha-Am* and wrote *Conclusions on the Jewish Problem in the Light of Marxism.*

Sokolow, Naḥum (1859–1936) Polish Zionist leader. He was born in Wyszogrod, near Plock, Poland. He joined the editorial board of the journal *Ha-Tzephirah* in Warsaw in 1884, later becoming its manager. From 1905 to 1909 he served as secretary of the World Zionist Organization; during this period he edited the organization's journal *Die Welt* and also founded its Hebrew weekly *Ha-Olam.* At the outbreak of World War I he moved from Berlin to London, where he became involved in the negotiations concerning the Balfour Declaration. After the war he presided over the Comité des Délégations Juives during the Versailles peace conference in 1919. He was chairman of the executive of the Zionist Organization (1921–31), and president of the World Zionist Organization and the Jewish Agency. His writings include a study entitled *History of Zionism.*

Sola, David Aaron de (1796–1860) British rabbi. He was born in Amsterdam. He became ḥazzan of the London Sephardi community in 1818. His writings include *Forms of Prayer According to the Custom of the Spanish and Portuguese Jews* and *Eighteen Treatises of the Mishnah.*

Solis-Cohen, Solomon (1857–1948) American physician and poet. He was professor of clinical medicine at Jefferson Medical College, Philadelphia (1904–27), and was also active in Jewish and Zionist organizations. He translated Hebrew poetry into English, including **Ibn Ezra**'s *Selected Poems.*

Solomon (fl. 10th cent. BCE) King of Israel (965–931 BCE), son of **David** and **Bathsheba.** He became king before his father's death, through the influence of **Bathesheba** and **Nathan,** who promoted his accession to the throne in place of **Adonijah,** his elder brother.

Solomon built the Temple in Jerusalem, constructed fortresses, store cities and chariot cities, and built a harbour at Elath; he also made administrative innovations, including the division of the country into 12 districts. The biblical books Song of Songs and Ecclesiastes are attributed to him. According to the Bible, he was known for his wisdom.

Solomon, Bertha (1892–1969) South African politician. Trained as a barrister, she served in the Transvall Provincial Council. Later she was elected to the South African parliament.

Solomon, Solomon J. (1860–1927) English painter. Born in London, he studied at Heatherley's Art School and the Royal Academy Schools. Later he studied at the École des Beaux Arts. In 1918 he became President of the Royal Society of British Artists. He painted portraits and allegorical frescoes.

Solomon ben Jeroham (fl. 10th cent.) Palestinian Karaite scholar. He lived in Egypt and Jerusalem. His writings include Arabic commentaries on the Bible and a Hebrew polemic against **Saadyah Gaon**.

Soloveichik, Ḥayyim (1853–1918) Lithuanian talmudist, son of **Joseph Baer Soloveichik**. He was born in Volozhin, and taught at the yeshivah there from 1880 to 1892. Later he lived in Brest-Litovsk, where he served as a rabbi. He developed a new trend in talmudic study based on conceptual analysis. He also wrote novellae on talmudic tractates and on **Maimonides**' *Mishneh Torah*.

Soloveichik, Isaac Ze'ev (1886–1959) Lithuanian rabbi and halakhist, son of **Ḥayyim Soloveichik**. He was born in Volozhin, and became rabbi at Brest-Litovsk in 1918 after the death of his father. During World War II he feld to Vilna, and he later settled in Jerusalem, where he founded a kolel (academy for advanced study of the Talmud).

Soloveichik, Joseph (1903–96) American talmudic scholar, son of **Isaac Ze'ev Soloveichik**. He was born in Pruzhany, Poland, and grew up in Hasloviz, Belorussia. In 1932 he emigrated to the US, where he served as a rabbi in Boston. He became professor of Talmud at the Isaac Elhanan Yeshiva in 1941. He was also professor of Jewish philosophy at the university's Bernard Revel Graduate School. His writings include *Ish ha-Halakhah*, an explanation of his theological position.

Soloveichik, Joseph Baer (1820–92) Lithuanian talmudist. He lived in Volozhin, where he served as joint rosh yeshivah with **Naphtali Tzevi Judah Berlin**. Later he became rabbi of Slutsk, and after a period spent in Warsaw (1875–8), of Brest-Litovsk. His *Bet ha-Levi* contains novellae on the Talmud, responsa and sermons.

Sommerstein, Emil (1868–1946) Austrian soldier. He was born in Bukovina. He fought in Galicia during World War I, and later commanded the Austrian army that captured Burgenland. He served as head of the Austrian organization for Jewish war veterans. After the Anschluss he was put under house arrest, and in 1942 he was deported to Theresienstadt. He returned to Vienna at the end of the war; he later settled in the US.

Sommi, Leone de (1527–92) Italian dramatist and poet. He was born in Mantua. He wrote and staged plays for the Gonzaga court theatre. and eventually became renowned throughout Europe as a dramatist and director. In 1585 he bought property in Mantua on which he built a synagogue. His writings include plays, poems, canzones and satires. His greatest works are the *Dialoghi*, an exposition on stagecraft, and his Hebrew comedy of betrothal, *Zaḥut Bediḥ uta de-Kidushin*.

Soncino, Israel (d. 1492) Italian printer. He was a physician. He set up a Hebrew press in Soncino, Italy with his son. They produced a tractate of the Talmud in 1484. Later they produced a complete Hebrew Bible with illustrations. Moving to various towns in Italy, the family began to print in Latin and Italian.

Sonnino, Sidney (1847–1922) Italian politician. He was the son of a Jewish father and Protestant mother. He became prominent in Italian politics as an economist and financial expert. Before World War I, he served twice as prime minister. During the war he was foreign minister and headed the Italian delegation to the Paris Peace Conference.

Sonntag, Jacob (1905–84) British scholar and editor. He was born in Wiznitz, northern Bukovina, and grew up in Vienna; he emigrated to England in 1938. In 1953 he founded the scholarly journal *The Jewish Quarterly*, which he edited.

Sopher [Schreiber], Moses [Ḥatam Sopher] (1792–1839) Sloviam rabbi. From 1803 he served as rabbi where he founded a yeshivah. He was an influential preacher and halakhic authority. His *Ḥatam Sopher* contains responsa and novellae.

Soutine, Chaim (1893–1943) French painter. Born in Similovitchi, Lithuania, he studied in the School of Fine Arts in Vilna and later went to Paris. He shared rooms with **Amedeo Modigliani**. With the Nazi occupation, he fled to a small French village and continued painting.

Soyer, Raphael (1899–1988) American artist. Born in Borisoglebsk, Russia, he went to the US in 1913. He studied at the Educational Alliance School and at the Art Students League. He painted scenes of New York.

Spassy, Boris (b. 1937) Russian chess champion. Born in Leningrad, he was the son of a Jewish mother and gentile father. He became a grand master at the age of 18. In 1969 he became world champion.

Spector, Mordecai (1858–1925) Ukrainian Yiddish novelist and editor. He was born in Uman. Initially he wrote sketches and novels, including *Der yidisher muzhik*, which advocated the return of the Jews to productive labour in Palestine. In 1857 he settled in Warsaw, where he wrote travel sketches, short stories and novels, and also edited a series of anthologies; in 1894 he helped to set up the important anthology, *Yontev bletlekh*. He moved to New York in 1921, and shortly before the end of his life wrote a volume of memoirs, *Mayn lebn*.

Spektor, Isaac Elhanan [Isaac Elhanan] (1817–96) Lithuanian rabbi. He was born in the province of Grodno, Russia. He served as a rabbi in various towns, eventually settling in Kovno, where he officiated until his death. He established a yeshivah in Kovno, and organized aid for stricken communities; he was the only rabbi invited to attend the conference of Jewish leaders held in St Petersburg in 1881–2 to discuss the plight of Jewry. Subsequently he supported the Ḥibbat Zion movement.

Sperber, Manes (1905–84) Austrian author. He was born in Zabolotov, Galicia, and moved to Vienna in 1916. He taught in Berlin from 1927 to 1933 and then settled in Paris. His novels about shtetl life include *Like Tears in the Ocean* and *All Our Yesterdays.*

Spicehandler, Ezra (b. 1921) American Hebrew scholar. He was born in Brooklyn. He became professor of modern Hebrew literature at the Hebrew Union College in 1952, and later was dean of the Hebrew Union College in Jerusalem. He published works dealing with modern and medieval Hebrew literature, Zionism, Judeo-Persian studies and talmudic history.

Spiegel, Sam (1901–85) American film producer. Born in Jaroslaw, Galicia, his family went to Vienna. Influenced by **Theodor Herzl**, he went to Palestine as a pioneer. He went to the US in 1927 and worked at MGM. Later he worked at Universal. His films include *On the Waterfront*, *The African Queen*, *The Bridge on the River Kwai* and *Lawrence of Arabia.*

Spiegel, Shalom (1899–1984) American scholar and educator. He was born in Romania, and educated in Vienna. From 1923 to 1929 he taught in Palestine, but then settled in New York, where he was professor of medieval Hebrew literature at the Jewish Theological Seminary. His publications include studies of the biblical prophets, and an edition of the liturgical compositions of **Eleazar Kallir**.

Spiegelman, Art (b. 1948) American cartoonist. Born in Stockholm, he studied at Harpur College, New York. In 1980 he established the comic magazine, *Raw*. His works include *Maus*.

Spielberg, Steven (b. 1947) American film director. Born in Cincinnati, he studied at California State College. His films include *Jaws*, *Close Encounters of the Third Kind*, *Raiders of the Lost Ark*, *E.T.*, *Indiana Jones*, *Empire of the Sun*, *Hook*, *Jurassic Park* and *Schindler's List.*

Spielvogel, Nathan (1874–1956) Australian author. He was born in Ballarat, in the state of Victoria. He was a country schoolteacher and travelled frequently in the eastern Australian outback. In his writing he portrayed Jewish immigrants who arrived in Australia from England and Europe.

Spinoza [De Spinoza; Espinoza], Benedict (1632–77) Dutch philosopher. He was born in Amsterdam. He had a traditional education, but his heretical views led to his excommunication in 1656. From 1660 he lived away from Amsterdam, earning his living as a lens polisher. His *Theologico-Political Treatise* initiated modern biblical criticism. In his *Ethics* he applied Euclidean methods to demonstrate a metaphysical concept of the universe with ethical implications.

Spire, André (1868–1966) French poet and Zionist leader. He was born in Nancy. He became a member of the Conseil d'État in 1894, specialized in employment problems at the French ministry of labour (1898–1902), and served as inspector-general in the ministry of agriculture (1902–26). He played an active part in the Dreyfus Affair. He became an advocate of Zionism, and in 1919 represented the French Zionists at the Paris Peace Conference. During World War II he lived in the US. His writings include *Poèmes juifs* and *Quelque Juifs et demi-Juifs.*

Spitz, Mark (b. 1950) American swimmer. Trained as a dentist, he won seven gold medals at the 1972 Olympics.

Spitzer, Karl (1830–48) Austrian student agitator. In the 1848 revolt against the Hapsburg regime, he was a leader of students in Vienna. He was shot and killed on the barricades.

Sprinzak, Yoseph (1885–1959) Israeli politician. He was born in Russia, where he was one of the founders of the socialist youth movement Tzeire Zion. He settled in Palestine in 1908, where he became active in labour politics. A founder of the Histadrut and Mapai, he represented Mapai in the Knesset, and later became speaker of the Knesset.

Stampfer, Yehoshua (1852–1908) Palestinian pioneer. Born in Hungary, he went to Palestine in 1869. In 1878 he helped establish the first Jewish agricultural settlement, Petaḥ Tikvah. He served as chairman of the local council.

Starer, Robert (b. 1924) American composer. He was born in Vienna. He fled the Nazis in 1938 and settled in Palestine, where he became staff pianist for the BBC Palestine. Later he taught at the Juilliard School in New York and became professor of composition at Brooklyn College. His compositions include settings of the Psalms, and liturgical cantatas such as *Kohelet*, *Ariel* and *Joseph and His Brothers.*

Starr, Joshua (1907–49) American historian and communal worker. He was born in New York. He was secretary of the Commission for European Jewish Cultural Reconstruction in 1947–9. He published studies of Byzantine and post-Byzantine Jewish history.

Stein, Edith (1891–1942) German philosopher. She was born in Breslau. She converted to Catholicism in 1922; she was appointed lecturer at the Institute for Pedagogy at Münster in 1932, but in 1933 abandoned her post and entered the Carmelite convent in Cologne as Sister Theresa Benedicta of the Cross. In 1938 she moved to the Netherlands. Under the Nazis she was deported to Auschwitz where she died. Her collected works were published in five volumes.

Stein, Gertrude (1874–1946) American author. Born in Allegheny, Pennsylvania, she was educated in Europe. In 1902 she settled in Paris with her brother, Leo. She wrote novels, sketches, plays and poems. She was a patron of artists including Picasso, Braque and Matisse. Her works include *The Autobiography of Alice B. Toklas.*

Stein, Marc (1862–1943) British archaeologist, of Hungarian origin. Born in Budapest, he went to India to teach at a university and became superintendent of the Indian Archaeological Survey.

Steinberg, Ben (b. 1930) Canadian composer, conductor, organist and educator. He was born in Winnipeg. He taught music in public schools in Toronto, and from 1988 he served as director of music at the city's Temple Sinai. He wrote Jewish liturgical music, and *Echoes of Children* commemorating the children who died during the Holocaust.

Steinberg, Isaac Nachman (1888–1957) Russian revolutionary and writer. He was born in Dvinsk, and worked as a lawyer in Moscow before World War I. He was arrested and exiled because of his revolutionary activities, but returned to Russia in 1910. In 1917–18 he was commissar for law. Later he lived in Berlin, London and New York. He was prominent in the Yiddish and Territorialist movements, and published studies of the Russian Revolution and Jewish issues.

Steinberg, Judah (1863–1908) Bessarabian writer and educator. He was born in Lipkany. His early works include a writing manual, a book of proverbs and a children's storybook. In 1897 he became a teacher in Leovo, Moldavia, and later settled in Odessa, where he was the correspondent of the New York daily *Di warheit.* He published textbooks, children's stories, feuilletons and fables. A number of his stories deal with Ḥasidic life.

Steinberg, Milton (1903–50) American rabbi and novelist. He was born in Rochester, New York, and became rabbi at New York's Park Avenue Synagogue. His publications include *As a Driven Leaf, The Making of the Modern Jew, Basic Judaism, A Partisan Guide to the Jewish Problem* and *A Believing Jew.*

Steinberg, Yaakov (1887–1947) Hebrew author. He lived in Warsaw, Switzerland and Palestine. His stories, set in the Ukraine, illustrate the difficulties of life in the diaspora.

Steiner, George (b. 1929) British scholar. He was born in Paris. He became professor of comparative literature at Geneva University and a fellow of Churchill College, Cambridge. Many of his writings deal with Jewish themes. His works include *The Death of Tragedy, After Babel, In Bluebeard's Castle* and *The Portage to San Cristobal of AH.*

Steinhardt, Jakob (1887–1968) Israeli artist. He was born in Zerków, Poland, and in 1933 settled in Palestine, where he became director of the Bezalel School of Arts and Crafts in Jerusalem. He produced woodcuts dealing with Jewish and biblical themes, as well as Palestinian landscapes.

Steinhardt, Laurence (1892–1950) American diplomat. He was a lawyer in New York and an active Zionist. He worked for the election of Franklin D. Roosevelt in 1932; later he became minster to Sweden, ambassador to Peru, the USSR, Turkey, Czechoslovakia and Canada.

Steinheim, Solomon Ludwig (1789–1866) German philosopher. He was born in Bruchhausen, Westphalia, and practised as a physician in Altona from 1813 to 1845. Later he settled in Rome. His writings include *Revelation According to the Doctrine of the Synagogue* and *The Doctrine of the Synagogue as Exact Science.*

Steinitz, Wilhelm (1836–1900) British chess-master. Born in Prague, he settled in England where he was a leading authority on chess and world champion. His works include *The Modern Chess Instructor.*

Steinman, David (1886–1960) American engineer. Born in New York City, he became professor of civil engineering at the University of Idaho. He designed and built over a hundred steel bridges in the US and other countries.

Steinman, Eliezer (1892–1970) Israeli writer. He was born in Obodovka, in the Ukraine, and became a part-time Hebrew teacher in Odessa. In 1920 he left Russia, and settled in Warsaw, where he wrote stories, essays, articles and a novel; he also published collections of Yiddish essays and stories about the pogroms against Ukrainian Jews. In 1924 he settled in Tel Aviv, where he wrote for *Ha-Aretz* and *Ha-Olam* and published stories and novels. He later became a columnist for *Davar.*

Steinschneider, Moritz (1816–1907) German bibliographer and orientalist. He was born in Prossnitz, Moravia. He taught in Prague and Berlin, where he also preached, officiated at weddings, worked as a translator, and wrote Hebrew textbooks. He was appointed lecturer at the Veitel-Heine-Ephraimsche Lehranstalt in 1859, and taught there for 48 years. From 1869 he was also assistant librarian at the Berlin State Library. He produced catalogues of the Hebrew books at the Bodleian Library, Oxford, and of the Hebrew manuscripts at Leyden, Munich, Hamburg and Berlin. His other publications include studies of the history of Jewish literature and Hebrew typography. From 1858 to 1882 he edited the *Hebraïsche Bibliographie.*

Steinthal, Heymann (1828–99) German philologist and philosopher. He studied in Berlin and was appointed lecturer in philology and mythology at Berlin University in 1850. In 1872 he became professor of biblical studies and philosophy of religion at the Hochschule fur die Wissenschaft des Judentums. He and **Moritz Lazarus** were the originators of the science of racial psychology.

Stencl, Avrom-Nokhem (1897–1983) Polish Yiddish poet. He was born in Czeladzy, Poland. He went to the Netherlands in 1919, then moved to Germany, and eventually settled in England. His publications include *Londoner Sonetn* and *Vaytshelpl Shtetl d'Britn.*

Stern, Avraham (1907–42) Palestinian pioneer. He emigrated from Poland to Palestine in 1925 and became active in Irgun Tzvai Leumi. In 1940 he disagreed with the policy of co-operating with the British and established the Stern Gang (Loḥame Ḥerut Yisrael) which attacked British policy and army personnel. He was arrested and killed.

Stern, Irma (1894–1966) South African painter. She was noted for her studies of non-European races as well as flower paintings.

Stern, Isaac (b. 1920) American violinist. He made his debut with the San Francisco Symphony Orchestra at the age of 11. He became a world-renowned virtuoso.

Stern, Lina Solomonovna (1878–1968) Russian scientist. Born in Lithuania, she was head of the Physiological Scientific Research Institute in Moscow. During the Stalin regime, she was dismissed from her post and stripped of her honours. Later she was rehabilitated during the Khrushnev era.

Stern, Otto (1888–1969) German physicist. He worked with **Albert Einstein** in Prague and Zurich. In 1923 he became professor of physical chemistry at the University of Hamburg. When Hitler came to power in Germany, he went to the US and became professor of physics at Carnegie Institute of Technology in Pittsburg. He was awarded the Nobel Prize in 1943.

Stern, William (1871–1938) German pyschologist and philosopher. Born in Berlin, he studied at the University of Berlin. Later he became an assistant professor of philosophy and psychology at the University of Breslau. In 1919 he moved to Hamburg University where he subsequently became professor. He was expelled by the Nazis and went to Holland and then to the US where he was professor at Duke University.

Stern-Taübler, Selma (1890–89) American historian, wife of Eugen Taübler. She was archivist of the American Jewish Archives in Cincinnati from 1947 to 1959. She wrote about the history of German Jewry and about court Jews.

Sternberg, Joseph (1894–1969) American film director. Born in Vienna, he went to the US at the age of seven. He worked with a company in Fort Lee, New Jersey were he was an editor and title-writer. He made training films during World War I, and then returned to the film industry. He directed the *Salvation Hunters* and later worked for MGM and Paramount. In 1935 he went to Columbia Pictures.

Sternberg, Sigmund (b. 1921) Born in Hungary, he was president of the Reform Synagogues of Great Britain, patron of the International Council of Christians and Jews, governor of the Hebrew University of Jerusalem, president of the Sternberg Centre for Judaism and founder of the Three Faiths Forum. He received a knighthood in 1976.

Stieglitz, Alfred (1846–1946) American photographer. Born in Hoboken, New Jersey, he studied at the Berlin Polytechnic. He was a pioneer of photographic techniques and helped gain acceptance of photography as an art form.

Stone, Eihu D. (1888–1952) American Zionist. From 1922 to 1934 he was assistant attorney for Massachusetts. He founded a Zionist organization for the New England region.

Stone, I. F. (1907–89) American journalist. Born in Philadelphia, he studied at the University of Pennsylvania. From 1927 to 1932 he wrote for various newspapers; later he bought the New York *Post* and published *The Court Disposes.* In 1938 he became associate editor of the *Nation.* From 1942 to 1948 he was a columnist for the New York *Star* and

Daily Compass. In 1953 he began publication of *I. F. Stone's Weekly*.

Strasberg, Lee (1901–82) American actor. Born in Austria-Hungary, he went to the US at the age of seven. He grew up on the Lower East Side of New York. He joined the Chrystie Street Settlement House's drama club. He later studied at the Clare Tree Major School of Theatre. Subsequently he helped form the Group Theatre company. In 1948 he joined the Actor's Studio, becoming artistic director. He founded the Lee Strasberg Theatre Institutes in New York and Los Angeles.

Strashun [Zaskovitzer], Samuel (1794–1872) Lithuanian talmudic scholar. He was born in Zaskovitzer; he was initially named after his birthplace, but later adopted the name of his father-in-law David Strashun. He lived in Vilna, where he devoted himself to scholarship. He wrote annotations and glosses on almost all the tractates of the Mishnah and Talmud.

Straus, Nathan (1848–1931) American merchant and philanthropist, brother of **Oscar Solomon Straus**. He was commissioner first for parks then for health in New York, and a member of the New York Forest Preserve Board. He established a milk pasteurization laboratory and milk distribution stations in New York, an emergency relief system to distribute coal and food to the poor, and a chain of boarding houses for the destitute. He also established the Pasteur Institute in Palestine and endowed child welfare stations and health centres there.

Straus, Oscar Solomon (1850–1926) American diplomat and jurist, brother of **Nathan Straus**. He served as American minister in Turkey, and later was apointed to the International Court of Arbitration at The Hague. He was secretary of commerce and labour in the US (1906–9) and then ambassador to Turkey. He helped to found the American Jewish Committee, served as an officer of the Baron de Hirsch Fund, and was president of the American Jewish Historical society. In his writings he illustrated the impact of Hebrew concepts on American culture.

Strauss, Leo (1899–1973) American philosopher and political scientist, of German origin. After emigrating to the US, he taught at the New School for Social Reserach in New York (1938–49) and was appointed professor of political science at the University of Chicago. He wrote studies of political philosophy and the relations between philosophy and theology.

Strauss, Levi (1829–1902) American manufacturer, of German origin. Born in Buttenheim, Germany, he went to the US in 1847. He initially began peddling in New York City; later he went to Louisville, Kentucky. In 1853 he went to San Francisco and established a store, Levi Strauss and Company. In 1873 he became a partner with Jacob W. Davis, a tailor from Nevada. They developed Levi jeans.

Strauss, Lewis Lichtenstein (1896–1974) American government official. Born in Charleston, West Virgina, he initially worked selling shoes. In 1917 he joined Herbert Hoover's Belgian relief service. In 1919 he worked for the banking house of Kuhn, Loeb and Company and married a daughter of one of the partners. He became a partner in 1928. In 1941 he was called to active duty with the US navy; several years later he became rear admiral. He served on the Atomic Energy Commission.

Streisand, Barbara (b. 1942) American singer and actress. She was born in Brooklyn. She appeared in Broadway musicals and in films, some of which have Jewish subjects.

Stricker, Robert (1879–1944) Austrian Zionist leader and journalist. He was born in Brünn, and became an engineer for Austrian state railways. Before World War I he edited the Vienna *Jüdische Zeitung*, and in 1915 he founded the Jewish War Archives. He became president of the Jewish People's Party, and in 1919 was elected to the Constituent National Assembly of the Federal Austrian Republic. From 1919 to 1928 he edited the *Wiener Morgenzeitung* and later *Die Neue Welt*. In 1931 he joined the Union of Zionist Revisionists, then in 1933 was one of the founders of the Jewish State Party.

Stroheim, Erich von (1885–1957) Austrian film director and actor. He was the son of middle-class parents in Vienna. He went to the US in 1909, and first appeared on screen in 1914. His films include *Blind Husbands, Foolish Wives, Greed, The Merry Widow, The Wedding March* and *Hello Sister!*.

Stroock, Alan Maxwells (1907–85) American lawyer, son of **Solomon Marcuse Stroock.** He started his career as a law clerk to Supreme Court Justice **Benjamin Cardozo** (1934–6), then joined the Stroock family legal firm Stroock and Stroock, where he became a partner. He served as chairman of the board and later president of the corporation of the Jewish Theological Seminary in New York, and was also active in various other Jewish organizations.

Stroock, Solomon Marcuse (1874–1945) American communal leader. A specialist in constitutional law, he was the chairman of various legal committees. He served as president of the New York branch of the Young Men's Hebrew Association, the Federation for the support of Jewish Philanthropic Societies in New York, and the American Jewish Committee.

Stutschewsky, Joachim (1891–1981) Israeli cellist, composer and historian, of Ukrainian origin. He worked as a cellist in Switzerland and in Vienna, where he contributed essays on Jewish music to the periodical *Die Stimme.* In 1938 he settled in Palestine. He organized concerts of Jewish music in Tel Aviv. He composed works for cello, numerous songs, and arrangements of folk songs. He also engaged in historical research on Ḥasidic musicians.

Suarès, André (1866–1948) French author, of Portuguese Jewish descent. He was born near Marseilles. Although he adopted a negative attitude to Judaism, he rallied to the defence of the Jews after the advent of Nazism.

Sukenik, Eliezer Lipa (1889–1953) Israeli archaeologist. He was born in Bialystok, and settled in Palestine in 1912. He became professor of archaeology at the Hebrew University. He excavated the Third Wall of Jerusalem, the city of Samaria, and the synagogues in the town of Beth Alpha.

Sulzberger, Arthur Hays (1891–1968) American newspaper publisher. Born in New York City, he studied at Columbia University. From 1917 to 1919 he served in the US Army. In 1917 he married Iphigene B. Ochs, the daughter of **Adolph S. Ochs**, publisher of the *New York Times.* In 1919 he joined the *New York Times*, later becoming publisher and president of the New York Times Company.

Sulzberger, Mayer (1843–1923) American jurist and communal leader. He was born in Heidelsheim, Germany, and emigrated to the US in 1849. He became a lawyer in Philadelphia and in 1895 was elected a judge of the Court of Common Pleas. He lectured on Hebrew jurisprudence and government at Dropsie College and the Jewish Theological Seminary. He served as president of the American Jewish Committee and the Young Men's Hebrew Assocation of Philadelphia. His writings include *The Am-ha-Aretz – the Ancient Hebrew Parliament: A Chapter in the Constitutional History of Ancient Israel, The Policy of the Ancient Hebrews, The Ancient Hebrew Law of Homicide* and *The Status of Labour in Ancient Israel.*

Sulzer, Solomon (1804–90) Austrian cantor. He was born in Hohenems, in the Tyrol, and served as a cantor in Vienna from 1826. He sought to revive traditional cantorial music by incorporating modern musical innnovations. His *Shir Tziyyon* purified many melodies from their later embellishments and included recitatives in the original Polish tradition.

Summerfield, Woolfe (1901–76) English lawyer and author. He was born in Manchester. Under the pseudonym Ben Mowshay he published two novels set in Kidston (Manchester) about the life of a Jewish hero, Abraham Bear Davis.

Sussmann, Heinrich (1904–86) Austrian painter. He was born in Tarnopol, Galicia, and went to Vienna in 1914. He later lived in Berlin and (from 1933) Paris. His later work deals with themes of the Jewish diaspora, including memories of his childhood in Galicia.

Sutro, Adolph (1830–98) American engineer. He was born in Aachen, Prussia. He went to the US in 1848 and first worked as a miner. After moving to San Francisco he dealt in real estate; he later served as the city's mayor. He amassed a large library, including numerous Hebrew manuscripts.

Sutskever [Sutzkever], Avraham (b. 1913) Polish Yiddish poet. He was born in Smorgon, Belorussia. His family moved to Siberia then to Vilna. He belonged to the 'Yung Vilne' school of Yiddish poets. In 1941–3 he was incarcerated in the Vilna

Ghetto, but escaped and joined the partisans. He settled in Paris in 1949. Many of his poems deal with European ghetto life and the Holocaust.

Suzman, Helen (b. 1917) South African politician. She was a lecturer in economics and became a member of parliament in 1953. She spoke for non-white races who were not given representation.

Sverdlov, Yakov (1885–1919) Russian communist politician. Born in Nizhnii Novgorod. He became secretary of the All-Russian Executive Committee and was appointed first secretary of the central committee of the party.

Svevo, Italo [Schmitz, Ettore] (1861–1928) Italian writer. Born in Trieste, he was a bank clerk and manager of his father-in-law's paint factory. He converted to Catholicism. He used the pseudonym Italo Svevo for his first novel, *Una vita.*

Swope, Gerard (1872–1957) American electrical engineer and philanthropist. He was born in St Louis. He became president of the International General Electrical Company.

Swope, Herbert (1882–1958) American journalist. Born in St Louis, he was a staff correspondent of the *New York World.* He exposed the Klu Klux Klan, New York crime, and labour conditions in Florida.

Syrkin, Marie (1899–1988) American author and educator. She was born in Berne, Switzerland, and was taken to the US as a child. She became the editor of the Labour Zionist monthly *Jewish Frontier*, and taught English at Brandeis University.

Syrkin, Nachman (1868–1924) American leader of Socialist Zionism. He was born in Mohilev, Belorussia. In 1907 he settled in New York and became active in Zionist work; he also contributed to Yiddish journals. During World War I he helped to establish the American Jewish Congress.

Szenes, Hannah (1921–44) Palestinian poet and resistance fighter. She was born in Budapest, and moved to Palestine in 1939. She joined Kibbutz Sedot Yam, and began to write poetry. In 1942 she became one of a group of parachutists organized by the Haganah to rescue prisoners of war and organize Jewish resistance in Europe; she was dropped in Yugoslavia, and crossed the border into Hungary, where she was arrested and executed by the Nazis.

Szichman, Mario (b. 1945) Argentine novelist. In 1967 he went to Columbia, and later settled in Venezuela. He served as a foreign reporter for **Jacobo Timerman's** *La opinión* and as a correspondent for the Italian news agency. In 1980 he moved to the US, where he has continued to work as a correspondent.

Szigeti, Joseph (1892–1973) Violinist of Transylvanian origin. Born in Sighet, he studied at the Liszt Academy of Budapest. He taught at the Berlin Conservatory, and later at the conservatory in Geneva. In 1925 he settled in the US, but retired to Switzerland in 1960.

Szigetti, Imre (1879–1975) Australian graphic artist and illustrator, of Hungarian origin. He was born in Budapest, and emigrated to Australia in 1939. A number of his drawings depict Hungarian Jewish life.

Szilard, Leo (1898–1964) American physicist of Hungarian origin. He studied at the University of Berlin. With the rise of Nazism, he went to England and worked at Oxford University. He then went to the US. From 1960 he was professor at the Enrico Fermi Institute of Nuclear Studies.

Szold, Henrietta (1860–1945) American Zionist and philanthropist. Born in Baltimore. In 1912 she organized Hadassah, the Women's Zionist Organization of America. She was the first woman to become a member of the executive of the Zionist Organization, in which she took responsibility for education and health.

Szolsberg, Icchak (1877–1930) Polish composer. He began his career in Vilna at the age of 13. Later he studied at the Warsaw Conservatoire. He was a music director in Fiszzon's Jewish Theatre in Warsaw, and composed for numerous Jewish theatres.

Szomory, Dezsö (1869–1944) Hungarian writer. He trained as a musician, studying at the Academy of Music in Budapest, before turning to writing. He later settled in Paris.

T

Taamrat, Emmanuel (1898–1963) Ethiopian educator. Born in Gondar, he went with **Jacques Faitlovich** to France and later studied at the Rabbinical College in Florence. From 1921 he worked at a kibbutz in Palestine. In 1923 he went to Ethiopia with **Faitlovich** and established a teacher-training school in Addis Ababa. He later worked for the immigration of Ethiopian Jews to Israel.

Tabatznik, Mendel (1894–1975) South African Yiddish essayist and poet. He was born in Kletsk, in Belorussia, and became the director of a Yiddish elementary school in Mir. In 1927 he settled in Johannesburg, South Africa, where he taught Yiddish and published articles about pedagogical issues. He also wrote poetry and an autobiographical novel.

Tabenkin, Yizḥak (1887–1971) Palestine labour leader. He went from Belorussia to Palestine before World War I. He was a member of the collective settlement Kinneret. Later he joined the Guedud ha-Avodah and helped found kibbutz Ein Harod which became the nucleus of a federation of kibbutzim, Kibbutz Meuchad. He helped organize the Aḥdut ha-Avodah party, and subsequently was a founder of Mapai. In 1944 he led the Aḥdut ha-Avodah group that broke away from Mapai. He was also a founder of Histadrut and a member of the Knesset.

Tal [Grünthal], Yoseph (b. 1910) Israeli composer and teacher. He was born in Pinne, in the Poznań district. He moved to Palestine and in 1937 joined the faculty of the Academy of Music in Jerusalem. Later he became head of the department of musicology at the Hebrew University. Many of his compositions are based on biblical motifs and liturgical poetry.

Talmon, Jacob Leib (1916–80) Israeli scholar. He was born in Rypin Poland. In 1934 he went to Palestine, where he became professor of modern history at the Hebrew University. His writings include *The Origins of Totalitarian Democracy*, *The Nature of Jewish History: its Universal Significance*, *The Unique and the Universal*, *Romanticism and Revolt* and *Political Messianism: The Romantic Phase.*

Tamar (i) (fl.? 19th–16th cent. BCE) Israelite woman, wife of Er, the eldest son of **Judah**, and later wife of Er's brother, **Onan**. After **Onan**'s death, **Judah** refused to allow Tamar to marry his third son, Shelah. In protest she disguised herself as a prostitute and bore twins by **Judah** (Genesis 38).

Tamar (ii) (fl. 10th cent. BCE) Israelite woman, daughter of David. She was raped by **Amnon**, her stepbrother (II Samuel 13), who was killed in revenge by her brother **Absalom**.

Tamm, Igor (1895–1971) Russian physicist. He studied at the Moscow State University and was professor at the Moscow State University and later directed the Lebedye Physical Institute of the Soviet Academy of Sciences. During the 1920s and 1930s his work concerned the dispersal of light in solid bodies. He shared the Nobel Prize in Physics in 1958.

Tammuz, Benjamin (b. 1919) Israeli writer and journalist. He was born in Kharkov in the Ukraine, and went to Palestine in 1924. From 1965 he was the editor of the weekend literary supplement of *Ha-Aretz* for which he wrote art criticism. In 1971 he became cultural attaché at the Israeli embassy in London. He wrote short stories, novels and children's books, and translated several books into Hebrew.

Tanḥum ben Joseph of Jerusalem (c. 1220–91) Palestinian philologist and biblical exegete. He lived in Palestine and Egypt. He wrote a lexicon to **Maimondes**' *Mishneh Torah*.

Tanḥuma bar Abba (fl. 4th cent.) Palestinian amora. He developed the art of homiletics and, according to tradition, was the author of many midrashim which begin 'Yelammedenu Rabbenu' ('Let our teacher pronounce'), including those that make up the Midrash Tanḥuma.

Tarphon (fl. 1st cent.) Palestinian tanna. He served with his priestly family in the Temple, and studied with **Johanan ben Zakkai** and **Gamaliel I**. He was active in discussions at the academy at Jabneh. The Mishnah refers to differences of opinion between him and **Akiva** regarding the halakhah.

Tartakower, Aryeh (1897–1982) Israeli sociologist and communal leader. He was born in Brody, in eastern Galicia, and taught at the Institute of Jewish Sciences in Warsaw. In 1939 he went to the US where he was director of relief and rehabilitation for the World Zionist Action Committee. He settled in Palestine in 1946 and taught at the Hebrew University. From 1948 to 1971 he was chairman of the Israeli section of the World Jewish Congress. He wrote studies of the Jewish labour movement, migration problems, the history of Polish Jewry, anti-Semitism, and the Jewish communities of the diaspora.

Täuber, Richard [Seiffert, Ernst] (1892–1948) Austrian tenor. Born in Linz, he studied at the Frankfurt Conservatory and made his debut as Tamino in *The Magic Flute*. He then worked with the Dresden State Opera, and later with the Vienna State Opera. With the rise of Nazism, he went to London.

Täubler, Eugen (1879–1953) American historian and biblical scholar. He was born in Gostyn, in the district of Poznań. He taught at the universities of Berlin, Zurich and Heidelberg, where he was a professor from 1925 to 1935. He emigrated to the US where he taught at the Hebrew Union College in Cincinnati. He wrote various studies of Jewish history.

Tcherikover, Avigdor (1894–1958) Israeli historian of Russian origin. He settled in Palestine in 1925 and became professor of ancient history at the Hebrew University. He published studies of the Jews in Palestine and Egypt during the Hellenistic and Roman periods.

Tchernowitz, Chaim (1871–1949) American talmudic scholar. He was born in Sebesh, Russia. He founded a yeshivah in Odessa and adopted the pseudonym 'Rav Tzair'. In 1923 he settled in the US and taught Talmud at the Jewish Institute of Religion in New York. He published studies of rabbinic literature, an abridgement of the Talmud, and histories of Jewish law.

Teitel, Jacob (1851–1939) Russian jurist and communal worker. He was born in Cherny Ostrov, Podolia. He was one of the first Jews in Russia to be employed in the judicial service during the czarist regime. Devoted to communal work, he helped Jews who were oppressed by the authorities, and was a founder of a relief enterprise which supported Jewish youth. In 1921 he left the USSR and became president of the Union of Russian Jews in Germany. When the Nazis came to power, he moved to France, where his memoirs were published.

Teitelbaum, Moses (1759–1841) Galician Ḥasidic leader. He was born in Przemyśl and served as a rabbi at Sieniawa and Ujhely. He was among the first to spread Ḥasidism in the northern and central districts of Hungary, and became known as a wonder-working tzaddik. He wrote a homiletic work (*Yismaḥ moshe*) and responsa.

Teixeira, Abraham Senior (1581–1666) Portuguese marrano financier and diplomat. He was born in Lisbon, the son of Dom Francisco de Melo and

Donna Antonia de Silva Teixeira, lady-in-waiting to the Queen. In 1643 he moved to Antwerp, where he became consul and paymaster for the government of Spain. After moving to Hamburg, he and his sons were circumcised; this caused a scandal, and led to an (unsuccessful) attempt by the imperial Viennese court to confiscate his property. Teixeira established an international banking house in Hamburg and took a leading role in Jewish affairs there, serving as the head of the city's Sephardi congregation. From 1655 he was resident diplomatic and financial minister for the Swedish crown in Hamburg.

Teixeira, Isaac Ḥayyim Senior (1625–1705) Dutch communal leader, son of **Abraham Senior Teixeira**. He became head of the Portuguese community in Amsterdam. He was unsuccessful in his attempt to intercede on behalf of the Jews of Austria, when they were threatened with expulsion.

Tenenbaum, Mordechai (1916–43) Polish Zionist. He was a leading member of the Polish Hechalutz Zionist group. He was active in the Jewish resistance movement during the Nazi occupation and developed the Jewish fighting organization in Bialystok. He led the ghetto revolt there.

Tertis, Lionel (1876–1975) British violist. Born in West Hartlepool, his father was a rabbi. He studied violin at the Leipzig Conservatory and the Royal Academy of Music.He toured the US and Europe as a solo violist.

Thalberg, Irving (1899–1936) American flim producer. Born in Brooklyn, he became assistant manager of an export company. Later he became secretary to **Carl Laemmle**, founder of Universal Pictures and went to California. He subsequently became production chief for **Louis B. Mayer** and supervised production at Metro-Goldwyn-Mayer.

Theodora (fl. 14th cent.) Bulgarian czarina. She came from a Byzantine Jewish family, but was baptized and married Czar Ivan Alexander.

Theudas (fl. 1st cent.) Palestianian religious leader and pseudo-messiah. He persuaded the people to gather up their possessions and follow him to the Jordan, where at his comand he claimed the river would part. The Roman procurator Cuspius Fadus sent cavalary after them. Theudas was caught and decapitated, and his head was taken to Jerusalem.

Thomashefsky, Boris (1866–1939) American Yiddish actor, of Ukrainian origin. He went to the US in 1881. He produced, wrote, adapted and acted in many plays performed at New York's Yiddish theatres. He also initiated the visit of a Yiddish theatre company from London.

Thon, Osias (1870–1936) Polish rabbi and Zionist, brother of Yaakov Thon. He was born in Lemberg. He became an associate of **Theodor Herzl**, whom he assisted in preparing the First Zionist Congress. From 1897 he was a rabbi in Kraków. In 1919 he was appointed vice-president of the Comité des Délégations Juives at the Paris Peace Conference; in the same year he was elected to the Sejm, where he served until 1935 and was head of the Jewish members' organization. He wrote a biography of **Herzl** and essays on Zionism.

Ticho, Anna (1894–1980) Israeli artist. She was born in Brünn, Moravia, and went to Jerusalem in 1912. She made numerous drawings of the Judean landscape.

Tiktin, Gedaliah (c. 1810–86) German rabbi, son of **Solomon Tiktin**. He became Landrabbiner in Breslau in 1854. He joined his father in a feud with **Abraham Geiger**.

Tiktin, Solomon (1791–1843) German rabbi. He became a rabbi in Breslau. In 1838 he opposed the appointment of the Reformer **Abraham Geiger** as assistant rabbi, preacher and dayyan in Breslau. He and his son, **Gedaliah Tiktin**, engaged in a campaign against **Geiger**, which divided the community.

Timerman, Jacobo (b. 1923) Argentine journalist. He was born in Russia, and went to Argentina in 1942. He became a political journalist and founded *La opinión* in Buenos Aires. His *Prisoner Without a Name, Cell Without a Number* explores anti-Semitism in Argentina.

Tiomkin, Vladimir (1860–1927) Russian Zionist leader. He was born in Yelizavetgrad in the Ukraine. He was a founder of the Ahavat Zion Society in St Petersburg, and later became head of the executive committee of the Russian Ḥovevei Zion in Jaffa. He returned to Russia and joined the Zionist movement, participating in Zionist congresses. During World War I he directed relief projects in southern Russia; after the 1917 Revolution he resumed his Zionist activities. In 1920 he settled in Paris and joined **Vladimir Jabotinsky's** Revisionist Zionist movement.

Tirado, Jacob (c.1560–1625) Portuguese religious leader. He was born in Portugal into a family of Conversos. He settled in Amsterdam, where he returned to Judaism. In c.1608 he helped to found the first Sephardi community in the city. Before 1616 he went to Palestine and settled in Jerusalem.

Tishby, Isaiah (b. 1908) Israeli scholar. He was born at Sándor Schwartz in Sanislo, Hungary. In 1933 he settled in Palestine, where he became a professor at the Hebrew University. His publications include studies of the kabbalah.

Tobiah ben Eliezer (fl. 11th cent.) Bulgarian talmudist and poet. He wrote *Lekaḥ Tov* (or *Pesikta Zutarta*), a midrashic commentary on the Pentateuch and the Five Scrolls.

Tobiah ben Moses (fl. 11th cent.) Turkish Karaite scholar, biblical exegete and liturgical poet. After studying in Jerusalem under Yeshuah ben Judah, he lived in Constantinople. He translated the Arabic works of his sect into Hebrew. His writings include *Yehi Meorot* on the biblical commandments, *Otzar Neḥmad* on Leviticus, and *Zot ha-Torah* on the Pentateuch.

Tobias, Lilly (1887–1984) Welsh novelist. She was born in Swansea. Her works deal with various modern Jewish themes. Her publications include *The Nationalists and other Goluth Studies*, *My Mothers' House* and *The Samaritan*.

Todd, Michael [Goldbogen, Avrom] (1907–58) American film producer. Born in Minneapolis, Minnesota, he became a building contractor. He worked as a theatrical producer and later formed the Magna corporation. His first film was *Oklahoma!* and he also produced *Around the World in 80 Days*.

Toledano, Yaakov Mosheh (1880–1960) Israeli rabbi. He was born in Tiberias. He served as a rabbi in Alexandria, and in 1941 was appointed chief Sephardi rabbi of Tel Aviv. He served as minister for religious affairs in the Israeli government.

Toller, Ernst (1893–1939) German dramatist and poet. Born in Samotshin, he studied at the University of Grenoble. Later he studied at Munich and Heidelberg. He participated in strikes and was imprisoned. He later engaged in anti-war and revolutionary activities. He was involved in the Bavarian Soviet regime; after the murder of **Kurt Eisner**, he was sentenced to imprisonment and wrote *The Swallow-Book* and a number of plays. When he was released from prison he was active in various liberal causes.

Topol, Ḥayyim (b. 1935) Israeli actor. He was born in Tel Aviv. He appeared at the Haifa Municipal Theatre, and later in *Fiddler on the Roof* in Tel Aviv. Subsequently he starred in the film production of the play.

Torres, Luis de (fl. 15th–16th cent.) Spanish explorer. He was interpreter to **Christopher Columbus** on the expedition of 1492 which led to the discovery of the New World. Born a Jew Torres was baptized before the expedition set sail.

Touro, Abraham (1774–1822) American philanthropist, brother of **Judah Touro**. He was born in Newport, Rhode Island, and with his brother helped to support Newport's synagogue. His will made possible the building of residential units in what later became the new city of Jerusalem.

Touro, Judah (1775–1854) American philanthropist, brother of **Abraham Touro**. He was born in Newport, Rhode Island. He worked as a merchant and supported Christian and Jewish charities.

Touroff, Nissan (1877–1953) American educator. He served as director of the Bureau of Hebrew Education in Palestine from 1914 to 1919. He was dean of the Boston Hebrew Teachers' College

(1921–26), and taught at the Jewish Institute of Religion.

Trani, Isaiah di (fl. 12th cent.) Italian talmudist. He was born in southern Italy but lived in the north. His commentaries on the Talmud carried the conception of contemporary French tosaphists to Italy.

Trani, Joseph di (1568–1639) Palestinian rabbi and scholar, son of **Moses ben Joseph di Trani**. He was born in Safed, and founded a yeshivah there. Later he settled in Jerusalem, where he did research on the design and plan of the Temple. He returned to Safed and became head of the Sephardi community. Eventually he moved to Constantinople, where he directed a yeshivah, and became chief rabbi of Turkey.

Trani, Moses ben Joseph di (1505–85) Palestinian rabbi. He was born in Salonica. He was one of the four scholars ordained by **Jacob Berab** in his attempt to reintroduce ordination and establish an authoritative Jewish leadership. Trani served as a rabbi and dayyan for 54 years, eventually becoming spiritual head of the Safed community.

Trebitsch Lincoln, Ignaz (1879–1943) Hungarian political activist. Born in Hungary, he was bapitized and went to Canada and was ordained. Later he moved to England and became a curate, but left the ministry. He became a member of parliament in 1910. During World War I he became a double agent to England and Germany. When the British sought to arrest him, he fled to the US; he was later extradited to England and imprisoned. He later went to Berlin where he was involved in right- wing politics. Subsequently he lived in China where he was an advisor to warlords. He later became a Buddhist monk.

Treinin, Avner (b. 1928) Israeli poet. He was born in Tel Aviv and taught chemistry at the Hebrew University. His poems are concerned with the Holocaust and recent events in Jewish history.

Tremellius, John Immanuel (1510–80) Italian Hebraist. He was born in Ferrara. He became a Catholic, then a year later converted to Protestantism. In 1542 he was appointed professor of Hebrew at the University of Strasbourg. He moved to England, where he was King's Reader in Hebrew at the University of Cambridge, and then to Germany to take the position of professor of Old Testament at the University of Heidelberg. He published a Latin translation of the Bible from Hebrew and Syriac.

Trepper, Leopold (1904–82) Polish head of a spy network. Born in Novy-Targ, Galicia, he joined the Hashomer Hatzair youth movement and the Polish communist party. He became the head of Hashomer Hatzair in Silesia and participated in communist youth groups. In 1924 he went to Palestine and became secretary of the Haifa branch of the communist party. Later he went to Paris and joined the French communist party and established a Yiddish weekly, *Der Morgen*. He then went to Moscow where he was involved in political and revolutionary activities. In 1937 he went to Brussels and then to Paris where he established a Soviet spy network, the Red Orchestra.

Treves, Johanan (b. 1429) French rabbi, son of **Mattathias ben Joseph Treves**. When his father died he became chief rabbi of Paris. Later Isaiah ben Abba Mari claimed the sole right of appointing rabbis in France and of conducting a yeshivah. With the help of Meir ben Baruch of Vienna, he attempted to remove Johanan from his post. The expulsion of Jews from France in 1394 ended the dispute, and Johanan went to Italy.

Treves, Mattatias ben Joseph (c. 1325–c. 1385) French rabbi. He was born in Provence, and lived in Spain. He returned to France when the edict of expulsion of the Jews was repealed in 1361. He founded a yeshivah in Paris and in 1363 became the city's chief rabbi.

Trietsch, Davis (1870–1935) German Zionist writer. He was born in Dresden. During a period spent in the US (1893–9), he wrote several works on Jewish migration. He participated in the First Zionist Congress (1897), advocating Jewish settlement in Cyprus and the Sinai peninsula. Later he published schemes for Jewish settlement in Palestine. He himself moved to Palestine in 1932. he was a founder of the journals *Ost und West*, *Palästina* and *Jüdischer Verlag*.

Trilling, Leopold (1905–75) American critic. Born in New York, he was professor of English literature at Columbia University. His works include *The Liberal Imagination*, *The Opposing Self* and *Beyond Culture*.

Troki, Isaac ben Abraham (c.1533–c.1594) Lithuanian Karaite scholar. He was born in Troki. He wrote an apologia for Judaism *Ḥizzuk ha-Emunah* (Strengthening of the Faith).

Trotsky, Leon [Bronstein, Lev Davidovich] (1879–1940) Born in Yanovka in the Ukraine, he was involved in revolutionary groups and arrested in 1898 and exiled. He escaped in 1902 and went to London where he joined Lenin. He then moved to Geneva. In 1905 he returned to Russia and was again arrested and exiled in Sibera. He escaped and went to Vienna. During World War I he was in Paris; he then went to New York but returned to Russia in 1917. He was elected to the Central Committee of the Bolshevik party and was an organizer of the October revolution. Later he came into conflict with Stalin, and was exiled.

Trumpeldor, Joseph (1880–1920) Palestinian soldier. He was born in Pyatigorsk in the northern Caucasus. He volunteered for the Russian army and became an officer. In 1912 he moved to Palestine, where he attempted to found a co-operative agricultural settlement. In Egypt during World War I he and **Vladimir Jabotinsky** tried to establish a Jewish unit to fight against the Turks in Palestine. In 1917 Trumpeldor went to Russia to organize Jewish groups who would settle in Palestine. Two years later he returned to Palestine as leader of a pioneer group and organized volunteers to protect Jewish settlements in Upper Galilee.

Tschernikhovski [Tchernikohovski], Shaul (1875–1943) Palestinian Hebrew poet, of Russian origin. He was born in Mikhailovka, and during World War I served in the Russian medical corps. From 1922 to 1931 he lived in Germany, and later he moved to Palestine. He wrote poetry, stories, essays and philological studies, and translated ancient and modern verse. His poetry had an important impact on Jewish youth.

Tschlenow, Jehiel (1863–1918) Russian Zionist leader. He was born in Kremenchug in the Ukraine, and became a physician. Active in the Ḥibbat Zion movement, he was one of the leaders of the Tziyyone Zion group founded in opposition to the plan for a Jewish homeland in Uganda. In 1906 Tschlenow convened the Helsingfors Conference. He later lived in Copenhagen and London, where he was an active Zionist. After the 1917 Revolution, he returned to Russia and convened a Russian Zionist Conference. His writings include *The Second Zionist Congress*, *Five Years of Work in Palestine* and *The World and Our Prospects*.

Tsinberg, Yisrael (1873–1939) Russian literary historian. He was born in a village near Lanovits, Volhynia, and lived in St Petersburg, where he became head of a chemical laboratory. He published a popular science book in Yiddish, critical and literary-historical studies, and a history of Jewish literature.

Tuchman, Barbara (1912–89) American historian. She studied at Radcliffe College and was a research assistant at the Institute of Pacific Relations in New York. She then worked for the *Nation*. From 1943 to 1945 she worked at the US Office of War Information. Her works include *Bible and Sword*, *The Zimmerman Telegram*, *The Guns of August*, *The Proud Tower*, *Stilwell and the American Experience in China*, *Notes from Asia*, *The March of Folly* and *A Distant Mirror: The Calamitous 14th Century*.

Tucholsky, Kurt (1890–1935) German writer. Born in Berlin, he studied at the University of Jena. He later lived in Germany, France, Switzerland, and settled in Sweden. His works include *Rheinsberg: ein Bilderbuch für Verliebte* and *Schloss Gripsholm*.

Tucker, Richard (1916–75) American tenor. He was a successful synagogue cantor. From 1945 he made a career as an opera singer at the Metropolitan Opera in New York.

Tucker, Sophie (1889–1966) American entertainer. She was born in Russia, and went to the US as a child. The songs for which she was known included *My Yidishe Momma*.

Tugenhold, Jacob (1794–1871) Polish author. He was born near Kraków. He founded a modern

Jewish school in Warsaw, which alienated Orthodox Jews. He served as vice-censor of Hebrew books, and from 1856 to 1863 was head of the government rabbinical seminary in Warsaw.

Tumarkin, Yigal (b. 1933) Israeli painter and sculptor. He was born in Dresden, and went to Palestine as a child in 1935. Later he lived in Germany, the Netherlands and Paris. He constructed a number of sculptural monuments in Israel.

Tunkel, Joseph (1881–1949) Russian Yiddish humourist and cartoonist. He was born in Belorussia. In 1906 he went to the US, where he edited the comic magazines *Der Kibitzer* and *Der groyse Kundes*. He returned to Warsaw in 1910 and became editor of *Der moment*. In 1939 he fled to France and in 1941 to the US. He wrote under the pseudonym 'Der Tunkeler'.

Tur-Sinai, Naphtali Herz [Torczyner, Harry] (1886–1973) Israeli philologist and Bible scholar. He was born in Lemberg. In 1933 he went to Palestine, where he taught at the Hebrew University. He wrote commentaries to the book of Job, a study of Proverbs, essays on biblical texts, rabbinic Hebrew, and problems in the history of the Hebrew language, and a work on the Lachish Letters.

Tuwim, Julian (1894–1953) Polish writer. Born in Lodz, he studied at the Unversity of Warsaw. He wrote poems, satires and musical comedies.

Twersky, Isadore (1930–97) American scholar. Born in Boston, he studied at Harvard University and was a professor there and director of the Center for Jewish Studies from 1978 to 1993. His work focused on **Moses Maimonides**.

Twersky, Menaḥem Naḥum (1730–83) Lithuanian Ḥasidic leader. He was a pupil of Israel ben Eliezer **Baal Shem Tov** and **Dov Ber of Mezhirich**. He practised as an itinerant preacher, stressing the importance of purifying moral attributes. He was the founder of a dynasty of tzaddikim. His son, Mordecai of Chernobyl (1770–1837), lived in some splendour and was greatly revered.

Twersky, Yoḥanan (1900–67) Israeli novelist. He was born in Shpikov in the Ukraine. He went to the US in 1926 and taught at the Hebrew College in Boston. In 1947 he settled in Israel, where he served on the editorial staff of the Dvir Publishing House in Tel Aviv. His novels include *Uriel Acosta*, *Aḥad ha-Am*, *Alfred Dreyfus*, *Rashi* and *Rom u-Tehom*.

Tzara, Tristan (1896–1963) French poet. Born in Moinesti, Romania, his works include *Vingt-cinq*, *Cinéma*, *Calendriers du coeur abstrait*, *Où boivent les loups*, *L'antitête*, *Le coeur à gaz*, *La fuite*, *La face intérieure* and *Parler seul*. He was a founder of dadaism.

Tzarfati [Zafartti], Joseph (fl. 15th–16th cent.) Italian poet and physician. He was active in Jewish affairs in Rome. He wrote poetry about a wide range of topics and his translation of the Spanish comedy *Celestina* initiated Hebrew drama.

Tzarfati [Zarfatti], Samuel (fl. 15th–16th cent.) Italian physician. He was in the service of the Medici family in Florence, and of several popes in Rome. He was active in Jewish affairs.

Tzemaḥ, Naḥum David (1890–1939) Theatre producer. He formed a Hebrew dramatic group in Vienna, which became the Ha-Bimah company. From 1930 to 1937 he directed the Tel Aviv Bet Am.

Tzemaḥ, Shelomoh (b. 1886) Israeli author, of Polish origin. He lived in Palestine in 1903–9, and again from 1921. His stories describe life in Israel.

Tzur, Yaakov (b. 1906) Israeli diplomat and public figure. He was born in Vilna, and emigrated to Palestine in 1921. He worked in the head office of the Jewish National Fund from 1929 to 1948. After the estabishment of the State of Israel, he represented Israel in Argentina and other South American countries, as well as in France. He later returned to Israel, where he became director of the Jewish National Fund.

U

Ullendorff, Edward (b. 1920) British scholar. He was born in Zurich. He lectured in Semitics at the University of St Andrews and was later professor at the universities of Manchester and London. He published numerous works on aspects of Semitics, notably in the field of Ethiopian studies.

Ullstein, Leopold (1826–99) German publisher. Born in Fürth, he worked in his father's paper business and went to Berlin. He founded a newspaper empire.

Unterman, Isaar Yehudah (1886–1976) Israeli rabbi and scholar. He was born in Brest-Litovsk, Belorussia. He served as rosh yeshivah in Vishova, Lithuania, and later as a rabbi in various Lithuanian communities. After moving to England, he became rabbi of Liverpool in 1924. In 1946 he was appointed chief rabbi to the Ashkenazi community in Tel Aviv-Jaffa, and in 1964 Ashkenazi chief rabbi of Israel. His writings include *Shevet mi-Yehudah* on problems of Jewish law.

Untermayer, Louis (1885–1977) American writer. Born in New York City, he served as a consultant to the Library of Congress. He compiled anthologies, including *Modern American Poetry* and *Modern British Poetry*. His correspondence with Robert Frost was published in 1963.

Urbach, Ephraim Elimelech (1912–91) Israeli scholar. He studied at the Breslau Rabbinical Seminary and at the universities of Breslau and Rome; he later taught at the Breslau seminary (1935–8). In 1938 he settled in Palestine, where he became a schoolteacher and headmaster of grammar schools in Jerusalem. In 1958 he became professor of Talmud at the Hebrew University. His publications include a study of the tosaphists and their methods.

Uri, Aviva (b. 1927) Israeli artist. Born in Safed, her works are based on forms derived from nature and landscape.

Uri, Phoebus ben Aaron Levi [Witzenhausen, Joseph] (1623–1715) Dutch printer. In 1658 he established a press in Amsterdam, which published rabbinical and religious works in Hebrew and Yiddish. He also published the first Yiddish newspaper, *Dienstagishe und Freytagishe Kurant*, from 1680. In 1692 he moved to Zholkva, Poland, where he is supposed to have been invited by the king, John Sobieski, to print Hebrew books.

Uriah ben Shemaiah (fl. 7th cent. BCE) Israelite prophet. A contemporary of **Jeremiah**, he foretold the destruction of Jerusalem and Judah. He was persecuted by **Jehoiakim** and fled to Egypt. Later he was brought back and put to death (Jeremiah 26:20ff).

Uris, Leon (b. 1924) American novelist. He was born in Baltimore. His novels include *Exodus*, which tells the story of the birth of the State of Israel, and *Mila 18*, about the uprising in the Warsaw Ghetto.

Ury, Lesser (1861–1931) German artist. He was born in Birnbaum, Prussia, and went to Berlin at the age of 12. He studied art in Düsseldorf, Brussels, Paris and Italy, later returning to Berlin. Some of his paintings deal with Jewish themes.

Usque, Abraham [Pinhel, Duarte] (fl. 16th cent.) Portuguese printer. He fled from the Inquisition around 1543 to Ferrara, where he became associated with the Hebrew and Italian press established by Yom Tov ben Levi Athias. His name appears in connection with the 1553 translation of the Bible into Italian (*The Ferrara Bible*).

Usque, Samuel (fl. 16th cent.) Portuguese poet and historian. He was born in Spain, but his family emigrated to Portugal in 1492. His *Consolation for the Tribulations of Israel* was designed to persuade marranos to return to Judaism.

Usque, Solomon [Luistano, Salusque] (c. 1530–95) Portuguese poet. He lived in Italy and Turkey. In collaboration with Lazzaro di Granziano Levi, he wrote the earliest known Jewish drama in the vernacular, a Purim play in Spanish. He also published a Spanish translation of the final part of Petrarch's sonnets. In Constantinople he engaged in Hebrew printing.

Ussishkin, Menaḥem Mendel (1863–1941) Russian Zionist leader. He was born in Dubrovno in the district of Mohilev in Belorussia; he moved to Moscow in 1871. He was a founder of the Zionist youth group Bilu in 1882, and of the Bene Zion society in 1884; in 1897 he attended the First Zionist Congress as a delegate. He published a pamphlet, *Our Program*, in 1903, advocating a policy of political activity and practical work in Palestine. In the same year he convened an assembly of Palestinian Jews at Zikhron Yaakov and a teachers' conference. After returning to Russia, he organized the Tziyyone Zion (1904) in opposition to the proposal for a Jewish homeland in Uganda. In 1906 he went to Odessa, where he became leader of the Ḥovevei Zion. He later settled in Palestine, where he was appointed chairman of the Jewish National Fund.

Uziel, Ben Zion Meir Hai (1880–1954) Israeli rabbi. He was born in Jerusalem. He became Ḥakham Bashi at Jaffa in 1912, and Rishon le-Zion in 1939. His writings include studies of Jewish law.

Uziel, Isaac ben Abraham (fl. 17th cent.) Dutch rabbi. He was born in Gez, and in 1610 was appointed rabbi of the Neveh Shalom synagogue in Amsterdam. He wrote poetry, a Hebrew grammar, and a translation of legends and fables.

Uzziah [Azariah] (fl. 8th cent. BCE) King of Judah (c. 780–c. 740 BCE). He conquered Philistia and led a league of kings opposed to Tiglath-Pileser of Assyria; he also rebuilt the port of Elath. He eventually fell victim to leprosy and ceded power to his son **Jotham**.

V

Vajda, George (1908–1981) French Arabist and Hebraist. He was born in Budapest. In 1928 he settled in Paris, where he became professor of Bible and theology at the Séminaire Israélite. He also lectured at the École Pratique de Hautes Études, and was active in the oriental department of the Institut de Recherches et d'Histoire des Textes. From 1950 he edited the scholarly journal *Revue des Études Juives.* In 1970 he became a professor at the University of Paris. His writings include studies of Arabic and Jewish philosophy, the kabbalah and Arab manuscripts.

Vámbéry, Arminius (1832–1913) Hungarian orientalist and traveller. He was born in Dunajska, Streda, on the island of Schütt, and lived in Constantinople, where he worked as a tutor in European languages. After becoming a Muslim, he became secretary to Mehmet Fuad Pasha. In 1863–4 he travelled through Armenia, Persia and Turkestan, disguised as a Sunnite dervish; he published an account of his experiences as *Travels and Adventures in Central Asia.* He later became a Protestant and taught oriental languages at the University of Budapest. His writings include studies of oriental languages and ethnology.

Vas, István (b. 1910) Hungarian poet. Born in Budapest, he studied in Vienna and later converted to Catholicism. He translated English and French poetry and produced poems of a sensual and metaphysical nature as well as autobiographical writings: *Difficult Love* and *Why Does the Vulture Screech?.*

Vazsonyi, Vilmos (1868–1926) Hungarian politician and lwayer. He founded the club of Junior Democrats in Budapest around 1890. In 1894 he was elected to the Budapest municipal council, and in 1901 to the lower house of the Hungarian parliament; during World War I he served as minister of justice. He advocated assimilation of the Jews in the diaspora, and was an opponent of Zionism.

Vecinho, Joseph (fl. 15th cent.) Portuguese scientist and physician. A pupil of **Abraham Zucato**, he translated his teacher's astronomical tables (*Almanach perpetuum*) into Spanish. Together with Martin Behaim and the court physician Rodrigo, he participated in a commission investigating navigation. He was forcibly converted in 1497, adopting the name Diego Mendes Vecinho.

Veksler, Vladimir Iosifiovich (1907–66) Soviet nuclear physicist. Born in Zhitomir in the Ukraine, he worked as an apparatus assembler in a factory and later went to Moscow. His early research was in the field of X-rays, and in 1936 he was appointed to the Lebedev Institute of Physics in Moscow. Subsequently he became director of the high energy laboratory of the Joint Institute for Nuclear Research.

Venetianer, Lajos (1867–1922) Hungarian rabbi and historian. He was born in Kecskemét. He served as rabbi in Csurgó (1893) and Lugos (1896), and from 1897 as chief rabbi in Ujpest. He was also professor at the Budapest Rabbinical Seminary. His publications include studies of Christian liturgy and Judaism, the history of Hungarian Jewry, and the organization of Jewish communities.

Ventura, Rubino (1792–1848) Italian soldier. He served as a soldier in Napoleon's army and went to Persia. He then served with the maharaja of Lahore.

Veprik, Alexander (1899–1952) Russian composer. He was born in Balta. He taught orchestration at the Moscow Conservatory from 1923 to 1942. His works include *Songs and Dances of the Ghetto*, *Jewish Songs* and *Kaddish.*

Verbitsky, Bernardo (1902–79) Argentine novelist and academic. He was born in Buenos Aires. He wrote prose fiction and essays; some of his work deals with the problem of Jewish identity.

Vermes, Geza (b. 1924) British scholar, of Hungarian origin. He taught at the University of Newcastle, and later became professor of Jewish studies at the University of Oxford. He published studies of the Dead Sea Scrolls, Jewish exegesis, and the Jewish background to the New Testament.

Vidal-Naquet, Pierre (b. 1930) French historian. He was born into an assimilated Jewish family, but his attitude to Judaism was changed by the Holocaust, in which his parents were killed. He led a campaign against Revisionist historians, who claim that the Holocaust did not take place.

Viertel, Berthold (1885–1953) Austrian writer. He studied in Vienna and in 1923 was the founder of an experimental theatre group. He began directing in Germany and Hollywood. In 1933 he returned to Germany but later went to England. His films include *The Little Sister, The Passing of the Third Floor Back* and *Rhodes of Africa.*

Vigée, Claude (b. 1921) French poet and essayist. He was born in Bischwiller. He was active in the Jewish Resistance in France during World War II, but in 1942 escaped to Spain and the following year emigrated to the US. He taught at various American universities, before becoming a professor at the Hebrew University in 1963. He wrote poems, stories and recollections, many of which deal with Jewish themes.

Vinawer, Maxim (1862–1926) Russian politician. He was a lawyer in St Petersburg and a leader of the Constitutional Democratic Party in the Duma. After the 1917 Revolution he became foreign minister in the shortlived anti-communist Crimean regional government.

Vischniac, Roman (1897–1990) Russian photographer. Born in St Petersburg, he studied zoology at Moscow University. After the Russian Revolution he settled in Latvia and then Berlin. He later embarked on a sustained journey through the Jewish communities of Poland, Lithuania, Latvia, Hungary, Czechoslovakia and Germany recording the lives of Eastern European Jewry. Later he went to France and then to the US where he was a portrait photographer. His works include *A Vanished World.*

Visser, Lodewijk Ernst (1871–1942) Dutch jurist. Born in Amsersfoort. He studied law and became general prosecutor in Amsterdam and later judge of the district court. In 1915 he became judge of the high court of Holland and in 1939 president of the high court. When the Germans invaded Holland in 1940 he appeared in the high court in his full dress and opened the session with a speech in which he attacked the invasion.

Vital, Ḥayyim (1543–1620) Palestinian kabbalist. He was a student of **Moses Cordoverro** and **Moses Alshekh**, and was associated with **Isaac Luria** during his last years in Safed. After **Luria**'s death, Vital claimed that he alone had an accurate account of **Luria**'s teaching. He boasted that his soul was that of the Messiah, son of Joseph, and he became known in oriental countries as a miracle worker. His notes on Lurianic kabbalah were transcribed and published as *Etz Ḥayyim.* From 1590 he lived in Damascus, where he wrote kabbalistic works and preached the coming of the Messiah.

Vital, Samuel (fl. 17th cent.) Syrian rabbi and kabbalist, son of **Ḥayyim Vital**. He lived in Damascus and later went to Cairo. He edited his father's works on Lurianic kabbalah.

Viterbo, Carlo Alberto (1889–1974) Italian Zionist. He was born in Florence. He became president of the Italian Zionist Organization in 1931. He was imprisoned in the Sforzacosta concentration camp during World War II and released by the Allies in 1944. After the war he relaunched the periodical *Israel*, which continued until his death.

Vitkin, Yoseph (1876–1912) Palestinian Zionist pioneer. He was born in Mogilev, Belorussia. In 1897 he went to Palestine, where he worked as a labourer, and later as a schoolteacher and headmaster. His writings include a number of pamphlets on pioneering, such as *A Call to the Youth of Israel whose Hearts are with Their People and with Zion* and *A Group of Young People from Eretz Israel.*

Vogel, David (1891–1944) Russian Hebrew poet and writer. He was born in Satanov, Russia, and settled in Vienna in 1912. He suffered periods of imprisonment during World War I (to 1916) and World War II (in French detention camps, to 1941), before being arrested by the Nazis in 1944. He wrote novels as well as poetry and is regarded as an important forerunner of Hebrew modernism.

Vogel, Julius (1835–1899) New Zealand prime minster. Born in London, he studied at London University School and at the Royal School of Mines. In 1852 he went to Australia where he was an assayer. He then embarked on journalism and wrote for several Victorian newspapers. In 1861 he settled in the South Island city of Otago, New Zealand. He founded the *Otago Daily Times* which he edited. He became a member of the Otago provincial council in 1863 and later provincial treasurer. He subsequently was elected to the house of representatives and became prime minister in 1873.

Volterra, Meshullam [Meshullam ben Menaḥem of Volterra] (fl. 15th cent.) Italian financier. He inherited his father's loan bank in Florence. In 1481 he travelled to Palestine; after a month's stay he returned to Florence via Venice. His *Massa Meshullam mi-Volterra be-Eretz Yisrael* is an account of his voyage.

Volterra, Vito (1860–1940) Italian mathematician. Born in Ancona, he lived in Florence and became an assistant in the physics laboratory at the University of Florence. He later became a professor of mechanics at the University of Pisa, and later professor of mathematical physics at the University of Rome. He made contributions in the fields of higher analysis, mathematical physics, integral equations, celestial mechanics, calculus of variations, mathematical theory of elasticity and mathematical biometrics.

Voronoff, Serge (1866–1951) French physiologist. Born in Voronege, Russia, he went to Paris in 1884 and studied at the Paris medical school. He became chief surgeon at the auxiliary hospital, Paris and later director of the biological laboratory at the École des Hautes Études. In 1917 he became director of the experimental laboratory in surgery at the Collège de France in Nice.

Vriesland, Victor Emanuel van (b. 1892) Dutch writer. Born in Haarlem, he studied French literature in Dijon. He became editor of a number of Dutch literary journals and in 1931 literary editor of the Dutch newspaper *Nieuwe Rotterdamsche Courant.* He published poetry, a novel and critical essays.

W

Wahl, Meir (fl. 17th cent.) Lithuanian talmudist, son of **Saul Wahl**. He was rabbi of Brest and a founder in 1623 of the Council of Lithuania, and autonomous governing body for Lithuanian Jewry.

Wahl, Saul (1541–1617) Lithuanian financier. He was the son of Samuel Judah ben Abraham, who was rabbi at Venice and Padua. Wahl became court agent to Sigismund III, and used his influence on behalf of Jews in Poland and Lithuania. According to legend, he was chosen to be King of Poland for a day.

Waksman, Selman (1888–1973) American biochemist of Ukrainian origin. born in Priluka, in the Ukraine, he went to the US at the age of 22. He studied at the University of California and was a professor at Rutgers University. He received the Nobel Prize for Medicine and Physiology in 1952. His works include *Principles of Soil Microbiology, The Conquest of Tuberculosis* and *My Life with the Microbes.*

Wald, George (b. 1906) American biologist. He was professor of biological sciences at Harvard. He researched into the chemisty of the eye and its relationship to vitamin A. He received the Nobel Prize in Medicine and Physiology in 1967.

Wald, Herman (1906–70) South African sculptor. He was born in Cluj, Hungary. He went to Paris in 1933 and later to London; in 1937 he settled in South Africa. Some of his art is influenced by Jewish subjects.

Wald, Lillian (1867–1940) American pioneer of public health nursing. Born in Cincinnati, Ohio, she studied nursing in New York City. Encouraged by the philanthropist, **Jacob Schiff**, she established the Henry Street Settlement house in New York.

Waldman, Morris David (1879–1963) American communal worker. He was born in Bartfa, Hungary, and was taken to the US as a child. From 1908 to 1917 he was managing director of the United Hebrew Charities of New York. In 1921–2 he organized relief for central European Jewish communities, and from 1928 he served as executive secretary of the American Jewish Joint Distribution Committee. His writings include an autobiography, *Not by Power* and *Sieg Heil*, a study of Hitler's treatment of the Jews.

Waley [Schloss], Arthur (1889–1966) British orientalist. He was assistant keeper of prints and drawings at the British Museum. He translated classical Chinese poetry and Japanese romances including *The Tale of Genji.*

Waley, Jacob (1818–73) English lawyer and communal leader. He served as professor of political economy at University College, London (1953–60). He was a founder of the United Synagogue, president of the Anglo-Jewish Association, and president of the Jews Hospital and Orphan Asylum.

Walkowitz, Abraham (1878–1965) American painter. He was born in Siberia, and went to the US in 1889. His works include *Faces from the Ghetto.*

Wallace [Wallenchinsky], Irving (1916–90) American novelist. Born in Chicago, he grew up in Kenosha, Wisconsin. He studied at the Williams Institute,

Berkeley, and Los Angeles City College. His novels include *The Chapman Report*, *The Prize*, *The Word*, *The Fan Club*, *The Second Lady* and *The Miracle*.

Wallach, Otto (1847–1931) German chemist. He was professor at Berlin and later at Göttingen. He received the Nobel Prize for research into the molecular structure of a group of substances known as terpenes.

Wallant, Edward (1926–62) American novelist. He was born in New Haven, Connecticut, and worked in a New York advertising agency. His novels deal with Jewish characters.

Wallenstein, Meir (1903–96) British orientalist. He was born in Jerusalem. He taught in Palestine (1925–9), and Manchester (1932–8), then from 1946 was reader in medieval and modern Hebrew at Manchester University. He settled in Jerusalem in 1970. His publications include studies of Moses Judah Abbas and his contemporaries, hymns from the Judean scrolls, and piyyutim from the Cairo Genizah.

Walter, Bruno (1876–1962) German conductor. Born in Berlin, He was opera coach at the Municipal Opera of Cologne. Later he became assistant conductor of the Hamburg Stadt-Theatre. In 1896 he became second conductor in Breslau and the prinicipal conductor in Pressburg. In 1900 he became conductor at the Berlin Opera. Later he became assistant at the Vienna Opera. In 1923 he went to Munich where he conducted performances of Mozart operas. When the Nazis came to power, he conducted in Amsterdam, Salzburg and Vienna. He then went to France, and later to the US.

Warburg, Edward (b. 1908) American communal leader, son of **Felix Warburg**. He was involved in a variety of cultural, communal, and philanthropic activities. He served as chairman of the American Jewish Joint Distribution Committee (1941–66) and of the United Jewish Appeal. In 1967 he became president of the United Jewish Appeal of Greater New York.

Warburg, Felix (1871–1937) American banker and communal leader, brother of **Max Warburg**. He was born in Hamburg, and in 1894 went to the US, where he became a partner in the banking firm of Kuhn, Loeb and Co. in New York. He served as chairman of the American Jewish Joint Distribution Committee (1914–32) and supported Jewish educational institutions, including the Hebrew Union College, the Jewish Theological Seminary and the Graduate School for Jewish Social Work.

Warburg, Max (1867–1946) German banker, brother of **Felix Warburg**. He served as a German delegate to the Paris Peace Conference at the end of World War I and was active in Jewish affairs. He settled in the US in 1939.

Warburg, Otto (1859–1938) German botanist, cousin of **Max** and **Felix Warburg**. He was born in Hamburg. He became professor at the University of Berlin in 1892. An active Zionist, he was instrumental in founding the Palestine Office at Jaffa in 1908, and served as president of the World Zionist Organization from 1911 to 1920. From 1921 he was head of the Jewish Agency's experimental station at Tel Aviv, and he also taught at the Hebrew University.

Warburg, Otto Heinrich (1883–1970) German biochemist. He studied the respiratory mechanisms of cancerous tissue. He received the Nobel Prize in Medicine and Physiology.

Wasserman, Jakob (1873–1934) German novelist. He was born in Fürth, and from 1898 lived in Vienna. His works include *My Life as a German and Jew*, *The Jews of Zirndorf*, *Caspar Hauser*, *The Goose Man* and *The Maurizius Case*.

Wassermann, August von (1866–1925) German scientist. He worked with **Robert Koch** and **Paul Ehrlich** on serums. He is known for the Wassermann test for syphilis.

Wassermann, Oscar (1869–1934) German banker and communal leader. He was born in Bamberg. He became a director of the Berlin branch of his family bank, and in 1912 joined the board of directors of the Deutsche Bank, which later merged with the Disconto-Gesellschaft. Later he was appointed a member of the Council of the Reichsbank. In 1933 he was dismissed from these posts. An active

Zionist, he held various positions in the Jewish community including the presidency of the Keren ha-Yesod in Germany.

Waten, Judah (1911–85) Australian novelist, critic and essayist. He was born in Odessa. In 1914 he emigrated with his family to Perth, where later he worked as a literary critic. In the 1940s he served as a member of the Jewish Council to Combat Fascism and Anti-Semitism. Some of his work deals with Jewish themes.

Waxman, Meyer (1887–1969) American scholar. He was born in Slutsk in Belorussia. In 1905 he emigrated to the US, where he became principal of the Mizraḥi Teachers Seminary, and later director of the Mizraḥi Zionist organization. In 1924 he joined the faculty of the Hebrew Theological College in Chicago; he was later appointed professor of Hebrew literature and philosophy there. His writings include *A Handbook of Judaism*, *Judaism: Religion and Ethics* and *A History of Jewish Literature.*

Weber, Max (1881–1961) American painter and sculptor. He emigrated to the US from Russia in 1891. He studied at Pratt Institute in Brooklyn and later in Paris. After returning to the US, he exhibited at Alfred Stiegliz's Gallery in New York. His abstract paintings were cubist in orientation. After 1919 his work became representational. Beginning in the 1930s his interests turned to Jewish subjects.

Weidenfeld, George (b. 1919) British publisher. He studied at the University of Vienna and emigrated to Enlgand in 1939. He worked for the BBC, and in 1948 he founded Weidenfeld and Nicholson. He was created a life peer.

Weidman, Jerome (1913–98) American writer. He has written 200 short stories as well as plays and novels. In much of his work he draws on the conflict between Jewish and American culture. Among his better-known works are the novels *The Center of the Action* and *Fourth Street East.*

Weigl, Karl (1881–1949) Austrian composer. He studied at the Vienna Music Academy and later at the University of Vienna. He was a rehearsal conductor at the Vienna Hofoper under **Gustav Mahler**. Later he taught at the New Vienna Conservatory. In 1938 he settled in New York and taught at Hart School of Music, Brooklyn College and the New England Conservatory of Music.

Weil, Gotthold (1882–1960) Israeli orientalist and librarian of German origin. He was born in Berlin. He became director of the oriental department at the Berlin State Library in 1906, and in 1920 professor at Berlin University. He was appointed professor of Semitic languages at the University of Frankfurt in 1934. After moving to Palestine he served as head of the National and University Library in Jerusalem (1935–46) and was professor of Turkish studies at the Hebrew University. He published works on Arabic and Turkish subjects.

Weil, Gustav (1808–89) German orientalist. He was born in Salzburg, Baden. He worked as a French instructor at a medical school in Cairo, then, after returning to Germany, as a librarian and teacher in Heidelberg. He wrote studies of Jewish influences on the Koran, Muslim history and Arabic literature. He also translated the *Arabian Nights* into German.

Weil, Simone (1909–43) French religious writer. She was born in Paris. She gave up teaching philosophy to become a factory worker. In 1936 she joined the Republicans in the Spanish Civil War. After the Nazi invasion of France she worked as a farm labourer in the south. She spent a period in the US, but returned to France to join the Resistance. She was fiercely critical of Judaism.

Weiler, Moses Cyrus (1907–2000) South African rabbi. He was born in Riga, Latvia, and was educated in Palestine and later in the US. In 1933 he settled in South Africa where he founded the non-Orthodox progressive movement and served as a rabbi. He moved to Israel in 1958 to teach at the Hebrew Union College.

Weill, Alexandre (1811–99) French philosopher. After a talmudic education he abandoned traditional Judaism. A friend of Hugo, Balzac and Baudelaire, he was prominent in the literary world. In later life he returned to a study of the Bible.

Weill, Kurt (1900–50) German composer. Born in Dessau, he studied at the Hochschule für Musik in Berlin and became conductor of the municipal opera in Lüdenscheid. His early compositions include *Concerto for Violin and Wind Orchestra, Der Protagonist* and *Der Zar lässt sich photographieren.* Later he collaborated with Bertholdt Brecht. In 1933 he went to Paris, and later settled in the US.

Weinberg, Elbert (b. 1928) American sculptor. He was born in Hartford, Connecticut. Some of his works deal with biblical subjects and others with the Holocaust.

Weinberger, Jacob (1879–1956) American composer. He was born in Odessa, and taught there from 1915 to 1921. He emigrated to Palestine in 1922, and later settled in the US. His works include the opera *The Pioneers,* and a number of choral works, among them *Prayers for the Sabbath, Isaiah* and *The Life of Moses.*

Weinberger, Jaromir (1896–1967) American composer. He was born in Prague, and taught there and in various other cities. In 1937 he emigrated to the US, settling in St Petersburg, Florida. His compositions include works based on biblical themes.

Weingreen, Jacob (b. 1908) English Hebrew grammarian and biblical scholar. He was born in Manchester. He became professor of Hebrew at the University of Dublin. His works include *A Practical Grammar for Classical Hebrew, Themes of Old Testament Stories, English Versions of the Old Testament* and *The Concepts of Retaliation and Compensation in Biblical Law.*

Weininger, Otto (1880–1903) Austrian philosopher. He was born in Vienna into a Jewish family, but later converted to Protestantism. His *Sex and Character* deals with the nature of anti-Semitism.

Weinreich, Max (1894–1969) American scholar. He was born in Kuldiga, Latvia. He served as research director of YIVO in Vilna from 1925, and later at the institute's new centre in New York. From 1947 he was professor at City College, New York. He published studies of Yiddish linguistics, folklore, literary history, psychology, pedagogy and sociology.

Weinreich, Uriel (1925–67) American scholar of linguistics, editor and educator, son of **Max Weinreich**. He was born in Vilna, and emigrated to the US in 1940. He became professor of Yiddish language, literature and culture at Columbia University in 1959. His writings include *College Yiddish: An Introduction to the Yiddish Language and to Jewish Life and Culture, Language and Culture Atlas of Ashkenazic Jewry* and *Modern English-Yiddish, Yiddish-English Dictionary.*

Weinryb, Bernard Dov (b. 1900) American economic and social historian. He was born in Turobin, Poland. He worked as the librarian of the Breslau Rabbinical Seminary, before emigrating in 1934 to Palestine, where he lectured at the School of Economics. Later he settled in New York and held a succession of teaching posts – at the Herzliah Teachers' Seminary, the Jewish Teachers' Seminary, Brooklyn College, Columbia University and Yeshiva University. From 1949 he was professor of Jewish history and economics at Dropsie College. He wrote studies of Jewish life and history.

Weisgal, Meyer Wolf (1894–1977) Israeli Zionist. He was born in Kikol, Poland, and moved to the US in 1905. He served as national secretary of the Zionist Organization of America, and as **Chaim Weizmann**'s political representative in the US. Later he became secretary-general of the Jewish Agency for Palestine. He subsequently settled in Israel and became president and chancellor of the Weizmann Institute of Science at Rehovot.

Weisgall, Hugo (1912–97) American composer and educator. He was born in Ivančice (now in Czechoslovakia), and settled in the US in 1920. He taught at Queens College, New York, and served as chairman of faculty at the Cantors Institute of the Jewish Theological Seminary. He has lectured extensively on the subject of Jewish music.

Weiss, Ernst (1884–1940) German novelist. Born in Brünn, he studied medicine. Later he went to Berlin where he lived until 1933; subsequently he went to Prague. In 1934 he settled in Paris. His works include *Die Galeere, Tiere in Ketten, Die Feuerprobe, Georg Letham, Arzt und Mörder, Der arme Verschwender, Der Verführer* and *Ich-der Augenzeuge.* When the German army entered Paris, he committed suicide.

Weiss, Isaac Hirsch (1815–1905) Moravian talmudic scholar. He lectured at the Vienna bet midrash from 1961. His *Dor Dor ve-Doreshav* is a history of the development of the oral law down to the Middle Ages.

Weiss, Peter (1916–82) German playwright. He was born in Berlin. In 1939 he settled in Sweden, where he was active as a painter, film producer and writer. In his play *The Investigation* he made use of documentation produced at the Frankfurt trial of Nazi war criminals.

Weisz, Victor [Vicky] (1913–66) British cartoonist, of German origin. Born in Berlin, he settled in England in 1935. He was a cartoonist for the *News Chronicle*. Later he worked for the *Evening Standard*.

Weizmann, Chaim (1874–1952) Israeli Zionist leader and statesman. He was born in Motel near Pinsk, in Belorussia. He settled in England and in 1904 became a lecturer in biological chemistry at Manchester University. In 1916 he was appointed director of the British Admirality Chemical Laboratories. His Zionist activities began when he became associated with the Democratic Fraction in 1901; the following year he and Berthold Feiwel proposed the creation of the Hebrew University. In 1903 Weizmann opposed the plan for the establishment of a Jewish homeland in Uganda and became a supporter of synthetic Zionism. He was the prime mover behind the Balfour Declaration. At the Paris Peace Conference of 1919 Weizmann together with **Menaḥem Mendel Ussishkin** and **Naḥum Sokolow** represented the Zionist movement, and in the same year he became president of the World Zionist Organization. He later retired to Rehovot to work at the Weizmann Institute, which he had helped to found. In 1948 he became the first president of the State of Israel.

Weizmann, Ezer (b. 1924) Israeli military commander, nephew of **Chaim Weizmann**. He served as a pilot in the British Air Force during World War II, then in 1958 became commander of the Israeli air force. He was appointed chief of operations of the Israeli general staff in 1966, and played an important role in the Six Day War in 1967.

Wellesz, Egon (1885–1974) British musicologist and composer. He was born in Vienna. After moving to England in 1938 he was baptized and took up a teaching post at Oxford University. His work as a scholar demonstrated the affinity of early church music with ancient Jewish cantillation.

Wengeroff, Pauline W. (1833–1916) Russian writer. She was born in Bobruisk, Belorussia, and became the wife of Ḥanan Wengeroff, a banker and communal worker in Minsk. Her memoirs depict the life of a rich Jewish family in the period before and after the Haskalah.

Werfel, Franz (1890–1945) Austrian novelist, playwright and poet. He was born in Prague, and served in the Austrian army. From 1940 he lived in the US. Some of his writing deals with Jewish themes.

Werner, Eric (1901–88) American musicologist. He was born in Vienna. He lectured at the rabbinical seminary in Breslau before moving to the US in 1938. He became professor of liturgical music at the Hebrew Union College in Cincinnati and in 1948 founded the college's School of Sacred Music. From 1967 to 1971 he served as head of the department of musicology at Tel Aviv University. He wrote studies of early Christian, medieval and Renaissance music, and of the relationship between ancient Greek and Hebrew hymnology and musical theories.

Wertheimer, Joseph von (1800–87) Austrian educator and author. He was born in Vienna, where he later was active as a merchant. He founded the city's first kindergarten in 1830, and in 1843 set up a Jewish kindergarten. His other acts of philanthropy included the establishing of a society to assist released criminals and provide guidance for juvenile delinquents, and in 1860 the founding of the society for the Care of Needy Orphans of the Israelite Community. He also played a leading role in the struggle to achieve equal social and political status for Jews.

Wertheimer, Max (1880–1943) German founder of Gestalt psychology. Born in Prague, he studied in Prague, Berlin and Würzburg. He founded and edited *Psychologische Forschung* and became professor at the University of Frankfurt. With the rise of the Nazis, he went to the US and taught at the New School for Social Research in New York.

Wertheimer, Samson (1658–1724) German court Jew. He was born in Worms. In 1684 he went to Vienna to join the bank of **Samuel Oppenheimer**, and he eventually became a court banker. In 1719 Carl VI appointed him chief rabbi of Hungary. Wertheimer was active on behalf of Jewish communities, and in 1700 obtained an order from the Emperor Leopold which resulted in the withdrawal from circulation of Johann Eisenmenger's anti-Jewish book, *Entdecktes Judentum*. He also created a fund to help paupers in Palestine.

Wesker, Arnold (b. 1932) English playwright. He was born in London. He held various jobs, including kitchen porter and pastry cook, before becoming a full-time writer. His plays include *Chicken Soup and Barley*, *Roots*, *I'm Talking about Jerusalem* and *Chips with Everything.*

Wessely [Weizel], Naphtali Herz (1725–1805) German Hebrew writer and leader of the early Haskalah movement. He was born in Hamburg, and lived in Copenhagen; his business affairs also took him to Amsterdam and Berlin. His first work was a study of the origins of Hebrew words and synonyms in the Hebrew language. Later he published a commentary on Avot and an annotated Hebrew translation (from the original Greek) of the Wisdom of Solomon. He also participated in the writing of **Moses Mendelssohn**'s commentary on the Pentateuch. Wessely's *Worlds of Peace and Truth*, written under the influence of Joseph II's Edict of Toleration, advocated an educational programme for Jewish youth in the spirit of the Haskalah. Subsequently he published the epic story, *Shire Tipheret*, which relates biblical events from the Exodus to the revelation on Mount Sinai.

West, Nathanel [Weinstein, Nathan] (1903–40) American writer. Born in New York, he studied at Tufts University and later at Brown University. He then went to Paris, and returned to New York where he worked as an assistant manager in various hotels. His works include *The Day of the Locust* and *Miss Lonelyhearts.*

Whitman, Ruth (1922–99) American translator and poet. She was born in New York. She lectured on poetry at Harvard University and Radcliffe College. She edited and translated *An Anthology of Modern Yiddish Poetry* and has published several volumes of her own poetry.

Wiener, Leo (1862–1939) American philologist. He was born in Bialystok, Poland. In 1882 he settled in the US, where he became a professor at Harvard University. His publications include *History of Yiddish Literature in the Nineteenth Century.* He became a Unitarian.

Wiener, Norbert (1894–1964) American mathematician. Born in Columbia, Missouri, he was the son of Leo Wiener, a professor of Slavic studies at Harvard. He studied at Tufts and later at Harvard. He taught at Massachusetts Institute of Technology. His works include *Ex-Prodigy: My Childhood*, *The Human Use of Human Beings*, *Cybernetics* and *The Tempest.*

Wieniawski, Henryk (1835–80) Polish violinist and composer. Born in Lublin, he studied at the Paris Conservatory. He became solo violinist to the tsar in St Petersburg and taught at the St Petersburg Conservatory. In 1872 he embarked on a US tour with the pianist **Anton Rubinstein**. Returning to Europe, he toured extensively.

Wiernik, Peter (1865–1936) American Yiddish writer, of Lithuanian origin. He went to the US in 1885. He served as editor of the Yiddish daily *Morgen-Journal* from its foundation in 1901, and also of the weekly *Der Amerikaner.* His writings include *History of the Jews of America.*

Wiesel, Elie (b. 1928) American author. He was born in Sighet, Romania. A survivor of the concentration camps, he later lived in Paris and New York. He became a foreign correspondent for an Israeli daily newspaper, and from 1957 worked for the *Jewish Daily Forward*; in 1976 he was appointed professor of humanities at Boston University. His works include *Night*, *The Gates of the Forest*, *Legends of Our Time*, *The Jews of Silence*, *A Beggar in Jerusalem* and *The Trial of God.* In 1986 he was awarded the Nobel Peace Prize.

Wiesner, Jerome (b. 1915) American scientist. Born in Detroit, he was an electronic engineer and carried out high level radar development. From 1961 to 1964 he was special scientific assistant to President Kennedy and director of the US Office of Science and Technology. In 1971 he became president of the Massachusetts Institute of Technology.

Wigoder, Geoffrey (1922–99) Israeli scholar of British origin. Born in Leeds, England, he studied at Trinity College, Ireland and Oxford University. In 1949 he settled in Israel. He was the editor of the *Encyclopedia Judaica*.

Willstätter, Richard (1872–1942) German organic chemist. He was born in Karlsruhe. From 1902 he taught at the University of Munich, but in 1924 he resigned his chair in protest against the university's anti-Semitic policy. He received the Nobel Prize for Chemistry in 1915.

Winchell, Walter (1897–1972) American journalist. He was a vaudeville performer and later contributed gossip material to *Billboard* and *Vaudeville News*. Later he worked for the New York *Evening Graphic* and the New York *Daily Mirror*. He also had a weekly radio programme.

Winchevsky, Morris (1856–1933) Lithuanian Yiddish poet and essayist. His activities as a socialist agitator led to his being imprisoned and banished from Germany and Denmark. He moved to London in 1879, and later lived in New York. He wrote poetry for Yiddish periodicals; he is regarded as the founder of Yiddish socialist literature.

Winder, Ludwig (1889–1946) Moravian novelist. He was born in Schaffa. He worked as a journalist on the *Deutsche Zeitung Bohemia* in Prague until 1938. A number of his works deal with Jewish topics.

Winston, Robert (b. 1940) British obstetrician. He studied at London Hospital Medical School and became professor of fertility studies at Imperial College, London. He was created a life peer. His works include *Reversibility of Sterilization, Tubal Infertility, Infertility: A Sympathetic Approach* and *Human Instinct*. He appeared on various television programmes including *Your Life in Their Hands, Making Babies, The Human Body, The Secret Life of Twins, Child of Our Time, Superhuman* and *Human Instinct*.

Wischnitzer, Mark (1882–1955) Russian historian, sociologist and communal worker. He lived in Galicia, Vienna and Berlin. After returning to Russia, he lectured at the institute of Baron **David Günzburg** in St Petersburg (1909–12). From 1914 to 1916 he was the editor of the periodical *History of the Jewish People* in Moscow. He lived in London for a time, then moved to Germany and served as secretary to the Hilfsverein der Deutschen Juden; in the period 1933–7 he helped to organize the emigration of Jews from Germany. Subsequently he became professor of Jewish history at Yeshiva University in New York. His writings include studies of Eastern European Jewish history.

Wischnitzer, Rachel (1892–1987) Polish art historian. She was born in Minsk in Belorussia. A pioneer of the study of Jewish art, she edited some of the first periodicals on this subject. From 1934 to 1938 she served as director of the Jewish museum in Berlin. In 1940 she went with her husband to New York, where she published studies of synagogue art.

Wise, George S. (1906–87) Israeli administrator. He was born in Pinsk, Belorussia, and emigrated to the US in 1926. He was associate director of the Bureau of Applied Social Research from 1949 to 1952. After moving to Israel he served as chairman of the Hebrew University's board of governors (1953–62). From 1963 he was president of Tel Aviv University.

Wise, Isaac Mayer (1819–1900) American Reform leader. He was born in Steingrub, Bohemia, and emigrated to the US in 1846. He served as rabbi of Congregation Beth El in Albany, then in 1854 became minister of a congregation in Cincinnati. He founded an English-language weekly, *The Israelite*, and a German-language weekly, *Die Deborah*; he also published an American Reform prayerbook, *Minhag America*. In 1855 he attempted to found a rabbinical seminary, Zion College; though he was unsuccessful at that time he was later a prime mover in the establishing of the Hebrew Union College in 1875. He summoned rabbinic conferences in 1869 and 1871, helped to form the Union of American Hebrew Congregations in 1873, and in 1889 organized the Central Conference of American Rabbis.

Wise, James Waterman (1901–83) American editor and author, son of **Stephen S. Wise**. He served as director of the Stuyvesant Neighborhood House in New York, and national secretary of Avukah, the American student's Zionist Federation. He also was editor of *Opinion*. His writings include *Liberalizing Liberal Judaism*, *Jews Are like that*, *Legend of Louise* and *A Jew Revisits Germany*.

Wise, Louise Waterman (d. 1947) American communal worker, artist and translator, wife of **Stephen S. Wise**. She established the Free Synagogue's Child Adoption Committee in 1914, and in 1933 became president of the Women's Division of the American Jewish Congress. She translated various works, and painted works on the theme of persecuted Jewry.

Wise, Stephen Samuel (1874–1949) American rabbi and Zionist leader. He was born in Budapest, and emigrated to the US as a child. He served as rabbi of Congregation B'nai Jeshurun in New York, and later in Portland, Oregon. In 1907 he established the Free Synagogue of New York, and in 1922 founded the Jewish Institute of Religion. He was secretary to the Federation of American Zionists, which subsequently became the Zionist Organization of America, and chairman of the Provisional Committee for Zionist Affiars (1916–19). For many years he was president of the American Jewish Congress.

Wiseman, Adele (1928–92) Canadian novelist. She was born in Winnipeg. Some of her works, including *The Sacrifice* and *Crackpot*, deal with Jewish life.

Wissotzky, Kalonymos Ze'ev (1824–1904) Russian merchant, philanthropist, and Zionist. He was born in Zhagare. In 1858 he moved to Moscow and established a tea firm. An active supporter of Ḥibbat Zion, he visited Palestine, where he supported religious settlers, and contributed to the foundaton of the Haifa Technion. He founded the Hebrew monthly *Ha-Shiloaḥ* in 1896.

Wistrich, Robert (b. 1945) Israeli scholar of British origin. He studied at Cambridge University and the University of London. He was professor at the Hebrew University and University College, London. His works include *Trotsky, Socialism and the Jews, Who's Who in Nazi Germany, Hitler's Apocalypse, The Perdition, Antisemitism: The Longest Hatred, Weekend in Munich, Demonizing the Other: Antisemitism, Racism and Xenophobia* and *Hitler and the Holocaust*.

Wittels, Fritz (1880–1950) Austrian psychoanalyst. He was born in Vienna. He was the first biographer of **Sigmund Freud**. In 1904 he wrote *Der Taufjude* (The Convert Jew), which argued that Jews should resist the temptation to join the majority culture and should stand up for their own interests.

Wittgenstein, Ludwig (1889–1951) British philosopher of Austrian origin. His father was a Protestant and mother a Roman Catholic of Jewish origin. Born in Austria, he studied at Linz, Berlin, Manchester and Cambridge where he became professor. His works include *Tractatus Logico-Philosophicus* and *Philosophical Investigations*.

Wolf, Johann Christoph (1683–1739) German Hebraist. He was born in Wernigerode, Prussia, and became professor of oriental languages and literature at the Hamburg gymnasium. His *Bibliotheca hebraea* is a list of Hebrew books based on the collection of **David Oppenheim**.

Wolf, Lucien (1857–1930) English historian, journalist and communal worker. He was born in London. He was foreign editor of the *Daily Graphic* (from 1890) and editor of the *Jewish World* (1906–8), and also edited the periodical *Darkest Russia*. In 1917 he became Secretary of the Joint Foreign Committee of the Board of Deputies of British Jews and the Anglo-Jewish Association. After World War I he attended the Paris Peace Conference in 1919. He published articles and works dealing with the period between the expulsion and resettlement of English Jewry (c. 1290–1650) and with the mission of **Manasseh ben Israel** to Oliver Cromwell.

Wolf, Simon (1836–1923) American communal leader. He was born in Hinzweiler, Germany, and emigrated to the US in 1848. Living in Washington, he intervened with presidents and other government officials to obtain equity for Jews in America and abroad. From 1878 to 1911 he was chairman of the standing committee of the Board of Delegates of Civil and Religious Rights. He also served as consul-general to Egypt and as president of B'nai B'rith (1904–5).

Wolff, Joseph (1795–1862) German missionary. He was born in Weilersbach, Bavaria. He converted to Catholicism in 1812, but later he joined the Anglican Church, serving as a vicar in England. He travelled as a missionary to the Jews in Palestine, Kurdistan, Mesopotamia, Turkey, Persia, Khursasan, Bukhara, India, Yemen, Abyssinia, and various European countries.

Wolffsohn, David (1856–1914) German Zionist leader. He was born in Dorbiany, Lithuania, and lived in Cologne, where he was a timber merchant. An active Zionist, he was a co-founder of a society to promote Jewish agricultural work and handicrafts in Palestine. Later he became an assistant to **Theodor Herzl**, who entrusted him with the preparations for the founding of the Jewish Colonial Trust. In 1898 he went with **Herzl** to Palestine to meet Kaiser William II. Wolffsohn was elected to succeed **Herzl** as president of the World Zionist Organization.

Wolfskehl, Karl (1869–1948) German poet. He was born in Darmstadt. In 1934 he left Germany and lived successively in Italy, Switzerland and New Zealand. He was influenced by the poet Stafan George; his series of poems, *Die Stimme spricht*, gives expression to the German Jewish tragedy.

Wolfson, Harry Austryn (1887–1974) American historian of philosophy. He was born in Belorussia, and emigrated to the US in 1903. In 1925 he became professor of Hebrew literature and philosophy at Harvard University. His publications include studies of **Ḥasdai Crescas**, **Spinoza** and **Philo**.

Wolfson, Isaac (1897–1991) Scottish businessman and philanthropist. He was born in Glasgow. He became chairman of Great Universal Stores in 1946. After World War II he devoted himself to philanthropic activities. The Edith and Isaac Wolfson Trust provided funds for building the Supreme Rabbinical Centre in Jerusalem, 50 synagogues throughout Israel, and the Kiryat Wolfson housing project for new immigrants. Wolfson also served as chairman of the Joint Palestine Appeal of Great Britain and Ireland, and president of the United Synagogue.

Wolpe, David (b. 1912) South African Yiddish writer. He was born in Keidan, Lithuania. He went to Palestine in 1930, but in 1936 returned to Lithuania, where he joined the army. In 1942 he was confined in the Kovno Ghetto, and later he was sent to the concentration camp at Dachau. In 1951 he settled in South Africa, where he became editor of the journal *Dorem Afrike*. One of the central topics of his writing is the Holocaust.

Wouk, Herman (b. 1915) American novelist and playwright. He was born in New York. Initially he worked as a radio scriptwriter, but later served in the US Navy as a line officer. His writing includes *The Caine Mutiny*, *Majorie Morningstar* and *This Is My God*.

Wyner, Yehudi (b. 1929) American composer and educator. He was born in Calgary, Canada, and went to the US at an early age. He taught at Yale University, and at SUNY at Purchase. He wrote a number of compositions for the synagogue.

Y

Yaari, Avraham (1899–1966) Israeli scholar of Galician origin, brother of **Yehudah Yaari**. He settled in Palestine in 1920; after teaching at a school in Tel Aviv, he worked in the Hebrew National Library and Tel Aviv University Library. He published studies dealing with Hebrew bibliography and the history of Jewish settlement in Palestine.

Yaari, Yehudah (1900–82) Israeli writer and diplomat, of Galician origin, brother of **Avraham Yaari**. He emigrated to Palestine in 1920 and served in the head office of Keren ha-Yesod. He held a number of diplomatic posts – as cultural attaché to the Israeli legation in Scandinavia (1955–7), director of the department for cultural relations of the Israeli foreign ministry, and as consul-general in Amsterdam. He wrote stories and romances dealing with Eastern European life during the 20th century and with pioneer youth in Israel.

Yadin, Yigael (1917–84) Israeli archaeologist and soldier. He was born in Jerusalem. He became a member of the Haganah and served in various official positions: he was chief of operations during the Israeli War of Independence, and chief of staff of the Israeli army from 1949 to 1952. He then taught archaeology at the Hebrew University, where he became professor. He published studies of the Dead Sea Scrolls and directed excavations at Hazor and Masada.

Yahuda, Abraham Shalom (1877–1951) Palestinian orientalist. He was born in Jerusalem. He taught at the Hochschule für die Wissenschaft des Judentums, in Berlin, and at the University of Madrid. In 1942 he became professor at the New School for Social Research in New York. He published biblical and philological studies, attempted to establish correspondences between Egyptian texts and the Pentateuch, and edited the Arabic text of Baḥya ibn Pakuda's *Duties of the Heart.*

Yaknehaz [Goldberg, Isaiah N.) (1858–1927) Lithuanian and Yiddish author. He was a teacher in Lithuania from 1880, and served as permanent assistant on the Hebrew newspaper *Ha-Melitz.* He wrote stories and sketches for the Hebrew and Yiddish press.

Yannai (i) (fl. 3rd cent.) Palestinian amora. He was a pupil of **Judah ha-Nasi** and **Ḥiyya**. He established an academy at Akhbara in Upper Galilee, the teachings of which are cited in the Palestinian and Babylonian Talmuds as 'de-ve Rabbi Yannai' (school of Rabbi Yannai).

Yannai (ii) (fl. ?6th cent.) Hebrew liturgical poet. He probably lived in Palestine. He introduced rhyme into religious poetry, wrote piyyutim related to the weekly portion of the Torah, and determined the final form of the Kerovah. His piyyutim (with the exception of *Az rov nissim* in the Ashkenazi rite for the Passover Haggadah) were forgotten until the 19th century, when scholars discovered others of his poems. Further examples were found in the Cairo Genizah.

Yaoz-Kest, Itamar (b. 1934) Israeli poet and fiction writer. He was born in Szarvas, Hungary. He survived incarceration at the concentration camp at Bergen-Belsen in 1944–5. In 1951 he went to Israel where he became an editor in the publishing house Eked. Some of his work deals with modern Jewish history.

Yassky, Chaim (1896–1948) Palestine medical administrator. Born in Russia, he went to Palestine in the 1920s. He worked for the Hadassah Medical Organization and helped initiate the construction of the Rothschild-Hadassah University Hospital on Mount Scopus. In 1931 he became director of Hadassah.

Yavne'eli [Warshavsky], Shmuel (1884–1961) Israeli organizer of Yemenite aliyah. Born in the Ukraine, he went to Palestine in 1905 and was an agricultural pioneer. In 1911 he was sent to the Yemen by the Zionist Organization. Due to his efforts, about 1500 Yemenites emigrated to Palestine in 1911–12 and a Yemenite mosahvah, Mahane Yehuda, was established. A fourth and fitth Yemenite aliyah came between the wars, and in 1949 the Operation Magic Carpet brought 40,000 Yemenites to Israel.

Yehoshua, Avraham (b. 1936) Israeli writer. He was born in Jerusalem. He served in the Israeli army. After living in Paris for a time, he settled in Haifa. He published stories about heroes haunted by indecision.

Yehudai (fl. 8th cent.) Babylonian gaon. He was born in Pumbedita. He succeeded Solomon bar Ḥasdai as head of the Sura academy in 757 and served until 761. He entered into relations with Jewish communities in North Africa, and attempted to enforce Babylonian usages in Palestine. His code of the law, *Halakhot Pesukot*, was written down for him by his pupils, since he was blind.

Yehudi ben Sheset (fl. 10th cent.) Spanish grammarian. A pupil of **Dunash ben Labrat**, he wrote a reply (consisting of 150 verses of introduction and a prose section) to the polemic directed against **Dunash** by the pupils of **Menaḥem ben Saruk**. This was in response to a criticism levelled by **Dunash** against **Saruk**.

Yellin, David (1864–1941) Palestinian scholar. He was one of the organizers of the founding conference of the Teachers' Association at Zikhron Ya'akov in 1903; later he was the association's president. He served as deputy director (from 1912) of the teachers' seminary founded by the Hilfsverein der Deutschen Juden in Jerusalem, and also lectured on Hebrew poetry of the Spanish period at the Hebrew University. He published studies of medieval Jewish poetry and Hebrew philology, a Hebrew dictionary and grammar, and an edition of the poems of **Todros Abulafia**. Besides his scholarly work, he was deputy mayor of Jerusalem (1920–5) and head of the Vaad Leumi (1920–8).

Yevin, Shemuel (b. 1896) Israeli archaeologist, of Russian origin. He went to Palestine before World War I, participating in various archaeological explorations. He was secretary of the Vaad ha-Lashon, and from 1948 to 1959 was director of the Israeli government's Department of Antiquities. His publications include studies of the **Bar Kokhba** revolt.

Yezierska, Anzia (1885–1970) American novelist, of Russian origin. She went to New York at the age of 16 and worked in a tailor's shop; later she found better-paid work and ran away from home. Her short stories and novels deal with the adjustment of the Jewish immigrant to American life. Her publications include *Hungry Hearts*, *Salome of the Tenements*, *Children of Loneliness*, *Bread Givers*, *Arrogant Beggar* and *All I Could Never Be*.

Yomtov ben Abraham Ishbili [Ritba] (c. 1250–1330) Spanish talmudist. A student of **Aaron ha-Levi of Barcelona** and **Solomon ben Adret**, he became a ḥakham and dayyan in Zaragoza. His talmudic commentaries contain summaries of the views of previous authorities. He also wrote a defence of **Maimonides** and a commentary on the Passover Haggadah.

Yomtov ben Isaac of Joigny (d. 1190) Liturgical poet, of Spanish origin. He settled in York in c. 1180. He wrote commentaries on the Bible and engaged in anti-Christian polemics. He composed an elegy on the Blois martyrs of 1171 and the hymn *Omnam Ken* for the eve of the Day of Atonement. According to tradition, he inspired the heroic mass suicide of the Jews of York in 1190.

Yose ben Halaphta (fl. 2nd cent.) Palestinian tanna. A pupil of **Akiva**, he became the head of the academy in Sepphoris, and one of the leaders of the assemblies at Usha and Jabneh after the abolition of the Hadrianic decrees against the practice of

Judaism. According to tradition, he was the author of the chronological work *Seder Olam Rabbah*. In the Talmud he is referred to as 'Rabbi Yose'.

Yose ben Joezer (fl. 2nd cent.) Palestinian rabbi and nasi. He and Yose ben Johanan of Jerusalem were the first of the scholars known as the 'zugot'. A disciple of **Antigonus of Sokho**, he served as nasi (head of the Sanhedrin).

Yose ben Yose (fl.5th cent.) Palestinian liturgical poet (the first paytan known by name). He lived in Palestine. His poems were highly regarded by the Babylonian geonim, and some were incorporated into the high holy day liturgy (notably the Avodah of the Sephardi rite for the Day of Atonement).

Yose ha-Gelili (fl. 2nd cent.) Palestinian tanna. At an early age he went to Jabneh, where he engaged in discussions with **Tarphon** and **Akiva**. His halakhot are found throughout the Mishnah, especially in the order Kodashim. He was known for the efficacy of his prayers for rain.

Yoseph, Dov (b. 1889) Israeli public figure. He was born in Canada, and settled in Pelstine in 1921. From 1945 to 1948 he was a member of the executive of the Jewish Agency, and later (1957–61) he served as its treasurer. During the War of Independence he served as military governor of Jerusalem. He was elected to the Knesset in 1949 as a member for Mapai, and held several cabinet positions, as minister of commerce and industry (1951–3), of development (1953–5), and of justice (1961–6).

Young, David (b. 1932) British politician. Born in London, he was secretary of state for employment (1985–7), and secretary of state for trade and industry (1987–9).

Yugdhan (fl. 8th cent.) Persian religious leader. A disciple of **Abu Issa al-Isfahani**, he lived in Hamadan. He was influenced by the doctrines of Islamic Sufism: he maintained that he was a prophet, advocated a mystical interpretation of the Torah, and argued that all religious symbols are allegories; he also supported the prohibition of wine and animal food introduced by the Issavites. A group of disciples grew up around him, which became known as the Yugdhanites.

Yulee [Levy], David (1810–66) American politician. Born in St Thomas, he was the son of Moses Elias Levy. He was a lawyer in Florida and was elected to the US Senate for the state of Florida. During the Civil War, he was a member of the Confederate Congress.

Yushkevich, Semyon (1868–1927) Russian novelist and playwright. He was a physician in Odessa. In his plays and narrative works he contrasted poor and virtuous Jews with their vulgar, rich co-religionists. After the 1917 Bolshevik Revolution he settled in the US.

Z

Zach, Nathan (b. 1930) Israeli poet. He was born in Berlin, and went to Palestine in 1935. He has published poetry, translated Arabic folk songs, and edited the selected works of **Yaakov Steinberg**.

Zacuto, Abraham [Abraham ben Samuel Zacut] (1452–c. 1515) Spanish astronomer and historian. His ancestors were French Jewish exiles who went to Castile in 1306. He studied and taught in Salamanica. His *Ha-Ḥibbur ha-Gadol*, a Hebrew work on astronomy, was translated into Spanish and Latin. He was the first to make a metal astrolabe, and he also drew up astronomical tables, which were used by **Christopher Columbus**. When Jews were expelled from Spain in 1492, he became astronomer and astrologer at the court of John II of Portugal; he was consulted by Vasco da Gama before his journey to India. Eventually he settled in Tunis, where he completed his *Sepher Yuḥasin* on the history of rabbinic scholarship.

Zacuto, Moses ben Mordecai (c. 1620–97) Italian kabbalist and poet. He was born in Amsterdam. During a pilgrimage to Palestine, he was persuaded to go to Italy, where he served as a rabbi in Venice and Mantua. He composed mystical and devotional poetry, some of which was used in the Italian liturgy. He wrote responsa, a poetical vision of the after-life (*Topheth Arukh*), and a drama about Abraham (*Yesod Olam*).

Zadkine, Ossip (1890–1967) Russian sculptor. Born in Russia, he was influenced by primitive art and later in Paris by cubism. His work includes *The Destroyed City*.

Zadoc-Kahn (1839–1905) Chief rabbi of France. He was chief rabbi of Paris from 1869 and later chief rabbi of France from 1889. He was a founder of *La Société Juive* and *La Revue des Études Juives*.

Zamenhof, Ludwig Lazarus (1859–1917) Polish philologist. He was born in Bialystok, and lived in Warsaw. In 1887 he published a pamphlet that set out the fundamentals of Esperanto. In 1905 he convened the first international Congress of Esperantists. He translated the Bible as well as German, Russian and English literature into this new language.

Zangwill, Israel (1864–1926) English author. He was born in London, where he later taught at the Jewish Free School. His writings include *Children of the Ghetto*, *Ghetto Tragedies*, *Ghetto Comedies* and *The King of the Shnorrers*. He also produced essays on Jewish themes, and translations of Jewish liturgical poetry and the poems of **Solomon ibn Gabirol**. Initially an enthusiastic Zionist, he helped to found the Jewish Territorial Organizaton in 1905.

Zaritsky, Yosef [Zarfutti, Yossef] (1891–1985) Israeli painter. He was born in the Ukraine, and went to Palestine in 1923. He painted watercolours of Safed, Tiberias and Jerusalem, and his later works chiefly depict the Israeli landscape.

Zebulun (fl. ?19th–16th cent. BCE) Israelite, sixth son of **Jacob** and **Leah**. His descendants, the tribe of Zebulun, received territory in central Palestine.

Zechariah (fl. 8th cent. BCE) King of Israel (743 BCE), son of **Jeroboam II**. He was assassinated by

Shallum of Jabesh, who seized the throne (II Kings 15:8–13).

Zedekiah (i) [Mattaniah] (fl. 6th cent. BCE) King of Judah (597–586 BCE), son of **Josiah**. He was originally called Mattaniah, but took the name Zedekiah when he was appointed king by Nebuchadnezzar in succession to **Jehoiachin**. Initially he refused to join an anti-Babylonian coalition, but later conspired with Egypt against Babylonia; as a result, the Babylonians invaded Judah and captured Jerusalem. Zedekiah was subsequently imprisoned in Babylon (II Kings 25; Jeremiah 52).

Zedekiah (ii) (fl. 9th cent. BCE) Israelite false prophet. He incorrectly predicted that **Ahab** would be successful in his invasion of Ramoth Gilead. He made iron horns to symbolize **Ahab**'s victory (I Kings 22).

Zederbaum, Alexander [Tsederboym, Aleksander] (1816–93) Polish editor and author. He was born in Zamość, and lived in Lublin and Odessa. He founded the Hebrew newspaper *Ha-Melitz* in 1860, and in 1862 began to issue *Kol mevaser* in Yiddish. Later he settled in St Petersburg where he established the city's first Russian Jewish periodical (*Vyestnik russkikh yevreyev*) and first modern Yiddish periodical (*Yidishes folks-blat*).

Zeira (fl. 4th cent.) Babylonian amora. He was a pupil of Huna and after moving to Palestine became an important teacher himself.

Zeira, Mordechai (1905–68) Israeli composer. He was born in Kiev in the Ukraine, and went to Palestine after having been arrested as a member of a Zionist youth organization. He initially found employment as a construction worker and fisherman, but in 1927 he moved to Tel Aviv and joined the Ohel Theatre. Later he worked for the Palestine Electric Corporation. He wrote numerous songs, which were in part influenced by Eastern European cantorial and Ḥasidic idioms.

Zeitlin, Hillel [Cejtlin, Hillel] (1871–1942) Russian philosopher. He was born in Korma, Belorussia, and in the 1890s lived in Homel. Initially he was a Zionist, but in reaction to the Kishinev pogrom he became a supporter of territorialism. After settling in Vilna, he published works in Yiddish opposing assimilation and secularism. In the 1920s he returned to Zionism. He is an important representative of Ḥasidic thought in modern Yiddish literature.

Zeitlin, Solomon (1892–1977) American scholar of Russian origin. He emigrated to the US in 1915 and taught at Yeshiva College. In 1921 he became professor of rabbinics at Dropsie College. He wrote studies on rabbinics, **Josephus**, the Apocrypha, Christianity and the Dead Sea Scrolls. He also served as editor of the *Jewish Quarterly Review*.

Zellick, Graham (b. 1948) British lawyer. He studied at Cambridge University and Stanford University. He was a professor at the University of London, and later vice-chancellor and president. Subsequently he was chairman of the Criminal Cases Review Committee.

Zephaniah (fl. 7th cent. BCE) Judean prophet. He was a member of a noble Judean family, and his prophecies were uttered during the early part of **Josiah**'s reign. He described the Day of the Lord, when the wicked will be punished, the poor will inherit the land, and the Lord will be universally acknowledged.

Zephira, Bracha (1913–90) Israeli singer. Born in Jerusalem, she performed with the Philharmonic Orchestra and also composed her own songs, in traditional, oriental style.

Zerahiah Levi [Saldin, Ferrer] (fl. 15th cent.) Spanish scholar and poet. A disciple of **Ḥasdai Crescas**, he served as rabbi of Zaragoza and all the communities of Aragon. He was a talmudist, preacher, physician and translator, and also participated in the Disputation of Tortosa.

Zerubbabel (fl. 6th cent. BCE) Israelite leader, grandson of **Jehoiachin**. With the consent of Cyrus II of Persia, he returned to Judah from Babylon to help rebuild Jerusalem. Together with Joshua the priest, he set up an altar, re-establishing the festivals, and began the rebuilding of the Temple.

Zhitlovski, Chaim (1865–1943) Russian philosopher and essayist. He was born in a small town near Vitebsk, Belorussia. He initially was involved in the revolutionary activities of the Narodniki. Later he founded the Jewish section of the Socialist

Revolutionary Party, which advocated Jewish national emancipation and Yiddish as the language of national rebirth. In 1888 he left Russia and settled in Switzerland, where he edited *The Russian Worker*. He returned to Russia after the revolution of 1905 and helped to found the Seymist party. In 1908 he went to New York, where he edited *Dos neie leben*.

Ziegfeld, Florenz (1869–1932) American impresario. He was a leading producers in American show business and founded the Ziegfeld Follies.

Zilpah (fl. ?19th–16th cent.) Israelite woman, handmaid of **Leah**. **Leah** gave Zilpah to **Jacob** as a wife. She bore **Gad** and **Asher** (Genesis 30:9–13).

Zimra, David ben Solomon ibn Avi [David ben Solomon ibn Zimra; Radbaz] (fl. 16th cent.) Spanish talmudist and kabbalist. He was born in Spain, and studied in Safed, Fez and Cairo, where he became chief rabbi. He later returned to Spain and served as a dayyan. He composed responsa, a commentary on **Maimonides**' *Mishneh Torah*, kabbalistic works and talmudic novellae.

Zimri (i) (fl. ?13th cent. BCE) Israelite, head of a clan of the tribe of Simeon. He consorted with a Midianite woman, and with her was stabbed by **Phinehas**, the grandson of **Aaron**. This act ended a plague which had been visited on the Israelites for commiting harlotry with Midianite women and worshipping Baal Peor (Numbers 25).

Zimri (ii) (fl. 9th cent. BCE) King of Israel (855 BCE) A captain of half the chariots of the Israelites, he killed **Elah**, son of **Baasha**, when he had reigned for only a short time. After Zimri assumed power he executed all the male relatives and admirers of **Baasha** (I Kings 16:11). However, he reigned for only seven days. **Omri** was proclaimed king by his own men and besieged Tirzah the capital city. Zimri set his own palace on fire and died in the blaze, thus evading capture.

Zinberg, Israel (1873–1939) Ukrainian historian of Hebrew and Yiddish literature. He was born near Kremenets, Volhynia, and worked as a chemical engineer. He wrote eight volumes of a history of Jewish literature from the Spanish period (c. 10th century) to the end of the Russian Haskalah.

Zinoviev, Grigori (1883–1936) Russian communist leader. Born in Radomyslski in Kirovograd, he joined the Russian Social Democratic Party in Switzerland in 1901. He was a delegate to the party's congress in Stockholm in 1906. He was exiled in 1908 and became one of Lenin's close collaborators. In 1917 he and Lenin returned to Russia. After the revolution, he was a member of the party's central commitee, and became chairman of the Lenin soviet party. In 1922 he became a member of the Politburo. Following Lenin's death in 1924, he became part of the triumvirate that ruled the Soviet Union.

Zipporah (fl. ?13th cent. BCE) Israelite woman, wife of **Moses**. She was the daughter of Jethro, priest of Midian. She travelled to Egypt with **Moses** to plead with Pharoah for the release of the Israelites; on the journey she saved the life of her son Gershom by circumcising him (Exodus 4:24–26). She returned alone to her father, with her sons Gershom and **Eliezer**; Jethro later took them to rejoin **Moses** on Mount Sinai (Exodus 18:1).

Zirelsohn, Judah Löb (1860–1941) Romanian rabbi and communal leader. He was born in Kozelets in the Ukraine, and served as rabbi of Priluki and Kishinev. He initially was a supporter of Zionism, but later dissociated himself from the movement. In 1912 he was one of the founders of Agudat Israel. When Bessarabia was incorporated into Romania in 1920, he became chief rabbi of Bessarabia and the leader of Orthodox Jewry there. In 1922 he was elected a deputy in the Romanian parliament, and in 1926 a senator. His writings include responsa, homilies, eulogies, essays and poems.

Zitron, Samuel Löb (1860–1930) Russian writer. He was born in Minsk, Belorussia. He studied at Lithuanian yeshivot and became interested in the ideas of the Haskalah. In 1876 he went to Vienna, and later studied in Germany. He contributed to the Yiddish press and to Hebrew periodicals in the diaspora. His writings include studies of the Zionist movement and its precursors, and Hebrew literature.

Zondek, Bernhard (1891–1966) Israeli gynaecologist. He worked in Berlin, and left Germany with the Nazis' rise to power. He became professor of gynaecology and obstetrics at th Hebrew University in Jerusalem. He was head of the hormone research laboratory at the Hebrew University.

Zorach, William (1887–1966) American sculptor. He was born in Eurburg, Lithuania, and emigrated to the US in 1891. He studied art in Cleveland, New York and Paris. In his later works he utilized Jewish subject matter.

Zuckerman, Solly (1904–93) British scientist. Born in Cape Town, he went to England and became known for his research on apes and monkeys. He served as a scientific adviser to the RAF during the war. He was chief scientific adviser to the British government on defence matters, and on general and scientific and technological questions. He was knighted in 1956 and later created a life peer.

Zuckermandel, Moses Samuel (1836–1917) Moravian talmudist. He served as a rabbi in Moravia and Germany. He compiled what became the standard edition of the Tosephta, published in 1880.

Zuckmayer, Carl (1896–1977) German playwright. He was born in Nackenheim. Although he had a Jewish mother, he was raised as a Catholic. From 1919 he worked in the theatre and as a freelance writer. In 1924 he joined Bertholt Brecht at Berlin's Deutsches Theatre. He moved to Switzerland in 1938, and later settled in the US. Jewish characters play a role in a number of his dramas.

Zukofsky, Louis (1904–78) American poet. Born in New York City, his early poems examine the tension between Jewish values and modern education. His works include *A*, a poem in 24 sections.

Zukor, Adolf (1873–1976) American film executive. Born in Ricse, Hungary, he went to the US in 1888. He and Marcus Loew created the Loew Company. Later he merged with **Jesse Lasky** and formed Paramount Studios.

Zulay, Menaḥem (1901–54) Israeli scholar. He was born in Oschcianci, Galicia, and settled in Palestine in 1920. He worked at the Schocken Institute for the Study of Hebrew Poetry. He was an expert on early Palestinian piyyutim and edited the collection of such poems discovered in the Cairo Genizah.

Zunser, Eliakum (1836–1913) Lithuanian Yiddish poet. He was born in Vilna. He was conscripted into the military, and later worked in Kovno as a braider of gold lace for uniforms. He became Russia's foremost wedding bard. In 1889 he moved to New York. Many booklets of his poems were published.

Zunz, Leopold (1794–1886) German historian. He was born in Detmold. He helped found the Verein für Kultur and Wissenschaft der Juden in Berlin in 1819, and his work is regarded as having laid the foundations for the scientific study of Jewish history (Wissenschaft des Judentums). From 1840 to 1850 he served as principal of the Berlin Teachers' Seminary. His early writings include a biography of **Rashi**, a history of Jewish homiletics, and a survey of Jewish names from biblical times. Among his later publications are a history of Jewish geographical literature, a history of Jewish liturgy, studies of medieval piyyutim and their authors and Bible studies. He also edited the works of **Naḥman Krochmal**.

Zweifel, Eliezer Tzevi (1815–88) Russian Hebrew author and essayist. He was born in Mohilev, Belorussia. He wandered through Russia stopping in various towns, and worked as a preacher and teacher. In 1853 he was appointed lecturer in Mishnah and Talmud at the government rabbinical seminary in Zhitomir. Later he lived in Russia and Poland finally settled in Glukhov in the Ukraine. In his *Shalom al-Yisrael*, he defended Ḥasidism, and demonstrated the movement's kabbalistic roots.

Zweig, Arnold (1887–1968) German novelist and playwright. He was born in Gross-Glogau, Silesia. He worked as a freelance writer in Bavaria and Berlin, where he edited the Zionist journal *Jüdische Rundschau*. After moving to Haifa, he co-edited the weekly *Orient* in 1942–3. In 1948 he settled in East Berlin. A number of his works deal with Jewish themes.

Zweig, Stefan (1881–1942) Austrian author. He was born in Vienna and became a member of the Young Vienna group of Jewish intellectuals. In 1918 he wrote a pacifist play *Jeremiah*. His works include a number of biographies, *The Buried Candelabrum* and *Beware of Pity*.